AT THE VANGUARD OF VINYL

at the
vanguard
of vinyl

A Cultural History of the Long-Playing Record in Jazz

DARREN MUELLER

DUKE UNIVERSITY PRESS
Durham and London
2024

© 2024 DUKE UNIVERSITY PRESS

This work is licensed under a Creative Commons Attribution-NonCommercial 4.0 International License, available at https://creativecommons.org/licenses/by-nc-nd/4.0/.

Project Editor: Livia Tenzer
Designed by A. Mattson Gallagher
Typeset in Utopia Std, Work Sans, and Kepler Std
by Westchester Publishing Services

Library of Congress Cataloging-in-Publication Data
Names: Mueller, Darren, [date] author.
Title: At the vanguard of vinyl : a cultural history of the long-playing record in jazz / Darren Mueller.
Other titles: Cultural history of the long-playing record in jazz
Description: Durham : Duke University Press, 2024. | Includes bibliographical references and index.
Identifiers: LCCN 2023025121 (print)
LCCN 2023025122 (ebook)
ISBN 9781478030072 (paperback)
ISBN 9781478025818 (hardcover)
ISBN 9781478059073 (ebook)
ISBN 9781478094159 (ebook other)
Subjects: LCSH: Jazz—1951-1960—History and criticism. | Sound recordings—Production and direction—History—20th century. | Sound recording industry—History—20th century. | African American jazz musicians.
Classification: LCC ML3506 .M84 2024 (print) | LCC ML3506 (ebook) | DDC 781.65—dc23
LC record available at https://lccn.loc.gov/2023025121
LC ebook record available at https://lccn.loc.gov/2023025122

Cover art: Duke Ellington sitting at grand piano with Billy Strayhorn, Universal Recording Studios, Chicago, 1963. Photograph by Jeff Lowenthal. Bridgeman Images.

To my parents

Contents

ix   Acknowledgments

1   **INTRODUCTION**
       The LP Goes Live

1
35   **DO THE HUCKLE-BUCK**
       Jazz and the Emergent LP, 1949–1955

2
75   **MISTAKES, MISHAPS, AND MISCUES**
       The Early LPs of Prestige Records

3
122   **QUEST FOR THE MOMENT**
       The Audio Production of *Ellington at Newport*

4
152   **WORLD STATESMAN**
       The Ambassadorial LPs of Dizzy Gillespie

5
191   **CAPTURING THE SCENE**
       The Cannonball Adderley Quintet in San Francisco

6
230   *MINGUS AH UM*
       The Avant-Garde Record Making of Charles Mingus

270   **CONCLUSION**
       Jazz as a Culture of Circulation

281   Notes
377   Discography
395   Bibliography
413   Index

Acknowledgments

A book is much like a record: a single author appears on the cover, but it emerges from a much larger network of friends, colleagues, family, and collaborators. And so I begin with a few words of gratitude to those that have lent their support and assistance.

I am indebted to the librarians and archivists who generously offered their expert advice about which paths to follow and the best ways to do so. I especially want to thank Tad Hershorn at the Institute of Jazz Studies (IJS), who was an early advocate for this project and who helped shape my core research questions and methodologies. There are many others: Joseph Peterson at the IJS; Jessica Wood in the Music and Recorded Sound Division at the New York Public Library; Karen Fishman and Harrison Behl in the Recorded Sound Research Center at the Library of Congress; and Ricky Riccardi, director of research collections at the Louis Armstrong House Museum. Their knowledge, dedication, and creativity are an inspiration. Elizabeth Surles (IJS) and Lisa Wright (University of Rochester Libraries) kindly provided digital imaging during my final days of revising.

At the start of this project in 2012, Matthew Leskovic generously facilitated my work in George Avakian's archive in Riverdale, New York. The Avakian family—George, Anahid, and Anahid Jr.—welcomed me into their home with grace and warmth. The vibrant spirits of George and Anahid continue to be felt.

Rebecca Geoffroy-Schwinden and James Davies were essential running mates who kept spirits high and provided guidance in how best to untangle the knottiest of issues. The deep camaraderie and big ears of Matthew Somoroff and Dave Garner brought continuous insight, humor, and counsel.

Matthew also offered valuable guidance as an editor—his sharp eye and thoughtful observations have improved my thinking greatly.

The list of other scholars to thank is long. Louise Meintjes helped me adjust the right dials so that the signal stayed clear but had enough noise to remind me of other possibilities. The Humanities Corridor crew—Fritz Schenker, Celeste Day Moore, James Williams, Ben Baker, and Ben Givan—offered thoughtful and constructive feedback over the past few years. My thanks also to the late-night Jazz Studies Collaborative group: Mark McCorkle, Christopher Coady, Kimberly Hannon Teal, Kelsey Klotz, and Rami Stucky. During the project's early stages, Aaron Johnson and Kate Heidemann continually pushed me to refine and explore. For the planned (and unplanned) conversations that brought many joys and lasting epiphanies, I thank the amazing cohort of jazz scholars besides those already mentioned: Nate Sloan, Patrick Burke, Stephanie Doktor, Ken Ge, Michael Heller, Ken Prouty, Jay Hammond, Brian Wright, Marc Hannaford, Christi Jay Wells, Kwami Coleman, Alex Rodriguez, John Howland, Sean Lorre, Kevin Fellezs, Dale Chapman, David Ake, Tammy Kernodle, Mark Lomanno, and Dana Gooley. My thanks also to Paul Berliner, Philip Rupprecht, Lewis Porter, and Henry Martin for being early advocates.

Others beyond the jazz corner of the world provided essential input and perspective. These include Mary Caton Lingold, Kimberly Brown, Sarah Fuchs, Chelsea Burns, Dan Ruccia, Karlyn Forner, and D. Edward Davis. I was fortunate to attend the incredibly supportive junior faculty symposium in 2020 hosted by the Popular Music Study Group of the American Musicological Society. Along with the other participants, I want to thank Andrew Flory and Mark Burford for their insightful comments during and after the workshop. I am also grateful to Joan Rubin for the invitation to present at the Humanities Center at the University of Rochester.

I finished this book while working at Eastman, where I am surrounded by an incredible intellectual community. I especially want to thank Anaar Desai-Stephens and John Kapusta for their many insights that have helped sharpen my thinking. Many other Eastman colleagues offered their steadfast encouragement and timely advice: Lisa Jakelski, Michael Anderson, Reinhild Steingröver, Glenn Mackin, Holly Watkins, Roger Freitas, Melina Esse, Jennifer Kyker, Jonathan Baldo, Jean Pedersen, Dariusz Terefenko, Jeff Campbell, Clay Jenkins, Ben Baker, Mark Kellogg, Rick McRae, and Jim Farrington. I have also been fortunate to think alongside Ryan Blakeley, Emmalouise St. Amand, and Suraj Saifullah—their humor, wit, and inquisitiveness (and memes) brought much-needed perspective and energy. Emmalouise and Miles Greenberg also provided superb research assistance.

Additional thanks to the team at Duke University Press, especially Ken Wissoker for his guidance, for his perspective, and for finding such generous reviewers who helped shape the book for the better. For their quick and thorough responses to my many questions, I also thank Kate Mullen, Joshua Tranen, and Livia Tenzer. My research was generously supported by the IJS, the Graduate School and Music Department at Duke University, and the dean's office and professional development committee at the Eastman School of Music.

No one else has lived with this book more than Stephanie Westen. Since the beginning, she has listened with open ears and offered sound advice that kept me focused on the book's core mission. Most of my revisions and editing happened during the COVID era, when together (and at home) we juggled two jobs, two young children, two cats, and one sprawling book about jazz records—this book would not have been possible without her. Through it all, Joyce, Steve, and Danny (the other Westens) provided welcome company, amusements, and delicious meals, for which I am enormously grateful.

My last note is reserved for my parents, Buffie Rosen and Henry Mueller, to whom this book is dedicated. From the first moment I picked up a saxophone, they gave me the courage to dream big. Thank you.

INTRODUCTION

The LP Goes Live

DECEMBER 24, 1954
IN A SMALL RECORDING STUDIO IN HACKENSACK, NEW JERSEY

A few seconds into the first attempt of "The Man I Love," Thelonious Monk interrupts the slow introduction of vibraphonist Milt Jackson to pose a question: "When am I supposed to come in, man?" Monk's seemingly innocent inquiry grinds everything to an immediate halt. The rest of the band, apparently already frazzled from the long recording session, reacts with unintelligible words but in unmistakably frustrated tones. Without pause, Monk replies: "I wanna know when to come in, man. Can't I stop too? Everybody else [*trails off*]." Miles Davis, as leader of the session, intervenes and addresses engineer Rudy Van Gelder: "Shhh! Shhh! Hey Rudy, put this on the record. ALL of it."

In most historical accounts, this infamous exchange documents the underlying tension between Davis and Monk. These histories ignore how this contentious moment of studio informality first circulated on record: on a 1957 LP spinning at 16⅔ rpm (revolutions per minute), an unusual format used primarily for spoken-word recordings for the visually impaired. The slower rotational speed and smaller grooves of these 16⅔-rpm "talking books" afforded twice the capacity of the typical LP, but at a much lower fidelity. As a result, the format rarely contained music. Monk's question, in addition to Davis's response, appeared on one of only six such records issued by Prestige Records.[1]

The limited production run of Prestige's 16⅔-rpm discs marks a particular moment of commercial experimentation in how to present jazz on record, where "alternate takes" sounded alongside their more widely available counterparts. Such doubling suggests that Bob Weinstock, Prestige's owner, attached value to the messiness of music making and thought that his connoisseur-oriented consumers might too. Although moments of studio informality—interruptions, mistakes, and musician chatter—were commonplace during the recording process, they rarely appeared on commercial records at this time. This LP's mere existence cannot be separated from Weinstock's apparent desire to capture, document, and archive the process of recording and the impression of closeness it brings. Davis's comments to Van Gelder in the control room similarly reveal his acute awareness of how the social space of the studio interacts with the business of record making and the inscription of performance onto disc. After all, jazz musicians operated within industry structures that privileged certain presentations of Black male artistry over others: creative authority, technical facility, and authentic expression of the self. The inseparability of Black jazz musicking from wider perceptions of Black masculinity makes it impossible to ignore the acute power discrepancies between (Black) cultural producers and (white) industry executives. In the particularities and power dynamics of this circulation history, what else is it possible to hear?

DECEMBER 16, 1953
IN A FORMER CHURCH, TURNED RECORDING STUDIO, IN NEW YORK CITY

A collection of musicians led by trumpeter Buck Clayton gather for a jam session at Columbia's famed recording studio on East 30th Street in New York City. A number of invited guests join the eleven jazzmen and the Ampex tape recorders. Most had never met before; this is an intimate gathering of mostly strangers. The ensemble records several takes of two different pieces, each lasting between fifteen and twenty minutes. The arrangement of "Robbins' Nest" is conventional: a simply stated melody followed by an unhurried string of fifteen choruses. Nonetheless, many of the soloists are heard in multiple. For example, Clayton's two choruses (the fourth and tenth) are separated by five other soloists. Similarly, trombonists Urbie Green and Henderson Chambers split a thirty-two-bar chorus at the beginning of the recording (chorus three), take individual solos in the middle (choruses seven and nine), and return for another duet at the end (chorus fifteen). The result is a relaxed but entertaining performance from start to finish.

Informal jam sessions with lengthy improvisations have deep historical roots in jazz. Yet putting them on commercial record was relatively rare at this time, especially for a large firm such as Columbia. The result of this session-turned-record became Clayton's first 12-inch LP, issued in 1954: *The Huckle-Buck and Robbins' Nest: A Buck Clayton Jam Session*. The otherwise relaxed nature of "Robbins' Nest" hides a technological conundrum: the master take includes at least three choruses spliced in during postproduction, including the duet by Green and Chambers as well as Clayton's first solo. Surprisingly, the liner notes written by the producers do not hide but rather celebrate the addition of more than two minutes of music to the original performance. "There were two takes of Robbins' Nest," writes John Hammond, "and thanks to George Avakian's imaginative tape-editing, this record combines the best of both."[2]

Clayton's performance combined with Avakian's invasive editing exposes the complex relationship that recording technologies had to 1950s jazz. Whereas the front jacket highlights the "full length improvisations," the liner notes boast about the ability to edit improvised performances together with little aural disruption. The favorable, if unusual, acknowledgment of such technological manipulation points to the changing affordances of record making in the 1950s. It similarly reveals the tension between the desire to document jazz history in the making and the required mediation needed to create a commercial product. Within that tension more questions remain about how the interracial group of musicians might have felt about their performances being cut and spliced together, as if their music making was raw material in need of technological improvement by white record producers. Control over the sound during and after the performance happened along racialized and gendered lines in ways that most often went unmarked: the accompanying notes and marketing ephemera do not mention that the musicians and the record producers were all men. Issues of labor and power within a racialized industry again rise to the surface. By listening through the splice, what else is it possible to hear?

MAY 15, 1953

IN A LARGE, HALF-FILLED CONCERT HALL IN TORONTO, CANADA

LATER, IN A SMALL RECORDING STUDIO IN NEW YORK CITY (OR POSSIBLY NEW JERSEY)

There was no rehearsal, only a sound check. However, any resulting sloppiness was overshadowed by the presence and performances of the bebop royalty onstage: Dizzy Gillespie, Charlie Parker, Bud Powell, Max Roach, and Charles Mingus. The inspired playing on "All the Things You Are," a 1940s standby of Parker and Gillespie's, has a push-pull feel to it: the rhythm section's movement between swing and Latin during the melody, the competitiveness heard among the soloists, the harmonically adventurous accompaniment, and the impromptu (and sometimes overpowering) horn backgrounds during Mingus's bass solo all serve as evidence.

Two basses can be heard during the Mingus solo that appears on the 1956 LP *The Quintet: Jazz at Massey Hall*. The Mingus faintly heard in the background sounds like an echo, although he remains eerily unfaithful to the Mingus clearly audible in the foreground. The bassist apparently felt that he was too low in the initial mix, so he rerecorded himself sometime after. He created this ghostly duet by overdubbing himself onto the concert recording. Aural remnants nevertheless remain.

As if mirroring the doubled recording, two different versions of "All the Things" circulated simultaneously in the early to mid-1950s: a 10-inch LP with no additions and a 12-inch version with the "reparative" overdubs. Both discs appeared on Debut Records, the label that Mingus cofounded with his wife, Celia, and Max Roach.[3] The bassist chose to overdub and then release the recording in multiple versions, although it is unclear if he let any of his collaborators know. Because record companies owned and operated by Black musicians were rare, his experimentations are a statement about control over his intellectual property, over his sound on record, and over the art of record production. In this way, Mingus's reimagining of the Massey Hall concert is not about faithfulness to an original. Rather, his actions point toward the relationship between the creative agency of Black jazzmen like Mingus and the uneven racial dynamics of the mid-century record business. In Mingus's edits, overdubs, cuts, and splices, what else is it possible to hear?

These opening vignettes—each about a performance turned into a recording—occurred roughly within a year and a half of one another. Their differences are notable. Davis's group recorded in a small studio for a fledgling independent, jazz-focused record label. Clayton's jam session occurred in a large studio owned and operated by one of the largest and most powerful media conglomerates of the time. The Massey Hall concert produced a live but not quite live recording eventually released by a musician-owned record label. Each situation features musicians performing in distinct spaces and draws attention to the divergent approaches to and methodologies of making records. The results differently imagine what jazz records were at that moment and what they might be in the future.

Taken together, however, they exemplify how jazz musicians and their record companies were adjusting to the advent of the long-playing record (LP), a playback medium initially introduced by Columbia Records in 1948. Along with improved fidelity, the format's strong yet lightweight "vinylite" material could accommodate nearly three times the number of grooves per disc, allowing for longer uninterrupted playback: up to 22.5 minutes per side for a 12-inch disc. The increased capacity beyond the three-minute limitations of the previous era dramatically altered the business and artistry of making records. Even so, LPs were an emergent technology that required new infrastructures to record, manufacture, distribute, and sell them. These unknowns made change happen slowly. The ubiquitous presence of the 12-inch vinyl record in the decades since the 1950s has made the integration of the LP seem brief and even uneventful, obscuring the decade-long period during which record makers experimented with how best to leverage its potential. Davis's ironic call to put social disagreements on record, Mingus's reparative sound work, and Avakian's editing of Clayton's improvisations were, in fact, at the vanguard of vinyl's adoption. Their similarities thus reveal the underexplored complexities that surround the LP as a recording format, as an instrument of technological mediation, and as a medium for historical documentation.

From these perspectives, the LP also emerges as a medium of sound and culture, a dynamic object with embedded racial and gender politics. The LP, despite its newness, became another means to reinscribe the uneven power relations of a heavily segregated music industry that was not gender inclusive in its operational structures. Much like the rest of the jazz business, the recording studio was a male-dominated space on both sides of the glass, and therefore a technological refashioning of what Hazel Carby observed about the bebop scene: a perpetual site of "men reproducing men without women."[4] Moreover, Black musicians had enormous influence onstage but minimal control over their artistic representations on record. Such working conditions influenced jazzmen as much as they did jazz recordmen. Consider Avakian's tape edits to Clayton's "Robbins' Nest." Even if Clayton (or any of the other musicians) knew about the stitched-together performance, they would not have had any input into how such mediation unfolded, nor would they have had any influence over the cover design, liner notes, and other discursive ephemera. And although Avakian consistently advocated for the music and its practitioners in a race-neutral way, he did so through an inherited understanding of jazz history and Black musical genius that always centered great men working together. Even Charles Mingus, who co-owned an independent label with Celia, a white woman, kept firm creative control over Debut's sound on record. His edits and overdubs thus resisted the racialized logic of the industry while also expressing certain qualities of postwar masculinity: capitalistic risk taking, technological control, and artistic authority.[5] As Davis's quip to Van Gelder similarly suggests, cultural politics flow through the record-making process at every stage.

At the Vanguard of Vinyl interrogates the sonic entanglements of record making—that is, the choices made while performing, recording, producing, designing, and circulating music on record. These entanglements matter because they destabilize the idea that jazz recordings are simply a passive playback medium meant to deliver sonic content. Listening for and through the processes of record making further reveals the tactics and strategies by which Black musicians in the 1950s found agency within the racialized practices of an industry that systematically disadvantaged them. These musicians skillfully leveraged a moment of technological turmoil in their efforts to redefine prevailing notions of Blackness within the United States. Yet even as the music successfully crossed artistic and cultural boundaries, altering the ways in which Black expertise, Black labor, and Black capital circulated, these efforts often reaffirmed gendered hierarchies within US culture. Understanding the decisions that render jazz performance into a commercial product makes clear that the history of the LP cannot be untangled from the ideologies of social difference that surrounded its creation, adoption, and eventual dominance.

This book's principal argument is that jazz records are more than the product of a singular musician or ensemble from a particular time and location. Like all commercially produced sonic media, LPs came into being through decisions both small and large by historically situated cultural producers with different philosophies about music and individual approaches to the technology of sound reproduction. Within the jazz industry's broader matrix of creative agency, postwar ideologies about race and gender continued to affect the working conditions, artistic possibilities, and circulatory pathways of record making. To examine how musicians interacted with other industry professionals, I attend to the details of musical performance through audio production: tape edits, microphone placement, the mixing of sound levels and instrument balance, room sound, overdubbing, and other sound-processing effects. I connect decisions about sound to the visual and tactile attributes of various LPs to understand the sounds on record as the combined product of different kinds of technological and artistic labor. Through this method I assert that the relationship between audio production and musical performance is a central yet underexplored means of understanding mid-century jazz.

Many scholars have convincingly articulated how jazz musicians operated within a social system where tropes of cultural difference marked location, audience, and musical style. Much of this literature understands technological advances in commercial record making from a deterministic perspective. There is a general assumption that the transition to the LP format happened quickly and without controversy because the desire for such recordings (and the methods of production) already existed. As a result, the nascent record-making activities of the 1950s often become a means of looking forward to the 1960s, when jazz most explicitly intersects with the struggle for civil rights and social equality. This naturalized treatment of the LP, I suggest, does not account for the diverse approaches to record production and record making that characterized the early LP era.

In order to tell the multilayered story of how Black cultural producers sought greater control over how their musical expertise circulated and became represented on record, *At the Vanguard of Vinyl* examines the LP's adoption through a set of four interrelated theoretical frameworks: (1) contestations over recording format, (2) the reorientation of race within the record business, (3) new forms of technological mediation, and (4) the codification of jazz's historical narrative. The birth of the LP widely increased the availability of historical jazz recordings as labels reissued older recordings on newer formats, a process that involves several layers of mediation along the record-making supply chain. The affordances of a particular format and the technological capabilities of its associated equipment shaped these reissues at several levels. At the same time, the blossoming of the record industry enormously increased the number of jazz records being produced. The structures of commercial record making mediated this growth: label executives decided which artists to sign, what kinds of music to record, and how to represent those musical sounds on record. Within the mechanisms for making—and remaking—jazz history, technological capabilities of recording intersected with changing conceptions of race, gender, and other forms of social difference. The ever-increasing agency of Black cultural producers enormously altered the instruments of control over the production of recordings.[6] As such, the dynamic connection between the historiography of jazz on record and struggles over racial inequality comes into focus.

As a technology of culture, the LP maps onto the more expansive sonic terrain of Black modernity in the early Cold War era. Black musicians throughout the twentieth century took a multifaceted approach to the poetics, politics, and practices of what Guthrie Ramsey describes as Afromodernism: the fight for opportunity, liberation, and freedom in relation to the socioeconomic institutions of capitalism within the United States.[7] Through their record making in the 1950s, Black jazz musicians fought against structures of racism while simultaneously appealing to the sympathies of left-leaning political figures, placing an ethos of the Black vernacular in dialogue with "serious" European musical aesthetics, campaigning to perform the products of mass culture in hallowed concert halls, and leveraging strategies of racial uplift against white privilege.[8] Collectively, these actions produced a jazz-specific version of Afro-modernism that drew from multiple aesthetic streams, refused reductive definitions, and explicitly combined musical style with social practices. As forms of representation eventually shifted because of the LP, so too did jazz's existing relationship to white mainstream culture and entrenched structures of whiteness.

Recognizing that jazz sits within a much broader constellation of political and artistic practices of African American culture, my analysis begins with a set of questions: How does the adoption of new technologies intersect with concurrent contestations over representation, power, and cultural capital? How do changing conceptions of musical time and recording space intersect with Cold War politics as well as the ongoing fight for civil rights? Who are the agents of mediation with control over the sonic, graphic, and verbal modes of representation on record, and what sociocultural factors influence how they make decisions about these representations? How are Black and white cultural actors differently invested in the processes of record making? In what ways do the decisions of record makers reinforce the gendered social order of jazz in the postwar era? How do sonic media enable musicians to create new auralities and acoustemologies—ways of knowing the world through sound? Records result from specific kinds of musical labor, sonic artistry, and technical creativity, so the history of the format's adoption becomes a way in which to understand how mediated objects represent historical knowledge and differently affect cultural change.

The emphasis on improvisation in jazz—the high value ascribed to music made in the moment of performance—offers a particular vantage point on the questions above. Many issues were in a constant state of flux during the LP's adoption, including gendered constructions of public and private space, understandings of time and place, and beliefs about authenticity and simulacra. By examining the correlation between improvised performance and its reproductions during this period, this book asserts that the increased mediatization of performance via technological advances in recording was actually a mediatization of culture(s) writ large. The pathways that such mediatization took can be heard in the sonic entanglements of record making, especially in how decisions about sound relate to both intended and imagined uses of the resulting records. Who controlled which form of media (and its contents) mattered just as much as how that media (and its contents) circulated. Through the jazz LP, *At the Vanguard of Vinyl* interrogates the relationships of sound to culture, technology to power, and mediation to cultural agency.

Recording Format

In their materials as well as their design, jazz records encode the culture that surrounds their creation and use. For example, Clayton's *The Huckle-Buck and Robbins' Nest* was one of only a handful of 12-inch jazz LPs issued in 1954. Most jazz—including Mingus's unedited version of "All the Things You Are" on *The Quintet: Jazz at Massey Hall, vol. 1* (1953)—was available only on 10-inch disc, the standard size for all forms of popular music in the first five years of the LP's commercial life. I explore the many reasons for this in chapters 1 and 2, including how and why the production of jazz records changed to match shifting assumptions about audience preferences for Black popular music. Indeed, by the time that Mingus reissued the overdubbed "All the Things You Are" in 1956 and Prestige released the 16⅔-rpm experiment of Davis's "The Man I Love" in 1957, the record industry had already adjusted, such that both tracks appeared solely on 12-inch LPs. In only a few years, 10-inch LPs became one forgotten playback medium among many.

Although quite literally at the margins, these details reveal how a considerable amount of uncertainty and rampant experimentation defined the transitionary time as the LP took hold of the market in the 1950s. For nearly a decade after the LP's introduction, cross-industry standardization remained impossible, forcing record stores to sell numerous types of records that varied in size, speed, and sound quality. Eventually, producers and executives planned recording sessions specifically to take advantage of the LP format. Eventually, record jackets with artwork, photos, and liner notes replaced the blank paper sleeves of the 78-rpm era. Eventually, innovations in signal processing created new methods of editing, mixing, and mastering. Eventually, producers regularly took advantage of the longer playback duration to create concept albums.[9] However, it took time for failed experiments to evolve into viable pathways with commercial sustainability. This precarious history hides in plain sight on the ridged surface of a recording format like the LP.

By recording format, I mean the mode of encoding sonic data onto a specific medium, such as an LP, cylinder, cassette tape, or MP3. As a term, *format* encompasses specifications such as size, shape, material, and sonic properties of the medium as well as the visuals, graphics, and text of its container. In *MP3: The Meaning of a Format*, Jonathan Sterne convincingly outlines how such attributes contain a range of assumptions, logics, and practices embedded within historically specific notions of technology and listening. Recording format therefore holds power over the social and cultural transmission of audio content because it sets the parameters for storage, distribution, and consumption of recorded sound.[10]

Consider the pre-LP experiments in recording jazz that ran beyond the 78-rpm time restrictions in terms of format. In an effort to overcome the technological limitations of the 78 format, record companies would sometimes split lengthier pieces between the A side and the B side of a 78-rpm disc. This is the case with Duke Ellington's "Tiger Rag" (1929) and "Diminuendo and Crescendo in Blue" (1938), Tommy and Jimmy Dorsey's "Honeysuckle Rose" (1934), and Dexter Gordon's "The Chase" (1947), a cutting contest with fellow tenor saxophonist Wardell Grey. Other, more ambitious examples include Benny Goodman's nearly nine-minute "Sing, Sing, Sing" (1937), which took two sides of a 12-inch disc; Ellington's four-sided "Reminiscing in Tempo" (1935); and a seventeen-minute version of "A Good Man Is Hard to Find" issued by Commodore Records on *Jam Session at the Commodore, no. 3* (1940).[11] Producer Norman Granz was an early proponent of this technique. By recording his jam-session-style Jazz at the Philharmonic (JATP) concert series, Granz became one of the first to release live concerts in three- or four-disc album sets.[12]

These examples represent only a small percentage of commercially released jazz in the 78-rpm era, yet they demonstrate how format correlates with changing practices of listening and record making. For instance, the originally issued versions of Ellington's "Tiger Rag" and Goodman's "Sing, Sing, Sing" split the pieces between the sides of a 10- and 12-inch 78-rpm record, respectively. The silence between, usually timed to coincide with a musical transition, sonically marked the technological limitations of the format. This aural interruption was built into the recording process and, in some cases, influenced compositional and performance decisions as well.[13] In the early 1950s, Brunswick and RCA Victor reissued the Ellington and Goodman recordings on LP as an unbroken track without the musical gap caused by the need to flip the record.[14] *New York Times* columnist John Wilson singled out this innovation specifically, underlining how such continuous play made it possible to hear the "smooth flow" of musical performance as never before.[15] With the uninterrupted playback of the LP, one technological innovation silenced the limitations of another and allowed musical sounds to travel across time and space with increasing efficiency and efficacy.

Even as an emerging medium, the LP forced record labels to adjust their record-making infrastructures in other ways as well. Because a single LP side could hold multiple tracks without pause, producers began rethinking their content and programming. Columbia producer George Avakian, who released the first popular music LPs onto the market in 1948, looked toward other media. As he told Michael Jarrett many years later, "The concept that I used in making a 10-in LP—a pop LP—was thinking of it as a radio program in which the entire package has a purpose. It's programmed. You start with something that catches the attention of the listener on the outside first track. In fact, I did this deliberately on both sides. I'd try to find a real attention-grabber. Then I'd pace the program and end with something that makes the person want to turn the record over."[16] In his role as the mediator between artist and consumer—what Andrew Blake has described as a "first listener"—Avakian reoriented his approach in response to the new demands of the LP format.[17] Thinking about the entire listening experience, he adopted radio programming as a model. However, it was the physical properties of the record that afforded certain possibilities.

As the above discussion implies, the logics of capitalism are what give recording formats like the LP their inherent power and ability to control cultural discourse. Any change to the delivery formats or circulatory mechanisms of music consequently creates possibility, either to alter the underlying conditions of how power operates or to strengthen already existing power structures. It is notable, then, that all the different constituencies mentioned in the previous paragraphs are men: jazzmen, recordmen, and male critics. Although these cultural producers worked in increasingly multiracial and multigenerational spaces, and power flowed unevenly among them, their jazz work continued to be shaped by men and their relationships with one another. As I explore throughout, these social conditions would have enormous influence on jazz culture during the industry-wide adoption of the LP format.

As vinyl LPs came to replace the shellac discs of the previous recording era, consumers in the early 1950s faced a rapidly changing and uncertain market. Numerous options in terms of size and speed became newly available. Spinning at 33⅓ rpm, there were 12-, 10-, and 7-inch LPs. At 45 rpm, there were 7-inch singles and extended-play (EP) discs. Many record companies also continued to produce 12- and 10-inch 78-rpm discs well into the decade, along with other experiments that have been lost to history.[18] By the late 1950s, the industry had normalized, and most labels issued either 12-inch 33⅓-rpm albums or 7-inch 45-rpm singles. The consolidation of formats departed from previous conventions that rigidly matched genre to disc size.

In what Debra Spar describes as a phase of "creative anarchy," the record industry moved from innovation to unstable yet widespread commercialization, and eventually to standardization.[19] During this multitudinous period, several formats uneasily coexisted alongside one another.

The infrastructural changes happening within the industry forced consumers to reevaluate their listening habits and record companies to develop new approaches to marketing and manufacturing.[20] New technological capabilities required audio engineers to experiment with the finer details of the recording process, from microphone placement and editing techniques to studio layout and design.[21] The changing habitus of both professional record makers and consumers drove musicians to rethink their orientation to the industry as well, and to find additional spaces in which to make their voices heard. Even so, the kind of newness ushered in by the LP also corroborates the frequently made observation that the upending of certain cultural norms can result in progress for some but not necessarily equal progress for all.[22] Often, the male-dominated conditions of record making reinscribed notions of masculine privilege and control, especially in terms of which historical narratives about jazz came to circulate most widely.

In order to examine the LP as a medium of culture, *At the Vanguard of Vinyl* pays particular attention to format. The physical characteristics, visual design, and sonic properties of jazz records reveal much about the cultural valences of the jazz industry and its listeners, particularly in regard to what kinds of information different groups valued and how this information circulated. The particularities of format reflect the cultural practice of record making, providing a window into the mediation processes along the record-making supply chain. From the perspective of format theory, then, the LP is a form of structured communication, social in its creation and cultural in its circulation.[23]

Race and Record Making

In 1949, a year after Columbia introduced the LP, *Billboard* magazine renamed its category for music marketed toward African Americans from "race records" to "rhythm and blues," or R&B for short. Numerous styles fell under the catchall banner of R&B: blues, gospel, boogie-woogie, jazz, and any other popular music that originated in the Black community. Despite the change, the term nevertheless continued to differentiate Black music from white music, a segregational logic also imposed onto the industry's playback media: 12-inch discs for classical recordings and Broadway shows, and 10-inch records for popular, country, and jazz, and anything else that fell under the R&B banner. This differentiation would continue despite further changes in playback media, as I explore in detail in chapter 1. Regardless, record-making practices continued to mark difference through format, a physical manifestation of entrenched notions of race and class in the early LP era.

The dominant power structures of Jim Crow that aggressively limited African Americans are central to media histories like the adoption of the LP within the United States. At the time of the LP's introduction, mixed-race ensembles onstage were still rare and hotly contested, as were integrated audiences in many areas of the country. The recording studio offered greater flexibility, but record labels were nevertheless wary of any music that entered into cultural debates about race.[24] Jazz musicians experienced these politics on a daily basis and wherever they worked. Given jazz's origins, praxis, and reception, racial ideologies have enormously influenced the continued circulation of the music through recorded objects, both before and after the advent of the LP.[25] Producers and industry executives, each differently invested in jazz's cultural politics, continued to act as silent mediators during the industry's adoption of the LP, especially as various record-making innovations increased the impact of record-production and audio-editing techniques.[26] Even so, inherited notions of Black masculinity, especially essentialist depictions that so often circulated through mass media, continued to define the conditions and possibilities of Black popular music. This historical context makes clear that the LP is not simply a technology for the dissemination of music but is actually a determining factor by which ideologies about music and its cultures circulate.

Like their predecessors, LPs were carefully curated objects of political discourse that circulated multiple notions of race and identity.[27] The origin story of the format is evidence of this fact. Columbia's quest for uninterrupted playback via long play began in 1939 as part of a larger business strategy to make the label the preeminent record company for classical music, a market then dominated by RCA Victor.[28] In 1939 Columbia president Edward Wallerstein directed the CBS research lab to develop long play.[29] The research team's first version appeared at the end of 1946 with a playback duration of seven to eight minutes per side. Wallerstein demanded longer. "I timed I don't know how many works in the classical repertory," he later recalled, "and came up with a figure of seventeen minutes to a side. This would enable about 90% of all classical music to be put on two sides of a record."[30]

After two more years of further demands for capacity, the CBS engineers went above and beyond, expanding playback to 22.5 minutes per side. Later, Columbia boasted about this accomplishment in its 1948 report to stockholders without any mention of jazz or popular music: "[The LP] has ended the 50-year delay in finding a solution to the oldest challenge in recorded music: being able to hear entire symphonies, concerti, string quartets, as well as complete Broadway musical shows, on a single disc, with no interruptions in the music not planned by the composer himself."[31] The first LP in Columbia's Masterworks catalog, ML 4001, was Felix Mendelssohn's Violin Concerto, op. 64, played by Nathan Milstein with an orchestra conducted by Bruno Walter.[32] Although popular music did immediately appear on LP, the format was conceived of and designed for classical music. Jazz was not a consideration.[33]

This origin story exposes a wider truth about the early years of the LP: jazz on record remained defined by whiteness. Jazz historian Kelsey Klotz understands whiteness as a continuous performance of white-centered norms and values. Although such performances "include, intersect with, and incorporate other performances of identity, including gender, sexuality, class, religion, and able-ness," the entrenched repetition of whiteness most often renders it invisible and inaudible. By turning her attention to the iterative quality of whiteness, Klotz convincingly demonstrates how white racial identity works to afford certain social privileges or deny opportunities in the creation and circulation of jazz.[34] Applied to record making, her analysis brings clarity to how both race and gender functioned as crucial organizing principles of the postwar jazz industry. Most nonmusician record makers in jazz—record-label owners, artist-and-repertoire (A&R) executives, producers, recording engineers, graphic designers, marketers, and critics (among others)—were white men.[35] Moreover, the ones with the most power, such as those running independent record companies or making contract decisions at the major firms, imagined a consumer base that was primarily white and male. Such assumptions, however inaccurate, directly affected the musical aesthetics and repertoire selections in the studio, the techniques of audio production, the design of the resultant LPs, and the marketing of those same records.[36] Any history of record making in this era must account for such individual and collective performances of whiteness in their various forms.

One example of how whiteness operated within the commercial infrastructures of the mid-century record business is the heavy editing on *The Huckle-Buck and Robbins' Nest: A Buck Clayton Jam Session*. As mentioned above, Avakian cut up and spliced in several choruses on "Robbins' Nest," a process that Hammond celebrates in the liner notes to this 1954 LP. Control over the technology, as well as the discourse surrounding it, remained the domain of white men who worked as intermediaries between jazz musicians—especially Black ones—and the capitalistic structures of the industry. These men may have shared a workspace, but they were understood through different, historically situated cultural scripts of masculine authenticity and authority.[37] For example, as much as *The Huckle-Buck and Robbins' Nest* LP celebrated Clayton's spontaneous musical abilities (as I explore further in chapter 1), the record explicitly foregrounded the white expertise of Avakian and Hammond in choosing the musicians and repertoire, directing the recording session, editing the tapes, and recounting the day's activities. Such performances of whiteness were made possible by the power differentials inherent in the practice of record making during the early LP era, regardless of the intentions of various individuals.

The capricious nature of the 1950s music industry meant that record makers would continually reform and recast these social dynamics. Once again, the LPs from my opening vignettes help illustrate how both individuals and organizations adjusted. When Miles Davis first began recording with Prestige Records in 1951, the label largely ignored the jukeboxes and radio stations that sat at the aural center of Black public life.[38] Instead, Weinstock curated his catalog around music that appealed to a form of jazz connoisseurship defined by white male sensibilities and record collecting. By 1957, when Prestige issued Davis's alternate take of "The Man I Love," the label had reversed tactics, recognizing that Black audiences were essential to its sustainability as a creative and commercial entity.[39] Along with heavily investing in musicians who would appeal to Black audiences, Prestige increased its production of 45-rpm singles, the primary playback medium for those aforementioned jukeboxes and Black radio stations (see chapter 5). By the end of 1960, Prestige had created several subsidiaries, including the Tru-Sound label, which focused on gospel, R&B, and Latin American music.[40] As was the case with other independent labels, however, male instrumentalists continued to define the sound of jazz on Prestige, despite the label's racially integrated roster of musicians.[41]

During the same period, Charles Mingus struggled to make his independent record label commercially viable while also giving its musicians complete artistic freedom. It is not coincidental, as chapter 6 argues, that Mingus's music comes to more overtly confront racial inequities at the precise moment when he begins to have a heavier hand in editing recordings during postproduction.[42] From this perspective, his overdubbed bass solo on "All the Things You Are" is not a singular moment of mediation but part of a wider history about how the business and artistry of record making entwine with Black political action and expressions of Black agency.

I contend that the jazz industry's relationship to socially constructed notions of difference can be heard in the details of record production.[43] In order to analyze how sound processing mediates this difference, I consider how jazz record making in the 1950s was an activity of constant negotiation and contradiction, especially for African American artists who refused the restrictive structures of whiteness that defined the jazz industry. To understand these cultural dynamics, I listen. I listen to different practices of mediation. I listen through the particularities of media. And I listen for the ingenuity of jazz musicians performing and making records. Through this listening, *At the Vanguard of Vinyl* uses the adoption of the jazz LP and the attendant rapid rise in music's mass consumption to examine how jazz musicians redefined their social position on a national and often international stage.

Mediation of Performance and Time

Recorded sounds materialize from the infrastructures behind their creation—that is, the specific approaches to production, manufacturing, packaging, and distribution.[44] When Columbia issued the stream of improvised solos heard in "Robbins' Nest" on *A Buck Clayton Jam Session*, the record producers designed the jacket to highlight both the "full length improvisations" on the front and the "imaginative tape-editing" on the back. Discourses of technology's relationship to performance quite literally surround the sound on record. The three choruses spliced in during postproduction and celebrated in the liner notes make clear that processes of record making matter in how they relate to one another. Some individuals, like Avakian with "Robbins' Nest" or Mingus with "All the Things You Are," had a heavy hand. Others, like Bob Weinstock at Prestige, rarely edited recordings in postproduction, for a number of reasons both economic and aesthetic. Such decisions reveal differing philosophies about recording, especially regarding the cutting and splicing together of recorded performances.

The ability to edit performances in this way relied on the convergence of the LP with another new technology: electromagnetic tape. Before the introduction of tape in the late 1940s, music was recorded directly onto a master disc, where a stylus would physically cut grooves into a thickly coated wax disc. With tape, those sounds would instead be encoded onto a thin, magnetizable strip of plastic film. The medium captured clear, uninterrupted performances with hardly any background noise, a feature that had enormous appeal for radio stations interested in tape-delayed broadcasts. Tape was also easy to use, enormously flexible, and relatively inexpensive for professional broadcast companies. However, it was tape's ability to be cut, copied, and spliced—the possibilities of editing—that ushered in new practices of record making at every stage of the recording process.

The first commercial tape recorder in the United States, the Ampex model 200A, appeared in April 1948, only a few months before the LP's introduction. Full-scale adoption was not instantaneous, yet tape machines quickly found their way into recording and broadcast studios across the industry, especially after 3M began manufacturing affordable tape reels in 1948.[45] The simultaneous arrival of the LP and tape was historical happenstance, an unplanned but nevertheless significant fusion of playback and recording media. This combination merged two streams of media innovation for the first time: reproduction of sound through inscription into grooves on a flat disc (originally popularized in the 1890s) and the processes of encoding sonic data magnetically onto tape such that these data could be manipulated without loss of fidelity.[46] The cultural practice of editing was not new, of course. The ability to cut, copy, and paste exists in many other cultural artifacts, including wax tables, palimpsests, and chalkboards (to name only a few). For sound recording, however, tape introduced the revolutionary ability to splice, merge, distort, and otherwise alter the time of recorded performance.[47] If the LP was a triumph of playback in the home, then tape was a triumph of editing in the control room.

Both technologies must be understood in relationship to each other. The compression of performance time into a smaller space coupled with the increased malleability of those musical "data" not only reshaped what it meant to package and sell music but arguably also altered the very notion of music itself.[48] Within the cultural economy of music, which places high value on the synchronicity between creative events and their reproductions, issues of informational flow and exchange quickly point to the sociopolitical complexities of these sonic media.[49] More control over sound translated into more control over the perception of time as it relates to musical performance.

As technologies that mediate time and space, both the LP and magnetic tape fit into a much broader history of 1950s technologies that redefined perceptions of time and space in the United States. In 1951 President Harry Truman conducted the first transcontinental television broadcast announcing the official end of the US occupation of Japan. That same year also marked the first TV broadcast of a live sporting event and the Federal Communications Commission's approval of color TV. The first political TV ads appeared a year later. In the years following, the introduction of the vidicon pickup tube made it possible to construct portable TV cameras—notably RCA's "Walkie-Lookie" camera (1953)—and the invention of the transistor radio by Texas Instruments (1954) led to the mass production of pocket-size radio devices.[50] In 1956 President Dwight Eisenhower signed the Federal-Aid Highway Act, a law that authorized the construction of the interstate highway system and began the largest public-works project in US history to date. Russia's 1957 launch of Sputnik 1, the first Earth-made satellite, caused a panic in part because it made the possibility of space exploration and intercontinental ballistic missiles a reality. Images of airplanes and worldwide travel similarly filled popular magazines and newspapers as access to commercial airlines increased in the late 1950s, a sentiment immortalized on Frank Sinatra's 1958 LP *Come Fly with Me*.[51]

Other technologies enabled more rapid exchange of information. The first electronic computer, the Ferranti Mark 1, became commercially available in 1951. Three years later, scientists Harold Hopkins and Narinder Singh Kapany published a significant article in *Nature* that demonstrated the practical abilities of transmitting data using light (i.e., fiber optics).[52] After the installation of the first transoceanic coaxial cable in 1950, several companies from the United Kingdom, United States, and Canada constructed the first transatlantic coaxial network. The Transatlantic No. 1 (TAT-1) opened in 1956, ushering in a new telecommunication era between Europe and North America.[53] Along with the creation of solar cells and magnetic computer hard drives, other scientific breakthroughs of the mid-1950s included the invention of the digital modem (1958), the commercial copy machine (1959), and the integrated circuit, popularly known as the microchip (1959). Mass communication expanded alongside mass consumerism, whereby the economic strength of the middle class led to more leisure time and expendable income for millions of people nationwide.[54] It would be several years, or in some cases decades, before many innovations made their way into most homes or offices. However, such advancements in the speed and ease of information circulation reveal much about the prevailing impulses of this cultural moment, which could be described as the subjective compression of space and time.[55]

The middle of the twentieth century was certainly not the first historical period when notions of space shifted through technological advancement. Industrialization in the late eighteenth and early nineteenth century forced a broad reconception of what proximity meant. Later, telegraphy, telephony, and radio increased the exchange of information across wide geographic regions. Nevertheless, the efficiency of informational travel expanded exponentially during the 1950s through the combination of different media. An increased number of television broadcasts of news programs, sports, and political events dovetailed with the expanding capabilities of telephone networks and radio broadcasts. More expansive control over the distribution networks also brought about more invasive forms of mediation and greater power over reproduction and representation. Such changes happened across different levels of culture simultaneously.

It is difficult to overstate the significance that these changes had for the music industry.[56] As recordings began outselling sheet music for the first time in the early 1950s, records became one of the dominant media for musical distribution and consumption. Larger media conglomerates like CBS and its largest competitor, RCA, began to devote more financial resources to making and selling records.[57] At the same time, the growing popularity of television created more avenues for promoting music. *The Steve Allen Show*, eventually renamed *The Tonight Show*, premiered in September 1954 on the National Broadcasting Company (NBC) TV network to compete with CBS's popular *Ed Sullivan Show*, which had been on the air since 1948. Both shows regularly programmed music, especially because a company like CBS could cross-promote its recording artists on TV, radio, and film.[58] As avenues of personal entertainment became more affordable (and distribution networks more efficient), far-off musical events increasingly found their way into the homes of millions of people in real time. A nationalized musical culture became more of a reality.

The far-off events that instantaneously appear on a live television broadcast were made possible only by sophisticated machines that seamlessly connect to elaborate infrastructures of communication. To work, these technologies must project what Rebecca Schneider refers to as the "lure of synchronicity."[59] That is, more-synchronous media result directly from increased mediation that simultaneously becomes less visible. One way to understand the increased possibilities of manipulating recorded performance during this era is through what Mary Ann Doane theorizes as "unreal" time. "The very idea of a time that is real," writes Doane in her work on still photography, "presupposes an unreal time, a technologically produced and mediated time."[60] As the flip side of "real time," the concept of unreal time rests on the tension between the live event and its mediated representation.

Perceived synchronicity is foundational to recorded music. Listening to a recorded object is a cultural practice with an inherent latency between performance and reproduction.[61] In this respect, sonic technologies of the early LP era translated new ways of thinking about sound, time, and space into a discourse of real time that gave the impression of instantaneous access and synchronous witnessing. Certainly, the invention and commercial adoption of sound recording at the end of the nineteenth century caused a similar moment of rupture. Yet the advent of tape technology made the LP into something different: record making became more than point-to-point inscription.[62] That is, the LP is a cultural technology of unreal time and, as such, sits at the center of an enormous shift in the relationship between performance and its reproduction.

Examples of unreal time proliferate through recorded jazz of the 1950s. Mingus's overdubbed bass lines found on *Jazz at Massey Hall* as well as Avakian's editing of Clayton's jam session are clear examples. There are others. Lennie Tristano rerecorded piano parts on his eponymous 1955 LP, *Lennie Tristano*.[63] Avakian added crowd noise to cover up splices and other adjustments on *Ellington at Newport* (1956) and fabricated audience applause to music recorded in an empty concert hall on *Ambassador Satch* (1956).[64] Both records were, according to *Down Beat*, top-five sellers on the jazz charts for several months in 1956 and 1957, respectively.[65] Irving Townsend, who succeeded Avakian at Columbia, similarly fabricated live audiences on two Ellington LPs from the late 1950s: *At the Bal Masque* and *Newport 1958*.[66] With one or two exceptions, the accompanying liner notes and other marketing material characterized these recordings as real-time performances. Placed in the context of changing conceptions of musical time, these LPs should not be understood as simply counterfeits.[67] They were expertly crafted products using new technological capabilities.

It is perhaps not surprising but nevertheless significant that the public discourse surrounding music during the early years of the LP simply ignored the innovations of tape recording. The hundreds of articles, advertisements, and press accounts about the innovation of the LP that appeared between

1948 and 1950 generally mention tape only in passing, if at all.[68] This discursive absence extended to the records, where liner notes often celebrated the newness of the LP. Consider *Masterpieces by Ellington* (1951), Duke Ellington's first record on Masterworks, Columbia's premier classical series. The liner notes, written by George Dale, highlight long-playing technology as a driving force behind the record: "The complete, concert type arrangements that have consistently dazzled Ellington fans have simply been impractical for ordinary recording purposes. Thanks to Long Playing records, these great Ellington settings can now be heard at last in their entirety." Dale's account fails to mention that this record was one of the first made using Columbia's Ampex 200A tape machines and, indeed, one of the first jazz recordings ever made on tape at all.[69] Tape's invisibility here and elsewhere likely results from its position along the record-making supply chain: its capabilities and contributions are hidden from consumer view. But more than that, highlighting playback over production further obscured how the technologies of mediation were having an ever-more-increased role in how such music materialized into the world.

The concept of unreal time is not only useful as an analytic to understand ontological questions about performance and reproduction. It also provides a framework to delineate the various approaches to recorded sound during this moment in jazz history.[70] Record labels differently value certain kinds of music, expect certain habits from their listeners, and hire certain personalities for the studio and to be behind the control board. Enormous technological changes disrupt these values, expectations, and habits, thereby providing a window into the broader culture from which such media objects emerge. The aim of this book is to trace the history of the jazz LP as the convergence of two tracks: the medium of playback (how it sounds) and the medium of production (how it was made). A central premise is that the practices that circumscribe sound reproduction are inherently cultural. Because power flows through these practices in different but interlocking ways, it follows that any history of technology is inherently a cultural history as well.

My analysis throughout this book focuses on how specific technological innovations affected the structures of record producing and music making. As such, I am not interested in questions of authenticity or synchronicity in their own right because jazz records are never in real time—or are never *only* in real time.[71] Rather, I wish to use these blurred moments of un/real time to understand how the industry reimagined jazz on record and, in doing so, renegotiated this music's cultural position within the United States. Through a focus on the jazz LP during a moment of enormous cultural disruption, I interrogate what historically situated notions of recording and production reveal about performance and its mechanical representations.[72]

Re/making Jazz History

Dan Morgenstern, the illustrious jazz critic and historian, recalled the lengthy period of re-standardization around the LP: "It took a while for studio recordings to take advantage of this new format, because they were still locked into the three-minute thing. You know, the [jazz] record industry was basically conservative—it took longer than you might expect for the 12-inch to replace the 10-inch discs."[73] Having arrived in the United States in 1947, Morgenstern became a professional jazz writer while the LP was still a nascent technology.[74] He believed that the format was revolutionary, in part because it created new opportunities for musicians. This included sidemen who were able to take longer solos beyond the standard half chorus allowed on 78-rpm records.[75] Morgenstern continued:

> There is something that's often misunderstood when America is compared to Europe in terms of jazz audiences. The US is a huge country—it's enormous, as big as all of Europe. In a European country, take a country like Denmark or Holland, if you are a jazz fan and there is a significant player or jazz event in Rotterdam and you live in Amsterdam, you go on the train or you drive. It takes you, at most, an hour and a half. If you're in New York and there is a terrific jazz festival in Seattle, it becomes a little more complicated. So what happened with the LPs was that a lot of people who liked jazz, but were in places where first-class musicians were seldom heard, got a taste of what it's like to hear a live performance, to hear musicians stretching out. It changed the listening habits, and it became a much more—young musicians and students could study these recordings and analyze the solos. It was a big sea change, you know, it was.[76]

In his description, Morgenstern recites an oft-repeated belief about the jazz LP: the format's capabilities brought listeners closer to the act of performance. Yet the focus on fidelity to "live" performance obscures the increased mediation inherent in these same technologies. Any increase in realism was ultimately the result of more technological intervention, not less.[77] The compression of time and space via technology surfaces once again in Morgenstern's observations about how the adoption of the LP increased the circulation of jazz across different geographic locations and through different communities of listeners.

Perhaps as a result, more jazz styles coexisted in the mid-1950s than at any previous time. Traditional jazz in the New Orleans small-group style thrived alongside virtuoso stride pianists, big bands performing within the legacy of the swing era, and musicians furthering bebop's harmonic and improvisatory innovations. Crooners rooted in the jazz tradition dominated the radio airways at the same time that other musicians fused jazz with different streams of Black popular music. And some composers adopted compositional techniques from the Western classical tradition to create a new, so-called third stream. Though certainly a testament to musicians' collective creativity, the successful coexistence of these subgenres also resulted from the increased access to jazz through records. By the early 1950s, the record industry was selling more units than ever before, which included the recirculation of previously out-of-print recordings from earlier decades (see chapter 1). This diffusion of jazz history via records had enormous consequences for how jazz was listened to and understood. Recall Morgenstern's comment that the LP had "changed the listening habits." The result was not simply a practical change in the material circumstances of jazz listening but also an epistemological change in understanding how jazz had developed over time.

At the Vanguard of Vinyl argues throughout that the renewed circulation of older jazz records on LP helped codify jazz's historical narrative. Because those with control over the mechanics of production and circulation were generally white, middle-class men, the structuring of jazz history in the 1950s occurred through white masculine expressions of intellectual authority and aesthetic capitalism.[78] Most of the first LPs purporting to tell the history of jazz were made by white recordmen ardently dedicated to early jazz. They included blues women such as Ma Rainey and Bessie Smith in their histories, but only as a celebrated origin point that eventually gave rise to the male-dominated world of instrumental jazz.[79] The restricted inclusion of women jazz musicians on LP had long-ranging consequences for how the dominant jazz discourse—what Sherrie Tucker describes as a story of "great men, sudden stylistic changes, [and] colorful anecdotes about eccentric individuals"—would travel through the early LP era and into the future.[80] The aural remnants of this gendered practice of history making can, for example, be heard on the *Smithsonian Collection of Classic Jazz*

(1973), inside the numerous CD-reissue packages of the 1990s, in the metadata of streaming platforms, and within the musical information on Wikipedia and other born-digital platforms.[81] As others have argued, the jazz history created through commercial record making is only one version of jazz history that exists.[82] Nevertheless, records remain a powerful force in how they deeply encode certain historical values, narratives, and possibilities into jazz culture.

The specific type of historiographical refashioning that occurs through record making can usefully be described as remediation. In their widely cited work on the subject, Jay David Bolter and Richard Grusin define *remediation* as the "representation of one medium in another." Examples include digital images of fifteenth-century manuscripts, music videos, video games based on movies (some inspired by books), and nineteenth-century painted photographs. Bolter and Grusin argue that new media always present themselves as improved versions of what came before even as they absorb and reshape the conventions, forms, and logics of older media. In other words, media never operate in isolation and always function culturally, socially, and historically.[83]

Consider the very first LPs, issued in 1948. The first entry in Columbia's 10-inch pop album catalog, *The Voice of Frank Sinatra* (CL 6001), was a direct repackaging of a four-disc album originally issued on 78 rpm in March 1946. Columbia's first LP in its Masterworks catalog (ML 4001) featured a 1945 recording of Mendelssohn's Concerto in E Minor for Violin and Orchestra.[84] When Prestige and Blue Note Records began regularly producing LPs in 1951, both firms employed the same tactics. Prestige's first LP (PRLP 101) featured recordings by Lee Konitz and Lennie Tristano that originated in 1949 and first circulated on four separately issued 78-rpm records.[85] One of Blue Note's first LPs, *Mellow the Mood* (BL 5001), was a compilation of recordings made in 1941, 1944, 1945, and 1946.[86] As back-catalog assemblages, the first LPs reveal a strategy of remediation happening across the industry.

In jazz parlance, records that embed older recordings into newer media are known as reissues. As remediations by another name, reissues exist in relation to previous media of the recording industry. After all, the LP's very creation was contingent on the cultural logic of the 78-rpm record: listeners' belief in recordings as faithful representations, the operational logistics of disc playback technology, the economic structures of record buying and collecting, consumer interest in recorded music, and assumptions by producers about who those consumers were and how to market to them.[87]

Thus, remediation happens through a combination of technical and cultural mechanisms. The reinscription methods involved in moving musical sounds from one format onto another are a technical matter. However, the decisions made during this process result from particular beliefs and assumptions that industry professionals hold about recorded sound, the contents of their back catalog, and their consumers.

I use *remediation* to describe a technological process with human agency at its center. Racial and gender ideologies helped determine how that agency came to be expressed. Consider how record producers, journalists, musicians, and other professionals during the early LP era consciously and consistently framed jazz's development in relation to itself.[88] Inchoate liner notes of the early 1950s began to document the many particularities of a recording session and events leading up to it. It is no small coincidence that writers such as Marshall Stearns, André Hodeir, Martin Williams, and Leonard Feather published some of the first robustly researched jazz-history books around this time as well.[89] Although many of these authors describe the music as a foundational creation of Black America, their expertise rested on a form of white intellectual authority that had been passed down from previous generations of male writers, researchers, and critics. Such an orientation to the foundational narrative of jazz further calcified a gendered version of jazz history that—to adopt Eric Porter's phraseology—largely celebrates jazz artistry "as the province of men."[90]

The movement toward explicit historical documentation on the records themselves developed slowly and in different ways across the industry. Records became one of the primary locations in which this historiographical disruption materialized.[91] For example, Columbia's first 12-inch jazz record, from 1950, made Benny Goodman's famed 1938 Carnegie Hall concert available on record for the first time.[92] Bolstered by the record's success, George Avakian then repackaged the celebrated but out-of-print recordings of Louis Armstrong, Bessie Smith, and Bix Beiderbecke into multiple-volume sets of 12-inch LPs. *The Louis Armstrong Story*, *The Bessie Smith Story*, and *The Bix Beiderbecke Story* first shipped in late 1951 and early 1952.[93] A few years later, Riverside Records launched its 10-inch Jazz Archives Series (RLP 1000), soon followed by a 12-inch series with the same name (RLP 12-100). Both series included remediated recordings, a ten-volume "history of classic jazz," as well as newly conceived oral histories.[94] For example, *Coleman Hawkins: A Documentary* (RLP 12-117/118) featured spoken recollections by Hawkins rather than musical performances. "This is a new kind of jazz record album," the liner notes proclaim. "*It is as if Coleman Hawkins were sitting in your living room*" (emphasis in original). The promotional material further states the general purpose of the Jazz Archives Series: to offer "12-inch LP reissues of classic early recordings reprocessed and revitalized by the finest of modern audio-engineering techniques."[95] Like other LPs at the time, this release emphasized a kind of historical authenticity made possible only by technological advances in recording and playback fidelity.[96]

From such particulars, a general observation arises: the increased circulation of records via remediation and other record-making practices created a public archive of jazz history on record. Like media, publics are historically specific and multiple. And a public archive can be created only through the ways in which the data of culture continuously circulate. Hegemonic views of race and gender were a consequential mechanism in the creation of jazz's public archive, especially given the prevailing influence of whiteness and maleness on the means of production within the record industry and on the creation of discourse in the jazz press.[97] Even as the LP produced new knowledge structures about the music's history, long-held social beliefs and cultural practices continued to dictate how this newly refigured public memory came to be. The limited inclusion of women on the earliest LPs is thus part of a much longer trajectory of denial and masculine control built into the social structures of the jazz business.[98] Throughout the decade, record companies increasingly promoted their LPs as an unquestionable means of encountering the past through sound. The explanatory material within liner notes and other promotional material surfaced in order to contextualize how and why that sound mattered. That is, the introduction of the LP foregrounded a sonic rhetoric of jazz history always already in circulation.[99]

Contents and Containers

At the Vanguard of Vinyl understands the increased mediation of musical time, the modifications and convergence in format, the remediation of past performance, and the continued expressions of jazz Afro-modernisms as part of the same cultural mechanism and imbricated practice of record making. Throughout the book, I argue that LPs, and records more generally, are mutually influenced by and productive of social value based on historically specific notions of technology, inscription, listening, and difference. To make this argument, I focus on one kind of Black political aurality expressed during a moment of enormous change to the existing commercial infrastructures of record making. These infrastructures supported a multistep process that included performance and recording; audio postproduction, including editing, overdubbing, mixing, and mastering; navigating the legal structures around intellectual property and manufacturing supply chains; marketing and distribution; and consumption through broadcast media, point-to-point sale, and the creation of critical discourse. Record making was often nonlinear—marketing, manufacturing, and legalities often influenced choices made in the recording studio (and vice versa). As such, there are many ways to approach the advent of the LP. In both my method and approach to analysis, I emphasize sound with a belief that the cultural history *of the LP* is the sonic history *on the LP*.[100]

My focus on sound is also meant to unsettle the written archive that documents this era of record making. One of the largest challenges facing any scholarly investigation of this subject is that musicians at this time, including those who received regular press attention, were seldom asked about record making as an aspect of their artistic practice or asked to comment on the studio as a political space.[101] Although specific commentary rarely appeared in print, musicians who did speak openly showed a nuanced understanding of the racial and economic dynamics in the studio. In contrast, white record producers and record-label owners have always been given opportunities to discuss, write, and boast about their record-making accomplishments, especially as their everyday work in the 1950s increased in historical value during the subsequent decades. Their recollections, often taken at face value, remain a dominant presence as a result. With this project, I ask the sounds on record to tell a story about how the advent of the LP altered the various ways that jazz records functioned as social and semiotic objects. Attending to sound in this way becomes a means and method of listening to the jazz archive and a way to respond to the uneven discursive evidence that continues to circulate.

In my exploration of record making across a diverse network of musicians and industry professionals in the 1950s, I focus on records that give me access to particular sites and practices of record making as they change through the decade. In choosing my materials, I strove to capture a diversity of musical styles, record labels, techniques of record production, and approaches to cultural politics. In many ways this multiplicity is the argument. I do not seek a complete history of jazz on LP. If, as I assert, singular records cannot be disentangled from the media and cultural infrastructures from which they materialize, then other forms of historical listening and storytelling are always present.

My six chapters unfold chronologically between the LP's introduction in 1948 and the normalization of stereophonic playback in 1959.[102] These chapters exist in pairs, grouped by what I see as the three stages of the jazz LP in the 1950s: experimentation, standardization, and arrival. Part I (chapters 1 and 2) explores the earliest jazz LPs—roughly from 1948 to 1955—before and during the asymmetrical transition to the 12-inch format. During this period of experimentation, jazz occupied an ever-shifting position within the racial, economic, and cultural landscape of the record industry despite remaining a relatively inconsequential market category. Both chapters concentrate intently on commercial infrastructures, offering a view of the industry through the circulation of a single song (chapter 1) and the proliferation of jazz-focused record labels (chapter 2). I ask what it meant for Black performance to newly circulate on LP during a time of limited agency for Black cultural producers within the white-owned record industry.

Chapter 1 focuses on various renditions of "The Huckle-Buck," the top-selling R&B hit of 1949. The song's movement through the record industry occurred in tandem with the proliferation of the LP as a medium for popular music. During this period of growth, jazz became the only music played by Black musicians to appear on LP, despite having a comparatively small market share. As jazz moved into a more central position with adult listeners between 1952 and 1955, LPs began to circulate racially coded language about the social and economic value of jazz. I assert that the repackaging of Black artistry onto a new, prestige format is best understood as a contemporaneous form of cultural repackaging as well. My chronological account of the early jazz LP outlines one crucial way that jazz further decoupled commercially from other forms of Black popular music.

As the B side of part I, chapter 2 further investigates the jazz LP at its moment of newness through the activities of a single independent label, Prestige Records, and its owner, Bob Weinstock. Once again, I attend to the commercial aspects of record making but focus on the sounds within Prestige's catalog, listening in detail to the musical mistakes and miscues that circulated on the label's earliest LPs. Notions of white male control built into the segregational logic of the record business directed Weinstock's record-making practices, especially his desire to document jazz history by capturing such moments of informality on record. I listen at the edges of performance for the ways in which alternate histories continually emerge.

Part II (chapters 3 and 4) examines the standardization of the 12-inch LP in the mid-1950s, when the Black politics of jazz began to occupy a more central position in the record industry and in mainstream US culture more broadly. I use the movement of jazz through the festival grounds at Newport (chapter 3) and the US State Department (chapter 4) to explore the sonic and social mediation of Black musical expression in spaces where white cultural producers held the power. The changing relationship between jazz musicians and the industry built around their audiovisual representations provides an opportunity to analyze how Black artists increasingly found new avenues of cultural expression through multiracial collaborations. Throughout this section I approach the sound of jazz LPs historically as much as I approach this history sonically.

The subject of chapter 3 is Duke Ellington's celebrated recording from the 1956 Newport Jazz Festival and the invasive yet reparative postproduction of Columbia producer George Avakian. In telling this history, I trace how recording jazz in spaces of elite white culture and the expanded possibilities of postproduction contributed to the growth of a white, mainstream audience in the mid-1950s. Making jazz history on record necessitated a collaboration among artists, festival organizers, sound engineers, and producers, all differently invested in the cultural politics that made jazz's circulation possible. This chapter situates such mediation within theoretical discussions of "liveness" on record in order to lay the groundwork for understanding the wider stakes of audio production choices in the early LP era.

During the same year as Ellington's Newport success, trumpeter Dizzy Gillespie became the first jazz musician to participate in the State Department's Cultural Presentations program, a highly public aspect of the US government's Cold War propaganda efforts abroad. Seeking to capitalize on this historic moment, Gillespie's record label issued two LPs featuring his ambassadorial ensemble: *World Statesman* (1956) and *Dizzy in Greece* (1957). Chapter 4 investigates the ways in which both records sit at the contested intersection of jazz, the struggle for racial equality, and international Cold War politics. I focus on the collaboration of Gillespie (music), Marshall Stearns (liner notes), and Norman Granz (label owner) as recordmen who explored how jazz record making could use the sounds of Black performance to make a political argument.

The final part (chapters 5 and 6) examines two contrasting strategies of Black record making in 1959, at the cusp of stereophonic sound and at a time when the LP's adoption was no longer in question. I interrogate how jazz musicians approached the nightclub (chapter 5) and the recording studio (chapter 6) as interconnected sites of musical labor and Black cultural work. Taken together, these chapters also offer alternative perspectives on the stages of experimentation and standardization found in the previous chapters, positioning the stories of individual musicians (more prevalent in the later chapters) within the systems in which they operated (more prevalent in the first chapters). Through these individuals I consider the economies of attention that surround jazz performance and how the entrenched systems of whiteness within those economies enabled certain artistic pathways for Black men and not others.

Chapter 5 focuses on Cannonball Adderley's 1959 hit record, *Quintet in San Francisco*. Adderley's onstage announcements, pedagogical introductions, and audible interactions with the audience became some of the record's most-defining characteristics, helping him to expand his popularity beyond a core jazz listenership. I outline how Adderley's LP materialized out of a broader shift by independent labels in the mid-1950s to record hard-bop musicians on location at jazz nightclubs. Placed within this historical trajectory of live recording, I explore how Adderley's joyful record making foregrounded a form of sonic Black sociality and self-fashioned jazz masculinity that fit collaboratively within existing structures of the music business. A close listen to *Quintet in San Francisco* reveals how Adderley's jazz commercialism worked simultaneously as an expression of Black modernity.

My final chapter explores how Charles Mingus integrated studio production into his musical practices during the 1950s. I begin and end with *Mingus Ah Um*, his 1959 LP that contains at least seventeen splices that cut over eleven minutes from the initial duration of the performances. Listening through the splice exposes Mingus's larger network of musical entrepreneurs who actively used the process of making records to disrupt how the jazz industry conventionally valued Black labor and the artistry of Black jazzmen. Mingus reimagined the economics and cultural politics of jazz through his concern for sound on record, where control over that sound also meant control over the form, content, and representation of his music. I use activities that appear technological—splicing and overdubbing—to define Mingus's record making as a cultural practice that flows through differently situated individuals working in collaboration.

In total, *At the Vanguard of Vinyl* interrogates moments of performance, the mechanical inscription of those moments, and the mediating processes involved in making them into commercial records. My investigation relies on many different kinds of records, many of which contain the same music but differ significantly in their format, packaging, visual design, mastering processes, or other production techniques.[103] To avoid clutter, I include only the artist, record title, and date in the text, placing the other details in the book's discography. Each chapter also ends with a "playlist" that focuses on a particular aspect of record making explored within that chapter. These playlists connect seemingly disparate records through contemporaneous trends in record making and the self-referential network of cultural practices that surrounded them. Each addendum is analytically compiled though certainly never complete.

As will become clear, jazz records are inherently contradictory. They enable spontaneous moments of musical improvisation to be listened to again and again—as a result, the ephemerality of musical creation circulates widely. The tangled balance between repeatability and spontaneity is not a naturally occurring phenomenon but rather a historically situated negotiation over sonic media as a form of communication. As commercial objects made for mass consumption, records are the product of social structures and cultural schemas that surround the business and artistic creation of music making. Ideological underpinnings about sound, technology, race, gender, and performance guide the decisions of record makers. The eventual outcome often changes drastically from record label to record label, producer to producer, and musician to musician. Yet it is also a historical reality that the processes of record making have become naturalized. Jazz records are, from this view, a technology of erasure as much as they are a technology of sound and circulation. *At the Vanguard of Vinyl* tells the story of how these historical shifts happened.

Playlist: Experiments in Jazz Record Making, 1929–1957

Each record in this playlist is an experiment in the presentation of jazz on record, especially in how best to capture and format lengthy performances, compositions, and historical narratives. Together, these records depict the variety of approaches to record making before, during, and after the introduction of the LP. (Unless otherwise noted, recordings are LPs.)

Benny Goodman. *The Famous 1938 Carnegie Hall Jazz Concert*. Columbia Masterworks, 1950.
Benny Goodman. *Sing, Sing, Sing*. 78 rpm. RCA Victor, 1937.

Bessie Smith. *The Bessie Smith Story, vols. 1–4*. Columbia, 1951.
Bix Beiderbecke. *The Bix Beiderbecke Story, vols. 1–3*. Columbia, 1951.
Buck Clayton. *The Huckle-Buck and Robbins' Nest: A Buck Clayton Jam Session*. Columbia, 1954.
Buck Clayton. *Jumpin' at the Woodside*. Columbia, 1954.
Dexter Gordon. *The Chase, parts 1–2*. 78 rpm. Dial, 1947.
Dizzy Gillespie, Charles Mingus, Charlie Parker, Bud Powell, and Max Roach. *The Quintet: Jazz at Massey Hall*. Debut, 1956.
Duke Ellington. *Diminuendo in Blue/Crescendo in Blue*. 78 rpm. Brunswick, 1938.
Duke Ellington. *Ellington at Newport*. Columbia, 1956.
Duke Ellington. *Masterpieces by Ellington*. Columbia Masterworks, 1951.
Duke Ellington. *Reminiscing in Tempo, parts 1–4*. 78 rpm. Brunswick, 1935.
Duke Ellington. *Tiger Rag*. 78 rpm. Brunswick, 1929.
Edward R. Murrow and Fred W. Friendly. *I Can Hear It Now . . . vol. 1*. Columbia Masterworks, 1949.
Frank Sinatra. *The Voice of Frank Sinatra*. Columbia, 1948.
Lennie Tristano. *Lennie Tristano*. Atlantic, 1955.
Lennie Tristano and Lee Konitz. *Lennie Tristano and Lee Konitz*. Prestige, 1951.
Louis Armstrong. *Ambassador Satch*. Columbia, 1956.
Louis Armstrong. *The Louis Armstrong Story, vols. 1–4*. Columbia, 1951.
Miles Davis. *Miles Davis and the Modern Jazz Giants*. 16⅔ rpm. Prestige, 1957.
Tommy Dorsey and Jimmy Dorsey. *Honeysuckle Rose, parts 1–2*. 78 rpm. Decca, 1934.
Various. *Jam Session at Commodore, no. 3: A Good Man Is Hard to Find*. 78 rpm. Commodore, 1940.
Various. *Mellow the Mood*. Blue Note, 1951.
Various. *Norman Granz' Jazz at the Philharmonic, vol. 8*. 78 rpm. Mercury, 1948.
Various. *The Riverside History of Classic Jazz, vols. 1–10*. Riverside, ca. 1955.
Woody Herman. *Sequence in Jazz*. 78 rpm. Columbia, 1949.

1

DO THE HUCKLE-BUCK

Jazz and the Emergent LP,
1949–1955

The history of the early jazz LP reveals the shifting position of jazz within the racial, economic, and cultural logics of the 1950s record industry. Jazz became, as this chapter asserts, the only music played by and associated with Black performers to appear with regularity on LP. The record industry's repackaging of Black artistry onto a new, prestige format initially designed for classical music and a white adult audience amounted to a contemporaneous form of cultural repackaging as well. At the same time that jazz began to occupy a more central position with adult consumers in the mid-1950s, jazz LPs began to circulate information about the music and its history, actively constructing a system of cultural value based around prevailing notions of Blackness.

This chapter retells the history of jazz between 1949 and 1955 as a history of new musical media and new media infrastructures. I focus on several renditions of "The Huckle-Buck," 1949's largest rhythm-and-blues (R&B) hit, which originated with Paul Williams but circulated widely through the record marketplace during a moment of significant transition. The song's success as an early crossover has made it a notable part of popular-music history. Yet the song is hardly an afterthought in jazz historiography, even though several jazz musicians recorded it and half the melody was derived from Charlie Parker's "Now's the Time." Such interconnections make "The Huckle-Buck" an ideal way to explore the jazz LP during its moment of newness and proliferation. Three performances from three different years will help set the scene.

TRACK 1: PAUL WILLIAMS, 1949

"HEY! Not now! I'll tell you when!" Paul Williams ends "The Huckle-Buck" with this spoken instruction to the band that also serves to invite the audience to keep dancing (2:43).[1] The voice, presumably Williams's, urges his band to continue with the catchy melodic fragment derived from Parker's oscillating bebop blues. The typical mixture of arranged ensemble, improvised solos, and several repetitions of the two-part melody gives the song musical variation while retaining a clear sense of direction.

"The Huckle-Buck" was an enormous hit for Savoy Records. By the end of 1949, Williams's record ranked first in both retail sales and jukebox plays by a sizable margin.[2] Even as numerous covers and copies began to simultaneously travel along Black, mainstream, and country musical streams, jazz functioned as a through line. Paul Williams idolized Johnny Hodges and Benny Carter and, like many saxophonists, including Parker, first entered into the music business by touring with big bands.[3] The song's composer, Andy Gibson, also had a history with Duke Ellington (as a copyist), McKinney's Cotton Pickers (as a trumpeter), and Charlie Barnet (as an arranger), and this background helps explain the interpolation of Parker's oscillating bebop blues into "The Huckle-Buck."[4] Furthermore, many of the artists who covered the song had unambiguous associations with jazz even as they moved skillfully among the various parts of the music industry. Pearl Bailey recorded the song with Hot Lips Page, and Lionel Hampton's version featured Betty Carter. Andy Kirk, Cab Calloway, and Cozy Cole placed their own jazz-informed styles within the context of Black commercial music. The bands of Tommy Dorsey, Benny Goodman, and Frank Sinatra were the product of big-band swing, which filtered musical elements of Black popular culture through the commercial music industry.[5]

In his call for an inclusive definition of the term *jazz*, David Ake argues that the music known as jazz has been a "site of multiple, even contradictory, identities," including commercial ones, since its beginnings.[6] The economic dynamics that Ake refers to were clearly at play during the late 1940s, when the transition from swing to bop caused jazz's separation from the overtly commercial side of the entertainment business.[7] The music's ambiguous and ever-changing definition nevertheless remained hotly debated in trade magazines such as *Down Beat* and *Metronome*.[8] For musicians, however, crossing among jazz, swing, R&B, and pop was often a matter of professional success—most went wherever there was work. The same was true for record labels, which increasingly moved to diversify their catalogs in the 1950s to compete in a cutthroat business. Savoy Records, which first issued "The Huckle-Buck," was already active in both the R&B and jazz markets before starting the classical subsidiary Regent in October 1949.[9] Modern, Specialty, and Aladdin recorded every subgenre of Black music—especially R&B, gospel, and jazz—and King remained successfully active in R&B as well as country and western. By the end of the 1940s, most major labels were already invested in popular Black artists: Louis Jordan, Ella Fitzgerald, and Louis Armstrong all recorded for Decca, Nat King Cole for Capitol, and Dinah Washington for Mercury.[10] Within the industry, economic concerns often superseded genre definitions that were based solely on musical sound. Jazz was only one style among many. Not all musical genres would circulate on LP.

TRACK 2: LOUIS ARMSTRONG, 1951

Louis Armstrong and the All Stars performed "The Huckle-Buck" during a concert in Pasadena, California, on January 30, 1951. The song had been in the band's repertoire for well more than a year, since August 1949, when they first inserted its melody during their rendition of "C-Jam Blues."[11] Armstrong's jazz adaptation could be a cross-genre allusion resulting from the song's continued popularity—or perhaps it was the influence of the band's new drummer, Cozy Cole, who had recently recorded it for Decca.[12] Either way, the song eventually became a feature for Velma Middleton, who sang and danced, to the Pasadena audience's audible enjoyment.

Decca did not issue Armstrong's rendition until August 1952, on *Satchmo at Pasadena*, an LP that marked a moment of changing possibilities. Armstrong's musical performance became one of the first concerts recorded with the LP format specifically in mind.[13] By the end of 1952, there were hundreds of jazz LPs, diverse in terms of musical styles and market positioning. Major and independent labels alike mostly issued material from their respective back catalogs, although some new recordings appeared cross-issued on 78 rpm, which continued to be the dominant format. Such activity reveals a shift in conceptions of musical labor and its value. As labels began to recognize the economic worth of past recordings, artists such as Armstrong began to perform accompanied by their musical pasts, which were newly recirculating on LP. Here and elsewhere, the conditions of jazz performance were in productive tension with the infrastructures of the music industry.

TRACK 3: BUCK CLAYTON, 1953

Buck Clayton recorded "The Huckle-Buck" in December 1953 at Columbia's 30th Street studios in New York City. In Clayton's hands the song became a relaxed blues over sixty-five choruses in true Kansas City–swing style—indeed, many of the musicians could list Count Basie as a former employer. The notion of repetition with a difference continually unfolds through the shuffling of personnel and the intermittent return of the melody. The interplay between soloist and rhythm section drives everything, creating a cohesive balance. This twenty-minute rendition extended well beyond nearly every other jazz studio recording made to date, on Columbia or any other label.[14]

Columbia issued "The Huckle-Buck" in about April 1954 as the A side of a 12-inch LP titled *The Huckle-Buck and Robbins' Nest: A Buck Clayton Jam Session*. The record was part of the label's broader strategy to expand its jazz offerings on LP geared toward its white, middle-class audience. Although jazz had always been part of Columbia's catalog, it was not until 1953 that the label began recording jazz at this scale. It was no coincidence that unit sales for jazz records had increased 55 percent industry-wide between 1953 and 1954.[15] Clayton's LP thus signals a change in approach: jazz recordings were not simply on LP but were specifically made for it. Jazz performance and record making exist in the same commercial ecosystem.

The performative multiplicity of the "The Huckle-Buck" across labels and formats happened in tandem with the standardization and wide-scale adoption of the LP as the dominant format for jazz and popular music. Even though jazz continued to represent a relatively small market share compared to other forms of popular music, Black or white, the genre came to be overrepresented on the LP format. This new musical medium—and the recording, manufacturing, distribution, and marketing infrastructures that supported it—would also circulate racially coded language aimed at white audiences about jazz's inherent cultural value. This chapter scrutinizes this assertion, using the circulation history of "The Huckle-Buck" to decipher how the jazz LP emerged from the segregational logic on which the record industry had always operated.[16] I argue that jazz in the 1950s should be understood through its material history as well as its well-documented musical one.

The discographical minutiae presented in this chapter point to broader trends about race and the music industry during the early LP era. I operate along two registers. First, I trace "The Huckle-Buck" as it moved from an R&B hit into the white mainstream, outlining how economic segregation functioned within the record industry in the late 1940s. This commercial trajectory is typically—and I believe mistakenly—not part of conventional jazz narratives, even though it became an essential factor in the jazz LP's emergence. Next, I provide a broader overview of the changing economic conditions of the music industry between 1949 and 1955, using the proliferation of different playback formats as evidence of commercial instability. Taken together, this view of the industry reveals 1955 to be a significant hinge point in jazz history that often gets overlooked because of the overwhelming focus on individual artists and the developments of musical style.[17] I outline how the industry-wide adoption of the 12-inch LP for all popular music led to an exponential investment in jazz by many record labels.

The remainder of the chapter returns to "The Huckle-Buck" in order to give a more detailed and chronological account of the early jazz LP. From my discussion of recordings by Louis Armstrong, Buck Clayton, and Frank Sinatra, two other conclusions emerge. First, the overreliance on reissued recordings during this period exposes both a hedge against commercial unpredictability and a changing approach toward musical labor. More precisely, the business of storing Black sonic labor for long-term profits extended the segregational logic of the industry outlined earlier in the chapter. Second, the move to record music specifically for the LP further decoupled jazz from other forms of Black popular music, which circulated almost exclusively on the singles market. The repackaging of jazz onto a new format was not simply a technological experiment but also an experiment in what it meant to sell Black music as a form of artful expression.

My analysis of "The Huckle-Buck" explores how the hardware of circulation encodes assumptions about race, class, and gender, arguing (once again) that recording format is an under-recognized force in jazz history. By focusing on the material products instead of critical reception or musical style, I aim to reframe notions of cultural value in relation to commercial systems and forms of corporate attention. LPs were not only expensive to produce but also required an audience that could afford both records and playback equipment. The broad network of human actors within these economic systems had to make numerous decisions about how best to expand their current rosters of musical talent, manage their back catalog, and take advantage of industry-wide market trends in order to grow their audience. Such decisions could not be made lightly. As such, label output is one of the clearest indications of jazz's position in the much larger constellation of the 1950s music industry because it directly reflects how decision makers at these companies employed their limited resources. In telling the early history of LP through a single song, it becomes clear that the history of jazz is never just about the music.

The Pre-LP Industry Logics of the Late 1940s

Propelled by its accompanying dance craze, Williams's recording of "The Huckle-Buck" spent fourteen weeks at the top of the *Billboard* R&B charts, first reaching the number-one position in March 1949. The record's success placed the saxophonist in second place among the year's top R&B artists, finishing behind Amos Milburn but ahead of Charles Brown, Louis Jordan, Bull Moose Jackson, the Orioles, and Wynonie Harris.[18] As was typical for hit records, many adaptations soon hit the record stores, jukeboxes, and radio waves.[19] Between January and July 1949, no fewer than fifteen separate versions of "The Huckle-Buck" flooded divergent segments of the market (see table 1.1). Consider the song's pervasiveness in the April 30, 1949, issue of *Billboard*: three recordings (by Williams, Roy Milton, and Lucky Millinder) appeared in the best-selling retail and most-played jukebox categories on the "race" charts; a quarter-page advertisement for Savoy publicized Williams's record ("Despite the many imitations . . . it's still #1 coast to coast"); an RCA Victor ad announced Tommy Dorsey's rendition; and the reviews page included commentary on Big Sis Andrews and on Bob Marshall with Cozy Cole.[20]

Both the originals and the covers sold well. By the end of the year, Roy Milton's rendition (the first with lyrics) ranked nineteenth in R&B sales; Dorsey's ranked twenty-ninth in retail sales for popular records over the same period.[21] Lucky Millinder's "D'Natural Blues," the same song with a different name, reached number twenty-five in retail sales and number twenty-four in jukebox plays.[22] Likewise, by December 1949, Pearl Bailey's rendition with Hot Lips Page was approaching one million in sales.[23] Even the country and western (C&W) derivation, recorded by the Delmore Brothers as "Blues Stay Away from Me," finished seventeenth and twenty-first in the retail and jukebox categories, respectively, for folk records.[24]

"The Huckle-Buck" began with popular R&B recordings, crossed over with white popular-music stars, and then continued to percolate across the industry. This rapid movement across markets was part of a larger trend in the postwar music industry, where songs popularized by Black artists regularly traveled across the color line, even while the artists themselves could not.[25] The economic effects of racial segregation within the record industry were not new, of course. For example, the unparalleled success of Mamie Smith's "Crazy Blues" (1920) led to the formation of a race-based market segmentation in the 1920s which assumed that musical taste mapped directly onto consumer racial identity. Despite the nationalized proliferation of these "race records," historian Karl Hagstrom Miller argues, most labels refused to allow Black artists to record music outside a narrowly defined category of "race" music. Such commercial decisions continued to perpetuate racist stereotypes that had clear roots in minstrelsy.[26] When in 1921 Harry H. Pace founded Black Swan, the first major Black-owned record company, he constantly had to confront overtly hostile individuals and navigate many different forms of structural racism built into US society as a whole.[27] The structural inequities of the US culture industry continued to influence how artists navigated the record industry's collapse during the Great Depression, the influx of radio as a medium of mass communication, the nationwide rise of swing, shellac rationing during World War II, and labor conditions

Table 1.1. Versions of "The Huckle-Buck" issued in 1949 (10-inch 78-rpm records)

	Artist	Published title	
1st wave	Paul "Hucklebuck" Williams	The Huckle-Buck	
	Lucky Millinder	D' Natural Blues	
	Roy Milton	The Huckle-Buck	
2nd wave	Bob Marshall with Cozy Cole Orchestra	The Huckle-Buck	
	Big Sis Andrews and Her Huckle-Busters	The Huckle-Buck	
	The Pig Footers	The Hucklebuck	
	Jimmie Preston and His Prestonians	Hucklebuck Daddy	
3rd wave	Tommy Dorsey	The Huckle-Buck	
	Benny Goodman	The Huckle-Buck	
	Frank Sinatra	The Huckle Buck	
4th wave	Cab Calloway	The Hucklebuck	
	Delmore Brothers	Blues Stay Away from Me	
	Lionel Hampton Orchestra	The Huckle-Buck	
	Andy Kirk	The Huckle-Buck	
	Tito Burns	The Huckle-Buck	
	Pearl Bailey, Hot Lips Page	The Huckle-Buck	

[Source] Data compiled from label and artist discographies, trade magazines, secondary sources, and (when necessary) online photos of the actual labels. Issue dates are imprecise, but the estimates rely on Daniels, *American 45 and 78 RPM Record Dating Guide*, cross-checked with trade reports when possible. The slashes indicate late in the first month or early in the second.

Note: Of these recordings, Dorsey's version appears to be the only one concurrently cross-issued on 45 rpm (Vic 47-3028). The Big Sis Andrews disc is sometimes listed as

Recording date	Label	Issue no.	Issued (1949)
12/15/1948	Savoy	683	January/February
1/3/1949	RCA Victor	20-3351	January/February
2/22/1949	Specialty	328	March/April
3/2/1949	Decca	48099	April
3/2/1949	Capitol	57-70000	March
early 1949	Mercury	8130	April
early 1949	Gotham	G 175	April
3/22/1949	RCA Victor	20-3427	April
3/31/1949	Capitol	57-576	April/May
4/10/1949	Columbia	38486	May
5/5/1949	Hi-Tone	135	June/July
5/6/1949	King	803	July
5/10/1949	Decca	24652	June
5/13/1949	Vocalion (Decca)	55009	June
6/7/1949	Decca UK	F.9193	June (approx.)
6/23/1949	Harmony (Columbia)	1049	July

issue number 700000y; my number matches the ads in *Billboard*. Recording dates for The Pig Footers and Jimmy Preston remain unclear, but several sources confirm the April 1949 issue date. "Blues Stay Away from Me," a country derivative that poached the "The Huckle-Buck" melody, hit #1 in jukebox plays and #2 in retail sales on the C&W charts in early 1950. See "Music Popularity Charts, Part VII: Folk (Country & Western)," *Billboard*, January 14, 1950, 34-35. The song's success would inspire many C&W adaptations, not listed here. For further analysis, including King's unusual C&W crossover strategy, see Birnbaum, *Before Elvis*, 33-34, 223.

leading to recording bans in the 1940s. The record business would significantly grow during the postwar era, propelled by the musical ingenuity of Black performers and the popularity of Black artists. As an early crossover record, "The Huckle-Buck" sits at the intersection between calcified cultural logics and new commercial possibilities.

It is helpful to think of "The Huckle-Buck" and its movement through the music industry as four successive waves of covers and crossovers. The initial wave popularized the song, doing so through independent R&B labels: Williams on Savoy and Milton's vocal addition on Specialty. (Millinder, the song's originator, might be considered as first wave as well, even though he recorded with a major label.) The second wave includes R&B covers on major or semi-major labels: Bob Marshall with Cozy Cole (Decca), Big Sis Andrews (Capitol), and the Pig Footers (Mercury). With the third wave, "The Huckle-Buck" crossed over with white popular artists on major labels. Tommy Dorsey, Benny Goodman, and Frank Sinatra each recorded it in the commercial swing style that remained dominant. These versions sold well and rated well with disc jockeys.[28] The final wave reestablished the song in the R&B market. By the end of June 1949, Lionel Hampton, Andy Kirk, Cab Calloway, and Pearl Bailey (with Hot Lips Page) had all recorded their versions for a mixture of indies, majors, and budget subsidiaries. In September of that year, *Billboard* characterized the song as having a "charmed life" with "renewing vitality" from record to record.[29]

A half-page advertisement for United Music Corporation, the publisher of "The Huckle-Buck," illuminates how race operated as a key component in the record-making marketplace in the late 1940s (see figure 1.1).[30] Appearing in the April 30, 1949, issue of *Billboard*, the ad's largest element is, unsurprisingly, the name of the song. All the artists that had recorded the song up to that point (through wave three) appear in the bottom half. Tellingly, the design visually segregates the five Black R&B artists from the three white popular artists with a bordered text box and a large arrow: "And NOW! 3 New Ace Recordings that'll launch this tune in the 'pop' field." The economic realities of the music business clearly underpin this ad because the popular field had the greatest revenue potential.[31] The language of arrival ("NOW!") and ascendance ("launch") was thus a statement of cultural value and capital as much as it was a statement about the prosperity of the publishing company that paid for the advertising space. The overall design clearly accentuates a trajectory from Black artists toward white ones.

Such market segregation was not, of course, limited to "The Huckle-Buck" but was, rather, hardwired into the record business, as it was across most

Figure 1.1. United Music Corporation advertisement. From *Billboard*, April 30, 1949, 35.

industries within the United States. Black musicians belonged to different unions, performed on different radio stations, and often appeared in different venues across the country.[32] They also recorded on different labels or subsidiaries specifically designated and advertised as "race records," which in turn had different infrastructures for distribution: radio formats targeting Black audiences, jukeboxes placed in Black community spaces, and record stores within Black neighborhoods.[33] Industry trade magazines similarly divided their coverage using the "race" genre marker. In June 1949, precisely as "The Huckle-Buck" ripped through the industry, *Billboard* decided to rename its "race" category, adopting the term *rhythm and blues* (R&B) instead. As musicologist Andrew Flory describes, R&B continued to signify the race of the performer and the audience rather than the musical style—the actual music was incredibly diverse, with only a few overlapping characteristics. It was assumed that Black music was separate, made by and for Black people. As a result, few African Americans succeeded outside the race market, even as their musical sounds "crossed over."[34]

Seen this way, musical artists are only the most visible aspect of an otherwise enormous media infrastructure that surrounds them. After all, RCA Victor, Capitol, and Columbia recorded "The Huckle-Buck" multiple times for both popular and R&B markets. Such multiplicity allowed major labels to capitalize on popularity through an entire network of individuals involved in the record-making process.

In 1949 the song, not the record, determined the internal workings of this media infrastructure. Publishers generally had more power than individual labels because publishers controlled the exposure and promotion through broadcast media.[35] As the advertisement for United Music Corporation signifies, once a hit was recognized as potentially profitable, speed became essential: arrangements were written, royalty rights secured, recording sessions organized, masters made, labels printed, records pressed, marketing strategies enacted, and records distributed.[36] When Frank Sinatra went into Columbia's Hollywood studio on April 10, 1949, for example, he recorded just two tracks with no alternate takes: "The Huckle-Buck" and "It Happens Every Spring." Both appeared on the same 78-rpm record that began circulating the following month. As this example illustrates, major labels built their businesses to quickly coordinate the necessary musical, legal, technical, and marketing resources to earn profits across generic boundaries, even as the musicians remained segregated. Here as elsewhere, separate was never equal.

The LP's Rise: A Brief History of Format, 1949–1955

The repackaging of jazz on the LP in the 1950s hastened its decoupling from other forms of Black popular music, a process that had started in the previous decade. Propelled by the rising popularity of both radio and recordings, swing had widely increased the circulation of Black music in the 1940s, as David Brackett and others have argued.[37] After World War II, the shift to home entertainment and the rapid growth of independent record labels in the R&B field created a robust network of Black-oriented radio.[38] Black popular music under the R&B banner was poised to become the first Black cultural product to be supported by the defining feature of postwar America: mass consumerism. However, the rise of mass-marketed Black music occurred almost exclusively through the singles market. In contrast, jazz moved onto the LP, supported by a network of white male jazz enthusiasts turned record producers who sought to turn their musical knowledge into commercial profits.[39] A substantial ecosystem of both jazz-specific and prestige print media—especially publications with an affluent, white male readership—helped further propagate the music as a form of artful expression.[40] Not by coincidence, jazz moved into elite white spaces such as college campuses, festival grounds in wealthy cities, and diplomatic pathways of the US State Department. The value of jazz came to be measured in both sales and artistic merit. The LP was a perfect fit for this purpose.

Domestic musical entertainment at mid-century was a three-way contest among the piano, the radio, and the phonograph.[41] Recorded music was always a distant third until the early 1950s, when sales began to expand exponentially. Gross profits rose from $191 million in 1951 to over $500 million by the end of the decade, helped enormously by the rising popularity of the LP.[42] Between 1948 and 1957, unit sales for the LP went from 3.3 to 33.5 million (see table 1.2); by 1958, LPs accounted for 58 percent of industry profits (see table 1.3).[43] Despite this clear upward trajectory, these figures are actually deceiving because they do not account for the ever-present volatility of the industry. This section offers a view of this unpredictability by examining the numerous playback formats that came to market before 1955, yet always with an eye toward the emergence of the jazz LP. It is best to begin in 1949, just as "The Huckle-Buck" rippled through the record industry.

In July 1949, Paul Southard, vice president of merchandising at Columbia, reported that the volume of LP sales had increased steadily every month since October 1948.[44] (Recall that the LP came to market in August 1948.)

Table 1.2. LP unit sales, 1949–1956

Year	LP units sold
1949	3.3 million
1950	5.9
1952	9.2
1954	11.1
1956	33.5

[Source] Robert Shelton, "Happy Tunes on Cash Registers," *New York Times*, March 16, 1958, section 11, 14.

Note: These figures are estimates based on reports from the American Federation of Musicians and only include US sales. Although the actual unit sales were certainly greater, these numbers demonstrate the format's growth in popularity.

However, the optimism embedded within this report must be put into perspective. Despite the fanfare around the LP's announcement, most major trade publications did not make the format a point of focus. For example, it was not until June 1949 that *Billboard* began listing advance releases of LPs, a standard practice for all genres of 78 releases.[45] Moreover, when the *Schwann Long Playing Record Catalog* issued its first volume in October 1949, it listed only eleven LP-producing labels.[46]

By the end of 1949, Decca, Capitol, and Mercury had joined Columbia in issuing parts of their classical, popular, and Broadway catalogs on LP. The only major label to resist was RCA Victor. The firm chose instead to develop an alternative and intentionally incompatible vinylite system, the 45-rpm record, which was first made available to the public around March 1949.[47] RCA's refusal to adopt the LP and Columbia's counter-resistance to the 45 single set off an industry-wide depression in sales—this became known as the "war of the speeds."[48] The July 2, 1949, issue of *Cash Box* reported that "record distributors throughout the nation continued their current practice of 'wait and see' with regard to business conditions facing the entire phonograph recording industry." The article goes on: the "bulk of industry,

Table 1.3. Format unit sales and profits by industry percentage, 1958

Format	% Units sold	% Share of market
45	68.3	36.2
LP	24.4	58.0
EP	5.1	4.2
78	2.1	1.2

[Source] Robert Shelton, "Happy Tunes on Cash Registers," *New York Times*, March 16, 1958, section 11, 14.

sales execs, distributors, dealers and operators" all agree that three speeds is an "unhealthy condition."[49] Through most of the year, no record label manufactured records in all three formats; Capitol became first to do so in September 1949.[50] All told, record labels, equipment manufacturers, record shops, and consumers did not know where to put their resources.

In 1950 Columbia and RCA resolved their corporate warfare, ushering in wide-scale adoption of both 45 and LP formats. Even so, the 78-rpm record remained the dominant medium for some time. Figures for 1953 from the Recording Industry Association of America (RIAA) show that despite a downward trajectory overall, 78s still accounted for 66.5 percent of unit sales and 52 percent of retail sales value across the industry. With 122 million discs sold, 78s outsold all other formats combined by a factor of two to one (see table 1.4). In comparison, LPs represented only 5.5 percent of unit sales and 20 percent of retail sales value.[51] Regardless of the incremental trends seen in these numbers, wide-scale adoption of the LP was not a guarantee.

It is not surprising that some firms, especially RCA Victor, remained skeptical about the LP's future. On July 31, 1952, RCA introduced its extended play (EP) format as a direct challenge to the LP's growing popularity in the classical singles market. The EP had the same diameter (7 inches) and spindle hole (1.5 inches) as a 45 but with narrower grooves. As the "extended" moniker implies, these discs offered twice the capacity, about eight minutes

Table 1.4. Format unit and retail sales comparison, 1949–1953

SALES BY UNITS				
	78 rpm	%	45 rpm	%
1949	177,771,476	94.3	7,330,785	4.0
1950	145,628,476	79.2	32,498,926	17.6
1951	127,974,752	75.6	34,594,143	20.4
1952	126,331,410	71.8	40,272,792	23.0
1953	122,000,000	66.5	42,000,000	23.0
RETAIL SALES VALUE				
	78 rpm	%	45 rpm	%
1949	$132,544,665	88.0	$5,599,560	3.8
1950	102,987,611	68.1	23,957,588	16.0
1951	102,810,928	66.0	28,393,918	18.0
1952	98,055,527	60.0	35,152,420	21.4
1953	90,000,000	52.0	35,000,000	20.0

[Source] "RIAA Reports $205,000,000 Gross as All Time High for Record Industry," *Cash Box*, May 15, 1954, 16.

per side.[52] The EP did well, selling nine million units during its first year of production. About ten million LPs sold over the same period (see table 1.4). As a result, most labels began simultaneously issuing the same materials on both LP and EP.

The EP's potential for jazz and popular music became clear almost immediately. Shortly after RCA's national distribution campaign began, the firm announced that it would issue popular music on the format.[53] Jazz firms quickly followed. In February 1953, Good Time Jazz and Mercury both announced plans for a jazz EP line; Savoy and Pacific Jazz soon did the same.[54] Outlets like *Down Beat* began covering the EP with unmistakable interest.

45 rpm EP	%	33⅓ rpm	%	Total
		3,332,793	1.7	188,435,054
		5,909,958	3.2	184,037,360
		6,575,865	4	169,145,143
		9,171,173	5.2	175,775,375
9,000,000	5	10,000,000	5.5	183,000,000

45 rpm EP	%	33⅓ rpm	%	Total
		$12,457,405	8.2	$150,601,631
		24,095,312	15.9	151,040,513
		25,186,938	16	156,391,784
		30,568,333	18.6	163,776,290
$14,000,000	8	33,000,000	20	172,000,000

For example, the June 3, 1953, issue included several articles comparing EP and LP systems, including "The Future of EP Records" by Manie Sacks of RCA and "Our Trick, Your Treat, Says Columbia of LPs" by George Avakian of Columbia.[55] Although the EP's popularity would last only a few years (see the tables above), the format's short-lived ascendance points to the unsettled nature of the industry some five years after the LP's introduction.

Through the chaos, it became overwhelmingly clear that the future of jazz was on LP. One April 1954 article in *Billboard* noted that the "long-play record and its junior partner, extended play, have been found the ideal medium for jazz by practically all the major record manufactures and dozens of small independents."[56] To highlight this observation for jazz, the author described the "rarity" of R&B on either format. In the same magazine less than six weeks later, Bob Rolontz described the new sales trend for jazz in similar terms: "Jazz LP's which would have only sold a total of 2,000 or 3,000 copies back in 1950, now sell as many as 1,000 or 1,500 sets via a single distributor." He singled out the format's large capacity as an important driver of this change. "More and more jazz A&R heads are recording jazz artists on a jam session type of kick," he wrote. "Instead of waxing the men on three-minute selections which used to be standard on 78's, the artists will take one tune and stay with it for the entire length of the LP disk."[57] Year-end reports for 1954 revealed that retail sales for jazz records had increased by roughly $3 million. By 1955, the jazz field was, as Is Horowitz described it, "almost entirely LP now," with the jazz single "a distinct rarity." He continued: "The LP is the ideal exposure medium for those unable to listen to much jazz in live performance and, in a significant way, the growth in jazz disk sales has paralleled the boom in the packaged record business generally."[58]

As this activity suggests, LPs and EPs—what the industry trades referred to as "packaged goods"—became the largest segment of the industry in 1955 in terms of overall sales.[59] In a separate report, Horowitz attributed the estimated 22 percent growth in total record sales during this year to the popularity of the packaged market, especially the increased interest in 12-inch LPs. Somewhat unexpectedly, unit sales and dollar volume for the larger LPs had more than doubled during the year (see table 1.5). The unanticipated move toward 12-inch LPs points to a more generalized point: large-scale changes in media infrastructure are chaotic for many reasons, but one of the largest factors is that consumers do not behave as expected. After all, Columbia never intended for the 12-inch LP to become the predominant format for popular music and jazz, but by 1955, this was quickly becoming the reality. The unpredictability that made the record business so competitive also created opportunities, especially at the margins. It is through such chaotic possibilities that jazz moved from the margins into the mainstream.

The LP as New Media on Savoy Records, 1949–1952

"HEY! *Not now! I'll tell you when!*" As if heeding Paul Williams's call to carry on, record labels continued to circulate the "The Huckle-Buck" well into the early 1950s. For example, Savoy reissued Williams's version on both 45-rpm (mid-1951) and 10-inch LP (July 1952) as part of the label's broader strategy

Table 1.5. Record format sales and yearly trends, 1955

SHARE OF TOTAL 1955 SALES (BY RECORD TYPE)		
Record type	Unit volume (%)	Dollar volume (%)
12-inch LPs	12.2	37.6
45 singles	37.4	24.5
10-inch 78s	26.8	19.9
EPs	10.7	11.9
10-inch LPs	2.3	4.8
7-inch 78s	10.6	2.2
GAIN OR LOSS: 1955 VS. 1954 (BY RECORD TYPE)		
Record type	Unit volume (%)	Dollar volume (%)
12-inch LPs	Up 127.9	Up 111.9
45 singles	Up 38.4	Up 29.5
7-inch 78s	Up 22.2	Up 17.9
EPs	Down 4.2	Down 14.5
10-inch 78s	Down 17.2	Down 16.6
10-inch LPs	Down 17.4	Down 27.5
12-inch 78s	Down 61.7	Down 62.2
Total sales:	Up 14.7	Up 22.1

[Source] Is Horowitz, "RIAA Report Spotlights Expansion of '55 Record Biz," *Billboard*, March 17, 1956, 17.

to generate profits from its back catalog.⁶⁰ The aforementioned LP, titled *Rhythm and Blues, vol. 1*, was a R&B compilation featuring Williams alongside Bill Moore, Milt Buckner, Hal Singer, and Big Jay McNeely. This record was, in actuality, a telling abnormality: it was the only nonjazz LP that Savoy had issued to date.

Savoy was one of the most jazz-focused independent record labels. Founded in 1942 by Herman Lubinsky, the Newark-based label specialized in all kinds of Black music within the R&B field, including jazz, blues, and (eventually) gospel.⁶¹ Savoy was an early proponent of bebop, largely because of A&R head (and "Huckle-Buck" producer) Teddy Reig. Through the mid- to late 1940s, Reig recorded many of the genre's most defining musicians: Charlie Parker, Dizzy Gillespie, Dexter Gordon, Sonny Stitt, Miles Davis, Fats Navarro, Kenny Dorham, Tadd Dameron, and Howard McGhee. The label's strong roster of Black musical talent created a deep back catalog of Black popular music that continued to circulate on multiple formats through the 1950s. Most of these recordings circulated on 78 rpm, which continued to be the most-popular and highest-value format across the industry (see the previous section). As such, Savoy's activity provides a good case study for examining the early jazz LP in relation to other forms of Black popular music.

Savoy was among the first independents to adopt the LP, entering into the package field at the end of 1949 with *Erroll Garner at the Piano*.⁶² This activity was part of Lubinsky's expansion strategy that, in reality, amounted to a hedge in market position. In 1949 he started the Regent subsidiary to offer an extended classical catalog on 10-inch LP. Likewise, Savoy entered the 45 field in February 1950 with a mixed slate of forty releases.⁶³ Despite this activity, Savoy released LPs only sporadically until around July 1951, when it began regularly issuing 10-inch LPs in batches every four to six months. The firm prioritized Erroll Garner and Charlie Parker above all, although several releases featured Gordon, Navarro, Stan Getz, and Lester Young (among others). Nearly all of Savoy's offerings were back-catalog reissues with a clear emphasis on jazz, despite its activity in other fields.⁶⁴

By the start of 1953, Savoy had issued around thirty-five LPs, making it one of the most active labels producing jazz LPs during this time.⁶⁵ In comparison with other jazz-heavy labels, this output equaled Blue Note and outpaced Dial and Prestige. Therefore, "most active" in this context meant issuing a few dozen jazz LPs as only one part of a multilayered business strategy. For example, Savoy produced many more singles over the same period: around 230 total on both 78 and 45 formats. In contrast, a major such as Columbia issued well over seven hundred LPs and two thousand singles before 1953, not counting its many subsidiaries and international releases.[66] As the moniker implies, major record labels operated at an enormously different scale in terms of recording, manufacturing, distribution, and sales.

Savoy's activity nevertheless reveals how jazz was the only Black music to have a strong presence on the format in the early 1950s. Consider the comparable activity between 1949 and January 1953 of two other indie labels that had a successful roster of Black musical talent (and that also issued covers of the "The Huckle-Buck"). King, which had a dual focus on R&B and country and western (C&W), released around five LPs and more than four hundred singles. Over the same interval, Specialty, which predominantly recorded Black music, issued only a single LP and around 130 singles.[67] Jazz musicians appear throughout the discographies of King and Specialty; however, neither made jazz a point of emphasis. Beginning in 1953, King became one of the only nonjazz labels to substantially invest in the LP when it began issuing numerous LPs featuring rumba, square dancing, Jewish music, instrumental pop, and Latin American dance music. The firm began regularly issuing R&B on LP in 1954, making it an exception to an otherwise clear trajectory: labels with a regular R&B output did not prioritize the LP format, whereas firms with a stronger jazz emphasis plainly did.[68] Well-known jazz indies such as Prestige, Blue Note, Savoy, Commodore, and Dial—in addition to lesser-known firms such as Jolly Roger, Jazz Panorama, Discovery, and Viking—all issued multiple LPs during the early 1950s.[69]

Savoy's promotion of bebop was quite unusual. Between 1950 and 1953, most jazz-interested labels emphasized historical recordings of traditional jazz styles. New Orleans musicians such as Louis Armstrong, Jelly Roll Morton, and Sidney Bechet were especially well represented on LP, as were Pee Wee Russell and Muggsy Spanier, who were associated with the Chicago jazz style. Dixieland-revival musicians such as Turk Murphy, George Lewis, Eddie Condon, and Art Hodes received similar attention. By the start of 1953, at least twenty-nine LPs listed in the *Schwann Catalog* included "Dixieland" in the title.[70] These discs generally fell into two categories. Either they were artist retrospectives such as the Dorsey Brothers' *Dixieland Jazz 1934–1935* on Decca (August 1950) or reissue compilations such as Savoy's *Dixieland Series, vol. 1* (February 1952) and Commodore's *Dixieland Jazz Gems, vol. 1* (June 1950). The commercial success of George Avakian's "jazz story" series at Columbia—multiple-LP sets featuring Armstrong (May 1951), Bessie

Smith (December 1951), and Bix Beiderbecke (May 1952)—provided a clear pathway, especially in how to package previously out-of-print recordings.[71] Like Columbia, most labels chose to reissue back-catalog material, a convention that recirculated historically significant recordings to a new audience.

Even labels that prioritized bebop artists issued a mixture of historical and contemporary substyles. Dial and Savoy were quick to issue Charlie Parker on LP but filled out their catalogs with more historically focused selections.[72] When Blue Note began issuing LPs in late 1950, the label focused all of its energy on its "traditional" series, with selections by Bechet, Hodes, Lewis, and James P. Johnson. Several of these discs included "Jazz Classics" in the title, an emergent trend to ascribe artistic and historical value to jazz.[73] It was not until August or September 1951, nearly a year after its first LP, that Blue Note began issuing LPs of Thelonious Monk, Ike Quebec, James Moody, and Bud Powell in its "modern" series. The label would help define the sound of jazz during the 1950s, but its first entry into the LP market focused entirely on earlier styles.[74]

Despite this activity, jazz made up only a tiny fraction of the LP market and an even smaller fragment of the industry overall.[75] Yet jazz was overrepresented on LP. Gospel and R&B had more overall market value in terms of retail sales, jukebox plays, and unit volume, but these genres rarely appeared on the LP format. Savoy's LP reissue of Williams's "The Huckle-Buck" in 1952 is a telling irregularity. Apart from jazz performers, Black musicians appeared on 78 or 45 singles almost without exception. Jazz's move onto LP, regardless of its minority position, discloses a much more significant trend: to repackage the music as a form of artful expression—much more akin to classical music, which remained the dominant music on LP.[76] This trend would only continue as labels began recording music specifically for the format.

The LP as New Media on Decca Records, 1949–1952

Even during the most fleeting moments, Louis Armstrong always had a certain flair. Listen, for example, to his gravelly yet energetic voice as he welcomes Velma Middleton onto the Pasadena stage in January 1951 to "jump" that "new dance called the huckle-buck." Slightly off mic, he punctuates the phrase with a spirited "YES SIR!" (0:08). Like Williams, his phrasing doubles as an invitation to the audience (which laughs) and a signal for the musicians to begin. The band swings with continuous enthusiasm, which helps the ensemble overcome a few moments of mild confusion midstream. From start to finish, the performance remains informal yet comfortable, even as the bass levels remain noticeably high in the recorded mix.

The resulting LP from 1952, *Satchmo at Pasadena*, marked a moment of changing habits around what was possible for a jazz LP.[77] In a rare move for the time, Decca announced that the recording would appear on LP, perhaps in an effort to accommodate the length of the individual performances: five of the ten issued tracks were more than five-and-a-half minutes long, a duration that extended beyond the capacity of any other format.[78] The extra capacity of the LP made it possible to include announcements, applause, and moments of informality like those found in "The Huckle-Buck." The technical complexities involved in making on-site recordings—recall the balance issues—made jazz concerts on record a rarity even for major firms such as Decca. Although jazz was well matched to the LP format, Decca simultaneously cross-issued all ten tracks on two four-disc albums of 45s in edited form; "The Huckle-Buck" also appeared as a single on 78 and 45 rpm.[79] The strategy taken with *Satchmo at Pasadena* followed standard industry practices and makes clear that change was most often incremental during these years.

The circulation history of Armstrong's performance provides a parallel view of the jazz LP before 1953. Like Savoy, Decca was an early adopter of the format and had a strong catalog of Black music, including jazz. Although the firm operated at a much larger scale of production than an independent like Savoy, Decca's strategy was quite similar. It actively put jazz on LP, with an emphasis on reissued content, but relegated other forms of Black music to the singles market. Newly recorded material was made to fit the constraints of the 78 single, even though most recordings simultaneously circulated on multiple formats. Few companies, Decca and Savoy included, made recordings specifically for the LP. The abnormality of *Satchmo at Pasadena* usefully points to a future that, in the middle of 1952, was merely in a state of becoming.

Decca issued its first LPs in 1949, well before most other firms. Unlike Columbia, which prioritized the classical market, Decca oriented its output toward popular and Broadway music. Its large LP catalog included mainstream stars such as Bing Crosby (*Bing Crosby Sings the Song Hits from Broadway*) and Guy Lombardo (*The Twin Pianos*) as well as records featuring folk (*Songs of the South African Veld*), barbershop (Mills Brothers, *Famous Barber Shop Ballads*), theater productions (*Judith Anderson in*

Medea), original cast musicals (*Oklahoma!*), and light-classical or semi-classical music (*Jascha Heifetz Playing the Music of Gershwin*).[80] The label broadened its already diverse output strategy in late 1950 by entering into the serious classical LP field with its "Golden Label" series. Before 1953, Decca's total output was similar to Columbia's, with well over seven hundred LPs and nearly two thousand singles, not including its active subsidiaries.[81]

Decca began issuing jazz on LP in April 1950. In preparation, the firm hired noted jazz collector Marshall Stearns to consult on the label's jazz holdings. According to his March 1950 letter, Stearns estimated that Decca's deep back catalog of jazz recordings included roughly eighty albums of 78s fit for reissue on LP.[82] The label's diverse stock of jazz or jazz-adjacent music—Paul Whiteman, Bing Crosby, Lionel Hampton, Billie Holiday, and Ella Fitzgerald (among others)—should be credited to Milt Gabler, the head of popular music who joined the label in 1941 and had a keen ear for jazz.[83] At Gabler's direction, Decca quickly repackaged many of its 78-rpm albums with no change in title, content, cover design, or liner notes.

Overall, the jazz LPs issued during the label's first year of production emphasized early jazz styles. For example, LPs featuring James P. Johnson and Eddie Condon appeared alongside Pete Daily and Phil Napoleon's *Dixieland Jazz Battle, vol. 1*, and a number of Armstrong retrospectives, such as *New Orleans Days* and *Louis Armstrong Classics: New Orleans to New York*.[84] These discs followed a familiar two-part pattern, either artist retrospectives like Count Basie's *At the Piano* or compilations such as the two volumes of *Gems of Jazz*, with musicians such as Mildred Bailey, Meade Lux Lewis, Bud Freedman, Gene Krupa, and Bunny Berigan.[85] All were of the 10-inch variety, and the firm carefully avoided making new recordings solely for the LP format.

Even though jazz represented less than 3 percent of Decca's total LP output before 1953, Gabler and the other Decca executives clearly saw enough value—economic or otherwise—to continue investing their resources.[86] This activity clearly contrasts with the firm's approach to its successful roster of R&B talent, which regularly made the *Billboard* charts. Louis Jordan and Buddy Johnson, two of Decca's most reliable hit makers, were not issued on LP during this time; gospel star Sister Rosetta Tharpe made a brief appearance on two 10-inch LPs in late 1951 but not in the years after.[87] Decca also issued a handful of LPs by the Mills Brothers and the Ink Spots, two Black vocal quartets that regularly appeared on the R&B charts but whose musical approach more closely aligned with white popular sensibilities. Both groups had sold equally well with white and Black audiences since before World War II, an unusual market position that certainly influenced the firm's release approach.[88] In contrast, jazz-related artists such as Billie Holiday, Ella Fitzgerald, Louis Armstrong, and Lionel Hampton regularly appeared on LP. By any metric, jazz had a smaller market share in both sales and output than other forms of Black popular music, but jazz musicians were nevertheless overrepresented in Decca's LP catalog.[89]

Decca's divergent approach to jazz is also apparent in its advertising from around this period. For example, a full-page ad in the April 24, 1954, issue of *Billboard* publicized the label's Black music offerings with the tagline "Look to Decca for Great Rhythm and Blues and Jazz" (see figure 1.2). The top half of the promotion includes a list of single records (78s and 45s) for four of the label's top sellers: Sister Rosetta Tharpe and Marie Knight on the left, and Louis Armstrong and Ella Fitzgerald on the right. The middle section includes another list of records separated by subgenre. Jazz is the only category to specify "singles," presumably to differentiate this section from the list of "jazz albums" that appears at the bottom. Only four of the twenty-three records mentioned in the ad are LPs, and all four are plainly advertised as jazz.[90]

Significantly, this 1954 advertisement also reveals how Decca began taking advantage of the LP's larger capacity to document jazz in performance. Notice that two of the listed LPs are concert recordings from separate live events at the Civic Auditorium in Pasadena, California—the same location that resulted in *Satchmo at Pasadena*. Each of these LPs prominently displays the name of Gene Norman, a Los Angeles disc jockey and impresario known for his Just Jazz and Dixieland Jubilee concert series. Norman began recording his concerts in the 1940s, eventually issuing some of them as 78-rpm discs on a few different labels, including Black & White and Modern.[91] Decca issued four concert recordings made by Norman on LP, beginning with *Just Jazz Concert: Lionel Hampton* in early 1951. The firm would go on to issue five jazz concerts on LP before the end of 1952 (see table 1.6), including the two listed in the *Billboard* ad discussed above.[92] Of these, *Satchmo at Pasadena* was the only one to be recorded after Decca began issuing jazz on LP.

Norman was not the first to issue concert recordings, as Gabler knew from personal experience. In the late 1930s, Gabler had famously pioneered and then recorded jam-session concerts at Jimmy Ryan's on 52nd Street.[93] His own Commodore label issued six 78-rpm records under the title *Jam Session at Commodore* between 1938 and 1947. These 12-inch discs became

Figure 1.2. Decca Records advertisement. From *Billboard*, April 24, 1954, 39.

the blueprint for jam-session-style records, including those made by Rudi Blesh, Norman Granz, and John Hammond.[94] Granz's Jazz at the Philharmonic (JATP), which showcased lengthy performances by both swing and bebop musicians, was the most successful expansion of Gabler's innovation.[95] Granz began recording these performances as early as 1945, eventually issuing a series of influential 78-rpm albums.[96] After the introduction of the LP, he immediately recognized its commercial potential for jazz. Two JATP volumes, issued on Mercury, appear in the first issue of the *Schwann Catalog* in October 1949; another, on Stinson, would soon follow in early 1950.[97] By May 1952, Granz had made a total of fourteen volumes available

Table 1.6. Live jazz LPs issued by Decca before 1953, in order of issue date

Issue number	Title	Artist	Year recorded	Issue date
DL 7013	*Gene Norman Presents Just Jazz Concert*	Lionel Hampton	1947	March 1951
DL 8037, 8038	*Satchmo at Symphony Hall, vols. 1 and 2*	Louis Armstrong	1947	June 1951
DL 8041	*Gene Norman Presents Satchmo at Pasadena*	Louis Armstrong	1951	August 1952
DL 8046	*Gene Norman Presents a Charlie Ventura Concert*	Charlie Ventura	1949	December 1952
DL 7022	*Frank Bull and Gene Norman Present Dixieland Jubilee*	Various	1949	December 1952

on LP. The relative success of these records (and others) clearly influenced Gabler's approach to the jazz LP at Decca during this time.

Although recording jazz outside the studio remained a rarity, *Satchmo at Pasadena* nevertheless provides a window into jazz's gradual move to LP. Both major and independent labels chose to strategize around an uncertain market and its future by relying on their back catalogs, as a close look at Decca's activity reveals. At the same time, the industry's clear economic growth allowed for some experimentation. When Gabler decided to tailor newly recorded material for LP release on *Satchmo at Pasadena*, he was taking a calculated risk because Armstrong was already a proven talent. Moreover, several other producers had already successfully issued jazz concerts on LP, including Avakian at Columbia with Benny Goodman's *The Famous 1938 Carnegie Hall Jazz Concert* (late 1950) and Granz's multiple JATP volumes.

As clever record executives knew, there was always a balance to be struck between innovation and convention. It is no secret, then, why the growing investment in jazz on LP achieved a similar balance between those recordings both old and new.

Moments like Armstrong's offhanded declarations—"YES SIR!"—and the audience response to "The Huckle-Buck" pointed to the future of jazz on record, even as that path remained murky. Such fleeting moments have power not simply because they reveal new commercial trends but also for what they signify about the broader move to repackage jazz history on LP. Reissued historical recordings circulated alongside new interpretations of standard songs, transmitting forms of Black expertise and artistry to a new and growing audience. Such trends can be heard in the music surrounding Armstrong's "The Huckle-Buck," which appeared after a five-and-a-half-minute version of "Way Down Yonder in New Orleans" and before a rendition of "Honeysuckle Rose" with guest Earl Hines. These performances are striking in their informality and fluidity, even as the unevenness of the sound levels heard throughout—for example, the balance during the piano solo in "'Way Down Yonder" (1:53)—is a sonic reminder that the industry similarly remained imbalanced. After all, despite other forms of Black music having a much larger market share, there was no move to present the informality and historicity of nonjazz on LP. Jazz took a divergent path as record-making professionals increasingly began to see the music as a stable, long-term investment.

(Huckle) Buck Clayton and the Ascendance of Jazz, 1953–1954

Buck Clayton's lengthy version of "The Huckle-Buck" features seven different soloists, all backed by a rhythm section that has perpetual energy but never hurries. Several soloists appear more than once, broken up by a combination of ensemble choruses, background riffs, and solos by the other musicians. As might be expected, Clayton has the most solo space. He trades fours with Joe Newman (3:49) and takes two different improvisational flights: the first an energetic sprint (10:30), followed a few minutes later by a muted, subdued stroll (15:01). In the trumpeter's hands, "The Huckle-Buck" is merely a blank canvas for collaborative music making in the recording studio.

Clayton's twenty-minute rendition of the 1949 hit was as much a musical experiment as it was a technological and commercial one.[98] At the time, all of Columbia's jazz offerings came out of its popular-albums department, headed by Avakian. Jazz was, as Avakian later wrote, never his only focus but rather an "ever-growing part" of his work made possible by the financial success of the popular-album music division in the 1950s.[99] Among other things, Avakian's relative autonomy allowed him to sign several artists between 1953 and 1955 who would help define the sound of jazz during this period: Dave Brubeck, Erroll Garner, Buck Clayton, Chet Baker, Eddie Condon, Louis Armstrong, Miles Davis, and Duke Ellington, among others. At the same moment, and not by coincidence, Avakian began moving Columbia into the 12-inch jazz LP field beginning with *Erroll Garner*, issued at the end of 1953.[100] Next came a series of three jam-session-style records led by Clayton, Condon, and Turk Murphy that were simultaneously issued and promoted in the second quarter of 1954.[101]

Clayton's performance of "The Huckle-Buck" cannot be separated from the material conditions afforded by the LP. "The Buck Clayton jam session was intended to exploit the freedom from time-limits afforded by long-play," Avakian wrote in a 1954 promotional booklet, "and to see what would happen if a carefully-chosen group of swing musicians (some of whom had never met each other) were to stage an informal session with no preparations."[102] Although several other jam-session recordings were already in circulation on LP, Avakian's decision to record an extended performance for a single side of a 12-inch disc was a sign of jazz's growing appeal to general audiences.[103] The trend toward jazz helps explain why Columbia began investing greater capital and labor into recording jazz specifically for the LP in 1953. Economic considerations often surround musical ones.

This December 1953 recording date occurred a few months after the LP's five-year anniversary, a milestone effusively celebrated in the jazz trade press.[104] By this time, the LP already had an aura of prestige around it. As Keir Keightley convincingly argues, this aura resulted from the format's origins as a medium for classical music and the more expensive price point that white adult audiences could afford. This was a reliable buying demographic, so the LP format would eventually become the "core commodity" for the industry, providing steady sales and a "counterbalance" to the volatility of the singles market.[105] These trends had enormous consequences for the jazz record industry. As jazz sales of packaged goods (LPs and EPs) steadily increased in a way that all other music nominally under the R&B category would not, record labels began to reorient their jazz output toward the two most dependable market segments in terms of sales: middle-class white adults and college-age consumers.[106] The heightened symbolic capital of the LP that helped make jazz into a music for "serious" listeners was an extension of the segregational logic of the pre-LP record industry.

Jazz's divergent path on LP should then be understood in relation to the racial and gender ideologies that code how music becomes valued. This is true even (or especially) when neither is named explicitly. In his 1954 *Billboard* article "Jazz LP's and EP's Become Disk Industry's Solid Staple," Bob Rolontz asserts that there is "little question" that college students were "largely responsible for the current jazz boom" because of their interest in the younger, more progressive generation of musicians. All the progressive "jazz men" listed to prove this point were white men: Chet Baker, Gerry Mulligan, and Dave Brubeck. Rolontz goes on to mention the popularity on the packaged market by listing another dozen or so musicians—Louis Armstrong is the lone Black artist who merits attention.[107] Such a bifurcated focus was part of a generalizable pattern, as proven by the 1954 controversy over Brubeck's *Time* magazine cover as well as the recurring refusal by *Down Beat* and *Metronome* to put Black musicians on their covers.[108] As Kelsey Klotz convincingly details in relation to 1950s jazz, notions of musical value are both cultural and economic.[109] The racialized logic that persisted in the music industry was the major reason why Black musicians were often written out of the coverage even as the popularity of their records steadily increased.

From this broader vantage point, Clayton's "Huckle-Buck" is a clear expression of how systems of value within the industry entwine with the means of circulation and the changing cultural politics around race. In the same promotional booklet mentioned above, Avakian describes his theory and philosophy of production at length. Throughout the text, he continually seeks to legitimize jazz as a reputable form of music making, often deemphasizing jazz's historical connection to Black popular music. For example, his main concern when selecting personnel was to find musicians "capable of immediate understanding among themselves, so that an integrated, united ensemble can emerge without conscious effort." Although the "element of surprise" was important, he continues, the qualifications of the musicians "would command respect" and "live up to the high standard of that respect." In other words, Clayton's sessions were controlled and congenial, relaxed but professional. "Contrary to the opinion held by the uninformed or misled, a jam session is not a carving contest," Avakian concludes.[110] Neither this lengthy promotional booklet nor the LP's liner notes mention that most of the musicians on the date, Clayton included, had had success on the R&B charts on records with Lionel Hampton, Erskine Hawkins, Lucky Millinder, and Illinois Jacquet.[111]

Avakian designed his promotional booklet to give distributors, disc jockeys, trade journalists, and record-store owners—all presumed to be white men—the necessary language to sell jazz as a music with broad appeal.[112] As a result, Avakian's sentiments were closely echoed in *Billboard*. In a review of Clayton's LP, Rolontz praises the record through a similar lens: "What comes out is bright and sparkling jazz, in the quiet swing tradition—a jam session without the violent quality which has come to be associated with the word. This is swing with musical integrity and two outstanding performances."[113] Though never explicitly discussed, racialized assumptions about Black popular music and Black musicians clearly underlie his framing. The implication is that Columbia's music was made by respectable jazz musicians and was suitable for a white mainstream audience that could afford the higher-priced LPs.

When Columbia issued Clayton's version of "The Huckle-Buck," in 1954, the terrain of the record industry had shifted dramatically since the song had first appeared in 1949. The popularity of jazz and popular music on LP was growing, even as alternate formats such as the EP continued to proliferate. With some clear overlaps, jazz was becoming a distinctive market segment separate from the industry formations traditionally understood as "popular" and "R&B." Part of this distinction arose from jazz's movement onto LP, a format tied to racialized notions of prestige and musical value. Commercial investment in jazz necessitated a careful balance between inventive music making and the right marketing strategy to make these records economically viable. As a result, the jazz LP came to be an essential mechanism for how the music continued to move away from its Black working-class audience and its historical connections to Black popular music.[114]

This dislocation can be heard throughout Clayton's version of "The Huckle-Buck." The melodies, background riffs, and solos always swing, but they do so carefully: everything remains in balance. This is not the blues of Paul Williams or Lucky Millinder, but one that unfolds in the "quiet swing" of an in-studio jam session. Clayton's lengthy LP may have represented a new trend in recording, but it was also a conscious effort by Avakian and Columbia to culturally repackage jazz for a different audience. Consider how Clayton's work moved through Columbia's jazz catalog over the next year. His music appears on both *$64,000 Jazz*, a cross-promotion with the prime-time CBS TV show *The $64,000 Question*, and *I Like Jazz!*, a marketing LP specifically meant to "introduce jazz to a mass audience."[115] On both, Avakian makes mention of Clayton's jam sessions but does so on records with covers that depict a white audience—a white family of four appears on *$64,000 Jazz*, and an assortment of fourteen white individuals at different economic levels appears on *I Like Jazz!* These LPs did not contain Black popular music. They contained jazz.

The Standardization of the Jazz LP, 1955

Frank Sinatra's 1949 version of the "The Huckle-Buck" first circulated on LP at the end of 1955.[116] The disc, titled *Get Happy*, appeared on Columbia's newly inaugurated House Party series, a budget line of popular-music LPs aimed at teenage consumers.[117] Profit was clearly the inspiration for the design and conception of the series, but its existence also testifies to the central role that recordings had in a much broader reimagining of domestic life for white, middle-class audiences of all ages. Not only did the House Party logo consist of two white teenagers leaning in for a kiss, but the series name aptly signaled to the domesticity (house) as well as the sociality (party) contained within the promise of that kiss. Many of the titles and covers—*Soft and Sentimental*, *Prom Date*, *Lover's Laine* (a play on Frankie Laine's name), and *Alone at Last*—accentuated a particular view of domestic teenage sexuality and offered an accompanying soundtrack perfectly suited to the LP.[118] As much as the industry had changed since 1949, the recirculation of Sinatra's "The Huckle-Buck" confirms how the same segregational logic continued to define popular music during the early LP era.

The decision to direct the House Party series toward the teen market was a calculated risk by Columbia to find economic value within an increasingly segmented market. During the 1950s the white mainstream audience became generally stratified along what Keir Keightley describes as the "age-format nexus": 45-rpm singles for teen listeners and 33⅓-rpm LPs for adults.[119] Columbia's House Party series ran against industry trends in how it featured a format that seemed ill suited to its intended audience and on a size (10 inches) with a depreciating market value.[120] Even as the LP, along with music on it, moved into what Keightley further describes as a "legitimized taste position" with adult audiences, record executives and their marketing departments increasingly found ways to extract value from their company's back catalog.[121] A record like *Get Happy*, for example, contained older material reissued on LP for the first time and featured an artist who had found revived success with another major label (Capitol). Importantly, the LP also contained six rather than the usual eight tracks, which decreased royalty costs. Such an approach made the $1.98 budget price more affordable for teenage consumers and more economically viable for the label.[122] An LP like *Get Happy* demonstrates the rising value of Columbia's back catalog and helps explain why the firm eventually issued more than a hundred House Party LPs between 1955 and 1957.[123] As the LP grew popular with middle-class white audiences, forgotten songs like "The Huckle-Buck" retained their value across different market segments, even if they were used as filler for a budget LP.

According to Hal Cook, director of sales at Columbia, the inspiration for the House Party line came from the firm's success with 12-inch popular-music LPs.[124] Columbia was not alone in finding fortune with the 12-inch LP. By the time of Cook's comments at the end of 1955, the packaged-record market (LPs and EPs) was the most profitable category of recorded merchandise.[125] Most commentators in the trade press attributed this trend to the popularity of the larger, 12-inch size across the industry.[126] According to release data from the *Schwann Catalog*, most independent labels active in popular music either issued their first 12-inch LPs in 1955 or began to actively expand their offerings on the larger format. Such trends would only increase in 1956.[127]

The pivot toward 12-inch LPs led to more capital investment in jazz. An April 1955 editorial in *Billboard* directly linked the "technical developments of the LP and EP package business" and the advances in playback machinery to what the author describes as a "jazz renaissance."[128] A similar editorial in *Cash Box* titled "Jazz Comes of Age" outlined the transformation of the jazz market from a small, specialized segment into "a staple" of the record business. "Today," the March 1956 article continues, "almost every record company that deals in album material, has a catalogue of jazz works which it can count on to sell month after month and year after year."[129] Avakian similarly proselytized in *Down Beat* that the "combination of the 12" LP and the rising interest in jazz enabled Columbia to enter the jazz field seriously."[130]

The output from different competitors across the industry between 1954 and 1956 corroborates these observations. Jazz-specific labels noticeably increased their LP activity. Pacific Jazz, Bethlehem, Savoy, Prestige, and Roost all issued their first 12-inch LPs in 1955, followed soon after by Blue Note and Debut.[131] All of these labels, along with Riverside and Atlantic, greatly expanded their 12-inch catalogs through 1956 by offering a combination of newly recorded and reissued material.[132] Other labels created jazz-specific series or subsidiary labels. The classical label Vanguard began its Jazz Showcase series in March 1954, the same year that Mercury founded EmArcy as a jazz-specific subsidiary.[133] EmArcy quickly pivoted from its singles-only approach to one focused around LPs. Similarly, Concert Hall Society began offering mail-order LPs through its Jazztone Society in 1955, and Aladdin officially established Jazz West Records as an LP-only jazz subsidiary in February 1956.[134] Following Columbia and Decca, other firms chose to integrate jazz into already existing infrastructures for popular music. According to *Billboard*, Atlantic specifically hired Nesuhi Ertegun as partner and vice president in January 1955 to expand its LP and EP jazz offerings.[135] Some labels preferred to expand more carefully, issuing jazz LPs as only one part of newly established popular-music subsidiaries. This was the approach taken by Argo of Chess and Label "X" of RCA Victor.[136]

Taken together, the increased attention to jazz by these record companies should be understood as an investment in new record-making infrastructures. New names and logos had to be chosen, designed, trademarked, and announced. Newly contracted talent and their subsequent recording sessions led to the manufacturing of new records, which in turn had to be circulated through expanding networks of distribution. As competition grew, marketing plans had to be creatively imagined and then enacted across different print and broadcast media. It took time, energy, and resources to accomplish this work.

As the record-making infrastructures for jazz grew, so too did the need to educate record executives, disc jockeys, regional distributors, and point-of-sale dealers about the music. For example, the aforementioned "jazz renaissance" editorial in *Billboard* led to the magazine's first special issue dedicated to the buying, selling, and programming of jazz. Among the thirteen pages of "review and preview" for 1955 was a full-page feature outlining four areas of jazz history: modern, instrumental, swing, and Dixieland. The explicit goal of these articles was to "increase understanding of jazz merchandising" that would then "help dealers sell more jazz records."[137] The lists of top-selling jazz albums on more than twenty different record labels did similar educational work, as did the series of three articles written by differently situated recordmen with expertise in jazz. Orrin Keepnews and Bill Grauer of Riverside Records focused on the sales potential of reissued material from the 1920s and 1930s. As a follow-up, Bob Shad of Mercury wrote about the advantages of building a jazz roster with lesser-known stars. Avakian finished the series a few issues later, arguing that liner notes played an indispensable role in documenting individual recording sessions and in educating audiences about the music's history.[138] Read together, these articles offer a blueprint for success: balance a back catalog of older material (Keepnews and Grauer) with new recordings by rising talent (Shad) while also investing in the informational infrastructure that will communicate the music's value to different audiences (Avakian).

Although it had a commercial edge, this ongoing educational work was also a form of cultural advocacy from the perspective of (usually white) male enthusiasm and authority over jazz history. Industry professionals often emphasized historical longevity in their descriptions of jazz's sales potential. In 1953 Bob Weinstock of Prestige discussed his new plans to issue LPs and EPs because the formats were "more timeless, and certainly better sellers, than the standard 78rpm record."[139] Ralph Gleason Jr. used comparable language in his 1954 review of Buck Clayton's *How Hi the Fi*: "This LP is obviously going to remain on the jazz fan's shelf long after lots of the current surplus of jazz albums have gone."[140] In 1955 Keepnews and Grauer similarly described reissue material on LP as "the closest thing to deathless, steady-sales-pace items the record business has ever known."[141] The material conditions of the LP format and masculinist notions of how musical aesthetics produce economic value sit at the center of these three sequential assertions.[142] Within the 1950s record industry, economic longevity marked cultural prestige, and vice versa.

Many of the articles to appear in the trades during this time worked to communicate jazz's cultural value in language that would be legible to white, middle-class audiences. For example, the 1956 *Cash Box* editorial "Jazz Comes of Age" emphasized how much the "popularity and dignity" of jazz had grown since Goodman first appeared at Carnegie Hall (in 1938). In the past, "it was generally considered that listening to jazz music was a lesser pursuit than listening to classical music." But today, the editorial assuages readers, things have changed: "We no longer find the qualitative factor stressed, i.e., the opinion that one is better than the other or that one is more highbrow than the other. Jazz has almost reached the status where it is measured on its own terms rather than on moral terms."[143] From the emphasis on concert-hall success to the assurances of musical merit over morality, the editorial plainly relies on racialized assumptions about musical value to legitimize and elevate jazz as a reputable musical pursuit.[144] By connecting cultural relevancy to commercial success, notions of race and capital entwine even as the former is always put in language of the latter. In other words, the undeniable popularity of jazz in the mid-1950s ushered in a vocabulary that implicitly framed the music's value in racially coded terms.

The always present but often unspoken presence of race brings us back to the 1955 LP *Get Happy*. Sinatra's 1949 version of "The Huckle-Buck" is performed in a commercial swing style that intentionally smooths out the prominent backbeat accents heard on R&B renditions of the song. With its harmonized vocal ensemble, Sinatra's single was popular with disc jockeys at the time of its release and had little aesthetic overlap with the contemporaneous sound world of Black popular music.[145] (Compare Sinatra's to Pearl Bailey's version.) As the song went from a 78 single in 1949 to a budget LP in 1955, it traveled through a media infrastructure designed to privilege white artists and white audiences. And so did jazz.

Revisit the two nearly kissing white teens in the House Party logo. Revisit the statements in *Cash Box* and *Billboard* about jazz's ascendance from a "lowly" pursuit to a commercially viable genre, where the music would no longer be judged in "moral terms." Revisit the continuing refusal by *Metronome* and *Down Beat* to put Black musicians on their covers.[146] Revisit the covers of *$64,000 Jazz* and *I Like Jazz!* in order to consider the whiteness of Brubeck's first LP for Columbia, *Jazz Goes to College* (1954). Then consider the growing presence of jazz in magazines such as the *New Yorker*, *Saturday Review*, *Esquire*, *Good Housekeeping*, and *Playboy*.[147] The growing popularity of jazz in 1955 was a function of white male record executives selling jazz to a white audience on a prestige format that, not by coincidence, had a larger profit margin and more reliable sales projection. Such a strategy involved the material, cultural, and sonic erasure of Black bodies and Black aesthetics. The trajectory of "The Huckle-Buck" during this period is significant precisely because it is unexceptional.

Jazz History as Material History

The sound of jazz during the 1950s cannot be separated from its material history on LP. As sales steadily grew, the increased circulation of jazz would come to mediate cultural knowledge about the music in specific ways. Record makers found new ways of using their back catalogs, new approaches to finding talent, new strategies of marketing across market segments, and new language to talk about jazz history. Such active and creative decision making happened alongside the intentional marshaling of capital to arrange and record the music, secure the copyrights, design and press the records, and distribute and publicize the results. Racialized assumptions about music shaped these emergent vocabularies, media infrastructures, and systems of value. In other words, a material history of jazz is more than an account of physical items and economic flows. It also reveals the regimes of knowledge production.

The journey of "The Huckle-Buck" between 1949 and 1955 is one way to discern the shifting approaches and changing mechanisms of the record industry writ large. In 1949 the song traveled across the industry's color line but did so on 78-rpm singles. The first jazz LPs also arrived at this time, but mostly as a means of recirculating back-catalog material. This LP reissue tactic persisted for several years during a period of industry instability—the first reissues of "The Huckle-Buck" on LP encapsulate this point. As jazz began to move from commercial margins to a more central market position between 1952 and 1955, artists like Louis Armstrong and Buck Clayton recorded "The Huckle-Buck" specifically for LP and EP release. In contrast, music under the R&B category rarely appeared on LP, even though it accounted for roughly 10 percent of the industry's total sales.[148] These jazz renditions of "The Huckle-Buck" also demonstrated new possibilities for jazz on LP, even as the records circulated language and discourse about musical value coded for a white adult audience. The final appearance of "The Huckle-Buck" on a budget Frank Sinatra LP indicates how jazz paved the way for the format's adoption for popular music, both Black and white. The standardization of the 12-inch size for music beyond serious classical coincided with an industry-wide investment in jazz around 1955. As a result, this year proved pivotal for jazz in terms of its historiography, its economics, and its symbolic capital as a form of artistic expression. The LP may not have been designed for the music, but the format helped usher in large-scale acceptance of jazz with expanded listening publics in the United States.

The increased reliance on back-catalog material revealed during the travels of "The Huckle-Buck" should also be understood as a change in musical labor. Record labels were no longer only in the business of recorded music, but increasingly in the business of storing sonic labor with future plans to extract that labor for profits over the long term.[149] This change in approach had direct consequences for musicians. For example, the recirculation of out-of-print recordings created a public archive of jazz history that further helped to construct an aura of prestige around the music. This educational imperative that surrounded jazz history was one of the preconditions for Black jazz musicians to gain popularity with adult, middle-class consumers. When Armstrong walked onto the Pasadena stage in 1951 or when Clayton went into Columbia's studios in 1953, they did so accompanied by their own histories on record. In different ways, both charted new technological paths for jazz using a valorized musical tradition that was only then coming into the wider public consciousness. Both LPs were also a cultural experiment in how to sell Black musical artistry through an industry in which the segregational logic remained entrenched.

When *Cash Box* declared in March 1956 that "Jazz Comes of Age," the LP was approaching its eighth anniversary. However, any notion of jazz's arrival was a misnomer. As a musical practice, jazz already had a robust tradition. What had changed was the music's commercial appeal beyond swing and the full integration of jazz into the packaged market specifically aimed at adult listeners. A new media infrastructure that circulated both current and historically significant music on LPs had emerged, creating new possibilities for jazz musicians. A large portion of the rest of this book explores how these musicians navigated such changes, with recognition that the artful creation of jazz as a sonic practice remains inseparable from its economic and material conditions.

Playlist: The Emergent Jazz LP

This playlist chronicles the jazz LP during the late 1940s and early 1950s when the industry remained in a continual state of flux. It includes both early efforts to reissue back-catalog content and attempts to package material specifically recorded for LP release. Together, these records show how the standardization of the LP was not a linear trajectory. (All recordings are LPs.)

Art Tatum. *Gene Norman Presents an Art Tatum Concert.* Columbia, 1952.
Benny Goodman. *The Famous 1938 Carnegie Hall Jazz Concert.* Columbia Masterworks, 1950.
Bessie Smith. *The Bessie Smith Story, vols. 1-4.* Columbia, 1951.
Billie Holiday. *Lover Man.* Decca, 1951.
Bing Crosby. *Bing Crosby Sings the Song Hits from Broadway.* Decca, 1949.
Bing Crosby. *Collectors' Classics: Bing Crosby, vols. 1-8.* Decca, 1951.
Bix Beiderbecke. *The Bix Beiderbecke Story, vols. 1-3.* Columbia, 1951.
Bobby Sherwood. *Classics in Jazz: Bobby Sherwood.* Capitol, 1952.

Buck Clayton. *The Huckle-Buck and Robbins' Nest: A Buck Clayton Jam Session.* Columbia, 1954.
Buddy Baker and His Orchestra. *Stairway to the Stars.* Specialty, 1952.
Cecil Young. *Concert of Cool Jazz.* King, 1952.
Charlie Parker. *New Sounds in Modern Music: Charlie Parker, vols. 1-2.* Savoy, 1951.
Charlie Ventura. *Gene Norman Presents a Charlie Ventura Concert.* Decca, 1952.
Coleman Hawkins. *Classics in Jazz: Coleman Hawkins.* Capitol, 1952.
Count Basie. *At the Piano.* Decca, 1950.
Dave Brubeck. *Jazz Goes to College.* Columbia, 1954.
Dexter Gordon. *New Sounds in Modern Music: Dexter Gordon, vol. 1.* Savoy, 1951.
Eddie Condon. *George Gershwin Jazz Concert.* Decca, 1950.
Eddie Condon. *Jam Session Coast-to-Coast.* Columbia, 1954.
Eddie Condon. *Jazz Concert.* Decca, 1950.
Ella Fitzgerald. *Ella Fitzgerald Souvenir Album.* Decca, 1950.
Ella Fitzgerald. *Ella Sings Gershwin.* Decca, 1951.
Erroll Garner. *Erroll Garner.* Columbia, 1953.
Erroll Garner. *Erroll Garner at the Piano, vols. 1-4.* Savoy, 1949-51.
Fats Navarro. *New Sounds in Modern Music: Fats Navarro, vol. 1.* Savoy, 1951.
George Brunis, Miff Mole, and George Wettling. *Dixieland Jazz Gems, vol. 1.* Commodore, 1950.
Guy Lombardo and His Royal Canadians. *The Twin Pianos.* Decca, 1949.
James P. Johnson. *The Daddy of the Piano.* Decca, 1950.
Lester Young. *Tenor Sax Solos.* Savoy, 1951.
Lionel Hampton. *Be Bop.* Decca, 1952.
Lionel Hampton. *Gene Norman Presents Just Jazz Concert: Lionel Hampton All Stars.* Decca, 1951.
Lionel Hampton. *Hamp's Boogie Woogie.* Decca, 1951.
Lionel Hampton. *Moonglow.* Decca, 1951.
Louis Armstrong. *Gene Norman Presents Satchmo at Pasadena.* Decca, 1952.
Louis Armstrong. *Jazz Classics.* Brunswick, 1950.
Louis Armstrong. *Louis Armstrong and the All Stars, vol. 1, New Orleans Days.* Decca, 1950.
Louis Armstrong. *Louis Armstrong Classics: New Orleans to New York.* Decca, 1950.
Louis Armstrong. *The Louis Armstrong Story, vols. 1-4.* Columbia, 1951.
Louis Armstrong. *Satchmo at Symphony Hall, vols. 1-2.* Decca, 1951.
Mel Powell. *Mel Powell Septet.* Vanguard (Jazz Showcase), 1953.
Pete Daily and Phil Napoleon. *Dixieland Jazz Battle, vol. 1.* Decca, 1950.
Sidney Bechet. *Jazz Classics, vol. 1.* Blue Note, 1950.
Stan Getz. *New Sounds in Modern Music: Stan Getz, vol. 1.* Savoy, 1951.
Tommy Dorsey and Jimmy Dorsey. *The Dorsey Brothers' Orchestra, vol. 1, Dixieland Jazz 1934-1935.* Decca, 1950.
Turk Murphy and His Jazz Band. *When the Saints Go Marching In.* Columbia, 1954.

Various. *Classics in Jazz: Dixieland Stylists*. Capitol, 1952.

Various. *Classics in Jazz: Modern Idiom*. Capitol, 1952.

Various. *Classics in Jazz: Piano Stylists*. Capitol, 1952.

Various. *Classics in Jazz: Sax Stylists*. Capitol, 1952.

Various. *Classics in Jazz: Small Combos*. Capitol, 1952.

Various. *Classics in Jazz: Trumpet Stylists*. Capitol, 1952.

Various. *Decca Jazz Studio 1*. Decca, 1954.

Various. *Dixieland Series, vol. 1*. Savoy, 1952.

Various. *Frank Bull and Gene Norman Present Dixieland Jubilee*. Decca, 1952.

Various. *Gems of Jazz: A Series of Superb Jazz Classics, vols. 1–2*. Decca, 1950.

Various. *I Like Jazz!* Columbia, 1955.

Various. *Jazz at the Philharmonic, vol. 1*. Stinson, 1950.

Various. *Jazz at the Philharmonic, vols. 8 and 10*. Mercury, 1949.

Various. *Jazz, vol. 1, The South*. Folkways, 1950.

Various. *Jazz, vol. 2, The Blues*. Folkways, 1950.

Various. *Rhythm and Blues, vol. 1*. Savoy, 1952.

Various. *$64,000 Jazz*. Columbia, 1955.

Woody Herman. *Classics in Jazz: Woody Herman*. Capitol, 1952.

2

MISTAKES, MISHAPS, AND MISCUES

The Early LPs of Prestige Records

In a small New York City recording studio on October 5, 1951, Miles Davis and his sextet record a strolling, sometimes meandering blues. The nearly ten-minute track of "Bluing" ends with a looseness uncommon for commercially recorded jazz from this period. At the close of the final chorus, Sonny Rollins plays a cadential figure to initiate a seemingly conventional ritardando (9:40). Davis and his bassist, Tommy Potter, catch it easily, but Art Blakey continues, his ride cymbal oblivious to the rest of the ensemble. Davis and Potter attempt to salvage the confusion by playing a few more notes. This strategy fails. Blakey, eventually realizing his mistake, slows down with a few cymbal hits and concludes with his characteristic snare roll punctuated by a final rim shot. Reacting to the musical miscommunication,

Davis voices his frustration toward Blakey, saying something like, "Play the ending, man—you know the arrangement" (9:51). This recording session is anything but routine.

Prestige Records issued "Bluing" in 1953 on the A side of a 10-inch LP titled *Miles Davis: Blue Period*.[1] At nine minutes and fifty seconds, "Bluing" extends well beyond the three-minute limit of the 78-rpm era. As such, it was one of the first jazz records specifically conceived for and then recorded to take advantage of long-playing technology. The ensemble's imperfect ending, kept on record, brought listeners into the spaces of music making that were previously inaccessible.

The accompanying liner notes by Ira Gitler single out Blakey's mistake as a highlight of the disc:

> An album by Miles Davis represents modern jazz at its best. In this album, as in Miles' PRESTIGE LP 124, the length of time for each selection is not restricted to the usual limits except in the case of BLUE ROOM, which was cut at a more conventional session. BLUING, the high spot on this set, is over nine minutes of freedom of expression on modern blues chord changes. At the very end, Art Blakey continues playing after everyone else has stopped. If you listen closely, you will hear Miles say something like, "You know that ending man, let's do it again," but why do it again when you've captured the feeling in the solos of Walter Bishop, Miles, Sonny Rollins, Jack McLean, and the inventive drumming of Art Blakey. The advantage given by LP, of not having to make a "product" for the juke boxes, allowed us to keep this take. OUT OF THE BLUE (Miles' plea to get happy) was done at the same session and although not as lengthy as BLUING still provided ample time for relaxed improvisation.[2]

By contrasting the freedom afforded by the LP with the restrictions of conventional recording methods, Gitler celebrates the ability to record musical expression seemingly without restraint. The mistakes on "Bluing," he emphasizes, are not for mainstream, commercial jukeboxes but rather for listeners who understand "modern" musical expression. Gitler's use of the phrase *modern jazz at its best* echoes the view of Prestige's founder and owner, Bob Weinstock. Describing his approach to record making, Weinstock told *Down Beat* in 1954 that he was most interested in recording musicians "who are trying to advance jazz."[3] Recording jazz at its best, from this view, necessitates the use of new and innovative recording technology. The repetitive use of the word *modern* therefore points to an overlapping set of record-making practices during a time of cultural change, technological possibility, and musical exploration.

In the ten-year period after Columbia introduced the LP in 1948, jazz labels found numerous ways to reinvent the jazz record. Some labels began issuing live concert recordings made in small jazz clubs, in European concert halls, and at outdoor festivals. Others recorded in-studio jam sessions, extended improvisations, or exploratory compositions that combined jazz and art-music traditions. Albums based on a specific theme or concept became much more common, including sets of reissued recordings from iconic artists. Writing for the *New York Times* in 1958, the ten-year anniversary of the LP, columnist John Wilson wrote that for the first time, jazz records could feature "free-wheeling performances" that were "unrestricted by studio formality."[4] Like Gitler's comments above, Wilson's distinction between "free" and "formality" rests on social, musical, and technological lines: by implication, long-playing capabilities enabled musicians to improvise beyond the rigid three-minute conventions of the 78-rpm format, which brought recorded performances much closer to jazz's supposed "natural" state. Although new technological possibilities certainly created new avenues of musical exploration, it took several years to rethink entrenched business habits and restructure industry practices to make those explorations a musical reality. The mistakes heard on "Bluing," then, should be thought of as an experiment designed to capture jazz in process.

This chapter interrogates the LP in its moment of newness from the vantage point of Prestige Records, the small but influential jazz record label. As chapter 1 described in detail, record companies in the early to mid-1950s were always balancing old and new practices to adjust to rapidly changing economic trends. Everything from recording techniques and graphic design to market strategies had to be rethought and differently integrated. Yet during this era of unpredictability, the logics of white masculine authority continued to structure the record industry. Through a focus on the nascent production standards of the jazz LP at Prestige, this chapter moves from the industry-wide analysis given in chapter 1 to the relatively narrow perspective of a single record company. Doing so allows for a different mode of listening that attends much more closely to the sounds on the records themselves. Examining the rich sonic details within Prestige's catalog recenters my analysis on musical performance, with an ear toward the changing relationship between jazz musicians and the industry built around their sonic and visual representations. Such listening makes clear that the emerging praxis of record making at Prestige developed around contemporaneous notions of race and gender within the jazz industry.

In this account of the LP's newness, I focus on how Prestige chose to encode informal moments like the broken ending to Davis's "Bluing" into and onto its early LPs. As such, this chapter offers a particular history about musical mistakes. It is not the mere existence of these miscues and mishaps that animates my argument, however. Missed entrances, flubbed notes, or mishandled endings are an everyday part of jazz practice and deeply woven into the fabric of jazz improvisation in ways that often create opportunity for creativity and musical mastery. Within this context, mistakes come in many different forms and are treated differently depending on where and when they take place and who is onstage at the time. When inscribed onto record, mistakes reveal a complex set of philosophies regarding sound reproduction and its relationship to jazz performance at mid-century.[5] I focus on Prestige's first attempts to place moments of informal music making onto record as a means of understanding what this newly mediated reality for jazz records meant for the genre as a whole. As such, this chapter is not only about mistakes on record and the newness of a particular technology. It is that, but it is also a history about how jazz records came to tell particular kinds of stories about the music, its history, and the cultural politics that surround both.

The interwoven history of Prestige's formats, issue dates, graphic design, and musical content reveals how ideologies of race within the postwar record industry deeply informed the label's adoption of the LP. To begin, I outline how Weinstock's historically minded approach came to highlight Black expertise without naming it as such. I explore this erasure through Prestige's use of the word *modern* on its packages and in its marketing. Notions of white male control built into the segregational logic of the record business directed Weinstock's record-making practices, especially in his treatment of musical informalities. I then trace similar moments of spontaneity across different recording formats. From the first 10-inch LPs through Prestige's experiments with 7-inch extended play (EP) and its eventual adoption of the 12-inch LP format (and its variations), jazz history came to be a focal point of the label's activities. Still, even as jazz history became a valued cultural practice, it did so along the sonic color line—such expressions of economic power were not lost on musicians.[6] This conclusion serves as a prompt to re-listen to and re-situate Davis's voice on "Bluing" within this broader history of record making. Musical mistakes, miscues, and mishaps might seem to be at the margins of music, but as I argue, it is precisely at these edges where we must listen.

The Documentary Impulse of Prestige Records

The aesthetics of spontaneity heard on Prestige's early LPs resulted from several overlapping concerns about the economics and artistry of record making. Consider the following statements found on the backs of three Prestige records between 1951 and 1956:

> Neither the musicians nor the small group of listeners who were usually in attendance had access to a tape recorder. We often regretted this inability to preserve the type of unhindered, swinging music we felt never was captured at recording dates. (Liner notes to *Swingin' with Zoot Sims*, LP [10 in., 33⅓ rpm], 1951)

> Each album is an individual record session in itself, with actual dates of the recordings inscribed on the cover. This series will be invaluable to all students and fans of jazz as it will give them an accurate, documented, chronological picture of both the jazz scene as a whole and the important musicians as individuals. (Advertising copy for Prestige's Extended Play series, *Bennie Green with Strings*, EP [7 in., 45 rpm], 1953)

> In addition to bringing back the obsolete 78s, the LP had enabled us to hear, for instance, many of Charlie Parker's great passages through the issuance of his rejected takes which, because of their abbreviated nature, never would have found their way on to a 78 rpm disc. (Liner notes to Miles Davis's *Collectors' Items*, LP [12 in., 33⅓ rpm], 1956).[7]

As these statements suggest, Prestige's LPs encouraged and intensified what I will call the *documentary impulse* of the early 1950s jazz industry: the compulsion to preserve, to make an account, to circulate tradition, and to create history on record. Individual record makers each had their own overlapping sets of personal, professional, or economic concerns. I use *impulse* to account for the multifaceted motivations, those both implicit and openly declared, that helped guide this deeply felt desire to document jazz history. The quotations above, which were repeated verbatim or in similar fashion on dozens of LPs and EPs in the 1950s, work to advertise how Weinstock actively harnessed Prestige to *record* the music in every sense of the word.

By assuming the role as a steward of jazz history, Weinstock expressed a form of white masculine authority that was increasingly common among record makers during the early 1950s. In her exploration of jazz and gender in the postwar period, Nichole Rustin-Paschal uses the neologism *jazzmasculinity* to describe the spectrum of masculine expectations of jazz culture on and off the bandstand: risk taking, displays of virtuosity, claims of authenticity, and emotional dedication to the music.[8] Among many other topics, she dissects the ideological investments that white jazzmen, especially those who owned independent labels, used to justify their desire to nurture jazz history: "To nurture jazz was to instruct consumers on how to be fans, and to preserve and protect the music from unscrupulous people, those who were uncommitted to the ideals advocated by jazz culture."[9] Weinstock's documentary impulse was not simply a manifestation of his enthusiasm for the music; it was also a gendered expression of his economic power. By using the brand and operations of Prestige in this way, he joined a generation of white jazz connoisseurs who asserted their artistic and intellectual authority over the music through record making.

As the head of a fledgling label, Weinstock was creative and wide-ranging in his approach. With the advent of so many new formats during Prestige's formative years, he found ways to inventively repackage his catalog while reserving some capacity for experimentation. He was also notoriously impecunious and therefore frugal out of necessity. He did not pay for rehearsals. He did not invest in the highest-quality sound recording or manufacturing practices, especially before 1955. He signed young musicians, often those on their first record deal, to short contracts. At every step, however, Weinstock chose to engage in a particular kind of record making that documented jazz history.

Consider the slogan that appeared somewhere on every one of Prestige's early LPs, usually on the back jacket and set in capital letters: "PRESTIGE PRESENTS THE OUTSTANDING MODERN MUSICIAN ON LP."[10] The word *modern* appeared ubiquitously in promotional materials and anywhere else that the label could put it.[11] This included record titles from 1951 and 1952 such as the following:

> Kai Winding and J. J. Johnson, *Modern Jazz Trombones*
> Fats Navarro, Dizzy Gillespie, Miles Davis, and Kenny Dorham, *Modern Jazz Trumpets*
> J. J. Johnson and Bennie Green, *Modern Jazz Trombones, vol. 2*

Various other LPs from the same period used the word *new* to similar effect:

> Lee Konitz, *The New Sounds*
> Lee Konitz and Stan Getz, *The New Sounds*
> Gerry Mulligan and Allen Eager, *The New Sounds*
> Various, *New Sounds from Sweden, vol. 1*
> Bengt Hallberg and Lars Gullin, *New Sounds from Sweden, vol. 2*
> Red Rodney, *The New Sounds*
> Miles Davis, *The New Sounds*

The idea of the "new" had been with the label since Weinstock founded it in 1949 under the name New Jazz. The name change to Prestige Records a year later invoked a sense of progress and achievement, ideals that Weinstock increasingly relied on to situate the label and market its music within the broader ecosystem of the industry. The ten LP titles above point to the sometimes-contradictory nature of such positioning. After all, the overwhelming majority of the seventy-three tracks had already been issued on 78 rpm.[12] The more recent recordings were simultaneously cross-issued on both formats as a hedge against commercial unpredictability (see chapter 1). Only four of these tracks—all from *Miles Davis: The New Sounds*—were longer than four minutes.

In order to navigate the economic conditions of an industry in flux, Weinstock relied on a younger generation of musicians who were "advanc[ing] jazz," as he put it in 1954.[13] Like the use of "new" and "modern" in the titles of the firm's early LPs, the notion of advancement that Weinstock often invoked served to signal Prestige's investment in musicians at the vanguard of jazz experimentation. The marketing message was clear: Prestige sold modern music that played back at a modern speed (33⅓) and that was made for modern listeners. Adopting such phrasing was also a clever way to brand the inexpensive labor of aspiring musicians eager for their first record deal. That is, this modernist language helped to downplay the capitalistic concerns of record making. Crucially, the rhetoric of forward progression also assumes an already established tradition, one in need of documentation. As was common for white male record collectors interested in the "modern," Weinstock used this kind of finesse marketing as a form of economic power. Record making was a tautological solution to a problem identified and articulated by white record producers.

The notion of "modern" has also served various social and artistic functions throughout jazz history, especially in how jazz musicians associated themselves with or distanced themselves from European musical values.[14] Because the term operated on different aesthetic, political, and technological levels, it is useful to situate Prestige's use of *modern* in relation to the Black artists around whom the label built a large part of its business. As Guthrie Ramsey explores in depth, Black musicians within the United States continually explored what modernity, modernism, and modern life meant for them, especially in relation to their economic opportunity and political freedom. As record makers, Black jazz musicians were Afro-modernists who had to navigate a commercial enterprise that retained many resilient manifestations of Jim Crow economics.[15] For example, the drug charges that resulted in Billie Holiday, Charlie Parker, and Thelonious Monk famously losing their New York City cabaret cards between 1948 and 1953 were the product of a legal-economic system designed to control and limit the actions of African Americans.[16] Most jazz clubs in the 1950s remained segregated, and integrated bands onstage, or especially on film, sparked controversy. As Dizzy Gillespie observed, radio and Broadway orchestras refused to hire Black musicians.[17] Moreover, white musicians overwhelmingly dominated the readers' polls in *Down Beat* and *Metronome* in the late 1940s and early 1950s, results that directly influenced musicians' contracts and performance opportunities.[18] Even as the record industry grew, there were few Black bodies behind the mixing boards, in the control rooms, or in executive chairs. More opportunities became possible in the late 1950s, as jazz musicians found new avenues of expression and resistance through hard bop, soul jazz, and the New Thing.[19] Still, the entertainment business remained one of the only public venues in which African Americans had access to a mass audience. At mid-century, musical performance provided an opportunity to express alternate or even multiple kinds of identities not necessarily represented elsewhere.[20] Within the boundaries of the commercial marketplace (like everywhere else), Black performance was never confined by its material conditions.

Weinstock did not display an understanding of such concerns with Prestige. Even as he built his business around Black musical sounds, he continued to operate within a particular rubric of white modernism that refused, by omission, to equate jazz with Black expressive culture. Prestige's marketing rhetoric in the early 1950s reflected the cultural sensibilities of white male record collectors, especially in its portrayals of "modern" jazz musicians as male innovators who pushed the boundaries of harmony, form, and melody through instrumental improvisation.[21] The label's orientation to Black cultural politics would shift somewhat in the latter half of the decade, but Weinstock's strategy with Prestige in the early LP era continued to rely on a long-established script of white masculine authority. With its LPs, Prestige asked listeners to hear jazz as sophisticated music that ran against mainstream consumer culture and that just happened (sometimes) to be Black.[22] The complexities of this approach can be seen in the label's catalog, which included a cross-section of jazz styles and a diverse roster of musicians, often in interracial configurations. Prestige's first fifty LPs featured a profusion of styles, from bebop and the blues-infused playing of saxophonists James Moody and Gene Ammons to the experiments of Lennie Tristano and Lee Konitz. Other musicians to appear included Roy Eldridge, Stan Getz, J. J. Johnson, Fats Navarro, Zoot Sims, Sonny Stitt, Al Haig, George Wallington, Wardell Gray, Sonny Rollins, and Miles Davis. Prestige thus contributed to a pervasive white modernist discourse that was tenaciously color-blind in the way it presented jazz as an autonomous art form that transcended social categories.[23] Some musicians embraced this view. Many others did not. Yet all had to grapple with a business built around an essentialized understanding of Black culture that ignored, and often contributed to, the violent structures of racism meant to exploit Black expertise, Black labor, and Black capital.

Prestige's first LPs thus emerged from two overlapping conditions. The first was the uncertain market outlined in chapter 1, which necessitated a creative and nimble business approach. The second was the form of white modernism that emphasized "new" and "modern" styles without reference to jazz's Black cultural roots. Prestige's documentary impulse existed at the intersection, offering a means to market and sell records in a way that avoided nakedly capitalistic language. Because forward progress is, fundamentally, the mirror image of historical tradition, the value ascribed to jazz as a tradition cannot be separated from a particular Eurological formation of history that emerges from—and subsumes Blackness within—colonialist white supremacy.[24] Within the 1950s record industry, the logics of European music (and its history) determined what kinds of cultural work had value, regulated which communication networks circulated that value, and prescribed who had agency to shape that value. In other words, Eurological notions of historical tradition shaped the focus of critical and commercial attention in ways that normalized whiteness. And so, if the jazz LP was, as I have been arguing, an experiment in how to sell Black musical artistry within an industry with an entrenched segregational logic, then the documentary impulse was both a manifestation of these same cultural trajectories and also a reliable road map.

In many ways, the LP was perfectly situated, both technologically and culturally, to drive Prestige's documentary impulses. The increased capacity meant that more recorded minutes of music would circulate after a single point-of-sale interaction.[25] The format's uncertain future necessitated a strategically economical approach, and filling records with a combination of back-catalog and newly recorded material was a sensible solution. The new cardboard jackets had space for liner notes and other forms of discursive ephemera to justify this redundancy; such rhetoric opened new avenues for historical awareness and investments in the telling of that history. These were not simply changes in and at the margins but a part of a broader shift in the industry's impulse toward documentation, where jazz history became something to be valued, listened to, and collected—like all art. As I argued in the introduction, the proliferation of liner notes, the inclusion of session data, and the issuing of alternate takes materialize on record at the same mid-century moment when Marshall Stearns, André Hodeir, Martin Williams, and Leonard Feather wrote their intensely researched jazz history texts.[26] Having a history implies a tradition that must be documented.

The multidisciplinary trend toward documentation may have shaped the conditions in which Black artists had to operate, but it did not necessarily determine how they chose to express themselves during performance. In pushing against the racialized logics and structures of the record business, musicians found creative ways to express what Ingrid Monson calls "aesthetic agency": the crossing of cultural, geographic, and stylistic boundaries to consciously self-fashion one's musical persona.[27] For one, the ability to make lengthier recordings had the unintended effect of also circulating different kinds of musical labor that exist at the site of production—by which I mean at the site of record production. When Ira Gitler boasts about how LP technology gave Miles Davis "more freedom than he has ever had on record[,] for time limits were not strictly enforced" (1951), or when John Wilson writes that the LP allowed for recordings that were "unrestricted by studio formality" (1958), they were not referring to a new freedom of aesthetic agency.[28] Nevertheless, the impulse toward documentation meant that forms of Black expertise, both past and present, began to circulate more widely. Mistakes, miscues, and mishaps may have just been that. But their presence on record also meant that LPs, as emergent sonic media, became something more than a container for musical sound. Jazz records came to be a mechanism for aesthetic agency and cultural imagination.

1951: The 10-Inch LP, First Takes

On his 1951 recording of "East of the Sun" for Prestige, Zoot Sims plays the melody a total of three times: once at the beginning, another at the end, and two nonconsecutive halves in the middle. The quartet plays the thirty-six-measure, ABAC form without deviation through the eleven-minute track, rendering an up-tempo yet still relaxed version of Brooks Bowman's 1936 song. The two melodic halves in the track's middle are not by design but are the result of a few moments of confusion.

Sims plays the full melody at the top, in typical fashion, followed by solo choruses by each member of the quartet. Sims comes in again after Art Blakey's drum solo, improvising for a half chorus before stating the second half of the melody (5:18). This leads to a seemingly natural ending point. Sims plays a clear cadential figure, and pianist Harry Biss and bassist Clyde Lombardi hit the tonic chord together as if to conclude (5:45). Blakey, however, plays through the ending without pause. Unlike his continuation on Davis's "Bluing," the rest of the band proceeds without so much as a skipped beat, although there is clearly confusion as Sims improvises around the melody for a half chorus and unambiguously states the melody once again (6:05). At this point, the track is not yet half over—Sims plays two more solo choruses, trades fours with Blakey for another two, and finally signals the out chorus through his return to the melody for the third time (10:15). At the end, Sims repeats the same cadential figure, and the band concludes together without trouble.

Through the two choruses of melodic confusion and a false ending, the band plays on the edge of a breakdown. The ensemble's execution makes this record feel loose but not sloppy; the ability to make a mistake not necessarily feel like one is its own kind of virtuosity. Elsewhere, Lombardi's bass solo ends four bars too early and in the wrong part of the form. The rest of the ensemble quickly adjusts. Despite the uncertainty, the group never hesitates or sounds in danger of falling apart, even though Sims's broken melody was not business as usual in an early-1950s recording session. The performance's looseness can be heard elsewhere as well. The saxophonist's inventive playing—his nearly endless stream of ideas—makes the composite more than its imperfections.

"East of the Sun" resulted from Prestige's first recording session specifically designed to take advantage of the convergence between long-playing and magnetic-tape technologies. Sims's August 14, 1951, session produced two tracks, "Zoot Swings the Blues" (over eight minutes) and "East of the Sun" (eleven minutes), which both appeared on opposing sides of a 10-inch LP titled *Swingin' with Zoot Sims* (1951). To signal the LP's newness, the B-side label included the phrase "Uninterrupted Version recorded Exclusively for LP," a sentiment highlighted on the label's other promotional material as well. For example, the back jacket of *Stan Getz, vol. 2* informed potential buyers about the "special long record running 11:00 and 8:30 minutes" of *Swingin' with Zoot Sims* that was "recorded exclusively for this LP."[29] Like record companies in the late 1940s, customers had to be educated about the LP's potential. Such descriptions of the record marked the listening experience through such new technological means as not simply novel but something "special" and "exclusive."

In the weeks immediately after Sims's recording date, Prestige scheduled two similar sessions with Gerry Mulligan and Miles Davis for release on LP.[30] These sessions resulted in several LPs released between 1951 and 1953, including two from Davis (one with "Bluing") and another from Mulligan. *Gerry Mulligan Blows* (1953) contained "Mulligan's Too," a seventeen-minute blues split between two sides of the 10-inch LP. The record jacket similarly included the short phrase "Special LP recording" that advertised the label's experimentation to potential buyers. Years later, Weinstock recalled his desire to have the musicians play longer solos:

> I sensed that we were going to have LPs. I'd heard rumblings. And I did three sessions that were monumental. The first one was Miles Davis with Sonny Rollins and Jackie McLean. Art Blakey was on drums. I think it might have been Walter Bishop and Tommy Potter, but I'm not sure. Anyway, I just said, "Miles, we're going to stretch out."
>
> He said, "You mean we're just going to play?"
>
> I said, "As long as you want almost—within reason."
>
> He said, "Okay, who should I use?"
>
> I said, "You seem to love Sonny Rollins." If you look at the early ones, Sonny's on a lot of them. I said, "You love Sonny."

He said, "What about this young guy Jackie McLean? He's pretty good too, if we're going to stretch out."

I said, "Yeah, I heard him. He's good." If you listen, that session we did "Dig," "Bluing." Now Jackie doesn't play on all the tunes. He wasn't really that great at the time. He was good.

So Miles and Sonny stretched out. That's how it went. We'd always talked about the personnel, what we're going to do. A lot of times they'd have tunes. Other times, I'd have tunes. Our main emphasis was just to play and stretch out. We accomplished that there.[31]

Through this passage, Weinstock's use of "just play" and "stretch out" describes technological advances in terms of musical performance. But in practice, the LP format afforded new musical possibilities that required musicians and producer to reorient their relationship in the studio. This changing sociality went beyond telling musicians to simply play longer, as Weinstock recalled about the Mulligan session: "On the Gerry thing I had him stretch out. He played a long solo, and then him and Allen Eager would play. They'd look at me, if I wanted them to play more. I'd shake my head, 'Yeah,' 'no,' or whatever. Then they'd switch. I'd sort of 'cut my throat.' He'd know he'd be going out at the end of the chorus."[32]

The discussion of personnel, suggestions of repertoire, and signals to the musicians while recording suggest changes to the role of the producer. Musical creation in the coming years would increasingly occur in tandem with technological innovations such as multitrack recording, tape editing, and the successful commercialization of stereo sound.[33] However, the LP's introduction was one of the first technologies in several decades that enabled producers such as Weinstock to reimagine jazz record making. Keeping various kinds of mistakes on record is one way in which such experimentations manifested in sound.

Prestige's first LP experiments are best understood within the wider economic context of the record business as well as through Weinstock's own biography. As a teenager, he began a mail-order business by advertising in *Record Changer*, a hobby that eventually grew into a more substantial enterprise. He rented space at the Jazz Record Center on 47th Street in Manhattan and soon after began making his own records.[34] Prestige, then called New Jazz, began in January 1949 with a recording session featuring pianist Lennie Tristano. Like so many other white recordmen, Weinstock's background as a collector allowed him to claim intellectual authority over the music's history, even as he kept a careful eye on his balance sheet in order to sustain his fledgling company.

Prestige was one of many newly established independent record labels interested in music that fell under the rhythm-and-blues banner.[35] As the record industry expanded in the late 1940s and 1950s, competition was fierce. This meant that labels had to both strategize around and hustle within an uncertain market. Label owners like Weinstock had to be willing to experiment along several different trajectories, which helps explain why firms such as Dial, Savoy, Commodore, and Blue Note all issued their first LPs by the end of 1950. Prestige followed in the middle of 1951, along with Circle, Jolly Roger, Jazz Panorama, and Roost.[36] Clearly, these labels believed it was worth investing in the jazz LP, even though the format overall still only accounted for 16 percent of total retail sales in 1951.[37]

Weinstock filled Prestige's first LPs with reissued material from his back catalog, employing the same strategy used by numerous labels, including Savoy (see chapter 1). These discs were all the 10-inch size and had three or four tracks per side, each lasting the standard two-and-a-half to three minutes.[38] Such remediation enabled Prestige to offer music on both new and old formats without having to invest in costly recording sessions that did not necessarily guarantee sales. In 1951 the move to LPs represented a calculated risk.

Prestige's eventual growth into a leading independent jazz label coincided with the industry-wide transition to the LP in the 1950s. Within this context, the release of *Swingin' with Zoot Sims*—mistakes, mishaps, and all—represented something different, a sonic manifestation of the adage "Competition spurs innovation." The record was the first Prestige LP with a track longer than eight minutes. Not by coincidence, it was also the first of the label's LPs to include liner notes on the back jacket.[39] The sixteen prior LP releases had either a blank back or a list of the label's catalog, which included track titles and sometimes personnel if space allowed. Recording dates and locations were generally absent. Gitler's liner notes on *Swingin' with Zoot Sims* thus represented an experiment in record production that doubled as both a marketing tool and an expression of white masculine authority. The notes highlight the insider culture of "modern" jazz musicians, who would gather after hours for jam sessions in "a studio on West 47th Street known as 'Don Jose's.'" Gitler continues using the language of technological possibility:

Neither the musicians nor the small group of listeners who were usually in attendance had access to a tape recorder. We often regretted this inability to preserve the type of unhindered, swinging music we felt never was captured at recording dates.

A recording session has undertones of tension running through it. The jazz artist faces the problem especially when he must undertake the bulk of the improvisation. Mistakes cannot be too large even though they are an expected and human occurrence when a man is attempting impromptu innovations. Then, there is the restriction of the time limit. First a tune is "run down for time." One chorus is measured on a stop-clock and the soloist then knows how many choruses he may blow. Most 78 RPM records run from two and a half to three minutes. This stricture has always confronted the recording jazz artist, until August 14, 1951. On that afternoon, Jack "Zoot" Sims ambled into the Apex recording studios to do some sides. It was obvious from the moment Zoot started to play that he was in a relaxed mood and really wanted to blow. Immediately, much of the uneasiness created by the restrictions was nullified to a great extent.[40]

Beyond his description of the circumstances surrounding the session, Gitler emphasized how the technology, the province of white men, gave listeners access to musical performances that were, until this point, reserved for only a few. The description of the recording space and naming of a recording date—August 14, 1951—tied the recording process to the specifics of music making. Even though the notes stress artistic expression, they subtly told consumers not only how to listen to the new LP technology but also why they should value the lengthier track. The concurrent materialization of liner notes on the LP jacket and the first Prestige session to take advantage of LP technology should be understood as a shift in cultural value around the notion of documentation as much as a shift in listening and recording.

Linking claims of "new" and "modern" music to technological innovation was a business strategy that Prestige used throughout the early 1950s. Gitler's liner notes to *Miles Davis: New Sounds*, released soon after Sims's LP, describe Davis's music in terms of the new modes of technological representation. In particular, Gitler highlights the possibility of recording without limits:

> Of course, Miles is to be appreciated for bringing a new sound and conception to the trumpet but what really gives him greatness are the

intangibles he possesses, which enable him to transmit sweeping joy with his "wailing" solos and reflective beauty in the delicacy of his ballads.

This album gives Miles more freedom than he has ever had on record for time limits were not strictly enforced. There is opportunity to build ideas into a definite cumulative effect. These ideas sound much more like air-shots than studio recordings.

Upon the wonderful rhythmic foundation of Art Blakey's drums, Tommy Potter's bass, and Walter Bishop's piano, tenorman Sonny Rollins and alto-man Jackie McLean are able to enjoy some of the unlimited time for their solo efforts. Rollins demonstrated the impact of the intangibles, again, with his solo on "Paper Moon." . . . Here are New Sounds at greater length. Listen to them at great length.[41]

The technology, as Gitler narrates it, provides an opportunity for a more immediate listening experience, one closer to hearing the musicians in person or over the radio. Such claims about modern technology and listening echo in Gitler's liner notes to Davis's *Blue Period* LP: "This album is a must to those who appreciate our modern jazzmen. I know that the people who have missed hearing the musicians in person will be especially gratified, because this is what they have been missing."[42] As with other early LPs on Prestige, including *Swingin' with Zoot Sims*, the term *modern* glosses technological and musical possibility without reference to the Black expertise on which such claims were built. In this context, it is noteworthy that the word *freedom* is both repeated and used without reference to the cultural context of Jim Crow. Recall that *Blue Period* included the mistaken ending on "Bluing," which Gitler characterizes as the "high spot" and describes as "over nine minutes of freedom of expression on modern blues chord changes."[43] Mistakes on record were made possible by the "freedom" from the technological limits of the 78-rpm format, which enables a new kind of listening. Yet freedom brought about by technology has its limitations: cultural freedom and economic liberation remained an impossibility in the early 1950s. As Fred Moten's work on Davis might suggest, mistakes on record offer their own kind of freedom within a longer history of unfreedom, the kind that Black jazz musicians lived with on a daily basis.[44]

Placed in their historical context, the mistakes on Sims's "East of the Sun" result from refigured possibilities of recording, producing, and listening. Hearing jazz in process through musical mistakes created the illusion of intimacy. Yet this illusion was made possible only by technologies of mediation and the ever-present economies of record making—the domains of white recordmen. As one of the first recording sessions for the LP, the record was an experiment in how to present and market extended jazz improvisation. As the first Prestige record with liner notes, it helped guide listening in a particular direction, where mistakes are not errors but rather an "essential" character of jazz improvisation.

More generally, such mistakes reveal how the notion of a jazz record was in the process of changing because of the LP format. In the next few years, disc size, visual design, liner notes, and other elements of producing records would rapidly change and codify around specific industry and consumer needs. However, in 1951 and 1952, when Prestige issued the LPs of Davis, Mulligan, and Sims, LPs were still new and roughly three times as expensive as their 78-rpm counterparts. Their future remained unclear. During these years of uncertainty, musical mistakes began appearing on record with more frequency as a means of selling the format as a new listening experience. This shift in priorities was a change in cultural value, not simply one in technological capabilities. From the beginning, liner notes told a story about the music's creation and taught people how to listen to the technology from the perspective of white recordmen. In doing so, these notes connect to a value system of white jazz modernism that understood the music in relation to its "universal" appeal rather than as an expression of Blackness. This is the documentary impulse on record.

1953: Extended Play

During the transition from 78 rpm to LPs, the visual, physical, and sonic attributes of jazz records changed dramatically as record labels adjusted their existing record-making infrastructures to give listeners as many options as possible.[45] Trial and error characterized this shift, as different formats quickly came and went. As discussed in chapter 1, jazz record labels strategically issued the same content across a variety of formats that differed in size, material, and rotation speed. Prestige was no exception. The label's 78-rpm version of Davis's "Bluing," issued in three parts between two different discs, was an inelegant solution to the market-volatility problem facing all labels at this time.[46] These broken-apart sides further illustrate an industry in constant flux.

It is within this context that RCA Victor introduced the 7-inch "extended play" (EP) disc in 1952, as outlined in chapter 1. EPs quickly gained commercial traction with independent jazz labels, and by 1954 Clef, Savoy, Contemporary, Pacific Jazz, Debut, and Prestige had all issued parts of their catalog in this format.[47] The growth of the EP in the jazz field followed a path identical to that of the early LP, as labels continued to emphasize previously issued material. When Savoy announced its adoption of the EP in March 1953, reports focused on the label's plan to reissue recordings by Charlie Parker, Erroll Garner, and Lester Young.[48] Of the one hundred EPs eventually issued on Savoy, the vast majority reproduce key production elements of the label's initial jazz LP offerings. For example, Savoy's first EP, *New Sounds in Modern Music: Charlie Parker, vol. 1*, replicated the cover design, title, and some music from the label's first 10-inch LP.[49] The major labels—Columbia, MGM, Decca, and Capitol—released pop and crossover EPs but did not use the format for jazz except for the occasional discs featuring jazz-adjacent stars such as Frank Sinatra and Bing Crosby.[50]

Prestige began issuing EPs around 1953, eventually releasing a total of seventy-four discs in its PREP 1300 series.[51] Like its first LPs, the label used the EP to repackage and reissue recordings already in its catalog. Most EPs included four tracks, two per side. Lengthier recordings were split between the A and the B sides, using the same practice from the 78-rpm era, when technological limitations necessitated such an aural break. This was, for instance, how Prestige issued "Bluing" on an EP titled *In a Blue Mood: Bluing* (ca. 1954).[52] The simple two-toned graphics and marginalia on the EPs were similar to the first 10-inch LPs, but with one important difference: each EP prominently displayed the recording session date on both the front and back jacket. For example, *Miles Davis Quartet* (1953) prominently displayed the recording date (May 19, 1953) in block letters next to Davis's name. The back covers did not have liner notes but, instead, featured a list of discs in the series along with track listings and recording date.[53] The disc label usually included personnel.

Similar to the liner notes that began appearing on Prestige's 10-inch LPs, these EPs told a particular story about jazz history that foregrounded the process of record making. After all, it was not standard practice in 1953 for record companies to name specific session dates on the record, even though it would have been a relatively easy matter to have included this information somewhere in the marginalia of earlier formats.[54] The majority of the label's EPs displayed "Prestige Extended Play Documentary Series" somewhere on the cover (usually on the top right corner) and a tagline of "Each album represents an individual record session" on the back. Additionally, the first few discs had a short explanatory paragraph on the back jacket:

> PRESTIGE presents jazz for the modern collector on extended play. This series represents the best in modern music from 1949 up to today. Each album is an individual record session in itself, with actual dates of the recordings inscribed on the cover. This series will be invaluable to all students and fans of jazz as it will give them an accurate, documented, chronological picture of both the jazz scene as a whole and the important musicians as individuals, beginning with 1949 and continuing on as each new year brings new developments in jazz.[55]

With the phrase "actual dates inscribed on the cover," the label marked the record jacket as a future location for such documentation while also emphasizing the need to accurately chronicle the music's development. This "documentary series" claimed to give access to the most "modern" music while simultaneously allowing "modern" listeners to track jazz's trajectory over time. As a fitting manifestation of the documentary impulse, Prestige's EP documentary series attempted to create a collectable jazz archive. Such historical self-consciousness certainly connects to Weinstock's background as a collector, his identity position, and his efforts to direct the label's catalog toward a listenership of presumably white male insiders similarly invested in this formation of history.

Beyond a marketing approach to avoid redundancy, the remediation of older content onto a newer format like the jazz EP should also be understood as a technological answer to a cultural question about writing jazz into the historical record. The addition of session dates might appear to be a simple change in the margins, yet such historical specificity connects to a noticeable shift in how jazz records documented music making at the site of production. Prestige's EP format framed the music in relation to itself, thereby presenting jazz history as something to be valued, listened to, and collected. Although the popularity of jazz EPs would quickly fade, these discs nevertheless point to the dynamic nature of how record makers found new uses for emerging technologies of sound. Prestige's EPs emerge from a broader trend in which jazz records increasingly promoted and sold the music as a means of encountering the past through sound.

Within such depictions of the recorded past, ideologies of race remained ever present. Prestige's approach to record making generally deemphasized the connections between jazz and Black expressive culture, a position that became increasingly tenuous as the label's documentary impulse grew. A history of jazz was simply difficult to tell without highlighting Black expertise and artistry, a tension encoded directly onto the record jackets themselves. Most covers in the EP series were relatively simple: a two-toned cutout photo of the artist accompanied by a track listing, record title, and session date. Yet even as the lexical content simultaneously omitted Blackness while drawing attention to the record's documentary nature, the visual language could not avoid the corporeal presence of the musicians. Teddy Charles's EP featured a photo of an integrated band hovering over some sheet music, seemingly deep in conversation about the specifics of the upcoming performance.[56] Other records featured photos of Black artists such as Bennie Green, Milt Jackson, and Miles Davis playing their instruments. Such depictions showcased the musicians in the midst of music making, drawing attention to the physical labor of music.[57] Thus, the documentary impulse of these EPs, which supposedly brought listeners closer to the act of music making, highlighted Black expertise by extension, even without naming it as such.

In the changing landscape of the early-1950s jazz industry, many formats, like the 7-inch EP and 10-inch LP, had a relatively short life span. More formats failed than succeeded. With a market in flux, record labels strove to balance their production and manufacturing costs with customer preferences. With the EP Documentary Series, Prestige explored how new formats might meet new demands. Seemingly insignificant elements in the marginalia reflect larger shifts in the relationship between music making and recording technology. If "modern" listening was partially about hearing jazz as it happened, all aspects of the record needed to help construct a feeling of musical immediacy. Prestige's EPs further integrated the physical, visual, and aural elements of record making toward that end.

1955: The 12-Inch LP

The piano intro to "Disappointed," a track on James Moody's *Hi Fi Party* (1956), includes some extra accompaniment from the musicians in the studio as they talk, laugh, and joke while the tape rolls. The social atmosphere continues into the solos of saxophonist Pee Wee Moore, trombonist William Shepherd, and trumpeter Dave Burns. Though mostly unintelligible, the voices can be heard throughout the entire six-minute-and-twenty-second track. At the beginning of his solo, Burns enters with a forceful double-time phrase, and someone shouts "Whoa!" During James Moody's solo, several others react: "swing it" (2:35)—"nice!" (2:52)—"go ahead" (3:00)—"yeah" (3:33). Vocalist Eddie Jefferson begins his solo with a reference to Charlie "Bird" Parker, who had passed away about five months before the August 1955 record session: "Here's Bird—here's what Bird said [*starts singing*]: I got in trouble foolin' around with a pretty woman" (3:45). His solo continues, precisely replicating the melodic content of Parker's 1946 rendition of "Lady Be Good," but with the addition of Jefferson's newly composed lyrics.[58]

Weinstock later explained that "Disappointed" was based on a concept of "long-term airplay" that he had heard on Norman Granz's Jazz at the Philharmonic (JATP) recordings. Weinstock liked that "you could hear the musicians talking."[59] The Parker JATP recording of "Lady Be Good" that inspired "Disappointed" is a perfect example. Recorded in January 1946 at the Philharmonic Auditorium in Los Angeles, the recording begins with a piano solo and a brief exchange. One of the musicians can be heard asking, "What's this?," and someone else responds with "Lady Be Good."[60] In his liner notes to *Hi Fi Party*, Gitler explicitly connects Moody's LP with Parker's JATP performance and draws attention to the sociality among band members as well as the studio informality: "The boys in the band shout encouragement to the soloists who are Pee Wee Moore, Shepherd, Burns, and Moody. Then Eddie Jefferson comes in with Bird's solo from JATP and turns it into an amusing sad story." Earlier in the notes, Gitler mentions the "happy vitality" of the session: "The prime example of this is Disappointed where the 'Silence On the Air' goes unobserved."[61] Even as Gitler attempts to sell records by bringing listeners "inside" the studio, "Disappointed" is also an example of how Prestige's documentary impulses result in the circulation of new musical subjectivities. In particular, Jefferson's recasting of Parker's improvisation presents an alternative case for musicians having the ultimate authority over jazz history. The aesthetics of spontaneity result in the increased aural presence of the musicians at the site of production, where their sociality translates into musical connection and artful expression.

Hi Fi Party was one of the first 12-inch LPs released by Prestige. The label began using the format in 1955 and 1956, following clear industry trends (see chapter 1).[62] Elsewhere, on *Milt Jackson Quartet* (1955), Gitler outlined the company's plans to use the larger format as a form of historical documentation:

> It seems that sometimes 10 inch LPs do not suffice. When a musician is an important one (in the sense of having something to say) lovers of the jazz art cannot get enough of him [sic]. The 12 inch LP is the logical solution, that is until everyone can get a Rek-O-Kut turntable.
>
> Prestige will utilize the 12 inch series in two ways. One will be to bring up to date the best work of the important musicians recorded at the company's inception: Stan Getz, Lee Konitz, Miles Davis, and Gerry Mulligan. Remastering will be done by Rudy Van Gelder who will bring the sound up to 1955 standards. Each of these albums will contain significant recordings of the aforementioned musicians. The space afforded by the 12 inch LP will be used to present a collection of numerous short tracks (i.e., the 3 minute recording), and in the cases of Mulligan and Davis, the longer sides as well.
>
> In new recordings for the 12 inch series, although the short track will not be completely neglected, the main emphasis is on ample time for development of ideas by the soloist and composer. As in the case of the reissues the musicians are important ones—people who are contributing richly to the story of jazz.[63]

Along with advertising Prestige's past catalog, Gitler highlights the label's newfound attention to sound quality through the remastering work of Rudy Van Gelder.[64] (The word *important* appears three times in this passage alone.) Notice, too, the stress put on male innovators of the "jazz art" who have contributed "richly to the story of jazz." This 12-inch manifestation of the documentary impulse echoes each of the label's previous experiments in record making while also placing additional stress on a male-dominated understanding of jazz history that could now be heard in the highest possible fidelity.

The adoption and standardization of 12-inch LPs made Weinstock rethink Prestige's overall presentation in other ways as well. Nearly all of Prestige's record jackets began to feature lengthier liner notes that educated consumers about the music and new technologies. Even the record sleeves, once simply a blank piece of paper, became an additional place for advertising.[65] The label's cover art also became increasingly sophisticated, detailed, and creative. The augmented emphasis on visual design occurred in tandem with a greater emphasis on record production, all intended to take advantage of the "long-playing" aspect of the technology.

This transition did not happen overnight. Weinstock treated Prestige's early 10-inch LPs much like 78-rpm records, which were generally sold in blank paper sleeves and had only simple lettering on the label itself that indicated artist, song title, record company, and issue number. Prestige's first LPs included only the leader's name in block letters, a list of tracks, and issue number. For example, the unadorned cover of *Lee Konitz Quintet, Lennie Tristano Quintet* (1951) displays the album and track names in dark-blue block lettering with the Prestige logo beneath (see figure 2.1). The top left and right corners, respectively, included the issue number, PRLP 101, and the phrase "Long Playing Micro Groove Non-Breakable Record," a marketing slogan developed by Columbia in 1948. The back jacket was dark brown and blank, much like the typical sleeve of a 78-rpm disc. This approach was partly pragmatic: the costs of printing ornate graphics would increase the price of discs that were already more expensive than their 78-rpm counterparts.

Sometime soon after, Prestige began to place simple, two-toned images of the bandleader on its covers. The label even issued updated versions of LPs already in its catalog, including the same Konitz and Tristano LP pictured in figure 2.2. In 1976 Gitler recalled Weinstock's preference for such design during this time: "I can still visualize the front cover [of *Swingin' with Zoot Sims* (1951)], a photograph of Zoot blowing his tenor saxophone printed in blue on yellow paper. That was Prestige's version of a two-color job but Weinstock's attitude was: 'They don't buy it for the cover, man. If they dig the music...'"[66] (see figure 2.3). The move from block lettering to a simple, low-budget image was relatively minor but nevertheless a significant indicator of the many shifts that would soon come in Prestige's visual language.

Weinstock's stripped-down approach soon began to change. By 1953 the abstract designs of Leo Sharper and David X. Young appeared on several 10-inch LPs, including *Teddy Charles Quartet: New Directions* (1953) and *Jimmy Raney Plays* (1953).[67] Designs by Don Schlitten featuring his own photographs or the amateur snapshots of Weinstock appeared the following year.[68] Many of the 10-inch LPs after catalog number 156 showcase a much more varied visual language in terms of image quality, design, and abstraction—compare figures 2.1–2.3 to *Miles Davis Quartet* (1954) in figure 2.4. These trends continued during Prestige's expansion onto 12-inch LPs when Weinstock hired a rotating cast of freelance graphic designers, photographers, and artists. There was no unifying aesthetic but rather an unencumbered sense of experimentation, from the fractured typography

Figure 2.1. Original album cover of *Lee Konitz Quintet, Lennie Tristano Quintet*, Prestige PRLP 101 (1951), design by Ira Gitler.

seen on Gil Mellé's *Quadrama* and Red Garland's *All Kinds of Weather* to the enigmatic illustration of *Trombone by Three* (figures 2.5–2.7). During the same period, the abstract designs on LPs such as *Mal-1* and *Cookin' with the Miles Davis Quintet* (figures 2.8 and 2.9) appeared alongside covers with evocative photographs of musicians or scenery—Mose Allison's *Local Color* and John Coltrane's first album as a leader, *Coltrane*, are illustrative examples (figures 2.10 and 2.11). Together, the work of Bob Parent, Don Martin, Tom Hannan, Gil Mellé, Scott Hyde, Marc Rice, Reid Miles, and Esmond Edwards came to define the visual language of Prestige between 1956 and the end of the decade.[69]

Prestige's new focus on its visual design brought it closer to another leading independent label, Blue Note Records. Founded in 1939 by Alfred

Figure 2.2. Updated album cover of *Lee Konitz Quintet, Lennie Tristano Quintet*, Prestige PRLP 101 (1951), design by Ira Gitler.

Lion and Max Marguilis, Blue Note similarly targeted the niche listenership of jazz collectors. Although it initially focused on traditional jazz styles, the firm shifted its approach in 1947 when it signed musicians such as Thelonious Monk, Art Blakey, and Bud Powell. In the 1950s, Blue Note eventually became the largest proponent of hard bop, a substyle closely associated with Black popular culture and that drew from R&B, gospel, and blues (discussed in chapter 5). Its roster during this time featured young musicians on their first or second record deals—first-time leaders on Blue Note include Horace Silver, Lou Donaldson, Clifford Brown, and Wynton Kelly. Even more so than Weinstock, Lion felt that jazz should not be, as he said in a 1956 interview with Nat Hentoff, produced "like ball point pens" and that the music was "not the kind of commodity you can market in every candy store."[70] In the

Figure 2.3. Album cover of *Swingin' with Zoot Sims*, Prestige PRLP 117 (1951), design by Ira Gitler.

1940s, Blue Note made the unusual decision to release jazz on 12-inch 78s, a format generally reserved for classical music. Lion explained his feelings that "jazz often could not be constrained to fit 10 [inches]."[71] Thus, it is not surprising that Blue Note became an early adopter of the LP, issuing its first 10-inch records at the end of 1950.

Unlike Prestige, Blue Note emphasized the appearance of its LPs from the beginning. Under the direction of photographer and co-owner Francis Wolff, Blue Note became one of the first independent labels to use high-quality photos and artwork on its records, despite the accompanying financial burden.[72] Blue Note's early 10-inch LPs were often two- or three-toned like those of Prestige, but they featured eye-popping photos, elaborate artwork, and intricate graphic design.[73] This was a sharp contrast to Prestige's

Figure 2.4. Album cover of *Miles Davis Quartet*, Prestige PRLP 161 (1954), design by David X. Young.

initial text-only approach. The visual aesthetics of Blue Note continued to lead the way when the label, like all others, adopted the 12-inch LP as its standard format.

Even as Prestige came closer to its competitors in terms of graphic design on the 12-inch discs, the label maintained its distinctive sound. Prestige's informal production aesthetic remained through the 1950s, as Weinstock recalled: "It was all very loose. I hated charts. I hated arrangements. That's where me and Alfred [Lion, of Blue Note] differed. Alfred would have rehearsals. I never had a rehearsal. I didn't believe in it. I believed jazz had to swing and be loose."[74] Weinstock always maintained that minimal preparation, with little to no rehearsal, helped foster a creative environment in the recording studio. In doing so, he also reinforced a view of jazz masculinity that binds

Figure 2.5. Album cover of *Quadrama*, Prestige PRLP 7097 (1957), design by Reid Miles.

authentic emotional expression to improvised risk taking.[75] Miles Davis expressed a similar opinion in 1955 when he agreed with an observation initially given by Max Roach: "He said he'd rather hear a guy miss a couple of notes than hear the same old clichés all the time. Often when a man misses, it at least shows he's trying to think of something new to play."[76] Unlike Davis, who spoke as a musician, Weinstock's investment in the aesthetics of spontaneity emerged from the economic realities of owning a small record label: preparative rehearsals, additional takes, and extra studio time to edit the tapes were all expensive. Weinstock's documentary impulse served as a filter, allowing him to turn his own impecuniousness into an engaging record.[77] This seems to be one of the lessons learned from the inclusion of

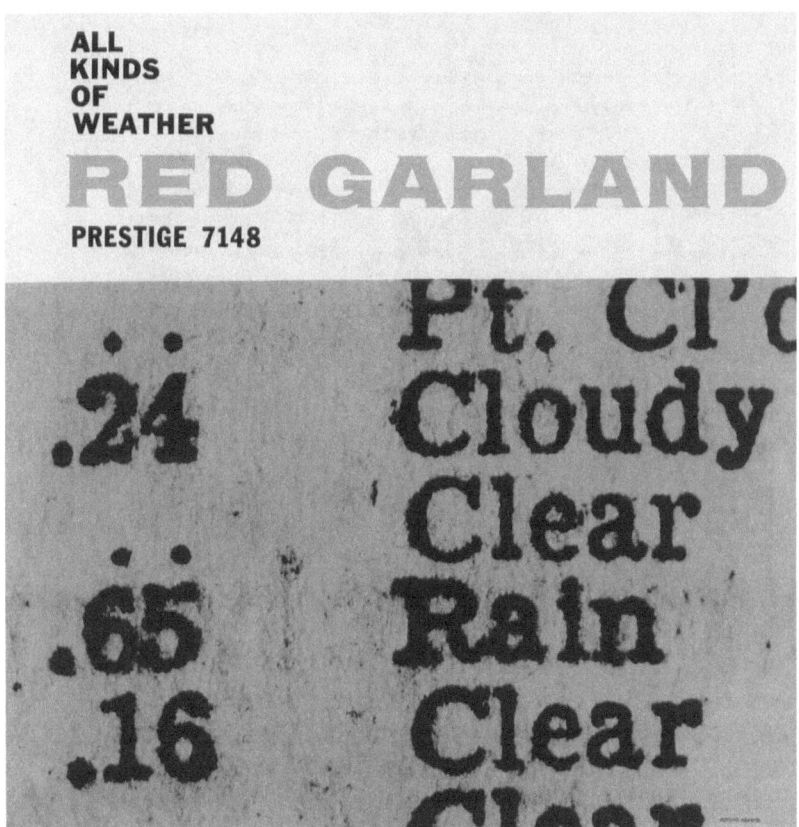

Figure 2.6. Album cover of *All Kinds of Weather*, Prestige PRLP 7148 (1959), design by Esmond Edwards.

musical mistakes, studio chatter, and other elements of informal music making heard on Davis's "Bluing" and Sims's "East of the Sun."

The extemporaneous sound world that Prestige continued to cultivate can also be heard on *Relaxin' with the Miles Davis Quintet,* recorded in 1956 but issued two years later. Davis's raspy voice opens the record as he communicates with those in the control room: "I'll play it and tell you what it is later" (0:00). He counts off the rhythm section with four measures of high-hat-like snaps that continue through Red Garland's piano introduction, based on the melody of "Westminster Quarters." Similar moments of informality occur on "You're My Everything," which includes a false start. An unaccompanied, descending scale by Davis begins this track. He stops

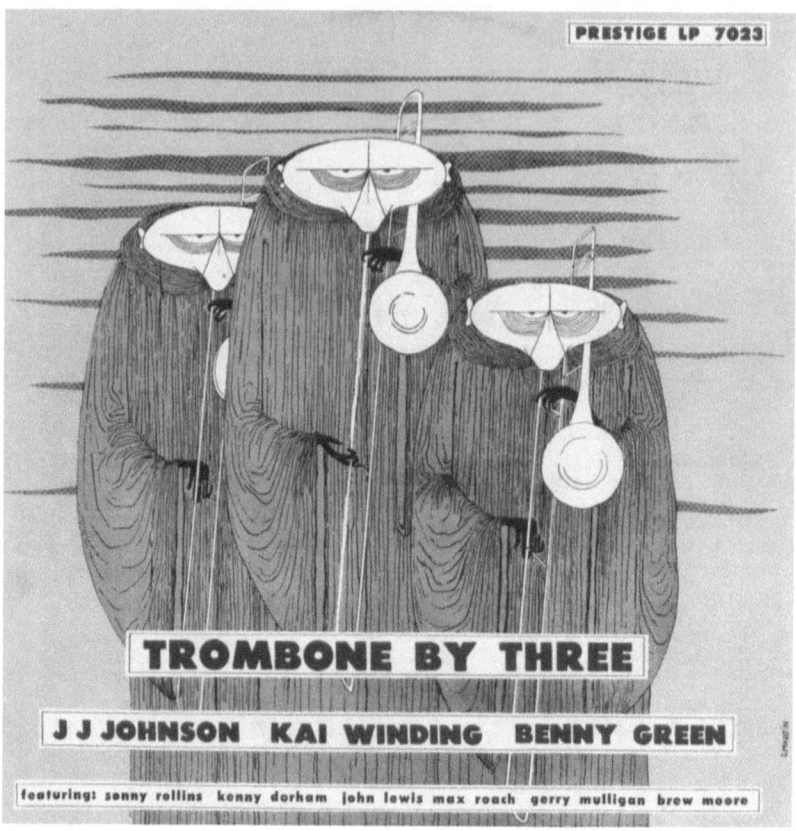

Figure 2.7. Album cover of *Trombone by Three*, Prestige PRLP 7023 (1956), design by Don Martin.

to call the tune and jokes with the musicians, "When you see a red light on, everybody's supposed to be quiet" (0:06). After a short back-and-forth with Van Gelder, Garland plays a melodic introduction that Davis soon interrupts with a whistle and then some instructions: "Play some block chords, Red." After a brief pause, they continue. "All right, Rudy? Block chords, Red" (0:28). The group runs down the track without further trouble. Like Prestige had done with Zoot Sims, the loose production aesthetic draws attention to the group's virtuosity through effortless execution.

Relaxin' was one of four LPs that featured Davis's quintet with saxophonist John Coltrane, pianist Red Garland, bassist Paul Chambers, and drummer Philly Joe Jones. After the 1955 Newport Jazz Festival, Davis signed a lucrative contract with Columbia Records. To fulfill his remaining contract

Figure 2.8. Album cover of *Mal-1*, Prestige PRLP 7090 (1957), design by Reid Miles.

with Prestige, Davis's quintet did two marathon-like recording sessions on May 11 and October 26, 1956, that produced enough material for a set of LPs titled *Cookin'*, *Relaxin'*, *Workin'*, and *Steamin' with the Miles Davis Quintet*. Prestige released the albums over the next four years, thereby taking advantage of Davis's continued success with Columbia.[78]

The high-level performance alone makes these LPs noteworthy. Equally significant for my purposes are the comparisons to concert performances that Gitler highlights in his liner notes. "Although this session was recorded in a studio," he writes on *Relaxin'*, "the tunes were done in the immediate succession of a nightclub-type set and there were no second takes." He goes on to describe the starts, stops, and chatter between musicians and engineer as adding to the "more personal" feeling of the recording.[79] Similar

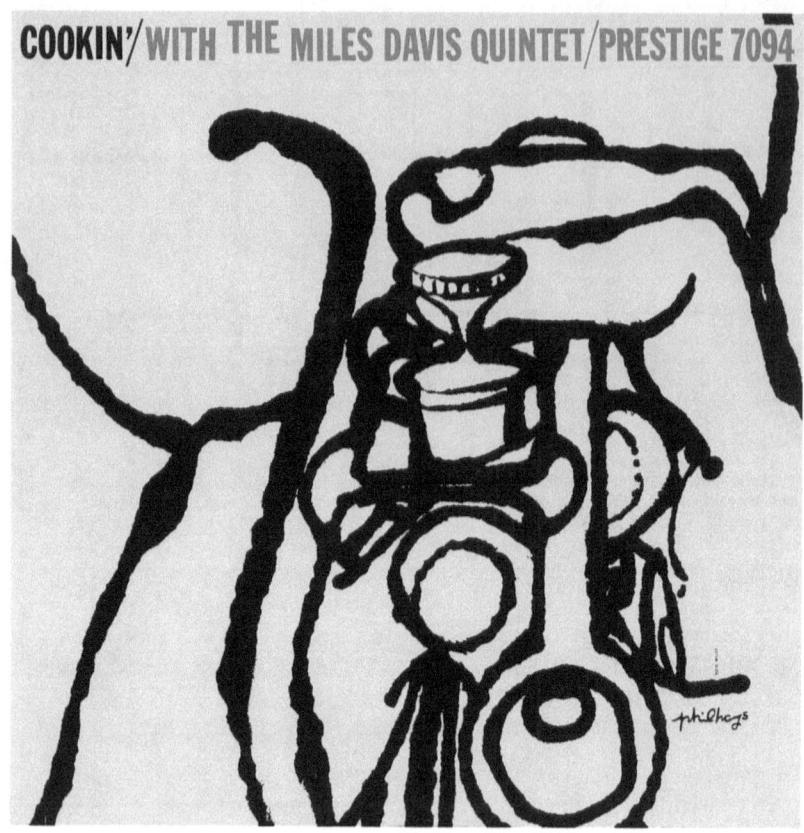

Figure 2.9. Album cover of *Cookin' with the Miles Davis Quintet*, Prestige PRLP 7094 (1956), design by Reid Miles and illustration by Phil Hays.

moments can be heard on Davis's other LPs. On "Trane's Blues" from *Workin'*, he audibly says "blues" at the start of the track. On *Cookin'*, Davis marks the end of "When Lights Are Low" with a quiet phrase: "Okay . . . all right. Okay" (13:00). Unlike on the LPs of 1951, these comments can be heard with clarity. Higher fidelity has social as well as musical significance.

These moments of informality on record appear during a time when record labels like Prestige were rethinking the possibilities of the studio and the purpose of jazz recordings. Record production was an essential component of both, although the promotional material surreptitiously focused attention away from the studio and toward the bandstand. In the notes to *Cookin'*, for example, Gitler attempts to close the phantasmic gap between musical performance and ears listening at home to a stereo: "Miles called tunes just

Figure 2.10. Album cover of *Local Color*, Prestige PRLP 7121 (1958), design by Marc Rice and photo by Esmond Edwards.

as he would for any number of typical sets at a club like [Café] Bohemia. There were no second takes."[80] Mentioning the Café Bohemia evokes a sense of place while also referencing several in-person recordings from that club issued in 1955 or 1956 on the Blue Note, Debut, Riverside, and Progressive labels.[81] Gitler's emphasis on first takes—on the music being made once and only once—also promises an unmediated listening experience. Such a promise hinges on assumed notions of race and gender: he is selling musical authenticity created by Black jazzmen in a high-stakes performance.

Such moments of social and musical interaction on record also reveal one way that Black jazz musicians in the mid-1950s increasingly found new forms of aesthetic agency. Musicians had always exerted power over the bandstand through repertoire, personnel, and stylistic decisions. However, the

Figure 2.11. Album cover of *Coltrane*, Prestige PRLP 7105 (1957), photo and design by Esmond Edwards.

studio was generally a location policed by record executives and sonically defined by recording engineers and their technologies. The label's desire to bring listeners into the studio through moments of recorded spontaneity allowed musicians to assert their authority over the recording session as well. When Davis says, "I'll play it and tell you what it is later" at the beginning of *Relaxin'*, he was not making a request but giving a command.[82] His interruption of Garland's piano introduction gives an immediate payoff—listeners are able to hear Davis's clear artistic vision in process. These moments of sociality have political import, no doubt bolstered by circumstances surrounding the sessions. After all, the loose production and marathon-like sessions resulted directly from Davis's decision to leave Prestige for Columbia. Davis's stock was rising, and he knew it.

Like all other companies, Prestige settled on the 12-inch LP as its primary format. Yet this outcome was not determined from the beginning but was the result of several years of trial and error as the label experimented with different disc sizes and rotation speeds. To a consumer audience listening to *Cookin'* in 1957 or *Relaxin'* in 1958, a 12-inch record with a visually appealing design, lengthy liner notes, and studio chatter was relatively new. The informality found on Moody's "Disappointed" and the casual studio conversations of Davis's "If I Were a Bell" must be understood in relation to these shifting modes of representation and production. By giving access to the spaces of music making typically kept private, these moments pushed the boundaries of what constituted musical performance on record and imagined a new era for the jazz LP. Unlike Weinstock's documentary impulse, which attempted to bring listeners closer to the act of music making through white masculine control, the aural presence of musicians on record accentuated Black artistry and expertise. This political aurality emerged during a period of media transition when jazz production was constantly in flux.

1956–1957: The 12-Inch LP (Take 2)

Recall the infamous false start to Miles Davis's 1954 recording of "The Man I Love," which I discuss at the start of my introduction. Only a few seconds into Milt Jackson's opening statement, Thelonious Monk abruptly ruins the take by asking a question: "When am I supposed to come in, man?" Monk's verbal intrusion audibly irritates the rest of the band—one musician remarks, "Man, the cat's cuttin' hisself." Monk responds immediately: "I wanna know when to come in, man. Can't I stop too? Everybody else [*trails off*]." Davis steps in with a directive to engineer Rudy Van Gelder, "Shhh! Shhh! Hey Rudy, put this on the record. ALL of it."

Davis's comments display a sharp awareness of the social dynamics within the studio and the work of the technicians behind the control board. But these are not the reasons why this outtake is so well-known. Rather, it is a disagreement between Monk and Davis that has made this session, as Monk biographer Robin Kelley puts it, "one of the most controversial in the history of jazz."[83] Kelley goes on to describe Monk's various disagreements with Davis after he asked the pianist to "lay out" (i.e., not play) behind all trumpet solos. Allegedly, Monk responded by purposefully sabotaging the session, which (as legend has it) nearly resulted in a physical altercation between the two musicians. Unsurprisingly, historians often use this exchange on "The Man I Love" to describe the underlying tension between Davis and Monk that ran through the session.[84]

To tell the cultural history of the jazz LP, circulation is just as significant as biographical intrigue. Initially, this 1954 session produced four tracks that Prestige released a year later on two 10-inch LPs titled *Miles Davis All Stars* and *Miles Davis All Stars, vol. 2*. However, Monk's interruption, along with Davis's comment to Van Gelder, did not appear on record until 1957, when Prestige issued the alternate take of "The Man I Love" on *Miles Davis and the Modern Jazz Giants*, a 12-inch LP spinning at the atypical speed of 16⅔ rpm (hereafter 16 rpm).[85] The 16-rpm format was initially adopted for spoken-word recordings, or "talking books," for the visually impaired. With a slower rotation speed and nearly twice the number of grooves per side, these discs had twice the playing time of a standard 12-inch LP but at the expense of a much lower playback fidelity. As a result, Prestige issued only six 16-rpm discs in total.

Each 16-rpm disc contained material previously issued on the label's regular 12-inch LP series (catalog numbers PRLP 7001 and above). For example, *Concorde* (1957) merged *Milt Jackson Quartet* (PRLP 7003) and *The Modern Jazz Quartet: Concorde* (PRLP 7005).[86] Similarly, the second disc in the 16-rpm series, Billy Taylor's *Let's Get Away from It All*, included direct reissues of *Billy Taylor Trio, vol. 1* (PRLP 7015), and *Billy Taylor Trio, vol. 2* (PRLP 7016), on the A side and B side, respectively.[87] The logo on the back jacket of both 16-rpm records included a tagline: "more modern jazz at the modern speed." Another phrase in small italics reads: "16, which actually stands for 16⅔-rpm, is the modern speed in phonograph records. The equivalent of two twelve inch 33 1/3-rpm recordings on one twelve inch disc is the result." Similar to the rhetoric used on Davis's *Blue Period* from 1951, the emphasis on "modern" glosses both musical style and Prestige's desire to give listeners different forms of access via new technological means of representation. Despite the change in format, past impulses of record making continue to linger.

Prestige answered Davis's call to put the broken-down take of "The Man I Love" on record by first issuing it on the B side of Davis's 16-rpm LP, *Miles Davis and the Modern Jazz Giants* (1957). Prestige had already issued an interruption-free version of "The Man I Love" on *Miles Davis All Stars, vol. 2* (1955). Davis's 16-rpm record from two years later included this incomplete take plus alternates of "But Not for Me" and "Bags' Groove."[88] Both record jacket and label differentiated the tracks from one another through a parenthetical after the song title (e.g., "take 2"), a lexical indication that Prestige standardized after its change to 12-inch LPs. Such was the case with the two recordings of "Zoot Swings the Blues" from the label's first LP recording session in 1951. The nearly nine-minute version of the song initially issued on 10-inch LP was itself the second take of an impromptu blues. Prestige issued the shorter "take 1" on 78 rpm under the name "Swingin' the Blues," even though the two versions share the same melody and overall approach. After its move to 12-inch LPs, Prestige reissued both takes in 1956 under the same name: "Zoot Swings the Blues."[89] Hidden within this seemingly minor change is the implicit suggestion to listen closely, which is to say historically.[90] The textual minutiae thus reveal a much more profound point about how Prestige asked its customers to value the music: in relation to its history.

Prestige's 16-rpm records should be understood as an extension of the documentary impulse that characterized the label's approach in the early LP era. These discs were, like other experiments before, a clear exploration of a potential revenue stream that also opened new avenues for historical understanding and awareness previously unavailable. From the addition of liner notes on 10-inch LPs and recording dates on EPs, to the increased sophistication of photos and graphic design, Prestige increasingly circulated new types of information along with the music. As a result, LPs came to tell a gendered version of jazz history that celebrated male instrumentalists. "Milt Jackson shows himself to be an exceptional jazzman," Gitler writes on the first 16-rpm record. "He is one of the **important** musicians whether considered in his own era or judged in relation to the overall history of jazz."[91] Elsewhere, Gitler riffs on the album title to Miles Davis's *Collectors' Items* (1956) to discuss how the LP has "enabled us to hear, for instance, many of Charlie Parker's great passages through the issuance of his rejected takes." Without the medium of the 12-inch LP, he continues, these takes "never would have been heard by the jazz public."[92] This particular LP includes two takes of "Serpent's Tooth," both of which feature Parker playing tenor saxophone (a historical oddity itself). Beyond the discographical minutiae, the doubled quality of such alternate takes articulated the value of instrumental improvisation as the location for musical innovation. This construction of jazz history became a constant refrain on record, making it into an indispensable commodity for Prestige.

Most media are historical by design, and sound recordings have always existed as part of a cultural compulsion toward preservation.[93] Yet Prestige's self-referential imagining of the record as a medium to document jazz history created a newly available archive of the music and the personalities behind its creation. Within such a public archive, at least three forms of expertise began to circulate with increased emphasis. Musical expertise is the most obvious example. Beyond the alternate takes mentioned above, consider James Moody's two versions of "It Might as Well Be Spring" recorded on September 29, 1954. Moody played tenor saxophone on the first take and alto on the second. Both takes simultaneously circulated on various formats for Prestige in 1955. The tenor take appeared on the 10-inch LP *James Moody's Moods* (PRLP 192) and on the EP *James Moody Band, vol. 2* (PREP 1369); the alto take was featured on the 10-inch LP *Moody* (PRLP 198) and issued as a 78-rpm single with "Faster James" (PR 903). As Prestige increased its 12-inch output in 1956 and 1957, both alto and tenor takes recirculated on the larger LP format as well.[94] This unusual doubling showcased Moody's instrumental flexibility and musical expertise. At the same time, the circulation history demonstrates the experimental context of the early LP era.

The second kind of expertise was the everyday business acumen that jazz musicians possessed. Davis's comments to Van Gelder during the broken take of "The Man I Love"—"Hey Rudy, put this on the record. ALL of it"— demonstrate an awareness of the recording studio as a place of business where the band performed not to a listening audience but rather to the network of commodity-making technologies that surrounded them.[95] As Davis seemed to imply, recording sessions were as much about labor and cultural negotiation as they were about musical events.

The records themselves displayed the third order of expertise: technical mastery. Each of Prestige's early 12-inch LPs included a small phrase repeated in the top corners of the back jacket: "remastered by Van Gelder."[96] This followed the proclamation, mentioned above, that the label's 12-inch LPs would be remastered by Van Gelder, "who will bring the sound up to 1955 standards."[97] The engineer's presence—in this case referred to by last name only—was certainly meant to advertise the sound quality of the new format. However, it also gestured toward the alternative kinds of technical labor and expertise that record making increasingly necessitated. Indeed, Van Gelder became an oft-invoked figure in this regard.[98]

The extremely limited production run of Prestige's 16-rpm discs, in one sense, marks a particular moment of commercial failure—that is, unless we listen along multiple frequencies. Between 1951 and 1957, Prestige released jazz on 45 singles and extended play, 10-inch LPs and 78s, as well as 12-inch LPs that spun at both 33⅓ and 16⅔ rpm. Davis's voice cuts across formats, thereby becoming a way to trace the shifting modes of representation and cultural value. The discographical details reveal Prestige's adaptive approach to new technologies and emerging consumer demands.[99] Through a process of trial, error, and experimentation within a dynamic and ever-changing commercial environment, Prestige's LPs came to tell particular stories about jazz in relation to itself. At the same time, the push toward documentation led to the circulation of different kinds of expertise and forms of musical labor at the site of (record) production. Alternate takes have the potential to reveal alternate histories as well, depending on how one chooses to listen.

1951: "Bluing" (Take 2)

Tension runs throughout Davis's 1951 recording of "Bluing." His soloing style, for example, simultaneously points in opposite temporal directions: his double-time, bebop-inspired lines recall his best playing in the 1940s as a sideman with Charlie Parker; his economic use of melodic fragments foreshadows his late-1950s style. The extended solo space allows Davis to deftly use the meandering tempo to his advantage, playing with, on top of, doubling up on, and stretching the time. Blakey's steadfast pulse remains constant. For his part, Sonny Rollins's tone often feels on the verge of splitting apart and often does, his squeaked notes a symptom of a mechanical problem with his reed, mouthpiece, embouchure, or some combination. Despite these issues, his style—part blues, part bebop—hints at Rollins's enormous potential. When Blakey shifts into a double-time feel partway through Rollins's solo, the saxophonist quickly follows, traversing the range of his instrument through long, sixteenth-note lines (5:25). Bassist Tommy Potter and pianist Walter Bishop Jr. stay in the original groove, setting up a playful yet uneasy juxtaposition between double time and single time. After a return to the original tempo during altoist Jackie McLean's solo, the ensemble returns to the same double-yet-single-time feel during Davis's second solo (8:50). Several times during his last two choruses, Davis sounds as if he is trying to signal a return to the original tempo, but the rhythm section does not follow his cues—a breakdown ensues.

The not-quite-double, not-quite-original time can be heard as a metaphor for jazz, which was similarly caught somewhere in the interstices of postwar America. The popularity of swing music in the prewar years made it possible to define jazz in relation to a rising consumer culture and white middlebrow values. White bandleaders such as Benny Goodman, Glenn Miller, Tommy

Dorsey, and Artie Shaw became international stars, even though Duke Ellington, Count Basie, Chick Webb, and Fletcher Henderson (to name only a few) were among the genre's greatest pioneers. In the 1940s, bebop emerged from the backroom jam sessions at Minton's and Monroe's, clubs that were embedded into the dynamic nightlife economy of Harlem and outside the white commercial spaces of the record business. The music's extreme tempos and extended chord structures required both technical virtuosity and an erudite understanding of melody, rhythm, form, and improvisational methods. The public face of bebop, at least in its early years, was Dizzy Gillespie, who, along with a cohort of other young, urban Black men, pushed the musical boundaries through intricate chord substitutions and highly variable melodies with angular contours and frequent chromaticisms. Rhythm sections with piano, bass, and drums were still the norm, but their accompaniment became increasingly interactive and rhythmically irregular.

Bebop musicians attempted a bold cultural transformation by remaking the musical language of jazz. Yet even as they worked to supplant the limitations placed on Black performers by the legacies of blackface minstrelsy, these musicians expressed a form of Black masculinity that reaffirmed the existing patriarchy of jazz culture. The Black male instrumentalists who led the movement valued virtuosity, intellectual authority, and emotional authenticity. As competitive as the scene was, these jazzmen also mentored one another in ways that built a homosocial community that excluded women.[100] Mastery of the music business became a crucial aspect of bebop's masculine expressions. As Guthrie Ramsey argues, bebop musicians actively sought economic viability in how they navigated the commercial geographies of New York City, especially during the downtown move from Harlem to 52nd Street. According to Miles Davis, "You went to 52nd to make money and be seen by the white music critics and white people."[101] To grow their audience, musicians had to rely on the white commercial infrastructures of the music business, including nightclubs, concert halls, and industry trade magazines, which regularly debated bebop's merits and lasting influences. Black jazzmen went into business with white managers, promoters, radio disc jockeys, and critics to procure the gold standard of masculine power: income, sexual appeal, and visibility within popular culture.[102] Ideologies of race and gender determined how jazz musicians chose to navigate the complex cultural topography of the late 1940s.

As a further extension of his cultural work, Gillespie turned toward record making when he established Dee Gee Records in 1951, the same year of

Davis's first LP recordings.[103] By becoming a label owner, Gillespie joined a long line of Black entrepreneurs in the record business, including W. C. Handy (Pace & Handy Music Co.), Harry Pace (Black Swan), Duke Ellington (Tempo Music), J. Mayo Williams (Black Patti Records), Don Robey (Peacock), and Mercer Ellington (Mercer Records).[104] In his autobiography, Gillespie described his record-making goals in terms of economic power:

> One alternative to just playing it cool was to make a lotta money—make all the money. I decided it would be desirable to own a record company. I'd have the record company, compose the tunes, and be an artist on the records, the whole thing.... People said I couldn't get a recording contract, which was untrue. I just wouldn't sign. They made offers, but I wouldn't sign because I wanted to make these records for myself. I felt I could produce my own records. With the objective of building a large record company, I invested my money and talent and tried to become a musical industrialist.[105]

On the surface, Gillespie's use of "cool" references the 1950s substyle of cool jazz that he previously discusses in relation to Miles Davis. But this also alludes to other, more elusive definitions. As Phil Ford, Scott Saul, and Joel Dinerstein explore in detail, conceptions of cool ran through US culture during the years after World War II, when the rise of a countercultural intellectualism, or white hipness, intersected with a form of Blackness that resisted the structures of everyday racism.[106] Although it came to mean something completely different in relation to the jazz industry, the cool aesthetic was rooted in Black culture. For Ralph Ellison, cool was a protective veil on segregated buses and a psychological "bullet proof vest" for Black people in the South. He writes about how keeping a "cool eye" was a "life-preserving discipline" and how "coolness" was a survival strategy used to endure the daily threats of racial violence.[107] This strategy was especially salient for Black men.[108] Amiri Baraka writes about cool as a social tactic to deal with "the horror the world might daily propose" and as the ability to "make failure as secret a phenomenon as possible" through calm detachment.[109] Gillespie's desire to become a "musical industrialist" emerges from a history of Jim Crow capitalism that denied aesthetic and economic power to Black musicians. He makes this point elsewhere, describing the music business in gendered terms: "All the big money went to the guys who owned the music, not to the guys who played it."[110] Becoming a record maker was an alternative yet risky approach, given the patent racism shown to Black businesses and the complex finances of record making in a crowded field.[111] Dee Gee closed shop in 1953, its short existence a testament to the risk inherent in deciding when not to play it cool in the immediate postwar period.[112]

As with the word *swing*, Baraka astutely points to the tension between *cool* as a "social philosophy" (as described above) and the commercial brand of jazz born in the early 1950s. To him, cool jazz was a "tepid new popular music of the white middle-brow middle class," a musical style that represented everything that Black "cool" stood against.[113] Like "swing" before, the *cool* of cool jazz traversed from verb to noun—from social philosophy to mass commercial category—along a historical trajectory of white (mis)appropriation of Black expression. Davis, once a Gillespie protégé, emerged as the paragon of 1950s cool by mid-decade, even though the word as an aesthetic and social strategy did not start or end with him.[114] The way he moved, spoke, dressed, and played left a striking impression with seemingly little effort and indefinite exactness—Davis used these qualities to reimagine Black male performance outside a primitivist dualism that split intellect from emotion along racial lines.[115]

Despite these attempts, Davis's cool persona in the early 1950s perfectly fit the white gaze of the jazz industry and the white male listeners who could afford to buy jazz LPs from Prestige. Consider the audiovisual modes of representation on Davis's first two LPs on Prestige, *The New Sounds* and *Blue Period*.[116] Both records resulted from a single October 1951 recording session that produced seven tracks split between two 10-inch LPs. Weinstock organized *Blue Period* around a clear theme: the tracks were titled "Out of the Blue," "Bluing," and "Blue Room." Gitler's notes primarily focus on long-playing technology, but he also describes the "modern blues chord changes" of "Bluing" in language that distances the LP's content from the socially rich history of blues praxis in African American culture.[117] In the notes to Davis's *New Sounds*, Gitler provides a similar message: "Of course, Miles is to be appreciated for bringing a new sound and conception to the trumpet but what really gives him greatness are the intangibles he possesses, which enable him to transmit sweeping joy with his 'wailing' solos and reflective beauty in the delicacy of his ballads."[118] Despite the underlying reference to African American musical practices, Gitler presents Davis's recording as modern music made with modern technology. At the same time, this passage repeats the primitivist trope that African American virtuosity is unquantifiable, what Adam Green and others have referred to as "naturalized genius."[119] In Gitler's reading, joy and beauty are outcomes heard through the technologies of whiteness.

More can be heard in the sound of Davis voicing his frustration at the end of "Bluing." Unlike the moments on *Relaxin'* and "The Man I Love," Davis's voice on the 1951 track is hard to distinguish with certainty. Utterances such as "ending" and "you know that" and "man" and "right?" are discernible, but the exact way that everything fits together escapes transcription. Still, his vocal exclamations replace the expected sense of musical resolution; the track builds to an unlikely conclusion. The intermedial musical texture and evasive vocalizations at the end of "Bluing" are a sonic microcosm for how jazz musicians were similarly caught somewhere among 78, 45, 33⅓, and 16⅔ revolutions per minute.

As the relationship between musicians and technologies of reproduction shifted, Davis's voice would come to appear and reappear on different formats. As such, his raspy expressions echo through the decade, often in greater fidelity, as he increasingly cultivated an unapologetic Black aesthetic to accompany his rising profile.[120] Davis's expansive presence on record was first made possible by the technological advancement of the long-playing record and the commodification of cool (as a noun) that Weinstock helped propel. Those factors did not dictate the conditions of Davis's circulation, however. The words on "Bluing" constantly escape, but they expose the musical unwieldiness of jazz as a marketing category and the cultural ruptures that technological change can bring. Davis's voice is a sonic manifestation of the alternate histories that were always present but were often not represented on record.

Alternate History at the Margins of Music

The prevailing image of a vinyl record is that of a 12-inch black disc, spinning at 33⅓ revolutions per minute. Although these discs—along with the 45 single—dominated the industry for several decades after the 1950s, there were many LP variations that came and went as small independent record companies such as Prestige experimented with different disc sizes and rotation speeds. Few had lasting impact, but these short-lived formats contain a great deal of information about the changing relationships between music making and the music industry's modes of circulation. Prestige's use of the 10-inch LP attempted to take advantage of the new capabilities of LP technology through the inclusion of musical mistakes. The label's "documentary" EP 45 series placed recording dates in the marginalia to help listeners construct a history of musical development. The 12-inch LP became a place for alternate takes to circulate. From one format to another, a sense of history in the making became a valued part of the label's strategy. The eventual standardization of a 12-inch record spinning at 33⅓ rpm saw the final blossoming of how the aural and visual elements worked together to define the sound of Prestige, and jazz more generally, in the years to come.

By the time Prestige issued its hundredth 12-inch LP in 1958, the label's strategy and overall output were changing. Like Davis, many of the label's most prominent musicians had signed deals with other labels: Monk moved to Riverside, Hank Mobley went to Blue Note, Milt Jackson and the Modern Jazz Quartet moved to Atlantic, and Sonny Rollins freelanced with Blue Note, Riverside, and Contemporary. Weinstock responded by signing John Coltrane, Mose Allison, Paul Quinichette, and Frank Wess. Prestige preserved its loose production style and jam-session recording dates with these artists, especially on LPs featuring saxophonist Gene Ammons.[121] Like Moody's "Disappointed" and Davis's *Relaxin'*, many of these LPs continued to include in-studio interactions and chatter among musicians. Preserving the looseness of jazz performance continued to be an inexpensive way for Prestige to produce records. But the informal aesthetics also fit the label's foundational ethos that celebrated these moments for their historical import.

Guided by his balance sheet and the white masculine scripts that structured his documentary impulse, Weinstock continued to be as inventive as ever. Reflecting on the legacy of Prestige in 1992, he wrote that "just as experimentation and improvisation is the essence of jazz, it is also the essence of running a label."[122] During the 1950s, these experiments took place at all levels of his business, from the musicians he selected to the tunes they played, and from the label's multiformat approach to the decisions made about liner notes, graphics, and other elements in and on the margins. Flexible business practices certainly ensured a sustainable future, but Prestige's documentary impulse offered a reliable strategy to employ the language of white modernism as a means of selling records. Seen through this lens, LPs are revealed to be a historiographical enterprise—a curated means of encountering the past through sound. Iconic moments encountered on record are, after all, products of music and marketplace, musical creation and record production. Put differently, LPs are media of cultural communication that help construct systems of value and discourses of history. The 1950s jazz industry continued to sonically encode the segregational logic of the industry and its attendant reliance on scripts of white masculine authority. Such expressions of power remained ever present.

As the record industry continued to grow, the sale of jazz records increasingly brought listeners into the spaces of spontaneous music making through the inclusion of mistakes, miscues, and mishaps. These moments of informality at the edges of performance vividly demonstrate the sociality of the recording process, bringing out the grain of performance through sound. Yet as Davis's early LPs evince, record making is never a politically neutral act. Prestige's rhetoric largely eschewed the connections between jazz and the history of Black expressive culture, even as Black musical labor and expertise continued to define the everyday of jazz. Across the aural and visual terrain of Prestige's catalog, it becomes possible to hear Davis voice his opinions, expand his musical possibilities, and create different spaces for artistic expression. Or, as Davis told Ralph Gleason in 1961, "When they make records with all the mistakes in, as well as the rest, then they'll really make jazz records. If the mistakes aren't there too, it ain't none of you."[123]

Playlist: Record Making at Prestige Records

Prestige took many approaches to record making in the early LP era. This playlist showcases the changing relationship between jazz musicians and their audiovisual representations on record. (Unless otherwise noted, recordings are LPs.)

Bengt Hallberg and Lars Gullin. *New Sounds from Sweden, vol. 2.* Prestige, 1952.
Billy Taylor. *Billy Taylor Trio, vols. 1–2.* Prestige, 1956.
Billy Taylor. *Billy Taylor Trio, vol. 3.* EP. Prestige, ca. 1954.
Billy Taylor. *Let's Get Away from It All.* 16⅔ rpm. Prestige, 1957.
Fats Navarro, Dizzy Gillespie, Miles Davis, and Kenny Dorham. *Modern Jazz Trumpets.* Prestige, 1951.
Gene Ammons. *Funky.* Prestige, 1957.
Gene Ammons. *The Happy Blues.* Prestige, 1956.
Gene Ammons. *Jammin' in Hi Fi with Gene Ammons.* Prestige, 1957.
Gene Ammons. *Jammin' with Gene.* Prestige, 1956.
Gerry Mulligan. *Gerry Mulligan Blows.* Prestige, 1953.
Gerry Mulligan. *The New Sounds.* Prestige, ca. 1951.
Gil Mallé. *Quadrama.* Prestige, 1957.
James Moody. *Disappointed, parts 1–2.* 45 rpm. Prestige, 1956.
James Moody. *Hi Fi Party.* Prestige, 1956.

James Moody. *It Might as Well Be Spring/Faster James*. 78 rpm. Prestige, ca. 1955.
James Moody. *James Moody and His Band: Moody* (10-in. LP). Prestige, 1955.
James Moody. *James Moody and His Band: Moody* (12-in. LP). Prestige, 1957.
James Moody. *James Moody Favorites, vol. 1*. Prestige, 1951.
James Moody. *James Moody's Moods*. Prestige, 1955.
Jimmy Raney. *Jimmy Raney Plays*. Prestige, 1953.
J. J. Johnson and Bennie Green. *Modern Jazz Trombones, vol. 2*. Prestige, 1952.
J. J. Johnson, Kai Winding, and Bennie Green. *Trombone by Three*. Prestige, 1956.
John Coltrane. *Coltrane*. Prestige, 1957.
Kai Winding and J. J. Johnson. *Modern Jazz Trombones*. Prestige, 1951.
Lee Konitz. *The New Sounds*. Prestige, 1951.
Lee Konitz and Lennie Tristano. *Lee Konitz Quintet, Lennie Tristano Quintet*. Prestige, 1951.
Lennie Tristano. *Lennie Tristano Quintet Featuring Lee Konitz*. EP. Prestige, ca. 1953.
Mal Waldron. *Mal-1*. Prestige, 1957.
Miles Davis. *Bags' Groove*. Prestige, 1957.
Miles Davis. *Blue 'n' Boogie*. EP. Prestige, ca. 1954.
Miles Davis. *But Not for Me, parts 1–2*. 78 rpm. Prestige, ca. 1955.
Miles Davis. *Collectors' Items*. Prestige, 1956.
Miles Davis. *Cookin' with the Miles Davis Quintet*. Prestige, 1956.
Miles Davis. *In a Blue Mood: Bluing*. EP. Prestige, ca. 1954.
Miles Davis. *Miles Davis All Stars, vols. 1–2*. Prestige, 1955.
Miles Davis. *Miles Davis and the Modern Jazz Giants* (12-in. LP). Prestige, 1959.
Miles Davis. *Miles Davis and the Modern Jazz Giants*. 16⅔ rpm. Prestige, 1957.
Miles Davis. *Miles Davis: Blue Period*. Prestige, 1953.
Miles Davis. *Miles Davis Quartet*. Prestige, 1954.
Miles Davis. *Miles Davis Quartet: May 19, 1953*. EP. Prestige, 1953.
Miles Davis. *Miles Davis Quintet*. Prestige, 1954.
Miles Davis. *Miles Davis with Sonny Rollins*. Prestige, 1954.
Miles Davis. *The New Sounds*. Prestige, 1952.
Miles Davis. *Relaxin' with the Miles Davis Quintet*. Prestige, 1958.
Miles Davis. *Steamin' with the Miles Davis Quintet*. Prestige, 1961.
Miles Davis. *Walking*. EP. Prestige, ca. 1954.
Miles Davis. *Workin' with the Miles Davis Quintet*. Prestige, 1960.
Miles Davis and His Band. *Bluing, parts 1–2*. 78 rpm. Prestige, 1952.
Miles Davis and His Band. *Bluing, part 3/Conception*. 78 rpm. Prestige, 1952.
Milt Jackson. *Concorde*. 16⅔ rpm. Prestige, 1957.
Milt Jackson. *Milt Jackson and the Modern Jazz Quartet*. EP. Prestige, ca. 1953.
Milt Jackson. *Milt Jackson Quartet*. Prestige, 1955.
Modern Jazz Quartet. *The Modern Jazz Quartet*. Prestige, ca. 1953.
Mose Allison. *Local Color*. Prestige, 1958.

Red Garland. *All Kinds of Weather*. Prestige, 1959.
Red Rodney. *The New Sounds*. Prestige, 1952.
Sonny Rollins. *Saxophone Colossus*. Prestige, 1957.
Sonny Rollins. *Sonny Rollins with the Modern Jazz Quartet*. EP. Prestige, ca. 1953.
Sonny Rollins and Thelonious Monk. *Sonny Rollins and Thelonious Monk Quartet*. Prestige, 1954.
Sonny Stitt, Bud Powell, and J. J. Johnson. *Sonny Stitt/Bud Powell/J. J. Johnson*. Prestige, 1956.
Stan Getz. *Stan Getz Quartets*. Prestige, 1955.
Stan Getz. *Stan Getz, vol. 2*. Prestige, 1951.
Stan Getz and Lee Konitz. *The New Sounds*. Prestige, 1951.
Teddy Charles. *New Directions: Teddy Charles Quartet*. Prestige, 1953.
Teddy Charles. *Teddy Charles West Coasters*. EP. Prestige, ca. 1953.
Thelonious Monk. *The Thelonious Monk Quintet*. EP. Prestige, ca. 1954.
Various. *New Sounds from Sweden, vol. 1*. Prestige, 1951.
Zoot Sims. *Swingin' with Zoot Sims*. Prestige, 1951.
Zoot Sims. *Zoot Sims Quartets*. Prestige, 1956.

3

QUEST FOR THE MOMENT

The Audio Production of *Ellington at Newport*

The opening moments of Duke Ellington's 1956 LP *Ellington at Newport* announce not only the band onstage but also the Newport Jazz Festival on record. It was the first time that a major label had attempted to record this (or any other) outdoor festival, and it was a difficult undertaking given the recording technology available at the time. The record begins with an introduction by emcee Father Norman O'Connor and then a few words by Ellington:

> O'CONNOR (0:00): Good evening, ladies and gentlemen. [*Applause.*] As you well know, one of the outstanding names in the field of jazz is that of Duke Ellington. And the group of men that are with him

are all musicians that are considered among the best and, certainly when working together under the direction and the very wonderful inspiration of Duke Ellington, one of the most capable groups in the field of jazz at the present moment. [*Cheers.*] I'm going to turn it over to the Duke and let him kind of introduce, because he does it very facilely and very easily. So it's Duke Ellington. [*Applause.*]

ELLINGTON (0:36): Thank you very much, Father O'Connor. [*Applause.*] We have prepared a new thing. And, of course, it's come especially for the Newport Jazz Festival, and so we'll call the, uh, first part of it, "Festival Junction." Jimmy Hamilton will state the theme. [*Solo clarinet begins.*]

Festival director George Wein had commissioned Ellington to compose a three-part suite for that year's event, the performance of which was to be recorded by Columbia and subsequently released as a special-edition LP produced by George Avakian.

Although Avakian's initial purpose was to record Ellington's *Festival Suite*, he happened to be on hand to document a performance of much greater significance—what Stanley Dance would later describe as "unquestionably one of the greatest individual triumphs in the entire history of jazz."[1] After an underprepared performance of the suite, Ellington called "Diminuendo and Crescendo in Blue," a two-part piece bridged by a solo from saxophonist Paul Gonsalves. During Gonsalves's improvisation, the crowd went wild when one of Newport's society women, Elaine Anderson, began exuberantly dancing in the aisle. Twenty-seven choruses later, Gonsalves ended to boisterous applause, so enthusiastic that festival director George Wein, fearing a riot, nearly ended the show. Ellington soothed the crowd by calling a feature for saxophonist Johnny Hodges, and the band continued to play into the early hours of the morning.

The 1956 performance at Newport, as the story goes, revitalized Ellington's career, which had been faltering in the previous few years. The postwar shifts in popular music, especially the arrival of rock and roll, had brought smaller audiences, shrinking recording contracts, and less overall public interest in the large-ensemble jazz that was Ellington's specialty. Despite the rising popularity of the jazz LP after 1955 (outlined in chapter 1), record labels were beginning to favor smaller ensembles because their improvisation-focused music was easier and more cost-effective to produce. Ellington's electrifying performance at Newport nevertheless became the subject of a cover story in *Time* magazine, and the resultant LP, *Ellington at Newport*, quickly rose up the jazz charts.[2] Purporting to give listeners access to a triumphant moment of a jazz icon, the LP became the composer's greatest-selling record and an oft-invoked piece of the Ellington mythology.[3] In the many years after, Ellington was reportedly fond of saying, "I was born in Newport 1956."[4]

In celebration of Ellington's hundredth birthday in 1999, Sony-Columbia's reissue label, Legacy, rereleased *Ellington at Newport* as a double CD that boasted a hundred minutes of previously unreleased and digitally remastered music from the 1956 Newport concert, in addition to extended liner notes by reissue producer Phil Schaap.[5] Besides issuing the concert in its entirety and in performance order, Schaap created a stereo recording by combining two mono tapes from the original Columbia masters and a broadcast of the concert from the Voice of America (VOA), the official international broadcast institution of the US federal government.[6] The composite recording offered Gonsalves's famous twenty-seven-chorus solo in far greater fidelity because in 1956 Gonsalves had mistakenly played into the wrong microphone. More than a mere LP-to-CD conversion, the 1999 CD reimagined Ellington's most mythologized moment on record through its production.[7]

Ellington at Newport (Complete), as the CD was titled, sparked controversy within jazz circles because it revealed how the original LP was not solely "Recorded in Performance on July 7, 1956," as the LP jacket states, but rather was a hybrid creation. Using newly available production techniques, producer Avakian had in 1956 inserted audience noise and studio overdubs onto the Newport tapes after the fact. The CD version of the festival concert revealed how Avakian restructured and condensed the tapes from Newport in order to create Father O'Connor's introduction that opened the 1956 LP. O'Connor's preamble from Newport was, as the transcription below shows, much longer and from a different part of the concert entirely (the bold text represents material kept by Avakian; the underlined text is material cut and spliced in elsewhere):

> O'CONNOR (0:00): **Good evening, ladies and gentlemen....** [0:53] **As you well know,** those of you who have been around jazz for a little while and even those who are a little new at this thing, **one of the outstanding names** is the very much and very important name **is that of Duke Ellington.** I hate to say how long he's been in the business,

but it hasn't been too long really, has it Duke? ([*Ellington off mike:*] Not too long, Father.) **And the group of men that are with him are all** a bunch and a wonderful group of individual **musicians that are considered among the** *best* in the field of jazz **and certainly when working together under the direction and the very wonderful inspiration of Duke Ellington, one of the most capable groups in the field of jazz at the present moment.** I think you know some of them; I'll run down real quick like.... [3:04] **I'm going to turn it over to the Duke and let him kind of introduce because he does it very facilely and very easily. So it's Duke Ellington.** [*Applause.*]

ELLINGTON (3:21): **Thank you very much, Father O'Connor.** Ladies and Gentlemen, our first selection brings Cat Anderson, Quentin Jackson, and Russell Procope to the microphone. One of our oldest, "The Black and Tan Fantasy." [*Piano begins.*][8]

The *Ellington at Newport* LP highlights the multiple perspectives that jazz musicians, industry professionals, and other jazz listeners have concerning audio production. Avakian's work in postproduction also brings up several fundamental questions about the nature of jazz history: How do records represent performance? How were records made to represent jazz history? In what ways do sound processing and record production construct such representations? How have philosophies and practices of record making changed over time? In what ways are these practices culturally situated? The discrepancies between the two versions of *Ellington at Newport* reveal historically specific ideas of what constitutes jazz on record, which further illuminates the imbricated relationship between musical performances and technical decisions behind the record console. Within this sonic and aural terrain, issues of labor and capital immediately surface.

The core concern of this chapter is the live record at mid-century. Unlike chapter 2, which examined new and refigured desires to capture the performative moment in the studio, here I am interested in the strategic manipulation of on-location recordings in postproduction. For several reasons, many economic, small labels like Prestige did not pursue the kinds of sonic mediation found on *Ellington at Newport*. As a firm with a greater commercial footprint, Columbia took a contrasting approach, investing time, effort, and resources into processes that increasingly collapsed the live event and its mediated representation. Control over the perception of musical time and space also became an economic tool that producers like

Avakian used to create a white mainstream market for jazz. Through a close examination of *Ellington at Newport*, this chapter explains how emerging methods of postproduction entwined with the political economy of the postwar record industry. Recorded in a space of elite white culture and then packaged and sold through a lens of popular music, *Ellington at Newport* necessitated a collaboration among artists, festival organizers, sound engineers, and producers, all differently invested in the cultural politics that made jazz's circulation possible.

In order to unravel the complex set of philosophies regarding sound reproduction, it is first necessary to unsettle the concepts of *liveness* and the *live record* as they were typically presented to mid-century jazz listeners. The ubiquity of the term *live* is a demonstration of its lasting power. Although I will sometimes use the term in its most normative way (e.g., "live record"), it will become clear that the meaning of *live* is historically contingent. As a result, my argument proceeds on both historical and philosophical grounds, moving between registers of political discourse and decision making during the recording and production process. To begin, I provide an overview of Avakian's approach to record making at Columbia, placing his passion for jazz history and his role at a major label within a longer trajectory of whiteness in the jazz industry. After then offering a theoretical framework in which to understand live jazz records, I consider Ellington's own position as a record maker in relation to the specific techniques used by Avakian to produce *Ellington at Newport*. Through this analysis, Gonsalves's solo is revealed to be both the LP's most famous moment and, in many ways, its most mediated. Finally, I reexamine Avakian's overall production methods, which attempted to simulate the experience of a jazz concert for 1950s consumers. This chapter thus situates the collaborative techniques of mediation within their historical moment and lays the groundwork for understanding the wider stakes of audio production during the LP era.

George Avakian, Columbia Records, and Whiteness

As the LP grew in popularity and became the industry's standard format, the so-called live jazz record proliferated. The commercial viability of on-location records was not an inevitable outcome and arose from several factors. Record companies had to invest their time in recording on location and then determine the artistic and financial value of that effort. To make live recordings part of their everyday business practice, A&R staff had to be sure that existing contracts and royalty agreements could accommodate these new venues for commercial music making. Producers also had to ensure that they had the right personnel to effectively record, edit, and master recordings into an attractive product for their market. The rise of the live jazz album resulted from the intersection of technological innovation and the expertise of individuals on the bandstand, behind the recording console, and in the front offices of record labels.

Avakian was the key player in the jazz industry's adoption of the LP. As someone who grew up in New York City, he was introduced to jazz through radio broadcasts as a teenager. This interest continued to grow during his time at Yale University, where he befriended a graduate student named Marshall Stearns and his group of (mostly male) jazz enthusiasts.[9] In 1939, while still a student, Avakian pitched Decca Records the idea of producing a 78-rpm album of jazz in the same format used for classical music: several discs organized around a theme (or group of pieces) and accompanied by lengthy, well-researched liner notes. *Chicago Jazz*, as it was eventually titled, became the first jazz album. A year later, Avakian began working for Columbia, where he launched the Hot Jazz Classics series to reissue out-of-print records by notable musicians such as Louis Armstrong, Bessie Smith, and Duke Ellington.[10] This series, which created a sense of newness through remediated content, was the first of its kind on a major label.

In 1948, the year of the LP's introduction, Columbia appointed Avakian head of international recordings and popular albums, where he oversaw the first albums of popular music issued on LP. Columbia did not prioritize the pop LP market during the format's early years, which meant that a sizable portion of his work involved the label's back catalog.[11] Among many other items, Columbia's corporate holdings contained a deep well of jazz, even though the firm had very few jazz artists, especially Black ones, on its active roster. An extensive understanding of popular music history was built into Avakian's job description as a practical matter. Such a professional orientation also extended outside the confines of his official role at Columbia. The same year as his promotion, he taught one of the first university courses about jazz at New York University and regularly published record reviews in the *Record Changer*, an influential magazine for collectors.[12] He also worked with Walter Schaap—Phil Schaap's father—to edit and expand Charles Delaunay's *Hot Discography* for US audiences.[13] Each of these activities was perfectly suited to support Avakian's desire and deft ability to document jazz's past through record making.

As I described in the preceding chapters, expressions of white masculine authority helped establish the dominant narratives of jazz history before, during, and after the adoption of the LP. Those with power over the mechanics of record making were typically white, middle-class men who were guided by their passions for jazz history and a perception of Black music that revolved around great men working together.[14] Like other enthusiasts turned recordmen, Avakian spent an inordinate amount of time writing about jazz, publicizing its value, and documenting its history.[15] His actions were those of a devoted individual with a successful working relationship with many musicians, including Duke Ellington and Louis Armstrong.[16] Even so, his ability to effectively advocate was also a function of the industry's segregational logic that made his expertise and authority especially legible to those with economic power: other white men. Within the confines of a major label, jazz advocacy traveled along a track of white aesthetic capitalism that supported the existing political economy by design. Avakian's various activities in the 1950s thus expose a particular record-making blend of whiteness that centered white male norms and values in iterative fashion.[17]

Turning jazz history into a viable commercial product took a multifaceted approach, including implicitly adopting a lens of white, Eurocentric values. This lens effectively distanced jazz from the broader history of Black popular music by emphasizing the music's greatness and lasting historical value. Recall the 1956 *Cash Box* editorial "Jazz Comes of Age," which described the newly found "popularity and dignity" of jazz. The article goes on to claim that jazz "has almost reached the status where it is measured on its own terms rather than on moral terms."[18] As I argued in chapter 1, this was the vocabulary of whiteness deployed to sell jazz LPs to the white, middle-class consumers who could afford the more expensive format. Such projections of whiteness served as a reliable marketing strategy for this kind of jazz record making.

Avakian relied on such tactics at various points in the years leading up to *Ellington at Newport*. The evidence for this assertion can be found in numerous places, including the Golden Era LP series that Avakian began in 1951 to "present and preserve some of the greatest of jazz performances of the past."[19] It can also be seen in Avakian's liner notes and promotional material for Buck Clayton's 1954 jam-session LP, discussed in chapter 1. And it can be observed in *I Like Jazz!*, a 12-inch compilation LP produced by Avakian as part of Columbia's first nationwide campaign, in June 1955, to promote

Figure 3.1. Album cover of *I Like Jazz!*, Columbia JZ 1 (1955).

its expanded jazz roster (figure 3.1).[20] The firm's full-page advertisement in *Billboard* described the LP as containing a "complete history of jazz" that was "specifically designed to pull in traffic and introduce jazz to a mass audience."[21] The LP was offered at a bargain price of $0.98, and its cover displays an assortment of people at various economic levels, including a gas station worker, police officer, secretary, chef, and farmer. A text bubble with the phrase "I like jazz" arises from each of the fourteen individuals. All are white, leaving no doubt as to who this imagined mass audience was. The free promotional material that accompanied the LP included a thirty-six-page booklet that placed each of the twelve tracks in its wider historical context.[22] Although Avakian's text clearly describes jazz as a form of African American expression, the booklet unambiguously attempts to legitimize the history of jazz through a value system most legible to a white public.

The live records produced by Avakian followed a similar trajectory. In 1950 Avakian produced Benny Goodman's *The Famous 1938 Carnegie Hall Jazz Concert*, one of the earliest commercial LPs of a live jazz concert and the first jazz album to sell more than a million copies. Albert Marx, husband of Goodman's vocalist Helen Ward, recorded the concert in 1938 as an anniversary present; Marx made copies for both Ward and Goodman on acetate records, a format used by collectors and bootleggers before the advent of tape recording. Although these recordings were not initially made for commercial use, Avakian decided to issue them on LP with the help of Columbia engineer Bill Savory.[23]

With Goodman's *1938 Carnegie Hall Concert* LPs, Avakian demonstrated the power that packaging and production held to create a market for jazz within postwar consumer culture. The 1938 concert marked the first time a jazz orchestra performed at the famed performance venue, and it was a notable event in Goodman's rise to stardom during the period.[24] The 1950 release of Goodman's LP set, issued twelve years after the original concert date, was a striking display of Columbia's new long-playing technology. Musically, the two-LP set included twenty-two tracks, six of which were more than five minutes long. Two of the tracks, "Honeysuckle Rose" and "Sing, Sing, Sing," ran more than twelve minutes. The physical design, similar to those of other Columbia LP sets from the era, was made to impress. The LPs came in a black box that, once opened, revealed extensive liner notes by Irving Kolodin extolling the significance of the concert and, by extension, the records. These elements came bound together within the box so that listeners could flip from page to page and record to record.

In 1950 Goodman's LPs were a remarkable experiment in the form and content of a jazz recording.[25] At this moment of technological transition, commercial big-band stars such as Goodman, Tommy Dorsey, and Frank Sinatra remained a dominant force in popular music. Still, popular LPs—jazz-adjacent or otherwise—were a small piece of the overall market, as I explored in my chapter 1 discussion of "The Huckle-Buck." It is significant that Goodman's transmuted recording appeared as 12-inch LPs and on Columbia's Masterworks series, attributes that were nominally reserved for classical music and an audience defined by its presumed (adult) whiteness. A large segment of the adult LP-buying market in 1950 would have been teenagers during Goodman's ascendance. As such, the documentary aspect of the LP set was perhaps its most meaningful quality. Kolodin's notes ask listeners to cherish the set as the truthful document of a significant historical event: "So has been preserved, in a representative way, one of the authentic documents in American musical history, a verbatim report, in the accents of those who were present, on 'The Night of January 16, 1938.'"[26] From the historicist tone put forth in Kolodin's notes to the date in the title, these LPs were designed to serve as evidence of a particular prewar moment. The live quality mattered, but only inasmuch as it mattered historically. Every level of Avakian's production accentuated this historical perspective, not as a novelty but as a means of placing the music and its history within Columbia's larger commercial footprint.

Avakian produced several other iconic live LPs between Goodman's *1938 Carnegie Hall Concert* and *Ellington at Newport*. Dave Brubeck's first album on Columbia, the acclaimed *Jazz Goes to College* (1954), was recorded on location at several different universities around the country. Brubeck's next Columbia LP, *Jazz at Storyville: 1954* (1954), was also live and produced by Avakian. Other top-selling live LPs include Armstrong's *Ambassador Satch* (1955) and Erroll Garner's *Concert by the Sea* (1956). The monumental success of *Ellington at Newport* has largely obscured how Avakian used his position at Columbia to document the Newport Jazz Festival in sound. Along with Ellington's disc, three other LPs came out of the 1956 festival: *Dave Brubeck and Jay & Kai at Newport*, *Duke Ellington and the Buck Clayton All-Stars at Newport*, and *Louis Armstrong and Eddie Condon at Newport*.

Columbia's live albums issued between 1950 and 1956 reveal a varied approach to this emerging genre. Some, like *Concert by the Sea* and *1938 Carnegie Hall Concert*, originated as bootleg recordings. In contrast, the four Newport LPs were purposefully made with the artists' knowledge well beforehand. *Ambassador Satch* included several performances that relied on manipulative postproduction techniques for their live sound. In total, these records portray concert halls, outdoor festivals, and jazz clubs; the original tapes came from a variety of sources, including enthusiasts, family members, and industry professionals. Despite the differences, Avakian remained the common thread as he experimented with different ways of producing (and reproducing) jazz performance on record.

Entrenched notions of whiteness shaped this history of jazz record making at Columbia. Consider the venues: Brubeck appeared on college campuses, Goodman at Carnegie Hall, Garner at a US military base in California, Armstrong in European concert halls, and the others in Newport, Rhode Island, a symbol of elite white culture and wealth made possible by the port town's central role in the slave trade of colonial America.[27] After exploding onto the national scene with *Jazz Goes to College*, Brubeck became the second jazz musician to ever be featured on the cover of *Time* magazine.[28] The 1954 article emphasized Brubeck's intellectual approach and his admiration of Bach, Beethoven, and Bartók. The accompanying photographs depict Brubeck as a happily married man and a devoted father, a clear contrast to national portrayals of jazz musicians as drug addicts and social delinquents.[29] Such projections of whiteness relate directly to the social depiction on the cover of *I Like Jazz!*, which was an invitation by implication: if a tailor, grandma, housewife, and young couple like this music, then "you" can too. Both the LP and Brubeck's *Time* article sought to legitimate jazz, but they did so by deemphasizing the music's historical connection to Black expressive culture.[30] As the person who signed Brubeck to Columbia, Avakian used the LP to make Brubeck into a mainstream musical star, and this rise to stardom happened through a particular lens of jazz and its history.[31]

Avakian's approach was not unique. At the time of the Newport Jazz Festival's inaugural event in 1954, jazz was achieving greater social prestige than ever before. Festival organizer George Wein explicitly drew on Newport's cultural capital as a summer resort town for many of the country's wealthiest families. In a *New Yorker* profile from 1954, Wein adopted an erudite persona and expressed a desire that his festival become for jazz what Salzburg was to Mozart, Bayreuth was for Wagner, and Tanglewood was for classical music within the United States.[32] Toward that end, Wein augmented the musical performances at Newport with educational events that featured notable critics, academics, and other intellectuals who discussed the music's social history and importance to US culture. The festival also invited the Voice of America to broadcast the event on its network overseas, tying jazz to Cold War constructions of democracy and American exceptionalism. The original name for the event, the American Jazz Festival, reflected Wein's aspiration to disseminate the serious side of jazz, both at Newport and around the world. It is not surprising, then, that the festivities often began with a rendition of "The Star-Spangled Banner." In 1956 none other than the Duke Ellington Orchestra had the honor of playing the national anthem to kick off the event.[33]

Avakian was no bystander during this cultural positioning. He was a charter member of the festival's advisory board and someone professionally invested in its success. As he told writer John Fass Morton years later, Avakian desired to record the 1956 event in part to help raise money for the festival, which was faltering financially at the time.[34] The annual event had also become a significant place to network and scout for talent. As saxophonist Cannonball Adderley wrote, "I am sure that to most [spectators] Newport means one big weekend jazz bash; but, to most of the jazz musicians, our annual convention has started."[35] And it was Miles Davis's 1955 Newport performance that convinced Avakian to sign the trumpeter to Columbia. As detailed in the previous two chapters, Davis's signing was made possible by the rising popularity of jazz on LP and Columbia's expansion into this market segment. Such trends would unexpectedly enable Black cultural producers to shape the record-making process in new ways. However, Avakian was simply attempting to take advantage of emergent commercial trends while also managing interpersonal relationships among differently situated record makers across racial lines.

When Avakian arrived at the festival grounds in 1956, he was there not only to produce records but also to actively participate in shaping jazz's future by pushing the music into white mainstream US culture. After all, Avakian was an Ivy League–educated New Yorker and one of the first industry professionals to package jazz in the same way as classical music—first in the form of 78-rpm albums and later on 12-inch LPs on Columbia's Masterworks series. His Hot Jazz Classics reissue series helped establish the early jazz canon, just as his New York University course brought the music into educational spaces of economic privilege. Moreover, his wife and sister-in-law, Anahid and Maro Ajemian, were active musicians in the contemporary art music scene, regularly performing and premiering the music of composers such as John Cage, Alan Hovhaness, Ernst Krenek, Lou Harrison, and Henry Cowell.[36] Avakian produced records from the perspective of a devoted jazz listener, although it cannot be ignored that his expertise was fostered within the halls of elite white culture and that his employer, Columbia Records, was heavily invested in both classical and white popular music. It was in this cultural milieu that Avakian pushed the boundaries of jazz record making with his production of *Ellington at Newport*.

Troubling the Live Record

Record companies often strive to present live recordings as a stable genre of record making, neatly delineated from those records made in the studio. However, the term *live* obfuscates the processes of recording, mixing, editing, mastering, and manufacturing through the reductive yet theoretically fraught language of real-time synchronicity. The term's continued use is unwieldy, even as it remains ubiquitous in everyday conversation about music. By placing it within the history of record making, I aim to add specificity to how the idea of "live" operates within the context of 1950s jazz, particularly how constructions of liveness intersected with contemporaneous ideologies of race. The convergence of LP playback and magnetic tape recording made live jazz events into a repeatable commodity. In this view, the so-called live jazz record is a product of record-making culture in midcentury, an invention contingent on the many social hierarchies that surround mechanical reproduction and cultural representation.

Commercially produced jazz recordings of this sort come in many different forms. Some were planned that way from the start, made under the direct supervision of a label and with the musicians' full knowledge of the recording in advance. Others were initially bootlegged by audience members with portable recording equipment and later prepared for release by record producers and audio engineers. Numerous live records have been made from radio or TV broadcasts, often years after the initial performance and without the musicians' knowledge. They also come from a wide array of locations: outdoor festivals, large concert halls, small jazz clubs, radio or TV studios, private homes, and regular recording studios with invited audiences. In total, live records come from different sources, make their way to market with different levels of intent, and demonstrate the varying amounts of control that record makers exercised over how and where the tapes were made.

One difficulty in discussing the live record genre as a coherent category is the slippery definition of *live*. According to the *Oxford English Dictionary*, applying the word to pieces of technology dates back to the Industrial Revolution, when the word described a movable part of a machine that imparts motion to another component—for instance, the axle of a wheel. This use was a form of personification because the word was also a popular descriptor for a person full of energy and activity, especially in the United States. Such conventions seamlessly translated into the electric age, when *live* came to designate an active electrical current. Not coincidentally, this terminology dates to the same period when Thomas Edison commercialized the light bulb and invented the phonograph. For nearly a century and a half, the word has meant motion and energy especially when applied to technology.[37]

Live came to reference sound beginning in the late 1930s, especially to identify an active microphone. The phrase *live mic* emerged precisely because the microphone was itself a product of the electric era of sound reproduction. When the field of acoustics adopted the term, *live* began to signify a space with a long reverberation time. Before then, however, the word was used to reference spaces in radio broadcasting, especially to contrast a "dead" or nonreverberant room.[38] A history of mass communication through sonic technology is thus embedded within the uses of *live*, especially in the early twentieth century, as sounds increasingly moved into different electronically mediated spaces.[39]

Beginning in the mid-1930s, *live radio* became a phrase that meant hearing a broadcast event at the time of its occurrence. A decade later, this terminology transferred directly to descriptions of television and other media.[40] In total, these examples demonstrate how the adjectival form of *live*, which would later be applied to the LP, implicates the historical intersection of sound reproduction, mass consumer culture, and expanding distribution networks of information. A "live" recording became appealing to consumers in part because technological innovation allowed new forms of contact with faraway events and the people there originally to witness them.

The word *live* did not appear in the titles or liner notes of jazz records until the late 1950s, when it soon became ubiquitous.[41] Still, it was common in advertisements for record players and other equipment to emphasize the "lifelike" quality of sound afforded by the LP.[42] As an August 1948 Columbia advertisement for the LP appearing in the *Los Angeles Times* proclaims, "Imagine a new tone quality so lifelike you'll scarcely believe you're listening to a record!"[43] Fred Reynolds, a *Chicago Daily Tribune* columnist, echoes this sentiment in the August 7, 1950, rendition of his "Platter Chatter" column: "The smooth, non-breakable record surfaces, together with the finest recording techniques, give you extraordinary lifelike reproduction."[44] Similar advertisements began appearing in jazz publications as well. A cartoon ad for Jensen Needles in the December 12, 1956, issue of *Down Beat* reads: "Gosh, Martha, these records sound so clear with this JENSEN NEEDLE that you'd swear those musicians were right here in this very room."[45] As soon as the LP went to market, descriptions of the technology adopted a discourse of fidelity that rested on claims of lifelike reproduction and notions of liveness.

I understand liveness to be a historically specific set of principles of reproduced sound.[46] Since liveness is contingent on its creators and producers, its qualities change over time. Liveness today does not mean the same thing that it did in the 1950s, even though there are significant overlaps in its central properties and definitions. One commonality is the idea of synchronicity, where all sounds on record (synthetic or otherwise) aurally appear to have occurred at the same point in time and in the same location.[47]

The impression of simultaneity entangles the past and present, closing the temporal gap between a performance at one time and listeners at another. Some examples include audience applause and conversation, onstage announcements, and the audible presence of musical mistakes. Such examples imbue a feeling of real-time interaction: a social aurality on record. The processes of encoding such moments into the grooves of a record are also historically specific, where record producers, audio engineers, and musicians have a particular idea of what matters to their listeners: what they hear, what they value in those sounds, and how they connect those aural elements to the world around them. Liveness implicates ways of knowing through sound, or what Steven Feld terms *acoustemology*.[48]

My conception of liveness on record follows musicologist Paul Sanden in many respects. In his *Liveness in Modern Music*, Sanden argues that the experience of liveness rests on the "perception of performance" rather than on the actuality of that performance.[49] Others, including Louise Meintjes and David Novak, further elucidate how the perception of liveness results from the network of social practices that surround record making at each stage of the process, from performing to recording, manufacturing, circulation, and listening.[50] Because the creation of liveness rests on the interaction of listeners with their respective listening technologies, the social networks behind the creative and technical decisions that go into making records matter a great deal. Moreover, audiovisual components affect the perception of liveness, including cover images and photographs, liner notes, advertisements, and other promotional ephemera that also changed with the adoption of the LP. Understood together, these elements reveal much about specific values and the use of these records in creating a sense of music happening in the here and now.

Jazz records are mediated at several levels. This includes the processes (and materials) of recording, sound processing, the editing of tapes, and the final mastering, in addition to the design of album covers and the creation of liner notes. Through such processes, many decisions are made about the presentation of the live event, often in a way that seeks to erase all of this collaborative labor.[51] Live records such as *Ellington at Newport* tell stories about themselves that obfuscate the methods of mediation. Although they often sell themselves as such, live jazz records are not documents of a specific event but are carefully curated representations of that event.[52] In the mid-1950s, when Columbia issued *Ellington at Newport*, liveness on record was something that had to be developed over time as listeners came to understand what live jazz records sounded like.

Producing Newport

Because their livelihoods often depend on records, musicians have always had reasons to be enormously invested in the sound quality of their recordings. African American musicians throughout jazz history have struggled to gain more commercial and financial control of their music and its representations.[53] This includes giving input about a variety of aspects during record production, marketing, and distribution. For example, Ellington attempted several times in his early career to have a major label issue his music on 12-inch 78-rpm records, a format unofficially reserved for classical music and that rarely featured African Americans. He was largely unsuccessful, although he did release several extended compositions on opposing sides of 10-inch discs, first with "Creole Rhapsody" (1931) and later with the four-sided "Reminiscing in Tempo" (1935), as well as the two-sided "Diminuendo and Crescendo in Blue" (1937).[54]

Ellington was also famously successful in maximizing his potential sources of revenue, and by the time of the 1956 Newport concert, his star power within the industry directly translated to control over decisions made in the studio. In his 2010 Ellington biography, historian Harvey Cohen describes a close working relationship between Avakian and Ellington beginning in the early 1950s, detailing how Ellington began approving final takes by listening to playbacks from the control room. "Ellington was so involved with sound," Avakian told Cohen, "to a degree that almost no one else was."[55] Columbia issued two LPs from this collaboration, *Masterpieces by Ellington* (1951) and *Ellington Uptown* (1952), on its Masterworks series. At the time, Ellington's Masterworks LPs were an unprecedented feat for an African American jazz musician.

Ellington was also aware of the commodity-making technologies contained within the studio. Consider a rehearsal excerpt from the post-Newport recording session on July 9, 1956.[56] The track opens with the band tuning, soon interrupted by a voice (possibly Avakian) from the control room: "OK, here we go. 'Festival Junction,' take one" (CD: 0:18). Jimmy Hamilton begins his solo introduction to the suite opener with a soft, extended B-flat before stating the main theme. Expecting a chord from Ellington, Hamilton holds a high D-flat before stopping to discuss the problem (CD: 0:36–0:40). Once everything is settled, Ellington sarcastically remarks, "That was real good; you shouldn't have messed that up." He then softly adds, "We're still liable to use it—we'll paste it on" (CD: 1:03). As with the early LPs of Prestige discussed in chapter 2, mistakes create their own possibilities. Ellington's comment "we'll paste it on" shows his awareness of the magnetic-tape technology in the control room and acknowledges its capabilities. Ellington's phrasing and word choice disclose his own involvement in the process—not *you* or *they* but *we*. Control over the technological mediation of those mistakes, as Ellington was likely aware, was another form of artistic agency and control.[57] The evidence, both in and out of the studio, suggests that Ellington was both a willing and savvy collaborator, even if that meant leaving the technical elements to producers like Avakian. Sometimes successful collaboration means knowing whom to trust and when to trust them.

Ellington's orientation toward record making, as well as his relationship with Avakian, was absent from the discourse surrounding the 1999 reissue of *Ellington at Newport*. Articles in trade publications, magazines, and newspapers championed Schaap's restoration of the concert tapes at the expense of Avakian's production of the 1956 LP. With headlines such as "What Really Happened at Newport? The Dimming of a Masterpiece" (*Coda*), "Repairing a Classic with an Ugly Secret" (*Fortune*), and "Setting the Record Straight: Reissue of *Ellington at Newport* a Lot More Live Than Original LP" (*Denver Post*), these articles (and others) portrayed the 1956 LP as a fraudulent document that had falsely represented the band's performance for more than four decades.[58] On one hand, listeners had a well-loved LP that they now knew to be heavily edited with overdubbed audience noises and added reverb. On the other, they had a CD claiming to restore the live performance to its unmodified state. Audio production was at the center of the debate about which recording sounded most accurate and representative of the Newport concert as it had happened onstage in 1956.

Avakian aggressively defended his production of the *Ellington at Newport* LP in 1999 by writing letters to various members of the jazz press, drafting newspaper editorials, speaking at conferences, and giving interviews about what he saw as a purposeful attack through misinformation.[59] He also began collecting various materials related to the reissue, including CD reviews, newspaper clippings, personal correspondences, letters to the editor, press releases, printouts of internet forum discussions, handwritten notes, and transcripts of conference presentations.[60] One such document contains a typed transcription of Schaap's liner notes extensively annotated by Avakian. Although at times Avakian's responses are reactionary, and obviously written decades after the initial event, a comparison between the 1999 CD and the 1956 LP through Schaap's and Avakian's words reveals changing ideologies of producing live jazz records, bringing greater clarity to Avakian's approach in 1956.[61]

Schaap's notes portray Avakian as the sole decision maker in the manipulation of the tapes in postproduction:

SCHAAP

Ellington at Newport intended to tell this story [of Paul Gonsalves's solo] to the record buying public. It did, but Columbia Records was convinced that post-production would be necessary to allow the music to deliver its message. The album *Ellington at Newport* doctored the music.[62]

AVAKIAN'S NOTES

*—But it was Duke who was so convinced that post-production would be needed for the Suite that he phoned me on July 6 to arrange [it], if possible.

*—"Doctored?" In order to release a viable album, highly professional editing was needed. And it was done at Duke's request. I gave the final acetates to Strayhorn to deliver to Duke, who then phoned to say, "I have only two things to say, George. One is, don't change a thing and the other is, thank you."[63]

Avakian inserts Ellington's and Strayhorn's involvement to highlight how the situation, from his perspective, involved close technological and musical collaboration in order to reconcile the difference between Ellington's artistic vision for the suite and the performance as recorded at Newport. As evidence, Avakian recalls that Ellington, fearing an underprepared performance, requested the studio reservation several days before the July 7 performance at Newport.[64] The aural proof heard on the Schaap-produced CD set (described above) suggests that Ellington was fully aware that the stage and the studio each contain their own possibilities.

The 1999 reissue unambiguously reveals an underprepared performance at Newport and of the *Festival Suite* in particular. Individual solos come off well, but ensemble passages are often sloppy, with missed entrances, flubbed notes, and other audible mistakes. In his annotations to Schaap's liner notes, Avakian writes that his intention was to correct mistakes played by the band on the Newport stage: "Duke was hugely grateful that something could be done to save the material, just as he had anticipated in asking me to reserve a studio on July 9.... Among the musicians, Cat Anderson and Johnny Hodges warmly expressed their gratitude that their several fluffs would not be permanently heard by the record-buying public."[65] Ellington was, according to Avakian, concerned about the reception of *Festival Suite* because it had been several years since his last long-form work.[66] However, Avakian's account of the time line is inexact. Two months before the festival—on May 16, 1956—Avakian wrote to Joe Glaser (Ellington's manger) about the plans to record at Newport, clearly stating that "in case of rain, high winds, equipment failure, low inspiration by the musicians, or just plain bad luck, I am preparing to do remakes in our studio immediately after the festival (beginning Monday, July 9)." He goes on to express that he hopes to avoid this solution because it "entails the difficult job of adding sound effects, as well as increasing our already very high cost of recording. But I will do everything necessary to insure good performance and good sound for all the musicians who participate."[67] Regardless of who was the original catalyst for the extra studio session, Avakian nevertheless makes his motivations clear: postproduction would be done if necessary to smooth out any mistakes so that they would not distract from the overall presentation of the music. Moreover, Avakian's letter also reveals how such editing was a regular if not expected part of the record-making process at Columbia, regardless of date or location. Ellington would have known this in advance.

In the early to mid-1950s, Columbia's listening demographic was a mainstream "America" largely defined by a white majority. A large portion of the label's jazz roster consisted of swing-era jazzmen such as Goodman and Ellington, who both rose to stardom in the 1930s and 1940s. Goodman's and Ellington's discs on the Masterworks series serve as evidence for how Columbia began intentionally blurring the aesthetic lines separating jazz, popular, and classical in the 1950s. Such an approach rested on long-established scripts of white masculine authority. Along with his regular stable of swing releases, Goodman recorded Aaron Copland's Concerto for Clarinet and String Orchestra and Mozart's Quintet for Clarinet and Strings in A Major (K. 581). Columbia issued these recordings on separate Masterworks LPs in 1951 and 1952, respectively.[68] *Masterpieces by Ellington*, a Masterworks LP from 1951, went out of its way to present Ellington as a "master" composer with lasting contributions. "Rarely in popular music does a composition earn the status of a masterpiece," writes George Dale in the liner notes. "There is so much that is ephemeral, and so much that is worthless, that the few lasting and memorable pieces shine like well-known stars in a singular naughty world. Duke Ellington's contributions to this small galaxy are among the brightest and most secure, and four of the finest have been chosen for this collection." Of Ellington, Dale asserts that "his place among the jazz immortals has long been assured."[69] By the middle of the decade, Avakian's treatment of rising male instrumentalists such as Dave Brubeck and Miles Davis pointed simultaneously to popular cultures of mass consumption (*Dave Digs Disney*, 1957) and white respectability through a mixture of jazz and classical (*Miles Ahead*, 1957).[70] In 1956 Avakian approached Ellington through a similar lens, where Black mastery and Black expertise existed within a commercial arena defined by white middlebrow sensibilities and the vocabularies of whiteness. The recording and production of Ellington's new composition for Newport 1956, *Festival Suite*, clearly fits within this broader trajectory of permanence through repeatability.

Louis Armstrong was also a key figure in Columbia's mainstream strategy. In 1955 he was "Ambassador" Satch, traveling in West Africa and performing in European concert halls. In July 1956, the same month of Ellington's Newport performance, the film *High Society* opened in US theaters. Starring Bing Crosby, Grace Kelly, and Frank Sinatra, *High Society* opens with several long overhead shots of the city of Newport accompanied by Armstrong's singing. His lyrics specifically reference the festival. The movie depicts an archetypical love triangle set within the confines of elite white culture, with Armstrong's music bookending the movie's plot. As a sign of the times, Black expertise exists at the edges but nevertheless frames the boundaries of heteronormative whiteness. As John Gennari argues, Armstrong's role was a typical Hollywood formula where a Black jazz musician was used to "authenticate a white star's knowing hipness."[71]

Columbia's audience for *Ellington at Newport* was a wide range of listeners. In this way, the label was quite different from a company such as Prestige Records, which catered to jazz aficionados by selling mistakes on record as a form of documentary evidence and technological novelty. For Columbia, a mistake-free performance and clean recording was the ideal end product. According to Harvey Cohen, Avakian recalls that Ellington was open to experimentation in the studio if it improved the end result.[72] The evidence again bears this out. For instance, Ellington's 1953 version of "The Mooche" on the *Ellington Uptown* LP (1953) features heavy amounts of reverb during a call-and-response clarinet duet between Russell Procope and Jimmy Hamilton (1:32–2:25). His LP *Blue Rose*, a 1956 collaboration with Rosemary Clooney, featured overdubbed vocals recorded in Los Angeles two weeks after the band laid down the initial tracks in New York City. From Avakian's perspective, the edits to the *Newport* LP were necessary in order to release a viable album that could be repeatedly listened to and sold to a wide consumer demographic. For Ellington, a mistake-free performance was also ideal in how it appealed to Ellington's sense of artistry and aesthetics.[73]

One example of a corrected mistake can be heard on the band's rendition of "I Got It Bad (and That Ain't Good)," a well-known Ellington standard, featuring saxophonist Johnny Hodges. Although the band played this piece immediately following "Diminuendo and Crescendo in Blue" during the concert, Avakian released "I Got It Bad" in 1956 on the A side of another LP recorded at Newport: *The Duke Ellington and Buck Clayton All-Stars*.[74] During the Newport concert, Hodges badly flubs the third note of the melody on two separate occasions (CD: 0:18 and 0:46). In an effort to correct such a prominent mistake, Avakian decided to splice in sixteen measures of music that came from the band's studio session. This insertion can be heard between Hodges's two misplayed notes.[75]

Jazz records circulate within a cultural economy based around moments of mastery and spontaneity during performance. Mistakes come to have different meanings depending on the circumstances. On the one hand, they are a valued aspect of jazz history, and many listeners champion jazz for being, as critic Ted Gioia has written, the "imperfect art."[76] Mistakes like Hodges's missed note, on the other hand, stand out in a way that weakens the performance. By splicing tape to include sounds not of *that* moment but of *another*, Avakian sacrifices the beginning-to-end integrity of the festival recording. However, such edits were done to create a listening experience that would stand up to repeated listenings by nonexpert listeners rather than with an intention to faithfully represent Hodges's playing that particular night in Newport. Avakian's annotation signifies that permanence via repeatability was the incentive for most, if not all, of his changes made in postproduction. If the performance at Newport was about the live moment, then the recording session was about the repeatability of that moment as it appealed to Columbia's listening demographic.

In the 1950s, as popular music scholar Albin Zak argues, records were not only about "truthful documentary" but also about the "aesthetic impact" rendered from the performance.[77] In the case of the *Ellington at Newport* LP, Avakian attempted to produce a particular kind of listening experience that was not about faithful representation but audile realism—hearing the event as live.[78] Agents of sound reproduction such as producers, engineers, and other professionals must be prepared, technologically and otherwise, for when such moments transpire onstage or in the recording studio. Producer

Bob Thiele succinctly summed this up when asked about recording saxophonist John Coltrane: "You gotta capture it when it happens. That's jazz."[79] If something goes wrong, however, jazz producers have to be technologically prepared. As Avakian recalled, "You had to know... the acoustical properties of a studio and... [have] a pretty good idea of what the engineer was able to do so you could... get the sound that you wanted."[80] Avakian's comment speaks to the intertwined and creative relationship between jazz performance and technological mediation. From the perspective of a producer, both studio and stage are creative spaces for music making that necessitate a skilled and inventive ability to render such moments repeatable on record.

Producing Gonsalves's Solo

A seemingly simple mistake made onstage by Paul Gonsalves has come to define the history of *Ellington at Newport*. In a draft of an unpublished letter from August 2004 to John McDonough of the *Wall Street Journal*, Avakian recalled his reaction at the 1956 Newport Festival after Ellington's band finished their performance of "Diminuendo and Crescendo in Blue": "Under ordinary circumstances, Paul's gaffe [of going to the wrong microphone] could have been forgiven or he could have been spliced out, but this solo was the absolute focus of what I instantly realized was surely the Ellington orchestra's most exciting performance ever, and that at all costs it must be released even though what I heard was seriously flawed."[81] Columbia's directional microphones were set up as carefully as possible to record a clean sound from all parts of the ensemble in order to give the mixing engineers the most control. Even so, when Gonsalves mistakenly stepped to the wrong microphone, there was little hope of accurately recording him in full: the mixing had to be done on-site and during the performance. Mixing engineer Adjutor "Pappy" Theroux did his best to adjust the balance, which audibly happens between twenty and thirty seconds into the solo (LP: 4:20 to 4:30).

After listening back to the tapes, Avakian felt that Gonsalves was still much too low in the mix and that "drastic steps had to be taken to restore some degree of what actually had happened."[82] He relied on his assistant, Calvin Lampley, and engineer George Knuerr to salvage the raw recordings using equalization, tape splicing, and an echo chamber. Beginning in the 1950s, recording engineers began creating echo and reverb by running sound through a speaker located in a reverberant space, using another microphone to pick up the room sound or "ambience." They would then feed this signal back into the mixing desk and blend it with the initial source.[83] Avakian describes how his team used this state-of-the-art technology in 1956 to repair, reconstruct, and eventually showcase a historic moment on LP:

> To rescue the great performance of "Diminuendo and Crescendo in Blue," the equalization (the ratio between high and low frequencies of sound) had to be changed, sometimes every few seconds, as Gonsalves's solo rose up and down in register, even though it also changed the sound of everything else on the tape. With no other means available to attempt corrections than a variable pitch oscillator and an echo chamber, re-recording engineer George Knuerr and I made dozens of splices, bringing the soloist forward as required, then splicing the solo together. Under the primitive conditions we were forced to work in 1956, it became necessary to hide these splices in order to maintain a continuous flow of the music and preserve the phenomenal drive that Gonsalves and the band had created. The only way was to hide those changes of equalization and sound level by masking them under additional crowd noise that distracted the ear from the otherwise noticeable cuts in the tape. The result was a steady flow of undistracted music which conveys the feeling of what actually took place.[84]

Avakian characterizes his editing and equalization as a creative and highly professional activity on the part of himself and his engineers to aurally reconstruct a feeling of what "actually took place." For him, the raw tapes were neither representative of nor faithful to the performance. As he writes elsewhere in this same document, "Musically, the original unedited recording did not sound like what the audience actually heard."[85]

In Avakian's hands, studio technology became a restorative vehicle based around an aesthetic of *sonic realism* and directed toward the LP's eventual listeners. He equalized, masked, added, and spliced a recording to sound like, in his words, "what the audience heard," which is a statement not about reality but about the perception of it. Avakian's initial editing and equalization made his mediation audible, destabilizing the record's believability as a "live" event. So it became necessary to distract the ear in order to sustain the affective reproduction of the music's "flow" and "drive," as well as the "feeling of what actually took place." Such an approach recalls Jonathan Sterne's argument that sound reproduction is not necessarily a "mimetic art" but rather about "crafting a particular kind of listening experience."[86] Avakian's heavily edited production demonstrates a dedication to an ideology of record making that privileges the perception of the live moment, the construction of liveness, rather than faithful representation.

The changing uses of studio technology within the industry during the 1950s that disrupted the beginning-to-end quality of a musical performance on record made it increasingly difficult to claim the existence of an authentic original. As producers' decisions about the sonic persona of records gradually came to depend on micro decisions about microphone placement, tape editing, equalization during mixing, and other forms of sound processing, records became less about real-life sonic representations and more about the sound aesthetics of high fidelity. As Albin Zak writes, these technological advances made it more and more difficult to answer the question "Fidelity to what?"[87] Avakian's *Ellington at Newport* LP hinges on its ability to create and capture the spirit of the event in sound, even if the LP was a reproduction of a performance in which there is no original.[88]

Listening to a concert at home with a record player is a culturally structured activity that can re/produce liveness, the quality of a recording that creates a sense of performance happening in the now. Believability arises because listeners allow it.[89] Liveness is not something that sound inherently possesses—it can neither "hold faith nor be faithful," as Sterne says—but a quality that listeners ascribe to it.[90] Avakian did his editing and studio manipulation with the assumption that his listeners' ears could and would make the perceptual leap to construct the sense (a "flow" or "drive," as he says) of the event with their record player at home. A producer does, above all, function as someone who mediates between artist and consumer using sonic technologies.[91] Avakian did his editing and studio manipulation, in other words, with certain assumptions about the listening habits of his consumers. He crafted a particular kind of listening experience meant to tap into feelings that audience members might get from a face-to-face encounter at a live jazz concert.

Making Records Live, Making Live Records

The strategy taken with the July 1956 events at Newport may have been novel, but *Ellington at Newport* contributed to a long arc of record-making experiments by Avakian. I have already mentioned the *Chicago Jazz* album, Goodman's *The Famous 1938 Carnegie Hall Jazz Concert*, *Masterpieces by Ellington*, and the series of in-studio jam-session records featuring Buck Clayton.[92] In the years after, Avakian would explore conceptual albums with long-form musical compositions and themes. These included Davis's work with Gil Evans on *Miles Ahead* (1957) and Brubeck's Jazz Impressions series, which began with a 1958 LP titled *Jazz Impressions of Eurasia*. With a cover depicting Brubeck in front of a Pan Am airplane, the *Jazz Impressions* LP features six original compositions that Brubeck composed in response to the quartet's three-month worldwide tour. Avakian also oversaw several LPs of extended concert jazz, including *Music for Brass* (1957) and *Modern Jazz Concert* (1958).[93]

Alteration of performance time through studio production and magnetic-tape manipulation played a large role in Avakian's trajectory. For example, "Robbins' Nest" from *The Huckle-Buck and Robbins' Nest: A Buck Clayton Jam Session* (1954) includes at least three choruses from a completely different take that were spliced in during postproduction.[94] On Miles Davis's first LP for Columbia, *'Round about Midnight* (1957), Avakian and Davis meticulously planned the session to include multiple run-throughs of each song. The issued version of "Ah-Leu-Cha" was made from two takes spliced together, with the edit point in the middle of Davis's solo.[95] The track "Atlanta Blues" on *Louis Armstrong Plays W. C. Handy* (1954) includes Armstrong playing a duet with himself, a feat accomplished by overdubbing a trumpet and scat solo onto the original track. Avakian used the same technique on *Miles Ahead*, where most of Davis's solos were later inserted.[96] *Ambassador Satch* included manufactured live performances, made by combining musical performances with audience sounds initially recorded at other live concerts.[97] In the years since, Columbia has become known for its heavy-handed production on its jazz records from this period, a regular practice of the day that has fallen out of favor with many of today's listeners.[98] At the time, however, Avakian was using the latest studio capabilities during a transitional moment, where the fundamental idea of recording jazz was in question.

Studio production is one link among many in the chain of mediation from performance to commercial record. Variables such as the location of microphones and public-address speakers, the natural acoustics of the venue, and any other form of electronic amplification transform, manipulate, and mediate the concertgoing experience as well. Media historian Philip Auslander argues that "in a sense, the mix, even when performed live, is a transformation of the actual performance produced by the musicians. In such a case, the audience has no access to the 'real' event, but only to its transformed version."[99] Although Auslander perhaps goes too far in collapsing *all* live performances into the category of mediatization, his argument nevertheless usefully unsettles any claims of authenticity regarding an unmediated live recording or performance.[100] Yes, the crowd noises on Ellington's LP were made through the manipulation of sonic characteristics in the studio, but several other technologies of sound reproduction were also present at the Newport concert. The public spaces of music making have similar characteristics of mediation and alteration.

Moreover, Columbia's target audience in 1956 was a wide demographic of music consumers. Throughout his tenure at Columbia, Avakian was the head of *popular* albums, and jazz was only a minor subset of the label's musical activity. A separate jazz division simply did not exist. With the rise of technological possibilities in the studio, effects such as overdubbing, echo, reverb, and others came to have a normalized presence in popular music during the 1950s. As Zak observes, "Records were no longer simply aural snapshots but deliberately crafted musical texts."[101] Although such effects were not widely used in jazz, records in this genre remained, as Andrew Blake argues, "largely in the world of simulation," even as it was becoming possible to emulate "the structure of the jazz concert itself."[102] Several Ellington recordings from the late 1950s produced by Irving Townsend, including *Newport 1958* and *Dance to Duke! at the Bal Masque* (1959), used studio recordings with audience overdubs. Despite this fact, both records claimed to be recorded "in performance" through their liner notes and other promotional materials.[103] It is unclear if Ellington ever knew about these specific manipulations, although his awareness of the record-making process is well documented.

On *Ellington at Newport*, Avakian used studio production to cultivate a sense of place of the Newport stage, most noticeable in the sounds of the audience. When asked about the 1956 LP, Avakian has long maintained that capturing the Newport audience was a primary concern. On-site recording for commercial purposes in 1956 was a new venture for a major label like Columbia, but Avakian and his team were prepared with several microphones, including two that were suspended above the stage for the express purpose of capturing the crowd noise and ambience of the event.[104] On the LP, Avakian's added crowd noise becomes increasingly noticeable about one minute and forty-five seconds into the solo (LP: 5:45), accompanied by shouts from Ellington at the piano bench. About a minute later (LP: 6:45), the crowd and drummer Sam Woodyard's propelling beat account for most of the sonic density, nearly overwhelming Gonsalves. The audience's sound, which has ebbed and flowed throughout, but in an upward trajectory overall, reaches its peak when Gonsalves holds a six-measure high note that introduces his final chorus (LP: 10:12). Just below the surface, nearly hidden beneath the excitement, Ellington shouts "Yeah, yeah, yeah" as the solo comes to a close.

The same moments on the CD reissue, without the added crowd noise, reveal a much more tempered audience. With few reflective surfaces at an outdoor venue like Newport, sounds dissipate quickly, even those of a large crowd. The audience reaction is clearly audible at points like Gonsalves's high note at the end of his solo (CD: 9:53), but the most discernible sounds are from individuals, such as the four distinctive cries of "whoo" that can be heard during an earlier part of the solo (CD: 9:15). Like Ellington's cries from the piano bench, such shouts express excitement, energy, and enthusiasm. These shouts are audible on the LP as well, but they blend in with the rest of the crowd, one vocalization among many.

The sounds of a large crowd, as opposed to individual voices, help the technology of sound reproduction bridge the fantastical gap between here and there, now and then. Avakian spliced, cut, copied, and edited in more voices—a crowd en masse—in order to cultivate the feeling of a performance for listeners not accustomed to hearing live jazz recordings. The audience on *Ellington at Newport* has a sonically rendered presence, where different sounds come to indicate different levels of engagement between the audience and performers onstage. In sound engineering, as ethnomusicologist David Novak details, *presence* refers to the upper midrange frequencies and the so-called critical band where most linguistic communication occurs. Accordingly, a high number of frequencies in this range create an effect of making sounds feel closer or more "present."[105] In the context of performance, presence can also refer to the quality or manner of performers and their interaction with the audience. Similar to the quality of liveness, this type of presence implies a feeling of immediacy that comes from face-to-face interaction where the audience has, as Paul Allain and Jen Harvie write, "a sense of the importance of being in that moment at the event."[106] The presence of the audience on record, similar to presence in audio engineering, relates to a feeling of proximity and a sense of "being there."[107] The complex layering of Avakian's additions creates a larger aural footprint of the audience and, like the touch of reverb added to the Newport tapes overall, allows a sense of place to resonate. The aggregation of shouts, yells, murmurs, and cries cultivates a particular idea of being "there," as being somewhere though not in the audience. Avakian produced an ideal place of listening specifically made for consumers at home with a stereo.

Documenting Duke

Reproductions of live jazz have existed since the music's earliest days in the form of radio broadcasts, some from remote locations such as nightclubs and concert halls. The adoption of the LP in combination with emergent electromagnetic-tape capabilities made these live moments repeatable and portable in new ways. The live recording became a viable commercial genre. During the ensuing adjustment period, record-industry executives, producers, engineers, and musicians all had to negotiate what it meant to put such live moments on record.[108] This network of creative individuals had to decide what kind of sounds, images, and design characteristics were necessary to make a sounded object feel live. Liveness on record, to put it another way, became a valued commodity that necessitated research and development.

During this time of experimentation, tape recording made it possible to splice, insert, overdub, and manipulate recordings in different ways. As more options emerged, musical time came to have a new commercial value. On-stage performance became more reproducible outside of the studio, which pushed the limits of what it meant to record jazz. It became feasible to record and produce lengthy performances, such as a twenty-seven-chorus solo by Paul Gonsalves at the Newport Jazz Festival. However, this control over time in the studio also created a need for specialists and expert technicians—it took costly studio resources to convert performance time into record time.[109] For *Ellington at Newport*, Avakian leveraged these new possibilities of time manipulation and on-site commercial recording to reproduce the feeling and ambience of a live event of historical import. Guided by an approach to record making that privileged sonic realism, he made creative decisions about the music to create a viable LP from flawed tapes. That is, this history on record would simply not exist without the manipulative techniques of audio production.

The site of Ellington's celebrated performance was anything but neutral. From its inception, the Newport Festival attempted to legitimize jazz by attaching itself to elite northeastern sensibilities and making the music into a symbol of sophistication and democratic public culture.[110] Similar to Prestige Records in the early 1950s, the Newport Festival presented jazz through a white cultural lens that marginalized the Blackness of African American musicians even as it celebrated their musical achievements. Jazz was a flexible enough category at the time to fit into the white spaces of Newport, but this project relied on preexisting scripts of white masculine authority and authenticity. Festival director George Wein and Columbia Records played their part, as did George Avakian through his corrective audio production. The *Ellington at Newport* LP, which contains an acclaimed moment of blues improvisation matched with a newly composed Ellington "suite," is a product of an aesthetic discourse of jazz whiteness.

Of course, *Ellington at Newport* was made possible through the collaborative efforts of many differently situated record makers, including Ellington. In his efforts to express his sonic Afro-modernity, Ellington might best be described as an enigmatic radical. He was famously slippery in offering some opinions but also fearlessly political in ways he chose to be, especially regarding his musical craft. These traits have been well documented, although the focus has rarely been on his relationship with sonic technologies. Yet Ellington clearly understood the technological aspect of his professional life, from the affordances offered by different recording formats to the purpose and possibilities of the studio. Although he left the technical execution to record makers like Avakian, he retained his aesthetic agency and seemed to know which kinds of relationships he could trust. There is no better example than the spoken introductions that begin the *Ellington at Newport* LP. Yes, Avakian heavily cut, copied, and spliced Ellington's voice. But the bandleader's aural presence remains. As before, the desire to document jazz history, an impulse so prevalent during the early LP era, meant that alternative forms of Black expertise and Black authority circulated anew.

Jazz records are as seductive as they are deceptive: seductive because they reproduce, repeat, and replay the values of spontaneity, individuality, and mastery at the center of the jazz aesthetic, deceptive because they present their contents as uninterrupted performances.[111] Live records give contemporary listeners the sense they are eavesdropping on lost moments of history, and do so by purposely misdirecting from the multilayered relationship between performance and its recorded Other. With this aural sleight of hand, the past is always in a state of becoming through listening. The 1956 *Ellington at Newport* LP assumes a date, a location, and a specific performance while at the same time bringing that moment to absent ears. Sound production helps to bridge the divide between here/now and there/then, whether through equalization, added crowd noise, or spliced-in corrections. These practices employ creativity, imagination, and expertise situated within overlapping, conflicting, and shifting approaches to rendering the live event in sound.

Playlist: Festival Stages, Studio Jam Sessions, and Other Lengthy Improvisations

Recording jazz festivals and jam sessions in the mid-1950s was a difficult and often messy undertaking, even for major labels like Columbia. This playlist explores several approaches to producing and designing records that feature lengthy jazz performances. (All recordings are LPs.)

Allyn Ferguson and Kenneth Patchen. *Allyn Ferguson and Kenneth Patchen with the Chamber Jazz Sextet*. Discovery, 1957.
Benny Goodman. *The Famous 1938 Carnegie Hall Jazz Concert*. Columbia Masterworks, 1950.
Benny Goodman and His Orchestra. *Benny Goodman in Moscow*. RCA Victor, 1962.
Buck Clayton. *All the Cats Join In: A Buck Clayton Jam Session*. Columbia, 1956.
Buck Clayton. *Buck Clayton Jams Benny Goodman*. Columbia, 1955.
Buck Clayton. *The Huckle-Buck and Robbins' Nest: A Buck Clayton Jam Session*. Columbia, 1954.
Buck Clayton. *Jumpin' at the Woodside*. Columbia, 1955.
Buck Clayton with Woody Herman. *How Hi the Fi: A Buck Clayton Jam Session*. Columbia, 1954.
Dave Brubeck. *Dave Brubeck at Storyville: 1954, vols. 1-2*. Columbia, 1954.
Dave Brubeck. *Jazz Goes to College, vols. 1-2*. Columbia, 1954.
Dave Brubeck, J. J. Johnson, and Kai Winding. *Dave Brubeck/Jay & Kai at Newport*. Columbia, 1956.
Duke Ellington. *At the Bal Masque*. Columbia, 1959.
Duke Ellington. *Duke Ellington and His Orchestra: Newport 1958*. Columbia, 1958.
Duke Ellington. *Ellington at Newport*. Columbia, 1956.
Duke Ellington. *Ellington Uptown*. Columbia, 1952.
Duke Ellington. *Masterpieces by Ellington*. Columbia Masterworks, 1951.
Duke Ellington and Buck Clayton. *The Duke Ellington and Buck Clayton All-Stars: At Newport*. Columbia, 1956.
Erroll Garner. *Concert by the Sea*. Columbia, 1956.
Kenneth Patchen. *Kenneth Patchen with Chamber Jazz Sextet*. Cadence, 1959.
Kenneth Rexroth and Lawrence Ferlinghetti. *Poetry Readings in the Cellar*. Fantasy, 1957.
Louis Armstrong. *Ambassador Satch*. Columbia, 1956.
Louis Armstrong. *Louis Armstrong Plays W. C. Handy*. Columbia, 1954.
Louis Armstrong and Eddie Condon. *At Newport*. Columbia, 1956.
Miles Davis. *Miles Ahead*. Columbia, 1957.
Miles Davis. *'Round about Midnight*. Columbia, 1957.
Various. *Modern Jazz Concert*. Columbia, 1958.
Various. *Music for Brass*. Columbia, 1957.

4

WORLD STATESMAN

The Ambassadorial LPs of Dizzy Gillespie

In 1956 trombonist Melba Liston regularly fronted Dizzy Gillespie's large ensemble as the featured soloist on her own arrangement of "My Reverie." Several historical remnants echo through her ensemble writing. Both melody and oscillating accompaniment come from Claude Debussy's *Rêverie*, a solo piano piece from 1890. Even so, her adaptation most closely follows Larry Clinton's "My Reverie," a 1938 hit that filtered Debussy through the swing-obsessed music industry of prewar America.[1] Taking inspiration, it seems, from Debussy, Clinton, and Glenn Miller—who made the song a trombone feature—Liston skillfully combines classical, popular, and jazz sensibilities into the sound of Gillespie's post-bebop big band. The subtle ebb and flow of her arrangement perfectly complements the fluidity of her playing, which can be heard throughout the ensemble's three-minute recording.

Liston's "My Reverie" appeared on *Dizzy Gillespie: World Statesman* (1956), one of two LPs purporting to document the first time that a jazz ensemble participated in the State Department's Cultural Presentations program. During two separate tours in 1956, Gillespie's big band took part in the program's multifarious initiative to positively influence public attitudes toward the United States around the world while simultaneously fighting communist propaganda.[2] Gillespie's ensemble, Liston included, performed more than one hundred concerts in eleven countries in Eastern Europe, the Middle East, and South America.[3] As one of two Black women and the only female instrumentalist on tour, Liston's role as a featured soloist doubly performed the narrative of racial equity and gender equality promoted by the State Department's programming.[4] By her own account, Liston's presence had quite the effect: "I had lots of women come to me in the Middle East tours to find out how life was over here for women and how in the world I could be running around there traveling and single when they were so subjected over there."[5] "My Reverie," then, should not be heard merely as a jazz versioning of Debussy but as a point where musical performance intersects with competing investments in Black expertise, Black labor, and Black capital during the 1950s. Jazz record makers definitely saw the convergence of musical and international politics as an opportunity.

Gillespie's record label, Norgran, run by impresario Norman Granz, released *World Statesman* a few months after the band returned from its second tour in South America. Along with a title that intimates political leadership, the liner notes, written by acclaimed jazz researcher Marshall Stearns, recount anecdotes from local newspapers and present the music as the "first half" of a tour concert. *Dizzy in Greece*, the follow-up LP, took a similar approach. The disc placed Gillespie in a location of specific political relevance and portrayed the music as a concert for the State Department.[6]

The LPs were well received by the jazz press. *World Statesman* appeared as a national best-seller in *Down Beat* four times between March and June 1957.[7] Despite criticizing the occasional lack of precision, reviewer Nat Hentoff characterized the band's music as "a collective storm" and Gillespie's playing in particular as "masterly."[8] *Dizzy in Greece*, issued in October 1957, received four out of five stars from *Down Beat*'s Don Gold. Gillespie's playing on the record, according to Gold, is "the epitome of creative jazz" and "glows with warmth and excitement." Gold further extols the "incomparable drive" of the band and the "fascinating" arrangements as "the best efforts of some of jazz' best writers." Although he recommends this album as one "worth owning and hearing often," he does remark that there is "no evidence that an audience is present for this concert performance, in Greece or anywhere else." He further observes that the title "seems to be justification for use of the cover photo, of Gillespie in Greek garb."[9]

Gold was right to question the name, discographical details, and motivations of this record. The material on both records resulted from two recording sessions in New York City in June 1956 and April 1957. Moreover, several surviving programs from the Middle East tour reveal that despite their claim to represent performances abroad, the LPs contain only a small cross section of the repertoire that Gillespie and his band played during the State Department tours. The records also omit Gillespie's humorous interactions with band members and the audience that were a regular part of the band's onstage performance, as concurrent live recordings evince.

Gillespie's LPs reveal a rupture between the act(s) of performance and the packaged commodity of its representation. Using the discrepancies between the tour performances and these LPs as a starting point, this chapter interrogates how the business of selling jazz records intersected with nationwide debates about cultural diplomacy, international affairs, and racial politics in the United States at mid-century. Unlike the tour concerts, which served a specific political purpose for international audiences, the LPs were specifically designed so that domestic consumers might imagine jazz as standing for the political ideals of the United States. I argue that these records were never meant to document the tours with veracity. Rather, the LPs were the product of a political, technological, and economic moment when Gillespie's record label could leverage musical diplomacy to both sell records and circulate an elevated vision for jazz within the country's cultural hierarchy.

In order to investigate the overlapping cultural logics of this moment, I focus on the collaborative record making of Gillespie, Stearns, and Granz. Each of these recordmen occupied a different position within the jazz industry, and each possessed distinct but complementary skill sets. It was also the normalization of the 12-inch LP format that heavily enabled and influenced their collaboration. In other words, the popularity of jazz on LP led to the proliferation of jazz-specific record labels (Granz), greater interest in historical writing about the music (Stearns), and more performance opportunities for charismatic musicians, including those at the request of the

State Department (Gillespie). As record makers each differently imagined the new purpose and potentialities of the jazz LP during this era, the musical politics of jazz came into contact with the geopolitics of Washington, DC. This created the possibility for social transformation, where the idea of jazz became just as powerful as the music.

As in my previous chapters, my exploration of Gillespie's LPs focuses on how record makers choose to curate, document, design, and market jazz on record. In this chapter, however, I move away from technological experimentation as the driver of change and instead ask a set of questions: What does it mean to make a political argument through jazz record making? What political work can the sound of Black performance do when captured on record? And what other modes of communication are necessary to effectively transmit the stakes of this political work? This chapter thus examines how the always emergent audiovisuality of the LP, nominally a commercial concern, relates to broader cultural discourses of which jazz was only a part.

Jazz as Cultural Diplomacy

From 1945 to 1960, the first fifteen years following World War II, more than forty countries containing roughly a quarter of the world's population (approximately 800 million people) gained independence. In the fight for political dominance in these decolonized states, race relations and the Jim Crow institutional discrimination laws in the United States became a major point of emphasis in Soviet propaganda efforts.[10] As early as 1946, Soviet propagandists distributed reports about lynchings and poor labor conditions in the southern United States. Senator William Benton warned Congress in 1950 that US race relations would hurt the country's efforts in most of the non-European areas of the Cold War.[11] It was no coincidence that Gillespie's tours focused on the Middle East and South America.

The inherent contradictions of sustaining Jim Crow policies while self-identifying as "leaders of the free world" presented a problem for the United States. Because it could not deny the realities of domestic racism, the State Department began emphasizing the moral imperative of democracy. It adopted a narrative that outlined a teleological future: the democratic process, however slow, would peacefully lead toward social justice and racial equality.[12]

The fight against the Soviet Union to gain political influence within decolonized states also led to aggressive anticommunist domestic policies within the United States, particularly those created by Republican senator Joseph McCarthy. Underwritten by fear of communism, such policies endangered prominent Black intellectuals with left-leaning ideals who publicly criticized the treatment of African Americans during their travels abroad. In an effort to control the international circulation of narratives about race relations within the United States, the State Department revoked the passports of activists such as Paul Robeson and W. E. B. Du Bois, whose actions, rhetoric, and writings challenged the state-sanctioned narrative of racial progress. At the same time, the FBI placed other African American artists under surveillance, including Richard Wright, James Baldwin, Josephine Baker, and Louis Armstrong.[13]

In response, many African American activists and community leaders began distancing themselves from figures like Robeson and Du Bois to avoid the negative attention of the US government. For example, the NAACP executive secretary Walter White, Council on African Affairs founding member Max Yergan, and US congressman Adam Clayton Powell Jr. rebuked communism while they simultaneously denounced racial violence and institutional inequality on moral grounds, placing their struggle in terms that fit within the language and logic of US democracy.[14] The mission statement of the Southern Christian Leadership Conference (SCLC), written in 1957, declared its desire to "redeem the soul of America."[15] In this way, Cold War civil rights extended beyond tangible political actions. As historian Waldo E. Martin argues, African American leaders fighting against social injustice adopted a discourse of morality in ways that allowed them to promote a vision of the nation built around diversity, complexity, and pluralism rather than one built around white dominant culture.[16] As a result, emerging debates about Black identity across different social strata increasingly focused on the degrees of overlap and difference between (white) American culture and African American culture.

At the same time, the State Department began increasing the visibility of African Americans abroad by sending distinguished authors, athletes, journalists, classical musicians, and other intellectuals on missions of cultural exchange. In the early 1950s, author J. Saunders Redding, journalist Carl T. Rowan, high jumper Gilbert Cruter, classical vocalist William Warfield, and the Harlem Globetrotters all toured on behalf of the US government.[17] The State Department also began placing African Americans in its embassies across the world and allowed prominent figures such as attorney Edith Sampson to speak at public events.[18] Powell, one of the few Black members of Congress, succinctly summarized this strategy when he told President Dwight Eisenhower in 1955 that "one dark face from the US is as much value as millions of dollars in economic aid."[19]

That same year, Powell helped persuade Eisenhower that jazz could be a useful tool in fighting Soviet propaganda abroad. Although many members of Congress considered jazz a lowbrow musical form, it had become undeniably popular in the Eastern Bloc, primarily through Willis Conover's *Music USA* radio show on the Voice of America network (VOA). Launched on January 6, 1955, *Music USA* played in prime-time slots before and after the evening news, dividing its airtime evenly between popular music and jazz. Historian Penny Von Eschen estimates that in 1955 the show reached around thirty million people in eighty countries.[20] Conover was fond of comparing jazz with the ideals of Western democracy: "Jazz is a cross between total discipline and total anarchy. The musicians agree on tempo, key, and chord structure but beyond this everyone is free to express himself. This is jazz. And this is America.... [People] love jazz because they love freedom."[21] Unlike Western art music, this thinking went, jazz was a singular product of the United States that could not be replicated by the Soviet Union.[22] Jazz was, as Vice Consul Ernest A. Nagy said, "one of the country's outstanding contribution[s] to the art forms of the world and perhaps our most popular export."[23] The jazz ambassadors tours, as they were later referred to, began through what came to be known as the Cultural Presentations program.[24]

Many scholars have examined jazz within the Cultural Presentations program and Gillespie's particular contributions. Most notably, Penny Von Eschen uses Gillespie to discuss how the US government chose to combat negative representations of Jim Crow worldwide. Cultural theorist Richard Iton places Gillespie's ambassadorial tours within the context of other Black entertainers navigating similar political terrain, tracing the relationship between national politics and Black popular culture.[25] Ethnomusicologist Ingrid Monson further locates the jazz tours within a musico-political trajectory, detailing how jazz musicians joined the struggle for social equality and civil rights as a means of battling entrenched structures of white supremacy. Von Eschen, Iton, and Monson all reveal how artists crossed social boundaries during a crucial time of political upheaval to enact cultural change through their popular appeal.[26] In what follows, I build on this work by considering Gillespie's ambassadorial music as a specific type of cultural work made possible by the systematic shifts of the recording industry and the rise of the jazz LP in particular. As I have been arguing throughout, the increased popularity of jazz with larger (and whiter) segments of the record-buying public in the mid-1950s coincided with record makers' attempts to reframe entrenched notions of cultural value that surrounded the music. It is not a coincidence that George Avakian planned Columbia's first Newport recordings (see chapter 3) at the precise moment when Gillespie toured the world at the behest of the State Department. The VOA's decision to record and broadcast from the Newport Jazz Festival is another convergence point of these overlapping trends.[27]

Questions nevertheless remain about how individuals operated within these broader trends and argued for the artistic and commercial relevance of jazz. Understanding how Gillespie's ambassadorial LPs shaped popular representations of jazz on the national stage puts the focus on record making as a cultural activity that must exist in collaboration. As a result, the often-contentious definition of jazz as a genre becomes much less important than the way that jazz musicians chose to leverage their skills as performers and the way that other individuals chose to package those performances for listeners. Record making is a commercial enterprise, to be sure, but it is also a regime of knowledge production that has tangible consequences for Black cultural workers.

Dizzy Gillespie as World Statesman

The American National Theater Academy (ANTA) oversaw the evaluation of participants for the Cultural Presentations program. With little knowledge about jazz, ANTA's music advisory panel sought the expertise of Marshall Stearns, who recommended Gillespie along with several other musicians.[28] Gillespie's dynamic ability and charismatic personality made him an ideal choice, although some policy makers in Washington still had concerns about sending jazz overseas. In a letter dated January 30, 1956, ANTA general manager Robert C. Schnitzer asked Stearns to accompany Gillespie's band and advised him that "every precaution must be taken to assure that America's popular music is presented in such a way as to achieve the best results for our national prestige." He continued: "We would also depend upon you to keep an eye on Dizzy's programs in order to see that he maintains the standards that have been set for them."[29] It is telling that ANTA solicited a white male academic to make jazz legible to cultural elites and to oversee a program intended to combat communist propaganda about racial inequality within the United States. Within the shifting dynamics of the early Cold War, jazz advocacy relied on and reinforced existing structures of white male authority for statesmen, recordmen, and jazzmen alike.

From Gillespie's perspective, the tours presented an enormous opportunity. Besides the chance to travel abroad extensively, the invitation allowed the trumpeter to lead a big band once again, something he had attempted several times previously with little financial success.[30] For most jazz musicians who grew up in the big-band era, fronting such a large ensemble was the gold standard of status and achievement. The support of the US government exponentially increased the power of such symbolism.

Agreeing to be the first jazz musician to represent America abroad nevertheless carried a degree of risk for Gillespie and his fellow musicians, especially given the treatment of Robeson, Du Bois, and others. The band members had to balance any opinions about the state of civil liberties for African Americans with their unwavering support of democratic ideals. While on tour, Gillespie both praised the progress in US race relations and spoke openly about Emmett Till, whose gruesome murder in 1955 made tangible the violent realities of African American life.[31] According to *Jet* magazine, local populations closely questioned Gillespie about Till's murder and about Autherine Lucy, the first Black student to attend (and be unjustly expelled from) the University of Alabama.[32] Gillespie, in Richard Iton's characterization, faced the challenge of having to be Black enough for foreign audiences but not so Black as to threaten the broader missions of the State Department.[33]

Gillespie states in his autobiography that he "wasn't going over to apologize for the racist policies of America" and also proudly acknowledges what he called an "'American assortment' of blacks, whites, males, females, Jews, and Gentiles in the band."[34] The presence of a racially mixed and gender-inclusive band onstage purposefully performed the narrative of progress pushed by the State Department. Gillespie recalled how the local people "could see it wasn't as intense [as they had been led to believe] because we had white boys and I was the leader of the band." He continues:

> That was strange to them because they'd heard about blacks being lynched and burned, and here I come with half whites and blacks and a girl playing in the band. And everybody seemed to be getting along fine. So I didn't try to hide anything. I said, "Yeah, there it is. We have our problems but we're still working on it. I'm the leader of this band, and those white guys are working for me." That's a helluva thing. A hundred

years ago, our ancestors were slaves, and today we're scuffling with this problem, but I'm sure it's gonna be straightened out some day. I probably won't see it, completely, the eradication of racial prejudice in the United States, but it will be eliminated.[35]

In this passage, Gillespie ties his activities to a narrative of economic progress and a future without prejudice, thereby adopting a perspective similar to that of the State Department's Cultural Presentations program. Jazz was, from this perspective, a tool for goodwill that could "bring people together."[36] In doing so, he also articulated a vision of the United States that was hybrid, mixed, and diverse, a position that echoed what many African American community leaders and public figures expressed at the time.[37] Onstage, this way of thinking translated into skillful performances that entertained and educated through a combination of humor, wit, and musical displays of virtuosity.

The Ambassadorial LPs in Context

Reports of Gillespie's activities abroad appeared in a wide array of print media. Jazz trades such as *Down Beat* and *Metronome* followed the tours closely, beginning with the official announcement from the State Department in November 1955. Coverage also appeared in the major newspapers of New York, Washington, Baltimore, Philadelphia, Salt Lake City, and San Francisco, in addition to media that catered specifically to African Americans. These periodicals included newspapers such as the *Pittsburgh Courier*, *New York Amsterdam News*, and *Arkansas State Press*, as well as magazines such as *Hue* and *Jet*. Between April 1956 and July 1957, *Esquire*, *Saturday Review*, *Variety*, *Newsweek*, and *Time*—magazines that generally targeted an educated, white, middle-class audience—similarly published articles about this new ambassadorial role for jazz.[38]

This exposure led to numerous performance opportunities for Gillespie's ensemble. Between its return from the Middle East and its second tour in South America in the summer of 1956, the band performed in New York City at Birdland and the Apollo Theater, at the White House for President Eisenhower, as well as at a civil-rights rally in Detroit. Gillespie also made an appearance on Edward R. Murrow's *Person to Person* TV show.[39] From the Apollo to the White House and from television to print media, Gillespie's role as a cultural ambassador circulated through all layers of US society, and his music was in high demand with audiences on both sides of the color line.

Within this mediascape, the owner of Gillespie's label, Norman Granz, issued two LPs featuring the State Department band, no doubt seeking to take advantage of this publicity. The first, *World Statesman*, featured ten tracks of the band's material. Recorded in a single session on June 6, 1956, in a New York studio, *World Statesman* began to circulate later that year on Granz's Norgran label.[40] Granz issued the second ambassadorial LP, *Dizzy in Greece*, at the end of 1957 on his newly formed Verve label. Of the disc's ten tracks, seven were from the same June 1956 recording session that produced *World Statesman*; Gillespie's band recorded the other three in April 1957 (see table 4.1).[41]

Gillespie infused his big band with the musical qualities of bebop, emphasizing individual and often virtuosic improvisation. The band's compositions and arrangements feature complex melodies, intricate harmonies, and swift tempos mixed with typical gestures in the big-band style: call-and-response figures between the brass and reed sections, melodies harmonized in four or five parts, full-band interludes between solos, and a chorus of through-composed material arranged for the entire ensemble in what is usually referred to as an "arranger's" or "shout" chorus. Tracks last between two-and-a-half and six minutes, with little variation in form. The typical arrangement includes an eight- to twelve-measure introduction, the melody orchestrated for a few soloists or the entire band, improvised solos (with band interludes), a shout chorus, and a restatement of the melody. As in bebop, the repertoire is a mixture of newly composed music and arrangements of standards from the Great American Songbook. Liston also contributed two arrangements that refigured music from the classical canon: "My Reverie" (Claude Debussy) and "Annie's Dance" (Edvard Grieg).[42] A hint of Gillespie's humor can also be heard on the novelty number "Hey Pete! Let's Eat More Meat."

The LPs emphasize their connection to the State Department tours at every level of design. One title portrays Gillespie as a diplomat, and the other places him in a location where he performed in his official capacity. The cover of *World Statesman* displays his silhouette with a plumed knight's helmet at his feet, a subtle allusion to a history of citizenship and military conflict in Europe and the United States (figure 4.1). On the cover of *Dizzy in Greece*, Gillespie leans against a fluted Doric column dressed in a white fustanella, the traditional Greek men's costume that functioned as a military

Table 4.1. Recording dates for all tracks on *World Statesman* and *Dizzy in Greece*

World Statesman			Recording date
Side 1		Dizzy's Business	June 6, 1956
		Jessica's Day	
		Tour de Force	
		I Can't Get Started	
		Doodlin'	
Side 2		Night in Tunisia	
		Stella by Starlight	
		The Champ	
		My Reverie	
		Dizzy's Blues	
Dizzy in Greece			
Side 1		Hey Pete!	
		Yesterdays	
		Tin Tin Deo	
		Groovin' for Nat	
		Annie's Dance	
Side 2		Cool Breeze	
		School Days	
		That's All	April 8, 1957
		Stablemates	
		Groovin' High	

uniform for centuries.⁴³ Against this foreign dress, Gillespie casually rests his trumpet in the crook of his elbow; he is at ease yet ready to play at a moment's notice (figure 4.2). This image presents him not as the young, urban Black revolutionary but as the confident ambassador unbothered (and perhaps a bit amused) by this costume. Bebop, the cover implies, is no longer a revolutionary act but as American as US statecraft.

The two unadorned back covers feature liner notes in the same organizational pattern. Written by Marshall Stearns, both notes recount the band's general activities in Eastern Europe and the Middle East through personal anecdotes and local newspaper reports, and then briefly describe the musical content on the LP.⁴⁴ The notes to *Dizzy in Greece* focus on a specific event in Athens, which Stearns describes as the band's greatest diplomatic moment:

> The band reached its peak, musically and diplomatically, in Athens where it out-rocked the rock-throwing Greek students. John "Dizzy" Gillespie and his ambassadors of jazz arrived just after the riots of May, 1956, and anti-American feeling was intense. Right or wrong, the Greeks felt that the United States should help them take Cyprus back from the British. Newspapers were asking why the Americans were sending jazz bands instead of guns. And the opening concert was staged for the same students who threw rocks at the windows of the United States Information Service.
>
> It was a tense moment and the students jeered as the band started to play. Then silence. And then, a complete and riotous switch—the roar of approval drowned out the big band; hats, jackets, and whatnot were tossed at the ceiling; and even the local gendarmes danced in the aisles. Between numbers, Gillespie miraculously kept the kids under control. After the concert, they carried him out on their shoulders, chanting "Dizzy, Dizzy, Dizzy," stalling traffic for a half hour and a dozen blocks. This music spelled out the happy, friendly, and generous side of American life with explosive force and, incidentally, siphoned off a Niagara of excess energy.⁴⁵

By locating the band in Greece, in both title and tale, the LP calls attention to the music's potential to dispel violent tendencies and overcome perceived differences.⁴⁶ Peaceful excitement is key to Stearns's narrative. The stories of the students dancing in the aisles with the authorities and then carrying Gillespie into the street portray a moment of shared jubilation. Placing these

Figure 4.1. Album cover of *World Statesman*, Norgran MG N-1084 (1956).

before the more typical descriptions of the musical content on the record, Stearns introduces the music through its supposed ambassadorial function to show the positive outcome of music merged with diplomacy.

The carefully crafted packaging of both LPs told a particular story about the value of jazz by highlighting the music's state-sanctioned status as well as its popularity with audiences abroad. Although unusual, these were not the first records to venture into such political terrain. At the beginning of May 1956, during the first leg of Gillespie's tour, Columbia issued *Ambassador Satch*, which contained several recordings from Louis Armstrong's fall 1955 tour in Western Europe.[47] Even though Armstrong was not on official state business, *New York Times* reporter Felix Belair Jr. wrote extensively about jazz as an untapped diplomatic resource: "America's secret weapon is a blue note in a minor key. Right now its most effective ambassador is

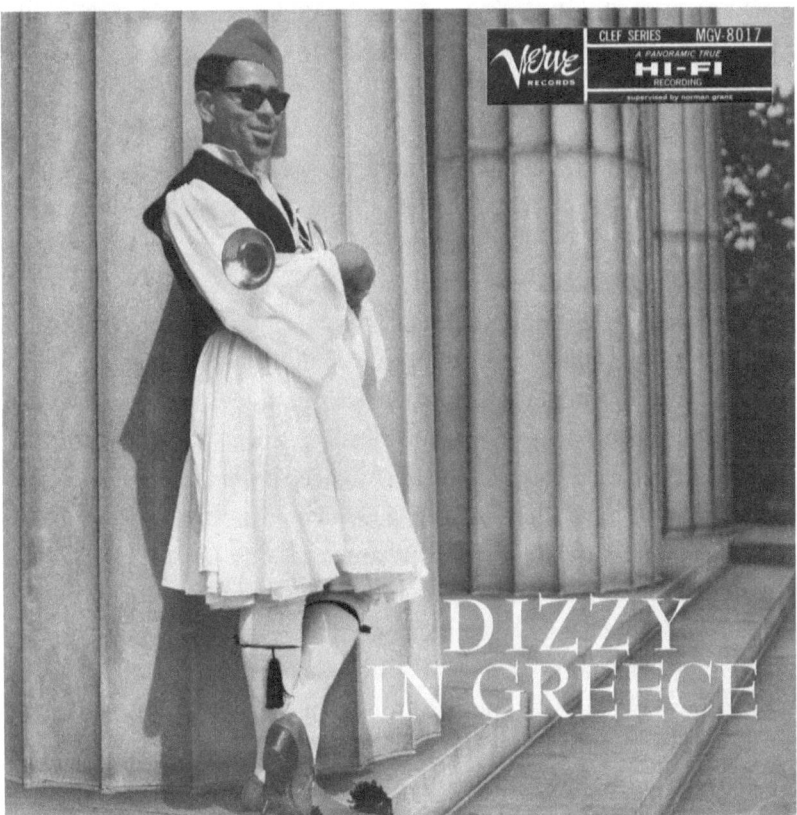

Figure 4.2. Album cover of *Dizzy in Greece*, Verve MG V-8017 (1957).

Louis (Satchmo) Armstrong. . . . American jazz has now become a universal language. It knows no national boundaries, but everybody knows where it comes from and where to look for more."[48] Taking his cue from such reports, Avakian accentuated the political value of jazz at every level of *Ambassador Satch*'s design and production, including the heavy-handed editing. The liner notes, written by Avakian, quote Belair's article at length in order to highlight the "international implication as well as the musical excitement of Armstrong's tour."[49] In both conception and design, Armstrong's record was meant to document the rising cultural power of jazz on the geopolitical stage.

Despite their similarities, the LPs of Armstrong and Gillespie emerged from commercial entities with vastly different resources. Unlike the single-session *World Statesman*, Armstrong's LP was made during three recording sessions in three different countries (Italy, Netherlands, United States), two of which required additional space, equipment, and engineers.[50] The substantial editing in postproduction required to manufacture some of the audience's reaction (think *Ellington at Newport*) and stitch together takes involved a significant amount of extra studio time. Avakian's extant notes from the Milan and Amsterdam recordings reveal detailed plans for editing: adding a drum kick to cover up a flubbed note or a cymbal crash to mask a splice, moving one portion of a take to another to highlight the best solos, incorporating extra audience reactions, and inserting additional vocalizations from Armstrong.[51] Without Columbia's vast economic and technological resources, *Ambassador Satch* would have sounded much different.

Granz took a very different approach out of both aesthetic preference and economic necessity. Like other white recordmen of his generation, including Bob Weinstock at Prestige, Granz embraced a view of jazz authenticity built around musical spontaneity. He relied on this conviction about the nature of jazz to justify his record-making decisions. Achieving a flawless record was not his goal, at least according to his comments about producing Ella Fitzgerald: "I've had conductors tell me that in bar 23 the trumpet player hit a wrong note. Well, I don't care. I wasn't making perfect records. If they came out perfectly, fine. But I wanted to make records in which Ella sounded best. I wasn't interested in doing six takes to come back to where we started. My position has always been that what you do before you go into the studio really defines you as a producer."[52] Gillespie's *World Statesman* perfectly encapsulates the tactics that Granz outlines in these comments. The unusual circumstances made for a compelling album, and the intensity of the tour and the timing of the recording session—two weeks after returning from the first trip—meant that the musicians were well rehearsed. The band does sound tightly knit and well balanced on the LP overall, yet there are small imperfections: listen closely for the lead trumpet flub on "My Reverie" (0:48), the sloppy ensemble work on "Dizzy's Blues" (0:25), and the recording-level imbalance on "Dizzy's Business" (opening), among others. Fixing such fleeting mistakes would have been expensive, given Granz's floundering finances at the time with his jazz-specific labels like Norgran.[53] Such repairs were also unnecessary. *World Statesman* would (and did) sell because it was a well-conceived LP that featured skilled performers and had free national publicity. In other words, sonic perfection was not necessary because the music alone would never have been enough to effectively communicate the outcomes of Gillespie's political work. Such an argument for jazz's political import had to happen through the LP's audiovisual design.

In many ways, the dynamic audiovisuality of Gillespie's records was made possible by the economic success of the jazz LP at a moment when record companies were selling more discs and making greater profits than ever before.[54] In response to growing consumer and market demands, including the industry-wide march toward the 12-inch format, record labels increasingly devoted more resources to visual design and layout. As discussed in chapter 2, more elaborate graphics and cover images began to replace the simple lettering and recycled visuals that were ubiquitous on records of the late 1940s and early 1950s. Record titles became progressively more poetic and evocative rather than simply descriptive.[55] These changes at and in the margins reflect a broader shift, where aural and visual elements on record worked to communicate the cultural value of jazz.

The covers of Gillespie's ambassadorial LPs reflect the industry's changing priorities. The silhouette image that appears on *World Statesman* is a recycled photo from a 1954 LP titled *Trumpet Battle*, featuring Gillespie and Roy Eldridge (figure 4.3).[56] Norgran's reuse of existing visual material, a common cost-saving practice, fit within the logic of the early-1950s record industry. So, too, did the predominantly unadorned white-and-blue background of *World Statesman*. In contrast, *Dizzy in Greece* features a vibrant edge-to-edge image of Gillespie that puts many other details on display: the direction of his gaze, the shape and placement of his sunglasses, the character of his smile, the folds of his white kilt, the black tassels across his calves, and the monochromatic texture of the stone columns.[57] Such visuals work with the other design elements to help evoke a sense of place and a purpose for being there.

Liner notes developed alongside the industry's adoption of the LP and came to have a ubiquitous presence on records in the 1950s and after. Many of the first liner notes mimicked the accompanying material found on classical 78-rpm albums, which focused on the biography of the composer or descriptions of the music and performance.[58] To those conventions, jazz records added personnel listings and other discographical information. As the genre developed, prominent white male critics such as Leonard Feather, Nat Hentoff, Martin Williams, and Whitney Balliett began to shape the dominant discourses about the music and its history on the packaging that surrounded the records themselves; LPs began working in a discursive feedback loop, with similar views expressed in the most widely known jazz publications. These trends coincided with increased attention to audio fidelity and recording technique as disc jackets began to display descriptions like

Figure 4.3. Album cover of *Trumpet Battle*, Clef MG C-730 (1954).

"high fidelity," "in living stereo," and "360 degree sound."[59] In accordance with these practices, both *World Statesman* and *Dizzy in Greece* prominently display the words "A panoramic true HI-FI recording" on the top left of the cover, placed next to the record-label logo and catalog number.

Two significant musical trends accompanied this industry-wide change in format and design. On the one hand, the rise of hard bop allowed musicians to challenge prevailing notions of white modernism by foregrounding the music's roots in African American expressive culture (see chapter 5).[60] On the other hand, white male cultural brokers such as a label owner like Granz, a producer like Avakian, and Newport Jazz Festival cofounder George Wein increasingly targeted middle-class audiences.[61] Granz issued records featuring Ella Fitzgerald singing popular standards accompanied by strings and placed his profitable Jazz at the Philharmonic (JATP) tours in large concert halls.[62] As the head of popular albums at Columbia Records, Avakian maintained an active jazz roster and successfully produced several crossover records featuring Dave Brubeck, Benny Goodman, Duke Ellington, Louis Armstrong, and Miles Davis. By cofounding the Newport Jazz Festival, Wein brought jazz to the affluent enclave of Newport Beach, Rhode Island. In 1956 the board of directors even changed the name of the festival (and its associated nonprofit) to the American Jazz Festival and began referring to jazz as "a true American art form" in its promotional materials.[63] Although jazz musicians, including Gillespie, regularly distanced themselves from white mainstream popular music, many were able to benefit from jazz's increasing acceptance by the American middle class.[64] The possibility of achieving popularity without yielding to blatant commercialism was, as I have argued in previous chapters, directly connected to the success of the jazz LP as a symbol of prestige.

Against this backdrop, Granz founded Verve Records in 1956 with an eye toward the popular-music market.[65] According to biographer Tad Hershorn, Granz's jazz-specific labels were financially viable only with support from his other activities, notably the JATP tours. A jazz-tinged release to the popular market was a chance for financial stability. Verve's first major project featured Ella Fitzgerald, whom Granz had been managing since the mid-1940s.[66] Fitzgerald's initial LPs on Verve each featured the repertoire of a different composer of the Great American Songbook. This organizational strategy took advantage of the 12-inch LP's capacity, which allowed for a single theme to be sustained through twenty-two minutes of uninterrupted music per side.[67]

Granz succeeded beyond expectation. *Ella Fitzgerald Sings the Cole Porter Song Book* (1956), one of Verve's first releases, became Fitzgerald's first top-selling record when it reached the number-one position on the jazz charts in August 1956, several months before the release of Gillespie's *World Statesman*.[68] Between July 1956 and June 1957, Fitzgerald's Verve records overwhelmingly occupied the top position on the jazz best-seller list, and her name started appearing alongside Harry Belafonte, Frank Sinatra, Elvis Presley, and Perry Como as a top "recording personality" of the day.[69] Verve's attempt to package jazz for a broader audience was largely a success, at least financially. The label had an estimated $2 million in sales in its first year.[70]

This period of significant change for the record business, and for Granz's labels in particular, coincided with a period of artistic exploration for Gillespie, who had signed with Granz's imprint Norgran in 1953. The label offered Gillespie flexibility and a large degree of artistic freedom with his recording projects. From 1953 to 1956, Gillespie recorded with strings, big bands, a large Afro-Cuban ensemble, and various small groups, often paired with other top-tier artists such as Stan Getz and Roy Eldridge.[71] Gillespie also took part in Granz's popular and profitable JATP tours.[72] The partnership with Granz offered Gillespie a regular stream of recordings, concert performances, and the opportunity to tour all over the world. After his success with Verve, Granz decided to unify his other labels, including Norgran and Clef, under the Verve banner in 1957.[73] All subsequent Gillespie titles, including *Dizzy in Greece*, appeared under the Verve imprint. The label also reissued many LPs from Norgran's catalog, usually with no changes except an updated logo on the top right corner of the album cover, as was the case with *World Statesman*.

The circulation of *World Statesman* and *Dizzy in Greece* coincided with Verve's founding, the record industry's total growth, and the rapidly expanding popularity of the LP format. The increased emphasis on the details of visual design—larger cover photos, more vibrant colors, the space for liner notes—contributed to the politicization of Gillespie's records. Using Norgran and then Verve as his platform, Granz took advantage of these industry changes to capitalize on Gillespie's role with the State Department and insert jazz into national debates about cultural diplomacy during the Cold War.

Gillespie's LPs and the Concert Tours

The liner notes of both LPs explicitly equate the musical contents of the discs to the concert tours. "This album," Stearns writes in the notes for *World Statesman*, "furnishes a sampling—volume two is yet to come—of the first half of the concert with Gillespie at his all-time best." He classifies two pieces as "encores" and eventually concludes, "So ends the first album and the first half of the concert." The notes on *Dizzy in Greece* take a similar approach: "This is the second album (the first was *Dizzy Gillespie: World Statesman*) of the music that piled up friends and momentum as it swung through the Middle East."[74] To introduce his discussion of the music, Stearns writes, "The concert begins with the novelty HEY PETE, a Quincy Jones arrangement of the blues." A draft of Stearns's liner notes to *Dizzy in Greece* concludes with a short statement: "The concert is over." Though eventually cut, that sentence was meant to parallel the end of the notes on *World Statesman*.[75]

Surviving programs from Gillespie's first tour make it clear that the LPs contain only a portion of the actual concert repertoire. Whereas the LPs feature bebop-inspired arrangements of standards and original compositions orchestrated for the entire band, the tour concerts presented a much more varied selection of styles and ensemble configurations.[76] The first half of the concert featured a succession of performances intended to present an overview of jazz's historical development (see figure 4.4).[77] The band's two vocalists, Dottie Saulters and Herb Lance, neither of whom appears on the LPs, sang African American spirituals, and Gillespie and drummer Charlie Persip demonstrated "African Drum Rhythms."[78] The ensemble also performed various examples of blues and early jazz styles, including a Dixieland rendition of "When the Saints Go Marching In" and several note-for-note transcriptions of pieces from the swing bands of Duke Ellington, Jimmy Lunceford, Benny Goodman, Roy Eldridge, and Count Basie.[79] "Groovin' High" concluded the concert's first half as an example of the bebop style that Gillespie had helped make famous. The second half highlighted the band's modern repertoire and included several Gillespie originals: "Cool Breeze," "The Champ," and "A Night in Tunisia." Along with various small-group tunes, presumably played in the bebop style, the band also performed swing-era vocal numbers such as "Seems Like She Just Don't Care" and "Gimme a Little Kiss."

This programming served several purposes, many of which dovetail with my previous discussion about the various ways that industry professionals leveraged the idea of jazz history during the 1950s. The historical material educated audiences unfamiliar with the many types of jazz and its development.[80] Presenting the wide variety of substyles and reenacting historical big-band charts told a musical story that started with jazz's earliest roots and arrived at Gillespie's modern style. Although jazz performance has always been historically self-referential, the explicit re-creation of earlier styles was unusual in the mid-1950s.[81] This concert programming, originally a suggestion of Marshall Stearns, taught audiences the various aspects of the music in an easily digestible narrative of progress and arrival.[82]

In South America, where the band traveled to Ecuador, Argentina, Uruguay, and Brazil, the ensemble abandoned the historical portion of the program and added several newly composed arrangements in Gillespie's Afro-Cuban jazz style.[83] Along with performing "Manteca" and "Tin Tin Deo," the ensemble's versions of "Begin the Beguine" and "Flamingo" also

```
        DIZZY  GILLESPIE  AND  HIS  ORCHESTRA
                        PROGRAM
St. Louis Blues  . . . . . . . . . . . . .       Orchestra
African Drum Rhythms  . . . . . . . . . .   Dizzy Gillespie
Spirituals  . . . . . . . . . . . . . . .      Herb Lance
     Sometimes I Feel like a Motherless Child
     Joshua Fit the Battle of Jericho
Oldtime Blues  . . . . . . . . . . . . .    Dizzy Gillespie
Dixieland: When the Saints Go Marching In  .   Small Band
New Orleans: Armstrog's Im Confessin  . .   Dizzy Gillespie
Swing:  Ellington's Mood Indigo. . . . . . .     Orchestra
        Lunceford s For Dancers Only  . . . .    Orchestra
        Goodman's King Porter Stomp . . . . .    Orchestra
        Eldredge's Rockin Chair . . . . . . .    Orchestra
        Basie's One O Clock Jump. . . . . . .    Orchestra
Bop:    Groovin High ne Whispering  . . Gillespie and Orchestra

                      INTERMISSION

Cool Breeze  . . . . . . . . . . . . . . . . .    Orchestra
Stella by Starlight  . . . . . . . . Dizzy Gillespie and Orchestra
Night in Tunisia  . . . . . . . . . . . . . . .   Orchestra
Vocals by Herb Lance accompanied by the Orchestra
     Lucky Old Sun
     Seems Like She Just Don't Care
The Gillespie Small Band
     Shoo Be Doo Be
     Begin the Beguine
     Sunny Side of the Street
The Champ  . . . . . Orchestra with drum solo by Charles Persip
Vocals by Dottie Saulters accompanied by the Orchestra
     Make Love to Me
     The Birth of the Blues
     Gabriel (a spiritual)
Gimme a Little Kiss  . . . . . Gillespie and Dottie Saulters
I Want You to My Baby  . . . . . . Gillespie and Orchestra
```

Figure 4.4. Program for Dizzy Gillespie and his orchestra, concert in Athens, Greece (May 1956). Courtesy of the Institute of Jazz Studies.

included newly arranged sections that heavily featured Afro-Cuban jazz rhythms. While on tour, the band also sought opportunities to play with famous tango artists in Buenos Aires and samba musicians in Rio de Janeiro. Argentinean pianist Lalo Schifrin and trumpeter Franco Corvini were invited to travel and perform with the band as well.[84] The hybrid musical styles showcased how jazz could be combined with other American musics, and the invitations for local artists to join the band demonstrated the musicians' propensity for inclusivity and diversity.

The band's activities in South America were not included on the commercially produced LPs from the late 1950s. Record producer Dave Usher, a friend and former business partner of Gillespie's, accompanied the band in South America and recorded every concert the band played using a portable suitcase tape recorder.[85] According to Usher, he and Gillespie had hoped the tapes might interest Granz on their return to the United States. Granz declined, but Usher kept the tapes, eventually issuing twenty-eight tracks across three CDs in 1999 and 2001.[86] The accompanying liner notes and credits include neither specific dates nor locations, yet the music remains consistent with several other live recordings of Gillespie's band from the same period, including a Verve LP from the 1957 Newport Jazz Festival. As such, Usher's recordings give a sense of how Gillespie's band likely sounded during both tours.

A version of "Groovin' High" recorded on location in South America illustrates how the band brought jazz history into the present through performance.[87] The ambassadorial band's arrangement pays tribute to Gillespie's bebop collaboration with Charlie Parker: the melodic content of the ensemble tags, solo transitions, and coda material, as well as the orchestration of the melody—unison trumpet and alto saxophone—originate from Gillespie and Parker's 1945 recording.[88] Gillespie based the harmony of "Groovin' High" on a well-known standard from 1920 titled "Whispering." The concert program alluded to this practice by expanding the title to "Groovin' High née Whispering."[89] To make this historical connection aurally explicit, the saxophone section overlaid the original melody of "Whispering" (played in unison) onto Gillespie's composition (beginning at 0:30). Although bebop musicians often employed the harmony of songbook standards in this way, it was unusual to perform both the original and newly composed melodies simultaneously.

In his demonstration of New Orleans jazz, Gillespie imitates the vocal and trumpet styling of Louis Armstrong on the band's version of "I'm Confessin.'"[90] During the spoken introduction and vocal scat breaks of the South American performance captured on Usher's tapes, Gillespie expertly mimics Armstrong's voice. For example, when Gillespie sings the word *but*, he places a strong attack on the *b* in an Armstrong-like gesture (0:54). At other points, he imitates the elder trumpeter's propensity to end phrases with a long, sung "mmmmm" (0:17). Gillespie's trumpet style also pays tribute through half-valve attacks, shakes at the ends of phrases, extended high notes, and quotations of the song's melody.[91] Fast bebop lines are notably absent. With its combination of humor and skill, the performance elicits laughter and strong applause from the audience.[92]

"I'm Confessin'" concludes with a lengthy call-and-response between soloist and band. Gillespie executes a series of rising high notes (2:15):

GILLESPIE: Ab-Ab-C-Ab-C
    PERSIP: Snare and bass drum hit. [*pause*]
BAND MEMBERS: "Higher!"
GILLESPIE: Ab-C-C#-A-C#

PERSIP: Snare and bass drum hit. [*pause*]
BAND MEMBERS: "Higher!"
GILLESPIE: A-C#-D-Bb-D
PERSIP: Snare and bass drum hit. [*pause*]
BAND MEMBERS: "Higher!"[93]

At this point, the melodic ascent ends, and Gillespie holds his high D. Responding to another call for "higher," he whistles the next note in the series; the audience laughs and cheers in response. Still in character, Gillespie starts chanting, "Gotta get one of those high Cs with the red beans and rice" and "high C, let's see, let's see where the high C is. Mmmmm" (2:52). He continues until the piano player answers a particularly loud outburst of "AHHHH" from Gillespie by playing the target one step above Gillespie's last-played note (3:32). After a few more moments of chatter, Gillespie asks the band, "You ready, boys? Go ahead." Another band member responds, "Are *you* ready?" and Gillespie nearly breaks character before repeating his question. This was standard showmanship. His final Ab–Ab–Db releases the built-up tension and concludes the performance. Gillespie reclaims his regular stage voice to announce the next tune.

Gillespie's comedic intelligence and exuberant, onstage charisma were major reasons why the musical advisory panel recommended him to the State Department in 1956.[94] With roots in the slapstick comedy of vaudeville, this jokester persona was an extension of the theatricality of other bandleaders such as Cab Calloway, who had employed Gillespie between 1939 and 1941. Such onstage antics were, in fact, what gave him the nickname "Dizzy" during his time in the Frankie Fairfax band in the mid-1930s. Gillespie's approach to his State Department program also displays the clear influence of Armstrong, beyond the mimicry heard on "I'm Confessin.'" As a veteran of the international touring circuit, Armstrong worked comedic bits into his performances with his band members. He regularly showcased both his vocal and instrumental talents despite employing another full-time vocalist. As a practical matter, the mixture of performance styles and ensemble configurations also allowed the trumpeters to rest their chops amid a demanding schedule. Gillespie's expertly crafted showmanship thus followed a well-worn path while also bringing levity to a performance that sat in the middle of a worldwide campaign against communism.

By matching novelty tunes, musical gags, and jokes with high-level musicianship, Gillespie offered an accessible and engaging performance to an audience unfamiliar with jazz. Several newspaper and magazine articles remarked on the overwhelming audience response. For example, the *Pittsburgh Courier* characterized the reaction in Abadan, Iran, as a "miracle" when the audience began "awkwardly" clapping along. "Soon," the article continued, "whistles and screams reached the stage."[95] Stearns similarly reported that in Aleppo, Syria, some audience members would yell phrases like "rock it and roll it," whereas others would "clap on the wrong beat, trying to figure out the proper response."[96] In Ankara, Turkey, the band was "drowned out by the roar of the audience," which was "a solid wall of sound."[97] Photos from the Middle East tour display large, over-packed concert halls with people visibly yelling, whistling, and dancing in the aisles.[98] Usher recalled a similar scene in South America, a claim substantiated by the audience on his recordings.[99]

Gillespie's skill and flexibility exhibited his authority over the concert hall. Stearns describes how the "pandemonium" of the audience "ground to a halt only when the band started the Turkish national anthem followed by the Star Spangled Banner."[100] The *New York Amsterdam News* and the *Pittsburgh Courier* similarly reported on the positive reaction to the band's performance of the Iranian national anthem.[101] Together, the paired anthems performed a notion of unity, a sentiment further accentuated by bilingual programs.[102] Writing for *Down Beat*, Stearns expressed the "pleased confusion caused by the fact that there are white as well as colored musicians in the band." He also characterized the reactions of people across a wide spectrum of age, ethnicity, and nationality as "something universal."[103] At various levels, the concerts challenged audiences to reevaluate any preconceived notions of institutional racism within the United States. After all, how were these audiences to understand a Black bandleader who spoke freely about racial politics and employed white musicians?[104]

Even as these onstage actions pushed a narrative of progress toward an egalitarian future, Gillespie's emphasis on blues traditions, church spirituals, and the styles of New Orleans, Dixieland, and swing placed jazz within a historical trajectory of African American music. At the same time, the "African drumming" demonstration overtly tied the music to the transatlantic movement of African peoples through slavery.[105] Repurposing jazz history into the present shrewdly told a story that tied US music to African American expressive culture. Through humor, playfulness, and musical expertise, Gillespie's onstage actions presented US culture as inherently hybrid, diverse, and multinational. In doing so, he skillfully navigated an ideological space layered with politically charged discourses about communism, racism, and democracy.[106]

The LPs served a different purpose, as evidenced by the reorganization of materials as well as the musical details. Unlike the State Department tour concerts, the LPs included neither small-group performances nor big-band vocal tunes.[107] Gone too were the demonstrations of jazz's historical development and Gillespie's antics, jokes, and displays of humor meant to engage with audiences. Although the back cover of *Dizzy in Greece* replicated the Greek lettering of Gillespie's name from the concert program (see figures 4.5 and 4.6), the LP shared only two titles with the actual Greek performance: "Cool Breeze" and "Groovin' High."[108] The arrangement of "Groovin' High" stayed mostly the same, except that the band omitted the "Whispering" melody meant to illustrate the song's origin.

Commercial considerations partially account for this difference because US consumers were the LPs' target market.[109] For example, potential buyers would not need to buy a record of Gillespie playing Count Basie when they could easily buy an LP of Basie's own band on the same record label. For their US performance in the middle of 1956, as Nat Hentoff wrote in *Down Beat*, the ensemble had to scramble for arrangements because "half of the band's overseas program was concerned with a historical recapitulation of jazz, a documentary which would not have been usable for American club dates."[110] The LPs' target audience paralleled that of the club date that Hentoff mentions.

Market factors do not completely explain the dissimilarities between Gillespie's ambassadorial LPs and the tour concerts, however. After all, another Verve LP from 1957 featuring the same ensemble, *Dizzy Gillespie at Newport*, includes several moments of Gillespie's musical humor and onstage antics.[111] For instance, the band's Newport rendition of "Doodlin'" ends with an impromptu call-and-response between band members. During the restatement of the theme at the end of the chart, baritone saxophonist Pee Wee Moore purposely misplays his highly exposed melodic line. Pianist Wynton Kelly responds with a jagged extrapolation of the melody; the band laughs, and Gillespie shouts, "Hey!" (5:23). Moore plays his melody again with an overexaggerated vibrato, as if mocking Gillespie. The rest of the band mimics this humorous vibrato, creating a noticeable reaction from the Newport audience (6:24).[112] When the song finally ends, the track continues long enough to catch someone from the audience requesting "Manteca." Gillespie dejectedly sighs before responding, "It's coming." "Manteca" is the next track

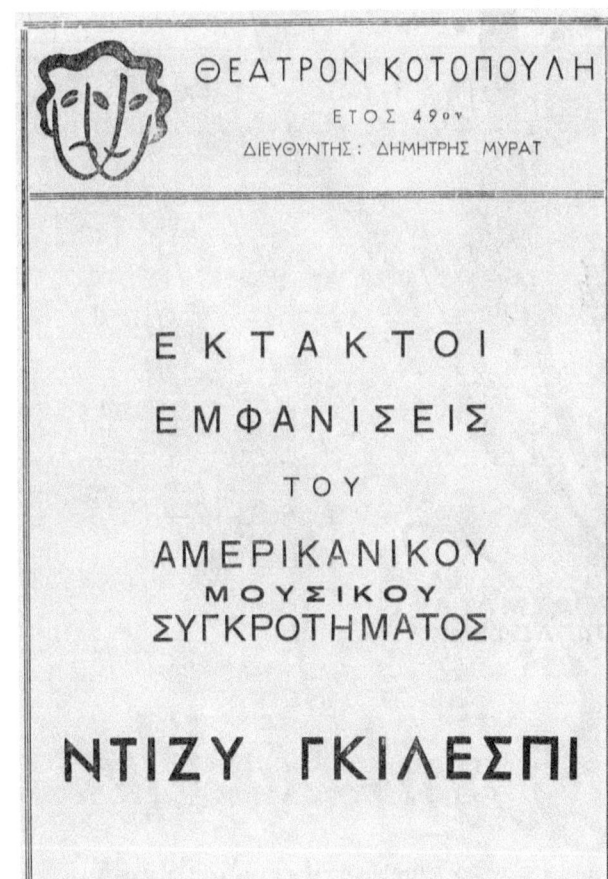

Figure 4.5. Title page, program for Dizzy Gillespie and his orchestra, concert in Athens, Greece (May 1956). Courtesy of the Institute of Jazz Studies.

on the disc, complete with its famous opening chant: "I'll never go back to Georgia." The lyrics were inspired by Gillespie's experience with segregation and Jim Crow as a traveling musician, and, as was typical, the band at Newport sings the phrase in unison with the iconic bass line. Although the State Department band also performed "Manteca" and its accompanying chant during the South American leg of the State Department tour, the song does not appear on either *World Statesman* or *Dizzy in Greece*.[113]

By omitting the moments of humor, spoken introductions, and interactions with the audience, *World Statesman* and *Dizzy in Greece* present Gillespie's music as serious political work. *Dizzy in Greece* accentuates this narrative by placing the band within the cradle of white European civilization. Whereas the tour concerts told a story about racial progress

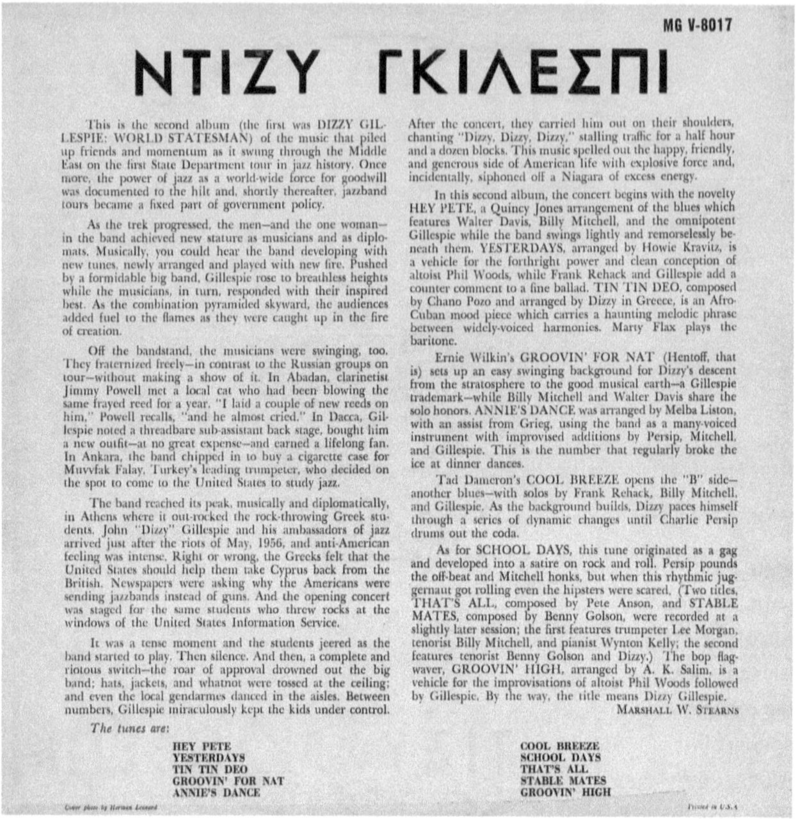

MG V-8017

NTIZY ΓΚΙΛΕΣΠΙ

This is the second album (the first was DIZZY GILLESPIE: WORLD STATESMAN) of the music that piled up friends and momentum as it swung through the Middle East on the first State Department tour in jazz history. Once more, the power of jazz as a world-wide force for goodwill was documented to the hilt and, shortly thereafter, jazzband tours became a fixed part of government policy.

As the trek progressed, the men—and the one woman—in the band achieved new stature as musicians and as diplomats. Musically, you could hear the band developing with new tunes, newly arranged and played with new fire. Pushed by a formidable big band, Gillespie rose to breathless heights while the musicians, in turn, responded with their inspired best. As the combination pyramided skyward, the audiences added fuel to the flames as they were caught up in the fire of creation.

Off the bandstand, the musicians were swinging, too. They fraternized freely—in contrast to the Russian groups on tour—without making a show of it. In Abadan, clarinetist Jimmy Powell met a local cat who had been blowing the same frayed reed for a year. "I laid a couple of new reeds on him," Powell recalls, "and he almost cried." In Dacca, Gillespie noted a threadbare sub-assistant back stage, bought him a new outfit—at no great expense—and earned a lifelong fan. In Ankara, the band chipped in to buy a cigarette case for Muvvfak Falay, Turkey's leading trumpeter, who decided on the spot to come to the United States to study jazz.

The band reached its peak, musically and diplomatically, in Athens where it out-rocked the rock-throwing Greek students. John "Dizzy" Gillespie and his ambassadors of jazz arrived just after the riots of May, 1956, and anti-American feeling was intense. Right or wrong, the Greeks felt that the United States should help them take Cyprus back from the British. Newspapers were asking why the Americans were sending jazzbands instead of guns. And the opening concert was staged for the same students who threw rocks at the windows of the United States Information Service.

It was a tense moment and the students jeered as the band started to play. Then silence. And then, a complete and riotous switch—the roar of approval drowned out the big band; hats, jackets, and whatnot were tossed at the ceiling; and even the local gendarmes danced in the aisles. Between numbers, Gillespie miraculously kept the kids under control. After the concert, they carried him out on their shoulders, chanting "Dizzy, Dizzy, Dizzy," stalling traffic for a half hour and a dozen blocks. This music spelled out the happy, friendly, and generous side of American life with explosive force and, incidentally, siphoned off a Niagara of excess energy.

In this second album, the concert begins with the novelty HEY PETE, a Quincy Jones arrangement of the blues which features Walter Davis, Billy Mitchell, and the omnipotent Gillespie while the band swings lightly and remorselessly beneath them. YESTERDAYS, arranged by Howie Kravitz, is a vehicle for the forthright power and clean conception of altoist Phil Woods, while Frank Rehack and Gillespie add a counter comment to a fine ballad. TIN TIN DEO, composed by Chano Pozo and arranged by Dizzy in Greece, is an Afro-Cuban mood piece which carries a haunting melodic phrase between widely-voiced harmonies. Marty Flax plays the baritone.

Ernie Wilkin's GROOVIN' FOR NAT (Hentoff, that is) sets up an easy swinging background for Dizzy's descent from the stratosphere to the good musical earth—a Gillespie trademark—while Billy Mitchell and Walter Davis share the solo honors. ANNIE'S DANCE was arranged by Melba Liston, with an assist from Grieg, using the band as a many-voiced instrument with improvised additions by Persip, Mitchell, and Gillespie. This is the number that regularly broke the ice at dinner dances.

Tad Dameron's COOL BREEZE opens the "B" side—another blues—with solos by Frank Rehack, Billy Mitchell, and Gillespie. As the background builds, Dizzy paces himself through a series of dynamic changes until Charlie Persip drums out the coda.

As for SCHOOL DAYS, this tune originated as a gag and developed into a satire on rock and roll. Persip pounds the off-beat and Mitchell honks, but when this rhythmic juggernaut got rolling even the hipsters were scared. (Two titles, THAT'S ALL, composed by Pete Anson, and STABLE MATES, composed by Benny Golson, were recorded at a slightly later session; the first features trumpeter Lee Morgan, tenorist Billy Mitchell, and pianist Wynton Kelly; the second features tenorist Benny Golson and Dizzy.) The bop flag-waver, GROOVIN' HIGH, arranged by A. K. Salim, is a vehicle for the improvisations of altoist Phil Woods followed by Gillespie. By the way, the title means Dizzy Gillespie.

MARSHALL W. STEARNS

The tunes are:

HEY PETE
YESTERDAYS
TIN TIN DEO
GROOVIN' FOR NAT
ANNIE'S DANCE

COOL BREEZE
SCHOOL DAYS
THAT'S ALL
STABLE MATES
GROOVIN' HIGH

Cover photo by Herman Leonard

Printed in U.S.A.

Figure 4.6. Greek lettering on the back of *Dizzy in Greece*, Verve MG V-8017 (1957).

and the importance of African American music to US culture, the LPs removed any direct ties to African American expressive culture by omitting the performances of African drumming, African American spirituals, blues practices, and New Orleans second-line traditions. Despite the projection of Gillespie's Black masculine cool—his seemingly effortless poise and self-assured charisma—the image cloaks his thick-rimmed sunglasses and goatee within the traditional Greek military dress. His persona is not presented on its own terms, either aurally or visually. Rather, it is put in costume and placed at a distance. The whitewashing of the band's activities on tour presented jazz to white, middle-class US audiences by adopting a language of class respectability. To do so, the LPs appealed to Western European values of whiteness at every level of their audiovisual production and design.

Marshall Stearns Drafts His Liner Notes

The Greek student riots mentioned in the liner notes to *Dizzy in Greece* made front-page headlines in the United States while Gillespie toured Southeastern Europe and the Middle East in May 1956.[114] The students were protesting British sovereignty in nearby Cyprus, then a British crown colony. Cyprus was seen as a strategic military and economic stronghold for Britain's Cold War operations in the Middle East. Separatists in Cyprus—in favor of uniting with Greece—had gained significant political power in the early 1950s, resulting in increased violence between 1954 and 1956.[115] Seeking to suppress the separatist movement, Britain announced its plan to execute two Greek Cypriots it labeled as "terrorists" on May 8, 1956, mere days before Gillespie arrived in Athens. The continued US support of Britain was already unpopular with the local population, and this announcement catalyzed riots on May 9 outside the British consulate in Salonika, as well as in Athens, where protesters threw rocks and attempted to storm the office of the United States Information Service, the overseas arm of the United States Information Agency (USIA). Undeterred, the British government executed the two men on the morning of May 10. Two days later, on May 12, Gillespie's band arrived in Athens to perform for an audience that largely supported Cypriot independence.[116]

Verve did not issue *Dizzy in Greece* until late 1957, but the story of Gillespie being carried into the street by former rioters first circulated in a July 14, 1956, article written by Stearns for the *Saturday Review* titled "Is Jazz Good Propaganda? The Dizzy Gillespie Tour."[117] Stearns argues for jazz's validity as a diplomatic tool, writing that the music could "communicate more of the sincerity, joy, and vigor of the American way of life than several other American creations inspired by Europe."[118] Although it was not directly apparent from the article's text, Stearns was proselytizing several different constituencies, including many who were actively campaigning against the continued use of jazz for cultural diplomacy.

The aggressively uneven political climate in which Gillespie operated at this time was on display during three congressional hearings in June and July 1956. Representative John Rooney and Senator Allan Ellender, in particular, forcefully questioned Theodore Streibert, director of the USIA and coordinator of the Cultural Presentations program, about the validity, effectiveness, and cost of the jazz programming.[119] During the House Appropriations Subcommittee meeting, Rooney pointedly asked Streibert, "Do you think it is a good expenditure of Government funds to allocate $5,000 in connection with Dizzy Gillespie?" After correcting the dollar amount, Streibert spoke positively about the first jazz tour: "$4,400, yes. Yes, sir, I think so. There is an enormous interest in American jazz bands, which is a great resource of this country."[120]

Unconvinced, the House committee voted to cut the project's proposed budget in half, from $9 million to $4.6 million. A few weeks later, on July 9, Streibert appeared before the Senate Appropriations Subcommittee and asked the Senate to restore the original budget. Resistance came from Senator Ellender of Louisiana:

ELLENDER: Now, I notice that you have also increased the amount for cultural activities; that is, to send orchestras abroad, and things like that.

STREIBERT: Yes, sir.

ELLENDER: Do you think that is beneficial? Let me have it straight.

STREIBERT: I will say this: I am in the business now of spending money to make an effect on public opinion abroad. I want to say that, in my opinion and from my experience, there is nothing we have spent that has produced such an effect per dollar spent as is sending of orchestras, of performers, of *Porgy and Bess*, of various kinds of individuals, particularly in the Near East, South Asia, and Far East, as this cultural program. It has paid off big dividends.

Now, I base that on reports from the posts, but I base it also on what our Ambassadors say, not what our own people in the Information Agency tell me, but what Ambassadors report back to the State Department.

ELLENDER: What reports did you get on the presentation of Dizzy Gillespie's orchestra? I heard it at one of the President's big dinners, I think, and I never heard so much pure noise in my life. They said that they played in Turkey and Rome and Paris, and I am wondering what good you got out of that.

STREIBERT: Well, sir, jazz is one of our resources. It is one of our assets. We are just starting to use it. We have been using it on the air very successfully in a program of music from America which has been widely listened to in Eastern Europe.[121]

Streibert went on to cite a positive press account as well as a glowing review from a Beirut dispatch.[122] Undeterred, Ellender continued his hard-line questioning:

ELLENDER: Did you get any criticism?

STREIBERT: No, sir.

ELLENDER: None whatever?

STREIBERT: No, sir. There has been criticism that people have been unable to get tickets and get in. They have been very generous in giving extra performances and playing at private affairs. I read the dispatches from Istanbul and they are similarly ecstatic. Not everybody likes jazz. Probably you are among those who do not.

ELLENDER: It is not a question of liking it. When I first voted for this measure, as you remember 2 years ago, the idea was to put forth that the people of England and France and Western Europe thought we were barbarians. That is in the record. I remember it. And it was brought out that we ought to counter that by sending in our own cultural orchestras and what have you.[123]

Ellender ends this portion of the discussion by unequivocally stating his view: "I say it does more harm than good to send some of this abroad, in my humble judgment."[124] In a press account soon after, he repeated his assertions regarding Gillespie: "To send such jazz as Mr. Gillespie, I can assure you that instead of doing goodwill it will do harm and the people will really believe we are barbarians."[125] Along with his description of Gillespie's music as "noise," Ellender uses racist language to differentiate jazz from orchestral music, which he finds to have more social and cultural validity.

As this testimony attests, disagreements over the funding for the Cultural Presentations program placed jazz and its practitioners in the middle of a cultural war over domestic and international Cold War policy. In August 1956 a group of senators led by Ellender voted to block the use of jazz in the USIA's programs, prompting a strong reaction from the Black press. In general, African American newspapers had been covering Gillespie's tours with enthusiasm and pride. For example, the *Pittsburgh Courier* ran a two-part series in June 1956 about Gillespie's travels abroad, noting that the band was doing "much more" than performing music: "[Gillespie] accomplished—perhaps better than all the ambassadors and envoys and ministers combined—the almost impossible feat of making genuine friends on an intimate, personal basis."[126] Calvin Delores in the *Arkansas State Press* encapsulated the general feelings about Congress's decision to cut the funds at the end of 1956: "Southern senators, headed by Ellender want other types of music and though they don't admit it publicly, they are really after keeping Negro talent from abroad."[127]

For his part, Gillespie had a keen awareness of these political stakes and embraced the public and highly political platform. In response to negative press reports about the congressional hearings, Gillespie sent a widely publicized telegram to President Eisenhower in August 1956:

> Shocked and discouraged by the decision of the Senate in the supplementary appropriation bill to outlaw American jazz music as a way of making millions of friends for the USA abroad. Our trip thru the Middle East proved conclusively that our interracial group was powerfully effective against Red propaganda. Jazz is our own American folk music that communicates with all people regardless of language or social barriers. I urge that you do all in your power to continue exporting this invaluable form of American expression of which we are so proud.[128]

Gillespie emphasized jazz's wide popularity across social strata as well as its inherent connections to US culture. He also stressed the "folk music" appeal to assert that the music could connect with world populations while remaining an art form unique to the United States. At the end of 1956, Gillespie similarly wired the chairman of the Senate Appropriations Subcommittee, Majority Leader Lyndon B. Johnson, asking for an audience in order to defend jazz's role in US activities abroad. His request was, unsurprisingly, not answered.[129] Nevertheless, Gillespie's comments echoed those of several proponents of the Cultural Presentations program. Streibert told the House committee that jazz is a "great resource of this country," and in a written statement to the same committee, Representative Frank Thompson depicted jazz as a "cultural weapon" for which the United States "has a copyright."[130]

Like Gillespie and Streibert, Stearns also advocated for jazz's place in the Cultural Presentations program through various channels of print media, including his liner notes to *World Statesman* and *Dizzy in Greece*.[131] As archival documents attest, Stearns presumably drafted these liner notes in conjunction with each other sometime between July and early September 1956 while debates raged over the State Department's use of jazz overseas. Several documents outline Stearns's overall strategy toward both LPs. *World Statesman*, as one handwritten note states, should take a "more general approach on Gillespie's effectiveness abroad." The same document also includes a track listing for *Dizzy in Greece* that includes seven pieces, all of which appear on the final LP.¹³² Significantly, the three tracks recorded at a later session in April 1957—"That's All," "Stablemates," and "Groovin' High"—are not mentioned here or on Stearns's typed draft of the *Dizzy in Greece* liner notes. The published version of the notes is identical to Stearns's draft with one exception: a parenthetical phrase was added to account for the three tracks not mentioned in the draft.¹³³ The 1956 date of these notes is further confirmed by a header in a separate document:

"Dizzy in Greece" 12 inch
Liner for Granz
Due Sept 7 airmail¹³⁴

Although no year is stated, the airmail due date likely refers to September 1956. Stearns's notes never mention material from the later session in April 1957 yet always accurately describe the other tracks in detail. Moreover, plans that outline the structure and contents of each LP often appear in the same document and seem to have been drafted at the same time.¹³⁵

Stearns conceived of both sets of liner notes as doing the same type of political work. A skeleton draft of the *Dizzy in Greece* liner notes makes it clear that Stearns wanted to foreground anecdotes from the band's tours in order to present Gillespie's travels as a triumph. Consider this brief outline:

1. range and overall success
2. Dacca—an example
3. Thru it all . . . Diz as diplomat: mixed band, Ankara, snake charmer
4. why they loved it—generous etc.
5. "   —real art
6. "   —freedom¹³⁶

By connecting the words *generous* and *freedom* to audience reception, Stearns aimed to show how jazz cultivated political goodwill for the United States, a common theme in both liner notes. In total, Stearns appears to be answering a question posed in a handwritten note found in the margin of one of these drafts: "Topic: Is jazz good propaganda?"¹³⁷

Not by coincidence, this rhetorical question is also the title of Stearns's *Saturday Review* article from July 14, 1956.¹³⁸ Published a few months after Gillespie's arrival in Greece and before the release of *World Statesman*, the article accentuates jazz's close connection to the "American way of life": "On the surface, everybody—even the old folks—seemed to want to love jazz, even before they heard it. They definitely associated jazz with the cheerful, informal, and generous side of American life and they were bowled over by its spontaneity and vitality."[139]

The article, in both tone and content, was the basis for Stearns's liner notes to *World Statesman* and *Dizzy in Greece*. Both documents link Gillespie's onstage performance to current events in order to argue for jazz's political relevance and convince listeners that jazz's value extends beyond US borders because of the music's ability to overcome cultural difference.[140] In the notes to *World Statesman*, for example, Stearns asserts that the band's "team-spirit" actively "spells out a new kind of freedom. Maybe that is why jazz is America's best-loved cultural export."[141] By metaphorically referring to the movement of goods across national boundaries, Stearns links jazz to the entrepreneurial spirit at the center of US capitalism, and his emphasis on the music's "vitality" associates the music with democratic ideals of progress, action, and freedom.[142]

Several stories appearing in both the liner notes and the *Saturday Review* article attempt to demonstrate the "generous side of American Life," a recurring phrase meant to explain how Gillespie's music reached local populations.[143] For example, saxophonist Jimmy Powell donated reeds to a local musician, and Gillespie apparently quoted phrases from "Ochi Chornia," a famous Russian folk song, as a nod toward the Russian Folk Ballet members in attendance at one performance.[144] Other stories directly addressed the tour's cultural politics. In one memorable anecdote, Gillespie invited a snake charmer into his room despite vigorous objections by hotel management; another describes Gillespie's refusal to play a concert in Ankara, Turkey, until the street children standing outside the gates were allowed to attend. Both *World Statesman* and Stearns's article quote Gillespie's explanation: "I came here to play for all the people."[145] Altogether, Stearns establishes that Gillespie's version of diplomacy included sharing his music with everyone, regardless of social, economic, or ethnic position. Jazz, in this view, unifies people through its capacity to engage peacefully across differences while also respecting individual forms of expression.

The idea of jazz's moral imperative can also be seen in Stearns's first monograph, *The Story of Jazz*, published in 1956, around the same time as *World Statesman*.[146] The book portrays jazz as a uniquely "American" contribution to the world. "Jazz," he writes in the introduction, "has played a part, for better or worse, in forming the American character."[147] One of the later chapters focuses on Gillespie's State Department tours and describes the music as a "secret sonic weapon" in the war against communism.[148]

In "win[ning] over the people," he writes, "the friendly and free wheeling band... led many people to abandon their communist-inspired notions of American democracy in the course of one concert."[149] In all instances, Stearns presented Gillespie as a symbol of national pride and racial harmony that both fit within his own worldview and offered a perspective similar to that of the State Department.

Dizzy the Diplomat

In spring 1957, more controversy erupted when a congressional appropriations subcommittee revealed the $141,000 cost of Gillespie's two tours.[150] Senator Styles Bridges, the senior Republican on the Senate Appropriations Committee, commented that he was "not very impressed" that jazz has "proven of real value in reaching important foreign audiences."[151] According to the *New York Journal-American*, Bridges made these comments in light of the exorbitant budget (in his view) that the USIA requested for the 1957 fiscal year.[152] Others, like Senator William E. Jenner, also publicly expressed criticisms of the USIA's use of government funds, naming Gillespie in particular: "We could not find any way to use the majestic power of America to give a little help to the Hungarians when they were fighting for their freedom. But now that their struggles are over, we are going to send them Dizzy Gillespie or another jazz band."[153] No controversy arose from similar ensembles, like the Los Angeles Symphony and Ballet Theater Company, whose tours cost $385,000 and $259,000, respectively.[154]

Many news sources, including the *New York Post* and the *Boston Herald*, reported that Gillespie's salary, quoted at $2,150, made him the highest-paid government employee during those weeks.[155] As one article put it, "President Eisenhower's $100,000 a year salary, exclusive of expense allowances, amounts to a little less than $2,000 a week."[156] These reports, as Ingrid Monson details, inaccurately described the allocation of fees and payment to Gillespie's band. Official documents reveal that during the Middle East tour the band *in total* was paid $1,950 per week (plus per diem), a figure raised to $2,500 (plus per diem) for the South American tour. Because this amount was split among members of the band—twenty-one for the first, twenty for the second—everyone, including Gillespie, made roughly the equivalent of union scale, or around $200.[157]

As Stearns had done in the pages of *Saturday Review*, Gillespie spoke out in defense through a June 1957 article in *Esquire* titled "Jazz Is Too Good for Americans." In it, Gillespie points to the music's increased popularity and acceptance all over the world, asserting that audiences within the United States were not giving jazz and jazz musicians enough support. He urged the middle-class readership of the magazine to change these economic and social dynamics. Using a metaphor of free speech, an ideological pillar of US democracy, he proposed that jazz be included in school curricula: "Let the children be aware, that no class distinction should exist between jazz and the classics. Let them be told that jazz is, in effect, free speech in music."[158] Referencing his tours with the State Department, he writes that the audiences in these countries have a healthier attitude toward the music than people do within the borders of the United States:

> They [foreign audiences] don't make a moral issue out of it, as we sometimes do. It's of no moment to them that jazz was first played in the whore houses of New Orleans, that it was heard in Prohibition speakeasies. Nor do they make a racial issue out of jazz. There is no significant amount of anti-Negro prejudice in their countries for them to holdout against this music.
>
> They are interested in jazz for jazz' sake. They listen to it for its musical message, not its sociological implications.[159]

Although Gillespie certainly paints a rosy picture of race relations abroad, he articulates a vision for a future in which jazz would be treated on its own musical merits and not be negatively judged because of its class and racial connotations. He also envisions governmental support for jazz through the establishment of a national archive and the continued patronage of jazz musicians performing abroad. If jazz were to rise in cultural status, he continues, "people like Senator Ellender of Louisiana would no longer come out publicly and say of jazz: 'I never heard so much noise in my life.'"[160]

Esquire targeted white, college-educated males interested in automobiles, travel, technology, sports, and politics, regularly portraying jazz as a music of male leisure.[161] To reach this audience, Gillespie adopted the moral ideals of American exceptionalism and Eurocentric musical aesthetics. Displaying a keen awareness of how to best translate his own Afro-modernist work toward economic and artistic liberation into language legible to a white, middle-class readership, he argued that accepting jazz within mainstream culture would be "better for America."[162] At several points in the article he emphasized that jazz is best appreciated through careful listening and urged readers to consider jazz as a serious art form that has reached many different populations. Other populations around the world understood this music in this way, argued Gillespie, and so too should people within the United States.

Within this context, Granz issued *World Statesman* and *Dizzy in Greece* in late 1956 and late 1957, respectively. Granz no doubt considered it savvy marketing to take advantage of Gillespie's national exposure and the cultural significance of the jazz ambassador tours. The political potential of this moment cannot be overlooked, however. Although it is unclear how Granz felt about jazz diplomacy as a political project, he had fought against racial segregation throughout his career. His activities in this realm reveal his belief in jazz's potential for enacting social change. Beginning in the 1940s, Granz included an antidiscrimination clause in his contracts that guaranteed desegregated audiences, even when traveling in the South.[163] When he first presented the jam-session-style concerts under the JATP banner in 1944, he did so as a benefit for twenty-one Mexican youths convicted of crimes committed during the Zoot Suit Riots of 1943. That same year he organized concerts to support the Fair Employment Practices Commission and other organizations fighting for antilynching legislation.[164] His business acumen provided a steady stream of concerts, recordings, and promotional opportunities for his musicians. Yet even as one of the jazz industry's most successful entrepreneurs, he always conducted his business with a politically conscious edge.[165]

The LPs present Gillespie as an active agent on the Cold War's front line. Granz also recognized how his primary business, selling records, could interact with the culture of print capitalism that, as Benedict Anderson famously argues, is vital to constructing the nation-state.[166] With these recordings, Granz seemingly took advantage of the moment to present Gillespie to a broad audience and place jazz on a national stage where discourses of racial discrimination and unequal citizenship were in continuous circulation.

Jazz Abroad, at Home

During an onstage moment in an unidentified South American city, Gillespie unexpectedly catches himself playing the straight man. "And now ladies and gentlemen," he begins a bit stiffly before pausing and commenting to himself, "Oh, I'm out of character."[167] This admission, however brief, testifies to his awareness of what it meant to be "in character" while onstage. Whether during a spoken introduction or while playing his trumpet in front of his big band, Gillespie's performance was not simply about music making; it was also a way to transmit cultural knowledge, memory, and citizenship through embodied action.[168] Indeed, his creativity on and off the bandstand helped him negotiate the shifting political landscape of jazz during a crucial time of upheaval on a worldwide stage.

As Gillespie and others clearly realized, the use of jazz to combat Soviet propaganda and the unprecedented support from the US government presented an opportunity to raise the music's profile and cultural positioning. Gillespie's LPs, as two small pieces of the puzzle, invariably engaged with domestic debates about civil rights within the United States. As a result, the LPs' contents became less about what actually took place on the tours and more about making the music legible to US audiences not already invested in jazz for its own sake. Here, the omission of any reference to the South American tour looms large. By including only Gillespie's activities in Eastern Europe and the Middle East, the LPs purposefully appealed to the cultural stature that Europe still maintained for US audiences. The records explicitly portrayed themselves as a jazz "concert" without Gillespie's vocal commentary or characteristic humor. This marketing strategy toward a political end can also be seen on the cover of *Dizzy in Greece*, with Gillespie leaning against the pillars of a temple that had resiliently stood the test of time. By implication, the music should as well.

The discrepancies in repertoire between the LPs and the tour concerts speak to the different kinds of political work each was attempting to accomplish. The tours' success depended on a collaboration between an interracial group of musicians and the nation-state that, onstage, performed a positive version of US culture for local populations. Gillespie used this opportunity to stage an inherently hybrid and diverse vision for the United States, one that foregrounded African American expressive culture. The LPs told a related but different story about jazz and its political effectiveness in the world. The jazz tours were a start, but it was equally important for US audiences to understand jazz as a participant in the serious business of diplomacy. The LPs rendered jazz as "American" music through their audiovisual design, depicting Gillespie as a dignitary fit for the resolute work of an ambassador.

Reading this political moment through the overlapping structures and networks of the music business makes clear how the circulation of performance on record attempted to shape the discourse surrounding jazz and musical diplomacy. The record industry's adoption of the 12-inch LP and the resultant increase of sales across a wide spectrum of consumers made the musical format into a mainstream medium for popular culture. These changes greatly influenced Granz as he positioned Verve within the already well-established channels of print capitalism, especially those publications aimed at middle-class white audiences. Recordings such as Gillespie's became visual, aural, and physical representations of the political moment, moving jazz into a contested arena of mid-century US culture. The consternation over jazz's place within this arena attests to its ascendancy. *World Statesman* and *Dizzy in Greece*, as two 12-inch black vinyl records, became objects through which the abstract connection between jazz and the nation-state could materialize.[169]

Both LPs adopted the same language and rhetorical strategies as other forms of print media covering Gillespie's ambassadorial tours. These records attempted to make Gillespie's music audible to the various strata of US culture by convincing listeners of jazz's import and relevance. Recall the first words of the notes for *Dizzy in Greece*: "This is the second album (the first was DIZZY GILLESPIE: WORLD STATESMAN) of the music that piled up friends and momentum as it swung through the Middle East on the first State Department tour in jazz history. Once more, the power of jazz as a world-wide force for goodwill was documented to the hilt and, shortly thereafter, jazz band tours became a fixed part of government policy."[170] Using Gillespie's activities as evidence, the LPs stress the historical significance of jazz's use in an official capacity by the State Department for the first of many times to come. Because the tours ultimately survived the public debates about the merits of jazz diplomacy, as well as a forceful pushback from Congress, the notes celebrate Gillespie as both a trailblazer and a political victor. In this way, the two LPs were not objects documenting the past but media that imagined jazz's future.

Playlist: The Record Making of Dizzy Gillespie

This playlist presents Gillespie's ambassadorial LPs in relation to his other record-making activities (both official and unofficial) in the mid-1950s. Gillespie's playlist is a reminder that all recordings should be understood as part of a much larger musical scene and a broader range of professional activities. (Unless otherwise noted, all recordings are LPs.)

Count Basie, Mary Lou Williams, Dizzy Gillespie, and Joe Williams. *At Newport*. Verve, 1958.

Dizzy Gillespie. *Afro: Dizzy Gillespie and His Orchestra*. Norgran, 1954.

Dizzy Gillespie. *Birks' Works*. Verve, 1957.

Dizzy Gillespie. *Dizzy and Strings*. Norgran, 1955.

Dizzy Gillespie. *Dizzy Gillespie at Newport*. Verve, 1957.

Dizzy Gillespie. *Dizzy Gillespie: World Statesman*. Norgran, 1956.

Dizzy Gillespie. *Dizzy in Greece*. Verve, 1957.

Dizzy Gillespie. *Dizzy in South America, Official U.S. State Department Tour, 1956, vols. 1–3*. CD. Consolidated Artists, 1999 and 2001.

Dizzy Gillespie. *Jazz Recital*. Norgran, 1956.

Dizzy Gillespie and Joe Carroll. *Blue Skies/Pop's Confessin' (I'm Confessing)*. 78 rpm. Dee Gee, 1952.

Dizzy Gillespie and Roy Eldridge. *Trumpet Battle*. Clef, 1954.

Dizzy Gillespie, Roy Eldridge, and Harry Edison. *Tour de Force: The Trumpets of Roy Eldridge, Dizzy Gillespie and Harry Edison*. Verve, 1957.

Dizzy Gillespie and Stan Getz. *The Dizzy Gillespie Stan Getz Sextet*. Norgran, 1954.

Dizzy Gillespie, Stan Getz, Coleman Hawkins, and Paul Gonsalves. *Sittin' In*. Verve, 1957.

Various. *Norman Granz' Jazz at the Philharmonic, vol. 18*. Clef, 1955.

5

CAPTURING THE SCENE

The Cannonball Adderley Quintet in San Francisco

For several weeks in October 1959, Julian "Cannonball" Adderley and his quintet were in residence at the Jazz Workshop, a club in San Francisco's North Beach district. The audience's vibrant reaction to the music—the whistles, yells, shouts, and applause that filled the space between numbers—inspired Orrin Keepnews at Riverside Records to record some of the performances on-site. The resulting LP, *The Cannonball Adderley Quintet in San Francisco* (1959), features an uncommon opening for the time: a lengthy address by Adderley to the gathered crowd:

[*Applause.*] Thank you very much, ladies and gentlemen. Now it's time to carry on some—if we could have lights out, please, for atmosphere. [*Pause.*] Now we're about to play a new composition by our pianist, Bobby Timmons. This one is a jazz waltz; however, it has all sorts of properties. It's simultaneously a shout and a chant, depending upon whether you know anything about the roots of church music and all that kind of stuff—meaning soul church music—I don't mean, ah, Bach chorales, and so that's different. You know what I mean? This is soul, you know what I mean? You know what I mean? All right. Now we're going to play this by Bobby Timmons. It's really called "This Here." However, for reasons of soul and description, we have corrupted it to become: "Dish Here." So that's the name: "Dish Here." [*Music begins.*]

During his monologue, Adderley pauses every now and then to acknowledge the presence of the audience. His tone is conversational and his comments informative. His announcement is peppered with questions to no one in particular yet spoken to everyone: "You know what I mean? All right."

Adderley's introduction also does significant cultural work. The purposeful "corruption" of the title, from "This Here" to "Dish Here," makes unequivocal connections to a history of Black expressive culture that grounds the quintet's musical approach. The word *soul*—"I don't mean, ah, Bach chorales, and so that's different"—distances Adderley's church-inspired music from white Anglican traditions and places his performance within an entangled set of ideologies surrounding late-1950s jazz. At the time of the Jazz Workshop recording, *soul* had become a buzzword within the jazz industry. Soul jazz was a burgeoning subgenre, a musical style that was greatly supported by Adderley's commercial success and his skills in communicating its value. His usage of *soul* thus operates in musical, cultural, and commercial spheres, and it points to the broader context of Adderley's music at the time. Like other records in the late 1950s, *Quintet in San Francisco* explicitly embraced Black popular culture on several levels, and it did so in a welcoming way.

Quintet in San Francisco, Adderley's first live recording, quickly became a sensation. According to a *Time* magazine profile, the LP had sold more than fifty thousand copies by May 1960, and the 45-rpm single of "This Here" was a surprise jukebox hit.[1] In comparison, contemporaneous Riverside albums by luminaries such as Thelonious Monk and Bill Evans reportedly sold around a thousand copies apiece.[2] The overwhelming sales of *Quintet in San Francisco* launched Adderley onto the national stage and into thousands of new homes. Although he was already well-known in jazz circles as a former Miles Davis sideman—and for his work on EmArcy and Riverside—the success of *Quintet in San Francisco* made Adderley the biggest-selling act on Riverside and a legitimate star in his own right. For the first time, he won the *Down Beat* critics' and readers' polls for top alto saxophonist of the year.[3] He also received increased media attention outside of jazz circles, including profiles in national magazines and newspapers. This success led to other commercial opportunities. In May 1960, for example, he recorded the music for a TV commercial for Prell Shampoo; in October the quintet appeared on a Debbie Reynolds TV special.[4] As a result, Adderley's next Riverside LP, *The Cannonball Adderley Quintet at the Lighthouse* (1960), received fifty thousand advance orders. In the years following, he went on to record a string of jukebox hits, including "Sack o' Woe," "Work Song," and "African Waltz." The latter became his first single to crack *Billboard*'s Hot 100, peaking at number forty-one.[5]

During this period of Adderley's career, his spoken announcements became an aural trademark and a memorable part of his artistic persona. His welcoming tone and overall jovial demeanor onstage gave listeners access to the stories behind the music. Yet Adderley's voice did not exist in isolation. Other elements in and on the records constructed the impression of an event unfolding at a particular time and place.[6] The liner notes of *Quintet in San Francisco*, written by renowned San Francisco jazz critic Ralph Gleason, similarly situate the music within the club through depictions of the capacity crowd, commentary on individual listeners, and descriptions of the audience's animated reactions to the music. The accompanying audience interactions reinforced a notion of proximity. Taken together, these textual and aural elements seemingly provide a window into the social spaces of music making. Such evidence also has a history linked to the ever-present racial politics at the sites of jazz performance.

My previous chapters have argued that jazz records act as objects of cultural communication, especially how certain inscription methods embed and circulate constructions of race. The mediation of liveness has been a key component of this investigation, which I have examined in relation to jazz's increased presence and popularity on the LP. By the end of the 1950s, the ubiquity of the jazz LP had created a much more stable market for the music, even as musicians continued to operate in contested cultural spaces with uneven power dynamics. In short, the media might have stabilized, but its meaning had not. Cannonball Adderley was a keen observer of these trends. Like Dizzy Gillespie before him, Adderley expertly used his humor and congeniality to present jazz as a form of Black expressive culture in ways often denied to Black record makers. Adderley was ever the entrepreneur: his salient form of Black sociality onstage welcomed listeners in as much as it opened new spaces for gainful employment outside the jazz-specific market. A close listen to *Quintet in San Francisco* reveals a form of sonic Afro-modernity that embraces, rather than rejects, jazz commercialism.

This chapter contextualizes Adderley's *Quintet in San Francisco* within the musical and technological history of the live record made in the jazz nightclub. Such records are a familiar analytic site for music scholars because of their supposedly documentary qualities. They do document, but they also construct. Because jazz history is, at its core, a story told through performance, the "live" moment on record comes to articulate cultural meaning through the interactions of sounds, texts, graphics, and other elements—what I will refer to in this chapter as the audiovisualities of the LP. *Quintet in San Francisco* provides entry into this historiographical terrain because it sits at the intersection of the jazz industry's experiments with on-site recording and the music's ever-evolving orientation to Black popular culture. This chapter therefore examines the live record at the jazz nightclub as an object of cultural memory that circulates multiple kinds of Black performance not always represented elsewhere.

The audiovisualities of *Quintet in San Francisco* require an analytic lens that places the development of musical style within a broader history of audio production, visual record design, and cooperative artistic labor at the nightclub. In order to parse these many cultural threads, I first outline how different approaches to live record production map onto divergent subgenres of jazz, especially hard bop. I then turn to the Jazz Workshop as a site of performance, situating Adderley's comments from the stage within San Francisco's cultural geography, the economics of the jazz club, and his own history as a pedagogue. This analysis sets up my discussion of the 1950s jazz club as a recording space with overlapping forms of musical and technical labor. Returning to *Quintet in San Francisco* in detail, I examine how the LP's audiovisual design constructs the who, what, when, where, and why of jazz performance—that is, how those elements define its scenes and scenarios.[7] Nightclub recordings during this period, I conclude, captured the interplay among music, musicians, and audience members, thereby producing—and in many respects defining jazz to be—a form of sonic Black sociality.

Hard Bop and the Long-Playing Record

"Hi-Fly," the first track on side 2 of *Quintet in San Francisco*, begins with a brief explanation of the composition from Adderley. Some indiscernible talking and other club noises serve as backdrop to his speech. During the cornet solo about halfway through the performance, someone—likely Cannonball himself—begins snapping on the backbeats, mimicking Louis Hayes's high hat (4:50).[8] At other moments, a "yeah" or different vocal exclamation pops into the foreground of the audio mix. The finger snapping continues into Timmons's piano solo, accompanied throughout by the undefined but plainly audible rustling sounds from the audience.

Live records simultaneously give access to exceptional performative moments and music as it happens in the everyday, outside the highly controlled environment of the recording studio. Because the audience has paid for the privilege of being there, the musicians are under pressure to perform while also adhering to the conventions of commercial exchange between artist and listener. Recordings made within this professionalized context give a sense of a performer's mastery over the musical moment, when the financial and artistic stakes are high and the musicians must rise to the occasion.[9] That is, live records construct the perception of synchronicity: no second takes, no false starts, and no chances to fix mistakes.[10] The aurality of the performance venue is vital to this construction: the interactions among musicians, music, and audience create an aural presence of a specific space and place.[11] They are the sounds of an everyday sociality. As live records proliferated in the 1950s as a direct result of the LP, the sounds of the jazz club also began circulating on records by Adderley and other hard-bop musicians.

I understand hard bop as a loosely defined category of jazz that thrived during a fifteen-year period between 1954 and 1969.[12] Although the majority of hard-bop musicians grew up listening to Charlie Parker, Dizzy Gillespie, and other bebop musicians, many of their first professional experiences were with bands operating in the Black popular sphere.[13] This experience had an enormous impact on jazz in the 1950s, as hard bop came to look both forward and back: forward in how musicians absorbed bebop's cultural politics and improvisatory musical language, backward in how they sought to reclaim musical sounds of the Black church and the Black working class, and place those sounds at the center of jazz.[14] And like bebop, the innovators of hard bop were typically young, urban Black men who embraced a form of masculinity defined by improvisational authority, intellectual freedom, and emotional authenticity as key expressions of Black masculinity. The style known as hard bop became closely associated with spaces of the Black community and could be heard in what Guthrie Ramsey has described as the "community theaters" of Black life: the casual gatherings and informal communal rituals where music's meaning in the world was regularly debated, negotiated, constructed, and felt.[15] Black audiences interacted with jazz during live performances, in their homes, and through jukeboxes located at local bars, nightclubs, juke joints, and venues on the so-called Chitlin' Circuit.[16] The bandstand was one location where social practices and cultural poetics met, circulating the music through Black popular culture. Hard bop is therefore a shorthand description for a musical style grounded in a Black social aesthetic.

As a well-trodden topic in jazz studies, hard bop in many ways continues to be at the center of the "constructed" jazz tradition among a diverse population of jazz listeners.[17] But much less attention has been given to how recording technology, record production, and the attendant rise of a new era of music consumerism affected the music's circulation.[18] For example, many iconic hard-bop records on Blue Note, Prestige, Riverside, and other independents emerged at the precise moment that the jazz industry fully adopted the 12-inch LP and 45 single as the dominant recording formats. This transition in musical media also coincided with the rise of live jazz records, especially those made by hard-bop musicians at small jazz clubs. Such trends in record making defined the terrain of the music's circulation and therefore how it became inscribed into jazz's historical record.

Mark Anthony Neal is one of the only scholars to explicitly connect the role of mass-market record making to the development of hard bop. Pointing to how R&B became the first form of Black popular music to benefit from the economic boom of mass-produced recordings, Neal describes hard bop as one of the few subgenres of jazz to portray urban Blackness within this market. With focused analysis on records from the 1960s, Neal further argues that the live aspects of such recordings presented the "intimate relationships" between Black artists and their audiences.[19] These artists can also be understood through what Alexander Weheliye formulates as "sonic Afro-modernity," the various Black cultural practices expressed and mediated through sonic technologies.[20] Weheliye does not consider record-making structures or hard bop in particular. However, his conception of sonic Afro-modernity is nevertheless useful for understanding Adderley's music as part of the technological formation and circulation of Black expressive cultures in the postwar era.[21]

Heard from this broader perspective, the ability to record on location in the jazz club also made it possible to encode hard bop's Black sociality into the vinyl grooves of the LP market. The increased sophistication of the packaging—the liner notes, advertising copy, photos, and other graphics—newly explored the tension between the ephemerality of music and the materiality of audio technologies. If the development of mass-produced recording at the end of the nineteenth century created a rupture between the sound and its source, then the increased attention to the visual design during the LP era signaled a re-materialization of that audiovisual relationship, but with a difference.[22] For jazz, this re-materialization happened within the boundaries of a white commercial marketplace that largely essentialized Blackness in terms of "vernacular" culture. Adderley's performance on his records challenged this essentialist construction through sonic means.

The three most important independent jazz record labels of the 1950s—Blue Note, Prestige, and Riverside—initially began as specialty labels catering to record collectors. Their respective owners were white collectors and enthusiasts turned recordmen, which meant that the popular music market did not drive their output or roster construction.[23] By the mid-1950s, roughly coinciding with the emergence of hard bop, these labels changed their approach and began issuing 45-rpm singles in order to target jukebox operators and Black radio stations.[24] Although only a few jazz records appeared on the national R&B or top 100 charts during this time, jukeboxes and Black radio stations increasingly featured the records of Jimmy Smith, Art Blakey, and Cannonball Adderley alongside popular artists signed to Atlantic, Chess, and Mercury. The increased attention given to African American consumers gave some jazz musicians more control over personnel and repertoire, even though most record producers remained white men from the United States or first-generation immigrants.[25] More control for jazz musicians increased the speed of hard bop's development and also created an influx of original jazz compositions now considered de rigueur.[26]

Live recordings proliferated throughout the jazz industry at the same time that independent record labels began targeting Black audiences. However, the types of live recordings changed drastically depending on the label and its position in the musical marketplace. Independent record labels featuring hard-bop musicians recorded almost exclusively in the small, intimate space of the urban jazz club because this was where these musicians primarily worked. Between 1951 and 1958, most small labels issued live records made in the New York City metropolitan area at clubs such as the Café Bohemia, the Five Spot, Birdland, Smalls Paradise, and the Village Vanguard.[27] Other records featured venues such as the Pershing Lounge and the London House (Chicago), the Spotlight (Washington, DC), Storyville (Boston), and the Blackhawk (San Francisco). Certain clubs, such as the Village Vanguard, became popular locations to record for many different labels, which in turn helped build a national reputation for those venues.[28]

In contrast, the mainstream swing artists who dominated the major labels in the mid-1950s—for example, Louis Armstrong, Benny Goodman, and Ella Fitzgerald—generally recorded in large concert halls in front of crowds that numbered in the thousands.[29] This is not a surprise, of course, because these theaters are where popular musicians most often performed. Filling a large venue was a reflection of one's star power. As a result, the presence of a large audience came to act as a sonic marker of a performer's broad commercial appeal. Examples include Armstrong's *Ambassador Satch* (1955), Fitzgerald's *At the Opera House* (1956), *Lena Horne at the Waldorf Astoria* (1957), and Erroll Garner's *Concert by the Sea* (1956), as well as the many records by Coleman Hawkins, Lester Young, Lionel Hampton, and Roy Eldridge as part of Norman Granz's Jazz at the Philharmonic (JATP).[30] Verve and Columbia took the same approach when recording the 1956, 1957, and 1958 Newport Jazz Festival, which led to the release of *Ellington at Newport* (1956), *Billy Holiday and Ella Fitzgerald at Newport* (1957), and *The Dave Brubeck Quartet: Newport 1958* (1959), among others.[31] During this time, labels recorded at Carnegie Hall (New York), the Shrine Auditorium (Los Angeles), Medina Temple (Chicago), and similar halls in other major US cities. By the early 1960s, recordings made in European concert halls also began appearing with greater frequency as popular jazz musicians found success with audiences abroad.

Production decisions about how to sonically represent the audience on record differed along similar lines. Mainstream artists recorded by the major labels generally featured a crowd en masse, heard only at the beginning and end of a particular track. Recall from chapter 3 that Columbia producer George Avakian's postproduction edits on *Ellington at Newport* created the perception of a much larger audience than what was on the original tapes. Onstage announcements from musicians were rare except in the case of vocalists, who on occasion would briefly introduce the upcoming song.

In contrast, live hard-bop records from this period foreground individual voices and audible exclamations of audience members reacting to specific moments of music making. Instrumentalists could be heard introducing the band members or telling anecdotes about the repertoire. Although these discrepancies were certainly the result of the acoustic differences between performance venues as well as the economic realities of editing in post-production, the contrasting sound worlds reflected an intentional variance in audio production values as well. Live hard-bop records reproduced the sociocultural relationships among listeners invested in the communal aesthetics central to many Black expressive cultures.

No company released more live records in the mid-1950s than Blue Note Records. This proliferation of live records coincided with the label's transition to the 12-inch LP, which began in 1956 with the launch of its Modern Jazz BLP 1500 series.[32] For example, nine of its first thirty 12-inch LPs in this series were live records from East Coast jazz clubs, primarily in New York City. These included *The Jazz Messengers at the Cafe Bohemia, vol. 1* and *vol. 2*; *Jutta Hipp at the Hickory House, vol. 1* and *vol. 2*; Art Blakey's *A Night at Birdland, vol. 1* and *vol. 2*; Kenny Dorham's *'Round about Midnight at the Cafe Bohemia*; and *The Incredible Jimmy Smith at Club Baby Grand, vol. 1* and *vol. 2*.[33] By 1957, when the label's 12-inch series reached one hundred discs, Blue Note had added several more, including Sonny Rollins's *A Night at the Village Vanguard* and Jimmy Smith's *Groovin' at Smalls' Paradise, vol. 1* and *vol. 2*.

These records included lively onstage announcements from musicians and club emcees, vocal interactions among band and audience members, and lengthy liner notes that described the makeup of the audience. During club dates it was common for jazz groups to play short, easily identifiable theme songs at the end of their set—these sonic tags doubly marked the sociality of the performance space. Many bandleaders used these moments to announce the group's personnel or to thank the audience members for their patronage. Blue Note often put these performance codas at the end of their LPs, which gave the record the impression of a live performance. By the end of the decade, nearly every independent jazz label had at least one live record from a jazz club: a feat, given the expense and economic risks involved. Many of these records copied Blue Note's production techniques and approach to sound.

Reflecting on the label many years later, Keepnews portrayed Riverside as the "feisty younger brother" of Blue Note and Prestige. In similarly gendered language, Keepnews recalled how Riverside had to fight for its "proper share of attention in a family of three aggressive New York-based independent jazz labels."[34] Like other labels started by white recordmen in the postwar era, Riverside initially focused on early jazz and reissues of out-of-print recordings. This orientation reflected the interests of the label's cofounders, Bill Grauer Jr. and Orrin Keepnews, who ran an influential magazine for record collectors called the *Record Changer* before establishing Riverside at the end of 1952.[35] The label's approach changed in the mid-1950s, when it began producing records by Thelonious Monk, Bill Evans, Abbey Lincoln, Wes Montgomery, Randy Weston, and Cannonball Adderley. This transition also coincided with Riverside's full adoption of the 12-inch LP as the label vied for its share of the jazz LP market. Keepnews later wrote that the "full-scale life" of Riverside began with *Thelonious Monk Plays the Music of Duke Ellington*, an album recorded in July 1955.[36] Released as the first disc in the label's Contemporary 12-200 series, the label's designation for its newly recorded artists, *Monk Plays Ellington* was also among its first 12-inch LPs issued.[37]

Riverside recorded its first live record in October 1956 at New York City's Café Bohemia, featuring pianist Randy Weston. The disc, titled *Jazz à la Bohemia*, followed in the footsteps of Blue Note, which had already issued three LPs recorded at the Café Bohemia in 1955 and 1956, two featuring the Jazz Messengers and the other with Kenny Dorham. Debut Records, a label co-owned by Charles Mingus, Celia Mingus, and Max Roach (see chapter 6), had similarly recorded at the Bohemia in December 1955, a session that produced *Mingus at the Bohemia*. The liner notes to Riverside's *Jazz à la Bohemia* include references to these records, showing the label's awareness of the industry trends at the time.[38] Riverside would not record another live LP until 1958, when it went into New York City's Five Spot to record Thelonious Monk and saxophonist Pepper Adams. From these sessions, Riverside issued three live LPs that same year.[39]

When Riverside went into the Jazz Workshop in October 1959 to record Cannonball Adderley, the live album had become an increasingly important genre within the jazz industry, and listeners had many options for consuming live jazz records. Blue Note, Columbia, Fantasy, Atlantic, Chess, Riverside, and Verve had all recorded and released their first on-location recordings from jazz clubs.[40] Many of these same companies had also issued LPs recorded in concert halls and jazz festivals. As the rest of the chapter explores, the changing audiovisualities that surrounded the adoption of and the adaptation to the long-playing record implicate a changing ideology of recording jazz. Parsing out the cultural forces at work behind the proliferation of commercial live recordings reveals the technological, musical, and entrepreneurial agency behind the circulation of jazz during this era.

The Jazz Workshop

Adderley's introduction to "Hi-Fly" quickly moves outward from the stage at the Jazz Workshop into the broader constellation of popular music: "Now we're going to do a piece by Randy Weston, a fine young jazz composer and jazz pianist, usually writes waltzes—sometimes known as a latter-day Wayne King. [*Faint audience chuckle.*] However, this one is 4/4 time. It's called 'Hi-Fly.'" The connection that Adderley makes between Weston and King here is unexpected and somewhat curious. Although Weston's most recent record at that time, *Little Niles* (1959), includes only pieces in 3/4 time—thus, "usually writes waltzes"—the sounds on the LP spring from the musical roots of the Black diaspora.[41] King, the eminently popular bandleader known for his gentle, "sweet" waltzes, operated exclusively in the white popular-music sphere in the mold of Paul Whiteman and Lawrence Welk. King had been a regular presence on radio and television programs since the 1930s and was often referred to as the "Waltz King."[42] Adderley's reference, even if in jest, was not a musical one but rather a loose gesture of welcome. It situates Adderley's audience within his music from the broadest possible perspective, inviting those who may not know Weston to listen. It is a gesture of and for attention.

Time and again, Adderley demonstrated a keen awareness of how different economies of attention drive key aspects of the music business. In May 1960, not long after Riverside issued *Quintet in San Francisco*, he authored an article for the *Jazz Review* titled "Paying Dues: The Education of a Combo Leader." Attention is a key theme in Adderley's perceptive descriptions of his working conditions, from the economic value of mainstream press attention to how audience behavior determines a gig's financial success. Noting that alcohol sales dictate a club's profits, he explains that awareness of one's working environment is a key to success: "A leader, by the way, doesn't have to depend on an owner's figures to tell how much business is going on. He can tell by the activity of the waiters and by seeing whether the people are drinking. A place can be packed, but if the waiters aren't busy, nothing's happening. It's very simple."[43] The message is clear: patron attention creates capital, so a successful leader must come to know the audience. In terms of his own audience, Adderley consistently looked beyond the jazz connoisseur, observing that critical devices such as polls have an outsized influence on "potential customers who don't know much about jazz."[44] These are the same potential customers that might, for instance, know Wayne King but not recognize Randy Weston.

Nightclubs like the Jazz Workshop operated through an economy of attention that both was racially coded and extended well beyond the performance stage. Club owners, the majority of whom were white men, knew that feature articles, interviews, polls, reviews, and successful recordings increased attendance, which in turn generated profits. Because most jazz musicians made their living through live performance, the commercial attention from mainstream press mattered. Again, as Adderley explains, "Economically, the reviews of critics in *The New Yorker*, *Saturday Review*, or *Hi-Fi/Stereo Review* mean more than those in *Down Beat* or *Jazz Review*. The musicians, however, respect the trade paper writers, by and large, more than the others. A review in *Playboy* means nothing in contrast to a vote for me in the Critic's Poll but it may mean more money eventually."[45] It was no coincidence that Adderley only mentions publications that were intended for a majority-white, middle-class, and male audience. The racialized and gendered infrastructures that produced such publications had enormous (yet unpredictable) power. Such conditions meant that Black jazz musicians had to depend on a capricious form of white critical attention and, simultaneously, contend with white desires for selective representations of Black masculinity and femininity. Adderley knew this and still chose to present the Black sociality of his music. He did so by paying attention to who was in his audience, including at the Jazz Workshop.

The Jazz Workshop was one node in a vast network of San Francisco jazz clubs at the end of the 1950s. A wide variety of styles could be heard seven nights per week, from the bebop-inspired sounds on display at the Black Hawk, Bop City, and the Jazz Workshop to New Orleans–style Dixieland at Burp Hollow, Earthquake McGoon's, On the Levee, and Club Hangover (among many others).[46] By 1959 the strong interest in jazz in the city supported weekly jazz columns in three major newspapers, including the *Chronicle* (Ralph Gleason), *Examiner* (C. H. "Brick" Garrigues), and *Oakland Tribune* (Russ Wilson).[47] Additionally, *Down Beat* and *Metronome* both regularly featured news reports and a summary of musician appearances, as they did with other jazz-friendly metropolises.[48] In 1960 Gleason credited the thriving club scene with making jazz central to the "cultural life of the city," specifically highlighting the area where the Jazz Workshop was located: "Friday and Saturday night on Broadway in North Beach can be equaled only in memory by 52nd ST in its heyday, a mob moving up and down the street dropping in and out of clubs, bars, and restaurants."[49]

The Jazz Workshop stood directly on Broadway, an east-west thoroughfare that ran through the entertainment epicenter of North Beach. This densely populated and ethnically diverse neighborhood had a high concentration of immigrants, especially Italian Americans. Despite the enormous influx of African Americans to San Francisco after World War II, racist redlining practices concentrated the city's Black population in the Western Addition to the southwest.[50] Nevertheless, jazz found a comfortable home in both the Western Addition—particularly in the eastern portion known as the Fillmore district—and North Beach, even though the two areas had vastly different racial politics.[51] The Fillmore supported a thriving network of Black-owned businesses and nightclubs; North Beach became a safe haven for white beatniks and bohemians, groups that tended to problematically appropriate the aesthetics of Black art as a means of affirming their own countercultural white identities.[52] Indeed, violent forms of structural racism were ever present in North Beach. For example, the district police regularly persecuted interracial couples as well as the businesses and social institutions that supported them.[53] Furthermore, tensions between the city's racially divided unions had led to geographic segregation, blocking Black musicians from working in the high-earning hotels, bars, and other venues downtown—North Beach and the Fillmore were on opposite sides of this color line (Van Ness Avenue).[54] For a variety of reasons, including the start of union amalgamation, Black music in North Beach began appearing much more frequently in the late 1950s. Despite the absence of a Black population, a minimal Black clientele, and continued restrictions on local Black musicians, jazz clubs in North Beach began to thrive.

When the Jazz Workshop opened its doors at 473 Broadway in 1956, the club primarily featured local talent.[55] A shift toward hard bop began in late 1958, as nationally known musicians increasingly appeared interspersed with local groups. The Jazz Workshop's emphasis on hard bop came to fill a niche within an otherwise crowded club scene. The Black Hawk booked the A-list jazz acts, which in 1958 and 1959 included Billie Holiday, the Modern Jazz Quartet, Miles Davis, and Oscar Peterson. Mainstream pop celebrities like Tony Bennett, Nat King Cole, and Doris Day appeared at the Venetian Room in the plush Fairmont Hotel; Black pop-music stars such as Dinah

Washington, Louis Jordan, and Ray Charles appeared across the bridge in Oakland (see table 5.1). After hours, touring musicians usually found their way to Jimbo's Bop City, one of many bustling clubs in the Fillmore district that supported local Black talent and welcomed both Black and white clientele.[56] The Jazz Workshop's reorientation toward hard bop happened in the months prior to Adderley's October 1959 arrival, when the club welcomed Johnny Griffin, Horace Silver, Red Garland, J. J. Johnson, and Benny Golson.[57] Entering into the 1960s, the Jazz Workshop had established itself as one of the city's premier jazz venues by welcoming a Black sociality—in particular, the Black male sociality of hard bop—onto its stage.

This prehistory helps situate Adderley's introductory comments heard on *Quintet in San Francisco* even as the racial makeup of his audience at the Jazz Workshop on a nightly basis remains unclear. The evidence points to a racially mixed and gender-inclusive congregation that was majority white. In 1956, during the club's early days, Mort Sahl sardonically observed the audience to be "bearded and sandaled, paints and writes and, lo and behold, jazz has become its folk music."[58] Although such comments imply a bohemian whiteness, the reality was much more complex. In his work on liberalism and policing in San Francisco, Christopher Agee argues that Black denizens were active participants in the North Beach beat culture, a historical reality erased by the majority-white media outlets actively covering the scene.[59] In a memorable *Down Beat* column describing Dmitri Shostakovich's visit to the Jazz Workshop during Adderley's residency, critic Ralph Gleason offhandedly mentions a "mixed group of Negro and white patrons in the front seats" who refused to move for the Russian delegation.[60] A photo from the quintet's follow-up visit in May 1960 similarly shows a racially mixed audience of men and women packed around the bandstand.[61] These observations should be read alongside the story of Otis Rauls, a Black insurance agent who was beaten by the police after leaving the Jazz Workshop in May 1958.[62] This history is multiracial but also telling: the jazz club may have embraced Black art, supported integrated bands, and welcomed mixed-race audiences, but no individual business could guarantee safety for Black patrons or, for that matter, its musicians. The economy of attention running through the Jazz Workshop must be understood in relation to the racial politics of the space and its geography.

Regardless of how much Adderley knew about this history, he still chose to educate his audience about the Black sociality of his music. Adderley was, after all, an educator by training. After graduating from college at Florida

Table 5.1. Comparison of Bay Area music venues, 1958–1959 (artists in order of appearance)

	Jazz Workshop	Black Hawk	Fairmont	Clubs in Oakland
1958	Paul Bley	Cal Tjader	Tony Bennett	Carmen McRae
	Freddie Gambrell	Max Roach	The Mills Brothers	Earl Bostic
	The Mastersounds (summer residency)	Billie Holiday		
	Sonny Rollins	Leroy Vinnegar		
	Virgil Gonsalves	Jimmy Giuffre and Mitchell-Ruff Duo		
	Sonny Stitt (into January)			
1959	Johnny Griffin	Modern Jazz Quartet	Carol Channing	Dinah Washington
	The Mastersounds (Vince Guaraldi on Mondays)	Ahmad Jamal	Nat King Cole	Louis Jordan
	Horace Silver	Gerry Mulligan	Jimmie Rodgers	T-Bone Walker
	Red Garland	Dizzy Gillespie	Édith Piaf	Ray Charles
	J. J. Johnson	Miles Davis	Tony Bennett	
	Benny Golson	Shelly Manne	Dennis Day	
	Cannonball Adderley	Oscar Peterson	Doris Day	
	Wes Montgomery	André Previn		
	The Mastersounds	Barney Kessel		

[Source] Data gathered from the "Strictly Ad Lib: San Francisco" sections of *Down Beat*, which were authored by either Ralph Gleason or Dick Hadlock and appeared roughly once per month throughout 1958 and 1959. This table is a representative sample rather than a complete listing.

A&M at the age of eighteen, he became a music instructor and the band director at Dillard High School in Fort Lauderdale.[63] Although he left his position in 1955 to pursue performing, Adderley retained what musicologist Ryan Patrick Jones calls a "long-term pedagogical commitment" to his audience. Using a variety of sources, including comments from the Jazz Workshop, Jones demonstrates how this pedagogical commitment enabled Adderley to effectively bridge the "gap between jazz aficionados and popular music enthusiasts" while also "demystif[ying] the inner workings of a professional jazz unit."[64] Adderley was clearly comfortable speaking to all kinds of audiences—he knew how to maintain their attention. Sometimes this meant humorously distancing himself from Bach chorales, as he did with "This Here." At other times, this meant making a waltz-based comparison between Wayne King and Randy Weston. Adderley welcomed audiences into his process, thereby attempting to make those in the room feel at ease with the Blackness at the center of his musical approach. Adderley already seemed to know that within the attention economy of the jazz club, a pedagogical edge is not required, but it can be an asset. His record producer, Orrin Keepnews, soon came to recognize this as well.

Recording the 1950s Jazz Club

Seconds into the first track of *Quintet in San Francisco*, Adderley begins to speak. His voice, though clearly audible, is faint and sounds like it is in the background. Individual and group laughter, some applause, and other murmurs from the club accompany Adderley's speech, revealing a lively feeling among those present at the Jazz Workshop. Recall his introduction to "This Here" that opened the set:

> [*Applause.*] Thank you very much, ladies and gentlemen. [*Audience murmurs continue beneath.*] Now it's time to carry on some—if we could have lights out, please, for atmosphere. [*Pause. Murmurs continue.*] Now we're about to play a new composition by our pianist, Bobby Timmons. This one is a jazz waltz; however, it has all sorts of properties. It's simultaneously a shout and a chant, depending upon whether you know anything about the roots of church music.

Asking to dim the lights ("for atmosphere") signals a moment of transition as the club moves from a gathering space to a performance venue. As the audience's presumed focus shifts from socializing to listening, the volume of Adderley's voice increases. This change is technological, an adjustment in the audio signal by the sound engineer at the mixing board. This audible shift lasts four seconds, beginning twenty-five seconds into the track—by the time he says, "It's simultaneously a shout and a chant," Adderley's voice has moved to the foreground and remains so through the rest of his address.

This adjustment in signal is unmistakably audible on record, although it is unclear how such sounds relate to the actual performance space. Did this adjustment accompany the lighting change? (Were there changes in lighting?) Did the audience at the club and the musicians hear this adjustment, or does it sound only on record? Who actually turned the knob to increase the volume, and at what point did he—and it was a "he"—realize the problem? How can the engineer's improvised adjustment be understood in relation to Adderley's music onstage? How did this moment of technological adjustment come to be kept on record?

Jazz clubs were not ideal locations in which to record. Acoustics varied wildly from location to location, as did the space available to set up the necessary recording equipment. When Argo went into the Pershing Lounge in 1958 to record Ahmad Jamal, for example, the only place to fit the equipment in the small lounge was in the liquor room, an enclosed space away from the stage.[65] When producer Michael Cuscuna recorded Dexter Gordon's US homecoming at the Village Vanguard in 1976, he set up his equipment in the tiny kitchen, a strategy he learned from previous producers and engineers who cut records at the iconic club.[66] Orrin Keepnews created a control room at the Keystone Korner in San Francisco—"not the most convenient place to record"—by running cables from the stage to a rented recording truck out on the street.[67] These small, out-of-the-way places were also chosen because they enabled the engineers (or producers) to clearly hear the mix through their headphones and properly adjust the audio signal being recorded. Still, the inability to see the stage, to control the acoustics of the performance space, or to anticipate the spontaneous and noisy interventions of the audience made recording difficult, especially compared to a professional recording studio. In most studios the producer and engineers sat in a control room behind a glass wall, sonically isolated but with a clear view of the musical space. The studio simply provided more control over all aspects of the recording process.

The limitations of recording equipment in the 1950s meant that on-location recording sessions had to be planned well in advance. Rudy Van Gelder, the engineer who recorded the first live recordings for Blue Note in the mid-1950s, recalled in a 2012 interview with Marc Myers how it took three days to set up, record the performance, and then break down his equipment. Van Gelder described how he brought a portable version of the Ampex 300-2 from his studio along with the necessary microphones:

> The Ampex allowed me to record musicians live—during concerts and at clubs. I started doing that for Blue Note during the club date we just discussed [Art Blakey at Birdland]. Alfred [Lion] always liked the energy and excitement of a live performance at night, but it would take me three days to record it. I'd have to take apart the studio and pack all the equipment into my car, drive to the venue, set up the equipment, record the musicians, and then break down everything and bring it all back to my studio in Hackensack—before my next session.[68]

There were several versions of the Ampex 300 mentioned by Van Gelder. First introduced in 1949, the regular-size Ampex 300 became one of the standard pieces of equipment in the early 1950s. The mono tape reels and recorder of this unit were roughly the size of a stackable washer and dryer— small enough to fit comfortably in a control room but certainly not portable by car. Ampex's portable version of the 300, released sometime in the early 1950s, came in two parts that were each the size of a large suitcase. Though certainly not convenient, the portable Ampex 300 was small enough to be packed into a car and set up on a regular-size table. The microphones, cables, stands, tape reels, and other equipment were easily portable as well, though time consuming to set up and take down, as Van Gelder describes.[69]

According to Keepnews, there were several issues that Riverside had to overcome during the making of *Quintet in San Francisco*. He initially planned to do a studio session of the Adderley quintet, but San Francisco had no professional recording studios at that time. Having already done several live recordings in New York, Keepnews decided to record Adderley on location at the Jazz Workshop, especially after hearing the audience's reaction to "This Here." Still, there were not many engineers in San Francisco who, in Keepnews's words, had "a command of the fledgling art of recording 'live' in a club." He eventually hired engineer Reice Hamel on the recommendation of Dick Bock of Pacific Records.[70]

The recorded sounds of *Quintet in San Francisco* tell a similar story, one that runs contrary to the claims of "high fidelity" that appear several times on the back jacket.[71] Along with the adjustment of Adderley's voice noted above, the record includes several moments of audible distortion. Such overloaded audio signal can be heard during Nat Adderley's long, high notes on "Spontaneous Combustion" (5:00), Louis Hayes's bass-drum hits on the melody to "Hi-Fly" (1:00), and the band's closing theme to "You Got It!" (4:30). During each of these moments, the sound distorts because the input signal exceeds the limits of the recording device, what audio professionals refer to as *clipping*. At several points on the disc, usually for just a moment, the sonic profile becomes muddy and distorted, making individual sounds much harder to identify. Several of Bobby Timmons's piano solos create a similar effect. On "Hi-Fly," for example, Timmons quotes the standard "I'm Beginning to See the Light" several moments into his solo, inspiring a heavy backbeat from Hayes (beginning at 7:30). Both Timmons's percussive touch and Hayes's accompaniment sonically overwhelm the equipment. Recording engineers usually adjust the input levels before recording to avoid such signal distortion. And like the outdoor festivals at Newport discussed in chapter 3, the mixing had to be done on-site with little room for error. For whatever reason, Hamel's recording levels were not properly set to account for the outbursts by Timmons or Hayes.

In some respects, these moments of distortion contribute to the record's liveness: the sounds at the limit of technological reproduction reveal a session in progress and hint at the experimental nature (and labor) of the record-making process. However, the mistakes made by a sound engineer connect to a more prevalent discourse about the technological difficulties of on-location recordings during the mid- to late 1950s. On Riverside's first live record from 1956, Randy Weston's *Jazz à la Bohemia*, the liner notes highlight the jazz club as a place of musical experimentation and artistic freedom. In doing so, Keepnews also notes the challenges of on-location recording:

> There is a growing (if still limited) tendency towards on-the-spot recording. This means sacrificing something of acoustics, freedom from distraction and overall control of the situation, in hopes of catching your performance on a good, truly live night. In the present case, the negative elements were minimized by the fact the Bohemia is an unhectic place and that Riverside's staff engineer, Ray Fowler, is an unhectic, highly skilled and sensitive technician. Also, the key musicians of the evening, Weston and baritone sax man Cecil Payne, are both exciting, inventive artists with a good deal to say.[72]

Chris Albertson's liner notes to Johnny Griffin's *Studio Jazz Party* (1960) echo the same sentiment:

In this era of the LP and of tape, the recording of jazz during actual club or concert performances has become a quite frequent occurrence. But while this can often result in a musically better and more exciting record, it can also often mean the quality of the sound has to be sacrificed at least to a degree, because of the difficulties of setting up microphones on location, the questionable acoustics of many clubs and similar technical pitfalls.[73]

Recording in a studio gave engineers and producers control over many variables of sound, from properly miking the drums to balancing the ensemble during a change between soloists. Flubbed notes and breakdowns could be more easily fixed, provided there was the time and money to do so. In contrast, on-location recording offered great potential for capturing an exceptional performance yet provided a technically more challenging recording environment. Limits of control over the recording situation were a common theme in the discussions of on-location recordings such as these. As Albertson points out, the musical result of such recordings had to make up for the difficulties of setup, uneven acoustics, and other unpredictable factors.

The musical and technological risks involved in recording jazz on location also became a selling point for record companies. On *Jazz à la Bohemia*, Keepnews includes a description of the equipment in the first paragraph of his liner notes: "One evening in the Fall of 1956 . . . Riverside unloaded a station-wagon full of recording equipment into the club and settled down to several hours of taping a live performance by Weston and his colleagues. The results of that evening make up this album."[74] Keepnews goes on to specifically name the engineer, Ray Fowler, as the creative agent and expert technician behind the technology. By accentuating the roles of such technological agents in overcoming the difficulties of capturing the "live" moments on record, the notes present the LP as a cooperative effort involving musician, engineer, producer, and record company, with the club as the common space of artistic labor. Keepnews finishes the notes by discussing the Café Bohemia as one of the top jazz clubs on the East Coast, but does so in relation to the other on-location recordings from the club on the Blue Note, Debut, and Progressive labels.[75]

One of these records, Kenny Dorham's *'Round about Midnight at the Café Bohemia* (1956), includes a similar description of technology and technician. Liner notes author Leonard Feather praises engineer Rudy Van Gelder in particular: "The session was recorded May 31, 1956 at the Café Bohemia, where Alfred Lion, armed only with the redoubtable Rudy Van Gelder and with a battery of microphones, tape reels, and recording equipment, stormed the Barrow Street citadel and won a bloodless victory in several hours of concentrated cutting."[76] The liner notes to Blue Note's *A Night at Birdland with the Art Blakey Quintet* (1954), also written by Feather, similarly describe Van Gelder as "an engineer who understands jazz and knows how to balance it" and praise him for creating a disc that "truly captures the spirit of the occasion and atmosphere on the world's most rhythmic aviary."[77] Feather's liner notes to Jutta Hipp's *At the Hickory House* (1956) similarly name the "masterful engineering job" of Van Gelder and credit the "ready assistance volunteered by Josh and Howard Popkin of the Hickory House."[78] Like those of Keepnews, Feather's description focuses on the technology and technician working together, a conception of record making that places technological possibility, engineering expertise, and commercial cooperation at its center.

Reproducing musical performance on record is a process with inherent contradictions, especially for a music like jazz, in which listeners both value the spontaneity of the performative moment and valorize the culture of records.[79] For this reason, the decision to capture and issue nightclub performances altered the ontology of the jazz record. Jazz labels began packaging their LPs not as objects to be collected but as a passport that gave listeners access to faraway acts of spontaneous music making.[80] Engineers also started building reputations around their ability to quickly adapt to circumstances unknown; their technical virtuosity became a part of the discourse just as their choices made behind the recording console constructed the sound of the jazz club on record. The channels of commerce that surrounded 1950s jazz worked to curate these narratives of technology and technician, music and musician, to appear as a storied encounter of a performance. The erasure of mediation thus happens through textual emphasis on the LPs themselves. This is a reminder that records always reflect the value systems that surround the sites of performance and the (economic) potential for record making.

Adderley's *Quintet in San Francisco* is an audiovisual reconciliation of such contradictions, a product of enormous technological and musical changes within the jazz industry that happened over the course of a decade. When Gleason writes that "I only hope that some portion of this comes through to you in hearing this album so that you may share this enjoyment," the technology becomes a vehicle for listening to and understanding the spaces of music making. The adjustment of Adderley's voice that begins the record, however brief, reveals a technological layer in the jazz club and the spontaneity of the recording process. Mistakes and imperfections, be it a misjudgment in recording level, an errant bass drum, or a fluffed note, become part of the story of how jazz musicians, producers, and engineers simultaneously negotiated the shifting landscape of the music business, the social dynamics of music making, and the acoustics of the space. As the first recording of his new quintet, the record was a musical experiment in Adderley's artistic sound. As a live record, it was a commercial experiment in how to package a form of music making that consciously drew attention to its Black aesthetic.

Sound, Image, Text, Technology

On the opening track of *Quintet in San Francisco*, there is a brief moment of respite after Cannonball Adderley finishes his solo and before his brother, Nat, begins improvising (5:25). In this break, a singular "yeah" emerges from the applause, filling the space left behind by Cannonball's exit. About a half minute later, with Nat in full swing, someone else intones, "That's right." Other individuals murmur in response. Later, someone starts clapping along, regularly hitting in rhythm to beats two and five of the catchy 6/4 vamp (6:50). The clapping returns during Bobby Timmons's piano solo, along with another sound: "ughhhhhhhhhhhhhh, huh"—"ughhhhhhhhhhhh, huh" (9:50).

These unidentified vocalizations articulate an interplay among music, musician, and audience. Other sounds also help create a sense of the shared musical moment: the rustle of the audience that opens the record, someone snapping along to the music, the vocal exclamations after a solo, and other indiscriminate sounds of the club. Taken together, these sounds cultivate a listening experience based around the interactions between people in a particular space and at a particular time. Live recordings, in this sense, are not only about the musical sounds but also about the sets of relationships that those sounds can be demonstrated to figure.[81] Even in relation to one another, such sounds only reveal so much. Consider Adderley's opening remarks: "[*Applause.*] Thank you very much, ladies and gentlemen. Now it's time to carry on some. If we could have lights out, please, for atmosphere. [*Pause.*] Now we're about to play a new composition by our pianist, Bobby Timmons." The first sounds heard on the record are not Adderley's words but the faint buzz of the audience, pointing to a moment of music making outside of the recording studio. Although they erase the nonspace of the studio, these sounds still do not place the music in a specific time or location. Despite their specificity, they remain anonymous.

Six words in the bottom left corner of the cover of *Quintet in San Francisco* add precision and fill in the details: "RECORDED LIVE AT THE JAZZ WORKSHOP." The small green lettering hovers right above the feet of Cannonball, who appears to be in mid-speech, standing with his saxophone hanging from his neck and looking down at his brother, Nat, seated in a chair. Even the LP's still photographs appear in motion. Written in the smallest font on the cover, the "recorded live" phrase places the record in a specific club and, along with the title, in a specific city. Credits on the back cover, placed just below the title, name the two recording dates as October 18 and 19, 1959. The first sentence of Ralph Gleason's liner notes adds further particulars: "When the CANNONBALL ADDERLEY QUINTET finished Hi-Fly—its closing number after a four week engagement at The Jazz Workshop in San Francisco in October of 1959—the audience stood and cheered and whistled and clapped for fifteen minutes."[82] Gleason then describes the scene in and outside the club, comparing the Jazz Workshop to the famous jazz venues along 52nd Street in New York City. Adderley's quintet, Gleason writes, filled the Jazz Workshop with "contagious" rhythms that, with so many bodies in motion, made the performance space resemble "a church as much as a jazz club." The specifics of these visual elements are not neutral but rather seek to construct this album as a ticket to an event where you just had to be there.[83]

These liner notes appear as a result of the commercial structures that surround this music and its consumption. Gleason, a nationally syndicated jazz critic from San Francisco, regularly contributed to the culture of print capitalism that made jazz a viable business in the 1950s. The small green letters naming the Jazz Workshop on the front cover appear as a result of design work by individuals named on the record: Paul Bacon, Ken Braren, and Harris Lewine. The name of producer Orrin Keepnews can also be found in small print on the back left corner, just above the production company, Bill Grauer Productions, Inc. Like the sounds of Adderley's quintet the elements in (and on) the margins are the result of creative decisions by record-company employees and executives, all of whom were men. Other creative agents responsible for the mixing and mastering—Reice Hamel and Jack Matthews—also appear alongside the graphic designers, all listed in a small paragraph that begins and ends with technical language about the recording technology: "A HIGH FIDELITY Recording...mastered by JACK MATTHEWS (Components Corp.) on a HYDROFEED lathe."[84] Discourses of technology quite literally surround the text that signals the collaborative labor of record making.

The audiovisual elements of the record attempt to bring the club into listeners' living rooms. Such audiovisuality did not appear by chance but resulted from the creative acts of historically situated individuals. Record-industry executives, producers, engineers, musicians, and other technicians had to develop and experiment with a way to make such a sounded object feel live. A new discourse of temporality and its relation to technology emerged as a result. Because the live qualities of recorded sounds meant different things to different companies, this process manifested itself in various ways. Through the 1950s, increased emphasis on the technological possibilities of on-location recording made liveness into a valued commodity.[85]

The audiovisual qualities of the 1950s live jazz LPs created a narrative that championed their very existence. The liner notes and other marginalia became the primary vehicle for these records to communicate to a listening audience how to understand this new genre of record making. The records specified the date and location of the original performance while simultaneously emphasizing the "in-person" or "on-the-spot" aspect of the recording. Jazz clubs, according to the logic the record presented, brought out something special from the musicians as compared to the studio environment.

Consider Blue Note's first on-location recording, which took place at New York City's Birdland in February 1954 and featured Art Blakey's quintet with pianist Horace Silver, bassist Curly Russell, saxophonist Lou Donaldson, and trumpeter Clifford Brown. The session produced enough material for three 10-inch LPs: *A Night at Birdland, vol. 1, vol. 2*, and *vol. 3*.[86] Following industry conventions at the time, Blue Note issued the three LPs in sequence and with the same title and cover design, with a slight change of accent color (blue, red, and green, respectively). The same liner notes, written by jazz critic Leonard Feather, appear on each disc and open with a quotation from Blakey:

> "Wow! First time I enjoyed a record session!"
>
> With these significant words, in a comment you will hear on one of these sides, Art Blakey offers an eloquent tribute to the motive that produced this unique series of recordings.

Because this material was by now familiar enough to the musicians, they were able to express themselves fully and freely. While they could avail themselves of the lack of any time limitation on the performances, they still took no undue advantage, never distorted liberty into license; as a result, there are no 20-minute voyages into tautophony.... Thus A Night at Birdland combines the three elements essential to an enjoyable evening of modern jazz: preparation, improvisation and inspiration.[87]

Feather goes on to depict the studio space as being characterized by the business of making records, contrasting it with the working conditions of the Birdland stage. Among other things, he mentions the time of a jazz-club gig (taking place between 11 p.m. and 3 a.m.) as a more natural environment that helped the musicians feel more comfortable and better able to express themselves. Invoking a similar sentiment found on the early LPs of Prestige (see chapter 2), Feather ties an idea of unencumbered expression to the possibilities afforded by the LP format.[88] His use of Blakey's statement further accentuates the technological possibilities of the format, connecting the liner notes to the sonic medium of the record.

Feather authored most of the liner notes for Blue Note's early live recordings. His texts often describe how the vitality of the club environment translated onto record. In the liner notes to Sonny Rollins's *A Night at the Village Vanguard*, the first live record at the acclaimed venue, Feather writes, "For the first time the Village Vanguard, one of New York's most proudly prescient night clubs, comes to life through the medium of an in-person recording."[89] On Jimmy Smith's *Groovin' at Smalls' Paradise*, recorded a mere twelve days after Rollins's set at the Vanguard, Feather also highlights the club environment while simultaneously promoting the recording technology: "I was lucky enough to be present the night it was recorded. It seems to me that some of the relaxed friendly atmosphere of the club is transfused into the grooves of this disc."[90] In each of these cases, Feather's description emphasizes the musical spontaneity and relaxed environment of the club that a studio recording could never duplicate. The jazz club, by this account, appears as the most natural environment for jazz performance—elsewhere he describes the nightclub as the "locus operandi" of jazz.[91] Recording technology, in Feather's account, becomes a crucial intermediary between jazz club and listener, something to be celebrated in how it transforms the "in-person" quality of the performance into the grooves of the disc. These records, like so many others, sold a listening experience uninhibited by technology yet at the same time beholden to it.

Riverside's first live record featuring Randy Weston at the Café Bohemia makes a similar distinction between stage and studio. In his liner notes Keepnews writes: "As recordings such as this sharply indicate, jazz as heard 'live' in actual club performance is inevitably more than a little different from the jazz recorded under studio conditions.... Most obvious, of course, is that the musicians are playing at and reacting directly to an audience, rather than just acoustically impeccable walls and two or three faces in the studio control room."[92] The notes continue to compare the studio to the live recording. Although the studios will continue to produce "a vast amount of lastingly excellent jazz," Keepnews believes that the jazz club is superior because it offers "certain important qualities of live performance at its best—warmth, spontaneity, vitality—that are only rarely duplicated in the studio." "Warmth" and "spontaneity" have a blended meaning, describing both the social environment of the jazz club and the music created on stage. Given that the sound quality of studio recordings was far superior to the quality of those made on location, such descriptions portray the sometimes messy and certainly noisier live recordings as being more revealing about the musicians' everyday experience. After all, the "faces in the studio control room" are nameless, bodiless technicians and businessmen who should not, by the logic outlined here, be mistaken for an audience.

The first live LP on Argo, a subsidiary of Chess Records, similarly emphasizes the difference between the studio and the spontaneous environment of the jazz club. Recorded in January 1958, *But Not for Me: Ahmad Jamal Trio at the Pershing, vol. 1* included notes by radio personality and Vee-Jay recordman Sid McCoy that emphasized Jamal's attachment to the Pershing Lounge:

> Miller Brown, the owner of the Pershing Lounge (of Chicago's Pershing Hotel), and Ahmad Jamal have a rare and wonderful thing going . . . these two men respect and regard one another very highly. So it is no wonder that Jamal has at the Pershing a suitable atmosphere and climate in which to swing freely. Away from the inhibiting pressure of the recording studio and with the stimulating warmth of a live audience to work before, plus relaxed familiar surroundings, Jamal has been allowed to give you—the listener, full benefit of his amazing skills and marvelous conception in a variety of modes, shades, and tones.[93]

The presence of the audience, here and elsewhere, is portrayed as a valuable asset to these recordings because of what it brings out in the musicians. Studio records are, by implication, incomplete and partial, despite their superiority in sonic fidelity. But "Fidelity to what?" then becomes the question.[94] Like similar examples above, this text uses "warmth" in conjunction with the "live" audience and as a justification for why this record should be considered special when compared to other releases. The atmosphere, along with the relationship between musician and club owner, creates the possibilities for uninhibited performance. The technological capability to record on location goes unnamed, but it nevertheless underwrites the potential to capture and circulate any such performance.

All told, live records emphasize the sociality of the bandstand as the authentic place for music making, especially through comparisons with the recording studio. By *sociality*, I refer to the intermingling interactions between audiences and musicians in a specific venue at a particular moment in time. Because such scenes are fleeting, the record's combination of sounds, images, and texts comes to redefine the *scenario* of jazz performance. Diana Taylor historicizes performance through the idea of scenario in order to account for both written and embodied practices. Like records, scenarios are repeatable and legible only through a set of epistemological beliefs that surround any given performance.[95] Live records of this era, then, are all examples of how beliefs about performance repeat through circulation.

Understanding live records as scenarios of cultural memory and historical imagining also points to what Taylor describes as the "social construction of bodies in particular contexts."[96] As such, the issue of race is never far beneath the surface: the structures of power within the industry did not favor African Americans jazz musicians.[97] With a few exceptions, record-label owners, producers, critics, engineers, and executives were not Black and were almost always male. The recording studio was space where control over technology meant control over audiovisual forms of representation.[98] In contrast, musicians had authority and control over the bandstand. For producers and record executives, deciding to make records of jazz-club performances meant less technological and musical control over the recording space, especially because manipulative processes in postproduction were expensive (and thus limited) during the early to mid-1950s.[99] The everyday musical sounds onstage translated onto record in a way that was directly related to who was performing onstage, what venue they were recording in, and who was producing the record.

Although producers still had the final say over how those sounds translated onto record, musicians had more control over the sound when recording, both in their musical performance and in the way they interacted with the audience. In a 1956 interview with *Down Beat*, Art Blakey described how he viewed the audience in relation to his performance onstage: "When we're on the stand, and we see that there are people in the audience who aren't patting their feet and who aren't nodding their heads to our music, we know we're doing something wrong. Because when we do get our message across, those heads and feet begin to move."[100] Here, Blakey outlines his ideal performance environment as one of high audience engagement and participation. His music-as-speech metaphor—"get our message across"—positions the music as a communication tool; he wants his audience to understand and react through bodily movement. Blakey's comments also reveal his attentiveness toward the audience while on the bandstand, revealing the centrality of social interaction to his mode of music making. Compare this with Dave Brubeck's description of his jazz-club audiences that appears in the liner notes to his Columbia LP *Dave Brubeck at Storyville: 1954, vol. 1*. Brubeck outlines how his group "play[s] differently for different kinds of audiences":

> A concert audience of college students isn't at all like a night club crowd. The youngsters want more excitement, whereas the night club audience usually consist of older people, which whom you can be more introspective. Just the size of the crowd has a special effect on me and the other fellows in the Quartet; playing for 2,000 or more people is not the same thing as playing for 200. . . . You'll notice that on JGTC [*Jazz Goes to College*] the tempos are faster and in general the playing is more explosive and more inclined to be purely emotional. In a night club, we're a little cooler, and things get more reflective.[101]

Brubeck characterizes his experience in the clubs as "introspective," hinting at Eurocentric tropes of artistic expression. His understanding of the interactions between audience and ensemble in a similar performance space reveals a stark contrast with Blakey's comments as well as those by others.[102] Around this time, Adderley described the nightclub as a vibrantly social space where the noisiness of an interactive audience sets the expectations for music making. He embraced this social environment.[103]

Different approaches to jazz audiences do not fit into strict racial categories, of course. However, such distinctions do reveal how different performance spaces in jazz intersect with concurrent ideologies of race, music, and technology. In the years leading up to *Quintet in San Francisco*, artists like Blakey and Adderley used their music to connect with audiences through musical decisions about melody, harmony, and rhythm as well as their announcements and overall demeanor onstage. Consider Gleason's comments in the liner notes to *Quintet in San Francisco* about the environment in the Jazz Workshop:

> The rhythm of this group is contagious and its overall effect might well cause the lame to walk and the halt to throw away their crutches. At times the atmosphere of the Jazz Workshop resembled a church as much as jazz club. The band quite obviously was having a ball ("I have never worked a job I enjoyed more" was the unanimous verdict of Julian and Nat) and there was no reluctance on their part to show it. When Bobby Timmons' exciting This Here ("it's part shout and part moan") would get moving, with Bobby in the midst of one of his full-fingered, rocking solos where he seems almost to be playing a duet with himself, the whole place would start rocking and stomping with the band.[104]

Gleason evokes biblical stories of Jesus—"the lame to walk and the halt to throw away their crutches"—and compares the participatory atmosphere in the Jazz Workshop to that inside of a church. This comparison connected the music to a growing commercial category of jazz associated with Black popular culture, as signaled by Adderley. It was not a coincidence that Riverside and other jazz labels at the time were targeting Black audiences like never before. The aesthetic values here cannot be separated from the economic structures surrounding Adderley's performance.

Quintet in San Francisco reflects these politics in sonic terms as well. Recall how Adderley solidifies the church metaphor in his opening announcement of "This Here": "It's simultaneously a shout and a chant, depending upon whether you know anything about the roots of church music and all that kind of stuff—meaning soul church music—I don't mean, ah, Bach chorales, and so that's different." He continues to talk about the "corruption" of the tune title from "This Here" to "Dish Here" for "purposes of soul," a reference to how his music entwines with Black popular culture. However, a disjuncture between the aural and the visual realms remains: the written representations of Timmons's composition on the record are still anglicized as "This Here." Like the politics of the studio space compared with the bandstand, the hard *T* and *H* that appear on the back of *Quintet in San Francisco* reveal how, despite their close interrelations, the aural and visual often have their own ways of making a record feel live.[105] Aural and visual elements have separate but related politics, layered with discourses of race, place, and technology.

Capturing the Sonic Sociality of the Jazz Club

The cutoff to "Spontaneous Combustion," the final track on side 1 of *Quintet in San Francisco*, ends with an extra punctuation from drummer Louis Hayes (11:30). The audience applauds and whistles; someone audibly says, "All right" and "uh huh." Adderley begins to address the crowd: "Thank you very much, ladies and gentlemen." (As he pauses, another voice jumps out: "Now that's what I'm talkin' about.") Adderley tries to continue, "Now we're going to—" but interrupts himself to let the applause die down. After another "thank you," he introduces the band members and closes out the set: "Now we gotta get another drink, because we have a whole lotta recording to do, so you gotta give us a break. We'll be back in a minute." Someone listening to this track would hear the quick fade-out yield not to silence but to the sound of their needle against the blank vinyl at the record's center.

If only for a moment, Adderley's voice can be heard on every track of *Quintet in San Francisco*, from extended announcements to brief thank-yous at the end of some tracks. Although the liner notes and other marginalia placed the music in a specific location, Adderley's voice and the accompanying sounds of the club present a particular kind of music making that foregrounds moments of sociality between musicians and audience members.[106] The sociality of venues that served Black clientele—nightclubs and other small venues—made its way onto live records as well. In other words, capturing the music in the club was about recording moments of social interaction between those on and off the bandstand as people experiencing an event together. The combination of sounds created a new musical aesthetic on record.

The conversational nature of Adderley's speech, combined with his light southern drawl and pedagogical disposition, enabled him to skillfully position his music as part of a longer trajectory of Black musical culture and do so in one of the most public forms available to jazz musicians. By leveraging his oration skills, he talked politics on the bandstand with a welcoming tone, rather than one of opposition.[107] Or as Keepnews described it many years later, Adderley did not talk "at" the audience but "to them."[108] Despite its overall impression of ease and effortlessness, his announcing style was a cultivated skill developed over time as a traveling musician fronting his own band. Biographer Cary Ginell details several press accounts that note Adderley's memorable onstage presence, especially in addressing the audience.[109] As leader, spokesperson, and representative, Adderley embraced the role in a way that translated so well onto record that Keepnews included an entire minute of his spoken introduction at the beginning of *Quintet in San Francisco*. This marked the first time that the sound of Adderley's spoken voice could be heard on record.

As his interactions on record reveal, Adderley embraced the nightclub environment for the opportunities it provided him as a performer. In 1964 he told Nat Hentoff, "Unlike Charles [Mingus], a joint [i.e., nightclub] has my favorite atmosphere. It's true that some people can get noisy, but that's part of it. It seems to me that I feel a little better when people seem to be having a good time before you even begin. And it gives me something to play on."[110] Such play was not necessarily about pure enjoyment but also a means of performing his self-assured intellect and expressive freedom—that is, a form of Black masculinity often denied to jazz musicians within the white infrastructures of the jazz industry. On record, these moments helped expand the sonic possibilities of Black expression in ways that were unavailable to a young Miles Davis at Prestige in 1951, to offer one example.

Adderley's presentation style also reveals a cultivated awareness of how the live moment interacted with the reproducible one. When Adderley comments that the band had "a whole lotta recording to do," he reveals the hybrid live and mediated nature of his performance. In essence, he was performing for two audiences in October 1959: one at the Jazz Workshop and another listening to the record at home. The stage and club exist as doubles of themselves, mediated through the expectations of on-location performance and the expectations of on-location recording.[111] The title, liner notes, and marginalia emphasize the club environment, whereas Adderley emphasizes the recording, at least during that moment.

Blue Note's first live record, *A Night at Birdland, vol. 1*, includes a similarly blurred moment between the live and mediated. The record opens with a minute-long monologue by emcee Pee Wee Marquette, who introduces the quintet and describes the hybrid quality of the performance turned recording session: "Ladies and gentlemen, as you know we have something special here at Birdland this evening, a recording for Blue Note records. When you applaud for the different passages, your hands go right on the records over there so when they play them over and over all over the country you may be some place and, uh, say well that's my hand on one of those records that I dug down at Birdland (0:00)."[112] Marquette emphasizes the expanded temporality and repeatability of the moment made possible by the technology of recording. By using the phrase "something special," his introduction informs the audiences both in the club and at home that they, too, are part of Blue Note records. Radio broadcasts from jazz clubs were common during the previous decades and often included announcements from the emcee or host speaking to the radio audience.[113] Marquette's introduction was an extension of this practice but also signaled a new form of repeatability, where musicians performed for audiences that were at once live and mediated. This form of meta-advertising repeats on *Jutta Hipp at the Hickory House*, where Leonard Feather introduces the performance as a recording session for Blue Note. Kept on disc, such moments serve as aural reminders of how technology mediates the stage during these performances.

Live records from this era required collaboration at the site of production. Musicians, record producers, club owners, and audience members all had different but overlapping levels of investment in the cocreation of these listening spaces. In addition, these records brought together two levels of commerce that, up until this point, had only been tangentially related to each other. The first was the club's physical space, a fixed boundary determined by a particular business at an exact time and a specific location. The second was the record-buying public, a diverse collection of listeners not bound to a physical location or clearly defined time but connected through the cultural activity of record collection. The ability to record on location collapsed both domains of commerce and attention into each other.

As one of the few labels to feature musicians' voices on its records, Blue Note recognized another potential way to draw listeners into the nightclub space: through audio production. Such voices on record established a feeling of social proximity because they brought the musician out from behind their instrument. Like *Quintet in San Francisco*, the three volumes of *A Night at Birdland* include Blakey introducing band members and the repertoire from the stage. Such announcements were more than informational; the LP's jacket also contained the same details. They give a sense of the spontaneous conditions at the site of performance and production. For instance, at the end of "Now's the Time," Blakey jokes about the youth of his band: "Yes sir, I'm going to stay with the youngsters. When they get too old, I'm gonna get some younger ones—it keeps the mind active" (8:45). During his introduction to "A Night in Tunisia," Blakey also details the circumstances surrounding

Gillespie's composition: "I feel particularly close to this tune because I was right there when [Gillespie] composed it, in Texas, on the bottom of a garbage can. [*Faint laughter.*] Seriously." Other examples included trumpeter Kenny Dorham's introduction to "Yesterdays" on *The Jazz Messengers at the Cafe Bohemia* (1956) and Sonny Rollins's preface to "Softly as in a Morning Sunrise" on *A Night at the Village Vanguard* (1958).[114] For many listeners, especially those not located in New York City, these announcements were one of the only times they would have been able to hear these Black men speak with such freedom and authority.

Announcements and other vocalizations from the stage were much rarer on other labels that did not emphasize hard bop.[115] Debut Records issued two 10-inch LPs recorded in September 1953 at the Putnam Central Club in Brooklyn, featuring a jam-session-style concert with trombonists J. J. Johnson, Kai Winding, Bennie Green, and Willie Dennis. Titled *Jazz Workshop: Trombone Rapport, vol. 1* and *vol. 2*, the discs included audience applause and other sounds of the club, but not a single musician announcement from the stage.[116] Louis Armstrong's voice can be heard throughout *Ambassador Satch* (see chapter 4), but Columbia Records generally did not include extended announcements from musicians on its live records. Consider the four 10-inch LPs featuring Dave Brubeck issued in 1954: *Jazz Goes to College, vol. 1* and *vol. 2*; and *Dave Brubeck at Storyville: 1954, vol. 1* and *vol. 2*. Although there is a brief announcement by radio host John McLellan at the end of *Storyville, vol. 2*, Brubeck's voice is never heard. In this way, Columbia followed Fantasy Records, which issued six live Brubeck records on 10-inch LP and EP beginning in 1953. No stage chatter appears on these records.[117]

Blue Note's co-owner Alfred Lion, who also produced most of the label's live records from this time, purposefully placed the musicians' voices on record. With the exception of Marquette's monologue on *A Night at Birdland*, Lion most often placed announcements at a track's end as an introduction to the record's next selection. The accompanying applause usually fades into the intervening silences, which are quickly broken by the music of the following track. In one sense, this organization provided an aural bridge between selections and presented a mostly seamless transition from one song to another. However, the sequence of the tracks on many of these LPs often does not match the actual performance order. In these instances, the seemingly seamless presentation was sometimes artificial: spliced and edited together in postproduction.[118] The aural presence of magnetic tape is often audible, as it is during Blakey's introduction to "Night in Tunisia" on

A Night at Birdland, vol. 2.[119] This set of LPs also includes a short musical tag that usually signaled the end of the set. At the end of "Mayreh" (5:50), Blakey's ensemble plays a quick version of George Shearing's "Lullaby of Birdland," the club's official theme song.[120] Unlike in the club, however, the record slowly fades out—a cymbal crash dissipating through an engineer's turn of a knob.

Hard-bop musicians such as Blakey, Adderley, Jimmy Smith, and others who closely aligned themselves with Black popular music created more live records during this time than did musicians in any other subgenre of jazz.[121] The first sounds on most of these records are a few seconds of club ambience: the murmur of voices, the clinking of dishes, the musicians warming up, or other interactions among band and audience members. These sounds were not of a crowd en masse but of individuals reacting to or creating the music. During Clifford Brown's trumpet cadenza on "A Night in Tunisia" from *A Night at Birdland, vol. 1*, someone (perhaps Blakey) shouts, "Blow your horn!" (8:55).[122] As the tapes continue to run after the band concludes "Where or When," the closing track on the A side of *The Incredible Jimmy Smith at Club Baby Grand, vol. 1*, someone calls to Smith: "Hey, Jimmy!" Soon after, someone else: "He went all the way out *that* time!" Then: "That cat is something else, ain't he" (9:05). By the time of this 1956 Blue Note record, Smith was exclusively performing on the Hammond B-3 organ, an instrument with roots in the Black church. Smith popularized the B-3 organ in jazz, although the instrument was already a mainstay in public gathering places within the Black community.[123] As live recordings of these artists began circulating in the mid-1950s, capturing the ambience of the club became a primary concern because it translated such community spaces onto disc along with the music.

Riverside's four live records that predate *Quintet in San Francisco*, recorded in 1956–58, include sounds of the club environment, although they do not include onstage announcements from the musicians.[124] Monk's *Thelonious in Action* and Weston's *Jazz à la Bohemia*, similar to some Blue Note LPs from this period, contain brief theme songs marking the end of the set. These tracks usually lasted around one minute apiece. The other records include moments of audience applause and the occasional snapped count-off to begin a performance. The applause at the track's end usually fades out quickly, an effect done in the studio after the fact. Thus, these records were similar to others from the period in how they captured aspects of the club environment, yet they were also quite different from Riverside's approach to recording and packaging Adderley's 1959 performance at the Jazz Workshop.

The presence of Adderley's voice on *Quintet in San Francisco* brought something different to listeners in how he asked them to contextualize his music on his terms. His skillfully delivered announcements infused a social aurality on record that, like Adderley's music overall, reflected the Black popular culture in which he was always already immersed. Its circulation on record was also the result of years of experimentation as independent jazz labels found ways to record on location and reproduce the interactive sounds of the club. Record production was key in crafting Adderley's socio-aurality on record.

In an era when jazz continued to distance itself from popular-music styles, musicians like Adderley welcomed the opportunity to produce music for Black communities. Adderley's approach, which became known as "soul" jazz, maintained its connections to the Black working class and other Black popular musics of the day.[125] Such development was not without controversy. Many writers and cultural critics—everyone from Martin Williams to Amiri Baraka (then LeRoi Jones)—criticized soul jazz for aligning itself with mass consumerism.[126] As would become clear in the years following *Quintet in San Francisco*, Adderley did not share these views and also had the opportunity, on record, to teach his audience about the many ways that his music celebrated the history of Black artistry and expression.[127] The spontaneous moments of audience and musician interaction featured on Adderley's live records combined musical poetics with forms of mass distribution and consumption. Adderley's awareness onstage and his mindfulness of the recording process—"we have a whole lotta recording to do"—are reminders of the role that technology played in jazz's sonic Afro-modernity.

The Joy of Cannonball Adderley

The commercial success of *Quintet in San Francisco* forced record makers to pay attention. By November 1960, the LP had sold nearly 100,000 copies, and the "This Here" single had surpassed the 75,000 mark.[128] No doubt seeking similar success, the heads of numerous labels decided to record at one San Francisco club or another: Dick Bock (World Pacific) at the Jazz Workshop, Norman Granz (Verve) at the Cellar, and Nesuhi Ertegun (Atlantic), who did a nonjazz date at the Hungry i. Keepnews remained active with Riverside as well, recording on location to issue *Barry Harris at the Jazz Workshop* (1960), *Thelonious Monk Quartet Plus Two at the Blackhawk* (1960), and *Bev Kelly in Person* (1960), a date with local saxophonist Pony Poindexter at the Coffee Gallery.[129] Others would follow. None matched Adderley's success, but the breadth of this activity speaks volumes about how the economics of attention entwine with jazz record making.

Onstage and on record, Adderley remained simultaneously casual and serious. His eloquently spoken introductions and rhetorical delivery encourage participation, offering entry into his music for listeners of all kinds. At the same time, he revealed with clarity the racial pride inherent in his music, foreshadowing the growing sentiment that would define soul, funk, and other forms of Black popular music in the 1960s. Adderley's emphasis on the words *soul* and *church* during his opening monologue to *Quintet in San Francisco* denotes an unmistakably Black musical aesthetic with roots in the Black vernacular, while not being reducible to it. Musicians like Adderley merged this with the improvisational styles of bebop, resulting in what Ingrid Monson has described as a "blackening of modernist aesthetics" in 1950s jazz.[130] Meanwhile, the presence of his voice on record testifies to how this Blackening translated onto commercial jazz recordings through Adderley's creative and critical music making.

Live recordings came to define Adderley in the years after, perhaps more than any other jazz instrumentalist during the period. He went on to record five live LPs on Riverside and another eight for Capitol Records, accounting for roughly half of his discography between 1959 and 1969.[131] Adderley's affable monologues became a defining characteristic, helping him to expand his popularity beyond a core jazz listenership. *Quintet in San Francisco* may have been responsible for catapulting him onto the national scene, but this LP materialized out of a deeper philosophical shift in record making during the 1950s. Magnetic tape recording and extended LP playback were technological possibilities that, among other outcomes, enabled independent jazz labels to capture the innovative sounds of hard-bop musicians on location and then package them for mass distribution. These musicians, in turn, used this new record-making approach to self-fashion a form of Black masculinity that centered on their intellectual authority, their emotional transparency onstage, and their confidence when speaking to any kind of audience.

Adderley actively participated in this process by embracing joy as a strategy for attention and artistic success. Many took notice. When Gene Lees, the managing editor at *Down Beat*, reviewed the band's appearance at the

Sutherland Lounge in Chicago, he noted Adderley's exuberance toward his band, the audience, and especially his brother Nat: "The rapport between the two brothers, aside from being a wonderful, warm, and occasionally amusing thing to watch (Cannonball sometimes looks so proud of Nat he could burst) contributes much to the cohesion of the group." Ralph Gleason agreed, going so far as to describe the "feeling of love" that "spread throughout the club night after night, set after set." Riverside's advertising copy went on to describe Adderley's new band as "the most stimulating, soulful, happy group you've heard in a **very** long time."[132] The musical chemistry between the brothers created a sense of joy onstage that celebrated Blackness through music. It was as if they were making an argument: we use Black joy to create meaningful music, we use Black joy to attract audience attention, we use Black joy to improve our working conditions, so Black joy should be on our records as well. The proof of concept appears in the liner notes to *Quintet in San Francisco*, where Gleason reports that the brothers expressed a unanimous sentiment: "I have never worked a job I enjoyed more."[133] In the end, Adderley's joyful approach garnered the attention of both Gleason and Keepnews, white recordmen who both chose to document it in print and in sound. Adderley's warm address toward his audience blurred boundaries between the live and recorded, and in doing so expanded the ways in which Black brotherhood could sound on record.

Adderley's joyful record making expressed a form of sonic Afro-modernity that recognized the possibilities for Black cultural producers within an increasingly mediatized world.[134] His productive working relationship with Keepnews and Riverside allowed him to take advantage of the commercial momentum created by *Quintet in San Francisco*. Along with regularly making other LPs, Adderley also began producing records for Riverside. In 1961 he narrated the commentary on *A Child's Introduction to Jazz* and wrote a regular column about jazz and the music business for the *New York Amsterdam News*.[135] He also started a production company called Junat Production with Nat; they envisioned Junat to be involved with concert promotion and television pilots.[136] Together, these activities evince an entrepreneurial approach that embraced cooperation with existing structures of the music industry. As Adderley put it in a 1959 *Down Beat* profile published during his Jazz Workshop residency, "When the public is aware of you, you can command better conditions for your efforts."[137] Adderley saw the power and possibility in an expanded jazz public. His record making was an extension of an approach already underway.

Playlist: Recording on Location at the Jazz Club

This playlist chronicles the history of record making in the 1950s jazz club. I have prioritized LPs that feature hard bop and that were recorded by independent labels. However, each of these records should be understood in relation to other live recordings of the era (such as those in the chapter 3 playlist). A handful of records from the early 1960s show how the practices developed in the early LP era continued into the next decade. (All recordings are LPs.)

Ahmad Jamal. *But Not for Me: Ahmad Jamal Trio at the Pershing, vol. 1.* Argo, 1958.
Anita O'Day. *Anita O'Day at Mr. Kelly's.* Verve, 1958.
Art Blakey. *The Jazz Messengers at the Cafe Bohemia, vols. 1–2.* Blue Note, 1956.
Art Blakey. *Meet You at the Jazz Corner of the World.* Blue Note, 1960.
Art Blakey. *A Night at Birdland with the Art Blakey Quintet, vols. 1–3.* Blue Note, 1954.
Barry Harris. *Barry Harris at the Jazz Workshop.* Riverside, 1960.
Bev Kelly. *Bev Kelly in Person.* Riverside, 1960.
Bill Evans. *Sunday at the Village Vanguard.* Riverside, 1961.
Bill Evans. *Waltz for Debby.* Riverside, 1961.
Buddy Rich. *Buddy Rich in Miami.* Verve, 1958.
Cannonball Adderley. *The Cannonball Adderley Quintet in San Francisco.* Riverside, 1959.
Cannonball Adderley. *Jazz Workshop Revisited.* Riverside, 1962.
Cannonball Adderley. *Quintet at the Lighthouse.* Riverside, 1960.
Cannonball Adderley. *Sextet in New York.* Riverside, 1962.
Charles Mingus. *Mingus at the Bohemia.* Debut, 1956.
Dave Brubeck. *Dave Brubeck at Storyville: 1954, vols. 1–2.* Columbia, 1954.
Dave Brubeck. *George Wein Presents Jazz at Storyville.* Fantasy, 1953.
Dave Brubeck. *Jazz at the Blackhawk.* Fantasy, 1956.
Dave Brubeck. *Paul and Dave: Jazz Interwoven.* Fantasy, 1954.
Dizzy Gillespie. *Dizzy Gillespie at Newport.* Verve, 1957.
Gene Krupa. *Gene Krupa at the London House: Big Noise from Winnetka.* Verve, 1959.
George Wallington. *Quintet at the Bohemia Featuring the Peck.* Progressive, 1955.
Gerry Mulligan. *The Gerry Mulligan Quartet.* Fantasy, 1953.
Jimmy Smith. *Groovin' at Smalls' Paradise, vols. 1–2.* Blue Note, 1958.
Jimmy Smith. *The Incredible Jimmy Smith at Club Baby Grand, vols. 1–2.* Blue Note, 1957.
John Coltrane. *"Live" at the Village Vanguard.* Impulse!, 1962.
Jutta Hipp. *Jutta Hipp at the Hickory House, vols. 1–2.* Blue Note, 1956.
Kenny Dorham. *'Round about Midnight at the Cafe Bohemia.* Blue Note, 1956.
Lee Konitz. *The Real Lee Konitz.* Atlantic, 1957.
Lennie Tristano. *Lennie Tristano.* Atlantic, 1955.

Les McCann. *Les McCann Ltd. in San Francisco*. Pacific Jazz, 1961.
Oscar Peterson. *On the Town with the Oscar Peterson Trio*. Verve, 1958.
Pepper Adams. *10 to 4 at the 5 Spot*. Riverside, 1958.
Randy Weston. *Jazz à la Bohemia*. Riverside, 1956.
Red Garland. *Red Garland at the Prelude*. Prestige, 1959.
Sonny Rollins. *A Night at the Village Vanguard*. Blue Note, 1958.
Thelonious Monk. *Misterioso*. Riverside, 1958.
Thelonious Monk. *Quartet Plus Two at the Blackhawk*. Riverside, 1960.
Thelonious Monk. *Thelonious in Action*. Riverside, 1958.
Thelonious Monk. *The Thelonious Monk Orchestra at Town Hall*. Riverside, 1959.
Wardell Gray. *Jazz Concert*. Prestige, 1952.
Will Holt and Dolly Jonah. *On the Brink*. Atlantic, 1961.
Willie Dennis, Bennie Green, J. J. Johnson, and Kai Winding. *Jazz Workshop, vols. 1–2, Trombone Rapport*. Debut, 1954 and 1955.

6

MINGUS AH UM

The Avant-Garde Record Making of Charles Mingus

In May 1959, Charles Mingus recorded at the famed 30th Street studio of Columbia Records in New York City. Despite his musical prominence and lengthy discography, the resulting LP, *Mingus Ah Um*, was the bassist's first LP issued by a major label.[1] It did not disappoint. Equal parts blues and bebop, and with a driving groove beneath, the music contains a focused impulsiveness that leaves plenty of room for spontaneous declarations. Throughout the seven-minute rendition of "Better Get It in Your Soul," for example, Mingus interjects vocally, shouting, humming, and singing with increasing density: "oh yeah" (0:26)—"yeah, I know" (2:20)—"yes Lord, I know what I know" (3:08)—"hallelujah!" (5:36)—"oh YEAAAAAHH!" (6:35). Unintelligible vocalizations can similarly be heard on "Jelly Roll," which also ends with a loose call-and-response between Mingus and his instrumental collaborators (3:33). A comparable moment of collective improvisation closes out "Boogie Stop Shuffle" (3:21). The aptly named "Bird Calls" includes several aleatoric sections where the musicians reach into the highest registers of their respective instruments with birdlike chatter (2:48).

A noticeable tape splice on "Jelly Roll" complicates the record's otherwise spontaneous aesthetic. At the end of Booker Ervin's one-chorus saxophone solo, the sudden return of the melody interrupts the final note of his descending double-time line (2:39). The full version of the track, issued decades later, reveals that Ervin resolves his line as expected (to the tonic). Yet the 1959 LP omits this final note as well as a short punctuation from pianist Horace Parlan and the entirety of Mingus's bass solo that follows. All told, the originally issued version of "Jelly Roll" excludes over two minutes of music from the complete studio take.[2] This lacuna opens up a greater truth about *Mingus Ah Um*: at least seventeen splices across six of the nine tracks removed over eleven minutes of music. The omissions include four melodic choruses, four complete solos, an eight-measure interlude, and portions of eight other solos across four different tracks (table 6.1).[3] In performance, Mingus deliberately cultivated a sense of organized chaos. *Mingus Ah Um* reveals a similar intentionality in the editing room during postproduction.

Beginning and ending with *Mingus Ah Um*, this chapter dwells on the splice as a place of rupture and possibility, closely examining how studio production became integral to Mingus's music in the 1950s even as his compositional aesthetic increasingly foregrounded spontaneity. To some, heavy studio production might seem incompatible, or at least at odds, with Mingus's brand of improvised music. However, a close examination of this entwined relationship exposes a larger network of musical entrepreneurs who actively used the process of making records to disrupt how the jazz industry traditionally valued Black artistry and labor. The splice thus offers a means to account for Mingus's various activities as a bassist, composer, record-label owner, and record producer as different facets of the same political activism. Although I start and end with issues that appear technological—for example, splicing and editing—I understand record making not as a machine-driven activity but rather as a cultural practice that flows through differently situated individuals working in collaboration. In doing so, I argue that Mingus reimagined the economics and cultural politics of jazz through a concern for the sound on record, where control over that sound also meant control over the form, content, packaging, and representation of his music. Examining

Table 6.1 Summary of postproduction edits on *Mingus Ah Um*, Columbia CL 1370 (1959)

Title	Track	Edits (C = chorus number)	Time cut	Total difference	
Better Git It in Your Soul	A1	[No edit]			
Goodbye Pork Pie Hat	A2	Melody C2	0:58		
Boogie Stop Shuffle	A3	Tenor sax C1-2, alto sax C1-4 (all), interlude A	1:16		
Self-Portrait in Three Colors	A4	[No edit]			
Open Letter to Duke	A5	Alto sax C1-2 (all)	0:52	Side A	−3:06
Bird Calls	B1	Melody C2-3, tenor sax C4-6, piano C2-3, alto sax C4-6, drums (all)	3:04		
Fables of Faubus	B2	[No edit]			
Pussy Cat Dues	B3	Melody C2, piano C2, clarinet C1, tenor sax C1	2:43		
Jelly Roll	B4	Melody C2, piano C2, bass (all)	2:12	Side B	−7:59
				Total	−11:05

Mingus's record making through the splice thus becomes a way to uncover stories of intellectual labor and artistic representation normally cut from the historical narrative.

As his career took off in the 1950s, Mingus operated simultaneously along multiple entrepreneurial trajectories. He became a record-label owner and a music publisher. He authored liner notes and an autobiography. He composed for and recorded with a wide variety of ensembles and a diverse set of musicians. And he produced records. Yet despite the sizable scholarship about the cultural complexity and political nuance of his music, his activities as a record maker remain underexplored.[4] This omission is even more curious given the heavy-handed approach to production that Mingus's discography reveals. He regularly spliced solos, stitched together takes, and overdubbed himself onto already completed recordings, some of which were made on location at concert halls or in nightclubs with an audible audience. The eleven minutes of missing music on *Mingus Ah Um* thus fits into a broader trajectory of Mingus's artistic practice in some unexpected ways.

Chronologically, this chapter focuses on the period between the founding of Debut Records in 1952 and the recording of *Mingus Ah Um* in 1959. This time line coincides with the record industry's adoption of the LP as the dominant medium for jazz as well as the period between Prestige's first LP experiments (chapter 2) and Cannonball Adderley's recording of *Quintet in San Francisco* (chapter 5). Accordingly, Mingus's story offers additional perspectives on the issues of format, production, jazz historiography, and Afro-modernities that have run through the preceding pages. Like Miles Davis, Mingus recognized the recording studio as both a place of business and a location of cultural power. Like Duke Ellington, he understood the role that postproduction has in fixing mistakes and creating records for repeated listenings. Like Dizzy Gillespie, he attempted to leverage performance toward social justice and civil rights. And like Adderley, he understood that jazz performance unfolds in contested spaces with constantly shifting cultural boundaries. Mingus moves alongside and sometimes in disagreement with these musicians, always fighting for greater control over the sound and design of his records. Together, their stories reveal the many ways in which Black musicians engage with the same record-making practices.

My investigation of Mingus is in open dialogue with the previous chapter about Adderley. Both chapters focus on LPs made in 1959 by Black record makers of the same generation who skillfully found ways to accentuate Black musical aesthetics both onstage and in the studio.[5] Adderley and Mingus also recognized that jazz performance, especially in the nightclub, takes place within an economy of attention where entrenched systems of whiteness created value around certain artistic pathways for Black men and not others. However, their approach toward these systems of musical labor and value differed enormously. For his part, Adderley worked within already existing structures, using his own brand of joyful musicianship, pedagogy, and record making. By fostering a meaningful relationship with Orrin Keepnews at Riverside and adopting an affable approach with club audiences, Adderley attempted to place jazz within the broader context of US popular music. Mingus took a more antagonistic stance, forcefully rejecting the accepted economics of the nightclub and the view that positioned jazz as a form of mass entertainment. He continually waged a kind of guerrilla warfare on the jazz industry along several fronts, including through his own record making. The contrasts between Adderley and Mingus act as a salient reminder that the cultural history of Black record making contains numerous perspectives, positionalities, and strategies.[6] Multiplicity once again emerges as a key element of jazz's sonic Afro-modernity during the LP era.

Mingus the Avant-Garde Entrepreneur

In a possibly apocryphal tale from 1957 or 1958, Mingus once used a record player as a form of protest. According to trombonist Jimmy Knepper, Mingus had become increasingly bothered by the clamorous environment at the Half Note, then a new club where he was working an extended contract. In an effort to cut through the noise and convince the audience to listen, Mingus set up his record player onstage one night. While the other musicians "relaxed" by reading books or playing cards, Mingus listened to his records.[7]

Mingus's protest attempted to recalibrate his relationship with his audience. As I explored in the previous chapter, nearly all jazz clubs operated through a racially coded economy of attention, where Black musicians exchanged their artistry for the attention of an audience that was often white and middle class. The audience's inattention toward Mingus onstage at the Half Note implicitly dismissed his music making as a form of expendable entertainment—not unlike a record. After all, a record player is as much a technology of mass culture as it is one of leisure, projecting sounds often relegated to the background. Inattention at the club was therefore a privilege, one normally inaccessible to Mingus. By focusing his attention on his record player, Mingus attempted to disrupt that privilege by turning the audience's inattention onto itself. He did this, one presumes, in hopes of refocusing the audience's awareness away from the club's social environment and back to what he seemed to value the most: artful music making.[8] Performance is always political, as Mingus knew well.

With a bit of theatrical flair, Mingus waged a guerrilla attack against the nightclub, one of the foundational institutions of white male control within the jazz industry.[9] Such a stunt was not unique. During a performance at the Village Vanguard, he supposedly reacted to an inattentive crowd by handing a newspaper to the pianist and a chess set to the drummer and saxophonist. Through the 1950s and into the 1960s, he often stopped mid-performance to reprimand the audience and demand their silence.[10] Later, in 1964, Mingus expressed his to desire to "never have to play in night clubs again," describing the environment as "not conducive to good creation." From Mingus's point of view, the noise created by an inattentive audience was a symptom of a much greater institutional problem within the jazz economy:

> I'll tell you where I'd like more of *my* future work to be. I'd like some Governmental agency to let me take my band out in the streets during the summer so that I could play in the parks or on the back of trucks for kids, old people, anyone. In delinquent neighborhoods in the North. All through the South. Anywhere. I'd like to see the Government pay me and other bands who'd like to play for the people. I'm not concerned with the promoters who want to make money for themselves out of jazz. I'd much rather play for kids.[11]

Mingus imagines a world in which the exchange between audience and musician happens without the club owners, promoters, managers, and other commercial brokers. He rejects the nightclub economy in favor of bringing jazz into disenfranchised communities for free and as a means of making intergenerational connection. His view of governmental involvement also sits in direct opposition to the US State Department, which was concerned only with jazz's capacity to serve as propaganda for the state. Significantly, Mingus's comments tacitly recognize that musical and cultural institutions determine the limits and possibilities of jazz performance. Once again, performance is shown to be entwined with its political surroundings.

Throughout his career, Mingus consistently attempted to reimagine the unequal power structures of the jazz industry.[12] As a young musician in Los Angeles, he spoke openly about the injustices and inequities that musicians of color faced. He participated in the early efforts to desegregate the musician unions through the merger of Local 47 (white and Latinx musicians) with Local 767 (African Americans).[13] Around the time that he moved to New York City, he also began campaigning for more equal representation in the jazz press. After his first writings—a reprint of a letter to Ralph Gleason—appeared in a June 1951 issue of *Down Beat*, Mingus regularly sought publication in trade magazines. He also regularly wrote his own liner notes. Both were forms of discursive representation not usually afforded to jazz musicians.[14] Onstage, he worked to establish several cooperative ensembles. This included the Jazz Composers Workshop in 1955 (a name he later adopted for his own groups) and the Jazz Artists Guild, which emerged from an anti-festival he co-organized in 1960 to protest the Newport Jazz Festival's treatment of African American musicians.[15] In 1959 Mingus even wrote to President Eisenhower about musician unemployment benefits and police corruption on the nightclub scene.[16] Through what Nichole Rustin-Paschal aptly describes as a "healthy disregard of white privilege in jazz culture," Mingus showed a level of institutional thinking that strove to resettle how economic and cultural ownership functioned within the industry.[17]

As part of his political activism to gain greater control over his musical labor and intellectual property, Mingus cofounded Debut Records in 1952 with his wife, Celia. Her initial $600 investment actually exceeded Charles's $500; drummer Max Roach became a third co-owner not long after.[18] Fittingly, Charles obtained his share of the capital through institutional means as well: New York State awarded him $500 after he successfully filed a grievance against the New York City musicians' union (Local 802) for wrongful termination from the Red Norvo trio.[19] Shortly after the formal incorporation of Debut in May 1952, Mingus also established Chaz Mar Inc., a publishing company that allowed him to collect any associated royalties.[20] Although Debut was active only from 1952 to 1957, Mingus continued to maintain the publishing rights to his music.[21]

Mingus's activities can be understood in a larger context through what Salim Washington describes as the "perpetual avant-garde" of jazz. Washington argues that the push in the 1980s and 1990s to establish the boundaries of an official jazz canon reduced the jazz avant-garde into a musical style rather than a set of cultural practices that imagined a more equitable future through music. He suggests a return to the notion of the perpetual avant-garde, "a certain attitude towards constant innovation, motivated in part by the desire for greater justice in the world."[22] Washington presupposes that the art form known as jazz describes the lived experience of African

Americans within a system of white supremacy that discredits their political agency and limits expressive possibilities. By striving to recapture the avant-garde from a narrowly defined history that reifies the "heroic" improviser, Washington reappropriates the term as a means of understanding musical praxis in a broader cultural context. Mingus is his primary example.

Washington's notion of the perpetual avant-garde makes it possible to consider Mingus's many professional activities as productively interconnected. As a bassist, composer, and businessman, Mingus constantly engaged in ideological battles surrounding the cultural production of jazz and continually strove to upset the political status quo. As Nichole Rustin-Paschal observes, a key aspect of this work was to adapt and redefine the figure of the Black jazzman—the racialized and gendered performance of jazz authority, artistry, and authenticity—without concern for the white men who held power within the jazz industry.[23] By lecturing his (often majority-white) audiences on their behavior, he critiqued the working conditions of jazz musicians. He expressed his intellectual and artistic authority through his public writing, including his liner notes. With pieces named "Haitian Fight Song," "Pithecanthropus Erectus," "Prayer for Passive Resistance," and "Original Faubus Fables," he unapologetically addressed the racial inequalities facing mid-century African Americans. In 1955 he again turned to the legal system by filing a claim against RCA Victor's use of Thad Jones, who was then exclusively contracted to Debut. The settlement was not a specified dollar amount, but a recording session: Mingus recorded what became *Tijuana Moods* for RCA Victor in 1957.[24] From this perspective, Mingus's record-player protest becomes not only a structural critique of the jazz industry but also one enactment of the perpetual avant-garde among many.

Mingus understood that institutional problems could not be solved through song titles and onstage actions alone. Part of his answer was to establish a record label within the inarguably oppressive system of the 1950s jazz industry, in what Scott Saul has convincingly described as Mingus's entrepreneurial activism.[25] Taking cues from both Saul and Washington, I find it productive to consider Mingus's activities with Debut as *avant-garde entrepreneurialism*. The avant-garde and entrepreneurship have much in common. Both push at accepted norms through creative means. Both attempt to rethink institutions, modes of circulation, and social models by assuming risk—artistic, economic, or a combination. And both demand collective action. In the age of mechanical reproduction, Black record making has often taken place where the avant-garde and entrepreneurship intersect. Black entrepreneurialism in the record business should thus be understood as part of the perpetual avant-garde: figures such as W. C. Handy, Harry Pace, Duke Ellington, Henry Glover, Ewart Abner, J. Mayo Williams, and Dizzy Gillespie each confronted the aesthetic, economic, and legal structures of white supremacy by acquiring capital and gaining control over the modes of production. These Black record makers were also part of a larger network of Black entrepreneurs within the entertainment industry who owned clubs, restaurants, theaters, dance halls, record stores, film-production companies, and so on.[26] As part of this trajectory within jazz, Debut attempted to create a more equitable world for jazz musicians by reimagining the business of jazz. At its core, the company embraced an entrepreneurial spirit that approached record making as a radical act.

Avant-garde entrepreneurialism is made possible only through collaboration. In jazz it often required both intra- and interracial collaboration. For example, even though Charles Mingus determined the musical direction of Debut, it was Celia Mingus who made the young label into a viable business. In many respects, Celia shaped Debut as much as, if not more than, Charles. As a record maker, Celia became many things: investor, bookkeeper, graphic designer, marketing agent, liner-note author, photographer, secretary, and negotiator. Again, I turn to the work of Rustin-Paschal, who argues that Celia sustained the label by assuming the guise of the jazzman: a performance of masculinity that women strategically adopted as a means of finding authority and agency within the male-dominated jazz ecosystem.[27] It was Celia's embrace of the jazzman persona that allowed her to cultivate the interpersonal relationships among those whom Debut depended on for its success. She took a hard line against distributors who were late on their payments, yet she also generously wrote letters to fans and disc jockeys all over the country. She befriended music critics, created regional distribution strategies, and made deals with various companies to press and ship Debut's inventory.[28] Like other record makers who were women—including Nicole Barclay (Blue Star and Barclay Records), Miriam Bienstock (Atlantic), and Vivian Carter (Vee-Jay)—Celia was tenacious, generous, calculating, and fearless.[29] In short, she was an avant-garde entrepreneur.

For a Black jazzman like Mingus, Debut was a means of claiming economic and cultural power through record making. His relentless approach to record production became a key aspect of this work. Throughout Debut's existence, Mingus embraced experimental uses of overdubbing, splicing, and other forms of editing.[30] His use of these production tools remained remarkably consistent even as his compositional style dramatically shifted from one based around notions of musical universals—creating music not bound by genre conventions—toward a more overt embrace of Black musical aesthetics such as swing, blues, and gospel.[31]

Placed within the wider context of Mingus's professional activities, such creative editing must be understood as a challenge to the accepted norms of what jazz sounded like on record. Overdubs, splices, and other edits were not only solutions to a musical problem but also statements of artistic authority and a way to take control over the means of production. Through creative record making, the studio became another way for Mingus to engage with the cultural politics and political economies of jazz performance.

Consider Mingus's use of overdubbing on *The Quintet: Jazz at Massey Hall*, a 1956 Debut LP featuring luminaries Dizzy Gillespie, Charlie Parker, Bud Powell, Max Roach, and Charles Mingus. Two basses can be heard during Mingus's solo on "All the Things You Are," creating a ghostly solo-turned-duet—the future Mingus heard in the foreground plays with and against the quieter past Mingus heard in the background. By most accounts, Mingus believed that his bass levels were too quiet in the overall mix, so he rerecorded himself onto the concert tapes sometime later. Overdubbed bass lines can be heard on all six tracks on the LP, including "Perdido," "Salt Peanuts," "Wee," "Hot House," and "A Night in Tunisia."[32] Mingus's technological reimaginings were not something that absolutely had to be done. In fact, Debut had already issued the same performance in 1953 on a 10-inch LP without these "reparative" ghostly overdubs.[33]

Mingus's creative additions were not unique, however. One of Debut's aforementioned 10-inch LPs, *Jazz at Massey Hall, vol. 2*, which featured Bud Powell, included "Bass-ically Speaking," a track not recorded during the famed concert but rather in the studio sometime later in 1953—the audience applause heard on the recording was later spliced onto the end of the track.[34] Although this type of studio production was relatively rare for jazz at this time, Mingus was already experimenting with such techniques in other contexts. During a December 1954 session for the Period label, Mingus recorded both piano and bass parts on "Four Hands" and "What Is This Thing Called Love?"[35] At the end of 1955, Mingus similarly overdubbed a second bass part onto "Percussion Discussion," a spontaneous duet with Max Roach recorded at the Café Bohemia. This duet-turned-trio appeared on *Mingus at the Bohemia*, a Debut LP from 1956.[36] Two years earlier, Mingus played on a 1953 recording session led by Teo Macero, the eventual producer of *Mingus Ah Um*. During the session, Macero overdubbed five saxophone lines to create "Explorations." Mingus did not play on the track, but his record company paid for and released it.[37]

Most of Mingus's studio work in the 1950s could be described as technical rather than creative, as biographer Brian Priestley does.[38] Yet by thinking about these activities as a matter of capital, capacity, and control, the terrain immediately shifts. Mingus's position at Debut enabled him to imagine the sonic possibilities afforded by studio technology. It is not coincidental that his most invasive uses of the studio technology occur on two 12-inch LPs issued by Debut in 1956: *Mingus at the Bohemia* and *The Quintet: Jazz at Massey Hall*. (Both happen to be live recordings.) The specialized equipment and technical expertise needed to use it made studio time incredibly expensive. Mingus nevertheless chose to spend precious resources on editing and overdubbing.[39] His ownership of Debut translated directly into control over the artistic direction of the session and the labor necessary to enact that vision. From this perspective, bass overdubs are not simply solutions to a technical problem but rather a form of avant-garde entrepreneurialism.

Another kind of creative artistic practice from this period further accentuates the links among studio production, music making, and entrepreneurialism. Mingus's first attempts at overdubbing began in the summer of 1953, about a year after the incorporation of Debut, and continued through the label's most active time, 1954 to 1957.[40] During this same period, Mingus began experimenting compositionally by superimposing standards onto one another. At an October 31, 1954, recording session, Mingus's arrangement of "Tea for Two" used the melodies of "Body and Soul," "Perdido," and "Prisoner of Love" in counterpoint. The surviving parts include an additional subtitle written in pencil: "Study in Lines." This view is echoed in the liner notes, where Mingus writes that this piece was "written to show that it is easy to listen to several lines at once—especially in this case where all the lines are already familiar to the listener." He goes on: "The results are simply counterpoint-one, -two, -three, and -four."[41] The same ensemble also recorded a separate version of "Body and Soul" that included John LaPorta playing "They Can't Take That Away from Me" as a countermelody.[42] During a December 1955 stint at the Café Bohemia, Mingus performed two similar arrangements: "Septemberly" was an amalgamation of "September in the Rain" and "Tenderly"; and "All the Things You C#" combined "All the Things You Are" with Sergei Rachmaninoff's Prelude in C#

Minor and Claude Debussy's "Clair de Lune."[43] Relatedly, his July 1957 version of "Laura" also included the melody of "Tea for Two" in counterpoint.[44]

Mingus's experimental superimposition of standards can be understood as an expression of his musical pluralism that transformed American Song Book standards through the polyphonic aesthetics of Western European classical music. From this point of view, Mingus derived his fugal subjects—and his counterpoint more generally—through the logic of jazz praxis. Indeed, this reading fits comfortably into the most accepted view of Mingus's musical activities of the early to mid-1950s: he composed score-based music that emphasized improvisational complexity; he operated under a belief in the universality of music separate and apart from audience or critical reception; he sought a synthesis of traditions in order to imagine a musical world in which jazz could be valued alongside all other musics.[45] Yet given the time line's overlap with Mingus's experiments in the studio, such experimental counterpoint might be rethought of as an extension of his technological practice—a kind of acoustic overdubbing. Both approaches require a form of imbricated sonic knowledge, the kind of musical imagination well suited to a composer like Mingus. And both are made possible through creatively recombining the musical, technological, or entrepreneurial. In short, Mingus's overdubs—those both acoustic and technological—were radical acts of jazz composition that reimagined the possibilities of jazz praxis.

In at least one instance, Mingus combined arranged superimposition and overdub techniques.[46] For the 1954 LP *Jazzical Moods*, he recorded a version of "What Is This Thing Called Love?" that included both "Hot House" and "Woody'n You" in counterpoint. During John LaPorta's alto saxophone solo, Mingus can be heard playing both piano and bass, the latter overdubbed sometime after. Although the combination of acoustic and technological techniques was uncommon, "What Is This Thing Called Love?" nevertheless demonstrates the close proximity of Mingus's techniques.[47] After all, Mingus's acoustic overdubbing of standards occurred at many of the same sessions in which he also used studio overdubbing.

Acoustic overdubbing needed only an arranger's touch. Studio overdubbing necessitated equipment that was not always accessible to musicians. Mingus did both, which required control over both composition and the record-making process. Mingus acquired such control by cofounding his own record company. As such, Mingus's entrepreneurship was not only about business acumen but also about imagining different musical possibilities onstage and in the studio. Debut thus allowed him to translate record making into cultural capital. It was an expression of Mingus's avant-garde entrepreneurialism.

Autobiography in Jazz

November 30, 1953, marked pianist Paul Bley's first recording session as a leader. Trying to squeeze in one last song at the end of his session for Debut, Bley had to balance an impatient engineer with a bass player, Charles Mingus, who needed further harmonic instructions for the AABA tune. As Bley narrates the chord changes to the bridge, singing to indicate how the harmony fits with the melody, the engineer impatiently interrupts: "Let's go!" (In response, one of the musicians—Mingus or Art Blakey—mutters something like "Somebody's pissed off.") Bley continues to sing his instructions, but the engineer persists: "Go! Go! I'm waiting." Through the chaos, Bley instructs "watch me" and counts off the tune with a few finger snaps. The trio launches into its rendition of "Santa Claus Is Coming to Town" as if they had known what to do all along.

To listeners who know Bley's future career arc, the brazenly commercial choice of "Santa Claus Is Coming to Town" stands out. Yet this song selection perfectly encapsulates the carefully balanced approach taken by Debut Records at the time: recording a relatively unknown musician with a propensity toward experimental jazz yet performing a commercial song in a straight-ahead bebop style. Given the end-of-the-year timing, a recording of "Santa Claus" might have had the potential to generate seasonal revenue for the fledgling label. Or perhaps it was simply ironic. In any case, the session was clearly done on a budget, which explains both the impatient engineer as well as the poor sound quality, even by 1953 standards. The balance of bebop, commercialism, and experimentation would equally apply to any number of sessions in Debut's early years.[48] Despite its lack of finances, or perhaps because of them, the label went out of its way to give rising musicians like Bley, Kenny Dorham, Thad Jones, Sam Most, John LaPorta, and Teo Macero their first opportunities to record under their own names.[49]

The November 30 session resulted in *Introducing Paul Bley*, a 10-inch LP issued in 1954. However, the trio's rendition of "Santa Claus," complete with studio chatter, did not appear until two years later, when Debut issued it on the A side of a 1956 promotional LP titled *Autobiography in Jazz*. Self-described as Debut's "own story" and released in celebration of the label's third anniversary, the LP featured various artists across the label's current catalog.[50] The disc appeared while Debut, much like the rest of the industry, was transitioning to the larger LP format.[51] The extra space allowed the label to issue fourteen tracks featuring thirty-five musicians across a wide variety of styles. "Orientation," "I've Got You," and "Kai's Day" are straight bebop. "Extrasensory Perception" presents a post-bebop experimentation similar to that of Lennie Tristano, who happened to serve as the date's recording engineer. The performance of "Notes to You" pays homage to Benny Goodman, while "Makin' Whoopee" and "Portrait" feature larger ensembles with strings and other orchestral instruments. Like "Santa Claus Is Coming to Town," the renditions of "Paris in Blue" and "Bebopper" aim toward the popular-music market. As if hinting at Mingus's future trajectory, "Eclipse" directly addresses the subject of interracial love in a Tin Pan Alley–like style and form. "Drum Conversation," a four-minute drum solo by Max Roach, attempts to capture improvisation in an experimental form. Mingus's artistic imprint was clearly a focus of the record: the bassist appears as a performer on nine of the fourteen tracks; four of the compositions are his as well. As the liner notes state, this LP "presents, at a price easily afforded [$1.98], a variety of artists and selections that will be pleasing to every modern jazz lover."[52]

The recording studio remains an uncredited contributor to *Autobiography in Jazz*, despite liner notes that detail personnel, session dates, and musical details. A splice in the middle of "Extrasensory Perception" merges two separate takes together. A studio-created fade-out at the end of "Medley"—a rendition of "You Go to My Head"—masks a modulation meant to lead into the second part of the medley that never comes. Like the twelve seconds of chaotic studio chatter on Bley's "Santa Claus," the audience sounds from the Putnam Central Club heard on "Kai's Day" create the impression of social informality. "Drum Conversation" includes a faked onstage announcement to introduce Max Roach. "Portrait" features a lengthy solo that Thad Jones overdubbed onto an orchestral track recorded a week earlier. Overall, pronounced edits and additions made in postproduction are consistently present through the wide variety of musical styles featured on the LP.

Featuring music recorded between April 1952 and September 1955, *Autobiography in Jazz* contains three-and-a-half years of experimental record making in the early LP era. Mingus was, as the liner notes state, the "masterminded" artistic director of the label who oversaw the recording and production. This 1956 LP thus encapsulates his approach toward the recording studio as not simply a place to make records but also as a location for artistry. After all, Debut's core mission was to have control over the music and its sonic reproductions, merging artistic process with commercial product. Generating musician-owned capital in the record business necessitated learning how to leverage the studio and its capabilities toward that end. As such, *Autobiography in Jazz* provides a window into how Mingus's trajectory as a producer developed alongside his development as a composer and bandleader.

"Extrasensory Perception" is one of several tracks on *Autobiography in Jazz* that document how Mingus's approach to record making progressed. The piece unfolds over three highly contrapuntal minutes (four times through the thirty-two-measure form). The first two choruses feature saxophonist Lee Konitz's melodic interpretation and his solo, which was supposedly written out by Mingus in the studio at the last minute.[53] The rhythm section and the bowed counterpoint of NBC symphony cellist George Koutzen accompanied both melody and solo. The thirty-two-measure solo by Mingus that follows provides contrast. Pianist Phyllis Pinkerton's improvisation and Konitz's return of the melody split the final chorus. Lennie Tristano's influence on the music is clear, beyond his presence as the recording engineer. The dense, contrapuntal interplay among the saxophone, bass, cello, and straight-ahead bebop rhythm section has all the markings of Tristano's early-1950s style. Konitz, Pinkerton, and drummer Al Levitt were well-known Tristano disciples.[54]

A splice occurs somewhere near the end of Mingus's bass solo, fusing the final chorus of an alternate take onto the master.[55] It is not entirely clear why the splice was made, although it was likely done to fix some minor issues at the end of the track. The unedited master included an ending that is a bit sloppy, with Levitt's drum solo extending well past the rest of the ensemble's cutoff. The issued master replaces the final chorus with a more focused piano solo and a simultaneously articulated ending.

"Extrasensory Perception" reveals how Debut both experimented with and relied on existing industry structures in terms of format, recording technique, and manufacturing. The April 12, 1952, session that produced the track was Debut's first official recording date.[56] Like the rest of Debut's early sides, the less-than-three-minute track was specifically made for the 78-rpm format; in fact, "Extrasensory Perception" appeared on one of only three 78-rpm records the label issued in 1952.[57] The format helps explain the track's abbreviated length, even as the splice discloses the presence of the Ampex tape machine installed in Tristano's studio, which was used for the date.[58] Debut's access to the most modern technology was much more limited than that of the major labels. The use of this musician-owned studio testifies to how the co-owners at Debut made use of a professional network formed around those with a similar entrepreneurial spirit. Even so, Debut had to offload certain steps in the record-making process; like other independent labels, the firm used RCA Victor to manufacture its records.[59] The splice on "Extrasensory Perception" thus materializes out of an overlapping web of commercial enterprise. As part of Debut's first recording session, the track also lets slip how early the label embraced sonic mediation as an inherent part of the record-making process.

Autobiography in Jazz contains several other instances of invasive editing like the splice on "Extrasensory Perception." The last seven-and-a-half minutes of the B side—tracks 13 and 14—are two unreleased recordings from the Massey Hall concert with Parker, Gillespie, Mingus, Roach, and Powell mentioned above. "Drum Conversation (Part 2)," a four-minute solo improvisation by Max Roach, includes announcements at both the start and end of the track.[60] The introductory remarks, surreptitiously made in the studio and later attached onto the recording, sound remarkably different from any other announcements from the concert. Loud clicks at the start give way to a squeezed and distant voice, as if recording in a tin can. The audible change in tape hiss reveals the splice. A few shouts from the Massey Hall audience and Roach's opening statement quickly follow. The enthusiastic applause at the solo's end leads to an announcement by the Massey Hall emcee: "Max Roach [*applause*]. I'm going to call the trio back on here now, if they care to join us. Charlie Mingus of course, on bass. Here he is [*applause*]. Bud Powell on piano. Bud [*applause*]." This oration introduces the trio's rendition of "I've Got You under My Skin."

The announcements, applause, and performance imply a sequential listening experience, one that runs counter to the May 15, 1953, concert. According to most sources, "Drum Conversation" opened the second set, followed by seven other selections played by the Roach, Powell, and Mingus trio. "Cherokee" immediately followed Roach's solo, and "I've Got You under My Skin" closed out the trio's portion of the concert.[61] The splices and added announcement on these two tracks collapse the concert's real-time experience into a false continuity on record.

By the time Debut issued *Autobiography in Jazz*, the label had already issued several LPs featuring carefully edited versions of the Massey Hall concert (as mentioned above). Editing notes in the Debut archives from June 1953 reveal numerous directions to lift levels during particular solos, to fade in (or out) at specific moments, or how to reorganize the original tapes to fit the material onto two 10-inch LPs.[62] Some of the editing, including the noticeable splices at the beginnings and endings of many tracks, is clearly audible. The quintet's version of "Wee," issued on *Jazz at Massey Hall, vol. 3* (1954), includes an appended "thank you" from Gillespie that clearly interrupts the lingering applause (6:45).[63] Both A-side tracks on *Jazz at Massey Hall, vol. 1* (1953) include similar edits. At the end of "Perdido," spliced-in applause abruptly interrupts the natural decay of the bass and drums (8:11).[64] The second cut begins with a few infamous remarks by Parker: "At this time we would like to play a tune that was composed by my worthy constituent, Mr. Dizzy Gillespie, in the year of 1942. We sincerely hope you do enjoy 'Salt Peanuts.'" The voluminous analysis of this moment as a sign of tension (or not) between the two artists has overshadowed the presence of a difficult-to-miss splice between "1942" and "we sincerely hope" of Parker's comments (0:08).[65] In order to fit the material onto the 10-inch format, this track was also split between the A and B sides.

The Massey Hall LPs include other moments of invasive editing that change the performance more dramatically. As described above, *Jazz at Massey Hall, vol. 2* (1953) includes a studio track called "Bass-ically Speaking" made to sound live—the spliced-in applause added in postproduction clearly cuts short the cymbal shimmer at the end (3:52).[66] The aforementioned renditions of "Wee" and "Perdido" each feature truncated melodic statements as well: "Wee" excludes one of the A sections at the top of the AABA form; the opening melody of "Perdido" is only eight measures rather than the standard thirty-two. Both tracks can be heard in full on subsequent CD reissues of the Massey Hall concert, revealing these omissions to be the result of editing in postproduction and not an abbreviated performance.[67] And Mingus, of course, later overdubbed bass parts to several tracks, including "Perdido," "Salt Peanuts," "All the Things You Are," and "52nd Street Theme."

If the splice on "Extrasensory Perception" demonstrates invasive editing to be part of Debut's foundational ethos, the postproduction on these Massey Hall recordings documents how these practices persisted through the label's activities in the early 1950s. Such experiments coincided with the label's trials with and adoption of the LP format. Between 1952 and 1954, the firm issued its output across eleven 78s, two EPs, and twelve 10-inch LPs.[68] Debut issued the Massey Hall material on three LPs as numbers two, three, and four in the label's 10-inch catalog, making them some of the label's earliest LPs.⁶⁹ As Debut transitioned to 12-inch discs in 1956—the same year as *Autobiography in Jazz*—the firm reissued most of the Massey Hall material on the larger format. In order to do so, Mingus felt that he needed to "clean up the tapes before remastering them," as he wrote to Norman Granz in June 1956.⁷⁰ By "cleaning up," Mingus meant increasing the degree of studio mediation. *The Quintet: Jazz at Massey Hall*, as the 12-inch LP was retitled, included Mingus's overdubbed bass parts, even on previously edited tracks like "Perdido" and "Salt Peanuts." This additional studio work included at least ten hours of additional editing done by Audiosonic Recording Company between June and October 1956.⁷¹ Through these additional edits and overdubs, the 12-inch LP thus presented a doubled reimagining of the Massey Hall concert.

A similar reimagining of the live moment can be heard on *Mingus at the Bohemia*, a 12-inch LP initially recorded at the Café Bohemia on December 23, 1955, and released about a year later. Issued in close proximity to *The Quintet: Jazz at Massey Hall*, the Café Bohemia LP shares more than a similar catalog number (DEB-124 and DEB-123, respectively). "Percussion Discussion," the closing track on its A side, is an impromptu duet between Mingus and Roach that echoes and expands on "Drum Conversation" from Massey Hall. And like the Massey Hall tapes, "Percussion Discussion" features a second bass part overdubbed onto the track at a later date.⁷² Mingus's duet-turned-trio is also accompanied by the sounds the club: applause, conversation, and a regularly occurring squeak that possibly originates from Roach's drum kit. Such technological intervention situated within the sociality of the nightclub can also be heard at the end of "Septemberly," where an audible splice abruptly interrupts the tapering musical ending to insert audience applause (6:55). Even as the label became among the first independent firms to issued live recordings from places like Massey Hall, Putnam Central Club, and Café Bohemia, Debut's output consistently featured splicing and overdubbing on those same recordings. The hybrid nature of these LPs, where the studio mediates the live moment, reveals how Debut embraced the technological aspect of record making.

"Portrait," the opening B-side track on *Autobiography in Jazz*, includes a similar mixture of studio techniques. Recorded a month before the Bohemia date, "Portrait" came together across two sessions in September 1955: the first to record the orchestra parts, the second to record Thad Jones, the featured soloist. The arrangement combines a standard jazz rhythm section with a heavily arranged chamber ensemble of strings, harp, woodwinds, and brass. Jones improvises through the melody in the legacy of *Charlie Parker with Strings*, his purely jazz style floating over the modernist orchestration.[73] The weighty dissonance of the arrangement on "Portrait" masks some of the particulars, but there appear to be two splices at the end of the form—around 2:21 and 2:35—when the brass and winds abruptly cut into the held notes of the strings. (However, the splices do keep the original arrangement intact.[74]) Jones's playing remains fluid and unbroken throughout, implying that he overdubbed his part onto an already edited ensemble track.

Musically, the merger of jazz and classical aesthetics on "Portrait" fit into Debut's varied stylistic approach, which ranged from Tin Pan Alley vocal tunes to experimental compositions.[75] The attempt to combine the prestige of classical and the experimentalism of bebop with elements of popular song allowed Debut's co-owners to correct two overarching problems they had with the music business: even as record executives required Black jazz musicians to put commercial considerations over artistic ones, those same musicians rarely received any profits arising from those artistic choices.[76] So if we understand Debut as an experiment in musician-centric capital, then the splicing and overdubbing sown through its catalog must also be considered part of the label's entrepreneurial pursuits for control over the musical product. The production on "Portrait" not only exemplifies Debut's overall approach to record making but also serves as a powerful indicator of how much control the label had over every aspect of sound.

By listening to the historical trajectories of record making, *Autobiography in Jazz* becomes more than Debut's "own story as told by many of the recording artists," as the liner notes state. From the splice on "Extrasensory Perception" to the overdubbed trumpet on "Portrait," the sounds on *Autobiography in Jazz* contain more than point-to-point inscription of real-time performances. Through the splice, it becomes possible to hear how the past and present punctuate one another, or what Rebecca Schneider describes as the "syncopated time" of performance.[77] Syncopation as a central analytic to describe the multi-temporality of performance resonates with jazz beyond its musical allusion. Jazz performance and jazz discourse constantly invoke the past, moving with or against it in various ways. For example, Charlie Parker does not appear on *Autobiography in Jazz*, yet he is present nonetheless. The liner notes mention his name several times; musically, he is invoked constantly, especially in the improvisational language of the musicians. From this point of view, the splice, cut, and overdub similarly testify to how jazz performance can be syncopated against other times. By listening through these examples, the moment of performance emerges as only one part of the creative process. Control over the studio meant a certain degree of control over the sounds of performance. Through the splice, the sonic and political merge.

Autobiography in Jazz contains a tangled history of format and postproduction. From this history, Mingus's "reparative" work in the studio becomes more than simply a question about fidelity to an original performance.[78] Mingus's studio creativity was not singular, but rather a pervasive form of experimentation using a variety of techniques and occurring over several years of record making. As a record producer, Mingus had the ability to purposefully compress and recombine spontaneous moments of musical performance. Debut's catalog is thus an implicit recognition that records are not documents of truth but inherently mediated experiences of listening.

The Plasticity of Performance

On September 18, 1953, trombonists J. J. Johnson, Kai Winding, Bennie Green, and Willie Dennis recorded for Debut at the Putnam Central, a club located in the Bedford-Stuyvesant neighborhood of Brooklyn. The session featured Mingus's newly formed Jazz Workshop, a loose collection of musicians who regularly gathered to play through new compositions and arrangements. During such sessions, the music was always a work in progress. For example, the trombonists' version of "Yesterdays" includes three piano introductions by John Lewis. Johnson interrupts the first two in order to get the tempo where he wants it (a touch faster). Before the third and final attempt, Johnson can be heard snapping his fingers and humming the melody as others chat idly in the background (0:23). Lewis's third attempt sticks. The other members layer into a lengthy version of the Jerome Kern standard.

The false starts and re-corrections appear in full on *Jazz Workshop, vol. 1, Trombone Rapport*, a 10-inch LP issued in 1954.[79] Debut's Putnam Central LP predates most of the on-location records made by Blue Note, Prestige, and Riverside (see chapter 5). Like most of those LPs, Rudy Van Gelder was trusted to work the recording console. As the LP's liner notes make clear, the main objective of the recording was to capture the work-in-progress atmosphere of the performance:

> In the summer of 1953, a Jazz Workshop was organized under the auspices of the Putnam Central Club in Brooklyn by its Manager Johnny

Parros in collaboration with Charles Mingus. The purpose of the workshop was to enable various jazz musicians to get together and to play new compositions written by the musicians themselves and other young composers. Some of the musicians to appear during the summer were Max Roach, Thelonius [sic] Monk, Art Blakey, Horace Silvers [sic] and many others. The musicians played for listening and dancing and had the cooperation of the audience in rehearsing new compositions prior to presenting them in final form. Arrangements were also made for several of the Workshop sessions to be recorded in this informal atmosphere. One such session was recorded by Debut Records and in this album we hear part of the results obtained from the assembling of four top jazz trombonists: J. J. Johnson, Kai Winding, Bennie Green, and Willie Dennis, aided and abetted by John Lewis on piano, Charles Mingus, bass, and Arthur Taylor, drums.

This first volume is devoted to the "jamming" portion of this particular Workshop presentation and attempts to reproduce the Workshop in action with the relaxed attitude of a session rather than the tension often present in the straight studio recording. YESTERDAYS carries out this idea by showing what actually happens. It begins, is stopped by J. J. who prefers a slightly faster tempo and sings a few bars so that everyone has the beat, and they begin again.[80]

As the club becomes a fluid, "informal" environment to work through musical ideas, the audience becomes another interlocutor. Accordingly, musical (and entrepreneurial) collaboration takes a prominent role in the creative process. The Jazz Workshop model rejects the notion of the heroic musical figure working in isolated struggle. Here, live performance is not the destination, but where some of the most exciting musical innovation occurs en route to a piece's "final form." Even as the bandstand becomes the workshop—that is, a celebrated place to experiment—the process of recording mediates the musical work. The double-natured essence of record making surfaces once again: the recorded informality of "Yesterdays" allows many listeners to hear the music making "in action" yet also transforms this performance into a reproducible commodity.

The Jazz Workshop soon became the hinge that Mingus's avant-garde entrepreneurship swung around. Most notably, it remained the name of his working group well into the 1960s.[81] Mingus also used the name for the second iteration of his publishing company—Jazz Workshop, Inc.—in addition to two short-lived record companies: the first released two bootleg recordings by Charlie Parker in 1957; the second issued records through mail order beginning in 1964. Notably, both labels transformed live performances into LPs.[82] The continual syncopation of the live and mediated makes it impossible to separate the Jazz Workshop—as both name and concept—from Mingus's activities as a record maker.

Along this historical trajectory, the Putnam Central Club was essential to the Jazz Workshop. The club had, after all, supported Debut in a literal sense. Not only did the fledgling record label record there on occasion, but Roach's mid-1950s studio sat right above the venue. Mingus and Roach ran rehearsals in the space and used one of the building's rooms for Debut-related storage.[83] As a result, the club became a narrative touchstone that appears on Mingus's records throughout the 1950s. The liner notes to *Autobiography in Jazz*, which included the never-released "Kai's Day" from the *Trombone Rapport* session, state that "the Jazz Workshop series materialized from an idea conceived by Charles Mingus while he was running sessions at Putnam Central Club in Brooklyn during the summer of 1953."[84] *Mingus Ah Um* repeats this story verbatim, closely echoing the notes to *Trombone Rapport*: "By 1953 [Mingus] had organized a series of jazz workshop concerts at the Putnam Central Club in Brooklyn. Some of the musicians who participated in the early days were Max Roach, Thelonious Monk, Horace Silver, Art Blakey, and the audience, who also had a hand in the working out of new compositions and arrangements."[85] This document once again signals how the sociality of the performance space, and especially the audience, materially affects the final outcome of the creative process.

With the Jazz Workshop, Mingus worked with, in, and around the moment of performance. This was true in 1953 as much as it was in 1959. On January 16, 1959, Mingus brought the Jazz Workshop into the Nonagon Art Gallery in Manhattan. The program notes to the event emphasize how the original compositions will "allow for ample jazz improvisation by the entire group." They go on to once again invoke the audience: "The specific works to be performed, as well as their order on the program, will be contingent on the rapport between performers and audience, and, subsequently, are not being listed in advance. In a sense, both the performers and the audience will help shape the program."[86] Whitney Balliett, the jazz critic for the *New Yorker*, gave a sense of how that sentiment translated into performance: "The concert was recorded on the spot, and although several selections were interrupted for brief retakes and admonitions by Mingus to his musicians (to his drummer: 'Don't get so fancy. This is my solo, man'), these diversions only accentuated the general vibrancy of the evening."[87] The stops and starts again echo the Putnam Central sessions, where the live moment was always a place of experimentation. In Balliett's words, a broken-down performance is not an embarrassing mistake but a "retake." Mingus's interruptions were not a lack of professionalism, we are told, but something that results from the recording process. The element of creative exchange between audience and ensemble, and the syncopation between performance and reproduction, were ideas born at the Putnam Central in the summer of 1953. At the Nonagon Art Gallery, it becomes possible to see how those ideas extend into 1959, less than four months before the Jazz Workshop recorded *Mingus Ah Um*.

Despite Mingus's continuity with the Jazz Workshop, his musical process went through a sweeping transformation in the mid-1950s. During this time, Mingus came to reject his previous approach of jazz uplift, striving to place jazz on an equal level with classical music. Instead, he came to closely embrace the more-traditional elements of Black expressive culture: blues, shouts, and groove.[88] As a part of this transformation, he moved from a heavily notated musical approach to a nothing-is-written mentality. As Mingus states in the liner notes to *Mingus Ah Um*, "Jazz, by its very definition, cannot be held down to written parts to be played with a feeling that goes only with blowing free." He continues to explain his process, detailing how he considers each musician's style. "In this way," he concludes, "I can keep my own compositional flavor in the pieces and yet allow the musicians more individual freedom in the creation of their group lines and solos."[89] Through this approach, Mingus found a way to musically experiment while continuing to rely on established traditions and influential figures. For instance, his compositions often point in several temporal directions at once. On *Mingus Ah Um*, four (of nine) tracks pay tribute to Charlie Parker, Duke Ellington, Lester Young, and Jelly Roll Morton: "Bird Calls," "Open Letter to Duke," "Goodbye Pork Pie Hat," and "Jelly Roll," respectively.

Here, once again, the musical merges with the mediated. The versions of each of these tracks first issued on the 1959 LP happen to feature substantial splices, proving how the moment of performance remained malleable for Mingus. Even as his music became more radical in terms of process and politics, his approach toward record making remained largely consistent. He continued to overdub, splice, and edit his recordings, despite the collapse of Debut. Without his own label, he had less control over every aspect of the record-making process, but his studio practices continued to reveal an element of Black experimentalism, just like his music. Andrew Homzy describes Mingus's mid-1950s compositional style as "plastic form": the abandonment of traditional structures (e.g., AABA song form) in order to accommodate spontaneous cues by the musicians. As Scott Saul elaborates, this approach allowed Mingus's compositions to be "elongated, compressed, or recombined," which gave more control to the musicians onstage.[90]

Such notions of recombination, elongation, and compression echo Mingus's technological practice of overdubbing in the studio. This correlation is a prompt to rethink Mingus's music making, bringing technological and musical praxis into conversation with each other. Both necessitated a combination of approaches that brought together vastly different kinds of knowledge. Both relied on collaboration and collective action. And more significantly, both syncopated time, working nonlinearly with the past in order to differently imagine what music was and how it operated in the world. That is, Mingus's approach onstage and in the studio understood the plasticity of performance.

Understanding the studio and stage as entwined, rather than divergent, activities is a prompt to revisit and reinterpret the eleven minutes of music edited out of *Mingus Ah Um*. Consider the treatment of saxophonist John Handy: of the seven musicians who appear on the record, Handy found himself edited out of the final LP more than anyone else. His entire solos were cut from "Open Letter to Duke" as well as "Boogie Stop Shuffle." Portions of his improvisations were also removed from the originally issued versions of "Bird Calls" and "Pussy Cat Dues." Some of these omissions most likely resulted from poor performances, such as the muddled solo on "Open Letter to Duke" or the lackluster improvisation on the back half of his "Bird Calls" effort.[91] But there were other perfectly fine performances cut too, like the first clarinet chorus on "Pussy Cat Dues."

One of the few instances that Handy's solo was left in full was in "Goodbye Pork Pie Hat," Mingus's immortal tribute to Lester Young. Although the second chorus of the opening melody was removed, Handy's two choruses remain intact even though he did not know the changes. According to the trombonist on the date, Jimmy Knepper, "[Mingus] never had music for the band. And we never rehearsed before recording. So John Handy didn't know the chords for 'Pork Pie Hat'; he didn't know about the flatted 10ths. I called 'em, beautiful chords. The song sounds like it's in a minor key, but it's not. But the effect of those chords was that you couldn't play a scale, you had to play blue notes. So John just played the blues, pretty much."[92]

By all accounts, Handy felt disrespected by Mingus throughout his tenure with the Jazz Workshop. Decades later, he willingly expressed frustration with Mingus's calculated sense of disruption: "Mingus was in the way so much, you couldn't play for it. The man would stop your solos... he was totally tyrannical."[93] Mingus seemed to thrive on the discomfort of his musicians, yet some saw the value of this approach. As Sy Johnson opined in 1979, "When he felt the band had become too facile, he'd destroy that ambience because he wanted us to *think* about what we were playing.... He never thought his function was to support the soloist, but rather to stir him up."[94] As Handy's comments evince, Mingus deliberately cultivated an aesthetic of spontaneity, sometimes uncomfortably so. He insisted that the musicians learn the music by ear in order to foreground individuality within a collaborative framework, even if this meant that some musical details were lost along the way.

On the stage or in the studio, the performative moment always had inspirational potential for Mingus. He often embraced the opportunity to start, stop, disrupt, and refigure the direction of a particular performance in real time. Mingus even composed this way on occasion, as the origin stories to three pieces featured on *Mingus Ah Um* attest. "Fables of Faubus," a piece initially conceptualized in 1957, found its name and subject matter after Dannie Richmond impulsively shouted the name of Orval Faubus, the Arkansas governor who had recently sent the National Guard to prevent the school integration in Little Rock. Mingus composed "Goodbye Pork Pie Hat" after the death of Lester Young in March 1959. "I was playing the Half Note Club the night we heard he died," Mingus later said, "and we went to the bandstand and played a Blues for Lester. I knew the guys would never do that again. I went home and wrote a blues the way I thought they were playing, with different types of chord changes—not just the regular blues—and it became part of the book."[95] Mingus created "Jelly Roll" in the middle of the *Mingus Ah Um* session for Columbia. The piece was not strictly a new composition but a loosely inverted version of "My Jelly Roll Soul," which Mingus had recently recorded on *Blues & Roots*. As the story goes, Mingus decided to reverse the direction of the two melodic parts on the spot. "Jelly Roll" was the result.[96]

"You could never relax with Charles," Handy told biographer Gene Santoro. "There was always unnecessary tension, unnecessary intimidation.... Worst of all was a lot of the music. I was right out of school, more academic about composition, but a lot of his stuff was raggedy, goddamn raggedy, not really put together. And that turned me off."[97] One man's "raggedy" is another's creative process. Mingus cultivated such raggedness toward an artistic end and did so with an understanding that the live moment was always something to be worked with—performance was never the end in itself. As Handy's comments allude, however, the spontaneous ethos never existed on an even playing field. Individual contributions were always in the context of Mingus's compositions, his ensembles, his gig, or his recording date. Ever the emotional jazzman, Mingus used anger as one of the ways to express his emotional honesty and sincerity.[98] With the Jazz Workshop, there was always a balance to be struck between working things out in real time and making a performance into something repeatable on record. He always sought control, even over the spontaneity inherent to his music.

Mingus's record making thus emerges as a continual oscillation between a desire for control and a desire to freely express. This observation raises more questions: Is it possible to hear the edits, overdubs, and other elements of postproduction as more than technological mediation? Is it possible to hear these moments as a form of artistic practice? Is it possible to hear this technological approach as musical expression? Is it possible to hear the splice as a remnant of a particular kind of sonic sociality?

Mingus Ah Um: Listening through the Splice

Two entrances interrupt Dannie Richmond's extended drum solo on "Bird Calls." The first occurs at the end of John Handy's solo when one of the alto saxophonists—either Handy or Shafi Hadi—mistakenly enters with a small snippet of the melody before yielding to the drums (4:24). Near the end of Richmond's improvisation, another unidentified alto saxophonist again accidentally enters with the first few notes of the melody, four measures too early (5:06). The version of "Bird Calls" issued on the 1959 version of *Mingus Ah Um* excludes both errors. Missing, too, are Richmond's entire solo and the back half of Handy's contribution. In total, three minutes of music was left on the cutting-room floor.[99] The splice that links Handy's first choruses with the return of the melody is subtle, barely detectable even when one knows to listen for it. The sudden interruption of the expected sustain in the bass and piano, and the somewhat abrupt ensemble entrance (2:06), are the only clues. But even these sonic characteristics might naturally occur in a Mingus composition.

A silent splice is an aural marker of audio professionalism. In 1959 this kind of seamless editing remained technically difficult and time-consuming. Major labels had a distinct advantage because they could afford the additional expense. Consider *Blues & Roots* (1960), which Mingus recorded for Atlantic three months before the *Mingus Ah Um* sessions with Columbia. *Blues & Roots* included a similar type of editing on four of the LP's six tracks.[100] Comparatively, these edits are much more clearly heard, although they are not nearly as disruptive as those that can be heard throughout Debut's catalog.[101] The silent splices on *Mingus Ah Um* result from the commercial record-making infrastructures at Columbia, which had the capital to purchase the specialized equipment, hire technicians with the right kinds of expertise, and staff the producers who knew where and when to make the correct edits. On *Mingus Ah Um* that producer was Teo Macero, a musician by training who had been hired at the label by George Avakian and who also had a long-standing musical relationship with Mingus (as I explore below).[102] Guided by a musician's ear, Macero chose to cut entire solos on "Jelly Roll" (Mingus), "Bird Calls" (Richmond), and "Open Letter to Duke" (Handy); edit out large portions of Parlan's and Ervin's solos on three tracks apiece; and condense the opening melodic statements on four different tracks (see table 6.1). The silence of these edits reinforces the expectation of an unbroken performance, even if that performance came into existence only for the purpose of selling records.

Despite his previous activities with Debut and his future postproduction work in the 1960s and 1970s, Mingus's involvement in the editing on *Mingus Ah Um* remains unknown and, admittedly, circumstantial.[103] Macero clearly welcomed Mingus into the control room: several photos from the May 5 recording session show Mingus surrounded by the recording equipment, smoking and laughing.[104] However, the tape editing did not take place with the musicians on the clock. Indeed, Macero's handwritten production notes, which show several iterations of the track sequence and timings, confirm that the edits for *Mingus Ah Um* took place in the nine days after the completion of the second recording session on May 12. Early drafts within these notes show plans to include only eight tracks in their unedited form and in a different order than they would appear on the issued LP (the tracks have different names as well). According to the timings next to each track name, the order of the final nine pieces was chosen before the editing took place. Macero submitted the official mastering instructions on May 21, although he revised these directions on June 2 to correct the track names, likely in consultation with Mingus.[105] Macero's production notes for Miles Davis's *Porgy and Bess* (recorded in 1958) show that he involved both Davis and Gil Evans in various parts of his editing process—he writes "sequence OK by Gil Evans" and "let Miles make decision" about a certain passage of an unknown track.[106] No such evidence, here or elsewhere, links Mingus to Macero's decision making on *Mingus Ah Um*.[107]

Listening through the splices nevertheless exposes Mingus's extensive network of record makers. For example, Mingus and Macero had an intensely musical relationship despite their dissimilar backgrounds. Macero was from New York, white, and highly educated, having both a bachelor's and a master's degree from Juilliard. Mingus was a transplant from Los Angeles, multiethnic yet nevertheless considered Black, and always somewhat sensitive about his education.[108] Even so, both musicians instinctually gravitated toward compositional methods that upset normative jazz praxis. In the early 1950s, they became founding members of the Jazz Composers Workshop, a group that attempted to integrate the harmonic and melodic sensibilities of jazz with the intricately written scores of classical music.[109] Macero would eventually appear on several of Mingus's early LPs for Debut, Savoy, and Period: "Eclipse," from an October 1953 Debut session, would end up on *Autobiography in Jazz*. In 1957 both also attended a series of jam sessions hosted by modernist composer Edgard Varèse, who was then beginning his experiments with music made solely through electronic means in the studio.[110] (Macero claimed to have patterned his own music after Varèse.) Several years before, Macero had used a series of overdubbing techniques to create a five-part solo saxophone composition called "Explorations." This piece appeared on Macero's first record as a leader, which Mingus issued on Debut in 1954.[111] Macero was also present for Mingus's own overdubbing experiments on "Four Hands" and "What Is This Thing Called Love?" (explored above).[112] They eventually went in different directions professionally, but Mingus nevertheless called on Macero in 1956 for some last-minute reparative work on *Pithecanthropus Erectus*. Though not officially on the date for Atlantic, Macero later explained: "When it was ready to come out, he [Mingus] needed somebody to overdub the squeaky notes on top that we had been associated with for a couple of years. So I went back and did that, overdubbed a lot of things for him."[113]

As Mingus's history with Macero attests, creative decisions happen in collaboration and at different levels of professional exchange. It was Macero, after all, who pushed for and eventually signed Mingus to Columbia in 1959.[114] If one listens at this collaborative register, it becomes possible to hear how *Mingus Ah Um* emerged out of a shared history of exploratory music making that simultaneously embraced the studio as a place of artistic possibilities. The careful mediation on the original LP retains the spontaneous nature of Mingus's music, regardless of who made which splice when.

Put differently, the editing on *Mingus Ah Um* is deeply musical. For example, the originally issued version of "Goodbye Pork Pie Hat" includes a single splice near the beginning of the track to remove the second melodic chorus, where the two tenor saxophones playing the melody split into unison octaves (table 6.2). With Handy's two-chorus solo left intact, the total number of melodic choruses drops from four to three, condensing the track by a little less than a minute. Potentially, any one of the melodic choruses could have been removed. As edited, however, "Goodbye Pork Pie Hat" foregrounds Handy's solo while also saving the compositional device used in the melody—moving from union to octaves—until later in the track, thus avoiding its repetition.[115] The structure remains unbroken, but the composition is effectively varied.

The rest of the edits were compositionally minded as well. Splices to condense solos always happen at structural markers and preserve a degree of balance to the tracks overall.[116] Of the eight instrumental choruses removed from "Bird Calls," two come from Parlan's solo and three each from Ervin and Handy. This condenses the track by about 1:45 of record time. "Pussy Cat Dues" contains one-chorus splices to the opening melody in addition to the piano, clarinet, and tenor sax solos. In a similar fashion, "Jelly Roll" omits single choruses of the melody, piano, and tenor saxophone. Altogether, the eleven minutes of missing material reshapes the LP, but the general form of each piece remains intact. No singular edit upsets the otherwise carefully managed equilibrium of Mingus's compositions (see tables 6.3–6.5).

Record making is an inherently messy process, but it nevertheless requires intentional action. Macero certainly could have issued *Mingus Ah Um* with seven or eight tracks instead of nine—a subpar solo or two would not have fundamentally changed anything. Because the two May 1959 record dates produced three additional tracks unissued until later, he also could have pushed to release two LPs instead of one.[117] But he did not because, I believe, he approached record production with a musician's ear and a keen awareness of the commercial landscape. "Being a musician myself," Macero later said when asked about his editing approach, "when I heard something bad, I had to cut it out. I couldn't stand to hear a bad solo. A guy plays eight

Table 6.2. "Goodbye Pork Pie Hat," comparison between 1959 LP and 2009 CD

Form	LP timing	CD timing	Details
Melody 1	0:00	0:00	2 tenor saxophones: unison
Melody 2	[cut]	0:54	2 tenor saxophones: unison in octaves
Tenor sax 1	0:54	1:49	Solo; first chorus
Tenor sax 2	1:47	2:42	Solo continues, flutter tongue for first four bars (Mingus echoes)
Melody 1	2:38	3:33	2 tenor saxophones: unison
Melody 2	3:34	4:29	2 tenor saxophones: unison in octaves
Final descent	4:25	5:20	Mingus bows, fermata in horns, change in chords beneath (E-flat minor, E major, E-flat minor); final sound is air blown through a saxophone
End	4:46	5:44	

bars or 12 bars that were bad, I'd just take it out." When discussing the role of the producer later in the same interview, he added that a producer should also make sure that a musician's "career was being taken care of with the major record company in terms of promotion and in the record clubs. You made sure that you made the right kind of records, and you were always looking out for their interests."[118] In this case, looking out for Mingus meant maintaining the sense of musical spontaneity that his music was so widely celebrated for. As a 1959 advertisement for *Mingus Ah Um* states, "Working from a musical skeleton, Charlie Mingus spontaneously makes music related to the moment. Mingus as the bass is strictly off-the-record, a jazzophile's dream."[119] The advertisement perfectly encapsulates the tension between

Table 6.3. "Bird Calls," comparison between 1959 LP and 2009 CD

Form	LP timing	CD timing	Details
Intro	0:00	0:00	Opening with free, overlapping, and descending melodies
Melody 1	0:12	0:12	18-measure form (8, 8 + 2), pedal at the tag
Melody 2	[cut]	0:25	16-measure form (8, 8), same melody but freer in B
Melody 3	[cut]	0:38	18-measure form (8, 8 + 2), same as melody 1
Tenor sax 1	[cut]	0:53	Solo begins over 18-measure form; 3 choruses
Tenor sax 2	0:27	1:35	Solo continues; 3 choruses
Piano 1	[cut]	2:17	Solo; 2 choruses
Piano 2	1:09	2:46	Solo continues; 1 chorus
Alto sax 1	1:24	2:59	Solo; 3 choruses
Alto sax 2	[cut]	3:42	Solo continues; 3 choruses
Drums	[cut]	4:24	Drum solo, alto sax false entrance at 4:24 and 5:06
Melodies 1–3	2:06	5:09	Same tripart structure as above; faint splice at 2:06 in LP version
Outro	2:48	5:50	Free and out of time, with aleatoric ascending figures and a fade-out
End	3:14	6:18	

Table 6.4. "Pussy Cat Dues," comparison between 1959 LP and 2009 CD

Chorus	Form	LP timing	CD timing	Details
Intro	4 measures	0:00	0:00	
1	Melody 1	0:14	0:14	12-bar altered blues
2	Melody 2	[cut]	0:55	Repeat
3	Trombone 1	0:55	1:37	Solo, no backgrounds
4	Trombone 2	1:38	2:17	Solo continues, backgrounds added
5	Piano 1	2:22	3:00	Solo, no backgrounds
6	Piano 2	[cut]	3:43	Solo continues, backgrounds enter tepidly
7	Clarinet 1	[cut]	4:24	Solo, no backgrounds
8	Clarinet 2	3:04	5:05	Solo continues, backgrounds added (with bass ostinato)
9	Bass 1	3:41	5:44	Solo, sparse texture in ensemble
10	Bass 2	4:20	6:23	Solo continues, backgrounds added
11	Tenor sax 1	[cut]	7:02	Solo, confusion in ensemble
12	Tenor sax 2	5:00	7:42	Solo continues, first four bars in double time, backgrounds added
13	Melody out	5:38	8:21	melody return + coda; implied double time in last four bars with an ending that recalls the opening
End		6:27	9:13	

Table 6.5. "Jelly Roll," comparison between 1959 LP and 2009 CD

Form	LP timing	CD timing	Details
Intro	0:00	0:00	1-chorus trombone solo, New Orleans 2-beat style
Melody 1	0:25	0:25	Alto sax/tenor sax descending lines, trombone ascending; trombone plays a tailgate-style rising figure in the last 4 measures
Melody 2	[cut]	0:51	Repeat
Alto sax 1	0:51	1:18	Solo, New Orleans 2-beat style continues in rhythm section
Alto sax 2	1:18	1:44	Solo continues, swing begins (in four)
Piano 1	[cut]	2:11	Single-line solo
Piano 2	1:45	2:40	Solo continues, begins with quotation of "Sonnymoon for Two" (another blues)
Tenor sax 1	[cut]	3:05	Solo, swing feel continues
Tenor sax 2	2:11	3:32	Solo continues, audible splice at 2:39 of LP version
Bass	[cut]	3:58	2-chorus solo
Melody 1	2:40	4:51	Played in same 2-beat style as opening melody
Melody 2	3:05	5:27	Repeat
Tag ending	3:33	5:46	Mingus call-and-response with himself: "I got one" [musical response], "I got two" [musical response]; bass and drums trade fills
End	4:01	6:17	

commercial record making and the idea that improvisation serves as the essential marker of jazz performance. Macero's understanding of this tension can be heard in the silent splice.

Mingus Ah Um exemplifies how specific relationships make record making possible. Yet this 1959 LP was only one node within Mingus's much more extensive professional network. Recall "Extrasensory Perception," which first appeared on *Autobiography in Jazz* but was made at Debut's inaugural recording session in 1952. On that date, Lennie Tristano makes an appearance as both recording engineer and owner of the record-making space: a studio on East 32nd Street in Manhattan that he had bought in 1951. Tristano initially planned to use the space to house a series of ventures: a record company, publishing firm, music school, and jazz club. As part of his own avant-garde entrepreneurialism, Tristano wanted to offer royalties at 5 percent for session leaders (above the usual 3 percent) and an unheard of 0.5–1 percent for sidemen (normally paid a flat rate).[120] His publishing company, jazz club, and music school never materialized, but he did use the space to teach private lessons, host jam sessions, and make the occasional record.[121] Tristano's label, Jazz Records, issued only one 45-rpm disc with two tracks: "Ju-Ju" and "Pastime," recorded in October 1951 and issued the following year. Like Mingus, Tristano desired to reimagine the jazz industry along several trajectories at once.

Tristano's East 32nd Street studio hosted many, including Charlie Parker, Leonard Bernstein, Max Roach, and Charles Mingus. "We spent a lot of time in his studio," Roach recalled about the early 1950s. "A lot of us. Mingus was involved in that as well."[122] Roach goes on to differentiate Tristano's downtown, "white" avant-garde style with Mingus and his uptown, "black" avant-garde approach.[123] Although it is clear that Roach's comments refer to musical style, there is clearly an overlap between their entrepreneurial activities. Mingus and Roach happened to have been enamored with Tristano during the time in which Debut came into being, which helps explain Tristano's enormous imprint on the label's first recording session. "Extrasensory Perception" uses his equipment, his current and former students, and his expertise behind the recording console. Eunmi Shim even posits that Tristano's failed venture with his own record company directly inspired Debut.[124] There is also the historical proximity of Tristano's experimental studio practices to Mingus's own embrace of such techniques during Debut's early years. After all, the splice and merger of two separate takes on "Extrasensory Perception" are suspiciously Tristano-like in terms of production: both "Ju-Ju" and "Pastime" feature a second piano overdubbed onto a previously recorded trio.[125] Given the rarity of these methods in 1952, Tristano seems like a likely point of contact who contributed to Mingus's technological imaginings.

Whereas Tristano may have helped inspire Debut, Celia Mingus actually ran the label's day-to-day operations. As discussed above, she gave her time and energy to the project, learning how to do multiple jobs at once and bringing a level of discipline that Charles could not. Importantly, she built relationships with disc jockeys and other professionals all over the country as a means of advancing Debut's goals. In doing so, Celia became a record executive operating in an industry where few women found success.[126] Her self-created network demonstrates her commitment to Debut as a commercial and cultural project, even as her individual agency remains ambiguous. Between Celia and Charles, it is difficult to specify who did what, when, and where. However, the why is clear: both understood that records operated economically (as a commodity), aesthetically (as sound and text), and communally (as a cultural object).[127] A key skill of record making is the ability to create relationships and sustain networks, a truth well understood by artists and producers but one that jazz historians often neglect in their analyses.

The collaborative and often messy relationship between Celia and Charles sat at Debut's center. So it is unsurprising that the effective end of the label in the middle of 1957 coincides with the collapse of their marriage.[128] Debut's untimely end testifies to Celia's fierce entrepreneurship and also highlights Charles's reliance on her as a business partner. As Rustin-Paschal persuasively argues, Charles was one of many jazz musicians who relied on the women in their lives to advance their professional activities.[129] This bit of biography helps contextualize Charles's future reliance on Diane Dorr-Dorynek, the author of the liner notes on *Mingus Ah Um*.

Charles Mingus initially hired Dorr-Dorynek in the fall of 1957 to handle the correspondences for Jazz Workshop, Inc., his new publishing company, established in April that year.[130] The often-problematic worldview of a jazzman like Mingus did not change easily. Dorr-Dorynek soon became Mingus's lover and personal assistant, eventually taking over many of Celia's tasks: writing letters and advertising copy, drafting liner notes, and typing up some of the handwritten notes that would eventually become Mingus's autobiography.[131] After the two moved in together, Dorr-Dorynek eventually invested in Debut by buying Harold Lovette's share of the company for $1,000. She also worked to lease Debut's catalog to a label in Denmark, a move that upset the other shareholders (including Celia), who were not consulted before the deal.[132] Dorr-Dorynek and Mingus ended their relationship in 1960, around the time that Columbia issued *Mingus Dynasty*. Mingus's musical portrait of her, "Diane," appeared on the LP. The description in the liner notes—credited to him, edited by her—is telling in its melancholy: "She was a painter I knew. It was written for her because I loved her at one time."[133] These liner notes were collaborative, like all of Mingus's activities from the late 1950s.

Even though he was no longer running his own label, Mingus actively sought control over elements of record making, especially the discursive framing that appeared in the liner notes. Dorr-Dorynek and Mingus coauthored the liner notes for his three LPs recorded in 1959: *Blues & Roots*, *Mingus Ah Um*, and *Mingus Dynasty*. The bylines for *Blues & Roots* and *Mingus Dynasty* both named Mingus as the author with a small addendum: "as told to Diane Dorr-Dorynek."[134] The notes to *Mingus Ah Um* are solely credited to Dorr-Dorynek, although she quotes Mingus extensively and his influence remains clear in every paragraph.

The decision to have Dorr-Dorynek author the liner notes was intentional, just like all the edits made in postproduction. Both had to be negotiated within existing industry structures and seamlessly integrated into existing logics of record making. This work took a kind of collaboration that Mingus had been involved with throughout many hard-fought years with Debut. Significantly, many of these collaborations were interracial: Tristano, Macero, Celia, Dorr-Dorynek, and Jimmy Knepper were all white, although each was differently situated within the industry. And of course, there were others as well, most notably musicians such as Dannie Richmond and Max Roach.[135] These relationships were often troubled, sometimes violent, and periodically exploitative. But they were also essential to Mingus's record making.

From the experimental studio techniques of Tristano and Macero to the coediting of liner notes with Celia Mingus and Dorr-Dorynek, Mingus understood how record production influenced both the musical process and the eventual reception of his work. As such, the splices on *Mingus Ah Um* may not have been made by Mingus, but they nevertheless must be contextualized within his avant-garde entrepreneurialism. Throughout the 1950s, especially with Debut, Mingus demonstrated a recognition that records were not unmediated performance but an artistic product enmeshed in a much larger network of professionals: the musicians performing, the engineer operating the equipment, the producer deciding the final order and contents, the author writing the liner notes, the designers making the cover and layout, the executives creating a marketing plan, the disc jockeys deciding on radio play, and others distributing and selling the final product. Recordings materialize from a network of individuals who have all built their expertise over time. Thinking about record making as a practice of avant-garde entrepreneurialism provides a nuanced understanding of this history without having to let go of the messiness. In a similar way, imagining a more egalitarian musical world is not a solo act but a messy, cooperative project. Relationships, in all their complexities, provoke action and hasten results. Such connections emerge by listening through the splices, even when they remain silent.

Mingus the Record Maker

In early 1960, Leonard Feather interviewed Charles Mingus as part of the long-standing "Blindfold Test" series in *Down Beat*. Mingus often directs his mostly negative commentary toward the business of making jazz records and the techniques of record production. While listening to Sonny Stitt's "Au Privave," Mingus homes in on a particular moment in Stitt's solo: "Well, you hear that thing he did on the second chorus, the bad note—he probably did that a whole lot of times on the record, and they spliced it out. There must have been a lot of splicing, or else they had an engineer who liked to twist the buttons, because the sound kept changing, it was as if a different soloist was coming up to the microphone." Later, while listening to Dizzy Reece's "The Rake," Mingus criticizes Feather's "blurry" equipment and complains that Hank Mobley is trying to copy the sound and style of Sonny Rollins. "I never heard Hank trying to sound like that," he continues. "Or else it's the way they're recording. Rudy Van Gelder makes those kinds of records. He tries to change people's tones. I've seen him do it. I've seen him take Thad Jones and the way he sets him up at the mike he can change the whole sound. That's why I never go to him; he ruined my bass sound."[136]

Mingus's listening with Feather reveals a musician intimately familiar with the ways in which record production affects playback: Van Gelder's technique can change the "whole sound"; Feather's equipment makes the music sound "blurry"; the unnamed engineer on Stitt's recording likes to "twist the buttons." Given his own history in the studio, Mingus's query about a possible splice is particularly revealing. After all, this "Blindfold Test" appeared in print mere months after the release of *Mingus Ah Um*. When read through the broader history of the LP, the interview acknowledges how technologies of recording mediate the live moment of performance in the studio. Such mediation does not happen passively, Mingus tacitly suggests, but is the result of decisions made by specific people along the record-making supply chain.

Mingus Ah Um could have existed only as a long-playing record. By 1959 it was no longer unusual to record music lasting over three minutes. Twelve-inch LPs and magnetic tape had been standard for years. Tape splicing was neither novel nor uncommon, although its relative silence remained a marker of professionalism. For many, Macero and Mingus included, editing via tape was simply one tool among many. Mingus developed his musical style within this mediated context. Because music increasingly existed within the conditions of recording—whether or not those performances made their way onto disc—record production became part of Mingus's musical practice. As a result, he developed a flexible notion of performance where the live moment was only one part of the creative process.

As a composer, Mingus drifted from the highly organized to the freely expressed. As much as he wrote for the personalities in his band, he also borrowed widely: from Western art-music traditions, from jazz history, and from Black church music. He was also sensitive to the working conditions of the gigging jazz musician and was never afraid to confront the racial injustices of the industry. By becoming a record maker, he increasingly found ways to gain artistic control, which necessitated both inter- and intra-racial collaboration. To think about Mingus as an avant-garde entrepreneur is therefore to recognize that not all political acts must be overt. From the details of recorded sound, splices in the tape can be understood as a form of radical Black practice. One of the enduring legacies of *Mingus Ah Um* is how such splices come into being not only through technological manipulation but also through a network of relationships.

Years later, in 1971, Mingus went back into the studio for Columbia to record *Let My Children Hear Music*. Macero produced the record, and Mingus wrote the liner notes. As one might expect, Mingus's essay is simultaneously gracious and critical, historically situated yet looking toward the future. At one point, he relates a story about Charlie Parker, who called one night and began improvising over a section of Igor Stravinsky's *Firebird Suite*. "I imagine he had been doing it all through the record," Mingus writes, "but he just happened to call me at that time and that was the section he was playing his ad lib solo on, and it sounded beautiful."[137] This short anecdote contains the convergence of media: self-authored liner notes on the back of an LP that tell a story of a mythologized figure who uses a telephone to share a moment of improvised performance over a classical recording. It also points to Mingus's plurality as a composer, musician, friend, entrepreneur, historian, author, and cultural critic. Simply put, he was a record maker through and through.

Playlist: The Record Making of Charles Mingus

The creativity of Charles Mingus is well documented on records from the 1950s and early 1960s. This playlist highlights Mingus's many activities as a record maker: musician, composer, arranger, producer, and executive. (Unless otherwise noted, recordings are LPs.)

Bud Powell. *Jazz at Massey Hall, vol. 2.* Debut, 1953.
Charles Mingus. *The Black Saint and the Sinner Lady.* Impulse!, 1963.
Charles Mingus. *Blues & Roots.* Atlantic, 1960.
Charles Mingus. *The Clown.* Atlantic, 1957.
Charles Mingus. *The Jazz Experiments of Charlie Mingus.* Bethlehem, 1956.
Charles Mingus. *Jazz Portraits.* United Artists, 1959.
Charles Mingus. *Mingus Ah Um.* Columbia, 1959.
Charles Mingus. *Mingus at Monterey.* Jazz Workshop, 1965.
Charles Mingus. *Mingus at the Bohemia.* Debut, 1956.
Charles Mingus. *Mingus Dynasty.* Columbia, 1960.
Charles Mingus. *Mingus Mingus Mingus Mingus Mingus.* Impulse!, 1963.
Charles Mingus. *Montage/Extrasensory Perception.* 78 rpm. Debut, 1952.
Charles Mingus. *The Moods of Mingus.* Savoy, 1955.
Charles Mingus. *Nostalgia in Times Square/The Immortal 1959 Sessions.* Columbia, 1979.
Charles Mingus. *Pithecanthropus Erectus.* Atlantic, 1956.
Charles Mingus. *Precognition/Portrait.* 78 rpm. Debut, 1952.
Charles Mingus. *Tijuana Moods.* RCA Victor, 1962.
Charles Mingus, Hampton Hawes, and Danny Richmond. *Mingus Three.* Jubilee, 1957.
Charles Mingus and John LaPorta. *Jazzical Moods, vols. 1–2.* Period, 1955.
Charlie Parker. *Bird at St. Nick's.* Jazz Workshop, 1957.
Charlie Parker. *Bird on 52nd St.* Jazz Workshop, 1957.
Dizzy Gillespie, Charles Mingus, Charlie Parker, Bud Powell, and Max Roach. *The Quintet: Jazz at Massey Hall* (12-in. LP). Debut, 1956.
Dizzy Gillespie, Charles Mingus, Charlie Parker, Bud Powell, and Max Roach. *The Quintet: Jazz at Massey Hall, vols. 1 and 3* (10-in. LPs). Debut, 1953 and 1954.

Max Roach. *Just One of Those Things/Drum Conversation*. 78 rpm. Debut, 1953.

Max Roach. *The Max Roach Quartet Featuring Hank Mobley*. Debut, 1955.

Paul Bley. *Introducing Paul Bley*. Debut, 1954.

Teo Macero. *Explorations*. Debut, 1954.

Various. *Autobiography in Jazz*. Debut, 1956.

Willie Dennis, Bennie Green, J. J. Johnson, and Kai Winding. *Four Trombones*. Debut, 1957.

Willie Dennis, Bennie Green, J. J. Johnson, and Kai Winding. *Jazz Workshop, vols. 1-2, Trombone Rapport*. Debut, 1954 and 1955.

CONCLUSION

Jazz as a Culture of Circulation

They gathered in Harlem on August 12, 1958. Dizzy Gillespie was on the outer edge of the crowd with his camera under his arm and joking with his idol, Roy Eldridge. At the top of the stairs, Buck Clayton stood in front of a few hard-bop musicians, including Benny Golson, Art Blakey, Art Farmer, and Wilbur Ware. Charles Mingus was, as usual, surrounded by history—he stood with Jay C. Higginbotham, Pee Wee Russell, Buster Bailey, Bud Freeman, and Red Allen. There were others, too: Lester Young in his porkpie hat, Mary Lou Williams standing with Marian McPartland, and Sonny Rollins casually posing at the back of the crowd. Louis Armstrong, Duke Ellington, and Miles Davis were notably absent, but many of their longtime collaborators were present. No photo like this—fifty-seven musicians across four decades—had ever been taken before.[1]

The chaotic yet joyful portrait of *A Great Day in Harlem* was taken on a nondescript Tuesday morning in August 1958, although it did not circulate until January 4, 1959, in a special edition of *Esquire* dedicated to the "Golden Age" of jazz.[2] In order to tackle the magazine's provocative declaration about the music's thriving state, *Esquire* included a series of essays about the past, present, and future of jazz. Art Kane's photo also offered its own answer. The location spoke to Harlem's significance as a communal gathering place. The sheer number of those involved demonstrated the musicians' continued investment in one another. The children sitting on the curb next to Count Basie were a hopeful promise of a cross-generational connection in the making. The demographics of the participants—interracial but mostly Black and primarily male—reflected the jazz scene more generally, at least in terms of performers. More abstractly, the spontaneity captured in the photo gestures to the many ways in which jazz musicians constantly perform and how those performances work to escape the technologies of documentation. All told, the photograph does manage to capture the vibrant, unwieldy, and dynamic quality of mid-century jazz.

I start with Kane's famous snapshot to revisit the year of its circulation, 1959, which has become a historical touchstone for jazz listeners and a year most remembered through records. Paul Bernays's 2009 BBC documentary, *1959: The Year That Changed Jazz*, epitomizes this view. The documentary concentrates on four LPs issued that year: Miles Davis's *Kind of Blue*, Dave Brubeck's *Time Out*, Ornette Coleman's *The Shape of Jazz to Come*, and Charles Mingus's *Mingus Ah Um*.[3] Others add John Coltrane's *Giant Steps* and the first release of *Spirituals to Swing*, a live recording from the momentous Carnegie Hall concerts in the late 1930s.[4] From this point of view, 1959 marked a breakout moment as well as a musical beginning. Coleman's collective improvisations and Davis's modal approach opened new avenues of harmonic and rhythm exploration. Brubeck's odd-meter experiments expanded the possibilities of form and musical fusions while also demonstrating a lucrative commercial pathway for jazz.[5] Mingus's wonderfully eclectic style and Coltrane's dense harmonic structure similarly looked forward to musical experiments of the 1960s and beyond. It is an inescapable conclusion that the music recorded in 1959 echoed through the decades to come.

At the Vanguard of Vinyl also ends in 1959, although I do not adopt the stance that it was the "year that changed jazz." Instead, I believe that 1959 represents a culmination of a decade-long transition where vinyl LPs moved from the vanguard to an unquestioned part of the center. By the end of the 1950s, the conventions of the 12-inch format and the use of magnetic tape were well established and an assumed part of record making. Because more music could fit into less space and at a dramatically higher fidelity than at any previous time, extended compositions and improvisations fit onto records with ease. Live records were no longer a novelty but an expected segment of the jazz market. Conceiving of 1959 as a breakout moment mistakenly celebrates records as objects of individual musical achievement and thereby erases the collective artistry, entrepreneurship, and creativity of record making.

Furthermore, a singular focus on instrumental improvisers too narrowly confines the multifaceted practice of jazz within the commercial marketplace. For example, how does *The Genius of Ray Charles*—which features Charles performing arrangements of Quincy Jones with members of the Basie and Ellington bands—fit into such a narrative? Does such a story have room for the many musical streams and influences heard on Nina Simone's *The Amazing Nina Simone*? The same could be asked of Sam Cooke's *Tribute to the Lady*, his homage to Billie Holiday. The history of jazz *on record* tells alternative stories if one is willing to listen.

The preceding chapters make the case that one of the most significant changes to jazz during the 1950s was the practice of record making. And so, on the vamp out, I offer three broad conclusions that draw from my earlier analysis. Because a core tenet of this book is that the cultural history of the LP is best understood through sound, I introduce these summations through three different recordings from 1959. My reflections are an attempt to listen historically and listen beyond singular moments of musical performance in order to consider how music on record moves through the world.

Records Make Meaning through Circulation

Abbey Lincoln's "Afro Blue" is a love song that crosses oceans and musical boundaries. The beginning horn riff—lifted from Cuban percussionist Mongo Santamaría's original version (also from 1959)—embraces the tension between Afro-Cuban and jazz sensibilities. Lincoln floats effortlessly atop the song's inherent cross-rhythms and Oscar Brown Jr.'s lyrics: "Dream of a land / my soul is from / I hear a hand / stroke on a drum." Ostensibly about the two lovers—"elegant boy" and "beautiful girl"— Lincoln's song transforms the blues into a diasporic imagining of jazz through Africa.[6] There is power, pain, and joy in her affirming imaginings of how musical practices

circulate. These moments also hint at the political aurality of Lincoln's future: "Rich as the night / afro blue."
—Reflection on *Abbey Is Blue*, LP, 1959

As an artistic and cultural practice, jazz exists in circulation. Much like media, circulation is plural, multilayered, and contingent on people with overlapping and often conflicting interests. In their essay "Cultures of Circulation: The Imaginations of Modernity," Benjamin Lee and Edward LiPuma understand circulation not as a manner of transmitting culture but as something that actually constitutes it. The circulation of media, they write, presumes and necessitates a community invested in what those media contain. Although such investment is always multifaceted, these "interpretive communities" rely on circulation to construct meaning, modes of understanding, and the terms of evaluation.[7] Circulation is, as ethnomusicologist David Novak sums up, a "culture-making process."[8]

This book has adopted an understanding of jazz as a culture created through circulation: the circulation of sounds on record, the circulation of written discourses, and the circulation of music made in performance. Some circulatory pathways, like those created by Charles and Celia Mingus at Debut, had to be built from scratch. In a similar fashion, Bob Weinstock traveled across the country by bus promoting Prestige to disc jockeys and jukebox distributors.[9] Musicians like Duke Ellington and Cannonball Adderley took a different approach, relying on established networks to find record makers that they could entrust with their music. As a Black man representing the State Department, Dizzy Gillespie charted a new route over worn diplomatic pathways and found multiple ways of connecting with different audiences. These examples are only a few that evince how record makers created, defined, and negotiated new paths of circulation for jazz.

Defining jazz as a culture of circulation acknowledges the essential though tangled relationship between music making and its reproductions. The multifaceted listenership of jazz depends on circulation just as the music's circulation depends on its listenership. This is one of things I hear in Abbey Lincoln's "Afro Blue," which begins to imagine alternative pathways of being and belonging through the merger of musical traditions. Such possibilities of listening otherwise are made possible by the music's circulation along multiple paths simultaneously. This is also what I hear in the spoken announcements of Adderley and Gillespie, which worked in close partnership with their musical performances. Both modes of engagement imagine alternative futures for jazz and do so in multiple registers. I hear something similar in the postproduction splices of Charles Mingus, which were also a function of the creative ingenuity and dedication of fellow avant-garde entrepreneurs like Celia Mingus. As I wrote in the introduction, a cultural history of the LP's adoption makes audible the ways in which Black expertise, Black labor, and Black capital increasingly circulated.

Through their circulation, jazz LPs have become an exemplary product of twentieth-century modernity: they materialize through commercial structures yet often disavow that connection, they are simultaneously beholden to technologies of mediation and reify live performance, and they serve as both locations of resistance and examples of how whiteness and white masculinity perpetuate the uneven power dynamics of the jazz industry. This perspective, I believe, makes clear that jazz LPs contain entire histories that reveal the social networks, musical practices, and political economies of jazz.

Record Making Is a Practice of Cultural Negotiation

No words are present on "Fables of Faubus," at least on the version recorded in May 1959 and issued on *Mingus Ah Um*. But the lyrics were always there during performance and can be heard on the October 1960 recording for Candid Records: "Ohhh Lord. Don't let 'em shoot us. Ohhh Lord. Don't let 'em stab us. Ohhhh Lord. Don't let 'em tar and feather us. Ohhh Lord. No more swastikas." The actions of Orval Faubus at Little Rock Central High School rang through the time-present of both sessions because the conditions that inspired Mingus's protest had not changed. Prosegregationists continued to march in Little Rock through 1959. Mingus was, as Ralph Ellison wrote about the bebop generation, "caught like the rest in all the complex forces of American life which come to focus in jazz."[10] Mingus chose to grapple with the violent and state-sanctioned denial of Black humanity with his music, no matter how, when, and in what way the lyrics circulated on record.

—Reflection on *Mingus Ah Um*, LP, 1959, and *Charles Mingus Presents Charles Mingus*, LP, 1960

On August 25, 1959, a white New York City police officer assaulted and arrested Miles Davis for refusing to clear the sidewalk while he was on break between sets at Birdland.[11] The attack happened eight days after the release of *King of Blue* and immediately after Davis had completed an Armed Forces Day broadcast. Davis's refusal was, in one sense, part of a national trend of resistance. Organized sit-ins were beginning to happen all over the country, although it was not until February 1960, when the Greensboro Four sat at the Woolworth lunch counter in Greensboro, North Carolina, that the collective power of these individual protests would start to become clear. These events would directly inspire the cover of *We Insist! Max Roach's Freedom Now Suite*, issued in late 1960 by Candid Records, the same label to issue Mingus's "Faubus" with lyrics. Within this context, jazz musicians would continue to use their music in the fight for economic opportunity, cultural liberation, and freedom within Jim Crow America.[12] On record and in performance, the music pushed the boundaries. It is difficult to imagine it on a three-and-a-half-minute shellac disc.

In parallel with the LP's adoption, many musicians made the effort to foreground the Black politics and poetics of jazz while simultaneously seeking greater power over the production of their music. The artists featured in the pages of this book went about such activism in divergent ways. Davis used his star power to reimagine and complicate assumed notions of Black male performance. Ellington and Adderley worked within industry structures to joyfully celebrate the history of Black music making while also exerting more control over the conditions of their artistic labor. Gillespie expertly used his charisma onstage to tell the Black musical story of jazz while also leveraging his ambassadorial position to influence national debates over civil rights. Like others before him, Mingus aggressively confronted the racial injustices of the record industry through his entrepreneurship, always seeking control over his sound on record. Record making is not politically neutral.

To date, jazz literature has skillfully investigated the many different stylistic developments of the 1950s and their underlying cultural politics. The dominant narrative about this period highlights musical innovations, struggles against the violent structures of racism, and the side-by-side (though often contentious) existence of bebop, traditional jazz, swing, cool jazz, hard bop, and soul jazz. The international profile of jazz's greatest stars helped the next generation enter these discursive and musical spaces. As jazz cut across various strata of US culture, it did so through the circulation of records. LPs are ever-present in jazz literature as objects of reference and recollection, but not often as a technology that shapes the terms of debate. Record making is a practice of cultural negotiation embedded within larger social systems, aesthetic schemas, and political economies. As I wrote in chapter 2, LPs are media of cultural communication that help construct systems of value and the discourses of history.

Records Are Unstable in Their Meaning

"So What" begins with a few notes in the bass, soon joined by the piano. The carefully arranged duet is a quiet beginning. Still, the subtle unintended sound of the resonating snare (0:10) can be heard if you listen for it. Irvin Townsend, the producer of *Kind of Blue*, warned of this: "Listen, we gotta watch it because of the, uh—there are noises all the way through this—this is so quiet to begin with that every click sounds" (1:27). He continues: "Watch the snare, too; we're picking up some of the vibration on it." Davis, undaunted, has a quick reply: "Well, that goes with it—[*Townsend from the control room: What?*]—All that goes with it." Townsend, resigned: "Alright. But not ... not, not all the other noises though. [*Pause.*] Take two."[13] Try to imagine hearing the subtle sounds of the buzzing snare on the low fidelity of a 78-rpm record. Try to imagine that quiet duet, that subdued melody, that nine minutes and twenty seconds of music without the high fidelity of magnetic-tape recording and LP playback. The possibility and promise of "So What" cannot be separated from the materiality of jazz history.
—Reflection on *Kind of Blue*, LP, 1959, and CD (legacy edition), 2008

Records are dynamic objects, unstable in their meaning because they are historically situated in their conception, design, and circulation. By tracking the emergent sound of jazz in the early LP era, *At the Vanguard of Vinyl* draws connections between seemingly disparate historical trends in order to reframe some well-known narratives of jazz history. I have, for example, linked the blossoming of independent jazz labels such as Prestige, Blue Note, and Riverside to the standardization of the 12-inch LP as a medium for middle-class adult listeners. I have also outlined how jazz became the only music played by Black musicians to primarily circulate on LP in the 1950s. As a result, jazz musicians increasingly gained more control over repertoire and personnel selections in ways that provided a counternarrative to the racially coded language that so often circulated alongside these LPs. These developments happened at the same time that jazz moved into the spaces of elite white culture, including large jazz festivals in places like Newport, Rhode Island, and the embassies of the US State Department. As the music increasingly circulated, jazz and its practitioners fearlessly crossed social and political boundaries. Approaches toward this form of Black record making differed as much as the music. As I wrote in the introduction, such multiplicity is the book's argument.

Defining jazz as a culture of circulation pushes many of the concepts outlined in this book forward in time. The documentary impulses that, as

I argue, are based on inherited scripts of white masculine authority and economic power (chapter 2) run through the *Smithsonian Collection of Classic Jazz* from 1973, the Original Jazz Classics reissue imprint founded at Fantasy in 1983, the CD reissue boom of the 1990s, and beyond. The tensions inherent in the aesthetics of sonic realism (chapter 3) can be heard in the formation of repertory ensembles and ghost bands, competitions like *Essentially Ellington*, the re-creations of famous records onstage, and transcription books that attempt to capture every detail in print. The concept of the jazz ambassador, born of the mid-1950s (chapter 4), lives on through the continued use of Black music for musical diplomacy today. Economies of attention (chapter 5) are still firmly ingrained into the jazz scene and can be observed in any number of places, from the jazz club and musical festival grounds to the use of jazz on public radio. Many avant-garde entrepreneurs (chapter 6) would go on to start their own labels (e.g., Strata-East Records, Black Jazz Records) and musical organizations (e.g., Union of God's Musicians and Artists Ascension, Association for the Advancement of Creative Musicians). These are only a few examples. Despite such Afro-modernist trajectories, however, notions of whiteness and white musical morality (chapters 1, 2, and 3) continue to influence the integration of jazz into prominent cultural organizations like Lincoln Center, the Kennedy Center, the Smithsonian, university music programs, and the Library of Congress. Finally, the business of storing Black sonic labor for long-term profits (chapter 1) continues to expand and proliferate, as the 2008 fire in the vaults of the Universal Music Group made clear to devastating effect.[14] A cultural history of the LP therefore reveals the integral position of sonic media in cultural debates about race and aurality within the United States in the 1950s and beyond.

As I stated at the outset, LPs are more than containers for sound. They are cultural objects that have helped to construct the historical, cultural, and social discourses of jazz. This cultural feedback loop throws the interactions between Black cultural producers and the structures of power within the jazz industry into sharp relief. Notions of and contestation over issues of labor, capital, and difference cannot be disregarded.

Postscript: Fragments and (Flamenco) Sketches

MILES DAVIS: Wait a minute, Irving. [*Bass sounds a few notes.*] Wait.

IRVING TOWNSEND: OK.

DAVIS: [*Unintelligible directions to the musicians, laughter.*] Oh yeah, alright. [*Addressing Townsend*] You know your floor squeaks, you know. You know what I mean? Can you hear me?

TOWNSEND: Yeah. [*Indistinct musician chatter. Cannonball Adderley's voice comes through.*]

DAVIS: Let's go.

CANNONBALL ADDERLEY: Surface noise, you know?

UNKNOWN: It's all part of the tune, man. [*Adderley chuckles.*]

—"Flamenco Sketches (sequence 1)," *Kind of Blue*, CD (legacy edition), 2008

In the midst of a conversation about the music, Davis pauses to call for the attention of Irving Townsend, the producer. Davis wants to discuss a squeak in the floor. Adderley, in a jocular mood, makes a parallel with record making—"Surface noise, you know?" The response, "It's all part of the tune," brings it back to the music. These sonic fragments were captured in 1959 but first circulated in 2008.[15] Despite the surface noise, it is always possible to listen again. Thinking of jazz as a culture of circulation is what I conclude from the record-making trajectory of the 1950s—the past, present, and future of it.

Playlist: The Many Records of 1959

Nineteen fifty-nine defined each of the following LPs in different ways. Many were recorded and issued within the year's twelve-month calendar boundaries. Others were recorded well before but then began to circulate that year. A few were issued either the year before or after, but were nevertheless tied to 1959 through a recording date or the publication of critical praise.[16] (All recordings are LPs.)

Abbey Lincoln. *Abbey Is Blue*. Riverside, 1959.

Ahmad Jamal. *Jamal at the Penthouse*. Argo, 1959.

Annie Ross with the Gerry Mulligan Quartet. *Annie Ross Sings a Song with Mulligan!* World Pacific, 1959.

Art Blakey. *Art Blakey and the Jazz Messengers* (later retitled *Moanin'*). Blue Note, 1959.

Bill Evans. *Everybody Digs Bill Evans*. Riverside, 1959.

Billie Holiday. *Billie Holiday* (later retitled *Last Recording*). MGM, 1959.

Cannonball Adderley. *The Cannonball Adderley Quintet in San Francisco*. Riverside, 1959.

Cecil Taylor. *Love for Sale*. United Artists Records, 1959.

Charles Mingus. *Blues & Roots*. Atlantic, 1960.

Charles Mingus. *Charles Mingus Presents Charles Mingus*. Candid, 1960.
Charles Mingus. *Mingus Ah Um*. Columbia, 1959.
Coleman Hawkins. *Soul*. Prestige, 1959.
Dave Brubeck. *Time Further Out*. Columbia, 1961.
Dave Brubeck. *Time Out*. Columbia, 1959.
Dave Lambert, Jon Hendricks, and Annie Ross. *Sing Along with Basie*. Roulette, 1959.
Dizzy Gillespie. *Have Trumpet, Will Excite!* Verve, 1959.
Dizzy Gillespie, Sonny Rollins, and Sonny Stitt. *Sonny Side Up*. Verve, 1959.
Duke Ellington. *Anatomy of a Murder*. Columbia, 1959.
Duke Ellington and Johnny Hodges. *Back to Back: Duke Ellington and Johnny Hodges Play the Blues*. Verve, 1959.
Ella Fitzgerald. *Ella Fitzgerald Sings the George and Ira Gershwin Song Book*. Verve, 1959.
George Lewis and His New Orleans Stompers. *Concert!* Blue Note, 1959.
Hank Mobley and Lee Morgan. *Peckin' Time*. Blue Note, 1959.
Horace Silver. *Blowin' the Blues Away*. Blue Note, 1959.
Jimmy Smith. *The Sermon!* Blue Note, 1959.
John Coltrane. *Giant Steps*. Atlantic, 1960.
Langston Hughes. *The Weary Blues*. MGM, 1958.
Max Roach. *We Insist! Max Roach's Freedom Now Suite*. Candid, 1960.
Melba Liston. *Melba Liston and Her 'Bones*. MetroJazz, 1959.
Miles Davis. *Kind of Blue*. Columbia, 1959.
Miles Davis. *Porgy and Bess*. Columbia, 1959.
Milt Jackson. *Bags' Opus*. United Artists Records, 1959.
Nat King Cole. *To Whom It May Concern*. Capitol, 1959.
Nina Simone. *The Amazing Nina Simone*. Colpix, 1959.
Oliver Nelson. *Meet Oliver Nelson*. New Jazz, 1959.
Ornette Coleman. *The Shape of Jazz to Come*. Atlantic, 1959.
Oscar Peterson. *On the Town with the Oscar Peterson Trio*. Verve, 1958.
Randy Weston. *Little Niles*. United Artists Records, 1959.
Ray Charles. *The Genius of Ray Charles*. Atlantic, 1959.
Sam Cooke. *Tribute to the Lady*. Keen, 1959.
Steve Lacy. *Reflections: Steve Lacy Plays Thelonious Monk*. New Jazz, 1959.
Sun Ra and His Arkestra. *Jazz in Silhouette*. El Saturn, 1959.
Thelonious Monk. *The Thelonious Monk Orchestra at Town Hall*. Riverside, 1959.
Various. *From Spirituals to Swing*. Vanguard, 1959.
Various. *Smithsonian Collection of Classic Jazz*. Smithsonian, 1973.
Yusef Lateef. *The Fabric of Jazz*. Savoy, 1959.

Notes

Introduction: The LP Goes Live

1   The December 1954 session initially produced four musical tracks that Prestige issued in 1955 on two 10-inch LPs: *Miles Davis All Stars, vol. 1* and *vol. 2*. The alternate take of "The Man I Love," complete with Davis's comment to Van Gelder, first circulated in 1957 on a record titled *Miles Davis and the Modern Jazz Giants*. Prestige released the alternative take of "The Man I Love" on a standard 12-inch LP in May 1959 as the last track of a different record also titled *Miles Davis and the Modern Jazz Giants*. The book's discography includes a complete citation for each record I mention in the text or in the notes. Citations for liner notes are found in the book's discography as well.

2   John Hammond and George Avakian, liner notes to *The Huckle-Buck and Robbins' Nest: A Buck Clayton Jam Session*, LP, 1954. Avakian goes on to detail which solos were spliced in and where. Relatedly, he also joined two separate recordings of "Jumpin' at the Woodside" to make a single track for the 1954 Buck Clayton LP of the same name.

3   Debut initially released the Massey Hall concerts in 1953 and late 1954 across three 10-inch LPs: *The Quintet: Jazz at Massey Hall, vol. 1*; Bud Powell, *Jazz at Massey Hall, vol. 2*; and *The Quintet: Jazz at Massey Hall, vol. 3*. The 12-inch LP version began to circulate in 1956.

4   Carby, *Race Men*, 139. I came to this observation and quotation through Rustin-Paschal, *Kind of Man I Am*, 17.

5   Expressions of masculinity in postwar jazz, especially Mingus's, are broadly explored in Rustin-Paschal, *Kind of Man I Am*.

6   My approach follows Stuart Hall, who argues that cultural change often happens through contestations over discourse—that is, over who gets to tell what kind of story. Hall, "What Is This 'Black' in Black Popular Culture," 24–25.

7   Ramsey, *Race Music*, 97-101, 106-8. For the intellectual genealogy of Afro-modernism, see Magee, "Kinds of Blue," 6-9.

8   For more on how Afro-modernist ideals functioned in different jazz styles throughout the 1950s, see Monson, *Freedom Sounds*, 66-106. Alexander Weheliye's exploration of sonic Afro-modernity is also relevant, particularly his attention to how Black subjects "structure and sound their positionalities within and against Western modernity." Weheliye, *Phonographies*, 5-8.

9   For further discussion on the early history of concept albums in 1950s jazz, see Decker, "Fancy Meeting You Here," 98-108. Singular themed collections of popular music (broadly defined) also existed as a small market segment during the 78-rpm era.

10 Sterne, *MP3*, 7.

11 Commodore's recording is discussed in Horning, *Chasing Sound*, 108-9. John Howland makes a provocative and convincing argument that the music on side 4 of Ellington's "Reminiscing in Tempo" was added only to accommodate the four-side record format. Howland, *"Ellington Uptown,"* 171-72. Victor first issued "Sing, Sing, Sing" as a 12-inch record as part of *A Symposium of Swing* (1937), a four-disc album featuring Goodman, Tommy Dorsey, Fats Waller, and Bunny Berigan. The label then issued a shorter, edited version of the track as a 10-inch single under Goodman's name in 1938.

12 Hershorn, *Norman Granz*, 78-98. Granz issued the JATP concert on multiple formats and labels, including Mercury's Jazz 11000 series of 78-rpm discs. For example, a lengthy 1947 recording of "Perdido" from Carnegie Hall appeared across three 78-rpm discs on *Norman Granz' Jazz at the Philharmonic, vol. 8* (1948).

13 Some examples can be found in Horning, *Chasing Sound*, 108.

14 Although LPs still necessitated flipping the record, this action rarely interrupted a track in progress. For more on the cultural significance of the "flip," see Katz, *Capturing Sound*, 77. As I explore in chapter 1, most of the first LPs in 1948-51 were sets of reissued recordings like the Ellington and Goodman tracks mentioned here.

15 John Wilson, "Unbound Jazz: Invention of LP Gave Jam Session Space," *New York Times*, March 16, 1958, section 11, 22. In reflecting on ten years of the LP, Wilson was writing specifically about Woody Herman's extended suite, "Summer Sequence," although it is clear from context that he is speaking about the genre as a whole. "Summer Sequence" first appeared on two 78-rpm discs (four sides total) as a part of Herman's *Sequence in Jazz* (1949).

16 Jarrett, "Cutting Sides," 329.

17 Blake, "Recording Practices and the Role of the Producer," 39.

18. According to Andre Millard, many labels used disc recorders—conventional disc-cutting methods in the 78-rpm era—until the late 1950s. Millard, *America on Record*, 207. *Down Beat* reported that 24.6 million 78-rpm records, worth over $18 million, sold in 1958. "78 Disc Sales Still Up," *Down Beat*, August 6, 1959, 11.

19. Spar, *Ruling the Waves*, 17.

20. In particular, the invention and adoption of the LP created an ecological shift in supply chain and waste streams as the industry moved from shellac (78s) to plastic (LPs and 45s). See especially Devine, *Decomposed*, 81–128.

21. For specific information about the technological and technical innovations of the control room during this period, see Horning, *Chasing Sound*, 104–39.

22. See, for example, Gray, "Black Masculinity and Visual Culture," 402; Kelley, "'We Are Not What We Seem,'" 88; Ramsey, *Amazing Bud Powell*, 124; and Porter, *What Is This Thing Called Jazz?*, 81–82.

23. For more on media as a form of structured communication, see Gitelman, *Always Already New*, 7.

24. Columbia's refusal to record Billie Holiday's performance of "Strange Fruit" is one example among many. See Griffin, *If You Can't Be Free, Be a Mystery*.

25. Among others, scholars such as Ingrid Monson, Scott DeVeaux, Scott Saul, Eric Porter, Penny Von Eschen, Mark Anthony Neal, and Guthrie Ramsey describe different ways that racial politics figures into music making and jazz musicians' wide-ranging political activity during the 1950s and surrounding decades. See Monson, *Freedom Sounds*; Neal, *What the Music Said*; Ramsey, *Race Music*; Saul, *Freedom Is, Freedom Ain't*; Porter, *What Is This Thing Called Jazz?*; Von Eschen, *Satchmo Blows Up the World*; and DeVeaux, *Birth of Bebop*.

26. My observations about audio production and the early LP draw from documents found in the private archives of George Avakian during my initial research in 2012. My citations include folder names from his filing cabinets, which generally correspond to Subseries 1B: Alphabetical Files in the collection's current home at the New York Public Library. For example, information about audio production at the beginning of the LP era (late 1940s) is discussed in Howard Scott and George Avakian, "The Birth of the Long Playing Record," printed interview with Avakian corrections, LP History file, George Avakian private archives (GAA), Riverdale, NY.

27. For more on the power structures of race in the pre-LP era, see K. Miller, *Segregating Sound*; and Gitelman, "Recording Sound."

28. In his capacity as the first president of Columbia Records, Edward Wallerstein urged William Paley (president of CBS) to buy the American Record Corporation (ARC) for $700,000 in 1939. ARC's catalog included Columbia Phonograph

along with Brunswick, Vocalion, and Okeh. CBS reorganized this side of their business under the name Columbia Records shortly after with a goal of also moving into the classical market. According to Howard Scott, who as music coordinator for the Masterworks label oversaw the transfer of Columbia's first LPs, Wallerstein hired several new employees in each division in the years immediately after the war, specifically with long-play ambitions in mind. Howard Scott, "The Beginnings of LP," typed document (draft), LP History file, GAA. This document is a draft of Howard H. Scott, "The Beginnings of LP," *Gramophone*, July 1998, 112–13. After serving as music coordinator during the LP's launch, Scott went on to produce many records for Columbia, including Glenn Gould's famed LP, *Bach: The Goldberg Variations* (1956).

29   Peter Goldmark, lead engineer on the LP project's first stage, directly contradicts Wallerstein's account. Goldmark claims credit for coming up with the idea for the LP in 1945 after listening to an interrupted version of Johannes Brahms's Second Piano Concerto. He further describes Wallerstein's attempts to submarine the project at every turn. See Goldmark, *Maverick Inventor*, 127–47. I have chosen not to adopt Goldmark's perspective because of several inconsistencies in his time line, as well as contradictions found in several unrelated sources. Regardless, classical music remains central to Goldmark's account of the LP's origin story. For support of Wallerstein's account, see "LP Time Line," printed document with Avakian corrections, LP History file, GAA; and Horning, *Chasing Sound*, 109–10.

30   Edward Wallerstein with Ward Botsford, "Creating the LP Record," *High Fidelity Magazine*, April 1976, 58.

31   Columbia Broadcasting System, Inc., "Annual Report to Stockholders for the Fiscal Year Ended January 1, 1949," March 22, 1949, ProQuest Historical Annual Reports, 7.

32   The next record in the catalog (ML 4002) features Bach. The ten after that spotlight a single composer: Beethoven.

33   According to Avakian, who produced the popular-album catalog at the time, Columbia initially prepared one hundred records in each of the company's popular and classical series. (The latter was a mixture of light and serious works.) Classical LPs on the Masterworks label cost $4.85 (12-inch, ML 4000 series) or $3.85 (10-inch, ML 2000). Ten-inch popular records cost $3.00 (CL 6000). Avakian outlines these details in "LP Time Line," p. 5, LP History file, GAA; and George Avakian to Floyd Levin, January 28, 1998, LP History file, GAA.

34   Klotz, *Dave Brubeck and the Performance of Whiteness*, 13. On the same page, Klotz underlines how whiteness is never singular: "Whiteness is performed differently by white people in unique circumstances, based on their intersecting identities and particular locations." The remainder of Klotz's book explores

whiteness as a vital category for understanding jazz and its circulation. A related discussion about whiteness, exclusion, and historical discourse can be found in Lewis, "Improvised Music after 1950," 100–105.

35 Although I focus on jazz, the same observation is true for the rest of the record industry. See Horning, *Chasing Sound*, 9. White men were overrepresented in other parts of the music business, including as managers, booking agents, club or venue owners, national magazine editors and writers, disc jockeys, and record-store owners.

36 Unsurprisingly, record-buying consumers were a complex, multifaceted segment of society not defined by race, gender, class, ethnicity, or location alone. This social fact is explored in Brooks, *Liner Notes for the Revolution*, 316–47; Klotz, *Dave Brubeck and the Performance of Whiteness*, 92–105; and Moore, *Soundscapes of Liberation*, 91–93. I describe how mid-century publishing companies oriented around top-selling white artists in chapter 1.

37 I draw from the discussions of masculine cultural scripts in jazz in Ramsey, *Amazing Bud Powell*, 121–42; Klotz, *Dave Brubeck and the Performance of Whiteness*, 9–16, 77–96; and Rustin-Paschal, *Kind of Man I Am*, 97–125.

38 For more on jukeboxes and radio stations in Black life, see Ramsey, *Race Music*, 4, 117.

39 See Rustin-Paschal, *Kind of Man I Am*, 97–104, for the wider historical context of white recordmen and expression of white masculinity. For more on Prestige's changing approach to Black audiences, see Rosenthal, *Hard Bop*, 62–65.

40 Other subsidiaries included Bluesville (featuring well-seasoned bluesmen), Moodsville (soul jazz), and Swingville (swing-era jazz musicians). A full listing of these labels can be found in Ruppli, *Prestige Label*. Although jazz dominated its catalog in the early 1950s, Prestige offered a limited number of R&B records as well (like most other independent jazz labels).

41 Prestige did hundreds of recording sessions in the 1950s. Only a handful were led or partially headlined by women, including Annie Ross (several in 1950–53), Dorothy McLeod (1952), Mary Lou Williams (1953), Barbara Lea (1957), Dorothy Ashby (1958), and Shirley Scott (1958).

42 For an overview of Mingus's change in musical approach, see Porter, *What Is This Thing Called Jazz?*, 124–25.

43 My thinking about technological mediation and forms of resistance in relation to constructions of race and difference is influenced by Meintjes, *Sound of Africa!*; K. Miller, *Segregating Sound*; Gitelman, "Recording Sound"; Weheliye, *Phonographies*; and Moten, *In the Break*.

44 I am influenced by Nicole Starosielski's investigation of the fiber-optic cables that facilitate worldwide information exchange. Starosielski pushes for an

understanding of media that accounts for modes of consumption in relation to underlying infrastructure. Starosielski, *Undersea Network*, 3-12. About recording technology, Susan Horning points to the improvement of microphones, mixing consoles, amplifiers, equalizers, compressors, limiters, cutting styli, lathes, cables, vacuum tubes, and loudspeakers during the early LP era. Horning, *Chasing Sound*, 111. For more on the manufacturing turn from shellac to plastic, see Devine, *Decomposed*, 81-128.

45 For a detailed account, see Jack T. Mullin, "Creating the Craft of Tape Recording," *High Fidelity Magazine*, April 1976.

46 As Peter McMurry details, the early use of tape for delayed broadcasts merged the ephemeral nature of radio with the repeatability of tape technology. McMurry, "Once Upon Time," 36. Jack Mullin further points out that the first use of tape within the United States was for soundtracks. Mullin, "Creating the Craft of Tape Recording."

47 McMurry describes tape as creating a "different kind of temporality" for sound recording. McMurry, "Once Upon Time," 37.

48 For more on the history of compression as it relates to musical distribution, see Sterne, *MP3*, 5-6.

49 My interest in the relationship between music making and its reproduction connects to long-standing debates in performance studies that attempt to make sense of these complexities. See Auslander, *Liveness*; Moten, *In the Break*; Schneider, *Performing Remains*; Phelan, *Unmarked*; and D. Taylor, *Archive and the Repertoire*. Although history figures prominently in this literature (albeit in different ways), the development and use of specific technologies of mediation is not the main focus. As a result, these authors largely do not address issues of power and control over the apparatuses of mediation, although they would likely all agree that mediation does not happen passively.

50 Howett, *Television Innovations*, 47. In a related development, the first commercial instant camera came to market in 1948. In the 1950s, artist Andy Warhol (who also made art for jazz record labels during the period) famously used instant photos to make instant portraits.

51 Matthew Somoroff first suggested to me the connection of Sinatra's album to the broader cultural imagination of an ever-expanding world within the United States. For a look at the transnational implications of changes to technology, art, and culture at the end of the 1950s, see Guilbaut and O'Brian, *Breathless Days*.

52 Hopkins and Kapany, "Flexible Fibrescope."

53 The 1950 cable connected Florida and Cuba. The TAT-1 carried telephone conversations, text-based messages, still images, and some television signals. These networks were part of a much larger expansion of telecommunication networks around the world. See Starosielski, *Undersea Network*, 38-44.

54 L. Cohen, *Consumer's Republic*, 112-64.

55 David Harvey discusses the compression of space and time in relation to postmodernism. Harvey, *The Condition of Postmodernity*, especially part 3. Here I wish to suggest a connection between the compression of musical data, following Sterne and others, and the perceived compression of time and space happening through technological advancement. Sterne, *MP3*, 5-6.

56 As Kyle Devine observes, the phrase *music industry* encompasses several industries, including recording, manufacturing, publishing, merchandizing, live performance, and so on. My use of this term, as will hopefully become clear throughout the text, is meant to evoke the wide constellation of these commercial activities, even as I continue to use the term in its conventional sense for ease of reading. Devine, *Decomposed*, 12-14.

57 As their names suggest, Columbia Broadcasting System (CBS) and Radio Corporation of America (RCA) were both similarly invested in other forms of mass communication, including radio and television.

58 The close relationship between commercial interests and music can also been seen in 1930s radio programming. See T. Taylor, *Sounds of Capitalism*, 80-90.

59 Schneider, *Performing Remains*, 93-94. I adopt Schneider's reading of Mary Ann Doane in this paragraph.

60 Doane, "Real Time," 24.

61 On the use of "latency" as it relates to the supply chain of musical production and the technologies of audition, see Bates, *Digital Tradition*, 134-36.

62 For the commercial adoption of recordings, see Sterne, *Audible Past*, 215-86. The close connections between the early history of sound recording and the history of writing and inscription are explored in Gitelman, *Always Already New*, 16-21. Lisa Gitelman points out that even the earliest production of sound recording depended on worldwide trade and the increasingly global economy. For a related discussion about inscription and sound, see Bohlman and McMurry, "Tape," 8.

63 More than a decade earlier, Sidney Bechet had overdubbed the instrumental parts for his 1941 recording "The Sheik of Araby." My thanks to Jeremy Smith for reminding me of these examples.

64 I discuss each of these recordings in chapters 3 and 4, respectively.

65 The 1956 sales ranking for *Ambassador Satch* was as follows: #4 (September 19), #3 (October 3 and 17), #2 (November 14). In the months before and after, Armstrong's LP ranked in the top twenty. In 1957 *Ellington at Newport* went in and out of the top five: #2 (February 6), #3 (March 6), #5 (May 2), #4 (May 20), #3 (June 27 and July 25). In April, September, November, and December of 1957, Ellington's LP remained in the top ten for nationwide sales. For full listings,

consult *Down Beat*'s "Best Sellers" report during the months listed above (usually around page 20).

66   For discussion about the simulation of "real-time" performance in relation to on-location recording, see Solis, "Unique Chunk of Jazz Reality."

67   In making this observation, I draw from jazz-fusion scholarship that examines the ontological crisis about jazz brought about by heavy studio production used in the 1970s. See Fellezs, *Birds of Fire*; Pond, *Head Hunters*; and Smith, "'Sell It Black.'" Despite my focus on the 1950s, I see an epistemological connection in how the uses of technology in the studio influenced musical performance.

68   One exception can be found in the coverage of Columbia's *I Can Hear It Now* LP, a 1948 collection of political speeches, interviews, and radio broadcasts emceed by Edward R. Murrow. Otto Mack's widely syndicated column mentions the eleven miles of magnetic tape of raw material that were eventually edited "with razor and paste" into a forty-five-minute final LP. See Otto Mack, "Record Parade," *Atlanta Daily World*, November 23, 1948, 3. Columbia's promotional materials—including its reports to stockholders—do not mention tape.

69   George Dale, liner notes to *Masterpieces by Ellington*, 1951. This LP also happened to be one of the first jazz records made at Columbia's 30th Street studio, and one of the first sessions recorded specifically for the LP format. The point about the Ampex machines is made in the promotional material for the 2014 reissue of *Masterpieces* by Analogue Productions: "Duke Ellington—Masterpieces by Ellington (Mono)," Acoustic Sounds, accessed December 21, 2017, http://store.acousticsounds.com/d/98200/Duke_Ellington-Masterpieces_By_Ellington-200_Gram_Vinyl_Record.

70   For more on the ontology of performance, see Phelan, *Unmarked*, 146–66; and D. Taylor, *Archive and the Repertoire*, 142–43.

71   I take this formation from Rebecca Schneider, who usefully questions the naturalized sense of linear time with respect to theatrical performance. Writing about the way that history figures into onstage performance through temporal "syncopation," she writes that theater "can never be 'live.' Or, never only live." Schneider, *Performing Remains*, 92.

72   My approach to the creative and aesthetic choices of mediation at the site of production, especially regarding the global circulation of recorded objects, relies heavily on Meintjes, *Sound of Africa!*; Feld, "Pygmy Pop"; and Feld, *Jazz Cosmopolitanism in Accra*.

73   Dan Morgenstern, interview with the author, March 8, 2012. For more on the particulars of 12- versus 10-inch records, see Myers, *Why Jazz Happened*, ch. 4.

74   Born in Munich, Germany, in 1929, Morgenstern grew up in Denmark and Amsterdam, where he became a devoted jazz listener. His enthusiasm for music

would carry him through a lengthy career as the editor of *Down Beat* and *Metronome*, a Grammy Award-winning author (for liner notes), and the eventual director of the Institute of Jazz Studies at Rutgers University-Newark.

75 For example, on the famed Charlie Parker and Dizzy Gillespie recording of "Groovin' High" from February 1945, each musician solos for only a half chorus (sixteen measures). Compare this with the sheer number of sidemen who came to prominence in the LP era because of their improvisational talents highlighted with Art Blakey's Jazz Messengers outfit: Wayne Shorter, Lee Morgan, Clifford Brown, Freddie Hubbard, Benny Golson, Curtis Fuller, Cedar Walton, and many others.

76 Dan Morgenstern, interview with the author, March 8, 2012.

77 Media theorist Paul Duguid generalizes this phenomenon, describing it as a "futurological" trope where new media are assumed to be more transparent and less mediated when, in fact, the opposite is true. I adopt this reading of Duguid from Gitelman and Pingree, *New Media*, xiii-xiv. For more on the idea of "transparency" in new media, see Bolter and Grusin, *Remediation*, 21-31.

78 See Rustin-Paschal, *Kind of Man I Am*, 100-104, for further discussion about expressions of white masculinity and record making during this period.

79 This historical incongruity is discussed in Porter, *What Is This Thing Called Jazz?*, 31; and Pellegrinelli, "Separated at 'Birth,'" 33-39. The restrictive inclusion of women vocalists as jazz founders can be found in the Jazz Archives Series on Riverside: Ma Rainey, Bessie Smith, and Ida Cox (among a few other vocalists) appeared with regularity, usually described as "great" or "legendary" voices of the blues.

80 Tucker uses this phrase to describe the dominant jazz discourse promulgated by the documentary by Ken Burns, *Jazz*, although clearly it applies more broadly. Tucker, "Big Ears," 376.

81 On the *Smithsonian Collection* and Martin Williams, see T. Jackson, *Blowin' the Blues Away*, 27-28. On the political economy of reissues, CDs, and digital platforms, see Pond, "Old Wine, New Bottles"; Chapman, *Jazz Bubble*; and Mueller, "Review: Wikipedia."

82 See Rasula, "Media of Memory"; Heller, *Loft Jazz*, 4-10; and Schuiling, "Jazz and the Material Turn," 88-91.

83 Bolter and Grusin, *Remediation*, 14-15, 45-49.

84 According to Avakian, all of the first hundred popular LPs were either direct transfers from 78-rpm albums or new collections assembled from existing singles. After the June 1948 announcement, these records shipped in batches of twenty (or so) in rough numerical sequence. Avakian to Floyd Levin, January 28, 1998, LP History file, GAA. Sinatra's four-disc 78-rpm album is catalog

number C112; Nathan Milstein's interpretation of Mendelssohn can be heard on Masterworks M-577, issued in 1946.

85   Konitz and Tristano's LP includes tracks from recording sessions on January 11, June 28, and September 27, 1949. Prestige originally issued these recordings as New Jazz 807, 808, 813, and 832. A full listing for each release can be found in the discography. When the label changed its name from New Jazz to Prestige, the company reissued all records in its Prestige 800 series with the same titles and issue numbers.

86   Blue Note first issued these recordings as 78-rpm records (both 10- and 12-inch) under the names of Edmond Hall, John Hardee, Benny Morton, and Ike Quebec with the following catalog numbers: 17, 37, 38, 47, 510, 521. See the discography for complete details. One track from *Mellow the Mood*, Ike Quebec's "I Surrender, Dear," was never issued on 78 but originates from a July 1945 recording session. Relatedly, Blue Note issued its first LP in 1950 as part of its BLP 7000 series, which focused on reissues of Dixieland from the 1930s and 1940s.

87   As Sterne reminds us, such cultural logics did not emerge neutrally but were themselves contested and negotiated. This is one of the major arguments in Sterne, *Audible Past*. See also Bolter and Grusin, *Remediation*, 55.

88   The idea of self-referentiality, which has a long history in all Western musics, can also be understood as remediation. See Bolter and Grusin, *Remediation*, 49. As Susan Horning points out, there was an increased interest in the history of technology in the 1950s. For example, the first issue of the *Journal of the Audio Engineering Society* appeared in January 1953. Horning, *Chasing Sound*, 75. See also Millard, *America on Record*, 115.

89   Stearns, *Story of Jazz*; Hodeir, *Jazz*; Feather, *Encyclopedia of Jazz*; Williams, *Art of Jazz*. The original, French version of Hodeir's work appeared in 1954. These authors were neither the first jazz historians nor the first to care deeply about the music's origins. Rather, the publication of these more academically leaning books is part of a broader moment when prestigious cultural institutions began to recognize the importance of jazz history. I understand these publications as acts of legitimacy even as the specific motivations of each author differed. For related commentary, see Gennari, *Blowin' Hot and Cool*, 146–55.

90   Porter, *What Is This Thing Called Jazz?*, 92. Although Porter's statement refers to writers in the 1940s, his observations are equally relevant in the 1950s. Several other scholars make similar points about masculinity and jazz historiography, including Rustin-Paschal, *Kind of Man I Am*, 101–2; and Gennari, *Blowin' Hot and Cool*, 180–83.

91   Because media are, as Lisa Gitelman argues, inherently historical by design, they force an encounter with the past through their use: Gitelman, *Always*

Already New, 5. The dual meaning of the term *record* is a legacy of this cultural mechanism. Relatedly, Ludovic Tournè argues that the increased availability of music brought about by the LP led to a revival of baroque music in the 1950s. This, in turn, influenced musicians' interest in mixing baroque genres with jazz. (Tournè uses the Modern Jazz Quartet as an example.) See Tournè, "Redefining the Boundaries of Culture," 90-91.

92   The success of Goodman's *The Famous 1938 Carnegie Hall Jazz Concert* (1950) soon led to other LPs, including *The Benny Goodman Combos* (1951) and *Benny Goodman and His Orchestra* (1951). A detailed examination of this concert can be found in Hancock, *Benny Goodman*; and Tackley, *Benny Goodman's Famous 1938 Carnegie Hall Jazz Concert*.

93   Columbia issued Goodman's concert and the *Armstrong Story* series on the Masterworks label. At the end of 1951 (or start of 1952), Columbia began producing its first 12-inch popular music line, the GL 500 series, which then housed the others. The initial GL prefix lasted for twenty-four records, until the label changed the prefix to CL in 1953 (likely in August). Details about the release history can be found in Avakian to Floyd Levin, January 28, 1998, LP History file, GAA. These details are confirmed by Mike Callahan and David Edwards, "Columbia Main Series, Part 1: GL 500 to CL 599 (1951-1954)," accessed August 16, 2017, https://www.bsnpubs.com/columbia/columbia12/columbia500.html.

94   The first record in the 10-inch series, *Louis Armstrong Plays the Blues* (1953), was a collection of recordings from 1924 and 1925. Other records in the Jazz Archives Series include *Ma Rainey, vol. 1* (1953)—a collection of 1920s recordings—and *Ragtime Piano Rolls, vol. 1* (1953), which featured piano rolls made by various ragtime pianists. The 12-inch series followed a similar format, except for the ten-volume *Riverside History of Classic Jazz* (ca. 1955), one of the first attempts to package the complete recorded history of early jazz.

95   Orrin Keepnews, liner notes to *Coleman Hawkins: A Documentary*. Riverside issued a similar spoken-word record featuring Lil Armstrong: *Satchmo and Me: Lil Armstrong's Own Story* (1959). This was the only LP in the Jazz Archives Series (either 10- or 12-inch) to feature a women instrumentalist as a headliner, and here she appears only as a conduit to Louis Armstrong.

96   Bolter and Grusin discuss such rhetorical emphasis as the "transparency of media." Bolter and Grusin, *Remediation*, 5, 30-31.

97   Michael Warner argues that the creation of a public happens through "reflexive circulation of discourse" over time. Adding to this line of inquiry, Lisa Gitelman outlines how the medium of sound recording in the late nineteenth century created an "abstract sense of publicness" that, while more inclusive, was still generally created around "whiteness and masculinity." See Warner, "Publics and Counterpublics," 62-68; and Gitelman, *Always Already New*, 12, 15-16. For

more on the way in which race figured into the jazz press, see Gennari, *Blowin' Hot and Cool*.

98 Many scholars who write about the construction of music history connect masculine control to the marginalization of women. In this passage I draw from Baade, "'Battle of the Saxes.'" Christina Baade quotes Susan McClary: "One of the means of asserting masculine control over [music] is by denying the very possibility of participation by women." McClary, *Feminine Endings*, 151-52. See also Porter, *What Is This Thing Called Jazz?*, 219; Rustin-Paschal, *Kind of Man I Am*, 17; and Porter, "Born Out of Jazz," 218.

99 Steph Ceraso defines "sonic rhetorics" as the ways in which "sound, in conjunction with other elements of an environment or interaction, operates as a material, affective force that influences (not determines) listeners' bodily states, moods, thoughts, and actions." Ceraso, *Sounding Composition*, 11-12. See also Ceraso and Stone, *Sonic Rhetorics*.

100 I borrow this phrase (and its theoretical underpinnings) from Gitelman, *Always Already New*, 21.

101 Discographers have regularly asked musicians for information about specific recording sessions. Though nominally about record making, these documentarians sought a specific set of data that did not account for the social and cultural practices of the studio.

102 The complicated history of stereophony encompasses a convergence of media in radio, film, and home audio that can (depending on one's definition) be traced back to the nineteenth century. However, stereophonic sound on LP dates to the late 1950s and a series of milestones: Audio Fidelity Records producing the first mass-produced stereo LPs in 1957, the arrival of affordable stereo cartridges and the growth of stereo catalogs at most labels in 1958, and wide-scale commercial acceptance of the technology in 1959. The normalization of stereophonic home sound combined with the regularity of multitrack recording techniques marked a new ontological era of the LP. This book ends at the cusp of this transition, which is explored in Théberge, Devine, and Everett, *Living Stereo*; Barry, "High-Fidelity Sound," 115-38; and Read and Welch, *From Tin Foil to Stereo*, 426-37.

103 This research relies on many published discographies. These include Michael Cuscuna and Michel Ruppli's discography of Blue Note Records, as well as Ruppli's equally thorough reference work about Prestige Records. See Cuscuna and Ruppli, *Blue Note Label*; and Ruppli, *Prestige Label*. There are several excellent (and accurate) websites as well: Peter Losin's Miles Ahead, a richly detailed discography of Miles Davis (http://www.plosin.com); the expansive Jazz Discography Project compiled by Nobuaki Togashi, Kohji Matsubayashi, and Masayuki Hatta (https://www.jazzdisco.org); the visual discography of

Torbjörn Sörhuus's Birka Jazz Archive (https://www.birkajazz.com/archive/prestige.htm); the deep dives found in London Jazz Collector (https://londonjazzcollector.wordpress.com/); and the indispensable Both Sides Now Publications (https://www.bsnpubs.com/discog.html).

Chapter 1. Do the Huckle-Buck

1. There are various spellings and hyphenation patterns for the song's name. For consistency, I use the original spelling and hyphenation throughout.
2. "Fourth Annual Music-Record Poll," *Billboard*, January 14, 1950, 16-17. As of the November 9, 1949, issue of *Cash Box*, "The Huckle-Buck" had been on the charts for twenty-three weeks.
3. Both Parker and Williams worked with producer Teddy Reig at Savoy Records. For more about Williams's history, see Reig and Berger, *Reminiscing in Tempo*, 98; and Birnbaum, *Before Elvis*, 29, 257-58.
4. In the 1930s and 1940s, both Cab Calloway and Count Basie performed Gibson's music. For Gibson's history, see Birnbaum, *Before Elvis*, 258; and "Happy Birthday Andy Gibson," Jazz Museum in Harlem, accessed April 26, 2020, http://jazzmuseuminharlem.org/today-in-jazz/happy-birthday-andy-gibson.
5. On jazz and swing in relation to the music entertainment industry, see Ennis, *Seventh Stream*, 87, 194, and (more generally) chs. 3 and 7; Brackett, *Categorizing Sound*, 149-91; and Ake, *Jazz Cultures*, 42-61.
6. Ake argues that the historiographical emphasis on the rise of bebop has had the effect of distancing jazz from the commercial marketplace. Ake, *Jazz Cultures*, 60-61. David Brackett similarly critiques jazz historians for favoring an evolutional model that excludes the complex commercial interaction among musical styles, categories, and identity. Brackett, *Categorizing Sound*, 185-86. See also Ennis, *Seventh Stream*, 196-97; and DeVeaux, *Birth of Bebop*, 8-17.
7. See Brackett, *Categorizing Sound*, 151, 180-81, 185-86; and Ramsey, *Race Music*, 48, 56-73.
8. For example, see the three letters that discuss the positives and negatives of bebop: "Chords and Discords," *Down Beat*, June 3, 1949, 10. Two articles in the same issue also discuss the merits of bebop: Pat Harris, "Admire Dis, Claims Mole," 4; and Sharon A. Pease, "Bop Man Haig Serious and Well-Schooled," 12. Also see Armstrong's response to hearing Bunk Johnson: "You can give that four stars right off. You can dance to it! In bebop, they don't know which way they're going to turn." Louis Armstrong with Leonard Feather, "Lombardo Grooves Louis," *Metronome*, September 1949, 18.
9. "Savoy Waxery Goes Longhair," *Billboard*, October 22, 1949, 15. Regent would eventually issue around fifty LPs beginning in mid-1950, according to Ruppli

and Porter, *Savoy Label*. Throughout this chapter I cite approximate LP issue dates using the *Schwann Long Playing Record Catalog*, a comprehensive monthly listing of new and existing LPs—cited hereafter as *Schwann Catalog*. Started in October 1949 by record-store owner William Schwann as a means of tracking LP availability, the *Schwann Catalog* quickly became an invaluable source for store owners, distributors, executives, and collectors. Sometimes new LPs appear a month or two late, so I corroborate dates in the trade magazines whenever possible. So, for example, the first Regent LP appears in *Schwann Catalog* 2, no. 7 (July 1950).

10   Andrew Flory describes an "unmistakable shift in corporate agency" in how majors approached the R&B market during this time. Flory, *I Hear a Symphony*, 18-20. See also Kennedy and McNutt, *Little Labels, Big Sound*, xvi; and Broven, *Record Makers and Breakers*.

11   The All Stars would go on to perform the song (in full) during concerts and broadcasts on October 15, 1949 (Geneva, Switzerland); November 8, 1949 (Marseille, France); and January 26, 1951 (Vancouver, Canada). This is likely a partial list. See Willems, *All of Me*, 193, 200, 202, 212, 214. Ricky Riccardi, director of research collections for the Louis Armstrong House Museum, includes useful commentary about this date in Riccardi, "60 Years of 'Satchmo at Pasadena.'"

12   Cole joined Armstrong after Sid Catlett's departure in spring 1949. I reference Cole's recording below.

13   "Music as Written: Decca Tapes Satchmo Concert at Pasadena," *Billboard*, February 10, 1951, 8.

14   A handful of jam-session 12-inch LPs predate Clayton's. A month or so before Clayton's LP came to market, Decca issued *Decca Jazz Studio 1* (1954), with one track per side. Norman Granz had produced a few jam-session recordings for 12-inch LP release in 1953. See Norman Granz, "How LP Changed Methods of Waxing Jazz Sessions," *Down Beat*, September 23, 1953, 2. John Hammond had recorded Clayton during a similar session with Mel Powell for 10-inch release on Vanguard's new Jazz Showcase series. See *Mel Powell Septet* (1953).

15   As a result, retail sales grew about $3.3 million in 1954. Is Horowitz, "Jazz Disks, Paced by LP, Hit Cool 55% Jump in Hot Year," *Billboard*, April 23, 1955, 1, 13. The same *Billboard* issue reported a correlated increase for jazz box-office sales in nightclubs and concert halls: "Fields Get Shot in Arm from Jazz Boom," *Billboard*, April 23, 1955, 13.

16   My use of "segregational logic" builds on the work of many cultural historians and sound scholars who examine the centrality that race has had in creating commercial structures, circulation pathways, generic constructions, and musical discourses in the United States since Reconstruction. In particular, I draw from Karl Hagstrom Miller's exploration of how "music developed a color

line" and Jennifer Stoever's assertion that the "sonic color line" has variously produced, coded, and policed "racial difference through the ear." Relatedly, Matthew Morrison's formation of "Blacksound" usefully describes how "sonic and corporeal ideas of race" flowed through commercial entities and legal structures. Though historically situated earlier than the advent of the LP, the structures of race, gender, and class analyzed by these scholars clearly echo through the commercial ecosystem of the 1950s record industry, as Ingrid Monson discusses at some length. See K. Miller, *Segregating Sound*, 2–6; Stoever, *Sonic Color Line*, 6–13; Morrison, "Race, Blacksound, and the (Re)Making of Musicological Discourse"; and Monson, *Freedom Sounds*, 29–31. For more on these issues in blackface minstrelsy, see Lott, *Love and Theft*; and Rogin, *Blackface, White Noise*.

17 Okiji, *Jazz as Critique*, 11–31. A related critique of individualism and notions of history can be found in Crawley, *Blackpentecostal Breath*, 145–51.

18 "Fourth Annual Music-Record Poll," 16–17.

19 For an overview of such popular-music adaptations, see Flory, *I Hear a Symphony*, 19. For discussion about the versioning of "The Huckle-Buck" in relation to R&B history, see Birnbaum, *Before Elvis*, 257–58.

20 All appear in *Billboard*, April 30, 1949: "Music Popularity Charts, Part VII: Race Records," 34; Savoy Records, advertisement, 34; RCA Victor Records, advertisement, 25; "Record Reviews," 130. Chart rankings were Williams, #1 in retail and jukebox plays; Milton, #15 retail and #11 jukebox; and Millinder, #11 retail and #7 jukebox. The imitative "Hucklebuck Daddy," which shared a name but not the music, ranked #6 in retail.

21 "Fourth Annual Music-Record Poll," 14–17.

22 As is well documented, Andy Gibson initially wrote the song for Lucky Millinder under the title "D'Natural Blues." Williams heard and adapted it as "The Huckle-Buck," a name taken from a new dance he learned from some unknown audience members in Devons, Pennsylvania. See Williams's account in Reig and Berger, *Reminiscing in Tempo*, 100. Williams's recorded version hit the market first, and Millinder later filed suit to be added as a cowriter: "Lucky Would Extract Bucks from Out 'The Hucklebuck,'" *Billboard*, September 3, 1949, 34.

23 Kay C. Thompson, "Kansas City Man," *Record Changer*, December 1949, 9.

24 "Fourth Annual Music-Record Poll," 18–19. This movement from rhythm and blues to country was extremely rare. See Ennis, *Seventh Stream*, 200. Henry Glover arranged "Blues Stay Away from Me" for the Delmore Brothers at the direction of label-owner Syd Nathan, who explicitly wanted to capitalize on the financial success of "The Huckle-Buck."

25 Several scholars have explored the new trend in how hits from the Black market moved onto the white popular charts during this time. Flory, *I Hear a*

Symphony, 15-22, presents an industry overview, including some discussion of "The Huckle-Buck," an early crossover success. Brackett, *Categorizing Sound*, 170-73, 185-86, explores mainstream swing in relation to Black popular music, genre categories, and industry infrastructures. Ennis, *Seventh Stream*, 194, focuses on the role of artist and repertory professionals. Birnbaum, *Before Elvis*, 29, examines Sinatra's versioning specifically. This literature distinguishes between crossover hits and the few Black artists—e.g., the Ink Spots, the Mills Brothers, Louis Jordan, Ella Fitzgerald—that appeared on the pop charts before the LP era.

26 K. Miller, *Segregating Sound*, 187-97, 206-8.

27 Suisman, *Selling Sounds*, 207-39. As David Suisman argues, Black Swan was a project of racial uplift and economic justice, and its brief existence between 1921 and 1923 demonstrates the many difficulties that Black-owned businesses faced during the period.

28 The versions consistently appear in *Billboard*'s jukebox and retail charts as well as disc-jockey polls throughout the second half of 1949, though never in the top positions.

29 "Lucky Would Extract Bucks," 34.

30 United Music Corporation, advertisement, *Billboard*, April 30, 1949, 35.

31 Music-publishing firms generated revenue by securing multiple recordings of a song, often across different genres. See Ennis, *Seventh Stream*, 208-10; and Brackett, *Categorizing Sound*, 177-78.

32 Guthrie Ramsey points out that in the late 1940s, gospel played in same arenas, venues, and halls that jazz and R&B did. Moreover, many labels recorded all three styles. Ramsey, *Race Music*, 117.

33 For more on the circulation of records within Black communities, see Brooks, *Liner Notes for the Revolution*, 331-47. When asked directly about racial divisions at big firms, George Avakian (of Columbia) described a "cleavage in distribution" without offering details. "George Avakian Interview" (with Michael Jarrett), summer 1994, p. 7, box 13, folder 14, George Avakian and Anahid Ajemian papers (AAP), New York Public Library. Distribution networks remain an under-researched area in jazz studies.

34 The history of crossovers has been well documented in popular-music scholarship, including in Flory, *I Hear a Symphony*, 16-21. Before 1950, only a few Black artists could be found outside of the "race" market—these included Louis Armstrong, Nat King Cole, Ella Fitzgerald, the Mills Brothers, the Ink Spots, and Louis Jordan.

35 A "recording director" (producer) at the label coordinated with these publishers, which George Avakian (of Columbia) described as "call[ing] most of the

shots" at the time. "Avakian Interview" (with Jarrett), p. 2, box 13, folder 14, AAP. Milt Gabler (of Decca) adds that publishers "controlled the business" because they dictated and managed live broadcasts. "Milt Gabler Interview: Fall, 1995 and Summer, 1998," pp. 5-6, digital folder DF-20510/2, Series 1: Interviews and Transcripts, Michael Jarrett Collection, Southern Folklife Collection.

36   For further context about the speed of crossover songs and the artistic, economic, and social relationships between music publishers and radio broadcasters, see Ennis, *Seventh Stream*, 20-22, 192. For more about the historical shift from song to recordings that happened along racial and economic lines, see Brackett, *Categorizing Sound*, 153-60.

37   Brackett, *Categorizing Sound*, 150, 153-62. Brackett argues that the 1940s music industry moved from a profit model built around the song (work concept) to one around the recording (sonic aesthetic), which allowed Black musicians to circulate with a broader musical public. My analysis expands into the 1950s, when Black musicians used the increased emphasis on records to take more control over their representations (in contrast to the swing era, for example). See also Neal, *What the Music Said*; and Ramsey, *Race Music*.

38   Ennis, *Seventh Stream*, 176-80.

39   The subject of white jazz connoisseurs turned recordmen is broadly explored in Rustin-Paschal, *Kind of Man I Am*, 97-104.

40   Ramsey, *Race Music*, 121-23; Ennis, *Seventh Stream*, 87-88. The jazz press is covered extensively in Gennari, *Blowin' Hot and Cool*.

41   Eventually, television would rise above all, but in 1949, 95 percent of US households had at least one radio; by 1954, 70 percent of all households had two. Ennis, *Seventh Stream*, 132. See also R. Sanjek, *American Popular Music and Its Business*; and T. Anderson, *Making Easy Listening*.

42   For these estimates, see R. Sanjek, *American Popular Music and Its Business*, 55. The record industry's growth cannot be separated from the mass consumer culture that arose in the immediate postwar era. See L. Cohen, *Consumer's Republic*.

43   Through the 1950s, 45s consistently outsold LPs in terms of unit sales (i.e., number of records sold), whereas LPs generally captured a greater percentage of total retail sales because they cost more per individual unit.

44   "Three Speed Disk Biz Continues to Caution Record Distributors in Buying," *Cash Box*, July 2, 1949, 16. In the article, Southard also emphasized that from 750,000 to a million families had purchased playback equipment.

45   See the editorial note "45's & LP's Listed," *Billboard*, June 4, 1949, 17.

46   *Schwann Catalog* 1, no. 1 (October 1949). This number is likely an underestimate, though not by much. The number of labels in the *Schwann Catalog* rose every single month between October 1949 and May 1952, and then steadily

thereafter. The count was 158 by the start of 1953, 209 by the start of 1954, and 243 by the start of 1955. My count differs slightly from R. Sanjek, *American Popular Music and Its Business*, 244.

47   "Victor Distribs Tee off Drive on 45 Disks" and "45 R.P.M. Prices Are Announced by RCA Victor," *Billboard*, March 12, 1949, 21, 28. Though made from the same vinyl material, RCA's 45s had a larger hole, rotated at a different speed, and were only 7 inches in diameter. With up to four minutes per side, these discs were well suited for pop singles and quickly found their way into jukeboxes all over the country.

48   For further historical context, see Ennis, *Seventh Stream*, 132-34; and Read and Welch, *From Tin Foil to Stereo*, 333-42.

49   "Three Speed Disk Biz," 16.

50   "Point and Counterpoint: Record Evolution," *Metronome*, September 1949, 9.

51   LPs represented a larger share of the retail sales because they were so much more expensive than either of the singles formats.

52   "Victor to Distribute Extended Play 45's," *Billboard*, August 9, 1952, 21. RCA's national distribution campaign began in August 1952, although the label had been using EPs for its classical albums series since April of that year. As the report further states, "Tho this new technique can be used in all fields of music, it is most adaptable for classical singles."

53   "Victor Plugs EP 45s for Distribs," *Billboard*, August 30, 1952, 20. See also "Manufacturers Gird to Meet Challenge of New EP Line," *Billboard*, September 20, 1952, 20, 48; and "Now It's EP—a New Groove," *Down Beat*, September 10, 1952, 2.

54   "Indie Jazz Labels Entering EP Field," *Billboard*, February 21, 1953, 55; "Savoy, Regent to Issue EP's," *Billboard*, March 28, 1953, 17; Pacific Jazz, advertisement, *Down Beat*, May 20, 1953, 14; Savoy Records, advertisement, *Metronome*, July 1953, 29.

55   Manie Sacks, "The Future of EP Records," *Down Beat*, June 3, 1953, 13; George Avakian, "Our Trick, Your Treat, Says Columbia of LPs," *Down Beat*, June 3, 1953, 13. The same issue also included Jack [Tracy], "Extended Play—and How It Stacks up against LP System," *Down Beat*, June 3, 1953, 13.

56   "Jazz Trend: Albums Move toward More Important Role," *Billboard*, April 24, 1954, 18. This issue was a special spotlight on R&B, but also included quite a bit of jazz coverage.

57   Bob Rolontz, "Jazz LP's and EP's Become Disk Industry's Solid Staple," *Billboard*, June 5, 1954, 15, 46. Rolontz goes on to mention fourteen labels, including all majors and several independent firms, that were actively producing jazz on both LP and EP.

58   Horowitz, "Jazz Disks, Paced by LP," 1, 13.

59 Paul Ackerman, "Roads Lead to Great Package Disk Days; It'll Be a Rough Trip," *Billboard*, October 1, 1955, 1, 25, 40. A good overview of the rising trend toward packaged goods, defined as "any recording [all speeds] sold in album form or in a display sleeve or jacket," can be found in Joe Martin, "$61,400,000 Projected for Disk Sales from Sept.-Dec.," *Billboard*, August 29, 1953, 1, 18. Despite the increase of jazz activity, classical music remained the focus for most LP-producing labels. Keightley, "Long Play," 375–91.

60 "The Huckle-Buck" appeared on the LP *Rhythm and Blues, vol. 1*, which first appears in *Schwann Catalog* 4, no. 7 (July 1952). Savoy issued the song on 45 opposite Wild Bill Moore's "Bubbles" and then again on EP in 1953.

61 A reassessment of Lubinsky's approach with Savoy in relation to the racial politics of the industry during this time can be found in Cherry and Griffith, "Down to Business," 1–24.

62 *Schwann Catalog* 1, no. 2 (December 1949). Although the LP's cover gives the title as "Erroll Garner Playing Piano Solos," I have listed it here as it appears most regularly. Savoy would eventually issue four volumes of *Erroll Garner at the Piano* between 1949 and 1951.

63 "40 on Savoy's 1st 45 Release," *Billboard*, February 25, 1950, 14. The article reports a "full-scale effort" that included instrumental standards, semi-classical, polkas, spirituals, and the piano music of Erroll Garner. The majority of Charlie Parker's Savoy output would eventually circulate on 45 on the label's 45-300 series.

64 My observations here and throughout this section were made by examining Savoy's month-by-month release schedule in *Schwann Catalog* from 1949 to 1953, cross-referenced with the label's past 78-rpm output and published discographies. Where possible, I confirm dates with industry trades, especially *Billboard*. Savoy issued the LPs by Parker, Gordon, Navarro, Getz, and Young on its bebop-focused MG 9000 series. See the chapter playlist for the names and dates of these LPs (the first six in the series). They first appear in *Schwann Catalog* 3, no. 7 (July 1951), although the actual release schedule may have differed somewhat.

65 This count, as well as the others in the paragraph, does not include LPs issued on Regent, the label's classical subsidiary.

66 I made these (informal) estimations using label discographies cross-referenced with *Schwann Catalog*. I calculated the number of issued singles for both Columbia and Savoy using sequential issue numbers, which is a quick but relatively inaccurate way of tracking output. My approximation of Columbia's output—715 LPs, 2,052 singles—does not account for the label's many subsidiaries or any international distribution. Nevertheless, these numbers are useful as a comparative (rather than a precise) accounting.

67   King's first two LPs—including *Concert of Cool Jazz* by the Cecil Young Quartet—first appeared in *Schwann Catalog* 4, no. 6 (June 1952). All issue dates for King LPs are unclear, so my estimated number of LP releases (five) is possibly low; because they appear to be direct clones, my count does not account for the Varsity LPs issued under the King label. King adjusted strategy and began issuing many more LPs in 1953, just after the period I emphasize here. Specialty's first LP was *Buddy Baker and His Orchestra's Stairway to the Stars*, issued in early 1952 as a 10-inch LP. Though not mentioned in the *Schwann Catalog*, the LP does appear in "Advance Record Releases," *Billboard*, January 19, 1952, 40. Pushing Little Richard in particular, Specialty would reorient toward the LP market in 1957.

68   The most-issued artist on King was Earl Bostic. See Ruppli and Daniels, *King Labels*. Atlantic, which issued a handful of jazz LPs during this period, is another minor exception. The label would move toward jazz in 1955, as I discuss below.

69   These observations were made by examining the release schedules of roughly five hundred jazz LPs across forty labels in the *Schwann Catalog* from 1949 to 1953. Coral, a Decca subsidiary (and thus not technically an indie), also issued a dozen jazz LPs before the start of 1953.

70   I base this count on the listings in *Schwann Catalog* 4, no. 12 (December 1952). For comparison, recall that Savoy's total output over the same period was thirty-five LPs.

71   All issue dates come from the first appearance of each LP in the corresponding issue of the *Schwann Catalog*. In some cases the true issue date might be a month (sometimes two) before. Several Armstrong LPs appeared before May 1951, including three on Decca and one on Jolly Roger (JR), a bootleg LP label.

72   Initially, Savoy had two 10-inch series differentiated by catalog number: its MG 15000 series leaned historical (but mixed), and its MG 9000 series focused on bebop (or related). Dial had three similar lines: its 200 series for "modern" jazz (read bebop), its 300 "historical jazz" series, and its 900 "collectors special" (12-inch LPs).

73   Blue Note's use of "jazz classics" on, for example, Sidney Bechet's *Jazz Classics, vol. 1*, followed Brunswick (a Decca subsidiary), which had issued an Armstrong LP titled *Jazz Classics* as part of its "collectors series" in early 1950. See "Coral Records and Brunswick Records Now Available in Long Play," advertisement, *Billboard*, March 24, 1950, 22. In early 1951, Decca reissued eight volumes of Bing Crosby material with the title *Collectors' Classics: Bing Crosby*. Capitol Records started its "Classics in Jazz" series in the spring of 1952 (all reissues of 78 albums under the same name). The chapter playlist includes nine examples featuring Coleman Hawkins, Woody Herman, Bobby Sherwood, and six compilations with various artists.

74 Blue Note's first LPs appear in *Schwann Catalog* 2, no. 11 (November 1950). Like others, the label used its catalog numbers to differentiate its "traditional" series (BLP 7000) from its "modern" one (BLP 5000). Blue Note had issued fourteen LPs in its traditional line before the first "modern" LP appeared around September 1951. I discuss the racialized underpinnings of the word *modern* in chapter 2.

75 According to the RIAA, LPs accounted for 18.6 percent of the total retail sales in 1952. See "RIAA Reports $205,000,000 Gross as All Time High for Record Industry," *Cash Box*, May 15, 1954, 16. Outdated formats often linger long past their peak—Michel Ruppli and Bob Porter state that Savoy issued its last 78 rpm in July 1959. See Ruppli and Porter, *Savoy Label*, 365.

76 A good resource that discusses format in relation to cultural value is Keightley, "Long Play," 375-91.

77 Despite the early-1951 performance-turned-recording date, Decca did not issue *Satchmo at Pasadena* until July or August 1952. The LP first appears in *Schwann Catalog* 4, no. 8 (August 1952), although Ricky Riccardi reports a July 1952 issue date. Riccardi, "Louis Armstrong." Riccardi's extensive notes here are a reposting of the liner notes to the Universal Music Group's digital-only issue of Louis Armstrong, *The Decca Singles: 1949-1958*.

78 See "Music as Written: Decca Tapes Satchmo Concert at Pasadena," *Billboard*, February 10, 1951, 8.

79 See the discography for all issued versions. The two volumes of 45 albums, a somewhat common format during this period, appeared at the same time as the LP. The singles seem to have been issued before the LP, likely in April 1952, at least according to the discographical listings in Ruppli, *Decca Labels*, which I cross-referenced with Daniels, *American 45 and 78 RPM Record Dating Guide*. This accounting contradicts Riccardi's statement that "Baby It's Cold Outside" (in edited form) was the only live material to get the "single treatment." See Riccardi, "Louis Armstrong." Circulation history often remains elusive.

80 Decca is well represented in the first *Schwann Catalog* on both 10- and 12-inch sizes, and with regular additions across series and genres thereafter.

81 As above, I made these (informal) estimations using label discographies cross-referenced with *Schwann Catalog*. My approximation of Decca's output—715 LPs, 1,946 singles—does not account for the label's many subsidiaries or any international distribution.

82 Marshall Stearns to David Kapp, March 20, 1950, Decca Folder, Record Company Files, Institute of Jazz Studies (IJS).

83 Gabler founded Commodore Records in 1938 using his acclaimed New York City radio and record shop as his operations hub. Commodore was the first

independent jazz label, the first label to successfully reissue out-of-print jazz recordings, and the first label to print complete musician credits on the record. For more on Gabler's record store, see Burke, *Come In and Hear the Truth*, 129–33.

84 Decca's early LP catalog included Johnson's *The Daddy of the Piano* as well as Condon's *George Gershwin Jazz Concert* and *Jazz Concert at Eddie Condon's*. Both Condon LPs were exact reissues of 78-rpm albums from 1946. The LPs mentioned here first appear in the May, July, September, and November issues of *Schwann Catalog* 2 (1950).

85 The aforementioned letter—Stearns to Kapp, March 20, 1950—confirms this specific reissue strategy. Decca issued its first jazz LPs the following month. Basie's *At the Piano* was a direct reissue of a 78-rpm album from 1948; the LP version first appears in *Schwann Catalog* 2, no. 4 (April 1950). The two volumes of *Gems of Jazz* first show up in *Schwann Catalog* 2, no. 5 (May 1950), although a review appears the month prior: "Album and LP Record Reviews," *Billboard*, April 22, 1950, 45. Folkways took a similar approach with its series of historical retrospectives under the titles *Jazz, vol. 1, The South* and *Jazz, vol. 2, The Blues*, beginning in October 1950 (and continuing). The first of these 12-inch LPs appears in *Schwann Catalog* 2, no. 10 (October 1950).

86 One *Billboard* article from January 1953 estimates that Decca had "more than 20 jazz albums in its active catalog." Twenty out of my estimated 715 LPs issued by Decca over the same period is 2.8 percent. It is unclear how either *Billboard* or Decca defined jazz within the context or what "active catalog" means, although the author does state the top sellers as Armstrong and Lionel Hampton. See "Decca Issues 5 New Jazz Sets," *Billboard*, January 31, 1953, 14. A broader (and more contemporary) view of how to define jazz places this number close to forty LPs, which would still be a small percentage of overall output.

87 The *Schwann Catalog* lists Tharpe's LPs under "Religious." Decca appears to have issued both Jordan and Tharpe on earlier 78-rpm albums and, in the early to mid-1950s, an assortment of EPs and 45-rpm sets—these remain a notable exception to the firm's overall strategy with Black markets. My discography includes only Tharpe's LPs: *Blessed Assurance* and *Wedding Ceremony*.

88 For more on the music of both groups at Decca, see Friedwald, *Jazz Singing*, 173–77. Decca issued two Mills Brothers LPs in 1949, two Ink Spots LPs in 1950, and a few others from both groups between 1951 and 1953. The first LPs of these artists are included in the discography.

89 I have included several of Decca's LPs featuring Holiday, Fitzgerald, and Armstrong in this chapter's playlist. In 1951 the RIAA estimated that R&B accounted for 5.7 percent of the industry's total output. Here are the other percentages for comparison: 18.9 classical, 13.2 country and western, 10.2

children's, 1.1 international, 1.0 Latin American, 0.8 "hot jazz." See R. Sanjek, *American Popular Music and Its Business*, 245.

90 "Look to Decca for Great Rhythm and Blues and Jazz," advertisement, *Billboard*, April 24, 1954, 39. Although tangential to my point here, this ad displays Decca's rather ambiguous approach to genre. The records of Leith Stevens—a white composer, conductor, and bandleader—appear under the headings of both R&B singles and jazz albums.

91 The release history of these records is unclear. One (unverified) report from March 1948 outlines plans from Sunset Records to release Norman's Just Jazz titles on 12-inch discs with distribution in New York, Boston, and Chicago. I could not find further details. In 1951 *Billboard* mentions in passing that Modern Records took over the issuing of Norman's Just Jazz recordings from the "now defunct" Black & White label; several titles from Modern's 78-rpm catalog do appear to have come from Norman. See "Bernay Returns to Platter Biz," *Billboard*, March 20, 1948, 16; and "Hamp's Jam: Decca Issue Out After He Leaves," *Billboard*, February 10, 1951, 16.

92 Hampton's LP first appears in *Schwann Catalog* 3, no. 3 (March 1951). As in the advertisement above, the record's cover prominently displays "recorded Civic Auditorium, Pasadena, California, August 1947." Somewhat confusingly, Decca also issued several compilation LPs with the word *concert* in the title even though they were, in fact, studio recordings. My table does not include these LPs. Note that four of the five items are from Norman, with *Satchmo at Symphony Hall* as the lone exception.

93 Gabler discusses the origins of these jam sessions in "Reminiscences of Milton Gabler: Oral History, 1959," pp. 1870–72, Popular Arts Project NXCP89-A30, Columbia Center for Oral History. For more on the cultural underpinnings of jam-session concerts, see DeVeaux, "Emergence of the Jazz Concert," 11–16; and Baade, "Airing Authenticity," 276–82.

94 The discography includes a detailed listing of these Commodore records. The most complete history of jam-session records can be found in Dan Morgenstern, liner notes to *The Complete CBS Buck Clayton Jam Sessions*, 3–4. The development of jam-session records—inclusive of both concert and studio recordings—follows this path: Gabler (Commodore), Blesh (Circle Records), Granz (Mercury, Clef), and then Hammond (Vanguard). By Morgenstern's account, one 1937 disc predates this development: *A Jam Session at Victor: HoneySuckle Rose/Blues*, featuring Tommy Dorsey, Bunny Berigan, and Fats Waller.

95 Granz held the first JATP concert on July 2, 1944, at the Philharmonic Auditorium, Los Angeles. See Hershorn, *Norman Granz*. Granz attended several of the sessions at Jimmy Ryan's, and Gabler would later take some credit for helping

to inspire JATP. See "Reminiscences of Milton Gabler," pp. 1870-71, Popular Arts Project.

96   Beginning in 1945, Granz began leasing his recordings to Asch, Disc, and Stinson Records. JAPT recordings later appear on various other labels, including Mercury, Norgran, and Clef (Granz owned the latter two).

97   These LPs are listed in *Schwann Catalog* 1, no. 1 (October 1949), and *Schwann Catalog* 2, no. 2 (February 1950). Eight more JATP Mercury LPs follow in *Schwann Catalog* 2, no. 4 (April 1950). Gabler reissued the Commodore sessions on LP around June 1952. Granz outlines his "special affection" for the LP in his 1953 *Down Beat* article: Granz, "How LP Changed Methods of Waxing."

98   Columbia simultaneously issued Clayton's "Huckle-Buck" on 12-inch LP, full EP set, and EP single (in edited-down form). Contemporaneous advertisements list all versions together—for example, "Columbia Keeps Sales Jumping with 12-Inch Hi-Fi Jazz," advertisement, *Billboard*, April 24, 1954, 49.

99   The "ever growing" statement, repeated in similar forms elsewhere, can be found in George Avakian to Peter [no surname], drafted letter with corrections, ca. 1990-93, p. 3, box 21, folder 6, AAP. In the early 2000s, Avakian also recollected that he had "a very attractive kind of autonomy there [at Columbia]—I didn't even have to write up a budget each year, because the money kept rolling in, and in effect subsidized the jazz operation." Richard M. Sudhalter, liner notes to *Columbia Small Group Swing Sessions 1953-62*, 2. Avakian's contemporaneous view of the economic restrictions of producing jazz can be found in George Simon, "Inside Jazz on Records," *Metronome*, January 1955, 18-19.

100 This record (CL 535) sometimes appears under the name *Erroll Garner at the Piano*. Avakian comments on the growing popularity of 12-inch LPs in "Columbia into High Gear on Long Play Jazz, Pops," *Down Beat*, July 28, 1954, 3. For more discussion about Garner's early LPs with Avakian, see Jarrett, "Cutting Sides," 330; and Jarrett, *Pressed for All Time*, 27-28.

101 Avakian's promotional book (discussed below) makes clear that he thought of these three LPs as a set to explore the 12-inch format for jazz. The other albums are Turk Murphy and His Jazz Band, *When the Saints Go Marching In*, and Eddie Condon, *Jam Session Coast-to-Coast*. See George Avakian, "Jazz at Columbia," promotional booklet, ca. 1954, Columbia Liners file, George Avakian private archives (GAA), Riverdale, NY. My citations include folder names that generally correspond to Subseries 1B: Alphabetical Files in the collection's new home at the New York Public Library.

102 Avakian, "Jazz at Columbia," Columbia Liners file, GAA. The booklet is undated, although the 1954 date is confirmed by the clear promotional function as well as the walking eye logo, which S. Neil Fujita designed to represent a stylus above

the grooves of a record. The logo was first introduced in 1954. The liner notes to Garner's aforementioned LP on Columbia express a similar logic about the possibilities of long-play recording: "I had only told him that I wanted him to record some double-length numbers for long-play and extended play release." Garner's trio went on to record thirteen numbers, with a close average of six minutes each. George Avakian, liner notes to *Erroll Garner*.

103   Various other jam-session LPs are discussed in Granz, "How LP Changed Methods of Waxing," 2. Avakian's promotional book obliquely references *Decca Jazz Studio 1* another jam-session LP issued just before Clayton's record.

104   For one example among many, see "LP, Boon to Music World, as Seen after 5 Years," *Down Beat*, September 23, 1953, 9.

105   Keightley, "Long Play," 375, 378, 380–86. My own research supports Keightley's assertions, although I believe he sometimes knits the early-1950s jazz and classical fields too closely together. Writing in 1997, Avakian also offers a slight corrective from the pre-LP era, stating that 78-rpm albums occupied a similar position as a stable commodity in comparison with singles. George Avakian to John [no surname], drafted letter (crossed out), May 19, 1997, box 22, folder 3, AAP.

106   Rolontz, "Jazz LP's and EP's Become Disk Industry's Solid Staple"; Sanjek, *American Popular Music and Its Business*, 338.

107   Rolontz, "Jazz LP's and EP's Become Disk Industry's Solid Staple." He mentions artists such as Shorty Rogers, Eddie Sauter-Finegan, Stan Kenton, Benny Goodman, Glenn Miller, and Artie Shaw.

108   See Crist, *Dave Brubeck's "Time Out,"* 16–22; Klotz, *Dave Brubeck and the Performance of Whiteness*, 117–55; and Gennari, *Blowin' Hot and Cool*, 173. The connections between formal criticism and cultural legitimacy around issues of race are also explored in Ramsey, *Race Music*, 121–23.

109   See especially Klotz, "On Musical Value," as well as Klotz, *Dave Brubeck and the Performance of Whiteness*.

110   Avakian, "Jazz at Columbia," Columbia Liners file, GAA.

111   John Hammond and George Avakian, liner notes to *The Huckle-Buck and Robbins' Nest: A Buck Clayton Jam Session*, LP, 1954. Of the musicians on Clayton's jam-session date, Julian Dash performed with Erskine Hawkins, Henderson Chambers with Lucky Millinder, and Joe Newman with Lionel Hampton. In the early 1950s, Clayton's recorded music foregrounded a variety of styles (beyond jazz) that would fall under the R&B heading.

112   In his concluding paragraph, Avakian writes: "Beginning with these remarks . . . you can now go into the matter more deeply—and we believe that you'll be glad you did, and so will your public!" Avakian, "Jazz at Columbia," Columbia Liners file, GAA.

113 Bob Rolontz, "Fine New Set Has Flavor of Jam Session," *Billboard*, April 10, 1954, 21, 47.

114 The relationship between jazz and Black working-class audiences is discussed (with no mention of the LP) in Neal, *What the Music Said*, 197; and Ramsey, *Race Music*, 56–73, 123–26. Ramsey points out that Leonard Feather's *Inside Be-Bop* (1949; reissued as *Inside Jazz* [1977]) overemphasized the connection between bebop and classical without mention of the blues or other forms of Black popular music.

115 Avakian produced both LPs. Columbia Records, "New LP a 98-Cent Jazz History," advertisement, *Billboard*, June 4, 1955, 25; "64G Jazz: Columbia Cuts Time to Tie-In," *Billboard*, October 15, 1955, 15, 18.

116 This record featured tracks recorded in 1946, 1949, 1950, and 1952 that had never appeared on LP. Further information can be found in Silva, *Put Your Dreams Away*.

117 "Col'bia to Jump Back into 10-in LP Field," *Billboard*, October 1, 1955, 16, 20. The House Party series launched in October 1955 with LPs retailing at $1.98—a typical 10-inch popular LP on Columbia sold for $2.98. In the article, Hal Cook, director of sales, described Columbia's strategy toward the teenage market.

118 For more on the aspirational domesticity circulating on LPs during the postwar era, see Borgerson and Schroeder, *Designed for Hi-Fi Living*.

119 Keightley, "Long Play," 377–78, 385.

120 Columbia had actually discontinued its entire 10-inch LP catalog in the summer of 1955, only to revive production of the size in October for this series. See "Col'bia to Jump Back into 10-in LP Field," 16.

121 Keightley, "Long Play," 385.

122 Columbia typically sold its 10-inch popular LPs for $2.98. For more on popular music and LP royalties, see Myers, *Why Jazz Happened*, 86–90.

123 The series ended officially in April 1957 as the last 10-inch line produced by a major label. "Columbia Writes Finis to 10"-ers," *Billboard*, April 27, 1957, 17. My thinking about market segmentation in the 1950s comes from L. Cohen, *Consumer's Republic*, 292–344.

124 "Col'bia to Jump Back into 10-in LP Field," 16, 20.

125 By the mid-1950s, LPs had become the backbone of the industry. For example, industry-wide profits for single records went from 80 percent in 1953 to 25–35 percent in 1957. See Keightley, "Long Play," 379.

126 Ackerman, "Roads Lead to Great Package Disk Days," 1, 25, 40.

127 The data, although quite noisy, show an obvious expansion of 12-inch offerings across all labels and genres. See volume 7 (1955) and volume 8 (1956) of

the *Schwann Catalog*. Before 1955, majors were already quite active in the pop LP fields of all sizes, and a small number of independents (e.g., Atlantic) had already issued one or two 12-inch LPs. Norgran was an outlier and was already well represented on the larger format by this time. These exceptions aside, the increased activity by (generally cash-strapped) independents in 1955 and 1956 signaled a much more meaningful shift.

128 "The Jazz Renaissance," *Billboard*, April 23, 1955, 13.

129 "Jazz Comes of Age," *Cash Box*, March 31, 1956, 3. The market position of jazz as distinct from other popular music is also discussed in Howland, "Jazz with Strings," 141.

130 Avakian finishes this statement by discussing the "flowering" of the Columbia jazz catalog. George Avakian, "The History of Columbia Is Saga of Jazz," *Down Beat*, December 12, 1956, 14. For further detail about Avakian's approach and Columbia's move to the 12-inch format for popular music, see Myers, *Why Jazz Happened*, 86–90.

131 The first 12-inch LPs issued by Pacific (May 1955), Bethlehem (June 1955), Prestige and Savoy (July 1955), Roost (December 1955), Blue Note (January 1956), and Debut (March 1956) appear in volume 7 (1955) and volume 8 (1956) of the *Schwann Catalog*. Actual issue dates might vary slightly from these listings.

132 This clear trend can be observed in volume 8 (1956) of the *Schwann Catalog*. Riverside had (like others) issued a small number of 12-inch LPs before this time but began regularly issuing the larger format beginning in January 1956.

133 Although its first recordings happened in 1953, Vanguard issued its first LPs (sponsored by *Down Beat*) in March 1954: "Reviews and Ratings of New Popular Albums," *Billboard*, March 27, 1954, 38. Despite being established around May 1954, EmArcy did not announce its plans for LPs and EP until July 1954: "EMARCY JAZZ: Label Plans LP, EP and Single Disks," *Billboard*, July 24, 1954, 14. EmArcy is first mentioned in the *Schwann Catalog* 7, no. 3 (March 1955).

134 The establishment of Jazztone is announced in Concert Hall Society, "10 All-Time Great Jazz Classics," advertisement, *Life*, July 11, 1955, 7. The history of mail-order labels—including Jazztone Society—is discussed in Wheeler, *Jazz by Mail*. According to *Billboard*, the owners of Aladdin officially formed Jazz West Records in February 1956 as a "package line featuring jazz only." See "Mesners Form New Co., Jazz West Records," *Billboard*, February 11, 1956, 15. The Jazz West moniker had previously been used on a handful of LPs issued by Aladdin in late 1954 and 1955.

135 "N. Ertegun Is New Atlantic Partner," *Billboard*, January 15, 1955, 10. The report mentions plans for Atlantic to focus on both contemporary and traditional jazz styles.

136 *Billboard* described Argo as a new "pop label" with plans to feature Ahmad Jamal and James Moody (among others). "New Pop Acts, Jazz LP's on Argo Agenda," *Billboard*, April 28, 1956, 24. Argo issued its first LPs in May 1956, eventually committing more fully to jazz in 1958, when the firm hired David Usher. See Collis and Guy, *Story of Chess Records*, 183-85, 214-17. According to the first reports about the subsidiary, in April 1953, Label "X" was similar to Coral (Decca) and OKeh (Columbia). Nev Gehman, "RCA Goes on a Multi-label Kick, Mulls Two New Ones," *Billboard*, April 25, 1953, 44, 72. Despite the date, the label did not issue records until early 1954. See Hannah Altbush, "A One-Year History of Label 'X,'" *Down Beat—Part 2* (special supplement), January 26, 1955, 3-4, 7.

137 "Categories of Jazz Disks," *Billboard*, April 23, 1955, 14. As early as 1950, Marshall Stearns suggested to David Kapp that Decca should compile a "book of jazz" to "educate the dealer and distributor, as well as the public" about the label's catalog. Stearns to Kapp, March 20, 1950, Record Company Files, IJS.

138 See Orrin Keepnews and Bill Grauer, "Re-issue Albums Have Solid Sale Potential," *Billboard*, April 23, 1955, 20, 24, 36; Bob Shad, "Building Jazz Catalog Is Major Undertaking," *Billboard*, April 30, 1955, 22; George Avakian, "Get All the Facts in No Space, but Interesting," *Billboard*, May 21, 1955, 42.

139 Bill Coss, "Jazz Label: Prestige," *Metronome*, August 1953, 22. This quotation is a paraphrase of Weinstock's comments.

140 Ralph Gleason Jr., "Buck Clayton Has a New LP with Woody Herman," *San Francisco Chronicle*, August 8, 1954, "This World," 17. *How Hi the Fi* was the follow-up to Clayton's jam-session record discussed above.

141 Keepnews and Grauer, "Re-issue Albums Have Solid Sale Potential."

142 Here I draw from Keightley, "Long Play," 382-83.

143 "Jazz Comes of Age," 3.

144 These same (unspoken) themes are also found in Avakian, "Our Trick, Your Treat, Says Columbia of LPs," 13.

145 Sinatra's version ranks #6 (and Goodman's #3) on this predictive survey by disc jockeys: "Music Popularity Charts, Part IX: Record Possibilities," *Billboard*, May 28, 1949, 34. Later that year, and on its tenth weekly appearance, Sinatra's record ranked #26 on the "records most played by disk jockeys" list: "Music Popularity Charts, Part III: Radio Popularity," *Billboard Disk Jockey Supplement*, October 22, 1949, 62.

146 Gennari, *Blowin' Hot and Cool*, 173.

147 Gennari, *Blowin' Hot and Cool*, 155-56, 172-73, 193-94. For more on the presence of jazz in *Good Housekeeping* and *Playboy*, see Klotz, *Dave Brubeck and the Performance of Whiteness*, 77-84, 96-115.

148 R. Sanjek, *American Popular Music and Its Business*, 340. The R&B field moved toward the packaged market in the 1960s. See Flory, *I Hear a Symphony*.

149 Keightley, "Long Play." This long-term extraction strategy continued, and it underlies the catastrophe of the 2008 fire at the vaults of the Universal Music Group; see Jody Rosen, "The Day the Music Burned," *New York Times Magazine*, June 11, 2019, https://www.nytimes.com/2019/06/11/magazine/universal-fire-master-recordings.html.

Chapter 2. Mistakes, Mishaps, and Miscues

1 This album also included "Out of the Blue" from the same session and "Blue Room" from an earlier session in January 1951.

2 Ira Gitler, liner notes to *Miles Davis: Blue Period*. Davis's group based "Out of the Blue" on the harmonic structure of "Get Happy," the well-known standard by Harold Arlen. Gitler references this connection within the parenthetical phrase: "OUT OF THE BLUE (Miles' plea to get happy)."

3 This quotation originates from a *Down Beat* article titled "Weinstock Judges Stars by Emotion, Musicianship," January 13, 1954, reprinted in the liner notes to *The Prestige Records Story*, 11.

4 Wilson also noted that these lengthy recordings "could not have been squeezed onto a 78-rpm disc even if anybody had thought of doing it at the time." John Wilson, "Unbound Jazz: Invention of LP Gave Jam Session Space," *New York Times*, March 16, 1958, section 11, 22.

5 Jazz offers a particular vantage point on these issues because it is a genre where listeners value both spontaneous improvisation and the reproducibility of records. Elsdon, "Jazz Recordings"; Rasula, "Media of Memory"; Tackley, "Jazz Recordings as Social Texts."

6 For more on the notion of the sonic color line, see Stoever, *Sonic Color Line*, 6–13.

7 Both quoted liner notes are by Ira Gitler.

8 Rustin-Paschal, *Kind of Man I Am*, 2–5, 98–104, 115–16, 128 (and elsewhere).

9 Rustin-Paschal, *Kind of Man I Am*, 97–104, 115–16. Here I extrapolate her quotation, which appears at the end of a section discussing the record making of Charles Mingus.

10 This chapter uses materials from the record collection at the Institute of Jazz Studies (IJS), housed at Rutgers University-Newark. The collection contains nearly 100,000 records, including multiple versions of the same record. Sometimes these copies differ dramatically in their visual design and layout. Traditional citation methods do not account for such differences because they

assume that a record with a unique catalog number (e.g., PRLP 104) equals another. To account for such differences, I cite some recordings multiple times in their different iterations. Whenever possible, I have accessed the physical media.

11   The discursive terrain would have been familiar to anyone who lived through bebop's rise during the years just before Prestige's founding. For example, the jazz press often described bebop musicians as "modernists," a label musicians chose to adopt, adapt, or reject for their own purposes. See Gendron, "'Moldy Figs' and Modernists"; Ramsey, *Race Music*, 96-130; and Monson, *Freedom Sounds*, 17-20, 66-106.

12   These tracks originate from about twenty recording dates in 1949, 1950, and 1951. All the LPs mentioned in this passage were among the first twenty-five issued by Prestige. In its use of "new" and "modern," Prestige closely followed other labels. For example, the back of Savoy's LP *New Sounds in Modern Music: Charlie Parker, vol. 1* (1951) includes the tagline "Savoy—The Greatest Name in Jazz, Modern Music, Rhythm and Blues." At the end of 1951, Blue Note started its "modern" BLP 5000 series, and Dial began its "modern" LP 200 series to feature their respective recordings with a bebop influence. For comparison, the music recorded by Davis on Prestige appeared on 78 rpm simply as "Miles Davis and His Band."

13   "Weinstock Judges Stars," 13.

14   See especially Monson, *Freedom Sounds*, 17-20; and Weheliye, *Phonographies*, 5-8.

15   Ramsey, *Race Music*, 97-101, 106-8.

16   Cabaret cards were required to perform in nightclubs. Monk lost his cabaret card in 1948 and again in 1951. Holiday lost hers in 1948, and Parker lost his in 1951. Clarke, *Wishing on the Moon*, 285; Kelley, *Thelonious Monk*, 155-57; Woideck, *Charlie Parker*, 43-44. A few years later, in 1959, a police officer violently beat Miles Davis outside of Birdland while he was on break between sets. For a related discussion about how this altercation intersected with the broader cultural politics related to record covers, see Cawthra, *Blue Notes in Black and White*, 125-27, 168.

17   On jazz clubs, see Burke, *Come In and Hear the Truth*; on jazz and film, see Knight, "Jammin' the Blues"; for Broadway orchestras, see Gillespie and Fraser, *To Be, or Not*, 411.

18   By a large margin, these same white musicians appeared more regularly on the covers of these periodicals than their Black colleagues. More exact figures regarding these readers' polls and magazine covers can be found in Monson, *Freedom Sounds*, 66-70.

19   In the first three chapters of *Freedom Is, Freedom Ain't*, Scott Saul details the parallels between these jazz subgenres and the fight for civil rights, particularly how musicians pushed back against this universalist notion of jazz. See Saul, *Freedom Is, Freedom Ain't*. Jazz's emerging Black aesthetic happened in parallel to other social contestations and political victories, including *Brown v. Board of Education* (1954), which declared state-sanctioned segregation illegal, and the State Department's decisions to use jazz in its Cold War propaganda efforts abroad (see chapter 4). Also see Porter, *What Is This Thing Called Jazz?*

20   Ramsey, *Race Music*, 77-78, 104-5, 127; Neal, *What the Music Said*, 27-32.

21   This aspect of Prestige's approach changed in the early 1960s as the label shifted its business model to reflect the popularity of hard bop and soul jazz. Weinstock also started several subsidiary labels that specifically focused on blues and folk music.

22   As several scholars point out, Prestige's racial politics followed Blue Note in many respects: Ramsey, *Race Music*, 117-20; Rosenthal, *Hard Bop*, 64-65. For a related discussion about modernism, commercialism, and the complexities of being an African American bebop musician, though with little concern for gender, see DeVeaux, *Birth of Bebop*, 13-17. For an analysis of gender and record making, see Rustin-Paschal, *Kind of Man I Am*, 95-125.

23   For more on the connections between modernism and colorblindness in jazz, see Monson, *Freedom Sounds*, 70-71, 78-80. My thanks to Kelsey Klotz, who helped me think through these issues.

24   See Lewis, "Improvised Music after 1950," 92-93, 99-103; and Crawley, *Blackpentecostal Breath*, 145-51, 195-96. Ashon Crawley's exploration of Black performance outside the notion of History (with a capital *H*) and Western philosophical thought points to the same mechanisms of cultural valuation that George Lewis also explores.

25   Many contemporaneous commentators note the increased circulation of historically important records, including the author of "Jazz Trend: Albums Move toward More Important Role," *Billboard*, April 24, 1954, 18.

26   Although these texts were not the first to take jazz's origins and development seriously, my aim is to put these academic jazz-history texts in conversation with the commercial structures that increasingly recognized the value of jazz history: Stearns, *Story of Jazz*; Hodeir, *Jazz*; Feather, *Encyclopedia of Jazz*; and Williams, *Art of Jazz*. A revealing analysis of this historiography can be found in Dunkel, "Marshall Winslow Stearns and the Politics of Jazz Historiography."

27   Monson, *Freedom Sounds*, 73-74.

28 Ira Gitler, liner notes to *Miles Davis: The New Sounds*; Wilson, "Unbound Jazz," which is from 1958. The seven-year separation reveals the lingering power that this discourse of technological freedom had during the 1950s.

29 *Stan Getz, vol. 2* (1951) was Prestige's fourth LP issued. The marketing copy found on this disc (found at the Institute of Jazz Studies) likely dates from after the initial print run for Getz's 1951 LP.

30 The sessions occurred on August 14, August 27, and October 5, 1951, by Zoot Sims, Gerry Mulligan, and Miles Davis, respectively. These recordings appear on *Miles Davis: The New Sounds* (1952), *Miles Davis: Blue Period* (1953), *Gerry Mulligan Blows* (1953), and *Swingin' with Zoot Sims* (1951).

31 Jarrett, "Cutting Sides," 331. Weinstock is correct about the personnel, although he misremembers Davis's session as the first. His time line about LPs is open to question: Prestige's first LP session occurred three years after Columbia's first LPs came to market.

32 Jarrett, "Cutting Sides," 331.

33 Commercial uses of stereophonic recording and playback began in the 1920s and 1930s. For instance, Disney's film *Fantasia* (1940) famously used stereo playback in theaters. The recording industry experimented with stereo in the 1920s, although it was not until the 1950s that labels began regularly recording in stereo. The first affordable stereo cartridges for LP players appeared in 1958, which helped stereophonic sound become a reality for consumer playback. See Théberge, Devine, and Everett, *Living Stereo*, 1–36.

34 Label owners with a background in retail founded several other record labels, including Commodore, HRS, Savoy, Dial, and Vee-Jay.

35 Approximately four hundred to six hundred labels with some interest in the R&B field issued records in the late 1940s, although only a handful found success on the *Billboard* or *Cash Box* charts. Ennis, *Seventh Stream*, 176. Other estimates are higher, believing that one thousand new labels formed between 1948 and 1954. Kennedy and McNutt, *Little Labels, Big Sound*, xvi.

36 The first LPs were in the following *Schwann Long Playing Record Catalog*: Dial (June 1949), Savoy (December 1949), Commodore (June 1950), Blue Note (November 1950), Circle (January 1951), Jolly Roger (February 1951), Prestige and Jazz Panorama (June 1951), and Roost (August 1951). At the time, Savoy, Commodore, Blue Note, Prestige, and Jolly Roger were the most active in the jazz field.

37 "RIAA Reports $205,000,000 Gross as All Time High for Record Industry," *Cash Box*, May 15, 1954, 16.

38 For example, Prestige's first LP, the 10-inch *Lennie Tristano and Lee Konitz* (1951), included six tracks recorded by Tristano and Konitz in 1949 at the label's first record session. Weinstock used this same strategy to fill the vast majority of

Prestige's first fifty LPs. For a full list of records, see Jazz Discography Project, "Prestige Records Catalog: 100, 200 Series," accessed January 6, 2023, https://www.jazzdisco.org/prestige-records/catalog-100-200-series.

39 Weinstock reportedly asked Gitler sometime at the end of 1951 to write the liners. As Gitler recalled, "Not only was it the first time Prestige had put anything but a catalog or blank space on the back liner of an LP but it was the first time I had been published, other than the high school and college newspapers." Ira Gitler, liner notes to *Zootcase*. Gitler eventually wrote hundreds of liner notes for Prestige. Benjamin Cawthra points out that the broader trajectory of liner notes on jazz recordings should be understood in relation to record collectors, many of whom became jazz producers and label owners during the LP era. Cawthra, *Blue Notes in Black and White*, 133.

40 Gitler, liner notes to *Swingin' with Zoot Sims*.

41 Gitler, liner notes to *Miles Davis: The New Sounds*. Other writers, such as Bob Rolontz at *Billboard*, made similar parallels between LP reproduction and jazz onstage: "Instead of waxing the men on three-minute selections which used to be standard on 78's, the artists will take one tune and stay with it for the entire length of the LP disk. This allows the musicians to play as tho they were at a regular live performance, instead of being held back by arbitrary record limitations." Rolontz, "Jazz LP's and EP's Become Disk Industry's Solid Staple," 46.

42 Gitler, liner notes to *Miles Davis: Blue Period*.

43 Gitler, liner notes to *Miles Davis: Blue Period*. *Freedom* does not appear in the liner notes of *Swingin' with Zoot Sims*. Rather, Gitler writes that "a blues was suggested. Zoot responded with an unaffected line that rose out of its swinging structure to emotional high notes. The first twelve bars were timed and Zoot was informed that he had room for twelve opening choruses. However, the music that followed the green light, was not to be contained within these boundaries."

44 Though nominally writing about Miles Davis, Moten analyzes issues of race, freedom, and emancipation within the writings of Theodor Adorno. Moten, "Taste Dissonance Flavor Escape," 84–85. Moten also states that "perhaps constant escape is what we mean when we say freedom."

45 I draw on Sterne, MP3: "All formats presuppose particular formations of infrastructure with their own codes, protocols, limits, and affordances. Although those models may not remain constant, aspects of the old infrastructural context may persist in the shape and stylization of the format long after they are needed" (15).

46 The label issued "Bluing" on three 78-rpm sides under the title *Miles Davis and His Band* (1952): Prestige 846 (*Bluing, parts 1 and 2*) and Prestige 868 (*Bluing, part 3/Conception*).

47 See Manie Sacks, "The Future of EP Records," *Down Beat*, June 3, 1953, 13; "EP's Move into Jazz, Classic, Polka Fields," September 5, 1953, *Billboard*, 13; and Rolontz, "Jazz LP's and EP's Become Disk Industry's Solid Staple," 15.

48 "Savoy, Regent to Issue EP's," *Billboard*, March 28, 1953, 17. This report outlined an initial plan for thirty-six discs (classical and jazz) with an additional twenty-four soon to follow. Savoy's first eighteen EPs issued did feature Parker (seven issues), Garner (nine), and Young (two). The full catalog can be found in Ruppli and Porter, *Savoy Label*.

49 All seven of Savoy's Parker EPs had the same design and musical content as the label's first four LPs featuring Parker (MG 9001, 9002, 9010, 9011), although the background colors and track order varied. One of the firm's rare nonjazz EPs, *Rhythm and Blues, vol. 1*, was a near-exact copy of Savoy's LP by the same name.

50 "EP's Move into Jazz, Classic, Polka Fields," 13. Other jazz labels such as Atlantic and Blue Note eventually released a few EPs, though not until the late 1950s, when the EP gained traction with R&B audiences. See Dawson and Propes, 45, 49.

51 My date, 1953, is an educated guess because EP release dates were not widely publicized. Prestige's first thirty EPs were all recorded in the first half of 1953 or before. The label recorded the first disc in the series—by vocalist Annie Ross—on October 9, 1952, and released it on 78 in January 1953, according to the January 24, 1953, issue of *Billboard*.

52 The label used the same approach with Davis's recordings of "Walkin'" and "Blue 'n' Boogie," both recorded on April 29, 1954, and issued on EP as *Walking* (ca. 1954) and *Blue 'n' Boogie* (ca. 1954) by the Miles Davis All Stars. According to the back jackets, the discs cost $1.58 each.

53 The back jackets of EPs issued later in the series included less information, presumably to list more recordings.

54 However, collectors had been documenting such information for years. See Epperson, *More Important Than the Music*.

55 This statement appears on the back matter on *Bennie Green with Strings* (1953). Later records in the series replaced this text with the tagline mentioned above.

56 See Teddy Charles, *Teddy Charles West Coasters* (ca. 1953).

57 Around half the discs in the series featured white artists, who were similarly depicted. Some records included more abstract graphic designs with no musician photos: *Lennie Tristano Quintet Featuring Lee Konitz* (1953), *Sonny Rollins with the Modern Jazz Quartet* (1953), and *Billy Taylor Trio, vol. 3* (1954).

58 The technique of composing lyrics over famous jazz solos is called *vocalese*. An overview of its history can be found in Grant, "Purple Passages of Fiestas in Blue?"

59 Bob Porter, liner notes to *The Prestige Records Story*, 47. Even though this recording was imagined for the LP, Prestige also released it as a 45: James Moody, *Disappointed, parts 1 and 2*.

60 Granz first issued this recording on *Jazz at the Philharmonic: Lady Be Good, parts 1 and 2* (1948), a 12-inch 78-rpm record.

61 Ira Gitler, liner notes to *Hi Fi Party*.

62 Prestige began circulating its first 12-inch LP, Billy Taylor's *A Touch of Taylor*, in June 1955. See Nat Hentoff, "Jazz Reviews: Billy Taylor," *Down Beat*, June 29, 1955, 16; and *Schwann Catalog* 7, no. 7 (July 1955). The firm issued several others in the coming months and committed more fully to the larger format in 1956. As detailed in chapter 1, Pacific Jazz, Bethlehem, Savoy, and Roost all issued their first 12-inch LPs in 1955 as well, followed in January 1956 by Blue Note. In perhaps a related move, Prestige also produced several hundred regular 45s with cross-issued content in the mid-1950s, although the specific details remain unclear (perhaps beginning in 1955 or 1956).

63 Ira Gitler, liner notes to *Milt Jackson Quartet*. This was Prestige's third 12-inch LP issued.

64 Several other early 12-inch LPs emphasized this same point. Prestige's second 12-inch LP, *Stan Getz Quartets* (1955), included a list of the label's first ten 12-inch discs, five of which have an asterisk next to their name and a note: "Reissues, remastered by Van Gelder." Prestige began regularly employing recording engineer Rudy Van Gelder during this period and rethought its manufacturing process. Critic Nat Hentoff wrote about Prestige's new commitment to sound quality in an August 11, 1954, review for *Down Beat*, noting the "better material" used in the label's pressings. "Believe me," he observed, "the difference is enjoyably noticeable." See Hentoff, "Miles Davis: Prestige 182," 194.

65 For a detailed account of Blue Note record sleeves, see London Jazz Collector, "The Blue Note Inner Sleeves," last modified July 22, 2021, http://londonjazzcollector.wordpress.com/record-labels-guide/labelography-2/the-blue-note-inner-sleeves.

66 Ellipsis in original. Ira Gitler, liner notes to *Zootcase*.

67 Young was responsible for many of Prestige's early abstract covers in 1954 and 1955.

68 For Schlitten's design work, see *Miles Davis Quintet* (1954) and *Miles Davis with Sonny Rollins* (1954), along with many of Prestige's EPs such as *The Thelonious Monk Quintet* (ca. 1954). A representation of his LP design with Weinstock's photography is *Sonny Rollins and Thelonious Monk Quartet* (1954). For more images, see "Prestige Records," Birka Jazz Archive, accessed January 29, 2023, https://www.birkajazz.se/archive/prestige.htm.

69 For more on these designers, see Gitler, "Introduction," 3, 5; and "Prestige Records," Birka Jazz Archive. For more on Prestige's LP covers and the racial politics of the era, see Cawthra, *Blue Notes in Black and White*, 130-31, 197-218.

70 Nat Hentoff, "No Mass Production for Blue Note," *Down Beat*, June 27, 1956, 12.

71 Hentoff, "No Mass Production," 11. Lion followed Milt Gabler, who had issued jazz on 12-inch 78s on his Commodore label in 1939 (see chapter 1).

72 Blue Note records sold for $1.50 per disc, a high price at the time. Lion strategized that collectors and other specialty listeners would pay a premium price for such records.

73 For more on the visual language of Blue Note, see Havers, *Blue Note*.

74 Jarrett, "Cutting Sides," 329.

75 This formation is discussed in Rustin-Paschal, *Kind of Man I Am*, 53, 100-103.

76 Nat Hentoff and Miles Davis, "Miles: A Trumpeter in the Midst of a Big Comeback Makes a Very Frank Appraisal of Today's Jazz Scene," *Down Beat*, November 2, 1955, 13-14. Davis offers these observations in response to a question about "West Coast" jazz. As such, there are clear racial and gendered undertones that deserve further analysis.

77 A later example of an engaging recording with clear and notable mistakes is Sonny Rollins's "Blue 7" from *Saxophone Colossus* (1957). As Benjamin Givan outlines in detail, bassist Doug Watkins misreads Rollins and becomes four measures out of phase with the rest of the group for around five choruses in the middle of the eleven-minute track. Givan, "Gunther Schuller and the Challenge of Sonny Rollins," 182-97, 226.

78 The release dates are as follows: *Cookin'* at the end of 1957, *Relaxin'* in February 1958, *Workin'* in February 1960, and *Steamin'* in August 1961. Prestige would use a similar strategy when Coltrane left for Atlantic (which returned the favor when Coltrane left for Impulse!).

79 Ira Gitler, liner notes to *Relaxin' with the Miles Davis Quintet*.

80 Ira Gitler, liner notes to *Cookin' with the Miles Davis Quintet*.

81 I discuss recordings made in jazz clubs in chapter 5.

82 For a similar reading of this moment that influenced my thinking and analysis, see Ake, *Jazz Matters*, 45-53. Ramsey also discusses musicians' authority over the final product in relation to recorded spontaneity and the shoestring budgets of most jazz labels. Ramsey, *Race Music*, 120.

83 Kelley, *Thelonious Monk*, 182.

84 See Kelley, *Thelonious Monk*, 182-84, for a full account. Relatedly, Gitler writes about this moment of tension in the liner notes to both *Bags' Groove* (1957) and *Miles Davis and Modern Jazz Giants* (1959). On the latter, he downplays

the fisticuffs between Davis and Monk while also pointing out the dialogue at the start of the track. Ira Gitler, liner notes to *Miles Davis and the Modern Jazz Giants*, LP, 1959.

85   Prestige released the alternative take of "The Man I Love" on a standard 12-inch LP in May 1959 as the last track of *Miles Davis and the Modern Jazz Giants* (same name, but different format). The liner notes to the 1959 record confirm the circulation history of this alternate take. Note that Kelley, in his account, mistakenly combines the 33⅓-rpm LP from 1959 (PRLP 7150) with the 16-rpm LP from 1957 (PRLP 16-3). Kelley, *Thelonious Monk*, 182.

86   For further details, see Jazz Discography Project, "Prestige Records Catalog: New Jazz 1100, Prestige 16⅔ rpm Series," accessed March 14, 2018, https://www.jazzdisco.org/prestige-records/catalog-new-jazz-1100-prestige-16-2-3-rpm-series/#prlp-16-1.

87   The two trio records in the PRLP 7000 series had similar covers and identical back jackets that listed the contents for both volumes. The notes significantly overlap with the 16-rpm record as well, a shortcut in the production time that suggests how all three records were thought of in relation to one another.

88   The release history of these different versions is complex. Alternate takes of "But Not for Me" and "Bags' Groove" appeared on Davis's 12-inch LP *Bags' Groove*, issued in 1957. Like most alternate takes issued by Prestige during this time, these versions did not include studio chatter or noticeable mistakes. The master recording of "But Not for Me" (take 1) appears on 78 rpm as *But Not for Me, parts 1 and 2*, as well as on the 10-inch LP *Miles Davis with Sonny Rollins* (1954). The master take of "Bags' Groove" appears on *Miles Davis All Stars, vol. 1* (1955).

89   Both alternates appear on *Zoot Sims Quartets* (1955), after which the standard title became "Zoot Swings the Blues." The 78-rpm alternate—released as *Trotting/Swingin' the Blues*, catalog number Prestige 751—is thus relegated to a historical footnote.

90   Dial's *Bird Blows the Blues*, the very first jazz LP issued by an independent record label (that I have found), offers another example of this kind of historically minded listening. The 12-inch LP included six reissues of well-known Parker tracks on one side and eight alternate takes on the other. The label's advertisements promise that these "never previously released" tracks contain some of "Parker's Most Amazing Solos." Dial Records, advertisement, *Down Beat*, June 4, 1949, 15. Similar advertisements appeared in *Billboard* (May) and *Record Changer* (June, November).

91   Emphasis in original. Ira Gitler, liner notes to *Concorde*.

92   Ira Gitler, liner notes to *Collectors' Items*. Side A includes previously unissued recordings from 1953 that feature Parker (thus Gitler's use of "rejected"). The

B side contains new recordings from March 1956, including a snippet of Davis addressing Van Gelder at the end of "In Your Own Sweet Way." Kelsey Klotz brought this use of Davis's voice to my attention.

93 As Lisa Gitelman points out, the "pastness" of media exists on several levels, including content, conception, and design. Gitelman, *Always Already New*, 5. For a related discussion about preservation at the dawn of the recording era, see "A Resonant Tomb" (chapter 6) in Sterne, *Audible Past*.

94 Moody's alto rendition can be found on the 12-inch LP *James Moody's Moods* (PRLP 7056). His tenor version is on the 12-inch LP *Moody* (PRLP 7072). I gathered this information from digital reproductions of these discs and their accompanying liner notes. The details about these recordings in most published discographies are often inaccurate, and Prestige's decision to give nearly identical names to different records exacerbates the confusion.

95 This point draws from Sterne, *Audible Past*, 225-37. Sterne situates the development of the recording studio within the social and cultural practices enabled by sound reproductive technologies more widely. As such, he argues that people performing within these spaces were in fact performing for the technological network even more than to an imagined audience.

96 This phrase can be found on the back of *Zoot Sims Quartets* (1956) and *Sonny Stitt/Bud Powell/J. J. Johnson* (1956), the latter of which included alternate takes of "Blue Mode" and "Fine and Dandy." Other LPs in the early PRLP 7000 series include the Van Gelder phrase as well.

97 Ira Gitler, liner notes to *Milt Jackson Quartet*. Blue Note also highlighted Van Gelder and the presence of unissued, alternate takes on its advertising for its new 12-inch LP series. Blue Note Records, "Blue Note Presents 12" LPs," advertisement, *Down Beat*, January 11, 1956, 27.

98 As I discuss in chapter 5, the invocation of Van Gelder's name became especially prominent as record companies began making on-location recordings in jazz nightclubs.

99 My analysis follows work in media studies about failed technologies, notably Matthew Kirschenbaum's analysis of computer hard drives and Jentery Sayers's exposition on the telegraphone. See Kirschenbaum, *Mechanisms*, 32; and Sayers, "Making the Perfect Record," sections 3-4, 28-30. Kirschenbaum examines antiquated technologies to understand the affordances and contemporary uses of computer storage devices. Sayers takes a similar approach, arguing that cultural discourses surrounding the now-forgotten telegraphone reveal much about the current usage of electromagnetic recording devices.

100 For further discussion of bebop and Black masculinity, see Ramsey, *Amazing Bud Powell*, 54-58, 85-91, 121-25; Carby, *Race Men*, 138-46; and Kernodle, "Black Women Working Together," 31-33.

101 Quoted in Ramsey, *Amazing Bud Powell*, 28. In this passage, Ramsey argues against the presumed position that bebop was anticommercial.

102 Ramsey, *Amazing Bud Powell*, 24-30, 60-66, 124-25, 133-34.

103 Dee Gee operated between 1951 and 1953. Although its first session took place on March 1, 1951, the first public announcement appeared a month later: "Gillespie Sets Up Dee Gee Disk," *Billboard*, April 14, 1951. The discographical details are spread between multiple sources and remain murky. The label ran at least fourteen sessions, most of them in 1951 (nine). There were no sessions in 1953, but the label continued to issue records through the year, at least according to coverage in *Billboard*. Following standard practices, Dee Gee cross-issued its catalog across various formats, including 78s (twenty-six), EPs (fourteen), 10-inch LPs (five), and 45 singles (unknown). Savoy Records bought the Dee Gee catalog in 1956 and reissued most of it on 12-inch LP.

104 These businessmen and companies were all active before Dee Gee's founding. I do not account for the many Black-owned regional labels or Black A&R personnel. Record labels relied on a broader constellation of Black-owned businesses, including clubs, theaters, record stores, and hotels. For wider histories of Black entrepreneurship, see Walker, *History of Black Business in America*; Rabig and Hill, *Business of Black Power*; and Green, *Selling the Race*. Also see D. Sanjek, "One Size Does Not Fit All," 535-62.

105 Gillespie and Fraser, *To Be, or Not*, 370. Although bebop appeared with some regularity on 78-rpm sides after 1945, record labels were slow to put the music on LP. Between 1949 and 1952, as outlined in chapter 1, Savoy, Dial, and a few labels associated with Norman Granz were among the only labels to issue bebop LPs—nearly all were reissues. This trend would change after 1953, as jazz labels moved increasingly toward the packaged market.

106 Ford, *Dig*; Saul, *Freedom Is, Freedom Ain't*; Dinerstein, *Origins of Cool in Postwar America*.

107 Ellison, "Extravagance of Laughter," 622, 631-32. My reading of Ellison draws from Saul, *Freedom Is, Freedom Ain't*, 60.

108 Majors and Billson, *Cool Pose*; Dinerstein, *Origins of Cool in Postwar America*, 169-73.

109 Baraka, *Blues People*, 212-13.

110 Gillespie and Fraser, *To Be, or Not*, 301.

111 The history of Black Swan, owned by Harry Pace, is an illustrative example. See Suisman, *Selling Sounds*, 207-39.

112 Dee Gee collapsed in 1953 when Gillespie's white business partner, David Usher, failed to properly manage the company finances. See the related discussion in D. Sanjek, "One Size Does Not Fit All."

113 Baraka, *Blues People*, 212–13. For a musicological examination of cool jazz and race within the United States, see Klotz, "Racial Ideologies." Klotz analyzes the discourse of Blackness and masculinity that surrounds Miles Davis's music of the 1950s in chapters 4 and 5.

114 Robert Farris Thompson, one of the first scholars to theorize about cool in relation to Black communities across the Americas, describes cool as an "antiquity" retained from West and Central Africa. R. Thompson, "Aesthetic of the Cool," 40–43, 64–67, 89–91. (His earlier 1966 essay in the same journal covers similar ground.) Within the context of jazz, Joel Dinerstein describes the origins of cool through Lester Young's musical style, obscure language, dress, and bodily movements. Dinerstein, *Origins of Cool in Postwar America*, 37–73.

115 For further analysis of Davis's "cool" aesthetic as it relates to his dress and body, see Klotz, "'Your Sound Is Like Your Sweat,'" 40–43.

116 Another clear example of these dynamics is Davis's *Birth of the Cool*, a 12-inch LP issued by Capitol in 1957. This LP featured recordings from 1949 and 1950 by Davis's famed nonet and with arrangements by Gil Evans, John Lewis, and Gerry Mulligan. Capitol had already issued some tracks on 78 rpm in the late 1940s and again on a 10-inch LP from 1954 titled *Classics in Jazz: Miles Davis*. The "Birth of the Cool" title first appeared in 1957 on the aforementioned LP. Capitol's 1957 LP featured a black-and-white photo of Davis playing his trumpet and wearing a pair of sunglasses (indoors). The word *cool* stands out in a bright red against the otherwise black-and-white design.

117 Among other places, the African American contexts of the blues are taken up in Carby, "It Jus Be's Dat Way Sometime"; Davis, *Blues Legacies and Black Feminism*; Griffin, *If You Can't Be Free, Be a Mystery*; Kernodle, "Having Her Say"; McGinley, *Staging the Blues*; Baraka, *Blues People*; and Murray, *Stomping the Blues*.

118 Ira Gitler, liner notes to *The New Sounds*.

119 Green, *Selling the Race*, 52. Also see Klotz, "'Your Sound Is Like Your Sweat,'" 35–36.

120 For more on Davis at the end of the 1950s, see Griffin and Washington, *Clawing at the Limits of Cool*, 109–15, 251–58. Prestige also reacted to this musical and cultural trend as Weinstock replaced the rhetoric of "modern" with the styles of hard bop and soul jazz, two related subgenres inspired by Black popular culture that I take up in chapter 5.

121 The four most illustrative examples are *The Happy Blues* (1956), *Jammin' with Gene* (1956), *Funky* (1957), and *Jammin' in Hi Fi with Gene Ammons* (1957).

122 Bob Weinstock, liner notes to Davis et al., *Prestige First Sessions, vol. 3*.

123 This statement is found in Chambers, *Milestones*, 236. For the original comments, see Ralph J. Gleason, liner notes to *In Person Friday and Saturday Nights at the Blackhawk, San Francisco*.

Chapter 3. Quest for the Moment

An earlier iteration of this chapter appears in *Jazz Perspectives* 8, no. 1 (2014).

1. Stanley Dance, liner notes to *Ellington at Newport* (Columbia Jazz Masterpieces), 2.
2. The January 9, 1957, issue of *Down Beat* ranked *Ellington at Newport* as number two on the jazz charts. "Jazz Best Sellers," *Down Beat*, January 9, 1957, 20. The LP remained a top-five best-seller for the rest of the year, except in April, when it ranked number eight.
3. A detailed account of the 1956 event can be found in J. Morton, *Backstory in Blue*. For an example of the dominant mythology that surrounds this event, see Burns, "Adventure," 16:30-22:00.
4. Although it has no specific origin, this oft-repeated statement can be found in Robert O'Meally, "Reborn and Going International," *New York Times*, January 17, 1999, AR32-33; and Fitzgerald, "Backstory in Blue," 83-85.
5. Legacy retitled this disc *Ellington at Newport (Complete)*.
6. Because the musicians were unpaid for the VOA broadcasts, the musicians' union barred those tapes from commercial use. Columbia negotiated the use of the tapes with the Library of Congress, which held the rights in 1999.
7. This chapter reworks my article on the same topic that situates the 1999 CD reissue and the 1956 LP within their respective cultural moments. I argue that the two versions of *Ellington at Newport* required expert technical skills and creativity behind the recording console and should be understood as different cultural artifacts. See Mueller, "Quest for the Moment."
8. Ellington, *Newport (Complete)*, disc 1, track 2. O'Connor's remarks came from the beginning of Ellington's set, temporally removed from the suite's performance at Newport. The rest of the material heard on the opening track of the LP—beginning with Ellington's statement "We have prepared a new thing"—can be heard on CD 1, track 8, beginning at 0:12.
9. As an extension of his jazz advocacy, Stearns founded the Institute of Jazz Studies in 1952. Throughout the 1950s he published articles about jazz in many prominent periodicals with a white middle-class readership. His 1956 monograph, *The Story of Jazz*, published by Oxford University Press, was among the first scholarly books about jazz history. I further consider Stearns's activities in chapter 4.
10. George Avakian, "The First Jazz Reissue Program: The Story behind the Original Hot Fives & Sevens Reissues and More," *JazzTimes* 30, no. 8 (2000).
11. I discuss the minority position of popular LPs in the introduction and chapter 1. For example, the first announcement of Columbia's LP catalog included a list of more than one hundred LPs in both sizes. Two-thirds of this initial catalog

comprised classical music, an output ratio that remained relatively consistent well into the early 1950s. See "Advance Information: Columbia's Initial LP Catalog," *Billboard*, July 3, 1948, 35-36. For more of Avakian's recollections about this time, see "George Avakian Interview" (with Michael Jarrett), summer 1994, pp. 2-5, box 13, folder 14, George Avakian and Anahid Ajemian papers (AAP), New York Public Library; and Mike Zwerin, "George Avakian, Godfather of the Pop LP," *International Herald Tribune*, March 27, 1997, 20.

12   From 1948 to 1951, Avakian's reviews of early jazz recordings regularly appeared in the "Records Noted" section of the magazine. One example (among others) includes George Avakian, "Bob Scobey," *Record Changer*, July 1948, 19. For more on the wider cultural context of the *Record Changer*, see Gennari, *Blowin' Hot and Cool*, 120, 144-45, 266-67.

13   These efforts were published as Delaunay, Schaap, and Avakian, *New Hot Discography*. The complex circulation history of Delaunay's volume is outlined in Epperson, *More Important Than the Music*, 41-47.

14   For sourcing and further discussion, see my introduction, chapter 1, and chapter 2.

15   Avakian's whiteness is not a clear-cut matter. Born in Armavir, Russia, in 1923, into an Armenian family, Avakian moved to the United States when he was three. By the time his professional career began in the early 1940s, the consolidation of American white racial identity afforded Avakian all the privileges of whiteness. My analysis thus considers him "white," with the recognition that such categories are historically and culturally constructed. For more on whiteness, immigration, and white privilege, see Jacobson, *Whiteness of a Different Color*. I am indebted to Kelsey Klotz for this resource.

16   For more on Avakian and Ellington, see H. Cohen, *Duke Ellington's America*, 291, 621n9 (among other places). Harvey Cohen points out that Ellington's Columbia contract, arranged by Avakian, included the highest royalty rate at the firm. Avakian's relationship with Armstrong is described in Riccardi, "Louis Armstrong." Aural evidence of their rapport can be found on "George Avakian Interviews Louis Armstrong" (disc 3, track 14), on *Columbia and RCA Victor Live Recordings of Louis Armstrong and the All Stars*.

17   My analysis of whiteness within the jazz industry draws from sociologist Joe Feagin's notion of the "white racial frame": a white-centered "worldview" created through a wide complex of passed-down beliefs, expressions of emotions, shared narratives, and social structures that form and maintain racial oppression in the United States. Feagin, *White Racial Frame*, 4. For applications to music studies, see Ewell, "Music Theory and the White Racial Frame," sections 2.1-2.5; and Klotz, *Dave Brubeck and the Performance of Whiteness*, 14-24, 48-51.

18 "Jazz Comes of Age," 3.

19 Uncredited author, liner notes to *John Kirby and His Orchestra*. Given the tone and content, especially the spotlight placed on the "painstakingly technical work" of the engineers and producers, I suspect that the anonymous author is Avakian. The Golden Era series included both 10- and 12-inch sizes and represented Columbia's initial entry into the 12-inch popular market. This line included the Avakian-produced "jazz story" collections—reissues of Louis Armstrong, Bessie Smith, and Bix Beiderbecke—that I discuss in the introduction and chapter 1.

20 "New LP a 98-Cent Jazz History," *Down Beat*, June 29, 1955, 7. Other discounted promotional samplers include EmArcy's *Jazz of Two Decades* (1955) and Debut's *Autobiography in Jazz* (1956), which I discuss in chapter 6. For more on the broader context of this trend, see R. Sanjek, *American Popular Music and Its Business*, 339.

21 Columbia Records, advertisement, *Billboard*, June 4, 1955, 25. Later that month, *Billboard* reported that this LP was "shaping up as the fastest selling LP in the history of the company." See "Col's 'I Like Jazz' a Fast Seller," *Billboard*, June 18, 1955, 24.

22 *I Like Jazz!* LP Catalog, 1955, box 22, folder 3, AAP. The booklet's text closely echoes Avakian's liner notes to *I Like Jazz!* For more on the LP's imagery in relation to Columbia's mainstream ambitions for jazz, see Cawthra, *Blue Notes in Black and White*, 137. Though outside the scope of this chapter, this kind of white middlebrow initiative around education echoes the approach of Columbia's highly successful record-of-the-month club.

23 I mention Savory to highlight the essential role of engineers and other technicians in the record-making process. Savory was known for his extensive collection of recordings made from radio broadcasts, as well as for his role in the development of the LP, along with fellow engineer William Bachman. Savory also oversaw the transfer of Columbia's back catalog onto LP in 1948. Savory's audio collection, some of which is available commercially, is now housed at the National Jazz Museum in Harlem.

24 Goodman's concert is the subject of two monographs: Hancock, *Benny Goodman*; and Tackley, *Benny Goodman's Famous 1938 Carnegie Hall Jazz Concert*. Neither source considers the physical attributes of the LP as a vital part of the history-making narrative as I do here.

25 In considering Goodman's LP as a jazz recording, I follow Avakian's own description as well as David Ake's inclusive imaginings of jazz. For more on genre and market distinctions, which I also discuss in chapter 1, see Ake, *Jazz Cultures*, 42–61; and Brackett, *Categorizing Sound*, 149–91.

26 Irving Kolodin, liner notes to *The Famous 1938 Carnegie Hall Jazz Concert*.

27 This point is made by Langston Hughes in his review of the 1956 Newport Festival: Langston Hughes, "Jazz Boys Whale in an Old Whaling Town," *Chicago Defender* (national edition), July 21, 1956, 9. I was directed to this article by H. Cohen, *Duke Ellington's America*, 321. Newport's broader history in relation to the slave trade is outlined in Brown University's *Slavery and Justice*.

28 Fellow Columbia artist Louis Armstrong was the first in 1949.

29 Issues of race, gender, and class were embedded within such depictions, a sentiment not lost on other jazz musicians at the time. See Klotz, *Dave Brubeck and the Performance of Whiteness*, 77–84, 121–44.

30 See Porter, *What Is This Thing Called Jazz?*, 119–20. Avakian's liner notes to *I Like Jazz!* do mention jazz as a form of African American expression, but only in passing.

31 A similar point about Avakian's use of the LP to try to mainstream jazz is made in Gennari, *Blowin' Hot and Cool*, 211.

32 Wein's comments are quoted in Gennari, *Blowin' Hot and Cool*, 226.

33 For one example, see the Ellington band's rendition on *Ellington at Newport (Complete)*, disc 1, track 1.

34 J. Morton, *Backstory in Blue*, 65–68.

35 Julian "Cannonball" Adderley, "Cannonball on the Jazz Scene: Newport Again," *New York Amsterdam News*, July 15, 1961, 15.

36 The Ajemian sisters deserve further scholarly attention. One place to begin would be Series II: Anahid and Maro Ajemian Papers, AAP. Some of this collection has also been digitized: see https://digitalcollections.nypl.org.

37 "Live, adj.1, n., and adv.," *OED Online*, last updated December 2022, Oxford University Press, https://www.oed.com/view/Entry/109299.

38 Rebecca Schneider points to the negative definitions of *live* found in many dictionaries, which tend to explain *live* as "not dead" or "not from a recording." Schneider, *Performing Remains*, 90. For a related discussion on deadness in relation to liveness, see Novak, *Japanoise*, 48–63; and Stanyek and Piekut, "Deadness."

39 "Live," *OED Online*.

40 In the 1940s the musicians' union fought against wide-scale adoption of recording for fear that recordings would take jobs away from their constituency. As Paul Sanden argues, recordings were "mechanical," whereas in-person performance was dynamic and "live." The term thus became associated with genuine music making and "truth" to a certain degree. Sanden, *Liveness in Modern Music*, 4. Sanden goes on to quote Sarah Thornton: "The expression 'live music' soaked up the aesthetic and ethical connotations of life-versus-death, human-versus-mechanical, creative-versus-imitative." Thornton, *Club Cultures*, 42.

41 There is disagreement among scholars surrounding the birth of "live" as a commercial category in music. Philip Auslander believes it to be in the 1930s, whereas Sarah Thornton dates it to the 1950s. In a sense, they are both correct. The growth and proliferation of radio in the 1930s and television in the 1950s led to new commercial categories for synchronous broadcasts in their respective milieus. For my purposes, the actual first usages of *live* in this respect are not as important as the cultural underpinnings that the term actually relied on, namely, the perception that mechanical reproduction of events and performances was possible. For example, Jonathan Sterne traces culturally constructed notions of "lifelike" reproduction to the nineteenth century, when the technologies of reproduction were being invented. See Auslander, *Liveness*, 39; Thornton, *Club Cultures*, 41-42; and Sterne, *Audible Past*.

42 Descriptions of "lifelike" reproduction were not new but rather the reanimation of a discourse that surrounded sonic technologies from the early twentieth century, particularly those surrounding public tone tests of the Edison phonograph. See E. Thompson, "Machines, Music, and the Quest for Fidelity," 156-58. Emily Thompson's related discussion of loudspeakers and electroacoustic reproduction in the 1920s home covers similar ground. E. Thompson, *Soundscape of Modernity*, 239-40.

43 Columbia Records, advertisement, "Now Demonstrating . . . the Record That Plays up to 45 Minutes!," *Los Angeles Times*, August 30, 1948, 12.

44 Fred Reynolds, "Platter Chatter," *Chicago Daily Tribune*, August 7, 1950, A2. Reynolds particularly lauds the LP for its increased fidelity.

45 Jensen Needles, advertisement, *Down Beat*, December 12, 1956.

46 The liveness of performance has been extensively debated in performance studies. Though somewhat tangential to my interest in the recorded sounds of liveness as they are historically situated, this literature (especially Diana Taylor) outlines some useful ways to consider the multilayered relationship between jazz performance and its recorded reproductions beyond a reductive discussion of "live" or "not live." See especially D. Taylor, *Archive and the Repertoire*, 141-46; Schneider, *Performing Remains*, 90-93; Phelan, *Unmarked*, 146-66; and Auslander, *Liveness*. For a related discussion from a media-studies angle, see Sterne's work on the social genesis of sound fidelity in *Audible Past*, 215-25.

47 For more on the idea of synchronicity in this context, see Schneider, *Performing Remains*, 90. Evan Eisenberg makes a similar point in his discussion of radio: "Radio puts its dispersed listeners under the spell of a shared event. The ritual aura of live performance—rhetorical, musical, what have you—is broadcast. This has nothing to do with radio waves or brain waves; it is a simple matter of simultaneity." Eisenberg, *Recording Angel*, 31.

48 Feld, "Waterfalls of Song," 97-98; Feld, "Acoustemology," 12-21. A related discussion about ways of knowing through the self-referentiality of jazz performance can be found in Katz, *Capturing Sound*, 80-94; and Berliner, *Thinking in Jazz*.

49 Sanden, *Liveness in Modern Music*, 6, 31. Although Sanden does not focus on jazz specifically, he does analyze how liveness functions in a variety of genres, including art music, experimental rock, live electronic music, mashup music, and hip-hop. Of course, other authors have written about liveness in music. Auslander addresses live music in his extensive discussion of rock: Auslander, *Liveness*, 61-111. Peter Elsdon briefly discusses liveness in his book on Keith Jarrett's *The Köln Concert*, although he offers no in-depth consideration of how liveness functions historically beyond Jarrett's 1975 record. Elsdon, *Keith Jarrett's the Köln Concert*, 8-10. Although he uses different terminology, John Mowitt writes about liveness, music, and the structures of listening, especially the sociohistorical factors that influence musical reception. Mowitt, "Sound of Music."

50 Meintjes, *Sound of Africa!*; Novak, *Japanoise*. For more on circulation and spaces of listening, see Novak, "2.5 × 6 Metres of Space."

51 For more on the labor of creating liveness, see Meintjes, *Sound of Africa!*; and Porcello, "Sonic Artistry."

52 This is true of all forms of reproduction, from the first mass-produced 78-rpm discs to radio broadcasts, from the images on a television or at the movie theater to the digital media streaming online today. See Sterne, *Audible Past*, 218.

53 Porter, *What Is This Thing Called Jazz?*, 42-43, 63-65, 177-82.

54 As Gabriel Solis argues, Ellington's technophilia heavily influenced his creative practice well before the LP era. Solis, "Duke Ellington in the LP Era," 198-205. For further discussion of Ellington's extended compositions in relation to "concert" jazz and contemporaneous ideologies of race, see Howland, "Ellington Uptown," 159-60, 167-76, 280. See also Porter, *What Is This Thing Called Jazz?*, 37-38, 49-52.

55 Against this background, Cohen concludes that it is "difficult to imagine" that Avakian demanded anything of Ellington to the extreme that Schaap implies. H. Cohen, *Duke Ellington's America*, 291, 621n9. John Gennari, writing about the 1956 Newport Festival, also describes Ellington as a "savvy operator who knew how to work with promoters like Wein to advance his own interests." Gennari, *Blowin' Hot and Cool*, 234.

56 Initially released on the 1999 CD, this excerpt can be found on *Ellington at Newport (Complete)*, disc 2, track 9.

57 Ellington's actions can also be understood through what Alexander Weheliye labels as "sonic Afro-modernity," whereby Black cultural producers gained greater control over their representations through technology. Weheliye, "'I

Am I Be,'" 100. For more on how audio production implicates politics of race and ethnicity, see Meintjes, *Sound of Africa!*; and Moten, *In the Break*.

58 Jack Chambers, "What Really Happened at Newport? The Dimming of a Masterpiece," *Coda*, May 2000, 39; Daniel Okrent, "Repairing a Classic with an Ugly Secret," *Fortune*, June 21, 1999, 52–56; Jeff Bradley, "Setting the Record Straight: Reissue of *Ellington at Newport* a Lot More Live Than Original LP," *Denver Post*, April 29, 1999, sec. Lifestyle, E5. Generally speaking, the information in these articles and most others came from Columbia's press release or Schaap's liner notes. The coverage sparked wide debate among jazz listeners about the mediated nature of jazz recordings, especially within circles of Ellington collectors. For example, see the lengthy discussion in the *Duke Ellington Music Society Bulletin*: "New Releases and Re-releases," DEMS *Bulletin* 99/4 (1999): 16–17. Most readers of and contributors to the DEMS *Bulletin* are collectors with highly specialized knowledge about Ellington's recorded history.

59 One illustrative example is Avakian to Gary Giddins, April 21, 1999, Duke Ellington file, Newport/Schaap, G.A. Correspondence on Topic, George Avakian private archives (GAA), Riverdale, NY. The rest of this chapter draws from materials collected in 2012 from Avakian's then-private archives. My citations include folder names that generally correspond to Subseries 1B: Alphabetical Files in the collection's current home at the New York Public Library.

60 Most of this material can be found in the Duke Ellington file, GAA. See in particular the "G.A. Correspondence," "Schaap Liners," and "P. Shukat" folders.

61 The details of the situation are even more complex and personal. Sources in Avakian's archive dating back to 1995 reveal that he was originally scheduled to produce the *Newport* reissue and was also responsible for beginning the negotiations with the Library of Congress to use the VOA tapes. "Jazz Release Overview 1995–1997," Sony Legacy Plans file, GAA; George Avakian, "Producing Discussion with Steve Berkowitz," typed document, November 9, 1995, Columbia/Epic Records, Reissues file, GAA; Avakian to Steve Berkowitz, September 27, 1996, Columbia/Epic Records, Reissues file, GAA. Additionally, Michael Ullman reported in 1996 on Avakian's discovery of a "better-balanced tape" for a reissue with "better sound." Michael Ullman, "The Jazz Column," *Fanfare: The Magazine for Serious Record Collectors*, September 1996, 464. In his liners, Schaap never mentions Avakian's involvement.

62 Phil Schaap, liner notes to *Ellington at Newport (Complete)*, 21. For similar comments from Schaap, see pages 19, 22, and 32 of that same document. For a detailed discussion of Schaap's sources, see H. Cohen, *Duke Ellington's America*, 621n9; and J. Morton, *Backstory in Blue*, 205.

63 George Avakian, "Ellington Newport CD Annotation," ca. 1999, pp. 6–7, Duke Ellington file, Newport/Schaap, Sony 1999 reissue of Ellington Newport 1956,

GAA. Teo Macero relates a similar story about Ellington responding positively to some edits done to *Anatomy of a Murder* (1959). "Teo Macero Interview," pp. 13-14, digital folder DF-20510/2, Series 1: Interviews and Transcripts, Michael Jarrett Collection, Southern Folklife Collection.

64. See H. Cohen, *Duke Ellington's America*, 621n9; and J. Morton, *Backstory in Blue*, 201-10. Avakian booked a New York studio on July 9—the Monday after the Saturday-night performance—to help patch up the concert recordings where necessary.

65. Avakian, "Ellington Newport CD Annotation," 7. Avakian was responding to comments that can be found in Schaap, liner notes to *Ellington at Newport (Complete)*, 21.

66. H. Cohen, *Duke Ellington's America*, 332.

67. George Avakian to Joe Glaser, May 16, 1956, Gösta Hägglöf Collection 2011.24.87, Louis Armstrong House Museum (LAHM).

68. See Copland and Goodman, *Concerto for Clarinet and String Orchestra*, 1951; Goodman, *Mozart: Quintet for Clarinet and Strings in A Major*, 1952. Goodman also performed and recorded the music of Igor Stravinsky, Darius Milhaud, Claude Debussy, and Johannes Brahms. He also commissioned works by Béla Bartók, Morton Gould, and Aaron Copland. See Tackley, *Benny Goodman's Famous 1938 Carnegie Hall Jazz Concert*, 156.

69. George Dale, liner notes to *Masterpieces by Ellington* (1951). A related discussion about this LP in relation to Ellington's wider output can be found in Solis, "Duke Ellington in the LP Era," 209-11.

70. The original cover of *Miles Ahead*, which featured a stylish white woman in a sailboat, is further evidence of a record-making approach at Columbia defined by whiteness. Famously, Davis objected to the cover, and Avakian changed it. See Cawthra, *Blue Notes in Black and White*, 148-53.

71. Gennari, *Blowin' Hot and Cool*, 227.

72. H. Cohen, *Duke Ellington's America*, 290-91. Avakian discusses his history with and approach to editing in "Avakian Interview" (with Jarrett), box 13, folder 14, AAP.

73. Ellington's early career can especially be viewed through a lens of racial uplift, from his nickname, the "Duke," to his interest in long-form composition, to his interest in concert jazz. For an in-depth discussion of Ellington's composition in relation to these ideals, see Howland, *"Ellington Uptown,"* 246-93.

74. Avakian writes elsewhere that he produced the four Newport LPs as a set. He released them concurrently, although they sold individually.

75. Hodges's mistakes are in measures 1 and 9 of the melody. For more discussion about the performance and editing, see Hoefsmit, "Duke Ellington at Newport 1956," 17.

76. Gioia, *Imperfect Art*.

77 Zak, *I Don't Sound Like Nobody*, 151.

78 I borrow the term *audile realism* from Sterne, *Audible Past*, 282. The kind of audile realism that Avakian was working toward in this moment exists very much at odds (philosophically) with the kind of historical fidelity guiding many jazz professionals in the late twentieth century, from Schaap's production to the proliferation of repertory ensembles and to the worldview of the jazz neoclassicists. The historically situated tension between Avakian and Schaap is the focus of my article Mueller, "Quest for the Moment." For an overview of the rise of jazz neoclassicism, see Chapman, *Jazz Bubble*, 9-12.

79 Quoted in Kahn, *Love Supreme*, 107.

80 H. Cohen, *Duke Ellington's America*, 290.

81 George Avakian, "Wall Street Journal Draft Letter," August 20, 2004, p. 3, John McDonough file, GAA.

82 Avakian, "Wall Street Journal Draft Letter," p. 4, GAA.

83 This room was called an echo chamber even though it could produce both echo and reverb. For specifics on Columbia's use of the technique, see Zak, *I Don't Sound Like Nobody*, 162.

84 Avakian, "Wall Street Journal Draft Letter," p. 4, GAA.

85 Avakian, "Wall Street Journal Draft Letter," p. 2, GAA.

86 Sterne, *Audible Past*, 242.

87 Zak, *I Don't Sound Like Nobody*, 152. For a lengthy discussion on how technologies of high fidelity were changing listening during this period, see T. Anderson, *Making Easy Listening*, 103-49.

88 In her discussion about the changing ontology of performance from the live moment to its reproduction, Diana Taylor points to various ways that the original "is never as whole as its representation" because of the ways that performance circulates within various cultural economies. D. Taylor, *Archive and the Repertoire*, 143-44. Relatedly, Sterne understands fidelity as a cultural phenomenon based around an ontological separation constructed between original and copy. This separation, he continues, obscures how the "original is itself an artifact of the process of reproduction. Without the technology of reproduction, the copies do not exist, but then, neither would the originals." Sterne, *Audible Past*, 216-19.

89 Cook, "Methods for Analyzing Recordings," 242.

90 Sterne, *Audible Past*, 282.

91 Blake, "Recording Practices," 39.

92 I discuss in chapter 1 the racialized notions of prestige and value that made this series commercially viable. There were five LPs total: *The Huckle-Buck and*

Robbins' Nest: A Buck Clayton Jam Session (1954), *How Hi the Fi: A Buck Clayton Jam Session* (1955), *Buck Clayton Jams Benny Goodman* (1955), *Jumpin' at the Woodside* (1955), and *All the Cats Join In* (1956).

93 Several other labels experimented with jazz on LP by issuing long-form poetry accompanied by jazz. This included Fantasy's *Allyn Ferguson and Kenneth Patchen with the Chamber Jazz Sextet* (1957) and *Poetry Readings in the Cellar* (1957), in addition to Cadence's *Kenneth Patchen with Chamber Jazz Sextet* (1959). Relatedly, Riverside issued two spoken-word, oral histories on LP during the same period: *Coleman Hawkins: A Documentary* (1958) and *Satchmo and Me: Lil Armstrong's Own Story* (1959). In 1957 Riverside also reissued Alan Lomax's 1938 interviews with Jelly Roll Morton on a series of twelve LPs: *Jelly Roll Morton: The Library of Congress Recordings, vols. 1–12*. (These recordings first appeared on LP in 1950 on Circle Records.)

94 As I mentioned in this book's introduction, John Hammond highlights this mediation in the liner notes: "There were two takes of Robbins' Nest, and thanks to George Avakian's imaginative tape-editing, this record combines the best of both." John Hammond and George Avakian, liner notes to *The Huckle-Buck and Robbins' Nest: A Buck Clayton Jam Session*. Avakian also joined two separate recordings of "Jumpin' at the Woodside" to make a single track for the 1955 Buck Clayton LP of the same name. For more on Avakian's editing during this time, see Jarrett, *Pressed for All Time*, 38–41.

95 Davis discographer Peter Losin reports that "Ah-Leu-Cha" is made from takes 4 and 5 with a splice point at 1:58. Avakian did the same with "Two Bass Hit" and "Little Melonae," although neither track was released on the 1957 LP. Peter Losin, "Miles Ahead Session Details: October 26, 1955," accessed January 2, 2023, http://www.plosin.com/MilesAhead/Sessions.aspx?s=551026.

96 For a detailed description of the studio techniques used on this record, and how they influenced subsequent reissues, see Phil Schaap, liner notes to *Miles Davis and Gil Evans: The Complete Columbia Studio Recordings*, 145–50. Avakian's extensive notes about Armstrong's W. C. Handy recording sessions show a highly involved editing process to splice, move, combine, and dub portions of the tapes. George Avakian handwritten notes, Satchmo Collection 2016.86.4, Louis Armstrong Plays W. C. Handy notes, LAHM.

97 George Avakian, interview with the author, July 2012. Avakian would continue such activities after he left Columbia. On *Benny Goodman in Moscow* (1962), he, along with Carl Schindler, simulated the calls of Soviet jazz fans shouting "Zoot! Pheel!" (for Zoot Sims and Phil Woods). Like *Ellington at Newport*, this simulation was done to mimic a concert experience that was not audible on the recording. Bill Crow, "To Russia without Love," accessed April 23, 2018, https://www.billcrowbass.com/to-russia-without-love.html. My thanks to Alex W. Rodrigues for this reference.

98 In his notes to the 2007 CD reissue of Ellington's *Newport 1958*, Michael Cuscuna heavily criticizes producer Irving Townsend's use of studio production. Michael Cuscuna, liner notes to *Duke Ellington and His Orchestra: Newport 1958*, 2007. Elsewhere, he criticizes Avakian's production of Buck Clayton's jam sessions: Michael Cuscuna, liner notes to *The Complete CBS Buck Clayton Jam Sessions*.

99 Auslander, "Musical Personae," 104. A detailed argument about the relationship of technology to onstage performance can be found in Connor, *Postmodernist Culture*, 153.

100 For a more developed notion of mediatization, see Auslander, *Liveness*, 5.

101 Zak, *I Don't Sound Like Nobody*, 162. Zak also argues that the "frank artifice" of popular records in the early 1950s "rendered the goal of real-life sonic depiction meaningless" (153).

102 Blake, "Recording Practices," 43.

103 The entirety of *At the Bal Masque* and eight of ten tracks on *Newport 1958* were studio recordings with overdubbed applause by producer Irving Townsend.

104 Ullman, "Jazz Column," 463; J. Morton, *Backstory in Blue*, 106, 113, 120, 155. Concert photos show an abundance of microphones onstage (ten or more) because Columbia and VOA each had their own system. For additional photos, see Schaap, notes to *Ellington at Newport (Complete)*, 23-25.

105 Novak, *Japanoise*, 53.

106 Allain and Harvie, *Routledge Companion to Theatre and Performance*, 193-94. For a nuanced discussion of the interrelated notions of audience, presence, and reproduction, see Auslander, *Liveness*, 66-69.

107 For more on the constructed yet deeply felt quality of presence and liveness on jazz recordings, see Ake, *Jazz Matters*, 45-48.

108 Historically, this process of introduction, experimentation, and eventual adoption accompanies any paradigm shift created by new technologies of mass media. For instance, Tim Taylor traces how the conventions of advertising jingles changed alongside the proliferation of radio and, later, television. See T. Taylor, *Sounds of Capitalism*, 65-99.

109 For more on how sound mixing moved from technical craft to artistic practice, see Kealy, "From Craft to Art."

110 I take the idea of democratic public culture as it relates to the Newport Jazz Festival from Gennari, *Blowin' Hot and Cool*, 210.

111 My description of records as seductive follows Rasula, "Media of Memory," 134-64. See also Okiji, *Jazz as Critique*, 87-94.

Chapter 4. World Statesman

An earlier iteration of this chapter is in *Journal of the Society for American Music* 10, no. 3 (2016).

1. "My Reverie" rippled through the white mainstream popular-music industry in 1938, with recordings made by Mildred Bailey, Bing Crosby, and Paul Whiteman, among others.

2. As a 1956 document prepared for a congressional hearing about the program states, "The primary objectives of the cultural (artistic and athletic) presentations program are (1) to improve the understanding in foreign countries regarding the cultural achievements of the United States and (2) to serve as a method for refuting Communist propaganda that the United States is a nation of cultural barbarians." *Supplemental Appropriation Bill, 1957: Hearings before the Committee on Appropriations, United States Senate*, 443.

3. From March to May 1956, Gillespie's ensemble traveled to Iran, Pakistan, Lebanon, Syria, Turkey, Greece, and Yugoslavia. The band then toured South America from July to August of the same year, performing in Ecuador, Argentina, Uruguay, and Brazil.

4. The first tour also featured vocalist Dottie Saulters. This narrative was, of course, a construction, complicated by the gender discrimination that Liston faced in Gillespie's State Department band. See Kernodle, "Black Women Working Together," 35-37, 41-42. Elsewhere and in more general terms, Liston describes her treatment by other male musicians as much more abusive. See Bryant et al., *Central Avenue Sounds*, 259-60.

5. Liston continues: "And it sorta seemed to inspire a bunch of the sisters over there to demand a little more appreciation for their innate abilities. Whatever it was. I had had many conversations with women, especially in the Middle East in that manner. They had things that they felt they were capable of doing and were not permitted to do. And they wanted to know how it happened that I could be out there doing such a thing." Quoted in Gillespie and Fraser, *To Be, or Not*, 415-16.

6. Marshall Stearns, liner notes to *World Statesman*; Marshall Stearns, liner notes to *Dizzy in Greece*.

7. A review of *World Statesman* appeared in the December 1956 issue of *Down Beat*, although the record did not appear on the best-seller list until the March 6, 1957, issue. The LP charted in four out of the next five lists: #13 (March 6), #12 (April 4), #13 (May 2), N/A (May 30), and #16 (June 27). See "Best Sellers" in the following issues of *Down Beat*: June 27, 1957, 24; May 30, 1957, 22; May 2, 1957, 24; April 4, 1957, 21; and March 6, 1957, 32.

8. Nat Hentoff, "World Statesman (review)," *Down Beat*, December 26, 1956, 30.

9   Don Gold, "Dizzy Gillespie: Dizzy in Greece (review)," *Down Beat*, November 28, 1957, 28-29. *Dizzy in Greece* never appeared on the best-selling jazz charts in 1957 or 1958. My issue date is based on "October Album Releases," *Cash Box*, October 12, 1957, 31.

10 Von Eschen, *Race against Empire*, 109, 116, 137; Monson, *Freedom Sounds*, 111.

11 Dudziak, *Cold War Civil Rights*, 37-39.

12 Dudziak, *Cold War Civil Rights*, 12-13.

13 Von Eschen, *Race against Empire*, 2-3; Dudziak, *Cold War Civil Rights*, 66-68.

14 Dudziak, *Cold War Civil Rights*, 56, 67.

15 The first president of the SCLC, established in 1957, was Martin Luther King Jr. Quotation found in Kelley and Earl, *To Make Our World Anew*, 470.

16 Martin, *No Coward Soldiers*, 31, 42-43. Martin also points out that there was substantial disagreement among the African American population about what exactly constituted Black culture(s) and how that related to US culture (white, Black, and otherwise) writ large.

17 Von Eschen, *Race against Empire*, 148, 197. For more details about the relevant congressional bills, see Monson, *Freedom Sounds*, 111-12. An excellent resource about music in the Cultural Presentations program is Fosler-Lussier, *Music in America's Cold War Diplomacy*.

18 Dudziak, *Cold War Civil Rights*, 59-61.

19 Von Eschen, *Race against Empire*, 148. Powell had close ties to the jazz scene through his wife, pianist Hazel Scott.

20 Von Eschen, *Satchmo Blows Up the World*, 14. Von Eschen estimates that by the middle of the 1960s, the show's reach had increased to nearly 100 million people. Shows were recorded in Washington, DC, and then broadcast a month later from VOA stations.

21 Quoted in Von Eschen, *Satchmo Blows Up the World*, 16-17. For similar quotations from musicians and critics that link jazz to notions of freedom and democracy, see Saul, *Freedom Is, Freedom Ain't*, 15; and I. Anderson, *This Is Our Music*, 38-43.

22 Von Eschen, *Satchmo Blows Up the World*, 20, 22.

23 Quoted in Davenport, *Jazz Diplomacy*, 45. References to jazz as a cultural and artistic "export" also appear in several other news sources during the mid-1950s, including *Time* magazine, which called jazz a "valuable exportable US commodity." See "Music: Jazz around the World," *Time*, June 25, 1956.

24 In August 1954, Congress authorized the president's Emergency Fund for International Affairs. This funding source was made permanent in 1956 by the International Cultural Exchange and Trade Fair Participation Act (PL-806), and

it was renamed the President's Special International Program for Participation in Internal Affairs, which was also known as the Cultural Presentations program. See Davenport, *Jazz Diplomacy*, 39. For more on the decisions to feature Western art music on these tours, see Fosler-Lussier, *Music in America's Cold War Diplomacy*, 9-13, 23-27. An overview of jazz as a diplomatic tool can be found in Von Eschen, *Satchmo Blows Up the World*.

25   My consideration of Gillespie follows Richard Iton, who defines *popular culture* as the subset of cultural practices filtered through various forms of mass communication and commercialism. Iton, *In Search of the Black Fantastic*, 291n1. Although Gillespie was not a popular artist in the sense that other 1950s icons were—Frank Sinatra, Elvis Presley, Guy Lombardo, and so on—he nevertheless had a regular presence in media discourses about Black popular music.

26   Von Eschen, *Satchmo Blows Up the World*; Monson, *Freedom Sounds*; Iton, *In Search of the Black Fantastic*. See also Davenport, *Jazz Diplomacy*.

27   Here I am referring to Avakian's letter (May 16, 1956) about his Newport plans, described in the "Producing Newport" section of chapter 3. Gillespie's official itinerary places him in Abdan, Iran, at the end of March and in Athens, Greece, in May. See Monson, *Freedom Sounds*, 115.

28   After attending several meetings of the advisory panel at the end of 1955, Stearns became a permanent member in January 1956. See H. Alwyn Inness, Vice Chairman, to Stearns, January 24, 1956, box 11, folder 28, Marshall Winslow Stearns Collection (MSC), Institute of Jazz Studies (IJS). Stearns initially named Louis Armstrong, Duke Ellington, Count Basie, Dizzy Gillespie, and Stan Kenton as top choices. The panel deemed their top choice, Armstrong, too expensive. Their second and third choices—Ellington and Basie—refused to fly, leaving Gillespie as the panel's recommended artist. For more, as well as a detailed listing of the panel, see Monson, *Freedom Sounds*, 112-14.

29   Robert C. Schnitzer, General Manager of ANTA, to Stearns, January 30, 1956, box 11, folder 28, MSC. For more on the broader context of Stearns's political activities in relation to jazz, see Dunkel, "Marshall Winslow Stearns and the Politics of Jazz Historiography." Although Dunkel does not discuss the specifics of Stearns's appointment, this article helps explain why Schnitzer might have recruited Stearns for such a task.

30   For an overview of Gillespie's activities with a big band, see Maggin, *Dizzy*, 197-214, 233-39; and Shipton, *Groovin' High*, 179-210, 275-92.

31   For a view of Gillespie's actions in relation to other Black entertainers navigating similar political terrain, see Iton, *In Search of the Black Fantastic*. A reading of Gillespie's activities as part of the "psychological" warfare of the State Department can be found in Carletta, "Those White Guys Are Working for Me," 115-34.

32 "Dizzy Gillespie, Nat Cole Entertain President," *Jet*, June 7, 1956. Like other magazines such as *Tan*, *Sepia*, and *Ebony*, *Jet* was generally thought of as a vehicle for projecting middle-class Black values, emphasizing Black achievement and other forms of cultural production generally ignored by the mainstream (i.e., white) press.

33 Iton, *In Search of the Black Fantastic*, 48.

34 Gillespie and Fraser, *To Be, or Not*, 414.

35 Gillespie and Fraser, *To Be, or Not*, 421.

36 Gillespie and Fraser, *To Be, or Not*, 414. While entertaining President Eisenhower at the 1956 White House Press Correspondents' dinner, Gillespie similarly told *Jet* that "my purpose in making the tour was to create goodwill for the U.S., and believe me, we sure need it over there." See "Dizzy Gillespie, Nat Cole Entertain President."

37 For an overview of the various, sometimes conflicting ways in which African American leaders promoted a pluralistic view of the United States, see Martin, *No Coward Soldiers*, 31–43.

38 See especially the 1956 and 1957 folders in the Dizzy Gillespie Clippings File, IJS.

39 Maggin, *Dizzy*, 282; Nat Hentoff, "Dizzy Gillespie Orchestra: Birdland, New York," *Down Beat*, July 11, 1956, 18; "Dizzy Gillespie, Nat Cole Entertain President"; "Dizzy Winds Up 'Person-Person' Show Friday," *Washington Afro-American*, June 26, 1956, 17.

40 Many discographies incorrectly list three studio dates—May 18 and 19, and June 6—that produced the ambassadorial LPs. For example, Gillespie biographer Alyn Shipton cites these dates based on studio sheets from Verve's archives. Shipton, *Groovin' High*, 285–86. Despite the paper trail, the May 18 and 19 studio dates are unlikely because the official State Department records place the band in Greece May 12–21. Monson, *Freedom Sounds*, 115. In his *World Statesman* review, Nat Hentoff describes the LP being made in one "nonstop, 90-minute" session. Hentoff, "World Statesman (review)."

41 Verve issued the other tracks recorded during the April 1957 session on *Birks' Works* (1957), another LP under Gillespie's name.

42 Coincidental or not, "My Reverie" had a renaissance in the years before the tours with artists such as Erroll Garner (1949), Sarah Vaughan (1951), Buddy Johnson (1951), Stan Kenton (1953), Carmen Cavallaro (1953), Bill Doggett (1955), and Sonny Rollins (1956). Liston based "Annie's Dance" on the third movement of Edvard Grieg's *Peer Gynt Suite* No. 1, op. 46. See Leonard Feather, "This Melba Is a Peach," *Down Beat*, September 16, 1956, 16.

43 Gillespie later revealed that the cover photo was taken on the front porch of Grant's Tomb, the mausoleum of Ulysses S. Grant located in New York City.

Harry Frost, "Dizzy and the Heckler: Dizzy Gillespie for President," *Down Beat*, October 19, 1963, 24, 42. The photo by Herman Leonard was most certainly taken after the tour. Surviving photos from Greece do portray Gillespie standing next to noticeably decaying columns, although none show him wearing a fustanella. See box 15, folder 6, and box 15, folder 10, MSC.

44 Stearns's personal papers about the State Department tours included several dozen newspaper clippings from the United States and from cities that the band visited. See box 11, folder 33, MSC.

45 Stearns, liner notes to *Dizzy in Greece*.

46 As historian Andrea Franzius details, official reports and dispatches from the US embassy in Athens contradict Stearns's characterization of Gillespie's reception, describing the concerts as a "relative non-success" that did not positively influence the political conflict. See Franzius, "Soul Call," 436. In his autobiography, Gillespie describes how Duncan Embry, a United States Information Service employee, sent in a "bad report" from Athens after a disagreement over an extra (unpaid) concert that Gillespie refused to play. Gillespie and Fraser, *To Be, or Not*, 425.

47 The LP was the brainchild of George Avakian, who traveled with Armstrong to oversee the recordings. Avakian's thinking is well documented in internal communications at Columbia and in letters to Armstrong's manager, Joe Glaser, which can be found in Satchmo Collection 2016.86.2, Correspondence, January–March 1956; and Satchmo Collection 2016.86.3, Correspondence April–September 1956, Louis Armstrong House Museum (LAHM). In a letter to Joe Moore, Avakian states that Columbia announced the LP to its distributors on April 24, 1956. (The first reviews appear a few weeks later.) See George Avakian to Joe Moore, April 25, 1956, Satchmo Collection 2016.86.3, Correspondence April–September 1956, LAHM. Gillespie was likely in Turkey during the release of Armstrong's LP.

48 Felix Belair Jr., "United States Has Secret Sonic Weapon—Jazz," *New York Times*, November 6, 1955, 1, 42. As mentioned above, Armstrong was initially the top choice of the ANTA's music advisory panel for the first jazz tour.

49 George Avakian, liner notes to *Ambassador Satch*.

50 The three recordings happened on October 30, 1955 (Amsterdam, Netherlands); December 20, 1955 (Milan, Italy); and January 24, 1956 (Los Angeles, California). Of these, only the Amsterdam recording included a full audience in attendance. In Milan, Armstrong recorded in a mostly empty hall with only a few spectators; the final date occurred in Columbia's Los Angeles studio. Avakian added most of the applause heard on the LP during postproduction. The most comprehensive account of the *Ambassador Satch* sessions is Ricky Riccardi, liner notes to *Columbia and RCA Victor Live Recordings of Louis Arm-*

strong and the All Stars, reposted online: https://dippermouth.blogspot.com/2018/10/liner-notes-for-columbia-and-rca-victor.html.

51 George Avakian handwritten notes, Satchmo Collection 2016.86.5, 1955 Concertgebouw concert notes, and Satchmo Collection 2016.86.7, Ambassador Satch editing notes and liner notes, LAHM.

52 Quoted in Hershorn, *Norman Granz*, 192-93.

53 The economic difficulties facing Granz at the time are discussed in Hershorn, *Norman Granz*, 190-93.

54 It is worth repeating the figures that I cite in chapter 1. Gross profits of the record industry rose from $191 million in 1951 to $360 million in 1957, helped enormously by the LP's popularity. In terms of overall sales, packaged goods (EPs and LPs) became the largest segment of the industry in 1955. By 1958, LPs alone accounted for 58 percent of total industry profits. See Robert Shelton, "Happy Tunes on Cash Registers," *New York Times*, March 16, 1958; and Paul Ackerman, "Roads Lead to Great Package Disk Days; It'll Be a Rough Trip," *Billboard*, October 1, 1955, 1, 25, 40.

55 Compare the titles of Blue Note's first two 12-inch LPs, *Miles Davis, vol. 1* (BLP 1501), and *Miles Davis, vol. 2* (BLP 1502), to two later titles: Sonny Rollins's *Newk's Time* (BLP 4001) and Horace Silver's *6 Pieces of Silver* (BLP 1539). Chapter 1 offers a historical account of this transition. For more on Blue Note specifically, see the numerical and title catalog listings in Cuscuna and Ruppli, *Blue Note Label*, 697-99.

56 *Trumpet Battle* was issued on Clef, another Granz label.

57 Within Granz's production work, there was precedent for this emphasis on visual design. In 1949 he produced a limited-edition 78-rpm album titled *The Jazz Scene* that matched carefully selected music with the striking photography of Gjon Mili and illustrations by David Stone Martin. The album, originally issued on Mercury, included six 12-inch 78-rpm discs.

58 Brian Priestley, liner notes to *The Jazz Scene*, 1994.

59 The term *Living Stereo* appeared on RCA discs in the late 1950s. Columbia Records displayed *360 degree sound* on its LPs beginning in the mid-1950s. The term *high fidelity*, or *hi fi*, became an industry buzzword during the same time. The wide use of the term led to, among other things, the adoption of this phrase for the well-known periodical *High Fidelity*, a magazine founded in 1951. For an overview, see D. Morton, *Sound Recording*, 129-40.

60 For more on how the racial politics of modernism figured into the commercial practices in jazz during the early 1950s, see Monson, *Freedom Sounds*, 12. On the rise of hard bop in relation to a developing Afro-modernity, see Neal, *What the Music Said*; and Ramsey, *Race Music*.

61 Davenport, *Jazz Diplomacy*, 43; Monson, *Freedom Sounds*, 12.

62 Granz began JATP in 1944 in Los Angeles. He expanded the concert series into a nationwide tour in the mid-1940s and, eventually, to Europe as well. The tours were also known for being racially integrated onstage and for Granz's insistence on desegregated audiences. See Hershorn, *Norman Granz*, 96–110.

63 Minutes, Special Meeting of the Members of The Jazz Festival of Newport, R.I., Inc., January 19, 1956, box 2, folder 4, Newport Jazz Festival Records, IJS. For a detailed account of the white mainstreaming of jazz at the Newport Jazz Festival, see Gennari, *Blowin' Hot and Cool*, 207–15, 225–49. For more on contestations over racial politics at Newport, see Saul, *Freedom Is, Freedom Ain't*, 123–43.

64 Gillespie openly criticized the commercial music of Elvis Presley, Guy Lombardo, and Liberace in 1957. See Dizzy Gillespie and Ralph Ginzburg, "Jazz Is Too Good for Americans," *Esquire*, June 1957, 143.

65 "Granz Forms Two Labels, Dickers for Mars Masters, Cuts EP Price," *Down Beat*, February 8, 1956, 8. The article quotes Granz describing the artists on this new label as ones with "commercial possibilities . . . if their pop sides were released on a label that has no association with jazz." The article also outlines Verve's strategy to target disc-jockey promotion, which Granz says is "necessary for a pop line."

66 Granz signed Fitzgerald away from Decca, the label that Fitzgerald had been with for twenty years. See "Fitzgerald to Granz Label," *Down Beat*, February 8, 1956, 8. The article describes Verve as Granz's "pop company." For more on Verve's founding, see Hershorn, *Norman Granz*, 190–91.

67 Granz's other early discs at Verve included another series titled *The Genius of Charlie Parker*, which arranged Parker's master recordings from the 78-rpm era into a single package. See Verve Records, advertisement, "Eight High Fidelity Albums by the Jazz-Immortal, Charlie Parker," *Down Beat*, May 30, 1957, 25. Granz's interest in creating concept albums went back to the early 1940s. For example, the first recordings of JATP concert series were placed in multi-disc 78-rpm albums that included detailed descriptions of the concert, including personnel and solo order: *Jazz at the Philharmonic: Presented by Norman Granz* (1945). Granz released JATP concerts on several labels, including Stinson, Asch, Disc, Clef, Norgran, and Verve. Tad Hershorn at the IJS pointed me to the Stinson discs cited here.

68 "Ella: It Took a Hit Album to Make Miss F. a Class Nitery Attraction," *Down Beat*, November 28, 1956, 13.

69 After several months at number two, Fitzgerald's Cole Porter record reached the top best-seller spot in August 1956. Her other best-selling records featured

the music of Richard Rodgers and her duets with Louis Armstrong. See "Best Sellers" in *Down Beat* between July 1956 and June 1957. The "recording personality" list comes from a disc-jockey poll. See "1957 Deejay Poll," *Down Beat*, May 30, 1957, 12. In the same poll, three of Fitzgerald's LPs ranked among the top ten vocal LPs of the year.

70 "Granz Unifies Four Disceries under Verve Banner," *Down Beat*, February 20, 1957, 10.

71 This chapter's playlist includes a cross section of Gillespie's many LPs from this time. Full citations can be found in the discography.

72 Notable musicians on the JATP tours included Coleman Hawkins, Lester Young, Ben Webster, Stan Getz, Roy Eldridge, Harry "Sweets" Edison, Charlie Parker, Benny Carter, Hank Jones, Oscar Peterson, Ray Brown, Louie Bellson, Gene Krupa, Buddy Rich, and Ella Fitzgerald.

73 "Granz Unifies Four Disceries," 10.

74 Stearns, liner notes to *World Statesman*. Notice also that both records mention the other despite being issued a year apart.

75 "Dizzy in Greece—Vol. II," typed draft, box 20, folder 1, MSC.

76 Greece Concert Program and "Dizzy Gillespie and His Orchestra: Program," box 24, folder 22, MSC. The May 2, 1956, issue of *Down Beat* gives a similar account. See "History of Jazz Big Feature of Gillespie Overseas Tour," 9. In the scholarly literature about Gillespie's tours, only Monson and Danielle Fosler-Lussier mention the content of the band's performances. Monson, *Freedom Sounds*, 115–16; Fosler-Lussier, *Music in America's Cold War Diplomacy*, 80–82.

77 This concert format was also described in the jazz press. See "History of Jazz Big Feature of Gillespie Overseas Tour."

78 Persip and Gillespie's demonstration was likely a variant of West African drumming styles that Gillespie had adopted into his playing via his interest in Afro-Cuban music and collaborations with Cuban percussionist Chano Pozo. For more on the cultural politics of Gillespie's Afro-Cuban styles, see Moreno, "Bauza-Gillespie-Latin/Jazz."

79 Gillespie's historical arrangements were transcribed from the recordings of famous big bands. Writing to *Down Beat* in 1956, Stearns praised such historical reenactments as having "zest and fidelity." Marshall Stearns, "Turkey Resounds, Reacts to Dizzy Gillespie Band," *Down Beat*, June 27, 1956, 16.

80 As *Down Beat* reported in May 1956, Gillespie did this to "demonstrate the evolution of big band" and "summarize several significant jazz trumpet styles."

See "History of Jazz Big Feature of Gillespie Overseas Tour." An April article in the *New York Amsterdam News* from the same year similarly describes how the band would "present a complete history of American Jazz from Blues to Modern." Stand-alone photo, *New York Amsterdam News*, April 7, 1956, 16.

81 The emulation of historical styles occurs throughout a jazz musician's training, though not usually as a note-for-note onstage performance. More on this practice and its history can be found in Berliner, *Thinking in Jazz*, 64–65, 101–9, 237–38.

82 Dave Usher first suggested to me that the idea of historical reenactment came from Stearns. Dave Usher, telephone interview with the author, July 9, 2015. This was later confirmed in a 1963 letter to the director at the Bureau of Cultural Affairs: Stearns to Glenn G. Wolfe, March 6, 1963, box 10, folder 29, MSC. The same argument can also be found in Fosler-Lussier, *Music in America's Cold War Diplomacy*, 79–84.

83 Although I have not been able to locate programs from South America, several recordings of Gillespie's tour in that region survive: Dizzy Gillespie, *Dizzy in South America, vol. 1* (1999); Dizzy Gillespie, *Dizzy in South America, vol. 2* (1999); Dizzy Gillespie, *Dizzy in South America, vol. 3* (2001).

84 Schifrin would go on to have a long Hollywood career, composing for TV and film. He is perhaps best known for composing the theme to the TV show *Mission Impossible*.

85 As discussed in chapter 2, Usher and Gillespie cofounded Dee Gee Records in 1951. Usher went on to become a producer at Argo, a subsidiary of Chess, in the 1960s.

86 For details, see the discography. Usher remembers using an Ampex 600 tape recorder, which came in two pieces surrounded by Samsonite luggage. Usher, interview with the author. These details are confirmed in Maggin, *Dizzy*, 283–84.

87 My reading of history and performance borrows from Diana Taylor's notion of the "historically charged" present of live performance. D. Taylor, *Archive and the Repertoire*, 143.

88 For more about the historical moment of Parker and Gillespie's recording, see DeVeaux, *Birth of Bebop*, 364–65.

89 Paul Whiteman's 1920 recording of "Whispering" became an enormous hit, paving the way for swing-era band leaders to record and perform their own versions of the song. As a result, "Whispering" became a jam-session standard in the 1940s. See DeVeaux, *Birth of Bebop*, 305, 330. Other arrangements in Gillespie's tour repertoire were derived from existing material, including Liston's "Annie's Dance" and "My Reverie" (as discussed above).

90 Gillespie, *Dizzy in South America*, vol. 2, track 6. In 1976 Gillespie described this rendition as "our tribute to Louis, of course." He continued: "I sent Pops a tape of that number from South America and man, he fell on the floor laughing." Leonard Feather, liner notes to Gillespie, *Dee Gee Days*.

91 This South American performance is nearly identical in both style and form to the July 1952 recording of "Pop's Confessin'," which features Gillespie and Joe Carroll (Dee Gee Records). The original "I'm Confessin'" was first made famous by pianist Fats Waller.

92 Two examples (of many) occur at 0:17 and 0:39.

93 The pitches I've listed here are as they sound (in concert pitch) on the recording.

94 Monson, *Freedom Sounds*, 113. In a 1956 concert review of the band, Hentoff similarly praised Gillespie's ability to combine "authority with good humor" while fronting the band. He goes on: "His unquenchable wit is still in welcome evidence in the introduction and often during the numbers, but now the wit is combined with the emotional and technical range that the Gillespie trumpet is so valuably capable of, and the result is some of the most rewarding Gillespie of his career." Hentoff, "Dizzy Gillespie Orchestra: Birdland, New York."

95 "Indians Dizzy over Gillespie's Jazz: Part 1," *Pittsburgh Courier*, June 2, 1956, 22.

96 Marshall Stearns, "Dizzy's Troupe Casts Spell over Mideast Audiences," *Down Beat*, June 17, 1956, 16; Stearns, "Turkey Resounds, Reacts to Dizzy Gillespie Band." The articles also include several lengthy passages from alto saxophonist Phil Woods, who similarly comments on the audiences' enthusiasm. Elsewhere, Stearns writes that the audience in Dacca "sat wide-eyed on the edge of their chairs at the first concert, and applauded politely as if the noise might interfere with the strange and wonderful music. By the third concert, however, they were participating fully—clapping on the right beat, yelling, and whistling like any college crowd at home." Marshall Stearns, "Is Jazz Good Propaganda? The Dizzy Gillespie Tour," *Saturday Review*, July 14, 1956, 29.

97 Stearns, "Dizzy's Troupe Casts Spell over Mideast Audiences," 17.

98 Concert photos, Istanbul and Athens, box 15, folder 10, MSC.

99 Usher, interview with the author.

100 Stearns, "Turkey Resounds, Reacts to Dizzy Gillespie Band." The liner notes to *World Statesman* similarly state that at the end of one concert, "a quick encore of the current country's national anthem was necessary to restore order." Stearns, liner notes to *World Statesman*. Note, too, that Ellington's big band played "The Star-Spangled Banner" to begin the 1956 Newport Jazz Festival.

101 "Indians Dizzy over Gillespie's Jazz: Part 1"; stand-alone photo, *New York Amsterdam News*.

102 Stearns's papers include concert programs and lecture notes in English, Turkish, Bosnian (and/or Croatian), Arabic, and Greek. See the lecture handouts, outlines, notes, and concert programs in box 11, folder 30; box 24, folder 22; and box 24, folder 23, MSC. Also see "Dizzy Gillespie and His All Stars Jazz Concert," concert program from Abadan, Iran (Taj Theater), March 1956, Gillespie Clippings, IJS.

103 Stearns, "Turkey Resounds, Reacts to Dizzy Gillespie Band"; Stearns, "Dizzy's Troupe Casts Spell over Mideast Audiences."

104 For more on Gillespie's view, see Gillespie and Fraser, *To Be, or Not*, 414.

105 Like others, Stearns and Gillespie were both heavily invested in the narrative of jazz being connected to Africa. For a detailed overview of this position and how the idea of "African retention" often assumes a historically unspecific sense of the continent, see Feld, *Jazz Cosmopolitanism in Accra*, 53–78; Kelley, *Africa Speaks, America Answers*; Moreno, "Bauza-Gillespie-Latin/Jazz"; and Radano, *Lying Up a Nation*.

106 My reading of Gillespie's humor as both a tool for relating across forms of cultural difference and a mode of social and political critique draws from Carpio, *Laughing Fit to Kill*, 7.

107 Vocalist Austin Cromer, who traveled with the band to South America, can be heard on the band's post-tour LP, *Birks' Works* (1957).

108 Other songs from the concert program appear on *World Statesman*, including "Stella by Starlight," "Night in Tunisia," and "The Champ." The concert program can be found in box 24, folder 22, MSC.

109 Granz's labels had a handful of international distribution deals, most notably with Barclay (France) and EMI under the Columbia name and logo (UK). A few of these European LPs, such as the UK release of *World Statesman*, closely mirrored the US version. It was much more common for these discs to have differences: the French version of *World Statesman* and the UK version of *Dizzy Gillespie at Newport* have the same covers as their respective US releases, but truncated liner notes. Other LPs were remarkably different. The UK version of *Dizzy in Greece* shares a cover but has vastly different content—seven tracks remain the same, but three tracks from the US version are left off and replaced by four other tracks from the *Birks' Works* LP issued in the United States. The liner notes, by Alun Morgan, mention but do not emphasize the political context of the music. Moreover, the UK *Dizzy in Greece* appears to have been issued nearly two years after the US disc with the same title. These details, which are difficult to confirm with certainty, reveal the international jazz LP market to have limited profitability and geographic restrictions within Europe. Although Granz did organize European JATP tours every year between 1952 and 1959, all the evidence suggests a US market focus in terms of record making. My discog-

raphy does not include international releases, although limited information can be found on discogs.com. The introduction of the jazz LP into the French record market is discussed in Moore, *Soundscapes of Liberation*, 82–87. Celeste Moore describes EMI as being slow to fully adopt the long-playing technology, which caused a lag in the European LP market.

110   Hentoff, "Dizzy Gillespie Orchestra: Birdland, New York."

111   On a disc titled *At Newport* (1958), Verve also issued three tracks of the band's Newport performance alongside performances by Count Basie, Mary Lou Williams, and Joe Williams.

112   An even longer recording of "Doodlin'" from South America has Gillespie yelling at the baritone sax player: "Get off. Out out out! Get off the stage." Someone else then adds, "and don't come back" (4:01). See Gillespie, *Dizzy in South America*, vol. 2, track 7.

113   "Manteca" is the last track on *Dizzy in South America, vol. 1*. There are no accounts in the press or in Stearns's papers of the band playing "Manteca" on the first tour in the Middle East.

114   This series of events made the front page of the *New York Times*. See "Rioters in Athens Stone US Office," *New York Times*, May 10, 1956, 1. See also Kay Lawson, "Hangings in Cyprus: Trouble in the Mediterranean—as Western Powers Seek to Curb New Nationalist Outbreaks," *New York Times*, May 13, 1956, 171.

115   In 1954 four thousand students aggressively protested the United States for refusing to support the Cyprus-Greek unity. See O'Malley and Craig, *Cyprus Conspiracy*, 3–34.

116   Gillespie remained in Athens until May 21. For a full schedule, see Monson, *Freedom Sounds*, 115. For more background about the conflict, see O'Malley and Craig, *Cyprus Conspiracy*.

117   Stearns, "Is Jazz Good Propaganda?" Published in July and, thus, between Gillespie's tours, the article predates the release of *World Statesman* by several months.

118   Stearns, "Is Jazz Good Propaganda?," 31.

119   For the full testimony, see *Supplemental Appropriation Bill, 1957: Hearings before the Subcommittees of the Committee on Appropriations, House of Representatives*, 702-16, 732-47; and *Supplemental Appropriation Bill, 1957: Hearings before the Committee on Appropriations, United States Senate*, 468-87.

120   *Supplemental Appropriation Bill, 1957: Hearings before the Subcommittees of the Committee on Appropriations, House of Representatives*, 736.

121   *Supplemental Appropriation Bill, 1957: Hearings before the Committee on Appropriations, United States Senate*, 482.

122 Danielle Fosler-Lussier points out that such reports often painted the cultural programs in a positive light because financial support depended on favorable accounts of progress. Fosler-Lussier, *Music in America's Cold War Diplomacy*, 3, 229n7.

123 *Supplemental Appropriation Bill, 1957: Hearings before the Committee on Appropriations, United States Senate*, 483.

124 *Supplemental Appropriation Bill, 1957: Hearings before the Committee on Appropriations, United States Senate*, 484.

125 Ellender's sentiments were widely reported, including in "Jazz Abroad—Gillespie's World Tour," *San Francisco Chronicle*, January 27, 1957, Gillespie Clippings, IJS. For the full statement, see Wagnleitner, *Coca-Colonization and the Cold War*, 212.

126 See "Indians Dizzy over Gillespie's Jazz: Part 1." Several months before, in an April 21, 1956, article, the *New York Amsterdam News* noted the enthusiastic reception by the crowd during a concert in Karachi, Pakistan, specifying how the State Department was "extremely pleased with all reports on the first lap of the tour and it is felt that the Gillespie orchestra is more than serving its purpose to promote goodwill in the tense area." See "1,000 Jam Karachi Theatre for Dizzy," *New York Amsterdam News*, April 21, 1956, 16.

127 Calvin Delores, "Seein' Stars," *Arkansas State Press*, August 10, 1956, 7.

128 "Dizzy Urges Ike to Back Jazz Tours: Jazz Diplomat," *Pittsburgh Courier*, August 4, 1956, 15. This telegram was widely reported in newspapers and jazz trade publications, likely because someone associated with Granz or Gillespie issued it as a press release.

129 "Gillespie in Bid to Defend State Dept. Program before Senate Critics," *Variety*, May 15, 1957, 59.

130 *Supplemental Appropriation Bill, 1957: Hearings before the Subcommittees of the Committee on Appropriations, House of Representatives*, 736, 747. For one view on jazz as an "American icon," see Gac, "Jazz Strategy." Of course, non-US musicians have been playing jazz throughout the music's history. See Starr, *Red and Hot*; A. Jones, *Yellow Music*; Atkins, *Blue Nippon*; Kater, *Different Drummers*; Dregni, *Gypsy Jazz*; J. Jackson, *Making Jazz French*; and Schenker, "Filipino Seekers of Fortune." Relatedly, the global politics of jazz historiography are explored in Moreno, "Imperial Aurality"; Phillips, *Shaping Jazz*; and Johnson, *Jazz Diaspora*.

131 Fosler-Lussier makes a similar argument about Stearns's use of print media, although she does not specifically mention these liner notes. Fosler-Lussier, *Music in America's Cold War Diplomacy*, 85–86. See also Dunkel, "Marshall Winslow Stearns and the Politics of Jazz Historiography."

132 "Liner 1: Dizzy Gillespie World Statesman," handwritten draft, box 20, folder 1, MSC.

133 "Tunes (2)," handwritten draft, box 20, folder 1, MSC. For a detailed discography of the sessions, see the accompanying notes to *Birks Works: The Verve Big-Band Sessions*, 1995.

134 "Dizzy in Greece 12 inch," handwritten draft, box 20, folder 1, MSC.

135 "Dizzy Gillespie: World Statesman—Volume 1," and "Dizzy in Greece—Volume II," typed drafts, box 20, folder 1, MSC.

136 Handwritten outline of *Dizzy in Greece*, box 20, folder 1, MSC. The anecdotes from Dacca and Ankara were featured in the final version of the liner notes.

137 "Dizzy in Greece—Volume II," typed draft with handwritten annotations, box 20, folder 1, MSC. Such rhetoric linking jazz to the notions of freedom and democracy was a significant part of legitimating the music. See Saul, *Freedom Is, Freedom Ain't*, 15; and I. Anderson, *This Is Our Music*, 38-43. For an overview of this practice in relation to the activities of the State Department, see Fosler-Lussier, *Music in America's Cold War Diplomacy*, 84-86.

138 Stearns, "Is Jazz Good Propaganda?"

139 Stearns, "Is Jazz Good Propaganda?," 28.

140 For an earlier example of liner notes explicitly relating jazz to Cold War politics, see Louis Armstrong's *Ambassador Satch* (1956).

141 Stearns, liner notes to *World Statesman*. As mentioned above, characterizations of jazz as a cultural export were common in the mid-1950s.

142 The appropriations request of the "President's Special International Program" for the fiscal year 1957 included funding for both the Cultural Presentations programs and international trade-fair participation run through the Department of Commerce and promoted through the USIA. It is doubtful that Stearns was referencing this bureaucratic link, but it nevertheless demonstrates how the Cultural Presentations programs were only part of a diverse diplomatic strategy. See the budget proposal reproduced in *Supplemental Appropriation Bill, 1957: Hearings before the Committee on Appropriations, United States Senate*, 441-70.

143 The phrase appears verbatim in both liner notes.

144 In his *Saturday Review* article, Stearns devotes several paragraphs to the exchange between the Russian dancers and Gillespie's ensemble, although it remains unclear about the specific Russian ensemble that was in attendance: "Backstage, members of the Russian Folk Dance troupe, which alternated with U.S. at the same theatre, were jitterbugging quietly, deadpan." Stearns, "Is Jazz Good Propaganda?," 30-31.

145 Stearns, liner notes to *World Statesman*; Stearns, liner notes to *Dizzy in Greece*; Stearns, "Is Jazz Good Propaganda?," 30-31.

146 Stearns, *Story of Jazz*. In his *Down Beat* review of the book, Nat Hentoff praises the book for giving "insight on a sociological body of attitudes and experiences that has so seldom been treated in writing on jazz." Nat Hentoff, "Marshall Stearns Writes Best-Yet History of Jazz," *Down Beat*, November 28, 1956, 17. For more on the cultural underpinnings of Stearns's historical work specifically related to *The Story of Jazz*, see Dunkel, "Marshall Winslow Stearns and the Politics of Jazz Historiography," 491-98.

147 Stearns, *Story of Jazz*, xi. Stearns was also the founder of the Institute of Jazz Studies, now located at Rutgers University-Newark (and where much of this research was conducted). In an October 1957 *Down Beat* article, Stearns wrote that by "foster[ing] an understanding of jazz," the institute would "serve an increasingly important function in the study of American culture." Marshall Stearns, "Institute of Jazz: A Discussion of Its Attempts to Foster an Understanding of Jazz," *Down Beat*, October 3, 1957, 26.

148 The phrase "secret sonic weapon" is a reference to Felix Belair, "United States Has Secret Sonic Weapon—Jazz," *New York Times*, November 6, 1955, 1, 42.

149 Stearns, *Story of Jazz*, 294-95.

150 The cost was $100,839 and $40,500 for the Middle East and South American tours, respectively. Only a small portion of this cost was made up by ticket sales, leaving the US government to pay for the remainder. See "Bop Notes Come High," April 10, 1957, Gillespie Clippings, IJS. Although no author or paper name appears on the document, the article comes from a Boston-area newspaper. My analysis through this section expands on Ingrid Monson's work on this controversy over Gillespie's pay. Monson, *Freedom Sounds*, 120-23, 355n38.

151 "It Cost 84G to Send Dizzy Culture Abroad," *New York News*, May 10, 1957. According to the *Boston Herald*, Stearns spoke at the committee meeting and championed Gillespie's tour as "one of the most successful cultural goodwill gestures the United States had made since the war." "Dizzy's Salary," *Boston Sunday Herald*, April 14, 1957. Donald B. Cook, head of the Special Projects Division for the State Department, also testified. According to the *New York Times*, Cook told the committee that the tours helped "offset reports of racial prejudice" by showing the possibilities of "attain[ing] eminence in the field of the arts." "U.S. Finds Unrest in Soviet Sphere," *New York Times*, April 11, 1957. All articles from Gillespie Clippings, IJS.

152 "Dizzy's Tour Hits Sour Senate Note," *New York Journal-American*, May 9, 1957, 4.

153 "Gillespie in Bid to Defend State Dept. Program before Senate Critics."

154 James M. Haswell, "State Department's Jazz Band Tour Costs $100,839," *Huntsville* (AL) *Times*, April 10, 1957, Gillespie Clippings, IJS. Monson makes a similar point about classical musicians being paid higher salaries. Monson, *Freedom Sounds*, 123.

155 "Dizzy's Salary."

156 "Bop Notes Come High."

157 The archival documents reveal that some band members were paid a little more than others. Monson suspects that these were Gillespie and the band's arrangers: Quincy Jones, Melba Liston, and Ernie Wilkins. Monson, *Freedom Sounds*, 120-23, 355n38.

158 Gillespie and Ginzburg, "Jazz Is Too Good for Americans."

159 Gillespie and Ginzburg, "Jazz Is Too Good for Americans."

160 Gillespie and Ginzburg, "Jazz Is Too Good for Americans."

161 The magazine's subtitle was "the magazine for men."

162 Gillespie and Ginzburg, "Jazz Is Too Good for Americans." My analysis of Gillespie's strategic use of European musical values as an expression of Afromodernism follows Ramsey, *Race Music*, 97-101, 106-8; Monson, *Freedom Sounds*, 17-20; and Weheliye, *Phonographies*, 5-8.

163 Granz biographer Tad Hershorn details how Granz actively encouraged other bandleaders—including Jimmy Dorsey, Duke Ellington, Stan Kenton, and Benny Goodman—to similarly place antidiscrimination language in their contracts. Hershorn, *Norman Granz*, 105.

164 Monson, *Freedom Sounds*, 37.

165 Hershorn refers to such actions in his subtitle, *The Man Who Used Jazz for Justice*. Although some musicians spoke out against Granz's preferred concert format, they generally praised him for his equitable business practices. Hershorn, *Norman Granz*, 195.

166 B. Anderson, *Imagined Communities*, 42-46.

167 This can be heard on "Stella by Starlight" (0:02) from Gillespie, *Dizzy in South America, vol. 1*, track 8.

168 For more on this view of performance, see D. Taylor, *Archive and the Repertoire*, xvi, 2-3, 20-21.

169 David Kazanjian's discussion of how the production, distribution, and consumption of goods structure political power informs my own reading of the LP as an object of cultural materialization within a rising global marketplace. Kazanjian, *Colonizing Trick*, 27.

170 Stearns, liner notes to *Dizzy in Greece*.

Chapter 5. Capturing the Scene

1. "Music: Cannonball," *Time*, May 30, 1960, 35. The 45-rpm single split the recording of "This Here" between the A side and B side. At the time, Adderley stated that the LP "went into five figures within five weeks" of release, making it easily his biggest seller (to date). Julian "Cannonball" Adderley, "Paying Dues: The Education of a Combo Leader," *Jazz Review* 3, no. 4 (May 1960): 15.

2. Orrin Keepnews, liner notes to *The Riverside Records Story*. Keepnews writes elsewhere that Evans's first Riverside record, *New Jazz Conception*, sold eight hundred copies its first year. The label's sales of Wes Montgomery numbered in the low single-digit thousands. Kennedy and McNutt, *Little Labels, Big Sound*, 107, 115-16.

3. For a more detailed look at the racial politics of *Down Beat* polls in the 1950s, see Monson, *Freedom Sounds*, 66-67.

4. Ginell, *Walk Tall*, 63, 80; "Cannonball Sales Boom," *Billboard*, November 14, 1960, 10. The report in *Billboard* states that *Quintet in San Francisco* was nearing 100,000 in sales.

5. Ginell, *Walk Tall*, 80.

6. My analysis in this chapter is influenced by Lisa Gitelman's discussion of records in relation to cultural practices of writing and speaking. See Gitelman, *Always Already New*, 29-44, 98-107.

7. As I explain below, my use of "scenarios" is indebted to D. Taylor, *Archive and the Repertoire*, 28-33.

8. Observing the Adderley group at the Jazz Workshop in 1960, an anonymous writer for *Time* noted Adderley's "hamlike right hand . . . with popping fingers" that "lined out the beat." See "Music: Cannonball," 35. Years later, Keepnews wrote that "[Adderley] was a player and a composer and a leader, and when someone else was soloing he was snapping his fingers and showing his enjoyment." Keepnews, *View from Within*, 202.

9. My understanding of the musical everyday and its relation to mediatized objects and structures of commerce is influenced by Lefebvre, *Rhythmanalysis*, 46-50.

10. For more on synchronicity as it relates to reproduction, see Schneider, *Performing Remains*, 93-94.

11. As discussed in chapter 3, George Avakian had such an aural presence in mind while editing Duke Ellington's performance at Newport in postproduction.

12. Several scholars have written about the shifting boundaries of hard bop. David Rosenthal prefers a four-tier taxonomy to account for the different styles of music and the musicians, who often had strong disagreements regarding musical aesthetics. Heavily influenced by Rosenthal's observations, but not necessarily his taxonomy, other scholars prefer to understand the porous

boundaries of hard bop as a cultural strategy of political resistance. For example, Scott Saul defines hard bop as a "web of affiliations" through record labels and performance venues. The social network, he believes, produced music relevant to the Black community by musicians' explorations and uses of musical characteristics at the "roots of the Black experience." Mark Anthony Neal reads hard bop in terms of the "Black Popular Sphere" (i.e., Black popular culture), accentuating how musicians were able to successfully leverage growing trends in mass consumerism to increase their cultural capital. Ingrid Monson defines hard bop in historical terms, as a development that places Black musical experience and cultural poetics at the center of its aesthetic. Pushing back against racialized assumptions about the singular importance of rhythm to Black music, she usefully advocates for the centrality of harmony to hard bop as well. Rosenthal, *Hard Bop*, 44; Saul, *Freedom Is, Freedom Ain't*, xii; Neal, *What the Music Said*, 29-31; Monson, *Freedom Sounds*, 12, 66-71, 99-106.

13 Neal, *What the Music Said*, 26, 29.

14 Saul, *Freedom Is, Freedom Ain't*, 2-3. Elsewhere, Saul characterizes the musicians as "profound jazz historians as well, lucid in ways that challenge the most assiduous listeners" (xii). For a thorough discussion of hard bop's racial and musical aesthetics in relation to other genres at the time, see Monson, *Freedom Sounds*, 69-78, 98.

15 Ramsey, *Race Music*, 4, 77-78. Ramsey further describes these theaters as sites of "cultural memory" based around the lived experiences of Black populations. See also Monson, *Freedom Sounds*, 97-98; and Rosenthal, *Hard Bop*, 40.

16 Rosenthal, *Hard Bop*, 63; Neal, *What the Music Said*, 30.

17 DeVeaux, "Constructing the Jazz Tradition."

18 For more on mass consumerism within the United States during this era, see T. Anderson, *Making Easy Listening*; and L. Cohen, *Consumer's Republic*.

19 Neal, *What the Music Said*, 77-84. Relatedly, David Ake uses the music of Louis Jordan to problematize the assumed binary between art and commerce central to the construction of the jazz canon. Ake, *Jazz Cultures*, 42-61.

20 Weheliye uses his notion of sonic Afro-modernity to question the ways that "authentic" and "vernacular" Black culture is produced, consumed, and disseminated. Sound and sonic technologies allow him to insert Black culture and its diverse practitioners into philosophical conversations about Western modernity. Weheliye, "'I Am I Be,'" 99-105. For more on the role of technology and mediation in the construction of race and ethnicity, especially in a globalized context, see Meintjes, *Sound of Africa!*

21 Rosenthal defines Adderley's music in relation to its popularity with Black audiences and his use of urban blues, gospel, R&B, and Latin American music. Rosenthal, *Hard Bop*, 44.

22 Here I follow Weheliye, who places the relationship between the material and aural at the center of his theory of sonic Afro-modernity. Weheliye, *Phonographies*, 5-8, 20, 29. A related discussion about sound, sight, and Black sociality can be found in "Visible Music," chapter 3 of Moten, *In the Break*, 171-231.

23 Blue Note was founded in 1939 by Alfred Lion and Max Margulis, who were soon joined by Francis Wolff. Lion and Wolff were Jewish émigrés from Germany who began record collecting as young men in Berlin. Although they were Jewish and were subjected to some forms of discrimination, these men were still afforded the privileges of whiteness within the United States. Prestige, established by Bob Weinstock, began its operations in 1949 (see chapter 2). Bill Grauer Jr. and Orrin Keepnews founded Riverside in December 1952 as passionate collectors, as I discuss below.

24 Record producer Michael Cuscuna told David Rosenthal that the average sales for Blue Note's singles were three thousand to jukebox operators and around a thousand to "individuals in Black neighborhoods." The label also sent discs to Black radio stations. Joe Fields, who worked for Prestige during this time, similarly said that most of that label's records were sold to Black audiences. Rosenthal, *Hard Bop*, 62-65.

25 This observation extends beyond the owners of Blue Note, Prestige, and Riverside. Ahmet Ertegun, an immigrant from Istanbul, Turkey, cofounded Atlantic Records with Herb Abramson (who was white) in 1947. Ahmet's brother, Nesuhi, joined Atlantic to run its jazz program in 1955. Chicago-based Chess Records was founded in 1950 by Leonard and Phil Chess, Jewish émigrés from Poland. Most of the A&R staff at the major labels were white men. As outlined in chapter 3, the head of popular albums for Columbia Records during this time, George Avakian, was born in Armavir, Russia. By mid-century, American white racial identity had expanded to include many immigrant populations. Immigration, whiteness, and white privilege are discussed in Jacobson, *Whiteness of a Different Color*.

26 Ramsey, *Race Music*, 119. Recordings of these originals usually fell between five and nine minutes, with a tendency toward minor keys and medium tempos.

27 Although Fantasy Records (based in San Francisco) was the major exception to this New York City focus, very few Black artists appeared on the label during this period.

28 There are many notable recordings from the Village Vanguard, including Bill Evans, *Sunday at the Village Vanguard* (1961) and *Waltz for Debby* (1961); and John Coltrane's *"Live" at the Village Vanguard* (1962). These records appeared on Riverside and Impulse!, respectively. For an in-depth discussion of liveness in relation to the Vanguard, see Teal, *Jazz Places*, 15-50.

29 Some exceptions are *Buddy Rich in Miami* (1958) and *Gene Krupa at the London House* (1959), both issued by Verve.

30 I discuss Granz's live JATP records in more detail in chapter 4. The JATP LPs (many of which were reissues of 78-rpm collections) also feature bebop musicians such as Dizzy Gillespie and Sonny Stitt, but not the hard-bop musicians discussed in this chapter.

31 Unlike Columbia, which released only four LPs from the 1956 festival, Verve took a more flexible approach: among the twelve LPs issued by the firm from the 1957 festival were discs featuring Dizzy Gillespie's big band (discussed in chapter 4), Cecil Taylor, the Gigi Gryce-Donald Byrd Jazz Laboratory, and Toshiko Akiyoshi.

32 Blue Note's first 12-inch LPs came to market in early 1956, meaning that planning began in 1955. As discussed in chapter 2, the use of *modern* here glosses an understanding of jazz that eschews racial difference.

33 Blue Note initially issued *A Night at Birdland* as three 10-inch LPs. The 12-inch discs mentioned here had the same content as their 10-inch counterparts. Both 10- and 12-inch versions had the same cover design and liner notes.

34 Keepnews, liner notes to *The Riverside Records Story*, 9.

35 I discuss the founding of Riverside in relation to early jazz on record in Mueller, "Early LPs of Louis Armstrong."

36 Keepnews, liner notes to *The Riverside Records Story*, 10.

37 The "12" in RLP 12-200 stands for 12-inch LP, a designation later dropped when Riverside stopped issuing 10-inch LPs. As I discuss in the introduction, the label had a concurrent 12-inch LP series titled the Riverside Jazz Archives RLP 100 series, focused specifically on reissues of artists such as Louis Armstrong, Fats Waller, Ma Rainey, and James P. Johnson.

38 Orrin Keepnews, liner notes to *Jazz à la Bohemia*.

39 This includes Monk's *Thelonious in Action* and *Misterioso*, as well as Pepper Adams's *10 to 4 at the 5 Spot*. The Five Spot is famous for its association with Monk. See Kelley, *Thelonious Monk*.

40 Some examples include *Lennie Tristano* (1955) and *The Real Lee Konitz* (1957) on Atlantic; *Buddy Rich in Miami* (1957) on Verve; and *But Not for Me: Ahmad Jamal Trio at the Pershing* (1958) on Argo (Chess). Prestige, which issued one of the first live jazz-club records in 1952, Wardell Grey's *Jazz Concert*, released its second live record in 1959: *Red Garland at the Prelude*.

41 Along with liner notes by Langston Hughes, Weston's LP features the arrangements of Melba Liston. Although Weston had won New Star Pianist in the *Down Beat* Critics' Poll in 1955, he was not a nationally known figure in 1959.

42 King, a Paul Whiteman alum, fronted a number of "sweet"-style dance bands that played a mixture of popular songs, waltzes, polkas, and light classics. He gained prominence through his radio show *The Lady Esther Serenade*, which ran from 1931 to 1938 on both NBC and CBS.

43 Julian "Cannonball" Adderley, "Paying Dues: The Education of a Combo Leader," *Jazz Review* 3, no. 4 (May 1960): 14. Elsewhere, he mentions that club owners, noticing the response to his playing while on tour with Miles Davis, regularly asked about booking an Adderley-led group in the future.

44 Adderley, "Paying Dues," 15.

45 Adderley, "Paying Dues," 15. Elsewhere, he writes: "That's why the *Playboy* poll is probably the most important of them all, which is why I get disgusted with some of the results." The jazz content of *Playboy* is discussed in Klotz, *Dave Brubeck and the Performance of Whiteness*, 105-15. For related commentary by Adderley—published during his Jazz Workshop residency—see Barbara Gardner, "The Tampa Cannonball," *Down Beat*, October 15, 1959, 20.

46 Several clubs were musician owned, including On the Levee (Kid Ory) and Earthquake McGoon's (Turk Murphy). The Jazz Workshop was owned by Art Auerbach, a lawyer.

47 For a contemporaneous overview of jazz in San Francisco, including its nightclubs, see "The West Coast Scene," *Down Beat*, November 12, 1959, 15-17, 56; and Ralph J. Gleason, "San Francisco and Jazz: Story of a Love Affair," *Down Beat*, November 10, 1960, 19-20. These articles also emphasize the close proximity of the Monterey Jazz Festival, which began in 1958. Gleason was a syndicated columnist, appearing in newspapers across the country and trade publications such as *Down Beat*.

48 City-by-city reports appeared in the "Strictly Ad Lib" section of *Down Beat* and the "Our Man in . . ." section of *Metronome*.

49 Gleason, "San Francisco and Jazz," 20. A useful retrospective of the city's jazz-club scene can be found in Sloane and Feinstein, *Keystone Korner*.

50 See Agee, *Streets of San Francisco*, 43-45, 60-62; and Broussard, *Black San Francisco*, 205-38, 239-42. For more on Black San Francisco in relation to other nonwhite populations, see Howell, *Making the Mission*, 123-26, 212-15, 239-43.

51 For the interconnections of music to the city's racial politics, see L. Miller, "Racial Segregation"; L. Miller, *Music and Politics in San Francisco*; and Hill, *San Francisco and the Long 60s*.

52 Herb Caen, a columnist for the *San Francisco Chronicle*, coined the term *beatnik* in 1958. For more on the racial politics of beat culture in relation to music, see Ford, *Dig*, 161-65; and Monson, "Problem with White Hipness."

53 Agee, *Streets of San Francisco*, 60-63. Among his many examples of overt racism, Christopher Agee describes specific worries from police that beat-supporting business would turn North Beach into a "little Fillmore." The legal battles over integrated housing in the district during the early 1950s are discussed in Broussard, *Black San Francisco*, 223-26.

54 L. Miller, "Racial Segregation," 186-99. The postwar growth of the Black community in the Fillmore district—west of Van Ness—led to a thriving club scene, which kept the geographic segregation but with less confrontation.

55 *Down Beat* first mentions the Jazz Workshop as a "new club" in its November 14, 1956, issue. Around the same time, Mort Sahl described the "recently established" club as a home for "formative minds and . . . self-described as a Bohemian rendezvous." Mort Sahl, "Some San Francisco Scenes," *Jazz Today*, December 1956, 24.

56 The Fillmore jazz scene is well documented in L. Miller, "Racial Segregation," 189-91; Chamberland, "House That Bop Built," 272-83; and Pepin and Watts, *Harlem of the West*. The social scene of the Fillmore clubs, which included mixed-race audiences, is succinctly described in Johns, *Moment of Grace*, 77-78.

57 Again, see the "Strictly Ad Lib: San Francisco" section of *Down Beat* in 1959.

58 Sahl, "Some San Francisco Scenes." Sahl's commentary referred to both the Jazz Workshop and the Cellar.

59 Agee, *Streets of San Francisco*, 47-48, 59-67.

60 Ralph Gleason, "Perspectives," *Down Beat*, December 24, 1959, 10. He further describes this refusal as "an appropriate demonstration of democratic individualism."

61 "Music: Cannonball," 35.

62 Agee, *Streets of San Francisco*, 62-63.

63 Gardner, "Tampa Cannonball," 18-19.

64 R. Jones, "'You Know What I Mean?,'" 170, 188. These page numbers refer to the specific quotations here, although Jones develops the argument throughout the article.

65 Cohodas, *Spinning Blues into Gold*, 153.

66 Michael Cuscuna, interview with the author, November 2011.

67 Keepnews, "Orrin Orates," 150-51.

68 Myers, "Rudy Van Gelder."

69 The "2" in Ampex 300-2 likely refers to the number of tracks available to record. Before the commercial adoption of stereophonic discs at the end of the 1950s, engineers often used two-track recorders to create the eventual monaural

70   Keepnews, *View from Within*, 202. Although Keepnews describes recording at Keystone Korner, another San Francisco club, Hamel's physical location at the Jazz Workshop remains unknown. Further recollection can be found in Orrin Keepnews, liner notes to *The Cannonball Adderley Quintet in San Francisco* (1989).

71   *Quintet in San Francisco* included the phrase *high fidelity* in two places: in the upper left-hand corner under the label name and at the end of the liner notes, among other technical notes about the producer, visual artist, and photographer. The bottom of the back jacket also had this phrase: "This record will provide highest quality sound reproduction on both standard long-play and Stereophonic playback systems."

72   Keepnews, liner notes to *Jazz à la Bohemia*.

73   Chris Albertson, liner notes to *Studio Jazz Party*.

74   Keepnews, liner notes to *Jazz à la Bohemia*. A similar description appears in the uncredited liner notes to *Lena Horne at the Waldorf Astoria* (1957): "On the evening of February twentieth RCA Victor set up microphone and equipment in the Empire Room and recorded the exciting performance you hear in this album. It is Lena Horne at her best—electrifying and dynamic as she sings for an audience—projecting all the fire and vibrance of her personality."

75   These records are *The Jazz Messengers at the Cafe Bohemia (vols. 1 and 2)*, *'Round about Midnight at the Cafe Bohemia*, *Mingus at the Bohemia*, and *George Wallington Quintet at the Bohemia Featuring the Peck* (1955). All the records were recorded in 1956 except where noted.

76   Leonard Feather, liner notes to *'Round about Midnight at the Cafe Bohemia*.

77   Leonard Feather, liner notes to *A Night at Birdland with the Art Blakey Quintet, vol. 1*.

78   Leonard Feather, liner notes to *Jutta Hipp at the Hickory House, vol. 1*. The full quotation is as follows: "Thanks to the ready assistance volunteered by Josh and Howard Popkin of the Hickory House, and a masterful engineering job by the indispensable Rudy van Gelder, two entire LPs were recorded in one highly productive evening at the club."

79   Elsdon, "Jazz Recordings"; Rasula, "Media of Memory"; Tackley, "Jazz Recordings as Social Texts."

80   Travel was a very common theme of LPs during the postwar era, as documented in part II of Borgerson and Schroeder, *Designed for Hi-Fi Living*.

81   My observations about hearing liveness as a set of relationships follow Rebecca Schneider's examination of synchronicity and Paul Sanden's understanding of the perception of performance on record. Schneider, *Performing Remains*, 90; Sanden, *Liveness in Modern Music*, 6, 31.

82   Ralph J. Gleason, liner notes to *The Cannonball Adderley Quintet in San Francisco* (1959). Emphasis in original.

83   In his discussion of format theory, Jonathan Sterne underscores how design elements (physical, textual, pictorial, and so on) never function neutrally. Sterne, MP3, 7–17.

84   *Lathe* is a general term for a tool that rotates an object against a stationary cutting tool. In the record-making process, a specially designed lathe was used to cut the grooves of the master disc during the tape-to-disc transfer. A hydro-feed lathe refers to a then-new technology where hydraulic pressure controlled the cutting stylus (moving radially), giving the cutting tool even and consistent pressure. Details about these machines can be found in magazine articles related to high fidelity—for example, Hubert Luckett, "This Record Checks Out Your Hi-Fi System," *Popular Science*, January 1957, 121–23.

85   I discuss the commodity of liveness more thoroughly in chapter 3.

86   The 10-inch format had room for three tracks of music per disc. The discs were issued in 1954 as part of Blue Note's Modern Jazz BLP 5000 series and were later reissued on two 12-inch LPs.

87   Feather, liner notes to *A Night at Birdland with the Art Blakey Quintet, vol. 1*.

88   Though an early adopter of the format, Blue Note had issued only a few dozen LPs by 1954. Blakey's discs, with catalog numbers BLP 5037, 5038, and 5039, were among the first forty LPs issued by the company.

89   Leonard Feather, liner notes to *A Night at the Village Vanguard*.

90   Leonard Feather, liner notes to *Groovin' at Smalls' Paradise, vol. 1*.

91   Leonard Feather, liner notes to *The Jazz Messengers at the Cafe Bohemia, vol. 1*.

92   Keepnews, liner notes to *Jazz à la Bohemia*.

93   Sid McCoy, liner notes to *But Not for Me: Ahmad Jamal Trio at the Pershing, vol. 1*. *But Not for Me* became an immediate sensation after its release. By August 1958, the record had sold nearly 48,000 copies. A 45-rpm single with "But Not for Me" and "Music, Music, Music" sold another 27,000 copies, bolstered by 11,000 unit sales of a 45-rpm EP made from the LP's material. By December, *But Not for Me* ranked as a *Down Beat* best-seller and was regularly charting on *Billboard*'s best-selling LPs in the country. Cohodas, *Spinning Blues into Gold*, 152–55.

94   In a similar context, Albin Zak asks the same questions. Zak, *I Don't Sound Like Nobody*, 152.

95 D. Taylor, *Archive and the Repertoire*, 28–33.

96 D. Taylor, *Archive and the Repertoire*, 29.

97 Gennari, *Blowin' Hot and Cool*; Monson, "Problem with White Hipness"; Baraka, "Jazz and the White Critic."

98 Jacques Attali argues that the commodification of music in the mid-twentieth century was the result of the "colonization of Black music by the American industrial apparatus." He also notes that the cultural terrain of "repetitive commodities" shifted at the end of the 1950s, although he gives few particulars. Attali, *Noise*, 103–4.

99 Columbia Records, as detailed in chapter 3, was an early adopter of these technologies. Independent jazz labels were forced to take a much different approach because they did not have the financial means to pay for either the studio time or the expert technicians required.

100 Quoted in Rosenthal, *Hard Bop*, 40. The original statement can be found in a 1956 *Down Beat* article titled "Jazz Messengers Blazing a Spirited Trail."

101 Dave Brubeck, liner notes to *Dave Brubeck at Storyville: 1954, vol. 1*. This 10-inch LP is one of the earliest live jazz-club records and Brubeck's first record with Columbia. The aural evidence confirms his observation. Whereas the audiences on the *Jazz at Oberlin* LP on Fantasy (1953) can be heard yelling, whistling, and clapping at various points and in the middle of songs, the audiences on Brubeck's LPs made at Storyville on both Fantasy and Columbia are much more reserved, faintly clapping only at the beginnings and ends of songs. The audience is there but is heard only quietly in the background.

102 During the mid-1950s, Brubeck was the subject of major criticism from Black jazz musicians, many of whom described his music as "cold" or "cerebral." For one example, see Hazel Scott's comments in A. Taylor, *Notes and Tones*, 261. Also see Klotz, *Dave Brubeck and the Performance of Whiteness*.

103 See Hentoff et al., "Jazz Summit Meeting," 266–67. Specific comments by Adderley about the nightclub appear below.

104 Gleason, liner notes to *Quintet in San Francisco*.

105 Here, my reading of the rupture between sound and text is influenced by Fred Moten's "phonographic encounters" with Eric Dolphy's *Last Date* and Marvin Gaye's *What's Going On*. See Moten, *In the Break*, 78–81, 224–29.

106 Such interactive moments can also be heard on one of the first live LPs from a jazz club: Wardell Gray's *Jazz Concert*, released in 1952. Recorded at the Hula Hut Club in Los Angeles, the 10-inch LP on Prestige included two tracks, "Jazz on Sunset" and "Kiddo," both also known as the bebop standards "Move" and "Scrapple from the Apple." The two tracks are similar to Gray's famous jam-session battle with Dexter Gordon titled *The Chase*, a 78-rpm record recorded

in June 1947. A lively audience can be heard throughout the nine-minute recording.

107   Contrast Adderley's approach with that of Charles Mingus, who took a more confrontational approach on- and offstage. In 1964 Mingus said that "I wish I'd *never* have to play in night clubs again.... The night-club environment is such that it doesn't call for a musician to even care whether he's communicating." Hentoff et al., "Jazz Summit Meeting," 266. Although recorded in the studio, *Charles Mingus Presents Charles Mingus* (1960) features Mingus announcing each composition and demanding that the imaginary audience be silent. For a reading of this record in relation to Black avant-garde practices at the time, see Washington, "'All the Things You Could Be by Now.'"

108   Keepnews, *View from Within*, 202.

109   For example, Nat Hentoff described Adderley as "Churchillian" onstage. See Ginell, *Walk Tall*, 21-22, 38-39.

110   Hentoff et al., "Jazz Summit Meeting," 267.

111   Jonathan Sterne argues that artists, musicians, and others in the early days of sound reproduction had to learn how to perform for the technology to take advantage of its possibilities. Sterne, *Audible Past*, 225-26, 235. Adderley's example demonstrates the saxophonist's virtuosity in this regard as he balances performing for both an audience and the technology.

112   Marquette, the emcee at Birdland from 1949 to 1965, can be heard on several recordings made at the club during this era. As a result, his voice instantly signifies a specific time, space, and musical happening. Marquette's distinctive vocal timbre also presents a different arrangement of race and gender compared with other jazz spokespeople such as Norman Granz (JATP records) or Father Norman O'Connor (from the Newport festivals).

113   Some examples can be heard on *The Complete Live Performances on Savoy*, a 1998 CD set of Charlie Parker's live recordings from the Royal Roost in 1948 and 1949.

114   Rollins can be heard saying, "Thank you, thank you. Elvin Jones on drums. [*Applause.*] Wilbur Ware on bass. [*Applause.*] We'd like to feature Wilbur right now on a little thing we hope you'll all be familiar with: 'Softly as in a Morning Sunrise.'"

115   Verve Records, run by Norman Granz, issued several records with onstage chatter, including two 1958 LPs: *Anita O'Day at Mr. Kelley's* and *On the Town with the Oscar Peterson Trio*. Some brief moments of musicians addressing the audience can also be heard on records with vocalists and mainstream jazz musicians: Armstrong's *Satchmo in Pasadena Auditorium* (Decca, 1951), Erroll Garner's *Concert by the Sea* (Columbia, 1956), *Ellington at Newport* (Columbia, 1956), *Dave Brubeck at Newport* (Columbia, 1956), *Louis Armstrong at Newport*

(Columbia, 1956), *Oscar Peterson at Stratford Shakespearean Festival* (Verve, 1956), *Ella Fitzgerald and Billie Holiday at Newport* (Verve, 1957), *Dizzy Gillespie at Newport* (Verve, 1957), and Fitzgerald's *At the Opera House* (Verve, 1958). In general, it was rare for voices of instrumentalists to be heard at length. One exception is Charlie Parker and Dizzy Gillespie's *Jazz at Massey Hall* (Debut, 1953).

116   Like other record labels, Debut later reissued the two volumes of *Trombone Rapport* on a single 12-inch LP (see chapter 6).

117   This included *The Dave Brubeck Quartet* (1953), *Jazz at Storyville* (1953), *Jazz at Oberlin* (1953), *Jazz at the College of the Pacific* (1954), *Paul and Dave: Jazz Interwoven* (1954), and *Jazz at the Blackhawk* (1956). Fantasy also issued *The Gerry Mulligan Quartet* (1953), an LP that featured live recordings on only the A side.

118   Compare, for example, the tracks as they appear on the three 10-inch LPs of *A Night at Birdland* to the discographical listing of these same recordings in performance order: Jazz Discography Project, "Blue Note Records Catalog: Modern Jazz 5000 Series (10 Inch LP)," accessed January 8, 2023, https://www.jazzdisco.org/blue-note-records/catalog-5000-series. The CD reissues often re-sequence the recordings in concert order. One example is the CD reissue of *Ellington at Newport*, the LP discussed in chapter 3.

119   Splices can also be heard on Evans's *Sunday at the Village Vanguard* and *Waltz for Debby*, issued by Riverside in 1961. Although they can clearly be heard on remastered versions of these records (issued in the 1990s and 2000s), such splices are much more difficult to identify on the original LPs played on modern-day equipment. Splices were rarely (if ever) written about in trade publications during the mid-1950s. Listener expectation regarding such mediation is a subject that deserves further research, but my sense is that splices and other forms of audio production received greater attention in the 1960s with the advent of stereo playback and regular use of multitrack recording.

120   Shearing composed the tune in 1952 for a series of live radio broadcasts from the club. Shearing, *Lullaby of Birdland*, 137–48.

121   Rosenthal creates a four-tier taxonomy of the music in his book about hard bop. Musicians inspired by urban blues, gospel, and R&B—e.g., Blakey and Adderley—have their own category. However, record making is not part of Rosenthal's analysis. See Rosenthal, *Hard Bop*, 44.

122   Several audience members also audibly react to Clifford Brown's trumpet solo on "Quicksilver" (2:43–2:50). The club environment is particularly audible throughout "Let's Cool One" and "In Walked Bud" on Monk's 1957 LP, *Misterioso*.

123   Neal, *What the Music Said*, 30; Crawley, *Blackpentecostal Breath*, 251–57.

124 The four jazz-club records are Weston's *Jazz à la Bohemia*, Adams's *10 to 4 at the 5 Spot*, and Monk's *Misterioso* and *Thelonious in Action*. In 1959 Riverside also issued *Thelonious Monk Orchestra at Town Hall*, recorded in a large concert hall in New York City. This LP also does not include onstage announcements.

125 Neal, *What the Music Said*, 29.

126 Monson, *Freedom Sounds*, 98.

127 Mark Anthony Neal describes Adderley as understanding "music's historical role in the everyday lives of everyday Black folks and, as such, fashion[ing] a jazz style that was both warmly received and culturally useful for the Black community." Neal, *What the Music Said*, 32.

128 "'Cannonball' Sales Boom," *Billboard*, November 14, 1960, 10.

129 Besides the Riverside LPs, the sessions mentioned here produced two LPs—*Les McCann Ltd. in San Francisco* (Pacific Jazz, 1961) and Will Holt and Dolly Jonah, *On the Brink* (Atlantic, 1961). Verve did not issue its recording from the Cellar with Ben Webster and Johnny Hodges. In 1960 Cal Tjader recorded without an audience at the Black Hawk. In his summary of this activity, Dick Hadlock also mentions Lester Koenig (Contemporary) recording Shelly Manne at the Black Hawk—these sessions took place in September 1959 and thus before Adderley's Jazz Workshop performance. Dick Hadlock, "Our Man In: San Francisco," *Metronome*, February 1961, 50-51. The Kingston Trio recorded at the Hungry i for Capitol Records in 1958.

130 Monson, *Freedom Sounds*, 71.

131 Riverside issued these LPs: *The Cannonball Adderley Quintet in San Francisco* (1959), *The Cannonball Adderley Quintet at the Lighthouse* (1960), *The Cannonball Adderley Sextet in New York* (1962), *Jazz Workshop Revisited* (1962), and *Nippon Soul* (1963).

132 Gene Lees, "Caught in the Act: Cannonball Adderley Quintet, Sutherland Lounge, Chicago," *Down Beat*, January 7, 1960, 42-43; Gleason, liner notes to *Quintet in San Francisco*; Riverside Records, advertisement, *Down Beat*, December 10, 1959, 45 (emphasis in original).

133 Gleason, liner notes to *Quintet in San Francisco*.

134 Weheliye, *Phonographies*, 5-8. See also Monson, *Freedom Sounds*, 71; and Ramsey, *Race Music*, 28.

135 The column ran from January to October 1961, beginning with Julian "Cannonball" Adderley, "Cannonball on the Jazz Scene," *New York Amsterdam News*, January 14, 1961, 13. I analyze the contents of these columns in Mueller, "On the Jazz Scene."

136 Ginell, *Walk Tall*, 77, 81.

137 Gardner, "Tampa Cannonball," 20.

Chapter 6. *Mingus Ah Um*

1. Mingus had recorded for RCA Victor in 1957, but the label delayed the release of the LP, *Tijuana Moods*, until 1962.

2. The unedited versions of all tracks can be found on the 2009 CD reissue of *Mingus Ah Um* (legacy edition). Columbia continued to issue the edited versions well into the 1980s, including on the 1987 CD version of *Mingus Ah Um* (Columbia Jazz Masterpieces edition).

3. LPs generally held forty-five minutes of music, although that constraint was sometimes expanded by cutting grooves into the extreme outside or inside of the surface (with some sacrifice in sound quality). The 1959 version of *Mingus Ah Um* includes just under forty-six minutes of music, 23:56 for side A and 22:03 for side B. The unedited content adds up to 27:02 for side A and 30:02 for side B.

4. There are four book-length monographs about Mingus that range from strictly biographical to more theoretical: Priestley, *Mingus*; Santoro, *Myself When I Am Real*; Gabbard, *Better Git It in Your Soul*; and Rustin-Paschal, *Kind of Man I Am*. Scott Saul and Eric Porter each have chapters about Mingus's cultural politics in relation to the Black freedom struggle (broadly defined). Saul, *Freedom Is, Freedom Ain't*; Porter, *What Is This Thing Called Jazz?* Brian Priestley's biography has the most detail about Mingus's record production (see the discography in particular), but the commentary does not connect such activities to broader trends in record making or musical practice.

5. Mingus (born 1922) was six years older than Adderley (born 1928). Both were also domestic émigrés to New York City, arriving in the early to mid-1950s from California (Mingus) and Florida (Adderley).

6. As various scholars have noted, Mingus regularly accentuated the multiplicity of his own identity through performance. See Rustin-Paschal, *Kind of Man I Am*; and Griffith, "Mingus in the Act." Griffith quotes an unpublished passage from Mingus's manuscript of *Beneath the Underdog* where he directly criticizes Adderley's views on race and hiring practices.

7. Like much of the mythology surrounding Mingus, the actual details remain opaque, even though the story appears in several sources: Priestley, *Mingus*, 92; and Santoro, *Myself When I Am Real*, 140. Priestley quotes Knepper, who was in Mingus's band at the time. A similar account focused intently on the idea of listening (and attention) can be found in Fr. Norman J. O'Connor, "Jazz Is to Hear, Not to Be Talked against, Says Charlie Mingus," *Boston Globe*, May 15, 1950, Charles Mingus Clippings File, Institute of Jazz Studies (IJS).

8. I am not the first to make this point or explore this issue. See Griffith, "Mingus in the Act," 354–60.

9   Saul describes Mingus's "guerrilla attacks" as high-concept, low-cost aggressions against different parts of the jazz industry. Saul, *Freedom Is, Freedom Ain't*, 150.

10 See Porter, *What Is This Thing Called Jazz?*, 133. In the 1960s Mingus became so well-known for such theatrical interventions that it became an expected element of his nightly performances. See Gabbard, *Better Git It in Your Soul*, 57; and Griffith, "Mingus in the Act," 357-58.

11 Hentoff et al., "Jazz Summit Meeting," 266-68.

12 Nearly all Mingus scholars discuss such activities, but the most in-depth analysis of Mingus's activism as it relates to 1950s cultural politics can be found in Porter, *What Is This Thing Called Jazz?*; and Saul, *Freedom Is, Freedom Ain't*.

13 The two unions merged in 1953 after Mingus had already moved to New York. Although Mingus was not part of the political organizing, Buddy Collette recalls that Mingus's outward resistance inspired others toward action. See Porter, *What Is This Thing Called Jazz?*, 108-9.

14 For a thorough discussion of Mingus's 1951 letter to Ralph Gleason, see Porter, *What Is This Thing Called Jazz?*, 102-12. I discuss Mingus's liner-note writing below.

15 For more on the origins of the Jazz Composers Workshop, see Gabbard, *Better Git It in Your Soul*, 55. The Jazz Artists Guild and the anti-festival are discussed in Priestley, *Mingus*, 117; Porter, *What Is This Thing Called Jazz?*, 134; Gabbard, *Better Git It in Your Soul*, 65-66; and Santoro, *Myself When I Am Real*, 168-70.

16 Porter, *What Is This Thing Called Jazz?*, 133-34.

17 Rustin-Paschal, *Kind of Man I Am*, 97.

18 Santoro, *Myself When I Am Real*, 99.

19 Debut was formally incorporated on May 7, 1952. For further details, see Gabbard, *Better Git It in Your Soul*, 40-45; and Santoro, *Myself When I Am Real*, 97-99.

20 See Priestley, *Mingus*, 47; and Porter, *What Is This Thing Called Jazz?*, 133. Mingus followed in the footsteps of Duke Ellington, who created his own publishing firm, Tempo Music, at the end of 1940. Gigi Gryce (Melotone Music) and Benny Golson (Totem Music) established publishing companies in 1955. In a 1961 interview, Cannonball Adderley mentions his own firm, as well as one owned by Quincy Jones. These musicians were increasingly not alone. Many other musicians soon did the same. See H. Cohen, *Duke Ellington's America*, 182-87; Lewis, *Power Stronger Than Itself*, 89-90; and Gould Maynard, "Two Rounds with Cannon," *Metronome*, September 1961, 13-16.

21 Saul points out that such activities were not always profitable but did empower other musicians to take collective action. Saul, *Freedom Is, Freedom Ain't*, 157.

After the collapse of Debut, Mingus established a second publishing company, Jazz Workshop, Inc., which remains active today. It took until 1960 for Mingus to make any sizable profits from his two hundred or so compositions. Priestley, *Mingus*, 123.

22   Washington, "'All the Things You Could Be by Now,'" 28-30. Washington further argues that the depoliticized framing of avant-garde jazz specifically enables the music to be placed within a broader framework of American nationalism that eschews Blackness.

23   Rustin-Paschal, *Kind of Man I Am*, 2-6, 13-14, 42-43, 50-53, 92-94. In my use, the jazzman is a persona. It relies on the construction of an identity, audience expectations for that identity to be performed, and investment in that identity by musicians and the people who surround them. As a construction, the jazzman persona is historically specific. As an identity, it relies on ideologies of difference: race, gender, class, sexuality, religion, able-ness, and so forth. As a performance, it brings expression of authority, artistry, and authenticity into being. A key theme of Rustin-Paschal's book is how Mingus complicated the jazzman figure in multiple registers.

24   *Tijuana Moods* was initially recorded in July and August 1957 for RCA Victor's short-lived jazz subsidiary, Vik, but the label did not release it until 1962. This delay likely resulted from the aforementioned legal dispute. Saul, *Freedom Is, Freedom Ain't*, 151. Always the trickster, Mingus skirted the very same laws when he recorded alongside "Charlie Chan" (Charlie Parker) for Debut and "Oliver King" (Thad Jones, of all people!) for Bethlehem. See Gabbard, *Better Git It in Your Soul*, 60; and Priestley, *Mingus*, 83.

25   Saul, *Freedom Is, Freedom Ain't*, 151. See also Washington, "All the Things You Could Be by Now," 35.

26   There are many sources that explore Black entrepreneurship across various fields. Two places to begin are Walker, *History of Black Business in America*; and Rabig and Hill, *Business of Black Power*.

27   Rustin-Paschal, *Kind of Man I Am*, 3-5, 15-19, 97-98, 128-29. In Rustin-Paschal's formation, the adoption of jazzmasculinity is not an aspiration to be understood as male, but rather to adopt the traits of masculinity that a particular community values. Her analysis explores how different women, including Celia Mingus, Hazel Scott, Mary Lou Williams, and Billie Holiday, adopted traits of jazzmasculinity to create space, express their freedom, and find success.

28   Rustin-Paschal, *Kind of Man I Am*, 98, 106-7, 112-25. For more on Celia's work with Debut, see also Porter, *What Is This Thing Called Jazz?*, 112-14.

29   For information about Nicole Barclay, who operated in the French record business, see Moore, *Soundscapes of Liberation*, 75-76, 95-98. Extensive information about Atlantic from Miriam Bienstock's perspective can be found

in Broven, *Record Makers and Breakers*, 60-72. For information about Vee-Jay, including a source list, see D. Sanjek, "One Size Does Not Fit All," 546-47, 559. Despite these examples, there was no substantial support system for women record makers. Rustin-Paschal describes how Celia learned the record business without a mentor, a testament to her determination and skill. Rustin-Paschal, *Kind of Man I Am*, 106.

30   In this way, Mingus moved alongside (and sometimes ahead of) the changes to audio production created by the introduction of multitrack recording. See Zak, *I Don't Sound Like Nobody*, 143-69.

31   For an overview of Mingus's change in musical style, see Porter, *What Is This Thing Called Jazz?*, 124-25. Porter does not discuss record production.

32   Ira Gitler, liner notes to *Charles Mingus: The Complete Debut Recordings*. Mingus was not the only one critical of the recording. The Toronto New Jazz Society (the organization that sponsored the concert) explored a lawsuit against the engineer, who, according to Dick Wattam, did an "abominable job" and "was responsible for depreciating the value of the tape." Dick Wattam to Charles Mingus, June 19, 1953, box 61, folder 18, Business Papers Series: Debut Records, Recording Projects, Jazz at Massey Hall, Charles Mingus Collection 2019 organization (CMC-2019). Note: My box and folder numbers refer to the organizational schema at the time of my initial research in May 2019 and not the reprocessed locations completed by the Library of Congress in 2020. To account for these differences, my citations include the series, subseries, and folder names.

33   In 1953 and early 1954, Debut released the Massey Hall concerts across three 10-inch LPs: *The Quintet: Jazz at Massey Hall, vol. 1*; *Jazz at Massey Hall, vol. 2*; and *The Quintet: Jazz at Massey Hall, vol. 3*. The 12-inch LP version discussed here began circulation in 1956.

34   Amazingly, this track also did not feature Bud Powell but Billy Taylor instead! Based on letters, data sheets, contracts, work orders, and receipts within the Debut archives, it appears that Celia and Charles removed Powell's recording of "I've Got You under My Skin" from the initial LP because of its poor recording quality, although they later issued it on *Autobiography in Jazz* (discussed in the next section). The use of "Bass-ically Speaking," fake applause and all, appears to be a hurried solution to fill out the record. See corresponding materials in box 61, folder 18, Business Papers Series: Debut Records, Recording Projects, Jazz at Massey Hall; and box 62, folder 12, Business Papers Series: Debut Records, Recording Projects, Discography, CMC-2019.

35   Music from this session first circulated on two 10-inch LPs for Period: *Jazzical Moods, vol. 1* and *vol. 2* (1955). Bethlehem issued the same content as a 12-inch LP titled *The Jazz Experiments of Charlie Mingus* (1956).

36 This session is discussed in Priestley, *Mingus*, 68; and Santoro, *Myself When I Am Real*, 117.

37 Debut released it as a 10-inch LP: Teo Macero, *Explorations* (1954). Macero discusses this session in Skea, "Rudy Van Gelder in Hackensack," 63.

38 Priestley, *Mingus*, 68.

39 The possibilities for Mingus shifted in the 1960s as his professional stature improved and more-invasive techniques of audio production became more normalized. "Passions of a Man," which appeared on the 1962 Atlantic LP *Oh Yeah!*, includes overdubbed voices speaking fake African languages. Two Impulse! records, *Black Saint and the Sinner Lady* (1963) and *Mingus Mingus Mingus Mingus Mingus* (1963), both include heavy layers of overdubbing and splicing as well. See Gabbard, *Better Git It in Your Soul*, 75; Priestley, *Mingus*, 131, 146–47; and Saul, *Freedom Is, Freedom Ain't*, 198.

40 Most sources point to the summer of 1953 as the most likely date for Mingus to have recorded his Massey Hall overdubs, even though they did not circulate on record until 1956. For one example, see Ed Michel, "Disc 4 [Discography]," liner notes to *Charles Mingus: The Complete Debut Recordings*. The evidence within Debut's archives, CMC-2019, remains inconclusive.

41 "Tea for Two: Study in Lines," manuscript in ink and pencil, box 30, folder 47, Music Series: Music by Others, CMC-2019; Charles Mingus, liner notes to *The Moods of Mingus*. The harmony is similarly combined, though more segmented: Mingus and George Barrow solo over the chords to "Tea for Two," and Teo Macero and Mal Waldron improvise over "Perdido."

42 Both tracks can be found on *The Moods of Mingus* (Savoy, 1955). These musical characteristics are discussed in Porter, *What Is This Thing Called Jazz?*, 116–17. Porter also describes a similar aesthetic created by improvised countermelodies on "Getting Together," "Purple Heart," and "Gregorian Chant," all from the same October 31, 1954, recording session. Mingus writes that he began such experiments in 1946 at the Down Beat Club in Los Angeles. Mingus, liner notes to *The Moods of Mingus*. Mingus is sincere in his note, but Gene Santoro suggests there may have been a satirical edge to Mingus's approach: Santoro, *Myself When I Am Real*, 69.

43 These two pieces can be found on *Mingus at the Bohemia* (Debut, 1956). For further details, see Porter, *What Is This Thing Called Jazz?*, 126.

44 See Priestley, *Mingus*, 83. This recording can be found on *Mingus Three* (Jubilee, 1957).

45 This view is eloquently described in Porter, *What Is This Thing Called Jazz?*, 124–25.

46 Other records include both techniques but not on the same tune. For example, the overdubs on "Percussion Discussion" appear on *Mingus at the*

Bohemia along with the melodic superimpositions of "Septemberly" and "All Things You C#."

47 Discographies sometimes list this version of "What Is This Thing Called Love?" as "Trilogy Pogo." The bebop tune "Hot House" is harmonically based on "What Is This Thing Called Love?" For more detail, see Priestley, *Mingus*, 60, 68.

48 Like other independent record labels, Debut began using Rudy Van Gelder at the end of 1953, which vastly improved the label's overall sound quality. These differences can be heard on the retrospective CD box set, *Charles Mingus: The Complete Debut Recordings* (1990).

49 More details on Debut's activities to support early-career or unknown musicians can be found in Priestley, *Mingus*, 55; Saul, *Freedom Is, Freedom Ain't*, 154; and Santoro, *Myself When I Am Real*, 97.

50 "Debut to Release 3rd Ann'y Album," *Down Beat*, December 14, 1955, 12. As a complete album, *Autobiography in Jazz* is not currently available in digital form. The individual tracks do appear on CD but are split between two box sets: *Charles Mingus: The Complete Debut Recordings* (1990) and *The Debut Records Story* (1997).

51 Debut issued *Autobiography in Jazz* in early 1956. The LP followed in the footsteps of Columbia, which issued the ninety-eight-cent sampler *I Like Jazz!* in the summer of 1955 as part of its first national advertising campaign to promote its expanded jazz roster appearing on 12-inch LP (discussed in chapter 3). Mingus mentions Debut's plans to convert its 10-inch catalog to the larger format, following industry trends, in a letter: Charles Mingus to Norman Granz, June 13, 1956, box 61, folder 18, Business Papers Series: Debut Records, Recording Projects, Jazz at Massey Hall, CMC-2019.

52 Liner notes to *Autobiography in Jazz*. In the mid-1950s, 12-inch classical LPs typically cost between $4.85 and $5.95, depending on the label. Popular and jazz records were sold at a slightly lower price, usually $1 less. The $1.98 price was specifically designed to promote the label's catalog. More information on pricing in the early LP era can be found in my introduction as well as in chapter 4 of Myers, *Why Jazz Happened*. According to the notes to *Charles Mingus: The Complete Debut Recordings*, eight out of the fourteen compositions remain under copyright by Mingus's publishing companies, Chaz Mar Inc. or Jazz Workshop, Inc.

53 Konitz's contract with Verve apparently covered only his improvised playing. Learning this at the session, Mingus wrote out a solo for the saxophonist on the spot. Santoro, *Myself When I Am Real*, 99. "Extrasensory Perception" was loosely based on "Idaho," a 1942 standard that had been recorded by Benny Goodman and Guy Lombardo. Priestley, *Mingus*, 49.

54 Mingus and Max Roach were also spending a significant amount of time with the pianist during this period. See Shim, *Lennie Tristano*, 80-81.

55 This is made clear through a comparison between the master take on *Autobiography in Jazz* and the unedited version found on the *Charles Mingus: The Complete Debut Recordings* box set.

56 Many discographies of Debut list two sessions before this date—Mingus obtained those recordings after Debut's collapse and issued them on his short-lived Jazz Workshop label. See the liner notes to *Charles Mingus: The Complete Debut Recordings*.

57 Santoro, *Myself When I Am Real*, 199-200.

58 Shim, *Lennie Tristano*, 78. An American Federation of Musicians (AFM) contract also lists a September 16, 1952, recording session at RCA Victor Studios, although all published discographies list this session as happening in Tristano's studio. AFM Contract (Local 802), September 12, 1952, box 62, folder 2, Business Papers Series: Debut Records, Recording Projects, Charles Mingus, CMC-2019.

59 Rustin-Paschal, *Kind of Man I Am*, 120-21. For more on independent labels and the economic challenges of manufacturing, see R. Sanjek, *American Popular Music and Its Business*, 223-24, 343-44.

60 The "Part 2" parenthetical on the *Autobiography in Jazz* track is not a mistake. On April 21, 1953, a month before the Massey Hall concert, Roach recorded a similar drum solo during a Debut session with Hank Mobley. Debut issued this earlier version of "Drum Conversation" on 78 rpm as *Just One of Those Things/Drum Conversation* (1953) and on 10-inch LP as *The Max Roach Quartet Featuring Hank Mobley* (1955).

61 All sources agree that "Drum Conversation" opened the second set, followed by "Cherokee." Some discographies then list "I've Got You under My Skin" as the next piece. Because it has the most detailed account of the concert order, here I adopt the version presented in the liner notes to *Charlie Parker: Complete Jazz at Massey Hall*. A different view can be found in Haydon, *Quintet of the Year*, 141.

62 Handwritten data sheet with editing notes, June 23, 1953, box 61, folder 19, Business Papers Series: Debut Records, Recording Projects, Jazz at Massey Hall, CMC-2019. There are no companies or technicians listed, but the notes clearly indicate the issue numbers (DLP 2 and 3) that correspond to the issued 10-inch LPs.

63 An identical version of this track can be heard on disc 2 of *Charles Mingus: The Complete Debut Recordings*.

64 The overdubbed bass on the 12-inch version of this track—from *Jazz at Massey Hall* (1956)—slightly obscures this cut. Both versions can be heard on disc 3 of *Charles Mingus: The Complete Debut Recordings*.

65 In his comments about the Massey Hall concert, Ira Gitler dedicates a full paragraph to disagreeing with Bill Cross, author of the original liner notes. Cross portrays Parker's comment as a sign of tension between Gillespie and Parker, but Gitler sees it differently: "Bird's introduction of Diz as 'my worthy constituent' is not sarcastic, but merely an example of Bird's full blown, poking-fun, put-on announcing style." Ira Gitler, liner notes to *Charles Mingus: The Complete Debut Recordings*, 25. A brief overview of this can also be found in Haydon, *Quintet of the Year*, 136.

66 It is difficult to confirm, but the appended crowd noise sounds like it is excerpted from the Massey Hall audience. *Charles Mingus: The Complete Debut Recordings* includes three alternate takes of "Bass-ically Speaking." Citing testimony from Billy Taylor, the liner notes state that Mingus likely overdubbed his bass parts to the other Massey Hall recordings at this session.

67 See disc 3 of *Charles Mingus: The Complete Debut Recordings*.

68 Debut issued its final 78-rpm disc in 1955. In 1956 the label issued one (and only one) 45-rpm single. The full listing of Debut's catalog can be found in the album and single index of Jazz Discography Project, "Debut Records Discography Project," accessed January 14, 2023, https://www.jazzdisco.org/debut-records.

69 According to the original royalty contracts, company receipts, and other correspondences, Debut initially planned to issue the Massey Hall concert as a 12-inch LP. Debut had even paid for mothers and stampers that would have been used to manufacture these discs. See box 61, folders 18 and 19, Business Papers Series: Debut Records, Recording Projects, Jazz at Massey Hall, CMC-2019. The 10-inch LPs sold well through Debut's early years, bringing attention and some revenue to the fledgling company. Priestley, *Mingus*, 55.

70 Charles Mingus to Norman Granz, June 13, 1956, box 61, folder 18, Business Papers Series: Debut Records, Recording Projects, Jazz at Massey Hall, CMC-2019. In this same letter, Mingus asks permission from Granz to use Parker's real name rather than "Charlie Chan," the name used on the initial 10-inch versions. A response from Granz's lawyers two weeks later sternly rejected this request.

71 Audiosonic Invoices, 1956, box 61, folder 19, Business Papers Series: Debut Records, Recording Projects, Jazz at Massey Hall, CMC-2019. The dates, hours, and pricing are as follows: June 20 (2.5 hours editing, totaling $20), September 26 (2 hours, $20), October 7 (4.5 hours, $45), and October 21 (1 hour, $10). It is unclear if this work included recording any overdubs.

72 Mingus apparently made these overdubs on a three-quarter-sized bass. See Priestley, *Mingus*, 68; and Santoro, *Myself When I Am Real*, 117.

73 Mercury Records issued the earliest LP version of *Charlie Parker with Strings* in 1950. (Clef reissued the same recordings in 1954.) The liner notes to

Autobiography in Jazz incorrectly credit Mingus as the arranger of "Portrait" and mistakenly give the date as September 1954, a year off. Alonzo Levister did the arrangement.

74 Compare the recording (disc 4 of *Charles Mingus: The Complete Debut Recordings*) with the original score: "Portrait," holograph manuscript in ink and pencil, box 20, folder 5, Music Series: Music by Charles Mingus, CMC-2019.

75 Debut first recorded "Portrait" on April 12, 1952, featuring vocalist Jackie Paris singing in a rather commercial style. Debut issued *Precognition/Portrait* in 1952 as a 78-rpm record. Mingus sent the record to Nat Hentoff, who wrote back that he preferred "Portrait" over "Precognition." He went on to ask: "What are your ideas on the 12-tone scale in jazz?" Hentoff to Mingus, July 1952, box 62, folder 2, Business Papers Series: Debut Records, Recording Projects, Charles Mingus, CMC-2019.

76 Several authors make this point, including Saul, *Freedom Is, Freedom Ain't*, 153-54; Santoro, *Myself When I Am Real*, 97; and Gabbard, *Better Git It in Your Soul*, 49.

77 Schneider, *Performing Remains*, 88-89, 92-93. Here Schneider applies Gertrude Stein's notion of "syncopation" to theatrical performance, although her discussion is suggestive of musical performance as well.

78 The cultural underpinnings of the original-versus-copy debates are taken up by Sterne, *Audible Past*, 216-23. In many respects, the CD reissues of this work—in particular, *Charlie Parker: Complete Jazz at Massey Hall* (2003) and *Charles Mingus: The Complete Debut Recordings* (1990)—implicitly argue for the originality of performance. Both CDs carefully include the nonedited tracks, thereby reifying the "original" performance both in their own production and in the inclusion of "complete" in the title.

79 Debut spread the recordings made at the Putnam across several records without overlap. Two 10-inch discs appeared first: *Trombone Rapport, vol. 1* (1954) and *vol. 2* (1955). Later, Debut released four more tracks on *Four Trombones* (1957). One final track, "Kai's Day," appeared on *Autobiography in Jazz*.

80 Liner notes to Willie Dennis et al., *Jazz Workshop, vol. 1, Trombone Rapport*. The uncredited notes were likely authored by Charles or Celia Mingus, or some combination thereof. See Rustin-Paschal, *Kind of Man I Am*, 106-7, 113.

81 Saul, *Freedom Is, Freedom Ain't*, 158-62; Porter, *What Is This Thing Called Jazz?*, 124-38.

82 The two Parker LPs are *Bird at St. Nick's* and *Bird on 52nd St.*, both from 1957 (after the collapse of Debut). In 1965 Mingus issued *Mingus at Monterey*, recorded at the Monterey Jazz Festival in the fall of the previous year.

83 Liner notes to *Charles Mingus: The Complete Debut Recordings*, 27. Roach grew up in Bed-Stuy, the neighborhood where the club was located.

84 Liner notes to *Autobiography in Jazz*.

85 Liner notes to Willie Dennis et al., *Jazz Workshop, vol. 1, Trombone Rapport*. Notice that the notes to *Mingus Ah Um* mention the same musicians in nearly the same order as the notes to *Trombone Rapport*, but the spelling has been corrected.

86 "Jazz Profiles: The Charlie Mingus' Jazz Workshop," concert program, January 16, 1959, Mingus Clippings, IJS.

87 Whitney Balliett, "Mingus among Unicorns," *New Yorker*, January 24, 1959. Later in 1959, United Artists released a recording of the performance as an LP titled *Jazz Portraits*.

88 For more on this stylistic change, see Porter, *What Is This Thing Called Jazz?*, 124-25.

89 Quoted in Diane Dorr-Dorynek, liner notes to *Mingus Ah Um* (1959). Mingus further narrates his approach in the liner notes to *Blues & Roots*, an Atlantic LP made the same year: "I decided to memorize the compositions and then phrase them on the piano part by part to the musicians. I wanted them to learn the music so it would be in their ears, rather than on paper, so they'd play the compositional parts with as much spontaneity and soul as they'd play a solo." Charles Mingus and Diane Dorr-Dorynek, liner notes to *Blues & Roots*.

90 For Homzy's description, see Mingus, *More Than a Fake Book*, 4. Saul's analysis can be found in Saul, *Freedom Is, Freedom Ain't*, 162-64.

91 For more on Parlan's and Handy's struggles on "Bird Calls," see Sy Johnson, liner notes to *The Complete 1959 CBS Charles Mingus Sessions*, 7.

92 Quoted in Santoro, *Myself When I Am Real*, 154.

93 Quoted in Johnson, liner notes to *The Complete 1959 CBS Charles Mingus Sessions*, 6. Handy's recollections also appear in Santoro, *Myself When I Am Real*, 146-47, 151, 154.

94 Quoted in Johnson, liner notes to *The Complete 1959 CBS Charles Mingus Sessions*, 6. Similar stories about working with Mingus exist throughout the bassist's biographies.

95 Quoted in Mingus, *More Than a Fake Book*, 53.

96 Johnson, liner notes to *The Complete 1959 CBS Charles Mingus Sessions*, 7. Tom Dowd, a recording engineer for Atlantic Records, also describes how Mingus would constantly change his compositions in the studio during the session. Tom Dowd, liner notes to *Passions of a Man: The Complete Atlantic Recordings 1956-1961*, 11.

97 Quoted in Santoro, *Myself When I Am Real*, 151.

98 Rustin-Paschal, *Kind of Man I Am*, 56.

99 These splices included the removal of two choruses of melody at the beginning, three choruses from the tenor saxophone solo, and also two choruses of piano solo. Among other places, the unedited track referenced here can be heard on the 2009 CD reissue: *Mingus Ah Um* (legacy edition).

100 Priestley, *Mingus*, 269. Unlike the edit-free tracks from *Mingus Ah Um*, which have been reissued several times since 1979, the unedited version of *Blues & Roots* has not been reissued.

101 Mingus's *Tijuana Moods*, which he recorded in 1957 for RCA Victor, also has sloppy editing. Priestley points to "Ysabel's Table Dance" in particular, which he describes as being haphazard, "like all remaining tracks on the album." Priestley, *Mingus*, 83. Though recorded for a large record company, this recording sat on the shelf until the early 1960s. Such neglect might account for the loose production.

102 Macero describes how he was hired at Columbia in Jarrett, *Pressed for All Time*, 74–75.

103 In addition to Mingus's history of using these technologies outlined above, John Goodman's lengthy interviews about the bassist's activities in the early 1970s include many details about *Let My Children Hear Music*, a 1971 LP for Columbia that Macero also produced. At one point, Macero says that Mingus was heavily involved with the editing process of this record. An accompanying photo shows both in the editing room at Columbia's studio. Mingus and Goodman, *Mingus Speaks*, 65, 69, 80, 99.

104 The context of these photos remains unknown. Two reissue box sets reproduce these images in their respective liner notes: *The Complete 1959 CBS Charles Mingus Sessions* (Mosaic, 1993) and *The Complete 1959 Columbia Recordings* (Columbia, 1998).

105 Teo Macero editing and mastering notes (handwritten) and mastering instructions (typed memo), May and June 1959, box 39, folder 15, Teo Macero Collection (TMC), New York Public Library. Although the handwritten notes are undated, the inclusion of tracks from both sessions and the use of uncorrected names strongly indicate that their date is between May 12 and 21. The uncorrected names on the mastering instructions, which also indicate many of the splices, place all documents within the same time frame. My assertion about the order is based on the clear iteration of track names and timings in addition to the various handwritten tables used to calculate the total timing per side.

106 Teo Macero editing and mastering notes (handwritten), ca. 1958, box 16, folder 1, TMC. Like Davis and Evans's other collaborations, *Porgy and Bess* was heavily edited, although neither musician appears to have been involved with the bulk of the editing.

107 My account relies on written accounts, so it is entirely possible that Mingus and Macero discussed the sequence and editing. In his commentary on the 1959 Columbia sessions, Sy Johnson largely skirts the issue, although he implies Mingus's involvement on several occasions. Only once does he explicitly say Mingus "edited out" one of the musicians. See Johnson, liner notes to *The Complete 1959 CBS Charles Mingus Sessions*, 10. Gene Santoro goes further, writing (without citation) that Mingus "spliced solos in and cut them, juxtaposing and moving sections." Santoro, *Myself When I Am Real*, 154. My analysis has not revealed the movement of one section to another location, although it is certainly possible.

108 For example, Mingus consistently asked the women in his life to edit and type his writing. As Santoro writes, he would "explain that he had no real education because of racism, and was embarrassed by his mistakes." Santoro, *Myself When I Am Real*, 154-55.

109 For more on the Jazz Composers Workshop, see Porter, *What Is This Thing Called Jazz?*, 116; and Rustin-Paschal, *Kind of Man I Am*, 199n41. Macero even figured into Mingus's earliest activities in New York City. Priestley, *Mingus*, 56.

110 See B. Cohen, "Enigmas of the Third Space."

111 Macero discusses the background of "Explorations" in Mingus and Goodman, *Mingus Speaks*, 100. For more about Macero's history at Columbia and his involvement with the Western art music scene in New York City, see Marmorstein, *Label*, 234-35.

112 These tracks can be found on the 1955 LPs *Jazzical Moods, vol. 1* and *vol. 2*.

113 Mingus and Goodman, *Mingus Speaks*, 100.

114 Priestley, *Mingus*, 101.

115 In the liner notes to the 2009 CD reissue, Priestley postulates that edits were done to make room on the LP. See Brian Priestley, liner notes to *Mingus Ah Um* (legacy edition), 20. Although Priestley's assertion is likely correct, my point here is that the splices can also be done in a musical way—both can be true, in other words.

116 The only exception might be "Boogie Stop Shuffle," which omits one eight-measure interlude along with two solo choruses by Ervin and Handy's entire solo.

117 Columbia issued the three tracks—"Pedal Point Blues," "GG Train," and "Girl of My Dreams"—in 1979 on a double LP titled *Nostalgia in Times Square/The Immortal 1959 Sessions*. Intriguingly, this LP also included reissues of five tracks from the *Mingus Ah Um* session in their unedited form. Further details about this reissue are included in the discography accompanying *The Complete 1959 CBS Charles Mingus Sessions* (1993).

118 "Teo Macero Interview," pp. 1-2, digital folder DF-20510/2, Series 1: Interviews and Transcripts, Michael Jarrett Collection, Southern Folklife Collection.

119 "New Cat in Town," advertisement, October 15, 1959, Mingus Clippings, IJS.

120 Shim, *Lennie Tristano*, 78.

121 The studio included industry-standard Ampex tape machines and Neumann condenser microphones made by the Telefunken company. Apparently, engineer Rudy Van Gelder helped build the recording studio. Shim, *Lennie Tristano*, 78.

122 Shim, *Lennie Tristano*, 81.

123 Shim, *Lennie Tristano*, 80-81.

124 Shim, *Lennie Tristano*, 82-83. Rustin-Paschal offers a slightly different account. She suggests that three fans—Bill Brandt Jr., Larry Suttlehan, and Joe Mauro—approached Mingus with the idea of starting the label but had to pull out because they were going into the armed services. She presents some further evidence that Mingus and Roach bought out the trio's shares of the company for $250 each. Rustin-Paschal, *Kind of Man I Am*, 199n36. It is possible that both origin stories are true.

125 Tristano's experiments were some of the earliest examples of creative postproduction using magnetic tape. Tristano biographer Eunmi Shim postulates that Tristano enlisted the help of Rudy Van Gelder. Later, Tristano would continue these multitrack experiments (with much controversy) on "Line Up," "East Thirty-Second," "Turkish Mambo," "Requiem," and "Descent into the Maelstrom." See Shim, *Lennie Tristano*, 81-82, 87-95, 180. Of these later tracks, all but "Descent" appear on the Atlantic LP *Lennie Tristano* (1955). "Descent" appeared much later, on a Japanese LP that also included reissues of "Ju-Ju" and "Pastime": *Descent into the Maelstrom* (1976).

126 A list of women executives in the US popular-music industry can be found in Broven, *Record Makers and Breakers*, 61.

127 A similar point is made in Rustin-Paschal, *Kind of Man I Am*, 104.

128 Debut's last two recording sessions—Jimmy Knepper in July and Shafi Hadi in September—produced quite a bit of material not released until decades later.

129 Rustin-Paschal, *Kind of Man I Am*, 97-98, 121-23. She points out that romantic partnerships shaped the careers of women artists as well, including Hazel Scott, Mary Lou Williams, Lena Horne, Carla Bley, and Abbey Lincoln. See also Robin D. G. Kelley, "The Jazz Wife: Muse and Manager," *New York Times*, July 21, 2002, 24.

130 Santoro, *Myself When I Am Real*, 131-32.

131 Mingus's autobiography, which he began to write in earnest around this time, was produced much like his records: a document spliced together in

collaboration within an industry (publishing) that had its own entrenched ideologies about race and artistic expression. His autobiography remains one of the most-written-about aspects of Mingus's career. See Porter, *What Is This Thing Called Jazz?*, 138-47; and Gabbard, *Better Git It in Your Soul*, 113-58.

132 Santoro, *Myself When I Am Real*, 132, 139, 146, 150.

133 Charles Mingus and Diane Dorr-Dorynek, liner notes to *Mingus Dynasty*. Admittedly, my description here avoids the issue of Mingus's many troubling abuses. For example, Mingus described Dorr-Dorynek to Jimmy Knepper as a high-class geisha and bragged to others that he planned to pimp her out. Toward the end of their relationship, the frequency of their fights increased, and, according to Santoro, these altercations "got physical." Santoro, *Myself When I Am Real*, 132, 158-59.

134 Mingus and Dorr-Dorynek, liner notes to *Blues & Roots*; Mingus and Dorr-Dorynek, liner notes to *Mingus Dynasty*. For more on the collaborative drafting of the *Blues & Roots* liners, see Porter, *What Is This Thing Called Jazz?*, 132-33.

135 For more on these relationships and those in the following decades, see Gabbard, *Better Git It in Your Soul*, 201-34; and Mingus and Goodman, *Mingus Speaks*.

136 At other points, Mingus shows a particular interest in the logistics of the business. About George Shearing's "Chelsea Bridge," he wonders if the arranger had "too much work to do and has to turn it out very fast." Regarding Johnny Hodges's "Big Show," he supposes that someone organized a group of Duke Ellington alumni to try and "figure out a way to make some money with some records." The magazine published the interview with Mingus across two issues: Leonard Feather, "The Blindfold Test: Charles Mingus," *Down Beat*, April 28, 1960, 49; and Leonard Feather, "The Blindfold Test: Charles Mingus," *Down Beat*, May 12, 1960, 39.

137 Charles Mingus, liner notes to *Let My Children Hear Music*. The essay was later retitled as "What Is a Jazz Composer?" See Mingus, *More Than a Fake Book*, 155-57.

Conclusion: Jazz as a Culture of Circulation

1 A fuller version of the story is told in Kane and Harari, *Art Kane, Harlem 1958*; and Bach, *Great Day in Harlem*. Also see Gabbard, "Evidence."

2 Art Kane, "A Great Day in Harlem," August 12, 1958, photo spread, in *Esquire*, January 4, 1959, 98-99.

3 The BBC first aired *1959: The Year That Changed Jazz* in 2009. See Phillip Lutz, "Evoking Jazz, through Film," *New York Times*, May 1, 2011, WE9. As of February 2023, the documentary could be viewed online.

4   See Brubeck, "1959: The Beginning of Beyond," 200. Darius, the eldest son of Dave Brubeck, describes 1959 as a "collective breakthrough" and jazz's "emancipation" from both popular entertainment and bebop. Although *Giant Steps* was recorded in 1959, Atlantic issued it in early 1960. The 1938 and 1939 Spirituals to Swing concert series was among the first times that Carnegie Hall featured African Americans as the headline act. For a reprint of the concert's original program, see Dugan and Hammond, "Early Black-Music Concert." Traditional jazz styles associated with New Orleans continued to be well represented on new releases as well. One example is George Lewis and His New Orleans Stompers, *Concert!* (1959).

5   For more on the commercial contexts of *Time Out*, see Crist, *Dave Brubeck's "Time Out."*

6   A similar reading of "Afro Blue" can be found in Porter, *What Is This Thing Called Jazz?*, 166–67.

7   Lee and LiPuma, "Cultures of Circulation," 192, 211. Among other things, I am persuaded by Lee and LiPuma's argument that circulation places issues of capital at the analytic center.

8   Novak, *Japanoise*, 17–18. Novak examines circulation on the "edges" of commercial networks to argue that the liminal spaces at those edges are often where change and transformation occur. I am most influenced by his use of feedback as an analytic for understanding circulation and culture.

9   For one version of this story, see Ben Ratliff, "Bob Weinstock, 77, Founder of the Jazz Label Prestige," *New York Times*, January 16, 2006, B7. Benjamin Cawthra points out that at that time, a national infrastructure for selling records did not exist. As a result, small record labels had to rely on regional sales charts, independent distributors, individual radio promoters, and jukeboxes in bars. See Cawthra, *Blue Notes in Black and White*, 196. Orrin Keepnews of Riverside once described his distribution method as a beat-up station wagon in which he hand-delivered records to various New York City stores. Orrin Keepnews, liner notes to *The Riverside Records Story*.

10 Ellison, "Golden Age, Time Past," 179.

11 This event is well documented, including in Natalie Weiner, "August 25, 1959," *The 1959 Project* (blog), August 25, 2019, https://the1959project.com/post/187258979442/august-25-1959. Of the many sources about 1959, Weiner's blog is one of the few to make an explicit argument that the significance of 1959 in jazz is not tied to individual records. For more on the racial politics of the accompanying photos of Davis's injuries, see Cawthra, *Blue Notes in Black and White*, 125–27.

12 Alongside the proliferation of sit-ins, numerous civil-rights organizations also continued to fight pro-segregation forces in the schools, organize campaigns

to combat voter suppression, and explore the merits of different tactics of nonviolence. Such activities are also not reducible to a singular calendar year. For more on the jazz contexts, see Monson, *Freedom Sounds*.

13   This studio chatter can be heard on "So What (Studio Sequence 1)" from *Kind of Blue* (legacy edition), disc 1, track 10. See the discography for a full listing.

14   Jody Rosen, "The Day the Music Burned," *New York Times Magazine*, June 11, 2019, www.nytimes.com/2019/06/11/magazine/universal-fire-master-recordings.html.

15   My transcription, *Kind of Blue* (legacy edition), disc 1, track 13.

16   For example, see the LPs listed in "Christmas Buyer's Guide," *Down Beat*, December 10, 1959, 30-32. The guide includes many LPs that were technically issued in 1958 but that received four- to five-star reviews "during 1959."

Discography

Adams, Pepper. *10 to 4 at the 5 Spot*. Riverside RLP 12-265. LP (12 in). 1958.
Adderley, Cannonball. *The Cannonball Adderley Quintet in San Francisco*. Riverside RLP 12-311. LP (12 in). 1959.
Adderley, Cannonball. *The Cannonball Adderley Quintet in San Francisco*. Original Jazz Classics OJCCD-035-2. CD. 1989.
Adderley, Cannonball. *Jazz Workshop Revisited*. Riverside RLP 12-444. LP (12 in). 1962.
Adderley, Cannonball. *Nippon Soul*. Riverside RLP 477. LP (12 in). 1963.
Adderley, Cannonball. *Quintet at the Lighthouse*. Riverside RLP 344. LP (12 in). 1960.
Adderley, Cannonball. *Sextet in New York*. Riverside RLP 404. LP (12 in). 1962.
Allison, Mose. *Local Color*. Prestige PRLP 7121. LP (12 in). 1958.
Ammons, Gene. *Funky*. Prestige PRLP 7083. LP (12 in). 1957.
Ammons, Gene. *The Happy Blues*. Prestige PRLP 7039. LP (12 in). 1956.
Ammons, Gene. *Jammin' in Hi Fi with Gene Ammons*. Prestige PRLP 7110. LP (12 in). 1957.
Ammons, Gene. *Jammin' with Gene*. Prestige PRLP 7060. LP (12 in). 1956.
Anderson, Judith. *Judith Anderson in Medea*. Decca DLP 9000. LP (12 in). 1949.
Armstrong, Lil Hardin. *Satchmo and Me: Lil Armstrong's Own Story*. Riverside RLP 12-120. LP (12 in). 1959.
Armstrong, Louis. *Ambassador Satch*. Columbia CL 840. LP (12 in). 1956.
Armstrong, Louis. *Columbia and RCA Victor Live Recordings of Louis Armstrong and the All Stars*. Mosaic MD 9-257. CD (9 discs). 2014.
Armstrong, Louis. *Gene Norman Presents Satchmo at Pasadena*. Decca DL 8041. LP (12 in). 1952.
Armstrong, Louis. *The Hucklebuck/Stardust*. Decca 28171. 78 rpm (10 in). 1952.
Armstrong, Louis. *The Hucklebuck/Stardust*. Decca 9-28171. 45 rpm (7 in). 1952.

Armstrong, Louis. *Jazz Classics*. Brunswick BL 58004. LP (10 in). 1950.

Armstrong, Louis. *Louis Armstrong and the All Stars, vol. 1, New Orleans Days*. Decca DL 5279. LP (10 in). 1950.

Armstrong, Louis. *Louis Armstrong Classics: New Orleans to New York*. Decca DL 5225. LP (10 in). 1950.

Armstrong, Louis. *Louis Armstrong Plays the Blues*. Riverside RLP 1001. LP (10 in). 1953.

Armstrong, Louis. *Louis Armstrong Plays W. C. Handy*. Columbia CL 591. LP (12 in). 1954.

Armstrong, Louis. *The Louis Armstrong Story, vol. 1, Louis Armstrong and His Hot Five*. Columbia ML 4383. LP (12 in). 1951.

Armstrong, Louis. *The Louis Armstrong Story, vol. 2, Louis Armstrong and His Hot Seven*. Columbia ML 4384. LP (12 in). 1951.

Armstrong, Louis. *The Louis Armstrong Story, vol. 3, Louis Armstrong and Earl Hines*. Columbia ML 4385. LP (12 in). 1951.

Armstrong, Louis. *The Louis Armstrong Story, vol. 4, Louis Armstrong Favorites*. Columbia ML 4386. LP (12 in). 1951.

Armstrong, Louis. *Satchmo at Pasadena, vol. 1*. Decca 9-336 (equivalent to A side of DL 8041). 45-rpm set (7 in, 4 discs). 1952.

Armstrong, Louis. *Satchmo at Pasadena, vol. 2*. Decca 9-337 (equivalent to B side of DL 8041). 45-rpm set (7 in, 4 discs). 1952.

Armstrong, Louis. *Satchmo at Symphony Hall, vol. 1*. Decca DL 8037. LP (12 in). 1951.

Armstrong, Louis. *Satchmo at Symphony Hall, vol. 2*. Decca DL 8038. LP (12 in). 1951.

Armstrong, Louis, and Eddie Condon. *At Newport*. Columbia CL 931. LP (12 in). 1956.

Baker, Buddy, and His Orchestra. *Stairway to the Stars*. Specialty SP 100. LP (10 in). 1952.

Basie, Count. *At the Piano*. Decca DL 5111. LP (10 in). 1950.

Basie, Count, Mary Lou Williams, Dizzy Gillespie, and Joe Williams. *At Newport*. Verve MG V-8244. LP (12 in). 1958.

Bechet, Sidney. *Jazz Classics, vol. 1*. Blue Note BLP 7002. LP (10 in). 1950.

Beiderbecke, Bix. *The Bix Beiderbecke Story, vol. 1, Bix and His Gang*. Columbia GL 507. LP (12 in). 1951.

Beiderbecke, Bix. *The Bix Beiderbecke Story, vol. 2, Bix and Tram*. Columbia GL 508. LP (12 in). 1951.

Beiderbecke, Bix. *The Bix Beiderbecke Story, vol. 3, Whiteman Days*. Columbia GL 509. LP (12 in). 1951.

Bernstein, Leonard. *What Is Jazz*. Columbia CL 919. LP (12 in). 1956.

Blakey, Art. *Art Blakey and the Jazz Messengers* (later retitled *Moanin'*). Blue Note BLP 4003. LP (12 in). 1959.

Blakey, Art. *The Jazz Messengers at the Cafe Bohemia, vol. 1*. Blue Note BLP 1507. LP (12 in). 1956.

Blakey, Art. *The Jazz Messengers at the Cafe Bohemia, vol. 2*. Blue Note BLP 1508. LP (12 in). 1956.

Blakey, Art. *Meet You at the Jazz Corner of the World*. Blue Note BLP 4054. LP (12 in). 1960.

Blakey, Art. *A Night at Birdland with the Art Blakey Quintet, vol. 1*. Blue Note BLP 5037. LP (10 in). 1954.

Blakey, Art. *A Night at Birdland with the Art Blakey Quintet, vol. 2*. Blue Note BLP 5038. LP (10 in). 1954.

Blakey, Art. *A Night at Birdland with the Art Blakey Quintet, vol. 3*. Blue Note BLP 5039. LP (10 in). 1954.

Bley, Paul. *Introducing Paul Bley*. Debut DLP-7. LP (10 in). 1954.

Brubeck, Dave. *Dave Brubeck at Storyville: 1954, vol. 1*. Columbia CL 6330. LP (10 in). 1954.

Brubeck, Dave. *Dave Brubeck at Storyville: 1954, vol. 2*. Columbia CL 6331. LP (10 in). 1954.

Brubeck, Dave. *The Dave Brubeck Quartet: Newport 1958*. Columbia CL 1249. LP (12 in). 1959.

Brubeck, Dave. *Dave Digs Disney*. Columbia CL 1059. LP (12 in). 1957.

Brubeck, Dave. *George Wein Presents Jazz at Storyville*. Fantasy FLP 3-8. LP (10 in). 1953.

Brubeck, Dave. *Jazz at Oberlin*. Fantasy FLP 3-11. LP (10 in). 1953.

Brubeck, Dave. *Jazz at the Blackhawk*. Fantasy FLP 3-210. LP (12 in). 1956.

Brubeck, Dave. *Jazz at the College of the Pacific*. Fantasy FLP 3-13. LP (10 in). 1954.

Brubeck, Dave. *Jazz Goes to College*. Columbia CL 566. LP (12 in). 1954.

Brubeck, Dave. *Jazz Goes to College, vol. 1*. Columbia CL 6321. LP (10 in). 1954.

Brubeck, Dave. *Jazz Goes to College, vol. 2*. Columbia CL 6322. LP (10 in). 1954.

Brubeck, Dave. *Paul and Dave: Jazz Interwoven*. Fantasy FLP 3-20. LP (10 in). 1954.

Brubeck, Dave. *Time Further Out*. Columbia CS 8490. LP (12 in). 1961.

Brubeck, Dave. *Time Out*. Columbia CS 8192. LP (12 in). 1959.

Brubeck, Dave, J. J. Johnson, and Kai Winding. *Dave Brubeck/Jay & Kai at Newport*. Columbia CL 932. LP (12 in). 1956.

Brunis, George, Miff Mole, and George Wettling. *Dixieland Jazz Gems, vol. 1*. Commodore FL 20.010. LP (10 in). 1950.

Charles, Ray. *The Genius of Ray Charles*. Atlantic 1312. LP (12 in). 1959.

Charles, Teddy. *New Directions: Teddy Charles Quartet*. Prestige PRLP 143. LP (10 in). 1953.

Charles, Teddy. *Teddy Charles West Coasters*. Prestige PREP 1307. EP (7 in). Ca. 1953.

Clayton, Buck. *All the Cats Join In: A Buck Clayton Jam Session*. Columbia CL 882. LP (12 in). 1956.

Clayton, Buck. *Buck Clayton Jams Benny Goodman*. Columbia CL 614. LP (12 in). 1955.

Clayton, Buck. *The Complete CBS Buck Clayton Jam Sessions*. Mosaic MD6-144. CD (6 discs). 1993.

Clayton, Buck. *The Huckle-Buck: A Buck Clayton Jam Session*. Columbia B-1836 (abbreviated). EP (7 in). 1954.

Clayton, Buck. *The Huckle-Buck: A Buck Clayton Jam Session*. Columbia B-397 (full length). EP (7 in, 2 discs). 1954.

Clayton, Buck. *The Huckle-Buck and Robbins' Nest: A Buck Clayton Jam Session*. Columbia CL 548. LP (12 in). 1954.

Clayton, Buck. *Jumpin' at the Woodside*. Columbia CL 701. LP (12 in). 1955.

Clayton, Buck, with Woody Herman. *How Hi the Fi: A Buck Clayton Jam Session*. Columbia CL 567. LP (12 in). 1954.

Cole, Nat King. *To Whom It May Concern*. Capitol W-1190. LP (12 in). 1959.

Coleman, Ornette. *The Shape of Jazz to Come*. Atlantic SD 1317. LP (12 in). 1959.

Coltrane, John. *Coltrane*. Prestige PRLP 7105. LP (12 in). 1957.

Coltrane, John. *Giant Steps*. Atlantic 1311. LP (12 in). 1960.

Coltrane, John. *"Live" at the Village Vanguard*. Impulse! A-10. LP (12 in). 1962.

Condon, Eddie. *George Gershwin Jazz Concert*. Decca DL 5137. LP (10 in). 1950.

Condon, Eddie. *Jam Session Coast-to-Coast*. Columbia CL 547. LP (12 in). 1954.

Condon, Eddie. *Jazz Concert at Eddie Condon's*. Decca DL 5218. LP (10 in). 1950.

Cooke, Sam. *Tribute to the Lady*. Keen S-2004. LP (12 in). 1959.

Copland, Aaron, and Benny Goodman. *Concerto for Clarinet and String Orchestra, Quartet for Piano and Strings*. Columbia Masterworks ML 4421. LP (12 in). 1951.

Crosby, Bing. *Bing Crosby Sings the Song Hits from Broadway*. Decca DL 5000. LP (10 in). 1949.

Crosby, Bing. *Collectors' Classics: Bing Crosby, vols. 1–8*. Decca DL 6008–6015. LP (10 in, 8 discs). 1951.

Daily, Pete, and Phil Napoleon. *Dixieland Jazz Battle, vol. 1*. Decca DL 5261. LP (10 in). 1950.

Davis, Eddie "Lockjaw," Dizzy Gillespie, Bennie Green, and Red Rodney. *Prestige First Sessions, vol. 3*. Prestige PRCD 24116-2. CD. 1992.

Davis, Miles. *Bags' Groove*. Prestige PRLP 7109. LP (12 in). 1957.

Davis, Miles. *Birth of the Cool*. Capitol T-762. LP (12 in). 1957.

Davis, Miles. *Blue 'n' Boogie*. Prestige PREP 1358. EP (7 in). Ca. 1954.

Davis, Miles. *But Not for Me, parts 1 and 2*. Prestige 915. 78 rpm (10 in). Ca. 1955.

Davis, Miles. *Classics in Jazz: Miles Davis*. Capitol H-459. LP (10 in). 1954.

Davis, Miles. *Collectors' Items*. Prestige PRLP 7044. LP (12 in). 1956.

Davis, Miles. *Cookin' with the Miles Davis Quintet*. Prestige PRLP 7094. LP (12 in). 1956.

Davis, Miles. *In a Blue Mood: Bluing*. Prestige PREP 1355. EP (7 in). Ca. 1954.

Davis, Miles. *In Person Friday and Saturday Nights at the Blackhawk, San Francisco*. Columbia C2L 20. LP (12 in, 2 discs). 1961.

Davis, Miles. *Kind of Blue*. Columbia CL 1355. LP (12 in). 1959.

Davis, Miles. *Kind of Blue* (50th anniversary legacy edition). Columbia/Legacy 88697 27105 2. CD (2 discs). 2009.

Davis, Miles. *Miles Ahead*. Columbia CL 1041. LP (12 in). 1957.

Davis, Miles. *Miles Davis All Stars, vol. 1*. Prestige PRLP 196. LP (10 in). 1955.

Davis, Miles. *Miles Davis All Stars, vol. 2*. Prestige PRLP 200. LP (10 in). 1955.

Davis, Miles. *Miles Davis and Gil Evans: The Complete Columbia Studio Recordings*. Columbia CXK 67397. CD (6 discs). 1996.

Davis, Miles. *Miles Davis and the Modern Jazz Giants*. Prestige PRLP 16-3. LP (12 in), 16⅔ rpm. 1957.

Davis, Miles. *Miles Davis and the Modern Jazz Giants*. Prestige PRLP 7150. LP (12 in). 1959.

Davis, Miles. *Miles Davis: Blue Period*. Prestige PRLP 140. LP (10 in). 1953.

Davis, Miles. *Miles Davis Quartet*. Prestige PRLP 161. LP (10 in). 1954.

Davis, Miles. *Miles Davis Quartet: May 19, 1953*. Prestige PREP 1326. EP (7 in). 1953.

Davis, Miles. *Miles Davis Quintet*. Prestige PRLP 185. LP (10 in). 1954.

Davis, Miles. *Miles Davis with Sonny Rollins*. Prestige PRLP 187. LP (10 in). 1954.

Davis, Miles. *The New Sounds*. Prestige PRLP 124. LP (10 in). 1952.

Davis, Miles. *Porgy and Bess*. Columbia CL 1274. LP (12 in). 1959.

Davis, Miles. *Relaxin' with the Miles Davis Quintet*. Prestige PRLP 7129. LP (12 in). 1958.

Davis, Miles. *'Round about Midnight*. Columbia CL 949. LP (12 in). 1957.

Davis, Miles. *Steamin' with the Miles Davis Quintet*. Prestige PRLP 7200. LP (12 in). 1961.

Davis, Miles. *Walking*. Prestige PREP 1357. EP (7 in). Ca. 1954.

Davis, Miles. *Workin' with the Miles Davis Quintet*. Prestige PRLP 7166. LP (12 in). 1960.

Davis, Miles, and His Band. *Bluing, parts 1 and 2*. Prestige 846. 78 rpm (10 in). 1952.

Davis, Miles, and His Band. *Bluing, part 3/Conception*. Prestige 868. 78 rpm (10 in). 1952.

Dennis, Willie, Bennie Green, J. J. Johnson, and Kai Winding. *Four Trombones*. Debut DEB-126. LP (12 in). 1957.

Dennis, Willie, Bennie Green, J. J. Johnson, and Kai Winding. *Jazz Workshop, vol. 1, Trombone Rapport*. Debut DLP-5. LP (10 in). 1954.

Dennis, Willie, Bennie Green, J. J. Johnson, and Kai Winding. *Jazz Workshop, vol. 2, Trombone Rapport*. Debut DLP-14. LP (10 in). 1955.

Dorham, Kenny. *Round about Midnight at the Cafe Bohemia*. Blue Note BLP 1524. LP (12 in). 1956.

Dorsey, Tommy, Bunny Berigan, and Fats Waller. *A Jam Session at Victor: Honeysuckle Rose/Blues*. Victor 25559. 78 rpm (10 in). 1937.

Dorsey, Tommy, and Jimmy Dorsey. *The Dorsey Brothers' Orchestra, vol. 1, Dixieland Jazz 1934–1935*. Decca DL 6016. LP (10 in). 1950.

Dorsey, Tommy, and Jimmy Dorsey. *Honeysuckle Rose, parts 1 and 2*. Decca 296. 78 rpm (10 in). 1934.

Ellington, Duke. *Anatomy of a Murder*. Columbia CL 1360. LP (12 in). 1959.

Ellington, Duke. *At the Bal Masque*. Columbia CL 1282. LP (12 in). 1959.

Ellington, Duke. *Diminuendo in Blue/Crescendo in Blue*. Brunswick 8004. 78 rpm (10 in). 1938.

Ellington, Duke. *Duke Ellington and His Orchestra: Newport 1958*. Columbia CL 1245. LP (12 in). 1958.

Ellington, Duke. *Duke Ellington and His Orchestra: Newport 1958*. Mosaic Records MCD 1014. CD. 2007.

Ellington, Duke. *Ellington at Newport*. Columbia CL 934. LP (12 in). 1956.

Ellington, Duke. *Ellington at Newport* (Columbia Jazz Masterpieces). Columbia CK 40587. CD. 1987.

Ellington, Duke. *Ellington at Newport (Complete)*. Legacy C2K 64932. CD. 1999.

Ellington, Duke. *Ellington Uptown*. Columbia ML 4639. LP (12 in). 1952.

Ellington, Duke. *Masterpieces by Ellington*. Columbia Masterworks ML 4418. LP (12 in). 1951.

Ellington, Duke. *Masterpieces by Ellington*. Acoustic Productions AAPJ 4418. LP (12 in). 2014.

Ellington, Duke. *Reminiscing in Tempo, parts 1 and 2*. Brunswick 7546. 78 rpm (10 in). 1935.

Ellington, Duke. *Reminiscing in Tempo, parts 3 and 4*. Brunswick 7547. 78 rpm (10 in). 1935.

Ellington, Duke. *Tiger Rag, parts 1 and 2*. Brunswick 4238. 78 rpm (10 in). 1929.

Ellington, Duke, and Buck Clayton. *The Duke Ellington and Buck Clayton All-Stars: At Newport*. Columbia CL 933. LP (12 in). 1956.

Ellington, Duke, and Rosemary Clooney. *Blue Rose*. Columbia CL 872. LP (12 in). 1956.

Ellington, Duke, and Johnny Hodges. *Back to Back: Duke Ellington and Johnny Hodges Play the Blues*. Verve MGV 8317. LP (12 in). 1959.

Evans, Bill. *Everybody Digs Bill Evans*. Riverside 12-291. LP (12 in). 1959.

Evans, Bill. *Sunday at the Village Vanguard*. Riverside RLP 376. LP (12 in). 1961.

Evans, Bill. *Waltz for Debby*. Riverside RLP 399. LP (12 in). 1961.

Ferguson, Allyn, and Kenneth Patchen. *Allyn Ferguson and Kenneth Patchen with the Chamber Jazz Sextet*. Discovery DS-858. LP (12 in). 1957.

Fitzgerald, Ella. *At the Opera House*. Verve MG V-8264. LP (12 in). 1956.

Fitzgerald, Ella. *Ella Fitzgerald Sings the Cole Porter Songbook*. Verve MG V-4001-2. LP (12 in, 2 discs). 1956.

Fitzgerald, Ella. *Ella Fitzgerald Sings the George and Ira Gershwin Song Book, vol. 1.* Verve MG V-4024. LP (12 in). 1959.
Fitzgerald, Ella. *Ella Fitzgerald Souvenir Album.* Decca DL 5084. LP (10 in). 1950.
Fitzgerald, Ella. *Ella Sings Gershwin.* Decca DL 5300. LP (10 in). 1951.
Fitzgerald, Ella, and Billie Holiday. *At Newport.* Verve MG V-8234. LP (12 in). 1957.
Garland, Red. *All Kinds of Weather.* Prestige PRLP 7148. LP (12 in). 1959.
Garland, Red. *Red Garland at the Prelude.* Prestige PRLP 7170. LP (12 in). 1959.
Garner, Erroll. *Concert by the Sea.* Columbia CL 883. LP (12 in). 1956.
Garner, Erroll. *Erroll Garner.* Columbia CL 535. LP (12 in). 1953.
Garner, Erroll. *Erroll Garner at the Piano, vol. 1.* Savoy MG 15000. LP (10 in). 1949.
Garner, Erroll. *Erroll Garner at the Piano, vol. 2.* Savoy MG 15001. LP (10 in). 1950.
Garner, Erroll. *Erroll Garner at the Piano, vol. 3.* Savoy MG 15002. LP (10 in). 1950.
Garner, Erroll. *Erroll Garner at the Piano, vol. 4.* Savoy MG 15004. LP (10 in). 1951.
Getz, Stan. *New Sounds in Modern Music: Stan Getz, vol. 1.* Savoy MG 9004. LP (10 in). 1951.
Getz, Stan. *Stan Getz, vol. 2.* Prestige PRLP 104. LP (10 in). 1951.
Getz, Stan. *Stan Getz Quartets.* Prestige PRLP 7002. LP (12 in). 1955.
Getz, Stan, and Lee Konitz. *The New Sounds.* Prestige PRLP 108. LP (10 in). 1951.
Gillespie, Dizzy. *Afro: Dizzy Gillespie and His Orchestra.* Norgran MG N-1003. LP (12 in). 1954.
Gillespie, Dizzy. *Birks' Works.* Verve MG V-8222. LP (12 in). 1957.
Gillespie, Dizzy. *Birks Works: The Verve Big-Band Sessions.* Verve Records 314 527 900-2. CD (2 discs). 1995.
Gillespie, Dizzy. *Dee Gee Days.* Savoy SJL 2209. LP (12 in, 2 discs). 1976.
Gillespie, Dizzy. *Dizzy and Strings.* Norgran MG N-1023. LP (12 in). 1955.
Gillespie, Dizzy. *Dizzy Gillespie at Newport.* Verve MG V-8242. LP (12 in). 1957.
Gillespie, Dizzy. *Dizzy Gillespie: World Statesman.* Norgran MG N-1084. LP (12 in). 1956.
Gillespie, Dizzy. *Dizzy in Greece.* Verve MG V-8017. LP (12 in). 1957.
Gillespie, Dizzy. *Dizzy in South America, Official U.S. State Department Tour, 1956, vol. 1.* Consolidated Artists CAP 933. CD. 1999.
Gillespie, Dizzy. *Dizzy in South America, Official U.S. State Department Tour, 1956, vol. 2.* Consolidated Artists CAP 934. CD. 1999.
Gillespie, Dizzy. *Dizzy in South America, Official U.S. State Department Tour, 1956, vol. 3.* Consolidated Artists CAP 935. CD. 2001.
Gillespie, Dizzy. *Have Trumpet, Will Excite!* Verve MG V-8313. LP (12 in). 1959.
Gillespie, Dizzy. *Jazz Recital.* Norgran MG N-1083. LP (12 in). 1956.
Gillespie, Dizzy, and Joe Carroll. *Blue Skies/Pop's Confessin' (I'm Confessing).* Dee Gee 3605. 78 rpm (10 in). 1952.
Gillespie, Dizzy, and Roy Eldridge. *Trumpet Battle.* Clef MG C-730. LP (12 in). 1954.

Gillespie, Dizzy, Roy Eldridge, and Harry Edison. *Tour de Force: The Trumpets of Roy Eldridge, Dizzy Gillespie and Harry Edison.* Verve MG V-8212. LP (12 in). 1957.

Gillespie, Dizzy, and Stan Getz. *The Dizzy Gillespie Stan Getz Sextet.* Norgran MG N-2. LP (10 in). 1954.

Gillespie, Dizzy, Stan Getz, Coleman Hawkins, and Paul Gonsalves. *Sittin' In.* Verve MG V-8225. LP (12 in). 1957.

Gillespie, Dizzy, Charles Mingus, Charlie Parker, Bud Powell, and Max Roach. *The Quintet: Jazz at Massey Hall.* Debut DEB 124. LP (12 in). 1956.

Gillespie, Dizzy, Charles Mingus, Charlie Parker, Bud Powell, and Max Roach. *The Quintet: Jazz at Massey Hall, vol. 1.* Debut DLP 2. LP (10 in). 1953.

Gillespie, Dizzy, Charles Mingus, Charlie Parker, Bud Powell, and Max Roach. *The Quintet: Jazz at Massey Hall, vol. 3.* Debut DLP 4. LP (10 in). 1954.

Gillespie, Dizzy, Sonny Rollins, and Sonny Stitt. *Sonny Side Up.* Verve MG V-8262. LP (12 in). 1959.

Gillespie, Dizzy, Stan Getz, Coleman Hawkins, and Paul Gonsalves. *Sittin' In.* Verve MG V-8225. LP (12 in). 1957.

Goodman, Benny. *Benny Goodman and His Orchestra.* Columbia GL 501. LP (12 in). 1951.

Goodman, Benny. *The Benny Goodman Combos.* Columbia CL 500. LP (12 in). 1951.

Goodman, Benny. *The Famous 1938 Carnegie Hall Jazz Concert.* Columbia Masterworks SL 160. LP (12 in). 1950.

Goodman, Benny. *Mozart: Quintet for Clarinet and Strings in A Major (K. 581).* Columbia Masterworks ML 4483. LP (12 in). 1952.

Goodman, Benny. *Sing, Sing, Sing, parts 1 and 2* (edited version). Victor 25796. 78 rpm (10 in). 1938.

Goodman, Benny, and His Orchestra. *Benny Goodman in Moscow.* RCA Victor LSO-6008. LP (12 in). 1962.

Gordon, Dexter. *New Sounds in Modern Music: Dexter Gordon, vol. 1.* Savoy MG 9003. LP (10 in). 1951.

Gordon, Dexter, and Wardell Gray. *The Chase, parts 1 and 2.* Dial 1017. 78 rpm (10 in). 1947.

Gould, Glenn. *Bach: The Goldberg Variations.* Columbia Masterworks ML 5060. LP (12 in). 1956.

Gray, Wardell. *Jazz Concert.* Prestige PRLP 128. LP (10 in). 1952.

Green, Bennie. *Bennie Green with Strings.* Prestige PREP 1304. EP (7 in). 1953.

Griffin, Johnny. *Studio Jazz Party.* Riverside RLP 338. LP (12 in). 1960.

Hall, Edmond. *Celestial Express/Profoundly Blue.* Blue Note 17. 78 rpm (10 in). 1941.

Hallberg, Bengt, and Lars Gullin. *New Sounds from Sweden, vol. 2.* Prestige PRLP 121. LP (10 in). 1952.

Hampton, Lionel. *Be Bop.* Decca DL 5222. LP (10 in). 1952.

Hampton, Lionel. *Gene Norman Presents Just Jazz Concert: Lionel Hampton All Stars.* Decca DL 7013. LP (10 in). 1951.

Hampton, Lionel. *Hamp's Boogie Woogie*. Decca DL 5230. LP (10 in). 1951.
Hampton, Lionel. *Moonglow*. Decca DL 5297. LP (10 in). 1951.
Hardee, John. *River Edge Rock/Sweet and Lovely*. Blue Note 521. 78 rpm (10 in). Ca. 1946.
Harris, Barry. *Barry Harris at the Jazz Workshop*. Riverside RLP 12-326. LP (12 in). 1960.
Hawkins, Coleman. *Classics in Jazz: Coleman Hawkins*. Capitol H 327. LP (10 in). 1952.
Hawkins, Coleman. *Coleman Hawkins: A Documentary*. Riverside RLP 12-117/118. LP (12 in). 1958.
Hawkins, Coleman. *Soul*. Prestige PRLP 7149. LP (12 in). 1959.
Heifetz, Jascha. *Jascha Heifetz Playing the Music of Gershwin*. Decca DLP 7003. LP (10 in). 1949.
Herman, Woody. *Classics in Jazz: Woody Herman*. Capitol H 324. LP (10 in). 1952.
Herman, Woody. *Sequence in Jazz*. Columbia C 177. 78 rpm (10 in, 3 discs). 1949.
Hipp, Jutta. *Jutta Hipp at the Hickory House, vol. 1*. Blue Note BLP 1515. LP (12 in). 1956.
Hipp, Jutta. *Jutta Hipp at the Hickory House, vol. 2*. Blue Note BLP 1516. LP (12 in). 1956.
Holiday, Billie. *Billie Holiday* (later retitled *Last Recording*). MGM E3764. LP (12 in). 1959.
Holiday, Billie. *Lover Man*. Decca DL 5345. LP (10 in). 1951.
Holiday, Billie. *Strange Fruit*. Commodore 526. 78 rpm (10 in). 1939.
Holt, Will, and Dolly Jonah. *On the Brink*. Atlantic 8051. LP (12 in). 1961.
Horne, Lena. *Lena Horne at the Waldorf Astoria*. RCA Victor LOC-1028. LP (12 in). 1957.
Hughes, Langston. *The Weary Blues*. MGM E3697. LP (12 in). 1958.
Ink Spots. *Ink Spots, vol. 1*. Decca DL 5056. LP (10 in). 1950.
Ink Spots. *Ink Spots, vol. 2*. Decca DL 5071. LP (10 in). 1950.
Jackson, Milt. *Bags' Opus*. United Artists Records UAL 4022. LP (12 in). 1959.
Jackson, Milt. *Concorde*. Prestige PRLP 16-1. LP (12 in), 16⅔ rpm. 1957.
Jackson, Milt. *Milt Jackson and the Modern Jazz Quartet*. Prestige PREP 1325. EP (7 in). Ca. 1953.
Jackson, Milt. *Milt Jackson Quartet*. Prestige PRLP 7003. LP (12 in). 1955.
Jamal, Ahmad. *But Not for Me: Ahmad Jamal Trio at the Pershing, vol. 1*. Argo LP-628. LP (12 in). 1958.
Jamal, Ahmad. *Jamal at the Penthouse*. Argo LP-646. LP (12 in). 1959.
Johnson, J. J., and Bennie Green. *Modern Jazz Trombones, vol. 2*. Prestige PRLP 123. LP (10 in). 1952.
Johnson, J. J., and Kai Winding. *Modern Jazz Trombones*. Prestige PRLP 109. LP (10 in). 1951.
Johnson, J. J., Kai Winding, and Bennie Green. *Trombone by Three*. Prestige PRLP 7023. LP (12 in). 1956.
Johnson, James P. *The Daddy of the Piano*. Decca DL 5190. LP (10 in). 1950.

Kelly, Bev. *Bev Kelly in Person*. Riverside RLP 12-345. LP (12 in). 1960.
Kirby, John. *John Kirby and His Orchestra*. Columbia GL 502. LP (12 in). 1951.
Konitz, Lee. *Marshmallow/Fishin' Around*. Prestige PR 807. 78 rpm (10 in). Ca. 1949.
Konitz, Lee. *The New Sounds*. Prestige PRLP 116. LP (10 in). 1951.
Konitz, Lee. *The Real Lee Konitz*. Atlantic 1273. LP (12 in). 1957.
Konitz, Lee. *Tautology/Sound Lee*. Prestige PR 813. 78 rpm (10 in). Ca. 1949.
Konitz, Lee, and Lennie Tristano. *Lee Konitz Quintet, Lennie Tristano Quintet*. Prestige PRLP 101. LP (10 in). 1951.
Krupa, Gene. *Gene Krupa at the London House: Big Noise from Winnetka*. Verve MG V-8310. LP (12 in). 1959.
Lacy, Steve. *Reflections: Steve Lacy Plays Thelonious Monk*. New Jazz PRLP 8206. LP (12 in). 1959.
Lambert, Dave, Jon Hendricks, and Annie Ross. *Sing along with Basie*. Roulette R-52018. LP (12 in). 1959.
Lateef, Yusef. *The Fabric of Jazz*. Savoy MG-12140. LP (12 in). 1959.
Lewis, George, and His New Orleans Stompers. *Concert!* Blue Note BLP 1208. LP (12 in). 1959.
Lincoln, Abbey. *Abbey Is Blue*. Riverside RLP 12-308. LP (12 in). 1959.
Liston, Melba. *Melba Liston and Her 'Bones*. MetroJazz E 1013. LP (12 in). 1959.
Lombardo, Guy, and His Royal Canadians. *The Twin Pianos*. Decca DL 5002. LP (10 in). 1949.
Macero, Teo. *Explorations*. Debut DLP-6. LP (10 in). 1954.
Mallé, Gil. *Quadrama*. Prestige PRLP 7097. LP (12 in). 1957.
Marais, Josef. *Songs of the South African Veld*. Decca DL 5014. LP (10 in). 1949.
McCann, Les. *Les McCann Ltd. in San Francisco*. Pacific Jazz PJ-16. LP (12 in). 1961.
Mills Brothers, The. *Famous Barber Shop Ballads, vol. 1*. Decca DL 5050. LP (10 in). 1949.
Mills Brothers, The. *Famous Barber Shop Ballads, vol. 2*. Decca DL 5051. LP (10 in). 1949.
Milstein, Nathan, and Bruno Walter. *Mendelssohn: Concerto in E Minor for Violin and Orchestra*. Columbia Masterworks M-577. 78 rpm (12 in, 4 discs). 1946.
Milstein, Nathan, and Bruno Walter. *Mendelssohn: Concerto in E Minor for Violin and Orchestra*. Columbia Masterworks ML 4001. LP (12 in). 1948.
Mingus, Charles. *The Black Saint and the Sinner Lady*. Impulse! A-35. LP (12 in). 1963.
Mingus, Charles. *Blues & Roots*. Atlantic 1305. LP (12 in). 1960.
Mingus, Charles. *Charles Mingus Presents Charles Mingus*. Candid CJM 8005. LP (12 in). 1960.
Mingus, Charles. *Charles Mingus: The Complete Debut Recordings*. Debut 12DCD-4402-2. CD (12 discs). 1990.
Mingus, Charles. *The Clown*. Atlantic 1260. LP (12 in). 1957.
Mingus, Charles. *The Complete 1959 CBS Charles Mingus Sessions*. Mosaic MQ4-143. LP (12 in, 4 discs). 1993.

Mingus, Charles. *The Complete 1959 Columbia Recordings.* Columbia C3K 65145. CD (3 discs). 1998.

Mingus, Charles. *The Jazz Experiments of Charlie Mingus.* Bethlehem BCP 65. LP (12 in). 1956.

Mingus, Charles. *Jazz Portraits.* United Artists Records UAL 4036. LP (12 in). 1959.

Mingus, Charles. *Let My Children Hear Music.* Columbia KC 31039. LP (12 in). 1972.

Mingus, Charles. *Mingus Ah Um.* Columbia CL 1370. LP (12 in). 1959.

Mingus, Charles. *Mingus Ah Um* (Columbia Jazz Masterpieces). Columbia CK 40648. CD. 1987.

Mingus, Charles. *Mingus Ah Um* (legacy edition). Columbia 88697 48010 2. CD (2 discs). 2009.

Mingus, Charles. *Mingus at Monterey.* Jazz Workshop JWS 001, 002. LP (12 in, 2 discs). 1965.

Mingus, Charles. *Mingus at the Bohemia.* Debut DEB-123. LP (12 in). 1956.

Mingus, Charles. *Mingus Dynasty.* Columbia CL 1440. LP (12 in). 1960.

Mingus, Charles. *Mingus Mingus Mingus Mingus Mingus.* Impulse! A-54. LP (12 in). 1963.

Mingus, Charles. *Montage/Extrasensory Perception.* Debut M 103. 78 rpm (10 in). 1952.

Mingus, Charles. *The Moods of Mingus.* Savoy MG-15050. LP (10 in). 1955.

Mingus, Charles. *Nostalgia in Times Square/The Immortal 1959 Sessions.* Columbia JG 35717. LP (12 in, 2 discs). 1979.

Mingus, Charles. *Passions of a Man: The Complete Atlantic Recordings 1956–1961.* Rhino R2 72871. CD (6 discs). 1997.

Mingus, Charles. *Pithecanthropus Erectus.* Atlantic 1237. LP (12 in). 1956.

Mingus, Charles. *Precognition/Portrait.* Debut M-101. 78 rpm (10 in). 1952.

Mingus, Charles. *Tijuana Moods.* RCA Victor LPM-2533. LP (12 in). 1962.

Mingus, Charles, Hampton Hawes, and Dannie Richmond. *Mingus Three.* Jubilee JLP 1054. LP (12 in). 1957.

Mingus, Charles, and John LaPorta. *Jazzical Moods, vol. 1.* Period SPL 1107. LP (10 in). 1955.

Mingus, Charles, and John LaPorta. *Jazzical Moods, vol. 2.* Period SPL 1111. LP (10 in). 1955.

Mobley, Hank, and Lee Morgan. *Peckin' Time.* Blue Note BLP 1574. LP (12 in). 1959.

Modern Jazz Quartet. *The Modern Jazz Quartet.* Prestige PRLP 160. LP (10 in). Ca. 1953.

Monk, Thelonious. *Misterioso.* Riverside RLP 12-279. LP (12 in). 1958.

Monk, Thelonious. *Quartet Plus Two at the Blackhawk.* Riverside RLP 12-323. LP (12 in). 1960.

Monk, Thelonious. *Thelonious in Action.* Riverside RLP 12-262. LP (12 in). 1958.

Monk, Thelonious. *The Thelonious Monk Orchestra at Town Hall.* Riverside RLP 12-300. LP (12 in). 1959.

Monk, Thelonious. *Thelonious Monk Plays the Music of Duke Ellington*. Riverside RLP 12-201. LP (12 in). 1955.

Monk, Thelonious. *The Thelonious Monk Quintet*. Prestige PREP 1352. EP (7 in). Ca. 1954.

Moody, James. *Disappointed, parts 1 and 2*. Prestige 45-141. 45 rpm (7 in). 1956.

Moody, James. *Hi Fi Party*. Prestige PRLP 7011. LP (12 in). 1956.

Moody, James. *It Might as Well Be Spring/Faster James*. Prestige PR 903. 78 rpm (10 in). Ca. 1955.

Moody, James. *James Moody and His Band: Moody*. Prestige PRLP 198. LP (10 in). 1955.

Moody, James. *James Moody and His Band: Moody*. Prestige PRLP 7072. LP (12 in). 1957.

Moody, James. *James Moody and His Modernists*. Blue Note BLP 5006. LP (10 in). 1952.

Moody, James. *James Moody Band, vol. 2*. Prestige PREP 1369. EP (7 in). Ca. 1955.

Moody, James. *James Moody Favorites, vol. 1*. Prestige PRLP 110. LP (10 in). 1951.

Moody, James. *James Moody's Moods*. Prestige PRLP 192. LP (10 in). 1955.

Moody, James. *James Moody's Moods*. Prestige PRLP 7056. LP (12 in). 1956.

Morton, Benny. *Limehouse Blues/My Old Flame*. Blue Note 47. 78 rpm (10 in). 1945.

Morton, Jelly Roll. *Jelly Roll Morton: The Library of Congress Recordings, vols. 1–12*. Riverside RLP 9001–9012. LP (12 in). 1957.

Mulligan, Gerry. *Gerry Mulligan Blows*. Prestige PRLP 141. LP (10 in). 1953.

Mulligan, Gerry. *The Gerry Mulligan Quartet*. Fantasy FLP 3-6. LP (10 in). 1953.

Mulligan, Gerry, and Allen Eager. *The New Sounds*. Prestige PRLP 120. LP (10 in). Ca. 1951.

Murphy, Turk, and His Jazz Band. *When the Saints Go Marching In*. Columbia CL 546. LP (12 in). 1954.

Murrow, Edward R., and Fred W. Friendly. *I Can Hear It Now ... vol. 1*. Columbia Masterworks ML 4095. LP (12 in). 1949.

Navarro, Fats. *New Sounds in Modern Music: Fats Navarro, vol. 1*. Savoy MG 9005. LP (10 in). 1951.

Navarro, Fats, Dizzy Gillespie, Miles Davis, and Kenny Dorham. *Modern Jazz Trumpets*. Prestige PRLP 113. LP (10 in). 1951.

Nelson, Oliver. *Meet Oliver Nelson*. New Jazz NJLP 8224. LP (12 in). 1959.

O'Day, Anita. *Anita O'Day at Mr. Kelly's*. Verve MG V-2113. LP (12 in). 1958.

Oklahoma! Decca DL 8000. LP (12 in). 1949.

Parker, Charlie. *Bird at St. Nick's*. Jazz Workshop JWS 500. LP (12 in). 1957.

Parker, Charlie. *Bird Blows the Blues*. Dial LP 1 (also listed as Dial 901). LP (12 in). 1949.

Parker, Charlie. *Bird on 52nd St*. Jazz Workshop JWS 501. LP (12 in). 1957.

Parker, Charlie. *Charlie Parker: Complete Jazz at Massey Hall*. Jazz Factory JFCD 22856. CD. 2003.

Parker, Charlie. *Charlie Parker with Strings.* Mercury MG-C-101. LP (10 in). 1950.

Parker, Charlie. *The Complete Live Performances on Savoy.* Savoy Jazz SVY-17021-24. CD (4 discs). 1998.

Parker, Charlie. *New Sounds in Modern Music: Charlie Parker, vol. 1.* Savoy MG 9000. LP (10 in). 1951.

Parker, Charlie. *New Sounds in Modern Music: Charlie Parker, vol. 2.* Savoy MG 9001. LP (10 in). 1951.

Parker, Charlie. *New Sounds in Modern Music: Charlie Parker, vol. 1.* Savoy XP 8000. EP (7 in). 1953.

Patchen, Kenneth. *Kenneth Patchen with Chamber Jazz Sextet.* Cadence CLP 3004. LP (12 in). 1959.

Peterson, Oscar. *On the Town with the Oscar Peterson Trio.* Verve MG V-8287. LP (12 in). 1958.

Peterson, Oscar. *Oscar Peterson at the Stratford Shakespearean Festival.* Verve MG V-8024. LP (12 in). 1956.

Powell, Bud. *Jazz at Massey Hall, vol. 2.* Debut DLP 3. LP (10 in). 1953.

Powell, Mel. *Mel Powell Septet.* Vanguard (Jazz Showcase) VRS-8004. LP (10 in). 1953.

Quebec, Ike. *Blue Harlem/Tiny's Exercise.* Blue Note 37. 78 rpm (10 in). 1945.

Quebec, Ike. *If I Had You/Hard Tack.* Blue Note 510. 78 rpm (10 in). Ca. 1944.

Quebec, Ike. *She's Funny That Way/Indiana.* Blue Note 38. 78 rpm (10 in). 1945.

Rainey, Ma. *Ma Rainey, vol. 1.* Riverside RLP 1003. LP (10 in). 1953.

Raney, Jimmy. *Jimmy Raney Plays.* Prestige PRLP 156. LP (10 in). 1953.

Rexroth, Kenneth, and Lawrence Ferlinghetti. *Poetry Readings in the Cellar.* Fantasy FLP 7002. LP (12 in). 1957.

Rich, Buddy. *Buddy Rich in Miami.* Verve MG V-8285. LP (12 in). 1958.

Roach, Max. *Just One of Those Things/Drum Conversation.* Debut M-107. 78 rpm (10 in). 1953.

Roach, Max. *The Max Roach Quartet Featuring Hank Mobley.* Debut DLP-13. LP (10 in). 1955.

Roach, Max. *We Insist! Max Roach's Freedom Now Suite.* Candid CJM 8002. LP (12 in). 1960.

Rodney, Red. *The New Sounds.* Prestige PRLP 122. LP (10 in). 1952.

Rollins, Sonny. *A Night at the Village Vanguard.* Blue Note BLP 1581. LP (12 in). 1958.

Rollins, Sonny. *Saxophone Colossus.* Prestige PRLP 7079. LP (12 in). 1957.

Rollins, Sonny. *Sonny Rollins with the Modern Jazz Quartet.* Prestige PREP 1337. EP (7 in). Ca. 1953.

Rollins, Sonny, and Thelonious Monk. *Sonny Rollins and Thelonious Monk Quartet.* Prestige PRLP 190. LP (10 in). 1954.

Ross, Annie, with the Gerry Mulligan Quartet. *Annie Ross Sings a Song with Mulligan!* World Pacific WP 1253. LP (12 in). 1959.

Sherwood, Bobby. *Classics in Jazz: Bobby Sherwood.* Capitol H 320. LP (10 in). 1952.
Silver, Horace. *Blowin' the Blues Away.* Blue Note BLP 4017. LP (12 in). 1959.
Simone, Nina. *The Amazing Nina Simone.* Colpix CP 407. LP (12 in). 1959.
Sims, Zoot. *Swingin' with Zoot Sims.* Prestige PRLP 117. LP (10 in). 1951.
Sims, Zoot. *Zootcase.* Prestige PR 24061. LP (12 in). 1976.
Sims, Zoot. *Zoot Sims Quartets.* Prestige PRLP 7026. LP (12 in). 1956.
Sinatra, Frank. *Come Fly with Me.* Capitol W920. LP (12 in). 1958.
Sinatra, Frank. *The Voice of Frank Sinatra.* Columbia C 112. 78 rpm (10 in, 4 discs). 1946.
Sinatra, Frank. *The Voice of Frank Sinatra.* Columbia CL 6001. LP (10 in). 1948.
Smith, Bessie. *The Bessie Smith Story, vol. 1, Bessie Smith with Louis Armstrong.* Columbia GL 503. LP (12 in). 1951.
Smith, Bessie. *The Bessie Smith Story, vol. 2, Bessie Smith, Blues to Barrelhouse.* Columbia GL 504. LP (12 in). 1951.
Smith, Bessie. *The Bessie Smith Story, vol. 3, Bessie Smith, with Joe Smith and Fletcher Henderson's Hot Six.* Columbia GL 505. LP (12 in). 1951.
Smith, Bessie. *The Bessie Smith Story, vol. 4, Bessie Smith, with James P. Johnson and Charlie Green.* Columbia GL 506. LP (12 in). 1951.
Smith, Jimmy. *Groovin' at Smalls' Paradise, vol. 1.* Blue Note BLP 1585. LP (12 in). 1958.
Smith, Jimmy. *Groovin' at Smalls' Paradise, vol. 2.* Blue Note BLP 1586. LP (12 in). 1958.
Smith, Jimmy. *The Incredible Jimmy Smith at Club Baby Grand, vol. 1.* Blue Note BLP 1528. LP (12 in). 1957.
Smith, Jimmy. *The Incredible Jimmy Smith at Club Baby Grand, vol. 2.* Blue Note BLP 1529. LP (12 in). 1957.
Smith, Jimmy. *The Sermon!* Blue Note BLP 4011. LP (12 in). 1959.
Smith, Mamie. *Crazy Blues/It's Right Here for You.* OKeh 4169. 78 rpm (10 in). 1920.
Stitt, Sonny, Bud Powell, and J. J. Johnson. *Sonny Stitt/Bud Powell/J. J. Johnson.* Prestige PRLP 7024. LP (12 in). 1956.
Sun Ra and His Arkestra. *Jazz in Silhouette.* El Saturn K7OP 3590/1. LP (12 in). 1959.
Tatum, Art. *Gene Norman Presents an Art Tatum Concert.* Columbia GL 101. LP (10 in). 1952.
Taylor, Billy. *Billy Taylor Trio, vol. 1.* Prestige PRLP 7015. LP (12 in). 1956.
Taylor, Billy. *Billy Taylor Trio, vol. 2.* Prestige PRLP 7016. LP (12 in). 1956.
Taylor, Billy. *Billy Taylor Trio, vol. 3.* Prestige PREP 1335. EP (7 in). Ca. 1954.
Taylor, Billy. *Let's Get Away from It All.* Prestige PRLP 16-2. LP (12 in), 16⅔ rpm. 1957.
Taylor, Cecil. *Love for Sale.* United Artists Records UAL 4046. LP (12 in). 1959.
Tharpe, Sister Rosetta. *Blessed Assurance.* Decca DL 5354. LP (10 in). 1951.
Tharpe, Sister Rosetta. *Wedding Ceremony of Sister Rosetta Tharpe and Russell Morrison.* Decca DL 5382. LP (10 in). Ca. 1951.

Tristano, Lennie. *Descent into the Maelstrom*. East Wind EW-8040. LP (12 in). 1976.

Tristano, Lennie. *Ju-Ju/Pastime*. Jazz 101. 45 rpm (7 in). 1952.

Tristano, Lennie. *Lennie Tristano*. Atlantic 1224. LP (12 in). 1955.

Tristano, Lennie. *Lennie Tristano Quintet Featuring Lee Konitz*. Prestige PREP 1308. EP (7 in). Ca. 1953.

Tristano, Lennie. *Progression/Retrospection*. Prestige PR 832. 78 rpm (10 in). Ca. 1949.

Tristano, Lennie. *Subconscious-Lee/Judy*. Prestige PR 808. 78 rpm (10 in). Ca. 1949.

Various. *Autobiography in Jazz*. Debut DEB-198. LP (12 in). 1956.

Various. *A Child's Introduction to Jazz*. Julian "Cannonball" Adderley, narrator. Wonderland RLP 1435 (Riverside). LP (12 in). 1961.

Various. *Classics in Jazz: Dixieland Stylists*. Capitol H 321. LP (10 in). 1952.

Various. *Classics in Jazz: Modern Idiom*. Capitol H 325. LP (10 in). 1952.

Various. *Classics in Jazz: Piano Stylists*. Capitol H 323. LP (10 in). 1952.

Various. *Classics in Jazz: Sax Stylists*. Capitol H 328. LP (10 in). 1952.

Various. *Classics in Jazz: Small Combos*. Capitol H 322. LP (10 in). 1952.

Various. *Classics in Jazz: Trumpet Stylists*. Capitol H 326. LP (10 in). 1952.

Various. *Columbia Small Group Swing Sessions 1953–62*. Mosaic MD8-228. CD (8 discs). 2005.

Various. *The Debut Records Story*. Debut 4DCD-4420-2. CD (4 discs). 1997.

Various. *Decca Jazz Studio 1*. Decca DL 8058. LP (12 in). 1954.

Various. *Dixieland Series, vol. 1*. Savoy MG 15005. LP (10 in). 1952.

Various. *Frank Bull and Gene Norman Present Dixieland Jubilee*. Decca DL 7022. LP (10 in). 1952.

Various. *From Spirituals to Swing*. Vanguard VRS 8523/4. LP (12 in). 1959.

Various. *Gems of Jazz: A Series of Superb Jazz Classics, vol. 1*. Decca DL 5133. LP (10 in). 1950.

Various. *Gems of Jazz: A Series of Superb Jazz Classics, vol. 2*. Decca DL 5134. LP (10 in). 1950.

Various. *I Like Jazz!* Columbia JZ 1. LP (12 in). 1955.

Various. *Jam Session at Commodore: Carnegie Jump/Carnegie Drag*. Commodore 1500. 78 rpm (12 in). Ca. 1938.

Various. *Jam Session at Commodore, no. 2: Embraceable You/Serenade to a Shylock*. Commodore 1501. 78 rpm (12 in). Ca. 1938.

Various. *Jam Session at Commodore, no. 3: A Good Man Is Hard to Find*. Commodore 1504, 1505. 78 rpm (12 in, 2 discs). 1940.

Various. *Jam Session at Commodore, no. 4: Lonesome Tag Blues/More Torilla B Flat*. Commodore 1510. 78 rpm (12 in). Ca. 1942.

Various. *Jam Session at Commodore, no. 5: Basin Street Blues/Oh Katharina!* Commodore 1513. 78 rpm (12 in). Ca. 1943.

Various. *Jam Session at Commodore, no. 6: When Day Is Done/At Sundown*. Commodore 1523. 78 rpm (12 in). 1947.

Various. *Jazz, vol. 1, The South.* Folkways FP 53. LP (12 in). 1950.
Various. *Jazz, vol. 2, The Blues.* Folkways FP 55. LP (12 in). 1950.
Various. *Jazz at the Philharmonic, vol. 1.* Stinson SLP 23. LP (10 in). 1950.
Various. *Jazz at the Philharmonic, vol. 8.* Mercury MG 35000. LP (10 in). 1949.
Various. *Jazz at the Philharmonic, vol. 10.* Mercury MG 35002. LP (10 in). 1949.
Various. *Jazz at the Philharmonic: Lady Be Good, parts 1 and 2.* Mercury 11075. 78 rpm (12 in). 1948.
Various. *Jazz at the Philharmonic: Presented by Norman Granz.* Stinson Records S453. 78 rpm (12 in, 3 discs). 1945.
Various. *Jazz of Two Decades.* EmArcy DEM-2. LP (12 in). 1955.
Various. *The Jazz Scene.* Mercury (limited edition, no issue number). 78 rpm (12 in, 6 discs). 1949.
Various. *The Jazz Scene.* Verve 314 521 661-2. CD (2 discs). 1994.
Various. *Mellow the Mood.* Blue Note BLP 5001. LP (10 in). 1951.
Various. *Modern Jazz Concert.* Columbia WL 127. LP (12 in). 1958.
Various. *Music for Brass.* Columbia CL 941. LP (12 in). 1957.
Various. *New Sounds from Sweden, vol. 1.* Prestige PRLP 119. LP (10 in). 1951.
Various. *Norman Granz' Jazz at the Philharmonic, vol. 8.* Mercury 11000, 11001, 11002. 78 rpm (10 in, 3 discs). 1948.
Various. *Norman Granz' Jazz at the Philharmonic, vol. 18.* Clef MG VOL. 18. LP (12 in). 1955.
Various. *The Prestige Records Story.* Prestige 4PRCD 44262. CD (4 discs). 1999.
Various. *Ragtime Piano Rolls, vol. 1.* Riverside RLP 1006. LP (10 in). Ca. 1953.
Various. *Rhythm and Blues, vol. 1.* Savoy MG 15008. LP (10 in). 1952.
Various. *Rhythm and Blues, vol. 1.* Savoy XP 8049. EP (7 in). Ca. 1953.
Various. *The Riverside History of Classic Jazz, vols. 1 and 2, Backgrounds/Ragtime.* Riverside RLP 12-112. LP (12 in). Ca. 1955.
Various. *The Riverside History of Classic Jazz, vols. 3 and 4, The Blues/New Orleans Style.* Riverside RLP 12-113. LP (12 in). Ca. 1955.
Various. *The Riverside History of Classic Jazz, vols. 5 and 6, South Side Chicago/Boogie Woogie.* Riverside RLP 12-114. LP (12 in). Ca. 1955.
Various. *The Riverside History of Classic Jazz, vols. 7 and 8, Chicago Style/Harlem.* Riverside RLP 12-115. LP (12 in). Ca. 1955.
Various. *The Riverside History of Classic Jazz, vols. 9 and 10, New York Style/New Orleans Revival.* Riverside RLP 12-116. LP (12 in). Ca. 1955.
Various. *The Riverside Records Story*, Riverside 4RCD 4422-2. CD (4 discs). 1997.
Various. *$64,000 Jazz.* Columbia B-777. EP (7 in). 1955.
Various. *$64,000 Jazz.* Columbia CL 777. LP (12 in). 1955.
Various. *Smithsonian Collection of Classic Jazz.* Smithsonian P6 11891. LP (12 in, 6 discs). 1973.
Various. *A Symposium of Swing.* Victor C-28. 78 rpm (12 in, 4 discs). 1937.

Ventura, Charlie. *Gene Norman Presents a Charlie Ventura Concert.* Decca DL 8046. LP (12 in). 1952.

Waldron, Mal. *Mal-1.* Prestige PRLP 7090. LP (12 in). 1957.

Wallington, George. *Quintet at the Bohemia Featuring the Peck.* Progressive PLP-1001. LP (12 in). 1955.

Weston, Randy. *Jazz à la Bohemia.* Riverside RLP 12-232. LP (12 in). 1956.

Weston, Randy. *Little Niles.* United Artists Records UAL-401. LP (12 in). 1959.

Williams, Paul. *The Huckle-Buck/Hoppin' John.* Savoy 683. 78 rpm (10 in). 1949.

Williams, Paul, and Wild Bill Moore. *The Huckle-Buck/Bubbles.* Savoy 45-799. 45 rpm (7 in). 1951.

Young, Cecil. *Concert of Cool Jazz.* King 295-1. LP (10 in). 1952.

Young, Lester. *Tenor Sax Solos.* Savoy MG 9002. LP (10 in). 1951.

Bibliography

Archives and Manuscript Collections

Columbia Center for Oral History, Columbia University Libraries, New York City
    Popular Arts Project, Oral History, 1958-1960

George Avakian Private Archives, Riverdale, NY (GAA)

Institute of Jazz Studies, John Cotton Dana Library, Rutgers University, Newark, NJ (IJS)
    Charles Mingus Clippings File
    Dizzy Gillespie Clippings File
    Marshall Winslow Stearns Collection, MC 030 (MSC)
    Newport Jazz Festival Records, MC 038
    Record Company Files

Library of Congress, Music Division, Washington, DC
    Charles Mingus Collection, 2019 organization (CMC-2019)

Louis Armstrong House Museum, Kupferberg Center for the Arts at Queens College, City University of New York (LAHM)
    Gösta Hägglöf Collection
    Satchmo Collection

New York Public Library, Music Division, New York City
    George Avakian and Anahid Ajemian papers, JPB 14-28 (AAP)
    Teo Macero Collection, JPB 00-8 (TMC)

Southern Folklife Collection, the Wilson Library, University of North Carolina at Chapel Hill
    Michael Jarrett Collection for the Study of Record Production #20510, https://finding-aids.lib.unc.edu/20510

Interviews

George Avakian, interview with the author, July 2012.
Michael Cuscuna, interview with the author, November 2011.
Dan Morgenstern, interview with the author, March 8, 2012.
Dave Usher, telephone interview with the author, July 9, 2015.

Newspapers, Magazines, and Other Periodicals

Arkansas State Press
Atlanta Daily World
Billboard
Boston Globe
Cash Box
Chicago Daily Tribune
Chicago Defender
Coda
Denver Post
Down Beat
Esquire
Fanfare: The Magazine for Serious Record Collectors
Fortune
Gramophone
High Fidelity Magazine
Huntsville (AL) Times
International Herald Tribune
Jazz Review
JazzTimes
Jazz Today
Jet
Life
Los Angeles Times
Metronome
New York Amsterdam News
New Yorker
New York Journal-American
New York News
New York Times
New York Times Magazine
Pittsburgh Courier
Popular Science
Record Changer
San Francisco Chronicle

Saturday Review
Schwann Long Playing Record Catalog
Time
Variety
Washington Afro-American

Books, Articles, and Other Sources

Agee, Christopher L. *The Streets of San Francisco: Policing and the Creation of a Cosmopolitan Liberal Politics, 1950-1972*. Chicago: University of Chicago Press, 2014.

Ake, David. *Jazz Cultures*. Berkeley: University of California Press, 2002.

Ake, David. *Jazz Matters: Sound, Place, and Time since Bebop*. Berkeley: University of California Press, 2010.

Allain, Paul, and Jen Harvie. *Routledge Companion to Theatre and Performance*. New York: Routledge, 2006.

Anderson, Benedict. *Imagined Communities: Reflections on the Origin and Spread of Nationalism*. 2nd ed. New York: Verso, 1991.

Anderson, Iain. *This Is Our Music: Free Jazz, the Sixties, and American Culture*. Philadelphia: University of Pennsylvania Press, 2007.

Anderson, Tim J. *Making Easy Listening: Material Culture and Postwar American Recording*. Minneapolis: University of Minnesota Press, 2006.

Atkins, Taylor. *Blue Nippon: Authenticating Jazz in Japan*. Durham, NC: Duke University Press, 2001.

Attali, Jacques. *Noise: The Political Economy of Music*. Minneapolis: University of Minnesota Press, 1985.

Auslander, Philip. *Liveness: Performance in a Mediatized Culture*. 2nd ed. New York: Routledge, 2008.

Auslander, Philip. "Musical Personae." *TDR: The Drama Review* 50, no. 1 (2006): 100-119.

Baade, Christina. "Airing Authenticity: The BBC Jam Sessions from New York, 1938/39." *Journal of the Society for American Music* 6, no. 3 (2012): 271-314.

Baade, Christina. "'The Battle of the Saxes': Gender, Dance Bands, and British Nationalism in the Second World War." In *Big Ears: Listening for Gender in Jazz Studies*, edited by Sherrie Tucker and Nichole Rustin-Paschal, 90-128. Durham, NC: Duke University Press, 2008.

Bach, Jean, dir. *A Great Day in Harlem*. DVD. Chatsworth, CA: MMV Image Entertainment, 2005.

Baraka, Imamu Amiri. *Blues People: Negro Music in White America*. New York: Morrow, 1963.

Baraka, Imamu Amiri. "Jazz and the White Critic." In *Black Music: Essays*, 15-26. New York: Akashic, 2010.

Barry, Eric D. "High-Fidelity Sound as Spectacle and Sublime, 1950–1961." In *Sound in the Age of Mechanical Reproduction*, edited by David Suisman and Susan Strasser, 115-38. Philadelphia: University of Pennsylvania Press, 2010.

Bates, Eliot. *Digital Tradition: Arrangement and Labor in Istanbul's Recording Studio Culture*. New York: Oxford University Press, 2016.

Berliner, Paul. *Thinking in Jazz: The Infinite Art of Improvisation*. Chicago: University of Chicago Press, 1994.

Birnbaum, Larry. *Before Elvis: The Prehistory of Rock 'n' Roll*. Lanham, MD: Scarecrow, 2013.

Blake, Andrew. "Recording Practices and the Role of the Producer." In *The Cambridge Companion to Recorded Music*, edited by Nicholas Cook, Eric Clarke, Daniel Leech-Wilkinson, and John Rink, 36-53. Cambridge: Cambridge University Press, 2009.

Bohlman, Andrea F., and Peter McMurry. "Tape: Or, Rewinding the Phonographic Regime." *Twentieth-Century Music* 14, no. 1 (2017): 3-24. doi:10.1017/S1478572217000032.

Bolter, Jay David, and Richard Grusin. *Remediation: Understanding New Media*. Cambridge, MA: MIT Press, 1999.

Borgerson, Janet, and Jonathan E. Schroeder. *Designed for Hi-Fi Living: The Vinyl LP in Midcentury America*. Cambridge, MA: MIT Press, 2017.

Brackett, David. *Categorizing Sound: Genre and Twentieth-Century Popular Music*. Oakland: University of California Press, 2016.

Brooks, Daphne A. *Liner Notes for the Revolution: The Intellectual Life of Black Feminist Sound*. Cambridge, MA: Belknap Press of Harvard University Press, 2021.

Broussard, Albert P. *Black San Francisco: The Struggle for Racial Equality in the West, 1900-1954*. Lawrence: University Press of Kansas, 1993.

Broven, John. *Record Makers and Breakers: Voices of the Independent Rock 'n' Roll Pioneers*. Urbana: University of Illinois Press, 2009.

Brubeck, Darius. "1959: The Beginning of Beyond." In *The Cambridge Companion to Jazz*, edited by David Horn and Mervyn Cooke, 177-201. New York: Cambridge University Press, 2002.

Bryant, Clora, Buddy Collette, William Green, Steven Isoardi, Jack Kelson, Horace Tapscott, Gerald Wilson, and Marl Young. *Central Avenue Sounds: Jazz in Los Angeles*. Berkeley: University of California Press, 1998.

Burke, Patrick. *Come In and Hear the Truth: Jazz and Race on 52nd Street*. Chicago: University of Chicago Press, 2008.

Burns, Ken, dir. "The Adventure." Episode 9 of *Jazz*. DVD. Washington, DC: PBS, 2001.

Carby, Hazel V. "It Jus Be's Dat Way Sometime: The Sexual Politics of Women's Blues." In *The Jazz Cadence of American Culture*, edited by Robert O'Meally, 469-82. New York: Columbia University Press, 1998.

Carby, Hazel V. *Race Men*. Cambridge, MA: Harvard University Press, 1998.

Carletta, David. "Those White Guys Are Working for Me: Dizzy Gillespie, Jazz, and the Cultural Politics of the Cold War during the Eisenhower Administration." *International Social Science Review* 82, nos. 3-4 (2007): 115-34.

Carpio, Glenda. *Laughing Fit to Kill: Black Humor in the Fictions of Slavery*. New York: Oxford University Press, 2008.

Cawthra, Benjamin. *Blue Notes in Black and White: Photography and Jazz*. Chicago: University of Chicago Press, 2011.

Ceraso, Steph. *Sounding Composition: Multimodal Pedagogies for Embodied Listening*. Pittsburgh: University of Pittsburgh Press, 2018.

Ceraso, Steph, and Jon Stone, eds. "Sonic Rhetorics." Special issue, *Harlot* 9 (April 2013). http://harlotofthearts.org/index.php/harlot/issue/view/9.

Chamberland, Carol P. "The House That Bop Built." *California History* 75, no. 3 (1996): 272-83.

Chambers, Jack K. *Milestones: The Music and Times of Miles Davis*. Toronto: University of Toronto Press, 1983.

Chapman, Dale. *The Jazz Bubble: Neoclassical Jazz in Neoliberal Culture*. Berkeley: University of California Press, 2018.

Cherry, Robert, and Jennifer Griffith. "Down to Business: Herman Lubinsky and the Postwar Music Industry." *Journal of Jazz Studies* 10, no. 1 (2014): 1-24.

Clarke, Donald. *Wishing on the Moon: The Life and Times of Billie Holiday*. New York: Viking, 1994.

Cogan, Jim. *Temples of Sound: Inside the Great Recording Studios*. San Francisco: Chronicle, 2003.

Cohen, Brigid. "Enigmas of the Third Space: Mingus and Varèse at Greenwich House, 1957." *Journal of the American Musicological Society* 71, no. 1 (2018): 155-211. doi:10.1525/jams.2018.71.1.155.

Cohen, Harvey. *Duke Ellington's America*. Chicago: University of Chicago Press, 2010.

Cohen, Lizabeth. *A Consumer's Republic: The Politics of Mass Consumption in Postwar America*. New York: Knopf, 2003.

Cohodas, Nadine. *Spinning Blues into Gold: The Chess Brothers and the Legendary Chess Records*. New York: St. Martin's, 2000.

Collis, John, and Buddy Guy. *The Story of Chess Records*. New York: Bloomsbury, 1998.

Connor, Stephen. *Postmodernist Culture: An Introduction to Theories of the Contemporary*. Cambridge, MA: Blackwell, 1989.

Cook, Nicholas. "Methods for Analysing Recordings." In *The Cambridge Companion to Recorded Music*, edited by Nicholas Cook, Eric Clarke, Daniel Leech-Wilkinson, and John Rink, 221-45. New York: Cambridge University Press, 2009.

Crawley, Ashon. *Blackpentecostal Breath: The Aesthetics of Possibility*. New York: Fordham University Press, 2016.

Crist, Stephen A. *Dave Brubeck's "Time Out."* New York: Oxford University Press, 2019.

Cuscuna, Michael, and Michel Ruppli. *The Blue Note Label: A Discography.* Westport, CT: Greenwood, 2001.

Daniels, William R. *The American 45 and 78 RPM Record Dating Guide, 1940-1959.* Westport, CT: Greenwood, 1985.

Davenport, Lisa E. *Jazz Diplomacy: Promoting America in the Cold War Era.* Jackson: University Press of Mississippi, 2009.

Davis, Angela Y. *Blues Legacies and Black Feminism: Gertrude "Ma" Rainey, Bessie Smith, and Billie Holiday.* New York: Pantheon, 1998.

Dawson, Jim, and Steve Propes. *45: The History, Heroes, and Villains of a Pop Music Revolution.* San Francisco: Backbeat, 2003.

Decker, Todd. "Fancy Meeting You Here: Pioneers of the Concept Album." *Daedalus* 142, no. 4 (2013): 98-108.

Delaunay, Charles, Walter E. Schaap, and George Avakian. *New Hot Discography: The Standard Directory of Recorded Jazz.* New York: Criterion, 1948.

DeVeaux, Scott. *The Birth of Bebop: A Social and Musical History.* Berkeley: University of California Press, 1997.

DeVeaux, Scott. "Constructing the Jazz Tradition: Jazz Historiography." *African American Review* 25, no. 3 (1991): 525-60.

DeVeaux, Scott. "The Emergence of the Jazz Concert, 1935-1945." *American Music* 7 no. 1 (1989): 6-29.

Devine, Kyle. *Decomposed: The Political Ecology of Music.* Cambridge, MA: MIT Press, 2019.

Dinerstein, Joel. *The Origins of Cool in Postwar America.* Chicago: University of Chicago Press, 2017.

Doane, Mary Ann. "Real Time: Instantaneity and the Photographic Imaginary." In *Stillness and Time: Photography and the Moving Image*, edited by David Green and Joanna Lowry, 23-38. Brighton, UK: Photoworks/Photoforum, 2006.

Dregni, Michael. *Gypsy Jazz: In Search of Django Reinhardt and the Soul of Gypsy Swing.* New York: Oxford University Press, 2008.

Dudziak, Mary L. *Cold War Civil Rights: Race and the Image of American Democracy.* Princeton, NJ: Princeton University Press, 2000.

Dugan, James, and John Hammond. "An Early Black-Music Concert from Spirituals to Swing." *Black Perspective in Music* 2, no. 2 (1974): 191-207.

Dunkel, Mario. "Marshall Winslow Stearns and the Politics of Jazz Historiography." *American Music* 30, no. 4 (2012): 468-504.

Eisenberg, Evan. *The Recording Angel: Music, Records and Culture from Aristotle to Zappa.* New Haven, CT: Yale University Press, 2005.

Ellison, Ralph. "An Extravagance of Laughter." In *The Collected Essays of Ralph Ellison*, edited by John F. Callahan, 617-62. New York: Modern Library, 1995.

Ellison, Ralph. "The Golden Age, Time Past." In *Keeping Time: Readings in Jazz History*, edited by Robert Walser, 171-79. New York: Oxford University Press, 1999.

Elsdon, Peter. "Jazz Recordings and the 'Capturing' of Performance." In *Recorded Music: Performance, Culture and Technology*, edited by Amanda Bayley, 146-63. Cambridge: Cambridge University Press, 2010.

Elsdon, Peter. *Keith Jarrett's "The Köln Concert."* New York: Oxford University Press, 2013.

Ennis, Philip H. *The Seventh Stream: The Emergence of Rocknroll in American Popular Music*. Hanover, NH: Wesleyan University Press, 1992.

Epperson, Bruce D. *More Important Than the Music: A History of Jazz Discography*. Chicago: University of Chicago Press, 2013.

Ewell, Philip A. "Music Theory and the White Racial Frame." *Music Theory Online* 26, no. 2 (2020). doi:10.30535/MTO.26.2.4.

Feagin, Joe R. *The White Racial Frame: Centuries of Racial Framing and Counter-framing*. New York: Routledge, 2020.

Feather, Leonard. *Encyclopedia of Jazz*. New York: Horizon, 1955.

Feather, Leonard. *Inside Jazz*. Reissue of *Inside Be-Bop* (1949). New York: Da Capo, 1977.

Feld, Steven. "Acoustemology." In *Keywords in Sound*, edited by David Novak and Matt Sakakeeny, 12-21. Durham, NC: Duke University Press, 2015.

Feld, Steven. *Jazz Cosmopolitanism in Accra: Five Musical Years in Ghana*. Durham, NC: Duke University Press, 2012.

Feld, Steven. "Pygmy Pop: A Genealogy of Schizophonic Mimesis." *Yearbook for Traditional Music* 28 (1996): 1-35.

Feld, Steven. "Waterfalls of Song: An Acoustemology of Place Resounding in Bosavi, Papua New Guinea." In *Senses of Place*, edited by Steven Feld and Keith H. Basso, 91-136. Santa Fe, NM: School of American Research Press, 1996.

Fellezs, Kevin. *Birds of Fire: Jazz, Rock, Funk, and the Creation of Fusion*. Durham, NC: Duke University Press, 2011.

Fitzgerald, Michael. "Backstory in Blue: Ellington at Newport '56." ARSC *Journal* 40, no. 1 (2009): 83-85.

Flory, Andrew. *I Hear a Symphony: Motown and Crossover R&B*. Ann Arbor: University of Michigan Press, 2017.

Ford, Phil. *Dig: Sound and Music in Hip Culture*. New York: Oxford University Press, 2013.

Fosler-Lussier, Danielle. *Music in America's Cold War Diplomacy*. Oakland: University of California Press, 2015.

Franzius, Andrea Georgia Marina. "Soul Call: Music, Race, and the Creation of American Cultural Policy." PhD diss., Duke University, 2006.

Friedwald, Will. *Jazz Singing: America's Great Voices from Bessie Smith to Bebop and Beyond*. New York: Charles Scribner's Sons, 1990.

Gabbard, Krin. *Better Git It in Your Soul: An Interpretive Biography of Charles Mingus.* Berkeley: University of California Press, 2016.

Gabbard, Krin. "Evidence: Monk as Documentary Subject." *Black Music Research Journal* 19, no. 2 (1999): 207-25.

Gac, Scott. "Jazz Strategy: Dizzy, Foreign Policy, and Government in 1956." *Americana: The Journal of American Popular Culture* 4, no. 1 (2005). https://www.americanpopularculture.com/journal/articles/spring_2005/gac.htm.

Gendron, Bernard. "'Moldy Figs' and Modernists: Jazz at War (1942-1946)." In *Jazz among the Discourses*, edited by Krin Gabbard, 31-56. Durham, NC: Duke University Press, 1995.

Gennari, John. *Blowin' Hot and Cool: Jazz and Its Critics.* Chicago: University of Chicago Press, 2006.

Gillespie, Dizzy, and Al Fraser. *To Be, or Not . . . to Bop.* Minneapolis: University of Minnesota Press, 2009.

Ginell, Cary. *Walk Tall: The Music and Life of Julian "Cannonball" Adderley.* Milwaukee, WI: Hal Leonard Books, 2013.

Gioia, Ted. *The Imperfect Art: Reflections on Jazz and Modern Culture.* New York: Oxford University Press, 1988.

Gitelman, Lisa. *Always Already New: Media, History and the Data of Culture.* Cambridge, MA: MIT Press, 2006.

Gitelman, Lisa. "Recording Sound, Recording Race, Recording Property." In *Hearing History: A Reader*, edited by Mark M. Smith, 279-94. Athens: University of Georgia Press, 2004.

Gitelman, Lisa, and Geoffrey B. Pingree. *New Media, 1740-1915.* Cambridge, MA: MIT Press, 2003.

Gitler, Ira. "Introduction." In *Prestige Records: The Album Cover Collection*, edited by Geoff Gans, 1-5. Beverly Hills, CA: City Hall Records and Concord Music Group, 2009.

Givan, Benjamin. "Gunther Schuller and the Challenge of Sonny Rollins: Stylistic Context, Intentionality, and Jazz Analysis." *Journal of the American Musicological Society* 67, no. 1 (2014): 167-237.

Goldmark, Peter. *Maverick Inventor.* New York: Saturday Review Press, 1973.

Grant, Barry Keith. "Purple Passages of Fiestas in Blue? Notes toward an Aesthetic of Vocalese." In *Representing Jazz*, edited by Krin Gabbard, 285-304. Durham, NC: Duke University Press, 1995.

Gray, Herman. "Black Masculinity and Visual Culture." *Callaloo* 18, no. 2 (1995): 401-5.

Green, Adam. *Selling the Race: Culture, Community, and Black Chicago, 1940-1955.* Chicago: University of Chicago Press, 2007.

Griffin, Farah Jasmine. *If You Can't Be Free, Be a Mystery: In Search of Billie Holiday.* New York: Free Press, 2001.

Griffin, Farah Jasmine, and Salim Washington. *Clawing at the Limits of Cool: Miles Davis, John Coltrane and the Greatest Jazz Collaboration Ever*. New York: Thomas Dunne, 2008.

Griffith, Jennifer. "Mingus in the Act: Confronting the Legacies of Vaudeville and Minstrelsy." *Jazz Perspectives* 4, no. 3 (2010): 337-68.

Guilbaut, Serge, and John O'Brian, eds. *Breathless Days, 1959-1960*. Durham, NC: Duke University Press, 2017.

Hall, Stuart. "What Is This 'Black' in Black Popular Culture." In *Black Popular Culture*, edited by Gina Dent, 21-33. Seattle: Bay, 1992.

Hancock, Jon. *Benny Goodman, the Famous 1938 Carnegie Hall Jazz Concert*. Shrewsbury, UK: Prancing Fish, 2009.

Harvey, David. *The Condition of Postmodernity: An Enquiry into the Origins of Cultural Change*. Cambridge, MA: Blackwell, 1989.

Havers, Richard. *Blue Note: Uncompromising Expression*. San Francisco: Chronicle, 2014.

Haydon, Geoffrey. *Quintet of the Year*. London: Aurum, 2002.

Heller, Michael C. *Loft Jazz: Improvising New York in the 1970s*. Berkeley: University of California Press, 2016.

Hentoff, Nat. "Miles Davis: Prestige 182." In *The Miles Davis Reader*, edited by Frank Alkyer, Ed Enright, and Jason Koransky, 194. New York: Hal Leonard, 2007.

Hentoff, Nat, Cannonball Adderley, Dave Brubeck, Dizzy Gillespie, Ralph J. Gleason, Stan Kenton, Charles Mingus, Gerry Mulligan, George Russell, and Gunther Schuller. "A Jazz Summit Meeting." In *Keeping Time: Readings in Jazz History*, edited by Robert Walser, 261-93. New York: Oxford University Press, 1999.

Hershorn, Tad. *Norman Granz: The Man Who Used Jazz for Justice*. Berkeley: University of California Press, 2011.

Hill, Sarah. *San Francisco and the Long 60s*. New York: Bloomsbury Academic, 2015.

Hodeir, André. *Jazz, Its Evolution and Essence*. Translated by David Noakes. New York: Grove, 1956.

Hoefsmit, Sjef. "Columbia/Legacy C2K 64932 Duke Ellington at Newport 1956 Complete." *DEMS Bulletin* 99, no. 4 (1999): 16-17.

Hopkins, Harold, and Narinder Kapany. "A Flexible Fibrescope, Using Static Scanning." *Nature* 173, no. 4392 (1954): 39-41.

Horning, Susan Schmidt. *Chasing Sound: Technology, Culture, and the Art of Studio Recording from Edison to the LP*. Baltimore: Johns Hopkins University Press, 2013.

Howell, Ocean. *Making the Mission: Planning and Ethnicity in San Francisco*. Chicago: University of Chicago Press, 2015.

Howett, Dicky. *Television Innovations: 50 Technological Developments*. Tiverton, Devon, UK: Kelly, 2006.

Howland, John. *"Ellington Uptown": Duke Ellington, James P. Johnson, and the Birth of Concert Jazz*. Ann Arbor: University of Michigan Press, 2009.

Howland, John. "Jazz with Strings: Between Jazz and the Great American Songbook." In *Jazz/Not Jazz: The Music and Its Boundaries*, edited by David Ake, Charles Hiroshi Garrett, and Daniel Goldmark, 111–47. Berkeley: University of California Press, 2012.

Iton, Richard. *In Search of the Black Fantastic: Politics and Popular Culture in the Post-Civil Rights Era*. New York: Oxford University Press, 2008.

Jackson, Jeffrey H. *Making Jazz French: Music and Modern Life in Interwar Paris*. Durham, NC: Duke University Press, 2003.

Jackson, Travis A. *Blowin' the Blues Away: Performance and Meaning on the New York Jazz Scene*. Berkeley: University of California Press, 2012.

Jacobson, Matthew Frye. *Whiteness of a Different Color: European Immigrants and the Alchemy of Race*. Cambridge, MA: Harvard University Press, 1998.

Jarrett, Michael. "Cutting Sides: Jazz Record Producers and Improvisation." In *The Other Side of Nowhere: Jazz, Improvisation, and Communities in Dialogue*, edited by Daniel Fischlin and Ajay Heble, 319–51. Middletown, CT: Wesleyan University Press, 2004.

Jarrett, Michael. *Pressed for All Time: Producing the Great Jazz Albums from Louis Armstrong and Billie Holiday to Miles Davis and Diana Krall*. Chapel Hill: University of North Carolina Press, 2016.

Johns, Michael. *Moment of Grace: The American City in the 1950s*. Berkeley: University of California Press, 2003.

Johnson, Bruce. *Jazz Diaspora: New Approaches to Music and Globalisation*. New York: Routledge, 2019.

Jones, Andrew F. *Yellow Music: Media Culture and Colonial Modernity in the Chinese Jazz Age*. Durham, NC: Duke University Press, 2001.

Jones, Ryan Patrick. "'You Know What I Mean?' The Pedagogical Canon of 'Cannonball' Adderley." *Current Musicology*, no. 79 (2005): 169–205.

Kahn, Ashley. *A Love Supreme: The Story of John Coltrane's Signature Album*. New York: Viking, 2002.

Kane, Jonathan, and Guido Harari, eds. *Art Kane, Harlem 1958: The 60th Anniversary Edition*. Alba, Italy: Wall of Sound Editions, 2018.

Kater, Michael H. *Different Drummers: Jazz in the Culture of Nazi Germany*. New York: Oxford University Press, 1992.

Katz, Mark. *Capturing Sound: How Technology Has Changed Music*. Berkeley: University of California Press, 2004.

Kazanjian, David. *The Colonizing Trick: National Culture and Imperial Citizenship in Early America*. Minneapolis: University of Minnesota Press, 2003.

Kealy, Edward R. "From Craft to Art: The Case of Sound Mixers and Popular Music." *Sociology of Work and Occupations* 6, no. 1 (1979): 3-29.

Keepnews, Orrin. "Orrin Orates." In *Keystone Korner: Portrait of a Jazz Club*, edited by Sascha Feinstein and Cathy Sloane, 147-54. Bloomington: Indiana University Press, 2012.

Keepnews, Orrin. *The View from Within: Jazz Writings, 1948-1987*. New York: Oxford University Press, 1988.

Keightley, Keir. "Long Play: Adult-Oriented Popular Music and the Temporal Logics of the Post-war Sound Recording Industry in the USA." *Media, Culture and Society* 26, no. 3 (2004): 375-91.

Kelley, Robin D. G. *Africa Speaks, America Answers: Modern Jazz in Revolutionary Times*. Cambridge, MA: Harvard University Press, 2012.

Kelley, Robin D. G. *Thelonious Monk: The Life and Times of an American Original*. New York: Free Press, 2009.

Kelley, Robin D. G. "'We Are Not What We Seem': Rethinking Black Working-Class Opposition in the Jim Crow South." *Journal of American History* 80, no. 1 (1993): 75-112.

Kelley, Robin D. G., and Lewis Earl. *To Make Our World Anew: A History of African Americans*. New York: Oxford University Press, 2000.

Kennedy, Rick, and Randy McNutt. *Little Labels, Big Sound: Small Record Companies and the Rise of American Music*. Bloomington: Indiana University Press, 1999.

Kernodle, Tammy L. "Black Women Working Together: Jazz, Gender, and the Politics of Validation." *Black Music Research Journal* 34, no. 1 (2014): 27-55.

Kernodle, Tammy L. "Having Her Say: The Blues as the Black Woman's Lament." In *Women's Voices across Musical Worlds*, edited by Jane Bernstein, 213-31. Boston: Northeastern University Press, 2004.

Kirschenbaum, Matthew. *Mechanisms: New Media and the Forensic Imagination*. Cambridge, MA: MIT Press, 2008.

Klotz, Kelsey A. K. *Dave Brubeck and the Performance of Whiteness*. New York: Oxford University Press, 2023.

Klotz, Kelsey A. K. "On Musical Value: John Lewis, Structural Listening, and the Politics of Respectability." *Jazz Perspectives* 11, no. 1 (2018): 25-51.

Klotz, Kelsey A. K. "Racial Ideologies in 1950s Cool Jazz." PhD diss., Washington University in St. Louis, 2016.

Klotz, Kelsey A. K. "'Your Sound Is Like Your Sweat': Miles Davis's Disembodied Sound Discourse." *American Studies* 58, no. 4 (2019): 33-51. doi:10.1353/ams.2019.0046.

Knight, Arthur. "Jammin' the Blues, or the Sight of Jazz, 1944." In *Representing Jazz*, edited by Krin Gabbard, 11-53. Durham, NC: Duke University Press, 1995.

Lee, Benjamin, and Edward LiPuma. "Cultures of Circulation: The Imaginations of Modernity." *Public Culture* 14, no. 1 (2002): 191-213.

Lefebvre, Henri. *Rhythmanalysis: Space, Time, and Everyday Life*. London: Continuum, 2004.

Lewis, George E. "Improvised Music after 1950: Afrological and Eurological Perspectives." *Black Music Research Journal* 16, no. 1 (1996): 91-122.

Lewis, George E. *A Power Stronger Than Itself: The AACM and American Experimental Music*. Chicago: University of Chicago Press, 2008.

Lott, Eric. *Love and Theft: Blackface Minstrelsy and the American Working Class*. New York: Oxford University Press, 1995.

Magee, Jeffrey. "Kinds of Blue: Miles Davis, Afro-Modernism, and the Blues." *Jazz Perspectives* 1, no. 1 (2007): 5-27.

Maggin, Donald L. *Dizzy: The Life and Times of John Birks Gillespie*. New York: Harper Entertainment, 2005.

Majors, Richard, and Janet Billson. *Cool Pose: The Dilemmas of Black Manhood in America*. New York: Lexington, 1992.

Marmorstein, Gary. *The Label: The Story of Columbia Records*. New York: Thunder's Mouth, 2007.

Martin, Waldo E. *No Coward Soldiers: Black Cultural Politics and Postwar America*. Cambridge, MA: Harvard University Press, 2005.

McClary, Susan. *Feminine Endings: Music, Gender, and Sexuality*. Minneapolis: University of Minnesota Press, 1991.

McGinley, Paige A. *Staging the Blues: From Tent Shows to Tourism*. Durham, NC: Duke University Press, 2014.

McMurry, Peter. "Once Upon Time: A Superficial History of Early Tape." *Twentieth-Century Music* 14, no. 1 (2017): 25-48. doi:10.1017/S1478572217000044.

Meintjes, Louise. *Sound of Africa! Making Music Zulu in a South African Studio*. Durham, NC: Duke University Press, 2003.

Millard, Andre. *America on Record: A History of Recorded Sound*. New York: Cambridge University Press, 1995.

Miller, Karl Hagstrom. *Segregating Sound: Inventing Folk and Pop Music in the Age of Jim Crow*. Durham, NC: Duke University Press, 2010.

Miller, Leta E. *Music and Politics in San Francisco: From the 1906 Quake to the Second World War*. Berkeley: University of California Press, 2011.

Miller, Leta E. "Racial Segregation and the San Francisco Musician's Union, 1923-60." *Journal of the Society for American Music* 1, no. 2 (2006): 161-206.

Mingus, Charles. *Charles Mingus: More Than a Fake Book*. New York: Jazz Workshop, 1991.

Mingus, Charles, and John F. Goodman. *Mingus Speaks*. Berkeley: University of California Press, 2013.

Monson, Ingrid. *Freedom Sounds: Civil Rights Call Out to Jazz and Africa*. New York: Oxford University Press, 2007.

Monson, Ingrid. "The Problem with White Hipness: Race, Gender, and Cultural Conceptions in Jazz Historical Discourse." *Journal of the American Musicological Society* 48, no. 3 (1995): 396-422.

Moore, Celeste Day. *Soundscapes of Liberation: African American Music in Postwar France*. Durham, NC: Duke University Press, 2021.

Moreno, Jairo. "Bauza-Gillespie-Latin/Jazz: Difference, Modernity, and the Black Caribbean." *South Atlantic Quarterly* 103, no. 1 (2004): 81-99.

Moreno, Jairo. "Imperial Aurality: Jazz, the Archive, and U.S. Empire." In *Audible Empire: Music, Global Politics, Critique*, edited by Ronald Radano and Tejumola Olaniyan, 135-60. Durham, NC: Duke University Press, 2016.

Morrison, Matthew D. "Race, Blacksound, and the (Re)Making of Musicological Discourse." *Journal of the American Musicological Society* 72, no. 3 (2019): 781-823.

Morton, David. *Sound Recording: The Life Story of a Technology*. Westport, CT: Greenwood, 2004.

Morton, John Fass. *Backstory in Blue: Ellington at Newport '56*. New Brunswick, NJ: Rutgers University Press, 2008.

Moten, Fred. *In the Break: The Aesthetics of the Black Radical Tradition*. Minneapolis: University of Minnesota Press, 2003.

Moten, Fred. "Taste Dissonance Flavor Escape (Preface to a Solo by Miles Davis)." In *Black and Blur*, 66-85. Durham, NC: Duke University Press, 2017.

Mowitt, John. "The Sound of Music in the Era of Its Electronic Reproducibility." In *Music and Society: The Politics of Composition, Performance, and Reception*, edited by Richard Leppert and Susan McClary, 173-97. New York: Cambridge University Press, 1987.

Mueller, Darren. "The Ambassadorial LPs of Dizzy Gillespie: *World Statesman* and *Dizzy in Greece*." *Journal of the Society for American Music* 10, no. 3 (2016): 239-69. doi:10.1017/S1752196316000201.

Mueller, Darren. "The Early LPs of Louis Armstrong and the Profits of Jazz History." In *The Oxford Handbook of Jazz and Political Economy*, edited by Dale Chapman. Oxford University Press, forthcoming.

Mueller, Darren. "On the Jazz Scene: The Publics and Counterpublics of Julian Cannonball Adderley." *Jazz and Culture* 6, no. 1 (2023): 1-26.

Mueller, Darren. "Quest for the Moment: The Audio Production of Ellington at Newport." *Jazz Perspectives* 8, no. 1 (2014): 3-23.

Mueller, Darren. "Review: Wikipedia: The Free Encyclopedia." *Journal of the American Musicological Society* 72, no. 1 (2019): 279-95. doi:10.1525/jams.2019.72.1.279.

Murray, Albert. *Stomping the Blues*. New York: McGraw-Hill, 1976.

Myers, Marc. "Rudy Van Gelder (Part 4)." *JazzWax*, February 16, 2012. https://www.jazzwax.com/2012/02/interview-rudy-van-gelder-part-4.html.

Myers, Marc. *Why Jazz Happened*. Berkeley: University of California Press, 2013.

Neal, Mark Anthony. *What the Music Said: Black Popular Music and Black Public Culture*. New York: Routledge, 1999.

Novak, David. *Japanoise: Music at the Edge of Circulation*. Durham, NC: Duke University Press, 2013.

Novak, David. "2.5 × 6 Metres of Space: Japanese Music Coffeehouses and Experimental Practices of Listening." *Popular Music* 27, no. 1 (2008): 15-34. doi.org/10.1017/S0261143008001517.

Okiji, Fumi. *Jazz as Critique: Adorno and Black Expression Revisited*. Stanford, CA: Stanford University Press, 2018.

O'Malley, Brendan, and Ian Craig. *The Cyprus Conspiracy: America, Espionage, and the Turkish Invasion*. New York: I. B. Tauris, 1999.

Pellegrinelli, Lara. "Separated at 'Birth': Singing and the History of Jazz." In *Big Ears: Listening for Gender in Jazz Studies*, edited by Sherrie Tucker and Nichole Rustin-Paschal, 31-47. Durham, NC: Duke University Press, 2008.

Pepin, Elizabeth, and Lewis Watts. *Harlem of the West: The San Francisco Fillmore Jazz Era*. San Francisco: Chronicle, 2006.

Phelan, Peggy. *Unmarked: The Politics of Performance*. New York: Routledge, 1993.

Phillips, Damon J. *Shaping Jazz: Cities, Labels, and the Global Emergence of an Art Form*. Princeton, NJ: Princeton University Press, 2013.

Pond, Steven F. *Head Hunters: The Making of Jazz's First Platinum Album*. Ann Arbor: University of Michigan Press, 2005.

Pond, Steven F. "Old Wine, New Bottles: Record Collecting, Jazz Reissues, and the Jazz Tradition." *Jazz Perspectives* 13, no. 1 (2021): 3-37.

Porcello, Thomas Gregory. "Sonic Artistry: Music, Discourse, and Technology in the Sound Recording Studio." PhD diss., University of Texas at Austin, 1996.

Porter, Eric. "'Born Out of Jazz... Yet Embracing All Music': Race, Gender, and Technology in George Russell's Lydian Chromatic Concept." In *Big Ears: Listening for Gender in Jazz Studies*, edited by Sherrie Tucker and Nichole Rustin-Paschal, 210-34. Durham, NC: Duke University Press, 2008.

Porter, Eric. *What Is This Thing Called Jazz? African American Musicians as Artists, Critics, and Activists*. Berkeley: University of California Press, 2002.

Priestley, Brian. *Mingus: A Critical Biography*. New York: Quartet, 1982.

Rabig, Julia, and Laura Warren Hill, eds. *The Business of Black Power: Community Development, Capitalism, and Corporate Responsibility in Postwar America*. Rochester, NY: University of Rochester Press, 2012.

Radano, Ronald M. *Lying Up a Nation: Race and Black Music*. Chicago: University of Chicago Press, 2003.

Ramsey, Guthrie P., Jr. *The Amazing Bud Powell: Black Genius, Jazz History, and the Challenge of Bebop*. Berkeley: University of California Press, 2013.

Ramsey, Guthrie P., Jr. *Race Music: Black Cultures from Bebop to Hip-Hop*. Berkeley: University of California Press, 2003.

Rasula, Jed. "The Media of Memory: The Seductive Menace of Records in Jazz History." In *Jazz among the Discourses*, edited by Krin Gabbard, 134-62. Durham, NC: Duke University Press, 1995.

Read, Oliver, and Walter L. Welch. *From Tin Foil to Stereo: Evolution of the Phonograph*. 2nd ed. Indianapolis: H. W. Sams, 1976.

Reig, Teddy, and Edward Berger. *Reminiscing in Tempo: The Life and Times of a Jazz Hustler*. Metuchen, NJ: Institute of Jazz Studies and Scarecrow, 1990.

Riccardi, Ricky. "Louis Armstrong: The Decca Singles 1949-1958." *The Wonderful World of Louis Armstrong*, December 30, 2016. https://dippermouth.blogspot.com/2016/12/louis-armstrong-decca-singles-1949-1958.html.

Riccardi, Ricky. "60 Years of 'Satchmo at Pasadena.'" *The Wonderful World of Louis Armstrong*, January 30, 2011. https://dippermouth.blogspot.com/2011/01/60-years-of-satchmo-at-pasadena.html.

Rogin, Michael Paul. *Blackface, White Noise: Jewish Immigrants in the Hollywood Melting Pot*. Berkeley: University of California Press, 1996.

Rosenthal, David. *Hard Bop: Jazz and Black Music, 1955-1965*. New York: Oxford University Press, 1992.

Ruppli, Michel. *The Decca Labels: A Discography*. Westport, CT: Greenwood, 1996.

Ruppli, Michel. *The Prestige Label: A Discography*. Westport, CT: Greenwood, 1980.

Ruppli, Michel, and Bill Daniels. *The King Labels: A Discography*. Westport, CT: Greenwood, 1985.

Ruppli, Michel, and Bob Porter. *The Savoy Label: A Discography*. Westport, CT: Greenwood, 1980.

Rustin-Paschal, Nichole. *The Kind of Man I Am: Jazzmasculinity and the World of Charles Mingus Jr*. Middletown, CT: Wesleyan University Press, 2017.

Sanden, Paul. *Liveness in Modern Music: Musicians, Technology, and the Perception of Performance*. New York: Routledge, 2013.

Sanjek, David. "One Size Does Not Fit All: The Precarious Position of the African American Entrepreneur in Post-World War II American Popular Music." *American Music* 15, no. 4 (1997): 535-62.

Sanjek, Russell. *American Popular Music and Its Business*. New York: Oxford University Press, 1988.

Santoro, Gene. *Myself When I Am Real: The Life and Music of Charles Mingus*. New York: Oxford University Press, 2000.

Saul, Scott. *Freedom Is, Freedom Ain't: Jazz and the Making of the Sixties*. Cambridge, MA: Harvard University Press, 2003.

Sayers, Jentery. "Making the Perfect Record." *American Literature* 85, no. 4 (December 2013). doi:10.1215/00029831-2370230.

Schenker, Frederick J. "'Filipino Seekers of Fortune': Jazz as Labor in 1920s Colonial Asia." *Popular Music and Society* 45, no. 4 (2022): 405-24.

Schneider, Rebecca. *Performing Remains: Art and War in Times of Theatrical Reenactment*. New York: Routledge, 2010.

Schuiling, Floris. "Jazz and the Material Turn." In *The Routledge Companion to Jazz Studies*, edited by Nicholas Gebhardt, Nichole Rustin-Paschal, and Tony Whyton, 87-96. New York: Routledge, 2019.

Shearing, George, and Alyn Shipton. *Lullaby of Birdland: The Autobiography of George Shearing*. New York: Continuum, 2004.

Shim, Eunmi. *Lennie Tristano: His Life in Music*. Ann Arbor: University of Michigan Press, 2007.

Shipton, Alyn. *Groovin' High: The Life of Dizzy Gillespie*. New York: Oxford University Press, 1999.

Silva, Luiz Carlos do Nascimento. *Put Your Dreams Away: A Frank Sinatra Discography*. Westport, CT: Greenwood, 2000.

Skea, Dan. "Rudy Van Gelder in Hackensack: Defining the Jazz Sound in the 1950s." *Current Musicology*, nos. 71-73 (2001/2): 54-76.

Slavery and Justice: Report of the Brown University Steering Committee on Slavery and Justice. Providence, RI: Brown University, 2006. https://slaveryandjustice.brown.edu/sites/default/files/reports/SlaveryAndJustice2006.pdf.

Sloane, Kathy, and Sascha Feinstein. *Keystone Korner: Portrait of a Jazz Club*. Bloomington: Indiana University Press, 2012.

Smith, Jeremy A. "'Sell It Black': Race and Marketing in Miles Davis's Early Fusion Jazz." *Jazz Perspectives* 4, no. 1 (2010): 7-33.

Solis, Gabriel. "Duke Ellington in the LP Era." In *Duke Ellington Studies*, edited by John Howland, 197-223. Cambridge: Cambridge University Press, 2017.

Solis, Gabriel. "'A Unique Chunk of Jazz Reality': Authorship, Musical Work Concepts, and Thelonious Monk's Live Recordings from the Five Spot, 1958." *Ethnomusicology* 48, no. 3 (2004): 315-47.

Spar, Debra. *Ruling the Waves: From the Compass to the Internet, a History of Business and Politics along the Technological Frontier*. New York: Harcourt, 2001.

Stanyek, Jason, and Benjamin Piekut. "Deadness: Technologies of the Intermundane." *TDR: The Drama Review* 54, no. 1 (2010): 14-38. doi:10.1162/dram.2010.54.1.14.

Starosielski, Nicole. *The Undersea Network*. Durham, NC: Duke University Press, 2016.

Starr, S. Frederick. *Red and Hot: The Fate of Jazz in the Soviet Union, 1917-1980*. New York: Oxford University Press, 1983.

Stearns, Marshall. *The Story of Jazz*. New York: Oxford University Press, 1956.

Sterne, Jonathan. *The Audible Past: Cultural Origins of Sound Reproduction*. Durham, NC: Duke University Press, 2003.

Sterne, Jonathan. *MP3: The Meaning of a Format*. Durham, NC: Duke University Press, 2012.

Stoever, Jennifer Lynn. *The Sonic Color Line: Race and the Cultural Politics of Listening*. New York: New York University Press, 2016.

Suisman, David. *Selling Sounds: The Commercial Revolution in American Music.* Cambridge, MA: Harvard University Press, 2009.

Supplemental Appropriation Bill, 1957: Hearings before the Committee on Appropriations, United States Senate, Eighty-Fourth Congress, Second Session, on H.R. 12138, an Act Making Supplemental Appropriations for the Fiscal Year Ending June 30, 1957, and for Other Purposes. Washington, DC: US Government Printing Office, 1956.

Supplemental Appropriation Bill, 1957: Hearings before the Subcommittees of the Committee on Appropriations, House of Representatives, Eighty-Fourth Congress, Second Session, Part 2. Washington, DC: US Government Printing Office, 1956.

Tackley, Catherine. *Benny Goodman's Famous 1938 Carnegie Hall Jazz Concert.* New York: Oxford University Press, 2011.

Tackley, Catherine. "Jazz Recordings as Social Texts." In *Recorded Music: Performance, Culture and Technology*, edited by Amanda Bayley, 167-86. Cambridge: Cambridge University Press, 2010.

Taylor, Arthur. *Notes and Tones: Musician-to-Musician Interviews.* New York: Da Capo, 1993.

Taylor, Diana. *The Archive and the Repertoire: Performing Cultural Memory in the Americas.* Durham, NC: Duke University Press, 2003.

Taylor, Timothy D. *The Sounds of Capitalism: Advertising, Music, and the Conquest of Culture.* Chicago: University of Chicago Press, 2012.

Teal, Kimberly Hannon. *Jazz Places: How Performance Spaces Shape Jazz History.* Oakland: University of California Press, 2021.

Théberge, Paul, Kyle Devine, and Tom Everett, eds. *Living Stereo: Histories and Cultures of Multichannel Sound.* New York: Bloomsbury Academic, 2015.

Thompson, Emily. "Machines, Music, and the Quest for Fidelity: Marketing the Edison Phonograph in America, 1877-1925." *Musical Quarterly* 79, no. 1 (1995): 131-71.

Thompson, Emily. *The Soundscape of Modernity: Architectural Acoustics and the Culture of Listening in America, 1900-1933.* Cambridge, MA: MIT Press, 2002.

Thompson, Robert Farris. "An Aesthetic of the Cool." *African Arts* 7, no. 1 (1973): 41-91.

Thornton, Sarah. *Club Cultures: Music, Media and Subcultural Capital.* Hanover, NH: University Press of New England, 1996.

Tournè, Ludovic. "Redefining the Boundaries of Culture: The French Experience of Jazz." In *Breathless Days, 1959-1960*, edited by Serge Guilbaut and John O'Brian, 82-98. Durham, NC: Duke University Press, 2017.

Tucker, Sherrie. "Big Ears: Listening for Gender in Jazz Studies." *Current Musicology*, nos. 71-73 (2002): 375-408.

Von Eschen, Penny. *Race against Empire: Black Americans and Anticolonialism, 1937-1957.* Ithaca, NY: Cornell University Press, 1997.

Von Eschen, Penny. *Satchmo Blows Up the World: Jazz Ambassadors Play the Cold War*. Cambridge, MA: Harvard University Press, 2004.

Wagnleitner, Reinhold. *Coca-Colonization and the Cold War: The Cultural Mission of the United States in Austria after the Second World War*. Chapel Hill: University of North Carolina Press, 1994.

Walker, Juliet E. K. *The History of Black Business in America: Capitalism, Race, Entrepreneurship*. New York: Macmillan Library Reference USA, 1998.

Walser, Robert, ed. *Keeping Time: Readings in Jazz History*. New York: Oxford University Press, 1999.

Warner, Michael. "Publics and Counterpublics." *Public Culture* 14, no. 1 (2002): 49–90.

Washington, Salim. "'All the Things You Could Be by Now': *Charles Mingus Presents Charles Mingus* and the Limits of Avant-Garde Jazz." In *Uptown Conversation: The New Jazz Studies*, edited by Robert G. O'Meally, Brent Hayes Edwards, and Farah Jasmine Griffin, 27–49. New York: Columbia University Press, 2004.

Weheliye, Alexander G. "'I Am I Be': The Subject of Sonic Afro-Modernity." *boundary 2* 30, no. 2 (2003): 97–114.

Weheliye, Alexander G. *Phonographies: Grooves in Sonic Afro-Modernity*. Durham, NC: Duke University Press, 2005.

Wheeler, Geoffrey. *Jazz by Mail: Record Clubs and Record Labels, 1936 to 1958*. Manassas, VA: Hillbrook, 1999.

Willems, Jos. *All of Me: The Complete Discography of Louis Armstrong*. Lanham, MD: Scarecrow, 2006.

Williams, Martin. *The Art of Jazz: Essays on the Nature and Development of Jazz*. New York: Oxford University Press, 1959.

Woideck, Carl. *Charlie Parker: His Music and Life*. Ann Arbor: University of Michigan Press, 1996.

Zak, Albin. *I Don't Sound Like Nobody: Remaking Music in 1950s America*. Ann Arbor: University of Michigan Press, 2010.

Index

Page numbers followed by *f* refer to figures.

16-rpm (16⅔) records, 2, 10, 110–12, 117, 317n85, 317n87
33⅓-rpm LPS, 12, 66, 117, 317n85; sales of, 51*f*
45-rpm records, 12, 42, 48–53, 66, 117, 192, 197, 348n1, 355n93; Black musicians and, 56; Debut Records and, 367n68; Decca Records and, 302n87; Dee Gee Records and, 319n103; "The Huckle-Buck" and, 57, 299n60; jazz industry and, 196; Jazz Records and, 263; Prestige Records and, 16, 112, 315n59; Savoy Records and, 54–55, 299n60, 299n63
78-rpm records, 12, 25, 49, 58–60, 91, 97, 117, 133, 282n12, 289n84, 367n68; bebop and, 319n105, 351n30; classical, 167; color line and, 71; Ellington and, 11, 137; era of, 10–11, 76, 92, 282n9, 283n18, 305n105; low fidelity of, 276; time restrictions of, 11, 23, 76–77, 90, 244

Adams, Pepper, 200; *10 to 4 at the 5 Spot*, 351n39, 359n124
Adderley, Julian "Cannonball," 31, 133, 193–97, 201–2, 204–6, 224–27, 273, 275, 349n21, 357n109, 358n121, 359n127, 360n5; *The Cannonball Adderley Quintet at the Lighthouse*, 193; Davis and, 278, 352n43; "Hi-Fly," 195, 201, 209, 213; Jazz Workshop and, 200, 204, 213, 225, 348n8, 352n45, 359n129; Mingus on, 360n6; on nightclubs, 218–19, 221, 233–34, 356n103, 3537n107; publishing firm of, 361n20; "Spontaneous Combustion," 209, 220. See also *The Cannonball Adderley Quintet in San Francisco*
Adderley, Nat, 209, 212–13, 219, 227
advertising, 44; copy, 197, 227, 264; Debut Records and, 365n51; Decca Records and, 59; jingles, 331n108; meta-advertising, 222; Prestige Records and, 96
aesthetic agency, 84–85, 107, 150
Afro-modernism, 8–9, 27, 282n7, 347n162
Agee, Christopher, 204, 353n53
agency, 26, 83, 201, 238, 264; aesthetic, 84–85, 107, 150; artistic, 138; Black, 7–8, 17, 29; corporate, 294n10; creative, 5, 7; cultural, 9; political, 237

Ake, David, 37, 293n6, 316n82, 323n25, 331n107, 349n19

Aladdin Records, 37, 68, 307n134

Allison, Mose, 118; *Local Color*, 98, 107*f*

"All the Things You Are," 4, 10, 17, 239–40, 246

alternate takes, 2, 46, 84, 113, 318n96; 12-inch LP and, 118; Davis and, 16, 110–12, 281n1, 317n85, 317n88; Mingus and, 367n66; on *Milt Jackson Quartet*, 318n97; Parker and, 317n90

Ambassador Satch (Armstrong), 131, 146, 164–65, 198, 233, 336n50, 345n140; Avakian and, 21, 165–66; sales rankings, 287n65

Ammons, Gene, 83, 118, 320n121

Ampex tape recorders, 3, 18, 22, 208, 244, 288n69, 340n86, 353n69, 372n121

Armstrong, Louis, 55, 64, 131, 141, 270, 296n34, 324n28, 334n28, 336n48, 336n50, 357–58n115; Armstrong, Lil, and, 291n95; Avakian and, 63, 127–28, 169, 322n16, 323n19, 336n47; on bebop, 293n8; Cole and, 294n12; Decca Records and, 37, 61, 300n37, 302n86, 302n89; FBI surveillance of, 156; Fitzgerald and, 338n69; Gillespie and, 173–74; "The Huckle-Buck" and, 37–39, 56–57, 62, 71; *Jazz Classics*, 300n73; *Louis Armstrong Plays the Blues*, 291n94; *Louis Armstrong Plays W. C. Handy*, 146, 330n96; *The Louis Armstrong Story*, 26; retrospectives, 58; Riverside Records and, 351n37; *Satchmo at Pasadena*, 38, 57, 59, 61, 72, 301n77. See also *Ambassador Satch*

Atlantic Records, 67–68, 118, 197, 200, 225, 238, 300n68, 307n127, 307n135; Coltrane and, 316n78, 374n4; EPs and, 314n50; Mingus and, 256–57, 364n39, 369n89, 369n96. See also Bienstock, Miriam; Ertegun, Nesuhi

At the Hickory House (Hipp), 199, 211, 222

audiences, 62, 69, 123, 161, 164, 171, 175–76, 341n96; Adderley and, 206, 219, 221, 234; Black, 16, 46, 59, 196–97, 219, 285n39, 306n114, 349n21, 350n24; desegregated (integrated), 14, 187, 338n62, 339n72; Gillespie and, 273; international, 154, 159, 185–86, 198, 356n101; jazz, 23, 218, 356n101; jazz-club, 217, 218, 222, 234; liner notes and, 69; live, 21, 134; middle-class, 168, 178, 189; Mingus and, 237; mixed-race, 204, 353n56; reissues and, 62; US, 127, 186, 188; white, 39, 63, 66–67, 69–70, 178, 189, 237

audio production, 7, 15, 30–31, 125–26, 199, 222; *Ellington at Newport* and, 138, 143–45, 149–50; Mingus and, 146–49, 363n30, 364n39; *Quintet in San Francisco* (Adderley) and, 194

aurality, 195; Black political, 27; political, 109, 273; race and, 277; social, 136, 225

Auslander, Philip, 146, 325n41, 326n49, 331n100, 331n106

authenticity, 9, 22, 80, 146, 237, 362n23; emotional, 114, 196; historical, 27; jazz, 166; masculine, 16, 150; musical, 107

authority: artistic, 6, 80, 237, 239; Black, 150, 223; creative, 2; Gillespie's, 175, 341n94; improvisational, 196; intellectual, 24, 26, 80, 87, 114, 226, 237; jazz, 237–38; jazzman persona and, 362n23; male, 69, 159; masculine, 16, 77, 80, 83, 88, 119, 128, 140, 149, 277; musicians', 95, 108, 217, 316n82

Autobiography in Jazz (Mingus), 242–43, 249, 323n20, 365nn50–51,

368n79; "Drum Conversation (Part 2)," 243, 245, 366n60; "Eclipse," 243, 257; "Extrasensory Perception," 243-45, 248, 263, 366n55; "I've Got You under My Skin," 243, 245, 363n34; "Kai's Day," 243, 251; "Portrait," 243, 247-48

Avakian, George, 12, 51, 63-67, 69, 129, 168-69, 289n84, 305n105, 328n74, 350n25; on 12-inch LPs, 304n100, 324n33; *Ambassador Satch* (Armstrong) and, 165, 336n47, 336n50; Armstrong and, 322n16, 330n96; audile realism and, 329n78; Brubeck and, 132; Columbia Records and, 62-63, 65, 127-28, 133, 284n33, 304n99, 304-5nn101-3, 305n112, 307n130, 322n11; Davis and, 63, 133, 141, 146, 169; Ellington and, 137-38, 322n16, 326n55; "jazz story" series, 26, 55-56, 323n19; liner notes to *I Like Jazz!*, 323n22, 3234n30; live records produced by, 130-31, 146, 158; Macero and, 256; *Miles Ahead* (Davis) and, 141, 146, 328n70; on publishers, 296n35; on racial division in record industry, 296n33; reviews of early jazz recordings, 322n12; tape-editing of, 3, 6, 16-17, 21, 328n72, 330nn94-97, 336n50, 348n11; whiteness of, 322n15. *See also* Clayton, Buck: *The Huckle-Buck and Robbins' Nest: A Buck Clayton Jam Session*; *Ellington at Newport*; Goodman, Benny: *The Famous 1938 Carnegie Hall Jazz Concert*

avant-garde (of jazz), 362n22; Black, 357n107; entrepreneurialism, 238, 240, 242, 252, 263, 265-67, 274, 277; perpetual, 236-38

Baker, Chet, 63-64
Balliett, Whitney, 167, 251-52

Baraka, Amiri, 115-16, 225
Barclay, Nicole, 238, 362n29
Barclay Records, 238, 342n109
Basie, Count, 38, 114, 171, 176, 271-72, 293n4, 334n28; *At Newport*, 343n111; *At the Piano*, 58, 302n85
beat culture, 204, 352-53nn52-53
bebop, 24, 113-14, 161, 163, 173, 195, 226, 242-44, 248, 275, 293n8, 319n101, 374n4; Black masculinity and, 311n22, 318n100; Dial Records and, 56, 300n72, 310n12, 319n105; generation, 274; Jazz at the Philharmonic (JATP) and, 60; Prestige Records and, 83; rise of, 293n6, 310n11; Savoy Records and, 54-56, 299n64, 300n72, 319n105. *See also* Gillespie, Dizzy; Parker, Charlie; Stitt, Sonny
Bechet, Sidney, 55-56, 287n63; *Jazz Classics Volume 1*, 300n73
Beiderbecke, Bix, 26, 56, 323n19
Belair, Felix, Jr., 164-65, 346n148
Bennett, Tony, 203, 205
Berigan, Bunny, 58, 282n11, 303n94
Bienstock, Miriam, 238, 362n29
Billboard, 13, 48, 51, 67-68, 70, 294n15, 299n64, 303n91, 307n134, 314n51; Argo and, 308n136; *The Cannonball Adderley Quintet in San Francisco* and, 348n4; charts, 40, 58, 296n28, 312n35, 355n93; Columbia Records and, 129, 323n21; Decca Records and, 59-60, 302n86; Dee Gee Records and, 319n103; Hot 100, 93; "The Huckle-Buck" and, 40-41, 43-46, 296n28. *See also* Rolontz, Bob
Birdland, 160, 198, 208, 214-15, 221-22, 224, 274, 310n16; Marquette and, 357n112
Bishop, Walter, 76, 86, 90, 113
Black artistry, 29, 35, 62, 94, 109, 225, 231

Black cultural producers, 2, 8, 29, 133, 227, 277, 326n57

Black entrepreneurs, 115, 238, 319n104, 362n26. *See also* avant-garde: entrepreneurialism; Debut Records; Gillespie, Dizzy: Dee Gee Records; Mingus, Charles

Black expertise, 7, 62, 90, 94, 121, 153; alternative forms of, 150; circulation of, 274; documentation and, 84; racism and, 83; Weinstock and, 78

Black Hawk, 198, 202-3, 205, 359n129

Black music, 13, 37, 40, 46-47, 62; colonization of, 356n98; Decca Records and, 57, 59; history of, 275; musical diplomacy and, 277; in North Beach, 203; rhythm and, 349n12; Savoy Records and, 54-55, 57; Specialty and, 55; white men and, 128

Blackness, 7, 35, 83, 91, 94; Adderley and, 206, 227; countercultural intellectualism and, 115; hard bop and, 196-97; Newport Festival and, 149;

Black performance, 29-30, 82, 155, 194, 311n24

Black popular music, 14, 24, 29, 40, 47, 54, 59, 66, 70, 224, 226, 306n114; audience preferences for, 10; history of, 128; jazz's historical connection to, 64-65; media discourses about, 334n25; soul jazz and, 225; swing and, 296n25. *See also* rhythm and blues (R&B)

Black sociality, 31, 194, 202, 204, 350n22; hard bop's, 197

Black Swan Records, 41, 115, 296n27, 319n111

Black working class, 195, 225

Blake, Andrew, 12, 147

Blakey, Art, 86, 90, 99, 197, 242, 250-51, 270, 358n121; audiences and, 218-19; Blue Note Records and, 355n88; "Bluing" (Davis) and, 75-76, 113; "East of the Sun" (Sims) and, 85; Jazz Messengers, 289n75; *A Night at Birdland*, 199, 208, 211, 214-15, 222-24

Blesh, Rudi, 60, 303n94. *See also* Circle Records

Bley, Paul, 205, 242-43

Blue Note Records, 25, 54-56, 67, 88, 98-101, 118, 197, 276, 290n86, 300n73, 315n62, 337n55, 351n32, 355n88; Café Bohemia and, 107, 200; EPs and, 314n50; Feather and, 215; hard bop and, 99, 196; *The Incredible Jimmy Smith at Club Baby Grand* and, 224; live records, 199-200, 207-8, 210, 222, 249; the modern and, 310n12; Modern Jazz BLP 5000 series, 199, 301n74, 355n86; *A Night at Birdland with the Art Blakey Quintet* and, 211, 214, 221-22, 351n33; pricing, 316n72; racial politics and, 311n22; record sleeves, 315n65; sales, 350n24; *Schwann Long Playing Record Catalog* and, 301n74, 307n131, 312n36; Van Gelder and, 318n97; visual language of, 316n73. *See also* Lion, Alfred; Wolff, Francis

blues, 13, 38, 54, 65, 75, 106, 111, 170-71, 272, 306n114; African American context of, 320n117; bebop, 36; chord changes, 76, 90, 116; Handy, John and, 253; hard bop and, 99; improvisation, 150; Mingus and, 239, 252, 254; *Mingus Ah Um* and, 230; Moody and, 83; practices, 178; Rollins and, 113; traditions, 175; urban, 349n21, 358n121; Weinstock and, 311n21; women, 24, 289n79. *See also* rhythm and blues (R&B)

Bolter, Jay David, 25, 289n77, 291n96

Brackett, David, 47, 293n6, 296n25, 297nn36-37
Broadway: music, 48, 57; orchestras, 82, 310n17; shows, 14-15
Brown, Clifford, 99, 214, 224, 289n75, 358n122
Brubeck, Dave, 63-64, 141, 169, 356n102, 358n117, 374n4; *Dave Brubeck at Storyville*, 131, 218, 223, 356n101, 258n117; *The Dave Brubeck Quartet: Newport 1958*, 198; *Jazz Goes to College*, 70, 131-32, 223; *Jazz Impressions*, 146; *Time Out*, 271, 374n5
Brunswick Records, 11, 284n28, 300n73
Burns, Dave, 94-95

Café Bohemia, 107, 198, 200, 210, 216, 239-40, 247
Calloway, Cab, 174, 293n4. See also "The Huckle-Buck"
The Cannonball Adderley Quintet in San Francisco, 31, 191-95, 201, 204, 206, 211-13, 219-22, 224-27, 233, 359n131; high fidelity and, 354n71; recording of, 208; sales, 348n1, 348n4
capital, 44, 63, 71, 125, 236, 240, 277; Black, 7, 83, 153, 274; circulation and, 374n7; cultural, 9, 132, 242, 349n12; investment, 67; musician-centric, 248; musician-owned, 244; patron attention and, 201; race and, 70; white supremacy and, 238
capitalism, 8; aesthetic, 24; Jim Crow, 115; logics of, 12; print, 187, 189, 213; US, 184; white aesthetic, 128
Capitol Records, 37, 48-49, 67, 92; Adderley and, 226; *Birth of Cool* (Davis), 320n116; "Classics in Jazz" series, 300n73; "The Huckle-Buck" and, 43-44, 46; Kingston Trio and, 359n129
Carter, Benny, 36, 339n72

Cash Box, 48, 67, 69-70, 72, 128, 293n2; charts, 312n35
CBS (Columbia Broadcasting System), 20, 66, 283-84n28, 287n57, 352n42; research lab, 14-15. See also Columbia Records
Chambers, Henderson, 3, 305n111
Charles, Ray, 204-5; *The Genius of Ray Charles*, 272
Charles, Teddy, 94; *Teddy Charles Quartet: New Directions*, 97
Chess Records, 68, 197, 200, 350n25; Argo, 68, 207, 216, 308n136, 340n85, 351n40
Chicago jazz, 55, 127
Circle Records, 88, 303n94, 312n36, 330n93
circulation, 20, 29, 64, 95, 113, 237, 374nn7-8; of Black expressive cultures, 197; of Black music, 47; Davis's records and, 117; of hard bop, 196; history, 2, 39, 40, 57, 112, 301n79, 317n85, 322n13; of jazz, 14-15, 24, 30, 70, 110, 126, 201, 272-74, 276, 278, 285n34; liveness and, 136; of LPS, 13, 24, 110, 112, 274; pathways, 294n16; of performance on record, 188, 217, 225; of records, 27, 32, 275-76, 288n72, 296n33, 311n25
civil rights, 8-9, 156-57, 233, 311n19; debates about, 188, 275
class, 14-15, 40, 186, 295n16, 324n29, 362n23; record-buying consumers, 285n36; respectability, 178
classical music, 24, 69, 252, 268, 305n105; 12-inch 78-rpm records and, 127, 130, 133, 137, 167; aesthetics, 248; bebop and, 306n114; Columbia Records and, 14, 22, 133, 140, 284n33, 322n11; Decca Records and, 58, 302n89; Liston and, 152, 161; LPS, 14-15, 35, 48, 56, 63, 71, 100, 133, 284n29, 299n59, 365n52; market, 57, 284n28; RCA Victor and,

classical music (continued)
14, 298n52; Regent Records and, 37, 54, 299n65, 314n48; scores, 257; singles, 49; Tanglewood and, 132; Vanguard and, 68. *See also* Davis, Miles: *Miles Ahead*

Clayton, Buck, 63, 72, 270; *How Hi the Fi*, 69, 308n140, 330n92; *The Huckle-Buck and Robbins' Nest: A Buck Clayton Jam Session*, 5–6, 10, 15–17, 29, 38, 63, 65, 128, 146, 281n2, 329–30n92; jam sessions, 3, 5, 21, 64, 66, 145, 294n14, 303n94, 305n111, 331n98; *Jumpin' at the Woodside*, 330n92, 330n94; "Robbins' Nest," 3, 6, 16–17, 146. *See also* "The Huckle-Buck"

Clef Records, 92, 170, 303n94, 304n96, 337n56, 338n67, 367n73

Cohen, Harvey, 137, 141, 322n16, 326n55, 327n62

Cold War, 8–9, 30; Britain and, 179; civil rights and, 156; Gillespie and, 187; jazz and, 132, 157–58, 170, 181, 311n19, 345n140; US race relations and, 155

Cole, Nat King, 37, 203, 205, 296n34

Coltrane, John, 104, 118, 143, 316n78; *Coltrane*, 98, 108*f*; *Giant Steps*, 251; *"Live" at the Village Vanguard*, 350n28

Columbia Records, 13–15, 22, 58, 147, 151, 284–85n28, 356n99; *Ambassador Satch* (Armstrong) and, 164, 166; Armstrong and, 324n28; Brubeck and, 70, 131–32, 218, 223, 356n101, 357n115; classical music and, 57; Davis and, 104–5, 108, 133, 146; East 30th Street studio, 3, 38, 72, 230, 288n69; echo chamber technique and, 329n83; Ellington and, 137, 140, 322n16; EPs and, 92; high fidelity and, 337n59; Hollywood studio, 46, 336n50; "House Party" series, 66, 67; *I Can Hear it Now* and, 288n68; *I Like Jazz!* and, 128, 129*f*, 365n51; jazz and, 62–63, 65, 67–68, 307n130, 323n22; jazz clubs and, 200; long-playing records (LPs) and, 5, 25–26, 47–49, 52, 55, 77, 97, 127, 130, 135, 284n33, 291n93, 306n117, 306n120, 306n122, 312n31, 321n11, 323n19; Macero and, 370nn102–3, 371n107, 371n111; Mingus and, 257, 265, 267, 370n103, 371n107; Newport Festival and, 158, 198, 351n31, 357n115; reissues and, 56; singles and, 48, 299n66; "Strange Fruit" (Holiday) and, 283n24; Voice of America (VOA) and, 321n6, 331n104; whiteness and, 328n70. *See also* Avakian, George; CBS; Clayton, Buck: *The Huckle-Buck and Robbins' Nest: A Buck Clayton Jam Session*; Cook, Hal; *Ellington at Newport*; Garner, Erroll; *Mingus Ah Um*; Savory, Bill; Southard, Paul; Townsend, Irving; Wallerstein, Edward

Commodore Records, 11, 55, 59, 88, 282n11, 301n83, 312n34, 312n36

communism, 156, 174–75, 184

concept albums, 10, 175, 282n9, 338n67

concert halls, 8, 69, 114, 175, 294n15; European, 77, 131, 141, 198; Jazz at the Philharmonic (JATP) tours and, 169; recording in, 21, 131, 134, 149, 198, 200, 233, 359n124

Condon, Eddie, 55, 58, 63; *George Gershwin Jazz Concert*, 302n84; *Jam Session Coast-to-Coast*, 304n101; *Jazz Concert at Eddie Condon's*, 302n84; *Louis Armstrong and Eddie Condon at Newport*, 131

consumption, 20, 28, 347n169; mass, 17, 32, 141, 225; music, 213; of recorded sound, 11

Contemporary Records, 92, 118, 359n129

Cook, Hal, 67, 306n117

cool, 115-17, 320nn114-16; Black masculine, 178
cool jazz, 115-16, 275; race and, 320n113
country/country and western (c&w), 36-37, 41, 43, 55, 295n24, 302n89
Crosby, Bing, 57-58, 92, 141, 332n1; *Collectors' Classics: Bing Crosby*, 300n73
cultural diplomacy, 154, 170, 179
cultural politics, 28, 83, 184; of hardbop, 195; of jazz, 14, 30-31, 78, 126, 231, 275; race and, 64; record covers and, 310n16; of record making, 6, 239
Cuscuna, Michael, 207, 292n103, 331n98, 337n55, 350n24

Dale, George, 22, 140-41
Davis, Miles, 54, 84, 94, 102, 114-16, 119, 233, 270, 275, 313n44, 316n76, 318n92, 320n113, 320n120; Adderley and, 193, 352n43; "Ah-Leu-Cha," 330n95; Avakian and, 63, 133, 141, 146, 169; *Birth of the Cool*, 320n116; Black Hawk and, 203, 205; "Bluing," 75-78, 85-87, 90-92, 103, 113, 116-17, 313n46; *Collectors' Items*, 111; Columbia Records and, 104-5, 108, 133, 146; *Cookin' with the Miles Davis Quintet*, 98, 105-6, 109, 316n78; cool aesthetic of, 116, 320n115; *Davis Digs Disney*, 141; *Kind of Blue*, 271, 274, 276, 278, 375n13; LPs and, 84; "The Man I Love," 2, 5-6, 10, 16, 109-10, 112, 117; *Miles Ahead*, 141, 146, 328n70; *Miles Davis*, 337n55; *Miles Davis All Stars*, 110, 281n1, 317n88; *Miles Davis: Blue Period*, 76, 90, 110, 116, 312n30; *Miles Davis and the Modern Jazz Giants*, 110, 281n1, 316-17nn84-85; *Miles Davis: The New Sounds*, 81, 89, 116, 312n30; *Miles Davis Quartet*, 92, 97, 101f; *Modern Jazz Trumpets*, 80; Monk and, 317n84; "Out of the Blue," 309n2; police beating of, 274, 310n16, 374n11; *Porgy and Bess*, 257, 370n106; Prestige Records and, 16, 83, 86, 91, 96, 108, 118, 221, 310n12, 314n52; *Relaxin' with the Miles Davis Quintet*, 103-5, 108-9, 117-18, 316n78; *'Round about Midnight*, 146; *Steamin' with the Miles Davis Quintet*, 105, 316n78; *Workin' with the Miles Davis Quintet*, 105-6, 316n78

Day, Doris, 203, 205
Debut Records, 5-6, 67, 92, 223, 237-40, 242, 247, 256-57, 265, 307n131, 362n24, 362n28, 365n49, 372n128; Café Bohemia and, 107, 200, 210; catalog, 249, 256, 367n68; circulation and, 273; collapse of, 252, 264, 362n21, 366n56, 368n82; *Explorations* (Macero) and, 364n37; "Extrasensory Perception" (Mingus) and, 244-46, 263; founding of, 233, 236, 361n19; Massey Hall concerts and, 245-47, 281n3, 363n33, 366n60, 367n69; "Portrait" (Mingus) and, 248, 368n75; Putnam Central and, 249-51, 368n79; Tristano and, 263-64; Van Gelder and, 365n48. See also *Autobiography in Jazz* (Mingus); Bley, Paul; Gillespie, Dizzy; *The Quintet: Jazz at Massey Hall*; *Mingus Ah Um*; Mingus, Charles; Mingus, Celia
Decca Records, 48, 55, 57-61, 68, 92, 294n14, 302-3nn84-90, 303n292, 308n137; Armstrong and, 300n71, 301n77, 357n115; Avakian and, 127, 305n103; Coral Records, 300n69, 308n136; Fitzgerald and, 338n66; "The Huckle-Buck" and, 37-38, 42-44; *Schwann Long Playing Records Catalog* and, 301nn80-81. See also Brunswick Records; Gabler, Milt
Delaunay, Charles, 127, 322n13

Delmore Brothers, 295n24; "The Huckle-Buck" and, 41–42
Dennis, Willie, 223, 249–50
desegregation: of audiences, 187, 338n62, 339n72; of musician unions, 235–36
Dial Records, 54–56, 88, 300n72, 310n12, 312n34, 312n36; bebop and, 56, 319n105; *Bird Blows the Blues* (Parker), 317n90
Dixieland, 68, 171, 175, 202, 290n86; revival, 55
Dizzy Gillespie: World Statesman, 30, 153, 161–62, 164f, 165–70, 177, 183, 187, 189, 342n108, 343n117; European versions of, 342n109; liner notes to, 182, 184, 341n100
Dizzy in Greece, 30, 153, 161–63, 165f, 167–68, 176–79, 187–89, 333n9; liner notes to, 170, 182–84; UK version of, 342n109
Doane, Mary Ann, 21, 287n59
documentation, 81, 84, 89, 113; historical, 6, 26, 95; record jackets and, 93; technologies of, 271
Donaldson, Lou, 99, 214
Dorham, Kenny, 54, 80, 200, 223, 242; *'Round about Midnight at the Cafe Bohemia*, 199, 210
Dorr-Dorynek, Diane, 264–65, 373n133
Dorsey, Tommy, 11, 37, 41–42, 44, 113–14, 130, 303n94, 347n163; *A Symposium of Swing* and, 282n11. See also "Honeysuckle Rose"
Down Beat, 21, 37, 135, 202, 204, 283n18, 307n133, 352n48; Black musicians and, 64, 70; extended play (EP) records and, 50; Gillespie and, 153–54, 160, 339n80; Jazz Workshop and, 353n55; polls in, 82, 193, 348n3, 351n41. See also Avakian, George; Gleason, Ralph; Hentoff, Nat; Morgenstern, Dan; Stearns, Marshall Winslow
Du Bois, W. E. B., 156, 159

Edwards, Esmond, 98, 103f, 107f–108f
Eisenhower, Dwight, 19, 157; Gillespie and, 160, 182, 185, 335n36; Mingus and, 236
Eldridge, Roy, 83, 167, 170–71, 198, 270; JATP European Tours and, 339n72
Ellender, Allan, 179–81, 186, 344n125
Ellington, Duke, 36, 114–15, 150, 171, 233, 238, 273, 275, 282n14, 326n54, 327n58, 328n63, 334n28, 347n163; *At the Bal Masque*, 21, 147, 331n103; Avakian and, 63, 127–28, 137, 139–41, 169, 322n16, 326n55; "Diminuendo and Crescendo in Blue," 11, 123, 137, 142–44; *Ellington Uptown*, 137, 141; *Festival Suite*, 123, 139–41; *Masterpieces by Ellington*, 22, 137, 140, 145, 288n69, 328n69; Mingus and, 252, 361n20; mistakes and, 142; *Newport 1958*, 21, 147, 331n98, 331n103; "Reminiscing in Tempo," 11, 137, 282n11; sonic Afro-modernity of, 326n57; "Tiger Rag," 11
Ellington at Newport, 30, 122–26, 136, 166, 287n65, 321n2, 321n7; audience for, 141, 148; Avakian and, 21, 123–26, 128, 131, 133, 138–45, 147–50, 198, 328nn64–65, 348n11; onstage chatter and, 357n115; reissue of, 124, 138, 321n5, 324n33, 326n56, 327n58, 327n61, 328n65, 358n118
engineers (audio/sound), 13, 134, 136, 144, 207, 209, 242, 265–66; mixing, 143. See also Fowler, Ray; Hamel, Reice; Knuerr, George; Tristano, Lennie; Van Gelder, Rudy
equality: gender, 153; racial, 30, 155, 158; social, 8, 157
Ertegun, Nesuhi, 68, 350n25
Ervin, Booker, 231, 256, 258, 371n116
Esquire, 70, 160, 185–86, 271, 347n161
Evans, Bill, 192, 200, 350n28, 358n119; *New Jazz Conceptions*, 348n2

Evans, Gil, 146, 257, 320n116, 370n106
executives, 2, 8, 10, 14, 266, 294n9; artist-and-repertoire (A&R), 15, 52, 54, 126, 319n104, 350n25; Decca Records, 58; record, 62, 66, 68, 70, 108, 149, 213, 214, 217, 248; women, 372n126
experimentation, 10, 29, 31, 61, 87, 155, 243, 331n108; commercial, 2; Debut Records and, 242–43; Ellington and, 141; jazz club and, 209, 225; Mingus and, 5, 249, 252; Prestige Records and, 80–81, 86, 97, 113, 118; tape recording and, 149
extended-play (EP) discs, 12, 49–51, 65, 78, 91–92, 94, 314n50; jazz, 93, 298n57, 314n51

Feather, Leonard, 167, 211, 214–15, 222, 306n114; jazz history and, 26, 84; Mingus and, 266; on Van Gelder, 210
Feld, Steven, 136, 342n105
fidelity, 2, 27, 96, 106, 110, 117, 124, 167, 217, 272, 276, 325n46, 329n88; high, 145, 168, 208, 214, 276, 329n87, 337n59, 354n71, 355n84; historical, 329n78, 339n79; improved, 5, 325n44; to live performance, 23, 135, 249
film, 20; integrated bands on, 82; jazz and, 310n17; production companies, 238; Schifrin and, 340n84; stereophony and, 292n102
Fitzgerald, Ella, 37, 58–59, 198, 296n25, 296n34, 302n89, 338–39n69; Granz and, 166, 168–69, 338n66, 339n72, 357n115
Five Spot, 198, 200, 351n39
Flory, Andrew, 46, 294n10, 295n19, 295n25, 296n34
folk music, 57, 182, 184, 204, 311n21
format theory, 10–13, 355n83
Fowler, Ray, 209–10

Gabler, Milt, 58–61, 297n35, 301–2n83, 303nn93–95, 304n97, 316n71. *See also* Commodore Records; Decca Records
Garland, Red, 103–4, 108, 204–5; *All Kinds of Weather*, 98, 103*f*; *Red Garland at the Prelude*, 351n40
Garner, Erroll, 63, 92, 299n63, 305n102, 335n42; *Concert by the Sea*, 131, 198, 357n115; *Erroll Garner at the Piano*, 54, 299n62, 304n100
gender, 6, 7–8, 15, 24–25, 27, 32, 324n29, 357n112; assumptions about, 40, 107; discrimination, 332n4; equality, 153; ideologies, 26, 64, 114; inclusivity, 159, 204; jazz and, 80; jazz industry and, 78; jazzman persona and, 238, 362n23; record buying and, 285n36. *See also* masculinity; men; women
genre, 37, 46, 239; categories, 296n25; Decca Records and, 59, 303n90; disc size and, 12, 56, 306n127; jazz as, 70, 158, 282n15, 309n5; live records as, 131, 133–34, 149, 200, 214
Getz, Stan, 54, 81, 83, 96, 299n64; Gillespie and, 170; JATP European tours and, 339n72; *Stan Getz Quartets*, 315n64; *Stan Getz, vol. 2*, 86, 312n29
Gibson, Andy, 36, 293n4, 295n22
Gillespie, Dizzy, 54, 82, 114–15, 152, 160, 165, 166, 169–70, 176–77, 233, 238, 270, 275, 334n25, 339n71, 341n94, 351n30; Adderley and, 194; African retention and, 342n105; Afro-Cuban music and, 339n78; Afro-modernism and, 347n162; bebop and, 114, 172, 195; big band and, 161, 334n30, 339nn79–80, 340n89; *Birks' Works*, 335n41; Black Hawk and, 205; commercial music and, 338n64; Davis and, 116; Dee Gee Records, 115–16, 319nn103–4, 319n112, 340n85, 341n91; *Dizzy*

INDEX 421

Gillespie (continued)
Gillespie at Newport, 176, 342n109, 358n115; "Groovin' High," 289n75, 335n40; humor of, 173, 175–76, 342n106; *Modern Jazz Trumpets*, 80; "A Night in Tunisia," 223; *The Quintet: Jazz at Massey Hall* and, 4, 239, 245, 246, 358n115, 367n65; *Trumpet Battle*, 167, 168*f*, 337n56; US State Department Cultural Presentations program and, 30, 153–55, 157–59, 161, 163–64, 170–75, 179–89, 273, 332nn3–4, 334nn27–28, 334n31, 335n36, 336n46, 339n76, 340n83, 343n116, 344n126, 346nn150–51, 347n157. See also *Dizzy Gillespie: World Statesman*; *Dizzy in Greece*; Granz, Norman; Stearns, Marshall Winslow

Gitler, Ira, 76–77, 84, 95–97, 98*f*-100*f*, 107, 111, 316–17n84; liner notes to *Blue Period* (Davis), 90, 116, 309n2; liner notes to *Charles Mingus: The Complete Debut Recordings*, 367n65; liner notes to *Collectors' Items* (Davis), 317n92; liner notes to *Cookin' with the Miles Davis Quintet*, 106; liner notes to *Miles Davis: New Sounds*, 89–90, 116–17; liner notes to *Relaxin' with the Miles Davis Quintet*, 105; liner notes to *Swingin' with Zoot Sims*, 88–89, 313n39, 313n43

Glaser, Joe, 140, 336n47

Gleason, Ralph Jr., 69, 119, 193, 202, 204–5, 352n47; Mingus and, 236, 361n14; *Quintet in San Francisco* (Adderley) and, 211, 213, 219, 227

Glover, Henry, 238, 295n24

Golson, Benny, 204–5, 270, 289n75, 361n20

Gonsalves, Paul, 123–24, 126, 139, 143–44, 147–49

Goodman, Benny, 37, 69, 113, 140, 171, 198, 243, 282n14, 305n107, 328n68, 365n53; Avakian and, 169; *The Famous 1938 Carnegie Hall Jazz Concert*, 61, 130–31, 145, 291nn92–93, 323nn24–25; Granz and, 347n163; "The Huckle-Buck," 42, 44, 308n145; "Sing, Sing, Sing," 11, 130, 282n11

Gordon, Dexter, 54, 207, 299n64; "The Chase," 11, 356n106

gospel, 13, 16, 37, 54, 56, 99, 239, 296n32; Adderley and, 349n21; hard bop and, 358n121

Granz, Norman, 11, 30, 60, 154, 161, 166, 225, 337n53, 342n109, 347n103, 347n165, 357n112; bebop and, 319n105; desegregated audiences and, 339n72; Fitzgerald and, 168–69, 338n66; Gillespie and, 172, 183, 187, 344n128; jam-session recordings and, 294n14, 303n94, 305n103; on LPS, 304n97; Mingus and, 247, 367n70; production work of, 166, 337n57. See also Clef Records; Jazz at the Philharmonic (JATP) concert series; Mercury Records; Norgran Records; Verve Records

Grauer, Bill, 68–69, 200

Gray, Wardell, 11, 83; *Jazz Concert*, 351n40, 356n106

Green, Bennie, 80, 94, 223, 249–50; *Bennie Green with Strings*, 79, 314n55

Griffin, Johnny, 204–5; *Studio Jazz Party*, 209

Grusin, Richard, 25, 289n77, 291n96

Hadi, Shafi, 255, 372n128

Half Note, 234, 254

Hamel, Reice, 208–9, 213, 354n70

Hamilton, Jimmy, 123, 137, 141

Hammond, John, 3, 16, 60, 294n14, 303n94, 330n94, 374n4

Hampton, Lionel, 58–59, 61, 65, 198, 302n86, 303n92. See also "The Huckle-Buck"

Handy, John, 253–56, 258, 369n91, 369n93, 371n116

Handy, W. C., 115, 238
Hawkins, Coleman, 198, 300n73, 339n72; *Coleman Hawkins: A Documentary*, 26-27, 291n95, 330n93
Hayes, Louis, 195, 209, 220
Hentoff, Nat, 99, 167, 221, 315n64, 346n146, 357n109; on Gillespie, 153, 176, 335n40, 341n94; Mingus and, 368n75
Hershorn, Tad, 169, 337n53, 338n66, 347n163, 347n165
Hodeir, André, 26, 84, 290n89
Hodes, Art, 55-56
Hodges, Johnny, 36, 123, 139, 142, 328n75, 359n129, 373n136
Holiday, Billie, 58-59, 82, 203, 205, 272, 302n89, 362n27; *Billy Holiday and Ella Fitzgerald at Newport*, 198, 358n115; cabaret card, 310n16; "Strange Fruit," 283n24
Homzy, Andrew, 253, 369n90
"Honeysuckle Rose," 11, 62, 130
"The Huckle-Buck," 36-44, 46-47, 54-57, 67, 71, 130, 293n2, 296n25, 299n60; Andrews and, 41-42, 44; Armstrong and, 62, 71; Calloway and, 36, 42, 44; Clayton and, 38-39, 62-65, 71, 304n98, 305n103; Cole and, 36-37, 41-42, 44, 294n12; Hampton and, 36, 42, 44, 305n111; Kirk and, 36, 42, 44; Marshall and, 41-42, 44; Millinder and, 41-42, 44, 65, 295n20, 295n22, 305n111; Milton and, 41-42, 44, 295n20; Nathan and, 295n24; The Pig Footers and, 42-44; Preston and, 42-43; Sinatra and, 39, 42, 44, 46, 66, 70-71, 296n25, 308n145; Williams and, 36, 40-42, 44, 52, 56, 295n20, 295n22
Hungry i, 225, 359n129

identity, 14-15, 93, 293n6; Black, 156; construction of, 362n23; multiplicity of, 360n6; racial, 15, 41, 322n15, 350n25

I Like Jazz!, 66, 70, 128-29, 133, 323n22, 324n30, 365n51
improvisation, 9, 76, 83, 95, 111, 118, 123, 215, 231, 243-45, 251; "Bird Calls" (Mingus) and, 253, 255; *Ellington at Newport* and, 150; Gillespie and, 161; jazz performance and, 263; mistakes and, 78, 89; records and, 32, 91
inequality: institutional, 156; racial, 8, 158
informality, 57, 62, 103, 106, 109, 119; on record, 29, 250; social, 243; studio, 2, 95
infrastructures, 5, 202; commercial, 15, 29, 114; of communication, 20; consumption and, 286n44; formats and, 313n45; informational, 69; media, 28, 36, 46, 52, 70-72; music industry, 38-39, 46, 68, 296n25; record industry, 221, 374n9; record-making, 11, 17, 28, 68, 91, 256
Ink Spots, 58, 296n25, 296n34, 302n88
intellectual property, 5, 28, 236
Iton, Richard, 157, 159, 334n25, 334n31

Jackson, Milt, 1, 94, 109, 111, 118; *Milt Jackson Quartet*, 95, 110
Jamal, Ahmad, 205, 207, 308n136; *But Not for Me: Ahmad Jamal Trio at the Pershing, vol. 1*, 216, 351n40, 355n93
jam sessions, 3, 52, 63-66, 77, 88, 151; bebop and, 114; concerts, 187, 223; Gabler and, 59-60, 303n93; Granz and, 187, 339n72; records, 60, 63, 128, 145, 294n14, 303n94, 305n103; Tristano and, 263; Varèse and, 257; "Whispering" as standard of, 340n89. *See also* Clayton, Buck: jam sessions; Gordon, Dexter: "The Chase"
Jarrett, Michael, 12, 330n94, 370n102
Jazz Artists Guild, 236, 361n15

Jazz at the Philharmonic (JATP) concert series, 60, 168-70, 187, 198, 303-4n95, 338n62, 339n72, 342n109; recordings of, 11, 60-61, 95, 282n12, 304n97, 315n60, 338n67

jazz clubs (nightclubs), 202-4, 207, 209-11, 215, 220, 250, 277, 294n15, 310n17; Adderley and, 206, 212, 221, 234, 356n103 (see also *The Cannonball Adderley Quintet in San Francisco*); ambience of, 224-25, 358n122; audiences, 218; Black audiences and, 196; Black entrepreneurs and, 238, 319n104; cabaret cards and, 310n16; Columbia Records' live albums and, 131; Davis and, 105, 107; live recordings and, 77, 134, 194, 196-201, 208, 212-13, 216-17, 222, 316n81, 318n98, 351n40, 356n101, 356n106 (*see also* Ampex tape recorders); Mingus and, 221, 233-36, 247, 357n107; musician-owned, 352n46; musicians and, 31, 114, 214, 217; owners of, 202, 217, 222, 235, 285n35, 352n43; radio broadcasts and, 149, 222, 358n120; record making in, 228; segregation and, 82. *See also* Birdland; Black Hawk; Café Bohemia; Five Spot; Jazz Workshop; Keystone Korner; Pershing Lounge; Putnam Central Club; San Francisco: jazz clubs; Storyville; Village Vanguard

Jazz Composers Workshop, 236, 257, 361n15, 371n109

jazz culture, 12, 25; masculine expectations of, 80; patriarchy of, 114; white privilege in, 236

jazz festivals, 23, 276; organizers of, 30, 126; recording at, 77, 122, 131, 134, 151, 200, 209. *See also* Monterey Jazz Festival; Newport Jazz Festival

jazz historiography, 8, 36, 71, 233, 290n90, 311n26; global politics of, 344n130

jazz history, 4, 8, 30, 68-72, 82, 111, 150, 171, 173, 175, 189, 276, 290n89; Avakian and, 6, 125-26; books, 26, 84, 311n26, 321n9; live performance and, 194; LPs and, 27, 62; materiality of, 276; Mingus and, 267; mistakes and, 142; musicians and, 95; Prestige Records and, 78-79, 92-93; recording format and, 40; record making and, 24-25, 27; Weinstock and, 29, 80; white masculinity and, 24, 69, 80, 96, 128

jazz industry, 7, 13, 94, 127, 154, 196, 211, 231; cool aesthetic and, 115; difference and, 17; documentary impulse of, 79; live recordings and, 194, 197, 200; Mingus and, 31, 234-36, 237, 361n9; power dynamics of, 274, 277; race and gender and, 15, 78, 237; soul and, 192; Tristano and, 263; white gaze of, 116; white infrastructures of, 221; whiteness in, 126, 322n17

jazzmasculinity, 80, 362n27

jazzmen, 5, 12, 64, 159; critics as, 12, 167; modern, 76, 90; race and, 31, 80, 107, 114

Jazz Panorama (record label), 55, 88, 312n36

jazz performance, 7, 38, 128, 131, 194, 217, 233, 235, 239, 248, 263, 325n46; economies of attention and, 31, 234; jazz clubs and, 215; racial politics and, 193; record making and, 39, 78, 118, 143; self-referentiality of, 171, 326n48

jazz press, 27, 138, 153, 236, 297n40, 339n77; bebop and, 310n11; race and, 292n97

Jazz Review, 201-2

Jazztone Society, 68, 307n134

Jazz Workshop, 202-3, 205, 225-26, 352n46, 353n55, 353n58; Adderley and, 191, 194, 200-201, 204, 206, 208, 213, 221, 225, 227, 248n8, 352n45, 359n129 (see also *The Cannonball Adderley Quintet in San Francisco*); Gleason on, 213, 219; hard bop and, 203-4; soul jazz and, 192

Jim Crow, 14, 90, 155, 157, 275; capitalism, 115; economics, 82; Gillespie and, 177

Johnson, James P., 56, 58, 302n84, 351n37

Johnson, J. J., 80, 83, 204-5, 223, 249-50; *Trombone by Three*, 98, 104f

Johnson, Sy, 254, 369n91, 371n107

Jolly Roger Records, 55, 88, 300n71, 312n36

Jones, Quincy, 170, 272, 347n157, 361n20

Jones, Ryan Patrick, 206, 353n64

Jones, Thad, 237, 242-43, 247-48, 266, 362n24

Jordan, Louis, 37, 40, 58, 204-5, 296n25, 296n34, 302n87, 349n19

jukeboxes, 16, 36, 40-41, 46, 76, 196-97, 273, 285n38, 298n47, 350n24; small record labels and, 374n9

Kane, Art, 271, 373n1

Keepnews, Orrin, 68-69, 191, 199-200, 206, 211, 213, 225, 348n2, 350n23, 374n9; Adderley and, 227, 234, 348n8; *The Cannonball Adderley Quintet in San Francisco* and, 208, 220-21; *Jazz à la Bohemia* (Weston) and, 209-10, 216; Keystone Korner and, 207, 354n70

Keightley, Keir, 63, 66, 301n76, 305n105

Kelley, Robin, 109, 317n85

Kelly, Wynton, 99, 176

Keystone Korner, 207, 354n70

King, Wayne, 201-2, 206, 352n42

King Records, 37, 43, 55, 300nn67-68

Klotz, Kelsey, 15, 64, 284n34, 305n109, 320n113, 352n45

Knepper, Jimmy, 234, 253, 265, 360n7, 372n128, 373n133

Knuerr, George, 143-44

Kolodin, Irving, 130-31

Konitz, Lee, 25, 83, 96, 244; *Lee Konitz Quintet, Lennie Tristano Quintet*, 97, 98f-99f, 290n85, 312n38; *Lennie Tristano Quintet Featuring Lee Konitz*, 314n57; *The New Sounds*, 81; *The Real Lee Konitz*, 351n40; Verve Records and, 365n53

Krupa, Gene, 58, 339n72; *Gene Krupa at the London House*, 351n29

labor, 4, 63, 81, 112, 125, 209, 240; artistic, 7, 194, 210, 275; Black, 7, 31, 40, 83, 119, 153, 231, 274, 277; collaborative, 136, 214; conditions, 41, 155; intellectual, 233; liveness and, 326n51; musical, 9, 31, 38, 40, 71, 84, 94, 113, 194, 234, 236

LaPorta, John, 240-42

Latin American music, 16, 55, 303n89, 349n21

Lee, Benjamin, 273, 374n7

Lewis, George, 55-56; and His New Orleans Stompers, 374n4

Lewis, George E., 285n34, 311n24

Lewis, John, 249-50, 320n116

Lincoln, Abbey, 200, 372n129; "Afro Blue," 272-73

Lion, Alfred, 98-11, 208, 211, 223, 316nn71-72, 350n23

LiPuma, Edward, 273, 374n7

listening, 6, 11, 17, 21, 27-28, 29, 77, 89, 94, 106, 148, 150, 206, 250, 273, 317n90, 360n7; experience, 12, 86, 90-91, 107, 142, 144-45, 212, 216, 245, 249; habits, 13, 23-24, 145; jazz, 24, 69, 186; liveness and, 136; mistakes and, 90-91; spaces of, 222, 326n50; splices and, 4, 31, 257, 266

Liston, Melba, 332nn4-5, 347n157, 351n41; "Annie's Dance," 161, 335n42, 340n89; "My Reverie," 152-53, 161

liveness, 126, 135-36, 148, 325n46, 326n49, 355n81; as commodity, 149, 214, 355n85; constructions of, 134, 145, 331n107; deadness and, 324n38; mediation of, 193; on record, 30, 136, 209; Village Vanguard and, 350n28

Lombardo, Guy, 57, 334n25, 338n64; "Idaho," 365n53

Lubinsky, Herman, 54, 299n61

Macero, Teo, 242, 265, 328n63, 370n102, 371n111; *Explorations*, 364n37; Jazz Composers Workshop and, 371n109; *Let My Children Hear Music* (Mingus) and, 267, 370n103; *Mingus Ah Um* and, 239-40, 256-58, 263, 267, 371n107; *The Moods of Mingus* and, 364n41

McLean, Jackie, 76, 86-87, 90, 113

Mal-1 (Waldron), 98, 105f

"The Man I Love" (Davis), 10, 110, 281n1

marketing, 4, 15, 21, 28, 68, 137, 266; Columbia Record's, 97; departments, 66; of Gillespie, 187-88; infrastructures, 39; jazz as category of, 117; liner notes and, 88; Prestige Records', 78, 81-82, 312n29; strategies, 46, 65, 70, 93, 128

Martin, Don, 98, 104f

masculinity, 238, 290n90, 362n27; Black, 2, 14, 114, 196, 202, 221, 226, 318n100; Blackness and, 320n113; jazz, 31, 101 (*see also* jazzmasculinity); postwar, 6, 281n5; white, 274, 285n39, 289n78. *See also* gender

mastering, 10, 28, 32, 133, 136, 213, 256, 370n105; remastering, 96, 247

media, 13, 17, 27, 111, 135, 189, 193, 196, 233, 268, 273, 286n44, 290n91, 318n93; broadcast, 28, 46, 68; conglomerates, 5, 20; of cultural communication, 118, 275; infrastructures, 36, 46, 52, 70-72; mass, 14, 331n108; new, 25, 36, 289n77; playback, 13-14; print, 47, 160, 182, 189, 344n131; sonic, 7, 9, 18, 32, 85, 277; transition, 109

mediation, 9, 13, 17, 20, 23, 30, 126, 144, 146, 147, 193, 258, 267, 288n72; Debut Records and, 245; of *Ellington at Newport*, 125, 136; erasure of, 211; *The Huckle-Buck and Robbins' Nest: A Buck Clayton Jam Session* and, 4, 330n94; Mingus and, 247; of musical time, 27; technological, 6, 8, 138, 143, 255; technologies of, 22, 90, 274, 286n49

mediatization, 9, 146, 331n100

Meintjes, Louise, 136, 285n43, 288n72, 326n51, 327n57, 349n20

Mellé, Gil, 98, 102f

Mellow the Mood, 25, 290n86

men, 4, 12, 26; bebop and, 6; Black, 31, 114-15, 195, 223, 234; record companies and, 213; white, 15-16, 24, 64-65, 89, 128, 197, 202, 237, 285n35, 350n23, 350n25. *See also Esquire*; gender; jazzmen; masculinity; recordmen

Mercury Records, 37, 43-44, 48, 50, 60, 197, 337n57; *Charlie Parker with Strings*, 367n73; EmArcy, 68; Jazz 11000 series, 282n12; JATP recordings, 304nn96-97. *See also* Granz, Norman

Metronome, 37, 64, 70, 82, 160, 202. *See also* Morgenstern, Dan

microphone placement, 7, 13, 145

middle class, 19, 116, 169

Middleton, Velma, 38, 56

Miles, Reid, 98, 102f, 106f

Miller, Glenn, 113, 152, 305n107

426 INDEX

Miller, Karl Hagstrom, 41, 283n27, 294n16, 352n51, 353n56
Millinder, Lucky, 41–42, 44, 65, 295n20, 295n22, 305n111
Mills Brothers, 57–58, 205, 296n25, 296n34, 302n88
Mingus, Celia, 5–6, 200, 236, 238, 264–65, 273–74, 362–63nn27–29, 363n34, 368n80. *See also* Debut Records
Mingus, Charles, 6, 16, 31, 233–43, 253, 255–56, 266–68, 274–75, 285n42, 360n5, 361n10, 363n31, 364n39, 369n96, 371n108; abuses by, 373n133; activism of, 361nn12–13; *A Great Day in Harlem* and, 270; "All the Things You Are," 10, 17; *Beneath the Underdog*, 360n6, 372–73n131; *Blues & Roots*, 254, 256, 265, 369n89, 370n100, 373n134; Chaz Mar Inc., 236, 365n52; "Four Hands," 239, 257; Gleason and, 361n14; *Jazzical Moods*, 241, 363n35, 371n112; Jazz Workshop, 249–52, 254–55; Jazz Workshop, Inc., 250, 264, 362n21, 365n52; *Let My Children Hear Music*, 267, 370n103; Macero and, 257, 371n107, 371n109, 371n111; *Mingus at the Bohemia*, 200, 239–40, 247, 354n75, 364n43, 364–65n46; *Mingus Dynasty*, 265; *Mingus at Monterey*, 368n82; *The Moods of Mingus*, 364n42; on nightclubs, 234–35, 357n107; "Perdido," 239–40, 246–47, 364n41; *Pithecanthropus Erectus*, 257; *The Quintet: Jazz at Massey Hall*, 4–5, 10, 21, 239–40, 247, 364n40, 367n66; RCA Victor and, 360n1; "Septemberly," 240, 247; "Tea for Two," 240–41, 364n41; *Tijuana Moods*, 237, 360n1, 362n24, 370n101; Tristano and, 263–64, 366n54; "What Is This Thing Called Love?," 239, 241, 257, 365n47. *See also Autobiography in Jazz*; Debut Records; Dorr-Dorynek, Diane; Jazz Artists Guild; Jazz Composers Workshop; Macero, Teo; *Mingus Ah Um*
Mingus Ah Um, 31, 230, 232–33, 240, 251, 257–59, 263, 266–67, 271, 360n3; "Bird Calls," 231–32, 252–53, 255–56, 258, 260, 369n91; "Boogie Stop Shuffle," 231–32, 253, 371n116; CD-reissue of, 360n2; "Fables of Faubus," 232, 254, 274–75; "Goodbye Pork Pie Hat," 232, 252–54, 258–59; "Jelly Roll," 230–32, 252, 254, 256, 258, 262; liner notes to, 264–66, 369n85; *Nostalgia in Times Square/The Immortal 1959 Sessions* and, 371n117; postproduction edits on, 232; "Pussycat Blues," 232, 253, 258, 261
mistakes, 2, 84, 87, 89–90, 119, 138, 141, 142, 209, 212; on "Blue 7" (Rollins), 316n77; on "Bluing" (Davis), 76–77; correcting, 139–40, 166, 195, 233; on "East of Sun" (Sims), 90; *Ellington at Newport* and, 139, 328n75; musical, 29, 78, 90–91, 103, 118, 136; *Swingin' with Zoot Sims* and, 88
mixing, 7, 10, 28, 133, 145, 331n109; *Ellington at Newport* and, 143–44; *Quintet in San Francisco* and, 209, 213
Mobley, Hank, 118, 266, 366n60
modern, 76, 80–82, 88, 90, 94, 110, 116, 320n120, 351n32
modernism, 82, 311n22; Afro-modernism, 8–9, 27, 282n7, 347n162 (*see also* sonic Afro-modernity); racial politics of, 82–83, 91, 118, 168, 337n60
modernity, 82, 274; Black, 8, 31; Western, 282n8, 349n20. *See also* sonic Afro-modernity
Modern Records, 37, 59, 303n91

Monk, Thelonious, 250, 251; Blue Note Records and, 56, 99; cabaret card and, 82, 310n16; Five Spot and, 351n39; "The Man I Love" (Davis) and, 1-2, 109-10, 316-17n84; *Misterioso*, 351n39, 358n122, 359n124; Riverside Records and, 118, 192, 200, 224, 226; *Thelonious in Action*, 224, 351n39, 359n124

Monson, Ingrid, 226, 283n25, 295n16, 310n18, 311n23, 333n17, 337n60, 375n12; on aesthetic agency, 84; on Afro-modernist ideals, 282n8; on hard bop, 349n12, 349n14; on jazz tours, 157, 185, 339n76, 346n150, 347n154, 347n157; on racial politics of *Down Beat* polls, 348n3

Monterey Jazz Festival, 352n47, 368n82

Montgomery, Wes, 200, 205, 348n2

Moody, James, 56, 112, 308n136, 318n94; "Disappointed," 94-95, 109, 118, 315n59; *Hi-Fi Party*, 94-95; Prestige Records and, 83

Moore, Bill, 54, 299n60

Moore, Pee Wee, 94-95, 176

Morgenstern, Dan, 23-24, 288n74, 303n94

Morton, Jelly Roll, 55, 252, 330n93

Morton, John Fass, 132, 321n3

Moten, Fred, 90, 313n44, 350n22, 356n105

Mulligan, Gerry, 64, 81, 86-87, 91, 96, 205, 312n30; *Birth of Cool* (Davis) and, 320n116; *The Gerry Mulligan Quartet*, 358n117

Murphy, Turk, 55, 63, 352n46; and His Jazz Band, 304n101

musical diplomacy, 154, 189, 277

music industry, 16, 20, 36-41, 44, 46, 117, 287n56, 297n37; Adderley and, 227; race and, 6, 39, 64; swing and, 152. *See also* "The Huckle-Buck"

Myers, Marc, 208, 288n73, 306n122, 307n130, 365n52

Navarro, Fats, 54, 80, 83, 299n64

NBC (National Broadcasting Company), 20, 244, 352n42

Neal, Mark Anthony, 196, 283n25, 306n114, 337n60, 349n12, 359n127

Newman, Joe, 62, 305n111

Newport Jazz Festival, 30, 104, 122-23, 131-32, 143, 149-50, 169, 172, 198, 341n100; Hughes on, 324n27; Mingus and, 236; Voice of America (VOA) and, 158; white mainstreaming of jazz and, 338n63. *See also* O'Connor, Norman; Wein, George

New Yorker, The 70, 132, 202, 251

Norgran Records, 153, 161, 166-67, 169-70, 304n96, 307n127, 338n67

Norman, Gene, 59, 61, 303nn91-92

North Beach, 191, 203-4, 353n53

Novak, David, 136, 148, 273, 324n38, 326n50, 374n8

O'Connor, Norman, 122-25, 321n8, 357n112, 360n7

on-location recording, 125-26, 207, 210, 214, 221; jazz clubs and, 200, 318n98; technological difficulties of, 209. *See also* record making: live recordings

overdubbing, 7, 28, 147, 247-48; "Atlanta Blues" (Armstrong) and, 146; Macero and, 257; Mingus and, 31, 238-41, 253, 364n39; *The Quintet: Jazz at Massey Hall* and, 4, 239

Pace, Harry, H., 41, 115, 238, 319n111. *See also* Black Swan Records

Pacific Jazz Records, 50, 67, 92, 315n62

Parker, Charlie, 4, 36, 54, 56, 79, 95, 111, 113, 195, 263; *Autobiography in Jazz* (Mingus) and, 245, 248; *Bird at St. Nick's*, 368n82; *Bird Blows the Blues*, 317n90; *Bird on 52nd St.*, 368n82; bootleg recordings of, 251; cabaret cards and, 82, 310n16;

Charlie Parker: Complete Jazz at Massey Hall, 366n61, 368n78; *Charlie Parker with Strings*, 367n73; *Collectors' Items* (Davis) and, 317n92; *The Complete Live Performances on Savoy*, 357n113; *The Genius of Charlie Parker*, 338n67; Gillespie and, 367n65; "Groovin' High," 173, 289n75, 340n88; JATP and, 339n72; Mingus and, 267, 362n24, 367n70; *Mingus Ah Um* and, 252; *New Sounds in Modern Music: Charlie Parker, vol. 1*, 92, 310n12; *The Quintet: Jazz at Massey Hall*, 239, 246, 358n115; Savoy Records and, 293n3, 299n63, 314nn48–49

Parlan, Horace, 231, 256, 258

Pershing Lounge, 198, 207, 216

Peterson, Oscar, 203, 205, 339n72

phonograph, 47, 49, 134, 266; Edison, 325n42; records, 110

playback, 5–6, 10–11, 14–15, 25; equipment, 40, 67, 297n44; fidelity, 27, 110; formats, 39, 47; LP, 134, 226, 276; media, 13–14, 16, 18, 22; stereophonic, 29, 312n33, 354n71, 358n119

Playboy, 70, 202, 308n147; poll, 352n45

popular (pop) music, 36, 37, 44, 55, 67–68, 157–58, 203, 234, 282n9, 307n129, 338n65; albums (LPs), 10, 12, 15, 25, 29, 39, 52, 65, 66–67, 71, 123, 127, 130, 291n93, 307n127, 307n130; cool jazz and, 116; *Ellington at Newport* and, 126, 142; EPS, 50, 92; LP royalties and, 306n122; market, 169, 197, 243; segregational logic of, 66; studio effects and, 147; white, 133, 169, 201, 372n126. *See also* Black popular music

Porter, Eric, 26, 283n25, 285n42, 289n79, 290n90, 360n4, 361n12, 363n31, 364n42, 374n6

postproduction, 28, 131, 199, 217, 223, 255; *Autobiography in Jazz* and, 243, 249; Avakian and, 3, 30, 125–26, 139–40, 142, 146, 166, 198, 336n50, 348n11; *Jazz at Massey Hall* and, 246; Mingus and, 16, 233, 256, 274; *Mingus Ah Um* and, 231–32, 265; Tristano, 372n125

Potter, Tommy, 75, 86, 90, 113

Powell, Adam Clayton, Jr., 156–57, 333n19

Powell, Bud, 4, 56, 99, 245, 363n34; *The Quintet: Jazz at Massey Hall*, 239, 281n3

Presley, Elvis, 169, 334n25, 338n64

Prestige Records, 29, 54–55, 81–82, 103–4, 106, 119, 125, 141, 149, 197, 199, 285n41, 290n85, 313n39, 350n23; 16-rpm (16⅔) records and, 2, 10, 110–11, 112–3; Black audiences and, 350n24; Davis and, 16, 105, 108, 110, 116, 221, 317n85, 317n88; "East of the Sun" (Sims) and, 85–86, 91; EPS and, 92–94, 314n51, 315n68; hard bop and, 196, 311n21; *Hi Fi Party*, 95; *Lennie Tristano and Lee Konitz*, 312n38; live jazz-club records and, 351n40; LPs and, 25, 67, 77, 79–80, 83–84, 87–88, 96–97, 109, 112–13, 117–18, 137, 215, 233, 276, 307n131, 312n36, 313n38, 315n62; *Miles Davis All Stars*, 281n1; *Miles Davis: Blue Period*, 76, 78; the modern and, 89–90, 310n12, 320n120; Moody and, 318n94; R&B and, 285n40; *Stan Getz Quartet*, 315n64; visual language of, 97–98, 100–101, 316n69. *See also* Gitler, Ira; Van Gelder, Rudy; Weinstock, Bob

Procope, Russell, 125, 141

producers, 10, 12, 14, 25, 26, 30, 125, 127, 145, 210, 212, 264, 323n19; of *The Huckle-Buck and Robbins' Nest: A Buck Clayton Jam Session*, 3, 17;

INDEX   **429**

producers (continued)
live recordings and, 134–36, 142–43, 149, 207, 214, 217–18, 222; LPs and, 61, 87; *Mingus Ah Um* and, 256; record collectors who become, 313n39, 350n23; white, 4, 15, 28, 47, 81, 197, 217. *See also* Avakian, George; Macero, Teo
Putnam Central Club, 223, 243, 247, 249, 251–52, 368n79

The Quintet: Jazz at Massey Hall, 4–5, 10, 240, 246, 247, 281n3, 363n33; overdubbing on, 239

race, 8, 14, 15, 27, 70, 107, 220, 285n30, 294–95n16, 305n108, 324n28, 357n112, 373n131; aurality and, 277; circulation and, 40, 64, 193; ideologies of, 7, 78, 93, 114, 134, 219; market, 46, 296n34; music industry and, 39, 116, 217; record making and, 32, 44, 78; relations during the Cold War, 155–56, 159, 186
race records, 13, 41, 46
racial uplift, 8, 296n27, 328n73
racism, 115, 155, 175, 353n53; structural, 8, 41, 83, 203, 275
radio, 12, 19, 20, 41, 47, 90, 127, 134, 297n41; Black, 16, 46–47, 197, 350n24; Black musicians and, 82; broadcasts from jazz clubs, 222; disc jockeys, 114, 266; King Records and, 201, 352n42; live, 135, 149, 325n41, 325n47; public, 277; tape and, 18, 286n46. *See also* CBS; National Broadcasting Company (NBC); Voice of America (VOA)
Rainey, Ma, 24, 289n79, 351n37; *Ma Rainey, vol. 1*, 291n94
Ramsey, Guthrie, 8, 82, 196; on bebop, 114, 306n114, 319n1011; on gospel, 296n32. *See also* Afro-modernism

RCA Victor, 11, 14, 20, 41, 48–49, 50, 91, 287n57; Debut Records and, 245; "The Huckle-Buck" and, 46; Label "X," 68; *Lena Horne at the Waldorf Astoria*, 354n74; *Tijuana Moods* (Mingus) and, 237, 360n1, 362n24, 370n101
realism, 23; audile, 142; sonic, 144, 149, 277
record companies, 11–14, 27, 68, 77, 86, 115, 167, 259; Black-owned, 41, 241, 251; independent, 15, 117; live recordings and, 126, 133, 210, 213, 318n98
record industry, 8, 10, 13, 24, 27, 29–30, 35, 63, 77, 78, 83, 126, 189, 233, 275; conservativism of, 23; economic longevity and, 69; executives, 149, 214; expansion of, 88, 119, 297n42; Gillespie and, 167, 170; "The Huckle-Buck" and, 47, 65, 71; profits, 337n54; segregation and, 39, 41, 64
Recording Industry Association of America (RIAA), 49, 301n75, 302n89
record jackets, 94, 167, 314nn52–53, 317n87; artwork on, 10, 100; liner notes on, 84, 96
record labels, 14, 15, 22, 28, 32, 37, 49, 91, 106, 123, 127; Black owned, 114–15, 319n103; consumers and, 63, 94; educational work of, 68; hard bop and, 349n12; independent (small), 16, 47, 54, 88, 102, 197, 317n90, 365n48, 374n9; jazz-focused, 5, 29, 54, 77, 154, 286n50; LPs and, 11, 39, 167, 319n105; major, 55; sonic labor and, 71. *See also* Blue Note Records; Capitol Records; Columbia Records; Commodore Records; Debut Records; Decca Records; Dial Records; Gillespie, Dizzy: Dee Gee Records; Mercury Records; Norgran Records; Prestige Records; RCA Victor; Regent Records; Riverside Records; Savoy Records; Verve Records

430 INDEX

record making, 2, 6-9, 13-18, 28-32, 39, 46, 81, 79, 125, 158, 196, 211, 214, 226, 258, 272, 275, 292n101, 342n109; Adderley and, 226-27, 233-34, 278; Avakian and, 126, 133, 140, 145, 149; Black, 237, 276; as cultural practice, 231; Debut Records and, 238, 242, 245, 247-48; Ellington and, 138, 147; Gillespie and, 114-16, 119, 154, 158, 189 (*see also* Gillespie, Dizzy: Dee Gee Records); Granz and, 154, 158; infrastructures, 11, 28, 68, 91, 256; jazz clubs and, 228; jazz history and, 25, 27, 92, 111, 127; live recordings and, 133-34, 136, 214; Mingus and, 233-34, 239, 241-44, 249-50, 252, 255, 263-65, 267; nonlinearity of, 28; Prestige Records and, 78, 93-94, 96; tape technology and, 21-22; Weinstock and, 76, 78, 80, 81, 87; whiteness and, 128, 131, 328n70

recordmen, 12, 30, 159; jazz, 6, 68, 128, 154, 197; white, 24, 87, 91, 166, 197, 200, 227,

record production, 5, 8, 14, 17, 96, 106, 118, 137; Adderley and, 225; circulation and, 196; decisions, 198; experimentation and, 88; live, 194; Mingus and, 238, 258, 265-67; site of, 84, 113; techniques of, 28, 266

Regent Records, 37, 54, 293-94n9. *See also* Savoy Records

reissues, 8, 25, 27, 55, 56-58, 62, 67-69, 71-72, 77, 96; Avakian and, 323n19; bebop, 319n105; Blue Note Records and, 290n86, 355n86; CD, 25, 277, 358n118, 368n78; Clef Records and, 367n73; Columbia Records and, 127, 133; Commodore Records and, 302n83, 304n97; Debut Records and, 358n116; Decca Records and, 57-58, 300n73, 302nn84-85; JATP LPs as, 351n30; Legacy (Sony-Columbia) and, 124; Original Jazz Classics and, 277; Prestige Records and, 88, 92, 110-11, 290n85, 315n64; Riverside Records and, 200, 330n93, 351n37; Savoy Records and, 54, 56, 92, 319n103; Verve Records and, 170. *See also Ellington at Newport*: reissue of

remediation, 25-27, 88, 93, 290n88

rhythm and blues (R&B), 13-14, 36-37, 46, 54, 65, 88, 296n32, 298n56, 309n148; Adderley and, 349n21; charts, 40-41, 58, 64, 197; Clayton and, 305n111; Decca Records and, 58-59, 60f; EP and, 314n50; hard bop and, 99, 358n121; King Records and, 55; labels, 44, 47, 312n35; LPs, 52, 71; markets, 44, 46, 56, 302n89; mass market and, 196; Prestige Records and, 16, 285n40. *See also* "The Huckle-Buck"

Rice, Marc, 98, 107f

Richmond, Dannie, 254-56, 265

Riverside Records, 26, 67-68, 197, 199-200, 276, 307n132, 330n93, 350n23, 351n37; Adderley and, 193, 226-27, 234, 359n131; Black audiences and, 219; Café Bohemia and, 107, 200, 209-10, 216, 224; early jazz and, 200; Evans and, 200, 348n2, 358n119; hard bop and, 196; Jazz Archive Series, 289n79, 291nn94-95; Monk and, 118, 192, 200, 224, 359n124; on-location records, 226, 249, 359n129. *See also The Cannonball Adderley Quintet in San Francisco* Grauer, Bill; Keepnews, Orrin

Roach, Max, 4-5, 102, 200, 205, 236, 263, 368n83; *Autobiography in Jazz* and, 243, 245, 366n60; Jazz Workshop and, 250-51; Mingus and, 265, 366n54, 372n124; *Mingus at the Bohemia* and, 247; *The Quintet: Jazz at Massey Hall*, 239; *We Insist! Max Roach's Freedom Now Suite*, 275. *See also* Debut Records

Robeson, Paul, 156, 159

Rollins, Sonny, 75–76, 83, 86, 90, 113, 118, 205, 266, 270, 357n114; "Blue 7," 316n77; *Miles Davis with Sonny Rollins*, 315n68, 317n88; "My Reverie," 335n42; *Newks Time*, 337n55; *A Night at the Village Vanguard*, 199, 215; *Sonny Rollins with the Modern Jazz Quartet*, 314n57

Rolontz, Bob, 52, 64–65, 298n57, 305n107, 313n41

Roost (record label), 67, 88, 307n131, 312n36, 315n62

Russell, Pee Wee, 55, 270

Rustin-Paschal, Nichole, 80, 237, 362n23, 372n129; Debut Records and, 372n124; on Mingus, Celia, 238, 363n29; on Mingus, Charles, 236, 281n5, 362n23. *See also* jazzmasculinity

Sahl, Mort, 204, 353n55, 353n58

Sanden, Paul, 136, 324n40, 326n49

San Francisco, 160, 194, 204, 208; African Americans in, 203; jazz clubs, 202, 225, 352n47. *See also* Black Hawk; *The Cannonball Adderley Quintet in San Francisco*; Gleason, Ralph; Jazz Workshop; Keystone Korner; North Beach

Santoro, Gene, 254, 364n42, 371nn107–8, 373n133

Saturday Review, 70, 160, 179, 183–85, 202. *See also* Stearns, Marshall Winslow

Saul, Scott, 311n19; on hard bop, 349n12, 349n14; on Mingus, 237, 253, 361n9, 361n21

Saulters, Dottie, 171, 332n4

Savory, Bill, 130, 323n23

Savoy Records, 54–57, 67, 88, 257, 299n64, 299n66, 300n70, 300n72, 301n75, 307n131, 310n12, 312n34, 312n36, 315n62, 319n103; bebop and, 54–56, 319n105; *Errol Garner at the Piano* and, 299n62; extended-play discs (EPs) and, 50, 92, 314nn48–49; "The Huckle-Buck" and, 36–37, 41–44, 52, 299n60; Parker and, 56, 92, 293n3, 299n63, 314nn48–49, 357n113; *Rhythm and Blues, Volume I*, 54. *See also* Regent Records

Schaap, Phil, 124, 127, 138–39, 326n55, 327n58, 327nn61–62,

Schifrin, Lalo, 172, 340n84

Schlitten, Don, 97, 315n68

Schneider, Rebecca, 20, 248, 288n71, 324n38, 368n77

Schwann Long Playing Record Catalog, 48, 55, 60, 67, 294n9, 297n46, 299n66, 300n69, 300n71, 307nn131–32, 312n36; Blue Note Records and, 301n74; Decca Records and, 301n77, 301nn80–81, 302nn84–85; EmArcy and, 307n133; King Records and, 300n67; Savoy Records and, 299n64, 300n70

segregation, 46, 47, 82, 115, 274, 294n16, 311n19, 374n12; Gillespie and, 177; Granz and, 187; in the music industry, 6, 13, 29, 39–41, 64, 66, 72, 78, 84, 119, 128; in San Francisco, 203, 353n54. *See also* desegregation

Shaw, Artie, 114, 305n107

shellac, 283n20, 286n44; discs, 12, 275; rationing, 41

Shepherd, William, 94, 95

Shim, Eunmi, 263, 372n125

Silver, Horace, 99, 204, 205, 214, 250, 251; *6 Pieces of Silver*, 337n55

Sims, Zoot, 83, 104, 330n97; "East of the Sun," 85–86, 90, 103; *Swingin' with Zoot Sims*, 86, 88–91, 97, 100f, 312n30, 313n43; *Zoot Sims Quartets*, 317n89, 318n96

Sinatra, Frank, 37, 92, 130, 169, 289n84, 334n25; *Come Fly with Me*, 19;

High Society, 141; "The Huckle-Buck" and, 39, 42, 44, 46, 66, 70–71, 296n25, 308n145; *The Voice of Frank Sinatra*, 25

Smith, Bessie, 24, 55–56, 127, 289n79, 323n19; *The Bessie Smith Story*, 26

Smith, Jimmy, 197; *Groovin' at Smalls' Paradise*, 199, 215; *The Incredible Jimmy Smith at Club Baby Grand*, 199, 224

Smithsonian Collection of Classic Jazz, 24, 277

sonic Afro-modernity, 196, 225, 227, 234, 282n8, 349n20, 350n22; Ellington and, 150, 326n57; *The Quintet in San Francisco* and, 194. *See also* Afro-modernism

soul jazz, 82, 192, 225, 275, 285n40, 311n21, 320n120

sound reproduction, 22, 134, 135, 142, 144, 354n71, 357n111; technologies of, 7, 147–48

Southard, Paul, 47, 297n44

Specialty (record label), 37, 43, 44, 55, 300n67

splice, 4, 31, 231, 233, 249, 255; silent, 256, 263. *See also Mingus Ah Um*

splicing, 17, 31, 142–44, 231, 238, 247–48, 266–67, 364n39. *See also Mingus Ah Um*

standardization, 10, 13; of 12-inch records, 71, 96, 118, 276; of the LP, 23, 29–31, 39, 72

Stearns, Marshall Winslow, 26, 30, 84, 182, 334nn28–29, 336n44, 342n102, 344n131, 345n142, 346n146; American National Theater Academy and, 158; Avakian and, 127; Decca Records and, 58, 308n137; Gillespie and, 153–54, 163–64, 170–71, 175, 179, 183–85, 336n46, 339n79, 340n82, 341n96, 342n105, 345n144, 346n151; Institute of Jazz Studies, 321n9, 346n147

Sterne, Jonathan, 10, 144–45, 287n55, 290n87, 313n45, 325n41, 329n88, 355n83, 357n11; on recording studios, 318n95

Stinson Records, 60, 304n96, 338n67

Stitt, Sonny, 54, 83, 205, 266, 351n30

Storyville, 198, 356n101

Streibert, Theodore, 179–81, 182

studio production, 31, 146–47, 231, 239–40, 288n67, 331n98

supply chain, 8, 13, 22, 28, 267, 283n20, 287n61

swing, 4, 37, 41, 60, 63, 65, 68, 72, 116, 175, 198, 239, 275; Black music and, 47, 296n25; commercial, 44, 70; era, 24, 140, 171, 285n40, 297n37, 340n89; Kansas City, 38; music industry and, 113, 152, 293n5

synchronicity, 18, 20–22, 133, 135, 195, 325n47

tape editing, 3, 6–7, 17, 87, 145, 256, 330n94

tape recording, 21, 130, 134, 149, 226, 276

Taylor, Billy, 110, 314n57, 315n62, 363n34, 367n66

Taylor, Diana, 217, 329n88, 340n87

technology, 9, 25, 27, 32, 78, 186, 217, 220, 244; of culture/cultural, 8, 21, 234; history of, 22, 290n88; listening and, 10–11; live, 134, 210; long-playing (LP), 16, 22–23, 76, 84, 89–91, 96, 116–17, 130, 343n109; performance and, 17, 219, 222, 288n67, 357n111; recording, 76, 94, 122, 144, 196, 210–11, 214–15, 222, 286n44; sonic Afro-modernity and, 225, 326n57; of sound reproduction, 12, 148; studio, 144–45, 240 television (TV), 19-20, 286n53, 287n57, 297n41, 326n52; Adderley and, 193, 227; Gillespie and, 160; King Records and, 201; live, 135, 325n41; live records and, 134; Schifrin and, 340n84. *See also* CBS; National Broadcasting Company (NBC); RCA Victor

Tharpe, Sister Rosetta, 58-59, 302n87

Townsend, Irving, 21, 147, 276, 278, 331n98, 331n103

Tristano, Lennie, 25, 83, 87, 243-44, 263-65, 366n58, 372n125; *Lee Konitz Quintet, Lennie Tristano Quintet*, 97, 98f-99f, 290n85; *Lennie Tristano*, 21, 351n40, 372n125; *Lennie Tristano Quintet Featuring Lee Konitz*, 314n57; *Lennie Tristano and Lee Konitz*, 312n38

Tucker, Sherrie, 24, 289n80

United Music Corporation, 44, 45f, 46

Usher, David, 172-73, 175, 308n136, 319n112, 340n82, 340nn85-86

US Information Agency (USIA) 179, 181, 185, 345n142; United States Information Service, 163, 179, 336n46. *See also* US State Department

US State Department, 47, 155-56, 159-61, 170, 174, 180, 182, 273, 276, 311n19; Cultural Presentations program, 30, 153; Mingus and, 235; tours, 154, 158, 176-77, 184-86, 189, 335n40, 336n44, 344n126 (*see also* Gillespie, Dizzy)

Van Gelder, Rudy, 6, 104, 109-10, 207-8, 266, 318nn96-98, 354n69; Davis and, 2, 112, 281n1, 318n92; Debut Records and, 365n48; *Jazz Workshop, vol. 1: Trombone Rapport* and, 249; remastering work of, 96, 112, 315n64; *'Round about Midnight at the Café Bohemia* (Dorham) and, 210-11; Tristano and, 372n121, 372n125

vernacular: Black, 8, 226; Black culture, 349n20; Blackness and, 197

Verve Records, 161, 169-70, 189, 198, 225, 338nn65-67, 351n29, 351n40, 357n115; *Birks' Works* (Gillespie) and, 335n41; *Dizzy Gillespie at Newport* and, 172, 176, 343n111; *Dizzy in Greece* and, 179; jazz club recordings and, 200, 359n126; Konitz and, 365n53; Newport Jazz Festival and, 351n31; *World Statesman* (Gillespie) and, 335n40. *See also* Clef Records; Granz, Norman; Norgran Records

Village Vanguard, 198, 207, 215, 235, 350n28

visual design, 13, 32, 91, 167, 170, 197, 309n10; Granz and, 337n57; Prestige Records and, 96, 98

Voice of America (VOA), 124, 157-58, 321n6, 327n61, 331n104, 333n20

Von Eschen, Penny, 157, 333n20

Wallerstein, Edward, 14, 283-84nn28-29

Wallington, George, 83; *George Wallington at the Bohemia Featuring the Peck*, 354n75

Ware, Wilbur, 270, 357n114

Washington, Dinah, 37, 203-4, 205

Washington, Salim, 236-37, 357n107, 362n22

Weheliye, Alexander, 196, 282n8, 326n57, 349n20, 350n22. *See also* sonic Afro-modernity

Wein, George, 123, 132, 150, 168-69, 326n55

Weinstock, Bob, 2, 16-17, 29, 69, 79-83, 86-88, 93, 101, 102, 109, 118, 166, 273, 311n121, 312n31, 312n38, 350n23; *Blue Period* (Davis) and, 116; cool and, 117; "Disappointed" (Moody) and, 95; Gitler and, 313n39; LPs and, 96-97; the modern and, 76, 78, 320n120; photography of, 315n68

Weston, Randy, 200, 201-2, 206; *Jazz à la Bohemia*, 200, 209-10, 216, 224, 351n41, 359n124

Whiteman, Paul, 58, 201, 332n1, 352n42; "Whispering," 340n89

whiteness, 15-16, 31, 83, 117, 130, 132, 141, 178, 204, 234, 350n23, 350n25; Avakian and, 128, 322n15; jazz and, 9, 15, 128, 131, 150, 277, 284-85n34; of *Jazz Goes to College* (Brubeck), 70; jazz industry and, 17, 126, 274, 322n17; record making and, 27, 128, 131, 328n70

white privilege, 8, 236, 322n15, 350n25

white supremacy, 83, 157, 237-38

Williams, J. Mayo, 115, 238

Williams, Martin, 26, 84, 167, 225

Williams, Mary Lou, 270, 285n41, 343n11, 362n27, 372n129

Williams, Paul, 54, 65, 293n3; "The Huckle-Buck," 36, 40-42, 44, 52, 56, 295n20, 295n22

Wilson, John, 11, 77, 84, 282n15, 309n4

Winding, Kai, 80, 223, 249-50

Wolff, Francis, 100, 350n23

women, 6, 114, 204, 264, 292n98, 332n5, 371n108; blues, 24; executives, 372n126; jazzmasculinity and, 362n27; musicians, 24, 27, 153, 285n41, 291n95, 372n129; record makers, 238, 363n29; vocalists as jazz founders, 289n79. *See also* gender

World War II, 41, 47, 59, 115, 155, 203

Young, David X., 97, 101*f*, 315n67

Young, Lester, 54, 92, 198, 252-54, 270, 299n64, 314n48, 339n72; origins of cool and, 320n114

Zak, Albin, 142, 145, 147, 331n101, 355n94

www.ingramcontent.com/pod-product-compliance
Lightning Source LLC
Chambersburg PA
CBHW031323230426
43670CB00006B/225